The main archaeological sites of ancient Central Asia
Ruins | ancient sites
Modern cities and towns
Scale (km)
0
250
500
750
1000
N
AREA OF MAP
SIBERIA
Ob' River
Yenisei River
Irtysh River
Ishim River
Krasnoyarsk
Sayan Mountains
Lake Baikal
Malt'a
Ulan-Ude
Bajkara
Salbyk
Anchil Chon
Minusinsk
TUVA
Tuekta
Bashadar
Pazyryk
Arzhan
Ak-Alacha
ZONE
TEPPE
Uskin Uver
Jargalant
Altan Sandal
Tsagaan Salaa
Altai Mountains
Khoit Zenger
Chilikta
Ke'ermuqi
Lake Balkash
KAZAKHSTAN
Dzungarian Desert
MONGOLIA
Gobi Desert
Bayan Zag
Tamgaly
Almaty
Besschatyr
Urumqi
Hutubi
Arpa Uzen
Issyk Kul
Tian Shan
CHINA
Xiaohe
Loulan
Tengger Desert
Cyropolis
Taklamakan Desert
Beijing
Sarazm
Shurali
Kashgar
Ayala Mazar
Zaghunluq
Pamirs
Shakty
Yamchun
Ai Khanum
Tashkurgan
Khotan
Hindu Kush
Kabul
Indus River
Mohenjo-Daro
INDIA

THE HISTORY OF
CENTRAL ASIA

VOLUME **ONE**

THE HISTORY OF CENTRAL ASIA

The Age of the Steppe Warriors

CHRISTOPH BAUMER

I.B.TAURIS
LONDON · NEW YORK

Published in 2012 by I.B.Tauris & Co Ltd
6 Salem Road, London W2 4BU
175 Fifth Avenue, New York NY 10010
www.ibtauris.com

Distributed in the United States and Canada
Exclusively by Palgrave Macmillan,
175 Fifth Avenue, New York NY 10010

Translated by Miranda Bennett

ISBN: 978-1-78076-060-5

A full CIP record for this book is available from the British Library
A full CIP record is available from the Library of Congress

Library of Congress Catalog Card Number: available

Designed by Christopher Bromley

Printed and bound in Italy by Printer Trento

FSC www.fsc.org MIX Paper from responsible sources FSC® C015829

Contents

Horse race at the winter Naadam festivity, Inner Mongolia Autonomous Region, northern China.

Introduction

We must welcome the future, remembering that soon it will be the past; and we must respect the past, remembering that it was once all that was humanly possible.

ADAPTED FROM **GEORGE SANTAYANA** (1863–1952)

Central Asia is a region of superlatives and extremes. In a huge, though mostly sparsely populated area of about 10 million km^2 hundreds of languages have developed and manifold cultures have blossomed. Because of its great distance from seas and oceans, Central Asia has a distinctive continental climate with often bitterly cold winters and torrid summer heat, and water shortages prevail in large regions – when water is available at all. Sudden climatic, ecological or tectonic events sometimes forced people to repeatedly take drastic action – such as developing new economic systems or leaving their homelands.

For these reasons life in Central Asia has often focused on survival, which has facilitated the discovery of vital technologies in such areas as metallurgy, transportation, trade and warfare. The people understood that they had to adapt themselves to challenging conditions and lived as hunters, gatherers, fishermen, settled or nomadic cattle breeders, farmers or specialised artisans. In southern Central Asia there developed very early proto-urban cultures and trade networks, which enabled contacts and the exchange of goods between widely distant cultures, such as Mesopotamia, the Indus Valley Civilisation in modern-day Pakistan, and China. The mobility necessary for life in large stretches of Central Asia clearly fostered the early trade in certain raw materials; long before the Silk Roads, there were jade, lapis lazuli and tin roads.

The attraction of Central Asian raw materials for the wealthy economic powers at the periphery of the Eurasian continent has not changed in the twenty-first century. On the contrary, natural gas and petroleum have taken the place of silk, and existing and planned pipelines, which connect the vast gas and petroleum reserves of Kazakhstan, Turkmenistan and Siberia to the energy-hungry economies of China and Western Europe, are modern-day Silk Roads.

We use the word 'culture' to describe those activities and achievements by people that can be of a material, spiritual, ethical, religious or political nature. A specific cluster of such activities forms a culture and sets it apart from other cultures for a certain time span. Cultures are often connected to a particular territory, which, depending on the dynamic of the culture's representatives at a given time, can expand or contract. Cultures tend to develop, to varying degrees, an ability to shape other cultures or to be influenced by them. Cultures are time-bound entities that go through several stages of development.[1]

In the case of the cultural history of Central Asia, however, the availability of sources for the pre-Christian era is inversely proportional to the territorial expanse and cultural riches of the area under study, as the peoples of that time did little or no writing. Thus, before the military expansion of powerful literate cultures such as Achaemenid Iran, China, the Northern-Indian Kushan or the Greek Macedonians, Central Asia resembles a prehistoric world. The only written sources come from the periphery of Central Asia. Among the most instructive are the 'Histories' of Herodotus (*ca.* 484–*ca.* 425 BC), the Greek reports of the campaigns of Alexander the Great in Sogdia and Bactria, the 'Shiji' chronicle of the Chinese historian Sima Qian (*ca.* 145–*ca.* 87 BC), and the 'Han Shu', the annals of the Western Han Dynasty (202 BC–9 AD) from the first century AD.[2] To these are added a few stone inscriptions from the realm of the Iranian Achaemenids. The Scythians, who lived north of the Black Sea, were in contact with Macedonia, the Bosporan Kingdom and Rome. Hence we are better informed about the Scythian culture than most other Central Asian cultures. Otherwise, the attempt at a reconstruction of the pre-Christian history of Central Asia is founded mainly on archaeological, ecological and linguistic evidence.

Among the most relevant archaeological sources are burial sites. Graves are sacred sites for nearly all cultures, as here the fundamental vulnerability of the human being to his inherent transience reveals itself abruptly and inescapably. Confrontation with the death of compatriots turns one's attention to one's own mortality and encourages, as a counterweight, ideas of some kind of survival after death and belief in supernatural powers, whether benevolent or threatening towards humanity. Insofar as members of a social group share these hopes and beliefs, they orient themselves to common ideals that give rise to normalised patterns related to death, such as burial ceremonies. Burial rites reveal not only the efforts to ensure the deceased have a smooth transition to the afterlife and thus the realm of the ancestors, but also the hope of remaining in contact with them and being watched over by them as guardians. Furthermore, these rituals express the hope of holding onto consciousness and continuing some mode of existence after one's own death. At the same time, the awareness of their own finite existence forces people to fashion their temporal lives with this in mind.

For these reasons, burial rites took on a culture-creating function, in that they motivated the living to consider and define their own responsibilities in this life. In the end, culture arises considerably from the conflict with death within the framework of burial and memorial rites, as well as from reflection on the unanswerable question of existence after death. In this sense the culture and society of the living are founded also in the world of the dead. The culture of the Egyptian pharaohs, with their elaborate death rites and enormous graves, which were undertaken even during the lifetime of the ruler, offers an outstanding example of this.

A second source for finding out the cognitive, emotional or spiritual life of a culture without written sources is its works of art, whether sacred or profane. These include two-dimensional works, such as cave painting and petroglyphs, and later murals and tapestries, as well as three-dimensional, figurative objects. In artworks the artist expresses particular values, hopes and fears, which are shared by a specific community, so they enable inferences to be made about the culture. Artworks are the most valuable 'books' of pre-literate cultures.

Regarding the timeframe under consideration, the intention of this four-volume work is to provide a well-grounded overview of the entire history of Central Asia, from the beginning of prehuman life to the twenty-first century present. Details and nuances can undoubtedly be lost, but a comprehensive view that does not content itself with the listing of events in a chronicle is able to reveal long-term trends and complex, interdisciplinary connections. The alternative to the aforementioned approach would be to entrust each chapter to a specialist as editor. The result would presumably be, as in the case of the seven-volume *History of Civilizations of Central Asia*,[3] produced by UNESCO, a lovely mosaic but not a complete, overarching picture. Admittedly, no work of history can be definitive, since history marches forward and new discoveries bring to light previously unknown facts and refine interpretation – each cultural history can only, like nomads, mark out a stage of the journey.

I

Geography, Climate and Prehuman History of Central Asia

Geography is the basis of history. It appears that the changes of climate have caused corresponding changes not only in the distribution of man, but in his occupations, habits, and even character. The climatic changes have been one of the greatest factors in determining the course of human progress.

ELLSWORTH HUNTINGTON, *THE PULSE OF ASIA*, 1907[1]

1. On the definition of Central Asia

The region of 'Central Asia' is shrouded in an aura of mystery. As much as it evokes dramatic images of endless steppes, life-threatening deserts, fierce horsemen and transcontinental Silk Roads, it tends to defy hard-and-fast analysis. The first person to use the term 'Central Asia' was the German explorer and naturalist Alexander von Humboldt (1769–1859) after returning from his research expedition of 1829. During this journey, at the behest of Tsar Nicholas I, he crossed Russia from St Petersburg in the west all the way to the Altai Mountains and the Chinese border[2] in the east. He was the first to recognise that Central Asia constituted a discrete entity within the Eurasian continent. The immense distance covered by Humboldt – the Russian-Chinese border is about 4,000 km from St Petersburg – gives a sense of how difficult it is to define Central Asia. It is as if one wanted to stake out a border in a borderless region.

One may attempt to define Central Asia in geographic, ethnic, economic-cultural or linguistic terms. In the linguistic sense it may be understood as the homeland of three great language families, namely Indo-European,[3] Altaic, and Uralic.

The Indo-European language family rapidly broke out of the bounds of Central Asia, developing into the Celtic languages in Western Europe, Hittite in Anatolia and proto-Tocharian in what is today north-western China, to name but a few. Speakers of the Iranian languages, especially the eastern Iranian subfamily, such as the equestrian nomadic Scythians, Sauromatians, Sarmatians and Alans in western Central Asia and the Saka in the east, played an important role until the first centuries of the Common Era.

From the sixth century AD, peoples of the Altaic language family shaped the history of Central Asia, beginning with the Turkic peoples and then, from the early thirteenth century, the Mongols. However, speakers of the Tungusic languages, which likewise belong to the Altaic language family, lived mostly in eastern Siberia and Manchuria and thus outside of Central Asia.

Finally, the presumed home of the Uralic language family lies in northern Eurasia, in the heart of the Urals. Within the largest, Finno-Ugric, language group, the Magyars were present in Eurasia before being driven from their then-homeland north of the Black Sea by the Turkic Pechenegs and fleeing to present-day Hungary. In summary, linguistic criteria are today inadequate to delimit Central Asia.

Economic-cultural aspects are also inadequate when it comes to delimiting the region of Central Asia. Large swaths of the Central Asian steppe belt were indeed home to stockbreeding peoples for millennia. Whether settled or, more commonly, mobile, these people developed their own individual cultures. The system of the semi-mobile livestock-raising economy began to develop first at the start of the third millennium BC in the heart of Eurasia as an adaptation to changing climatic and ecological conditions and does not represent an independent characteristic of Central Asia. In addition, agriculture began to advance in certain steppe and desert regions, thanks to irrigation systems along rivers.

It is geographic and ethnic factors that most accurately define Central Asia. Such a combination suggests itself because history deals not only with the cultural, economic, socio-political and military phenomena within a given geographic area. History, of course, also concerns the peoples who live there. These communities prospered, either within their ancestral lands or, having left them, in new homes at or even beyond Central Asia's peripheries, which they infiltrated, occupied, and enriched with their own cultures. On account of the economically driven mobility of many Central Asian cultures, such as the Scythians, the Turkic peoples, and the Mongols, the phenomenon of migration runs through the history of Central Asia as a leitmotif. The geographic permeability of the relatively flat steppe belt, stretching over 4,400 km on the east–west axis from the Mongolian Altai to the Danube basin without significant mountain or water obstacles, has for millennia invited the migration of peoples. The reverse migration of people and cultures from the fringes to the centre also occurred, if more rarely and often as part of a strategy developed for economic and military reasons. Among these were the campaigns of Alexander the Great to the east, the offensives of the Chinese Han and Tang Dynasties to Central Asia and into Mongolia, and the annexation of large parts of Central Asia by tsarist Russia in the nineteenth century. The history of the Eurasian continent resembles a pulsing interaction between Central Asia and the peripheries in west, east and south, so the cultural borders of Central Asia shifted frequently over the course of history. These permanent interactions of peoples, languages, cultures and states caused Central Asia to become a unique 'palimpsest of cultures'.[4]

In order to lend these naturally unstable borders a fixed framework it is best to give priority to geographic aspects. As with culture and language, Central Asia is geographically defined in different ways. In the political context, the term designates the five one-time Soviet republics of Kazakhstan, Kyrgyzstan, Tajikistan, Turkmenistan and Uzbekistan – a region that extends over 4 million km^2 and is home to 62 million people.[5] UNESCO uses a much broader definition, including in Central Asia all the countries and regions between the

The continental drift from the Carboniferous to a future position in 50 million years

Future Quaternary (In *ca.* 50 million years) – Africa will have fused with Eurasia forming a new northern supercontinent; the Mediterranean Sea has disappeared and is replaced by a new mountain range and South America drifts into the northern hemisphere.

Cretaceous (145.5–66.5 million years ago) – The continents approached their present positions about 100 million years ago, but India was still located relatively close to the Antarctic and Australia.

Triassic (251–199.6 million years ago) – East and north China have fused with northern Pangaea, south China and Indochina are still independent landmasses. At the end of the Triassic, initial fissures announce the separation of North America from Eurasia.

Carboniferous (358–299 million years ago) – At the end of the Carboniferous *ca.* 300 million years ago, the northern landmasses collided with Gondwana in the south to form the megacontinent Pangaea.

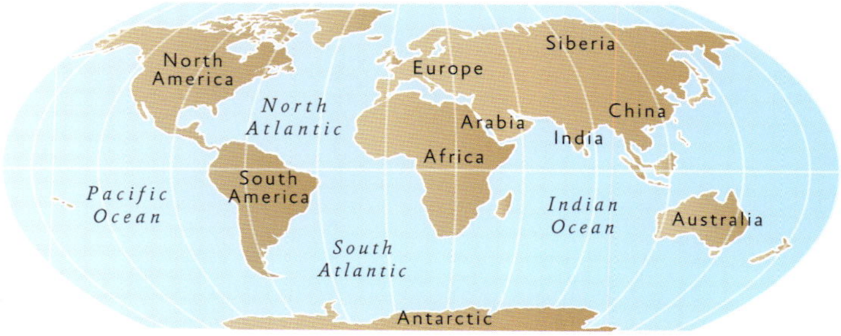

Quaternary (since 66.5 million years ago) – Also the present positions of the continents remain unstable and are changing.

Jurassic (199.6–145.5 million years ago) – Pangaea begins to break apart into the future continents.

Permian (299–251 million years ago) – Laurasia and Gondwana form the megacontinent Pangaea, which is separated from the narrow landmasses in the east by the Paleo-Tethys Ocean.

The dinosaur hunter Roy Chapman Andrews

'I always intended to be an explorer, to work in a natural history museum, and to live out of doors.'[6] The American Roy Chapman Andrews (1884–1960) had the perseverance and assertiveness to realise this vision of his life. During his early college years, however, he just indulged his desire for a life outdoors and was a mediocre student. After receiving his degree, he looked within himself: 'Mentally I took myself apart and examined the pieces. I didn't like what I saw. On that June [1906] afternoon I changed from an irresponsible boy to a man just as though one suit of clothes had been taken off and another put on.'[7] Andrews then took charge of his life, went to New York, and found a position, for a token wage, in the taxidermy department of the American Museum of Natural History. He soon undertook scientific expeditions to Borneo, Japan and Korea. In North Korea he spent months exploring densely forested mountains infested with bandits and, upon his much delayed return to Seoul, was surprised to read his own obituary in the newspapers!

Andrews' moment arrived in early 1920, when he proposed to the museum's president Henry Fairfield Osborn (1857–1935) that he test the latter's theory of the origin of dinosaurs, pterosaurs, and perhaps even human beings in Central Asia by means of fieldwork in the Gobi Desert in Mongolia. Andrews had decided to devote himself to this question as early as 1915, after reading one of Osborn's articles, and had undertaken a five-month reconnaissance of the Gobi with his wife Yvette in 1919. Although at the time there had been only a single official fossil discovery in that area, the tooth of a rhinoceros, northern China and the Gobi were very promising sites for searching, since Chinese apothecaries had for a long time sold the teeth and bones of unknown animals as medicine. Additionally, the first investigations of the Jesuit Emile Licent of 1916–20 had revealed a couple of potentially interesting fossil beds.[8] Still more promising was the fact that about 150 million years ago the Central Asian plateau was dry land and unlike, for instance, Europe, parts of it had not been flooded. Thus a fossil inventory stretching over many epochs could be anticipated.

The first expedition left Beijing in Dodge automobiles on 17 April 1922, after a camel caravan sent out several weeks earlier had placed fuel depots at regular intervals. After just a few days the expedition made two spectacular finds at Iren Dabasu in northern Inner Mongolia. The first were the teeth and bones of a powerful mammal, approximately 34 to 56 million years old and resembling a rhinoceros, from the family Titanotheriidae (Brontotheriidae). The excitement was great, since this was the first discovery of a titanotherium outside America. On the same evening the real sensation made itself known. Andrews reported:

> While dinner was being prepared, Granger [the chief palaeontologist] wandered off along the grey-white ridge that lay like a recumbent reptile west of the camp. Even in the failing light he found a few fossil bits and we realized that we had another deposit at our very door. The following morning ... Granger was at work, exposing the tibia of a large dinosaur! 'This means,' said Doctor Berkey [geologist], 'that we are standing on Cretaceous strata – the first Cretaceous and the first dinosaur known in eastern Asia [north of the Himalaya]!'[9]

Another important find followed about 800 km north-west of Iren Dabasu in Outer Mongolia, near the lake of Tsagaan Nuur, when the expedition discovered the skull and parts of the skeleton of a baluchitherium.[10] The baluchitherium, today called paraceratherium or indricotherium, looked like a gigantic, hornless rhinoceros and weighed more than 16 tons. This herbivore was the largest land mammal of all time and lived in the Oligocene (33.9–23.0 million years ago) and early Miocene (23.0 to 5.3 million years ago).

At the start of August 1922 two more thrilling discoveries were made, 220 km south-east of Tsagaan Nuur near the region of Shabarakh Usu, a formation of red sandstone. The second of these finds was the most sensational of all five of Andrews' Gobi expeditions but, ironically, was not recognised as such for an entire year. First the photographer Shackelford discovered the skull of an unknown reptile at the top of a sandstone chimney. This was an ancestor of the Ceratopsia, a group of herbivorous, beaked dinosaurs from the Cretaceous that had a snout similar to a parrot's beak and a neck frill in the form of a bony collar. In honour of Andrews this fossil of a relatively small, up to two-metre-long dinosaur genus bears the name *Protoceratops andrewsi*. Toward evening Granger encountered fragments of eggshells, which were at first classified as the relatively ordinary eggs of an extinct bird.[11]

A year later, in July 1923, the expedition returned to the 'Flaming Cliffs' of Shabarakh Usu, modern Bayan Zag, where they found more eggshells, among them 13 petrified eggs in a sandstone block. They had a cylindrical, elliptical shape and were up to 30 cm long. A few eggs were broken open and provided a glimpse of the delicate skeletons of embryonic dinosaurs. Now there was no doubt: 'it was evident that dinosaurs did lay eggs and that we had discovered the first specimens known to science.'[12] It was long assumed that these eggs were from protoceratops; today they are also associated with hadrosaurids, duck-billed dinosaurs.[13] Spherical dinosaur eggs were later also found in the Gobi and attributed to the powerful sauropods, which had long, snake-like necks and small heads. Another surprising find was made by the third expedition in 1925, 500 m from Bayan Zag, when they found hundreds

◂ Start of the fourth Mongolian expedition of Roy Chapman Andrews on 16 April 1928, north of Kalgan, now the city of Zhangjiakou, Hebei Province, northern China. American Museum of Natural History Library, New York.

of small stone tools and worked flints from the Mesolithic period (11,700–6000 BC), as well as countless rectangular pieces of dinosaur eggs bearing neatly carved holes – clearly these early human beings had crafted necklaces out of dinosaur eggs.[14] All these discoveries in the today pitilessly hot desert around Bayan Zag suggest that during the Mesolithic and at the time of the dinosaurs, mild, humid weather prevailed.

Andrews had to cancel the planned expeditions of 1926, 1927, and 1929 on account of an increasingly hostile stance toward foreigners among the Chinese authorities and because robber gangs were operating ever more boldly in northern China, but he was able to undertake two further expeditions, under difficult conditions, in 1928 and 1930. During the last trip Andrews came upon a graveyard of more than 20 platybelodons, colloquially called shovel-tuskers. These weighty herbivores, which had a shovel-like lower jaw, were presumably trapped in the quicksand of a swamp, from which they could not free themselves, some 15 to 20 million years ago.[15] After 1930 scientific work in China was no longer possible for foreigners; only Sven Hedin managed to work until 1935 in a region on the edge of Xinjiang plagued by civil war. Among the additional significant discoveries of the expeditions led by Andrews were parts of skeletons of three theropods, the bipedal dinosaurs velociraptor, oviraptor, and the small, nocturnal sauronithoides, as well as the armoured pinacosaurus, which was as long as 5 m and moved on all fours. All of these dinosaurs lived about 80 to 70 million years ago. At the completion of the five expeditions it was clear that the Gobi represented one of the richest regions of Asia for late dinosaurs and early large mammals.

In 1933 Andrews prepared for another expedition, this time to Soviet Central Asia, but fate had other plans. In 1934 the museum director Sherwood suffered a heart attack, whereupon Andrews was named interim director. Shortly thereafter he injured his back so badly in a fall from a horse that he had to give up riding forever, and the prospect of further expeditions dimmed. Andrews was persuaded to assume the post of director permanently. Though he initially enjoyed the work, he badly missed the outdoor life: 'For twenty-five years I had lived in the field, sleeping in the open, and I was like a wild animal suddenly put in a cage.'[16] Soon the Great Depression cast its shadow over the museum: generous sponsors saw their fortunes dwindle, scientific expeditions were cancelled, and Andrews' work became that of a promoter; on 1 January 1942 he resigned from the directorship.

Dinosaur eggs discovered in May 1925 by George Olsen at Shabarak Usu (Bayan Zag), Ömnögov Aimag, southern Mongolia. American Museum of Natural History Library, New York.

Chalk formation called 'Tchink' near Bozzhira on the Ustyurt Plateau, Mangyshlak Peninsula, western Kazakhstan.

Caspian Sea and Mongolia without access to an ocean; that is, the five former Soviet republics, central and eastern Russia south of the taiga, north-eastern Iran, Afghanistan, northern Pakistan, Kashmir, Ladakh, Tibet and Mongolia.[17] With this far-reaching definition, Central Asia becomes a very heterogeneous entity, climatically, economically and culturally, which is divided into two parts by the Hindu Kush, Pamir, Kun Lun and Himalaya mountains.

For the purposes of this book Central Asia is defined in geographic terms as the region that lies between the Caspian Sea to the west, Mongolia to the east, the southern Siberian steppe to the north, and the Hindu Kush and Kun Lun mountain chains to the south. It stretches from roughly 48° to 115° longitude and 35° to 55° north latitude and encompasses the five former Soviet republics, southern Russia from Lake Baikal to the Volga, northern Afghanistan, Xinjiang and Inner and Outer Mongolia.[18] The maximum distance along the east–west axis is approximately 5,000 km and along the north–south axis approximately 2,000 km. In terms of ethnicity and nomadic confederations or empires, however, the boundaries of Central Asia were temporarily enlarged when Central Asian peoples settled in peripheral regions and markedly influenced the culture there. The Scythians and Saka, whose territory extended from 32° to 100° longitude and from 42° to 55° north latitude, represent an outstanding example of such a process. Further examples are the Sarmatians, Alans and Huns in Eastern Europe as well as the Yuezhi/Kushan, and, more than a millennium later, the Timurids in the northern part of the Indian subcontinent. But most nomadic federations or empires were primarily defined by their rule over peoples, less over territories.[19]

2. The interdependence of geography, climate and history

Compared with the age of the planet, about 4 billion years, the 55-million-km^2 Eurasian continent, and with it Central Asia, is, in geological terms, a relatively 'young' formation. It grew out of the separations and collisions of various tectonic plates – more specifically, lithosphere plates – which support the oceans and continents and drift like rafts on the semi-fluid rock of the underlying mantle.

The current form of the Eurasian continent began to form in the geologic Permian age (299–251 million years ago), when the continents of Laurussia, Siberia and Kazakhstania came together and formed Laurasia, the forerunner of the Eurasian continent. At the same time, the Urals arose along the most significant junction of the colliding continents. The nearly 2,100-km-long mountain chain, which runs from north to south and rises to 1,895 m, marks the boundary between Europe and Asia. This border was established by the Swedish officer and geographer Philipp Johann von Strahlenberg (1676–1747) in 1730, after he explored Siberia geographically and anthropologically during his 13 years as a prisoner of war. For Strahlenberg the boundary ran along the Urals, then the Emba (Jembi) River, which empties into the Caspian Sea, and finally the Kuma-Manych Depression north of the Caucasus.[20] With his definition of the border, which was recognised by Russia, von Strahlenberg resolved a centuries-long dispute, in which the border was proposed to be along either the Don[21] or the Ob. As a result of this boundary placement, the western part of Central Asia as geographically defined above, stretching from the Urals to the Volga, actually falls within Europe.

Shortly before the formation of Laurasia, at the end of the Carboniferous (358–299 million years ago), Laurussia fused with the southern supercontinent Gondwana, consisting of South America, Africa, India, Australia and Antarctica, from which came the final global geological megacontinent, Pangaea. Somewhat later, at the start of the Triassic (251–199.6 million years ago), first eastern China and then northern China collided with the supercontinent Laurasia, which formed the northern part of Pangaea. The Indian subcontinent, or the Indian Plate, began to collide with Eurasia only much later, some 40 million years ago. As the Indian Plate slid under the Eurasian, the Himalayas were pushed up by tectonic forces. The Himalaya range is still growing today. The interface between the Indian and the Eurasian plates was discovered by the Swiss geologist Augusto Gansser in 1936 near Kailash in western Tibet.[22]

The contiguous landmass of Pangaea, extending from north to south, enjoyed a climate at least 3 °C warmer than today's, allowing for an unlimited flourishing of land animals. Reptiles in particular, among them dinosaurs and pterosaurs,[23] experienced phenomenal growth and dominated life on land and in the air during the Triassic and the subsequent epochs of the Jurassic (199.6–145.5 million years ago) and Cretaceous (145.5–66.5 million years ago), while mammals in the broadest sense played a subordinate role until the Cretaceous. At the end of the Cretaceous, half of all species died out, among them all non-avian dinosaurs.[24] Thanks to particular geological conditions, spectacular discoveries of dinosaur fossils were made in southern Mongolia in the 1920s.

Already in the Late Triassic the first cracks of the eventual splitting off of North America from Eurasia were becoming evident. About 150 million years ago the global megacontinent Pangaea broke into the supercontinents Laurasia and Gondwana, and then, 15 million years later, the middle Atlantic opened like a zipper and divided North America from Eurasia. While the arrangement of the continents was comparable in rough outline to their current positions even 100 million years ago, they clearly approximated the present arrangement 12 to 14 million years ago. Since the continents are never still, however, further tectonic shifts are foreseeable. Extrapolation from the current movements points toward a union of Africa with Eurasia and disappearance of the Mediterranean Sea in *ca.* 50 million years.[25]

Geographic and climatic peculiarities have decisively shaped the development of Central Asia.[26] As a consequence of its particular position as a northern inland region, the compensatory mechanisms of the maritime climate play only a small role, which leads to a distinctive continental climate with large temperature differences between the cold and hot seasons. Winters in Central Asia are mostly cold to extremely cold; the summers, by contrast, warm to unbearably hot. The relatively northern position of Central Asia influences both the amount of daylight and the level of precipitation. Photosynthesis, vital to the growth of plants, is directly related to the amount of daylight, which is drastically reduced in northern zones during the long winter season. In addition, the prevailing west winds from the Atlantic and Mediterranean lose much of their moisture and compensating effect when they encounter the Urals and sweep eastward as dry winds. As a result the climatic differences between summer and winter, as well as relative aridity, increase markedly toward the east.

In general the west winds streaming in from the Mediterranean and the Black Sea are the main source of winter and spring rainfall in Central Asia. For this reason the climate of Central Asia is particularly sensitive to the lessening of moisture in these winds, as, for instance, when ice crusts covered Northern and Central Europe. By contrast, during the late Pliocene and early Pleistocene (*ca.* 2.8–2.4 million years ago) Central Asia was less arid and less broadly exposed to the dry, dust-bearing winds, since at the time the Caspian Sea and the Aral Sea formed a single, large body of water.[27] In south-eastern Central Asia the trend toward aridity increases still further because the mountain chains of the Hindu Kush, Pamir, Kun Lun and Himalayas on its southern edge force the moist summer monsoon clouds that stream from the south to the north to rise and release their moisture as rain. Thus the temperature differences between the seasons are especially dramatic in the Taklamakan and Gobi deserts.

One of the most important ways of judging climatic conditions in a given region, as well as its suitability for agriculture, is to measure the effective moisture on the ground, that is, the relationship between precipitation and potential evaporation, which is a function of the prevailing temperature. Thus, for example, 100 mm of rainfall in the tundra or northern taiga on the northern edge of Central Asia can, on account of the very limited potential evaporation, lead to floods or the creation of new layers of silt, while the same amount in the Gobi Desert quickly evaporates because of the intense sunlight and high potential evaporation. In the tundra precipitation exceeds evaporation by more than 50 percent; in the Taklamakan Desert it is up to 170 times less. All these factors seriously limit the amount of land usable for agriculture, leading to a relatively low population density.

The Central Asian landmass forms an enormous rectangle that falls into four climatic zones, whose main axes run east–west. From the north to the south these are the tundra (which lies outside the scope of this work), the forested zone of the taiga, the grass steppes, and the deserts.

The tundra is a treeless zone, about 400 to nearly 1,000 km wide, north of the Arctic Circle.[28] It is characterised by extremely cold and dark winters; strong, freezing winds; frequent fog and cloudiness; and permafrost, so that the growing season is limited to about three months and snow covers the ground for nearly eight months of the year. This hostile zone is a kind of frozen desert. South of the tundra lies the taiga with its immense coniferous forests, which are interspersed with deciduous forests, such as those of birch, in its southern part. These forests appeared at the end of the last Ice Age, 12,000 to 10,000 years ago; they stand on permafrost whose surface thaws in early summer, leading to marshy conditions and an accumulation of mud. Until the exploitation of their rich natural resources of timber and minerals by the emergent Russia and the subsequent Soviet Union, both the taiga and the tundra played subordinate roles in the history of Central Asia.

On the southern edge of the taiga the forests merge first with a narrow band of steppe forests, which is followed by an entirely grass steppe, giving way in its southern part to a desert-like steppe. The Central Asian steppe is part of the Eurasian steppe, which extends from the lower Danube plain in the west over 7,800 km to the Pacific Ocean, interrupted only by the southern Siberian Altai and Sayan mountains. The climate of the grass steppe is semi-arid; it is not humid enough to allow the growth of forests and is largely unsuitable for agricultural use. Precipitation is low and results in a chronic moisture deficit; aeolian erosion is significant, and the salinisation of the soil is also a problem. These obstacles to arable farming were only overcome when agriculture was mechanised in the nineteenth century. Thus the steppe offered little in the way of immediate nourishment to human beings, the foundations of their economy were mostly hunting, fishing and animal husbandry. To avoid overgrazing, animal breeding was tightly controlled; the herds had to rotate their grazing areas within a designated perimeter.

The mobility of the steppe stockbreeders and their need for products and raw materials from settled agrarian cultures gave rise to a state of flux between peaceful trade and plundering raids. At the start of the tenth century BC the inhabitants of the steppe had at their disposal horses, two-part bits, and small recurve bows, a combination that not only gave them military superiority but also represented the goods most desired by the settled societies. This paradox was revealed especially clearly in the case of China, which could resist the steppe nomads on its northern border only by means of a cavalry but which, due to a lack of its own pastureland, had to acquire horses from the same nomads or, beginning in the sixth century AD, from the equally forbidding Tibetans. For the nomads the horse represented both their most valuable export and their strongest instrument of war. Finally, the flat topography of the Central Asian steppe greatly facilitated mobility. In fact, the peoples of the steppe enjoyed a freedom of movement almost on a par with that of seafaring nations – whether for purposes of trade or of war.

Since in Central Asia aridity always increases from north to south, on its southern edge the steppe opens out into wide stretches of desert devoid of vegetation. To the west the Mangyshlak Peninsula, which belongs to Kazakhstan, protrudes into the north-eastern Caspian Sea. The landscape here is marked by spectacular lime and sandstone formations, and is an important source of natural gas and petroleum. The peninsula is sparsely populated today, but more than 1,000 years ago it was the meeting point for different cultures. It is often considered part of the 180,000-km^2 Ustyurt Plateau, a tableland in Kazakhstan and Uzbekistan, which consists of clay regions in the west, salt regions in the north near the Aral Sea, sand dunes in the south-east, and marl in the east. At the southern end of the Aral Sea, the nearly 300,000-km^2 Kyzyl Kum Desert, whose name means 'red sand', lies in the western part of the Turanian Basin. The Kyzyl Kum, rich in such ores as gold, silver, copper, and uranium, covers central Uzbekistan and extends into southern Kazakhstan as well. In the north-eastern part of the Kyzyl Kum, the Syr Darya river, the ancient Jaxartes, separates the desert from the Mujun Kum desert. The Mujun Kum gives way in turn to the bleak, steppe-like semi-desert Betpak-Dala, whose Kazakh name means 'bad plain'. North-east of this 'bad steppe' stretches the sand desert Saryesik-Atyrau, which is split in its eastern part by the mountains of the Dzungarian Alatau from the Dzungarian desert. This approximately 50,000-km^2 desert, which lies in the north-western Chinese Autonomous Region of Xinjiang, is a plain of gravel and salt and has the distinction of being the furthest place in the world from any sea.

As the Syr Darya separates the Kyzyl Kum and Mujun Kum deserts, the river Amu Darya, the legendary Oxus, splits the Kyzyl Kum in its southern part from the sand and scree desert called Kara Kum. With an area of about 450,000 km^2, the Kara Kum covers more than 90 percent of Turkmenistan. From the fourth to the start of the second millennium BC, the desert, rich in petroleum and especially natural gas, was home to a proto-urban culture. Later, one of the most important routes of the so-called Silk Road ran through it, with the oasis city of Merv one of the most significant junctions. These sophisticated early cultures had economies based on irrigated agriculture, animal husbandry and interregional trade with the Indus Valley and Mesopotamia. They are outstanding examples of the fact that even thousands of years ago life flourished in the desert. A precondition for this was the existence of mountains on the edges of the desert, from which rivers flowed into the interior. Mountains force air to rise, cooling it, which lowers the saturation point and increases precipitation. In the case of the Kopet Dag Mountains on the border between Turkmenistan and Iran these rains, provoked by an orographic lift, directly feed the rivers.[29] The significantly higher mountains of Pamir and Kun Lun, by contrast,

Sand dunes more than 100 m high are a distinguishing feature of the Taklamakan Desert north of Qiemo, Xinjiang, north-western China.

A fisherman cuts a hole in the ice of the frozen Aral Sea in order to fish, western Kazakhstan.

function as enormous reservoirs for the snow and ice that swell the rivers during the annual snowmelt.

In north-western China the Tian Shan Mountains divide the Dzungarian Desert in the north from the Taklamakan Desert in the south. Spreading over 338,000 km^2, the Taklamakan is, after the Rub' al Khali in Arabia, the second largest purely sand desert in the world. Since it occupies an exceptionally continental location, is surrounded to the south, west, and north by high mountains that repel rain clouds and in the east meets up with the Kum Tag desert, its climate is hyper-arid, with less than 20 mm of annual precipitation and in parts up to 2,900 mm of potential evaporation. Although today the desert consists of shifting sand dunes, a glacial sea occupied the land until about 800,000 years ago, after which the climate dried up dramatically. As in the Kara Kum Desert, however, rivers running north from the Kun Lun Mountains once crossed the desert and provided the basis for life on both the southern edge and in the interior of the Taklamakan. At the turn of the third to the second millennium BC at the latest, there were Bronze Age settlements along the rivers and in the oases, which survived by means of livestock breeding and irrigated agriculture.[30] Because these rivers shifted significantly in the flat desert landscape and held gradually less water from about 1000 BC on, the oases and settlements moved southward in tandem, so that one could speak of 'wandering oases'.

North-east of the Taklamakan there are further deserts. First is the desert of Lop Nor, which can also be regarded as the eastern part of the Taklamakan, and the deserts of Gashun Gobi east of Xinjiang and Badain Jaran and Tengger in Inner Mongolia, with

the latter two belonging to the Gobi. Finally the Yellow River divides the Tengger Desert from the deserts of Mu Us in the centre and Kubuqi in the north of the steppe-like Ordos plateau. The largest of all the Central Asian deserts is the Gobi at just under 1,300,000 km^2. This desert forms a complex system of steppe, scree, sand, and stone deserts and occupies more than half of the Republic of Mongolia. Only 10 percent of Mongolia is forested and just one percent is arable, hence the extraordinarily low population density of just under two inhabitants per square kilometre, although this was higher in the Middle Ages. Though just three percent of the Gobi, whose Mongol name means 'stone desert', is made up of pure sand dunes, the winds that blast to the south and south-east allow these to advance further and, along with the deserts of Mu Us and Kubuqi, threaten Beijing in the medium term.

A few of the Central Asian deserts, such as the Kara Kum and Kyzyl Kum, expanded or appeared in the late Middle Pleistocene (*ca.* 400,000–126,000 years ago), which shrank the territory of hominins that are extinct today and limited their mobility. When one considers the simultaneous expansion of deserts in Arabia, Syria, Mesopotamia and Iran, this climatic development may have effectively separated Africa from Asia for about 300,000 years, with the consequence that human evolution during the second half of the Pleistocene may have developed independently on the two continents.[31]

The American geography professor Ellsworth Huntington (1876–1947) was one of the first researchers to recognise, in the early twentieth century, a close connection between climatic conditions and economic options and to perceive the powerful

At the Kyzyl-Art pass, 4,336 m above sea level, on the border between Tajikistan and Kyrgyzstan.

influence of climatic changes on the life circumstances of people within a given climatic zone. He carried out research trips to Turkmenistan in 1903–4 and the Taklamakan Desert and Lop Nor in 1905–6, studying the geology and archaeology of the region. This gave him insight into the causal relationship between an initial geological and geographical location, climatic changes and the effects on human history.[32] A river in the midst of an inhospitable desert enables life to flourish by making productive arable agriculture possible. The drying up of the river as the result of climate change brings about the slow death of this green oasis and the transition to animal husbandry. Without falling into mechanistic climate determinism, it is possible to see in the history of Central Asia connections between societal changes, crises and corresponding climatic changes that deprived people of their means of sustenance. Major examples are the transition from an agrarian economy to one based on livestock breeding on the steppes during the third millennium BC or the immense migration of people that took place between the third and sixth centuries AD.

Although people long for stable climatic conditions and today feel threatened by dramatic climate events, if seen over the long term climate and weather are fundamentally unstable things. Climate change represents normality in the history of the Earth, as can be seen from two extremes in our planetary climate: during the Cryogenian (*ca.* 850–635 million years ago) an ice crust covered the entire Earth, except for the Equator; during the Cretaceous, however, the poles were free of ice. For its part, temperature has direct effects on the expanse of the oceans, as cold binds up water as ice: during warm periods sea levels rise and during cold periods they sink. For instance, during the last cold period, 24,000 to 16,000 years ago, global sea level was 125 m below the present level. At this time the British Isles were connected to Europe, and North America was linked with north-eastern Asia via the Bering land bridge.[33]

3. The factors determining climate

The Earth's climate is determined by five factors:[34] the orientation of the Earth to the sun, the sun's activity, the concentration of greenhouse gases, volcanic activity, and the atmospheric and oceanic currents.

The particular orientation of the Earth to the sun means that the amount of solar energy that reaches the Earth is variable over the long term for three reasons. First, the orbit of the Earth around the sun does not form a circle but rather an ellipse, and the sun does not lie in the centre of this ellipse; secondly, the relative inclination of the Earth's axis to the plane of the orbit fluctuates; and thirdly, the orientation of the Earth's axis changes cyclically. The combination of these three cyclical factors – the eccentricity of the Earth's orbit and the slope and the precession of its axis – has led in the last 800,000 years in the northern hemisphere to a basic trend of ice ages lasting about 100,000 years each, peppered with periods of extreme cold. Between each ice age, however, warmer intervals have appeared, lasting 5,000 to 17,000 years. Since our current warm period began about 12,000 years ago, its end, statistically speaking, is perhaps soon overdue.

The second climate-determining factor is the activity of the sun, which is a variable star. Depending on the level of the star's activity and differences in its magnetic field, it transmits differing amounts of heat energy to the Earth. Since the late 1940s the Earth has been receiving an unusually high level of energy from the sun, which contributes to so-called global warming. Also with regard to this parameter, statistical data, according to researchers at the Max Planck Institute, indicate a decrease in the presently high level of solar activity in the coming decades, which could likewise contribute to global cooling.[35]

Without the third factor, the greenhouse effect, there would be no life on our planet. The French physicist and mathematician

Hominin or hominid?

Before the spread of DNA analysis beginning in the late 1980s, it was considered proven that human beings and their ancestors were clearly distinct from great apes such as the chimpanzee, gorilla and orang-utan, so humans were subsumed under the term 'hominids' and the great apes and their ancestors under the term 'pongids'. Genetic research has shown, however, that we humans stand much more closely genetically to chimpanzees and gorillas than all three of these do to orang-utans. Thus it follows that the ancestors of the orang-utan branched off long before the most recent shared ancestor of humans, chimpanzees and gorillas. For this reason the term 'hominid' now refers to human beings and their ancestors as well as chimpanzees and gorillas and their ancestors. The term 'hominin' was introduced in order to distinguish us from the two African great apes. 'Hominin' refers only to humans and their ancestors, while 'gorillini' is used for gorillas and their ancestors and 'panini' for chimpanzees and their ancestors.[36]

Jean Baptiste Fourier (1768–1830) discovered as early as 1822 that certain gases in the atmosphere absorb the Earth's long-wave radiation. Most of the penetrating, shortwave solar radiation reach the Earth's surface and cloud layers and gets reflected into the atmosphere as long-wave terrestrial radiation. There greenhouse gases such as water vapour, carbon dioxide, ozone and methane absorb this radiation and return them half to the Earth and half into outer space. This natural greenhouse effect results in a warming of the Earth's surface by currently 33 °C; without this effect the mean temperature on the surface of the Earth would be -18 °C, instead of the current average of 14 to 15 °C. The greenhouse effect is not in itself a catastrophe but rather a normal condition necessary for life. Humanity has also experienced epochs significantly warmer than our own, such as during the Eemian interglacial period (*ca.* 126,000–115,000 years ago), when the average temperature was 5 °C higher.[37] There have been much higher concentrations of CO_2 in the atmosphere than at present, and this did not per se represent an apocalyptic disaster. During the Permian (*ca.* 299–251 million years ago) the concentration of CO_2 was about 900 ppm,[38] compared to the maximum concentration in 2008 of 385 ppm, and during the Triassic (251–199.6 million years ago) it even reached about 1,750 ppm[39] – almost five times the amount in 2008! During the Triassic, however, reptiles, especially dinosaurs, experienced an extraordinary flourishing on the supercontinent of Pangaea. And 55.8 million years ago, the CO_2 level surpassed 1,500 ppm during the 'Palaeocene-Eocene Thermal Maximum' (PETM) when global temperatures soared by 5 °C and all major ice sheets disappeared. This dramatic global warming of an already warm environment led to the emergence of several major modern mammalian orders.[40] A future increase in global temperature would, however, lead to a rise in sea level, submerging low-lying coast regions and islands.

The fourth climate-influencing factor is represented by strong volcanic eruptions that release huge amounts of aerosols such as sulphur dioxide into the atmosphere. If such mega-eruptions occur in the tropics, they can influence the global climate as aerosols trapped in the stratosphere reflect sunlight and thus less solar energy reaches the Earth, temporarily cooling the climate. One of the most famous examples in modern times was the eruption of the Mount Tambora volcano on the island of Sumbawa, Indonesia, from April to July 1815. In 1816, the world suffered a 'year without a summer', with correspondingly widespread crop failures.[41] A comparable event happened in 535 AD when an enormous volcanic eruption took place in Indonesia, with negative consequences for the entire Eurasian continent. Thus the Byzantine historian Procopius (*ca.* 500–562) noted that in the years 535 and 536 the sun shone only weakly.[42]

The major ocean currents and the atmospheric currents, also called jet streams, represent the fifth factor. Both the cold currents directed toward the Equator and the warm currents flowing to the poles, as well as polar front and subtropical jet streams, balance the weather between extremely hot and extremely cold regions, in that they inhibit an unchecked heating of the tropics and a similar cooling of the polar regions.

In the following chapters and volumes we will encounter many dramatic historical events that were set in motion by global climate changes. These should be distinguished from similarly appearing, narrowly defined regional climate shifts caused by earthquakes, changes in river courses, or anthropogenic factors such as the overuse of soil or bodies of water, overgrazing, widespread felling of forests, etc. Because the eastern part of Central Asia is generally more arid than the west, changes in climatic conditions there tend to have more dramatic consequences, since the situation can become life-threatening more quickly. Thus the peoples of western Central Asia were better able to adapt to negative climate changes than those in the east, who often decided to migrate. There is, however, no climate determinism that directs the course of history. People and societies react differently to comparable changes in their natural environment, depending on their degree of mobility, the organisation of the society, the available technologies, their own and their foreign neighbours' military capabilities, and the prevailing ideology.

II

The Settlement of Central Asia in the Palaeolithic

On the Birthplace and Antiquity of Man. *It is, therefore, probable that Africa was formerly inhabited by extinct apes closely allied to the gorilla and chimpanzee; and as these two species are now man's nearest allies, it is somewhat more probable that our early progenitors lived on the African continent than elsewhere.*

CHARLES DARWIN, *THE DESCENT OF MAN*, 1871[1]

The motifs of the origin, purpose and transience of human life belong to the age-old fundamental questions of human beings. Prior to the Enlightenment, these three questions remained the purview of philosophy, ethics and religion, after which the natural sciences began to emancipate themselves from belief in the supernatural and turned to the first fundamental question, that of our origin. It was primarily Charles Darwin (1809–82) who began the radical breaking of taboo and in 1859 explained the development of human beings as the product of natural evolution. In the model proposed by evolution there are for living things only two options: adaptation and reinvention or extinction. Twelve years later Darwin put forth the hypothesis that all modern human beings descended from a shared African ancestor. Was Darwin right? Is Africa the cradle of humanity? Or is Asia?

1. 'Out of Africa' or 'Out of Asia'?

In the Early Pleistocene in Asia there were presumably only the hominins *Homo erectus*, whose name means 'upright man', but by the Middle and Late Pleistocene (781,000–12,000 years ago) perhaps six different species of the genus Homo (man) inhabited the region. These were: *Homo erectus*; the ancestors of *Homo floresiensis*; *Homo denisova*, discovered in Central Asia; Neanderthals; maybe an 'archaic *Homo sapiens*'; and modern *Homo sapiens*.[2] The small-statured *Homo floresiensis*, discovered in 2003, died out over 12,000 years ago, leaving only our species, *Homo sapiens*. The variety of human species in Central and Southeast Asia raises the question of whether modern human beings may possibly have developed in Asia.

By the second half of the twentieth century almost no one contested the African origin of the first hominins. There are, however, two opposing schools of thought regarding the origin of human beings themselves. The 'Out of Africa' hypothesis postulates two or three significant migrations of early human species out of Africa. The first, of *Homo erectus*, took place about 1.8 million years ago, first to Asia and then to Europe, after which these hominins developed independently of each other on account of the isolation of their individual groups. A dissenting thesis, propagated especially in the United States, holds that *Homo erectus* refers only to an Asian line of descent and calls the further development of the *Homo erectus* remaining in Africa *Homo ergaster*, 'working man,' from which emerged *Homo heidelbergensis*, who settled in Europe some 600,000 years ago. Much later, about 100,000 to 130,000 years ago, the modern human being called *Homo sapiens* spread in a second or third wave from East Africa – first to the eastern Mediterranean coast and from there to Asia and Europe. In the process *Homo sapiens* is thought to have displaced and superseded all the other hominin species, including the Neanderthals, without interbreeding with them. For this reason, this hypothesis is also called the 'Replacement Hypothesis'. According to this theory, all human races have formed in a relatively short time out of this *Homo sapiens*, 'wise' or 'knowing' man.

The multiregional model, by contrast, postulates that the regional descendants of *Homo erectus* in Africa, Europe and Asia developed separately into modern human beings, with a continuous 'gene flow' on the edges of the centres of development ensuring anatomical and reproductive commonalities and preventing the development of regional divergent species. There is believed to have been no extinction of human species such as the Neanderthals,

Geological and prehistoric anthropological timetable

GEOLOGICAL CHRONOLOGY	AGE IN YEARS
Pliocene	5.332 – 2.588 million
Pleistocene	2.588 million – 12,000
Lower	2.588 million – 781,000
Middle	781,000 – 126,000
Upper	126,000 – 12,000
Holocene	12,000 – Today

ANTHROPOLOGICAL CHRONOLOGY	AGE IN YEARS
Palaeolithic	2.6 million – 11,700
Lower	2.6 million – 300,000
Middle	300,000 – 40,000
Upper	40,000 – 11,700
Mesolithic	11,700 – 8,500/5,500, depending on area of Central Asia
Neolithic	8,500/5,500 – 6,000/3,200, depending on area of Central Asia

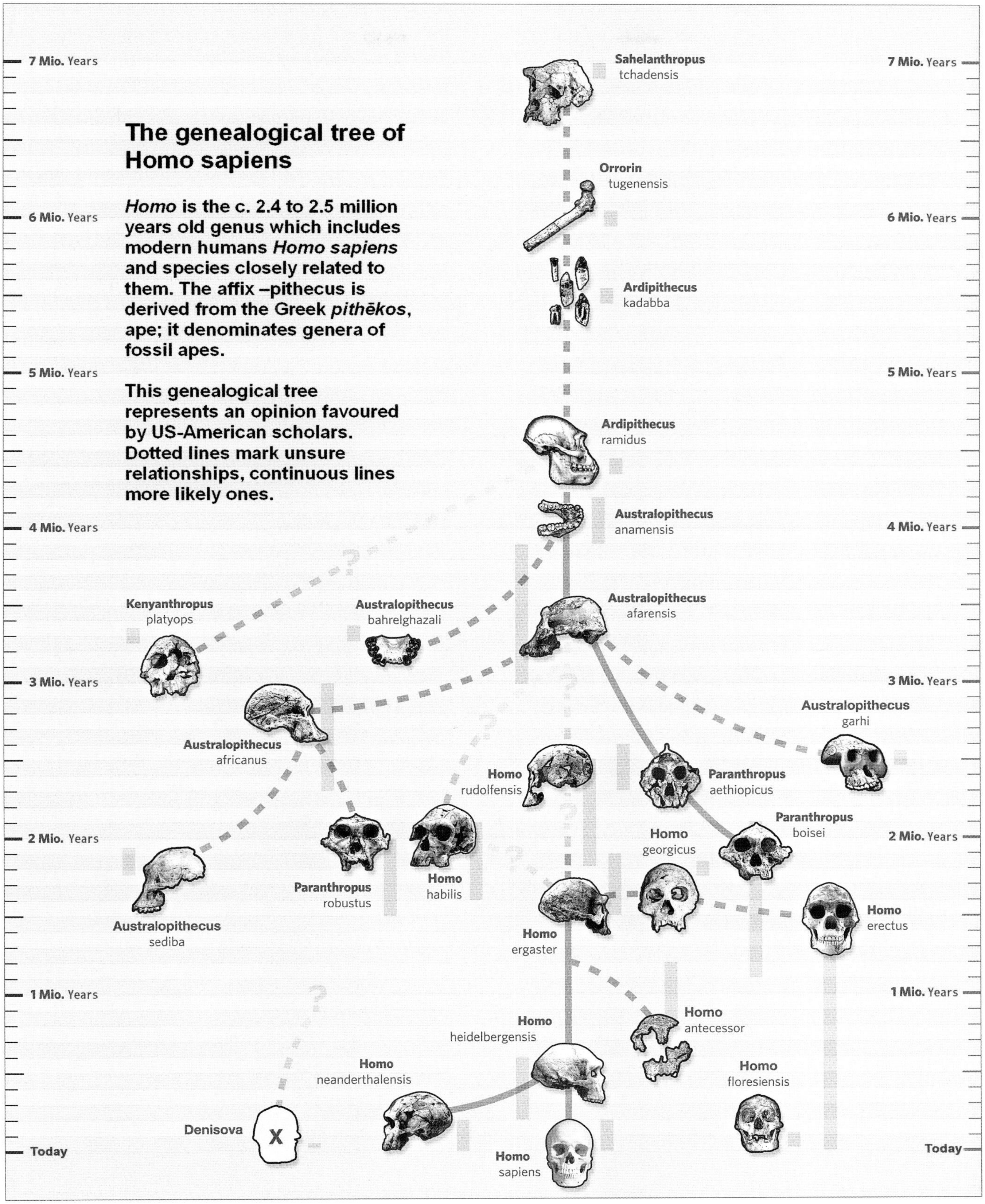

The genealogical tree of *Homo sapiens*.

but rather continuous interbreeding. Thus the individual human races arose hundreds of thousands of years ago, and different physical traits are in part a legacy of the different ways in which *Homo erectus* developed.[3] DNA analyses of modern human beings contradict this conclusion, however, as they show an overall strong uniformity of the human genotype of all races. The isolation of the individual hominin groups also makes the postulated gene flow unlikely. On the basis of additional genetic, anatomical and archaeological research, according to the current state of knowledge, the Out of Africa hypothesis has, broadly, prevailed.[4] However, the most recent DNA analyses of Neanderthals and two Denisova hominins from the southern Siberian Altai, as well as Chinese discoveries of a few skulls, more than 100,000 years old, which display characteristics of both *Homo erectus* and *Homo sapiens*, have called into question the 'Replacement Hypothesis'.

2. The earliest settlements of Central Asia

A global cold period led to an extreme drought in Africa 2.8 to 2.5 million years ago and the savannas rapidly expanded. In East Africa, out of the hominin *Australopithecus afarensis* developed the presumable ur-human *Homo rudolfensis*. Some 400,000 years later *Homo habilis*, the 'handy man', emerged. Since these hominins fashioned the first stone tools in the form of 'pebble tools', they freed themselves from direct dependence on their environment and began the Oldowan period. About 1.8 million years ago emerged *Homo erectus*, who used fire and began to make pear-shaped hand axes, worked on both sides, called bifaces, which made the butchering of meat much easier. The ability to use meat expanded the potential habitat for humans into non-tropical colder and drier regions where plant food was less abundant. These hand axes introduced the Palaeolithic era of the Acheulean, which slowly superseded the Oldowan period. With fire, protein sources could be cooked and stored frozen meat could be thawed. Fire also offered protection from cold and predators. Thanks to these capabilities, *Homo erectus* expanded its search for sustenance to the north and soon became the first hominin to leave Africa; the members of its species that stayed behind are also called *Homo ergaster*. In its migration to Asia *Homo erectus* proved to be a successful pioneer who met the challenges of new ecological surroundings with technological innovations.

Because the strongly continental and arid climate of Central Asia offered difficult living conditions even then, it is not surprising that the earliest traces of *Homo erectus* are found in the southern regions. In 1984 in south-western Eurasia in Dmanisi, Georgia, archaeologists came upon three mostly complete skulls and other fossils of a very early example of *Homo erectus*, who displayed a conspicuously smaller skull, with barely half the volume of ours. Nevertheless these early hominins possessed an exceptional social culture, since the toothless skull of an old man, no longer able to survive alone, indicates that the group living there cared for its old and impaired members. These 1.75-million-year-old fossils from the Lower Palaeolithic are among the oldest human discoveries found outside Africa.[5] Fossils up to 1.66 million years old from Java, Indonesia and northern China show that *Homo erectus* arrived in East and Southeast Asia not long after they reached Dmanisi in the Caucasus. Contemporaneous with the finds in Sangiran and Mojokerto on Java are those of Majuangou, which lies in the

Even today in mountainous regions of Central Asia the mountain goat is venerated as a symbol of life and fertility. Tashkurgan, Xinjiang, north-western China.

northern Chinese Nihewan Basin, 150 km west of Beijing; these are the oldest human fossils in East Asia.[6] Later discoveries of *Homo erectus* in China come from Yunxian in Hubei Province and from Lantian, Shaanxi, both of which are about 800,000 years old.[7]

Hand axes dated at 1.4 million years from Ubeidiya, in the valley of the Jordan River south of Lake Tiberias, are not only the oldest stone tools of the Acheulean outside of Africa but they also suggest that the Near East, perhaps together with the crossing of the then narrower and shallower Red Sea, was the most important route from Africa to Eurasia.[8]

The fossils from the famous archaeological site of Zhoukoudian, 50 km southwest of Beijing, are only half as old as those from Majuangou, but the rich trove provided significant knowledge about the development of humans in East Asia. The Swedish geologist Gunnar Andersson discovered the site and two apparently simian molars in 1921. Only five years later were they attributed to an unknown early human. A molar uncovered by the Swedish palaeontologist Anders Bohlin later laid the groundwork for the hypothesis of a new human species, *Sinanthropus pekinensis*, which was reclassified as *Homo erectus* in 1950.[9] A total of 28 sites in Zhoukoudian yielded human fossils, among them 14 skullcaps, from about 45 individuals, as well as animal fossils and tools made of stone, horn and bone. In the most important site, Locality 1, a former cave, the oldest tools were 720,000 years old. The human fossils showed that representatives of *Homo erectus* lived here with interruptions between about 690,000 and 420,000 years ago. It appears that these humans not only mastered fire but also engaged in violent conflicts, armed with clubs, which led to the death of inferior combatants; cannibalism was also not unknown to them. Likewise from Zhoukoudian, from Locality 4 and Locality 15 as well as the 'New Cave', come fossils as old as 250,000 years that serve for Chinese scholars as proof of the ostensible development of an archaic *Homo sapiens* within China.[10]

Slightly less than 1 million years ago, *Homo erectus* established a foothold in the heart of Central Asia, at least during times between ice ages.[11] As a precondition they must have adapted to the harsh continental climate, which required insulating clothing in the form of animal skins, protection from the elements, mastery of fire, and an economy based on hunting. Such an orientation toward the hunt, in turn, presupposed suitable weapons and the ability to plan, organise and successfully execute a hunt. Thanks to the prevailing winter cold, meat was easy to preserve and only had to be thawed with fire. Humans in Central Asia could survive only as adaptable and social beings. The oldest verifiable evidence from Central Asia comes from Kuldara in southern Tajikistan, where 880,000- to 995,000-year-old stone scrapers have been found. In addition, in the neighbouring site of Khonako II artefacts about 740,000 years old have been discovered. Lakhuti I, another nearby site, has yielded stone objects about 475,000 to 530,000 years old; of comparable age are the pebble tools from Karatau I south-east of Dushanbe.[12] Slightly more recent are the finds at Obi-Mazar (Lakhuti III), which are 380,000 to 425,000 years old, somewhat older than those from Kulbulak, at the western end of the Tian Shan mountains, where archaeologists discovered more than 70,000 (!) flint tools.[13]

Then, north-east of Tajikistan in the Kyrgyz part of Fergana, in the cave of Selungur 2,000 m above sea level, archaeologists came upon human fossils and stone tools that were dated to the Middle Palaeolithic and could be about 126,000 to 200,000 years old. It is unclear whether only descendants of *Homo erectus* lived in Selungur[14] or if Neanderthals, who left revealing traces in the cave of Teshik-Tash in southern Uzbekistan, did as well. Significantly older discoveries of stone implements have been made in the Karatau Mountains in southern Kazakhstan and on the western Kazakh peninsula of Mangyshlak, which have been attributed to the Early and Middle Palaeolithic.[15] In addition to over 100 Central Asian archaeological sites from the Lower and Middle Palaeolithic,[16] such as the Angara Culture's Makarovo IV west of Lake Baikal, the site in the basin of Issyk-Kul Lake in northern Kyrgyzstan, or the Bolshoi Gluchoj cave in the Urals,[17] Mongolia has yielded some informative finds. In 2006, for the first time, a well-preserved pre-Holocene skullcap of an archaic *Homo sapiens* from the Upper Pleistocene was discovered here. The skullcap is about 20,000 years old and was found near Salkhit in Mongolia, north-east of the capital Ulaan Baatar.[18]

In Mongolia, the cave of Tsagaan Agui in the Gobi Desert in the south of the country is especially outstanding, for here researchers have access to 700,000 years of stratigraphy. Belonging to the earliest layer are hand axes of the Acheulean type, worked on both sides. These clearly contradict the assertion found in older literature that such tools had not reached Central and East Asia. The theory of a so-called 'Movius Line', introduced in 1948 by the American archaeologist Hallam Movius, says that the ostensibly sophisticated technology of the Acheulean did not spread further north-east of a border stretching from the Caucasus to India and that the corresponding populations on this side of this boundary remained at a lower technological level. Further discoveries of bifaces from Central Asia, such as those from Mangyshlak in western Kazakhstan[19] and the 800,000-year-old sites of Yunxian and Lantian in China – both 200,000 years older than the earliest 'biface' of Europe – belie this theory.[20] In Tsagaan Agui layers from the Middle and Late Palaeolithic follow the Early Palaeolithic band. Buddhist votive gifts and a Chinese coin from the eleventh century[21] show that the cave offered people shelter into our own era.

2.1 Neanderthals and *Homo sapiens* – supersession or interbreeding?

The first fossils of *Homo neanderthalensis* were discovered in Belgium in 1829 and on Gibraltar in 1848, but only after the find in 1856 of a curious, flat skullcap with a pronounced supraorbital ridge in the Neander valley in Germany were these fossils recognised the following year as the now world-renowned early human. This realisation, two years before the seminal book *On the Origin of Species*, represents the advent of palaeoanthropology, and the Neanderthal was quickly seized upon as a kind of 'chief witness for the theory of evolution'.[22] The site in the Neander valley was 42,000 years old; as of today bones from more than 400 individuals of *Homo neanderthalensis* have been discovered worldwide.

From whom did the Neanderthals descend and how close do they stand to us genetically? Science was preoccupied with these questions, especially the latter, for more than a century. Because there is evidence that Neanderthals and *Homo sapiens* lived near each other for millennia in Europe and the Near East,[23] the questions arise of whether they interbred and whether their offspring were fertile. If such mixed offspring could reproduce, Neanderthals and sapiens do not represent two separate species; if they were infertile, however, Neanderthals and sapiens would be two distinct species, such as the horse and the donkey, which can interbreed but whose offspring are barren. Investigation of this palaeogenetic question is at the same time an investigation into our own ancestral heritage.

A widely accepted hypothesis assumes that some 800,000 to 900,000 years ago a speciation significant for human history took place in Africa, leading to two distinct lines of descent. *Homo heidelbergensis*, descended from *Homo ergaster*, migrated from Africa to Europe. Here he encountered the somewhat older hominins called *Homo cepranensis*[24] and *Homo antecessor*,[25] perhaps in Italy or Spain, and developed into *Homo heidelbergensis* more narrowly defined, from which came the Neanderthals.[26]

In Africa, by contrast, Heidelberg Man, more broadly defined, sometimes interpreted as a variation of *Homo rhodensiensis*,[27] evolved further into an archaic *Homo sapiens*, of which the 154,000- to 160,000-year-old Herto Man, discovered in 1997 in the Afar Triangle in Ethiopia, may be the earliest ancestor. This discovery attests to the Out of Africa theory in that, as genetic studies suggest, modern humans first appeared in Africa less than 200,000 years ago. This hominin not only possessed a skull volume of 1,450 cubic centimetres, at least equal to that of modern humans, but also appears to have performed post-mortem rituals. This can be deduced from the skull of a youth that was stripped of its flesh shortly after death and polished clean.[28] Modern *Homo sapiens* then emerged from this Herto hominin, advancing into the Near East some 100,000 to 130,000 years ago and starting to spread worldwide about 80,000 years ago. According to this hypothesis, three great human species lived in the prehistoric world at the start of the Middle Pleistocene: *Homo heidelbergensis/rhodesiensis* in Africa, *Homo heidelbergensis*, narrowly defined, in Europe, and *Homo erectus* in Asia, with these last two leading to evolutionary dead ends.

When modern humans advanced into Europe 45,000 years ago, two human species encountered each other after having been genetically separate for hundreds of thousands of years. The latest evaluations, based on DNA analyses of Neanderthals and *Homo sapiens*, show that the two evolutionary lines, one leading to Neanderthals and the other to modern humans, split about 516,000 years ago.[29] Until recently the overwhelming majority of researchers supported the idea that Neanderthals and modern humans did not interbreed. Since 2010, however, it has been shown that Neanderthals and sapiens interbred not just in isolated cases, which would result merely in infertile hybrids, but rather intermixed, since as much as 4 percent of the genetic material of the Neanderthals can be found in modern humans. This consistency can be found between Stone Age DNA and that of modern Europeans, Asians and peoples of Oceania, but not with African DNA; hence this intermixing must have occurred outside Africa, but before the ancestors of Europeans and Asians split off from each other. This intermixing presumably took place in the Near East, 50,000 to 100,000 years ago, when an ice age between *ca.* 115,000 and 65,000 BC forced Neanderthals out of Central Europe southward.

A study, published in March 2010, of the mitochondrial DNA[30] of a 30,000- to 48,000-year-old finger bone from a Denisova girl showed twice as much genetic separation from modern human *Homo sapiens* as the separation between Neanderthals and modern humans. The complete DNA analysis of the nucleus, published in December 2010, as well as an earlier study of an archaic-looking molar of another young Denisova adult, brought to light very surprising results: the Denisova hominins, whose remains were found in a cave in the southern Siberian Altai Mountains, were a sister group of the Neanderthals, from whom they branched off about 300,000 years ago. The Denisova genetic material is twice as far removed from that of today's European and Asiatic people as the Neanderthals are from modern Europeans and Asians, but it shows significant proximity to today's Melanesians of Papua New Guinea. The intermixing of Denisova hominins and the ancestors of the Melanesians presumably took place not in southern Siberia but in Southeast Asia. The researchers concluded: 'We estimate that 2.5% (+/- 0.6%) of the genomes of non-African populations derive from Neanderthals, in agreement with our previous estimate of 1–4%. In addition, we estimate that 4.8% (+/- 0.5%) of the genomes of Melanesians derive from Denisovans. Altogether, as much as 7.4% (+/- 0.8%) of Melanesians may thus derive from recent admixture with archaic hominins.'[31] The first complete decipherment of the genome of an Australian Aboriginal published in September 2011 showed a similar genetic proximity to Denisovians as do Melanesians.[32]

With regard to eastern Eurasia, the authors state 'These results show that on the Eurasian mainland there existed at least two forms of archaic hominins in the Upper Pleistocene. A western Eurasian form with morphological features that are commonly used to define as Neanderthals, and an eastern form to which the Denisova individuals belong.'[33] Interestingly, the Denisovan hominins did not contribute to the genetic makeup of the neighbouring Chinese and Mongols.

On the basis of these findings, the research team from the Max Planck Institute in Leipzig concluded that the Out-of-Africa theory remains valid insofar as the great preponderance of genetic variations that are spread outside of Africa originated in Africa: 'The vast majority of genetic variants that exist at appreciable frequency came from Africa with the spread of anatomically modern humans.'[34] The pure 'Replacement Hypothesis', however, cannot be sustained. It may be supposed that an 'Assimilation Out-of-Africa' theory will supersede the hitherto existing 'Replacement Out-of-Africa' theory.

The cave of Shanidar, inhabited by Neanderthals 80,000 to 60,000 years ago, northern Iraq.

Neanderthals were well adapted to a cold and harsh climate; they were of powerful, muscular build, somewhat smaller than modern Europeans but with a slightly larger brain. Their skulls were elongated, and the flat, projecting brow, as well as the pronounced supraorbital ridge, lent them an archaic appearance. Besides presumably cooked plants, meat was most prominent on the menu of Neanderthals, who, contrary to earlier ideas, did not eat carrion but instead actively hunted. During group hunts, which required planning and organisation, they used not only stones but also wooden lances and darts. Thanks to such long-range weapons, which were invented by *Homo heidelbergensis* about 270,000 to 400,000 years ago, it was possible to hunt large game such as wild horses, mammoths, woolly rhinoceroses and cave bears.[35] The animals were skinned, so that the Neanderthals could protect themselves from the cold with fur clothing. Contrary to general opinion, the Neanderthals were not pure cave dwellers, but also built a kind of tent at the entrances to their caves for protection and on the steppes probably constructed very simple shelters from mammoth tusks and bones. The remains of such shelters can be found on the western edge of Central Asia near Molodova in the Ukraine, among other places.[36]

It is unclear why Neanderthals left no traces after *ca.* 26,000 BC, after they had lived for nearly 10,000 years alongside *Homo sapiens* of the Cro-Magnon type. Presumably a combination of climatic, economic, technological and physiological factors led to the extinction of the Neanderthals. From 60,000 to 25,000 years ago the European climate oscillated rapidly several times between longer cold periods and short warm periods. This cycle peaked 30,000 to 26,000 years ago in a cold period, coupled with devastating loess storms, which damaged the vegetation layer.[37] The Neanderthals, who were dependent on eating meat, presumably could not adapt sufficiently to these volatile climate changes and their consequences, such as suddenly changed fauna that required new hunting weapons and tactics as well as preservation methods. In addition, the anatomical structure of Neanderthals meant they needed more calories than *Homo sapiens*, who, for their part, were more agile and mobile.[38] Analyses of comparable skeletons also suggest that modern Cro-Magnon humans were healthier and, in particular, suffered fewer broken bones than did Neanderthals, which indicates a greater life expectancy. Whether the Neanderthals' allegedly lesser speech abilities played a role is unknown.

The migration of *Homo sapiens* out of Africa

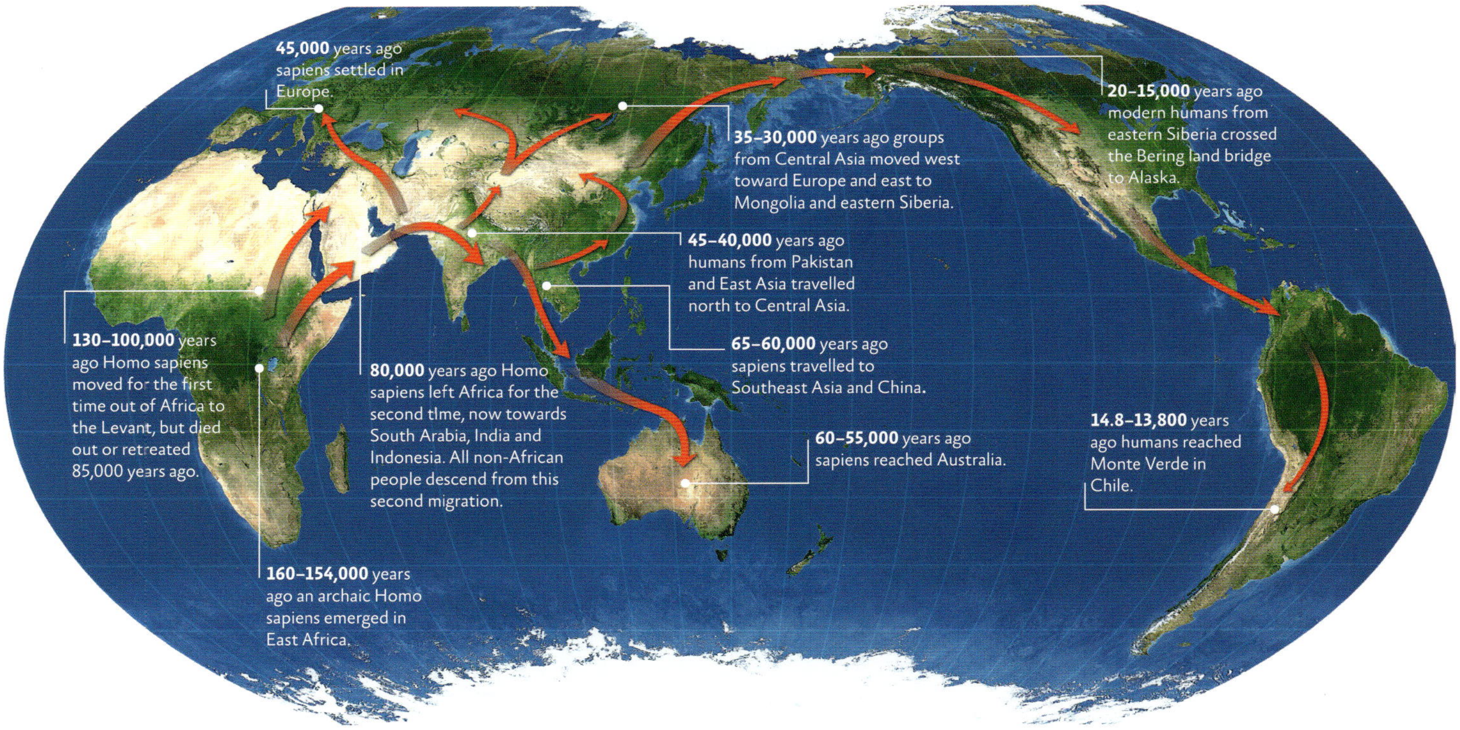

The latest research highlights two additional, related, factors that contributed to the extinction of the Neanderthals. These are their low reproductive ability – female Neanderthals matured later, gave birth only once every four years and had a relatively shorter life expectancy than *Homo sapiens*. As a result the Neanderthals had an extremely low population density. Presumably hardly more than 7,000 to at most 10,000 Neanderthals lived in Europe at one time, which meant they were highly vulnerable to epidemics, famine, or a more successful and probably better armed group of humans.[39]

Archaeological and palaeontological finds in Europe show that the geographic centre of the Neanderthal world lay between the Atlantic and the Black Sea. At times, however, it extended into the Near East, the Caucasus and Central Asia, as far as the Okladnikov cave in the Russian Altai. Presumably the Eemian interglacial period allowed the Neanderthals to settle in southern Siberia and Central Asia. Notably, the northern boundary of the Neanderthals' range in both Europe and Central Asia lies near the 52nd parallel, which bears witness to the adaptation of these prehistoric peoples to the harsh northern climate.

In Central Asia there have been over 100 discoveries from the period of the later Middle Palaeolithic and the early Late Palaeolithic (*ca.* 120,000 to 30,000 years ago) that include so-called Mousterian stone tools, which are characterised by sharp scrapers and flints with thin blades.[40] Although Neanderthals used Mousterian tools almost exclusively, one cannot automatically conclude that finds of such tools were necessarily associated with Neanderthals. This is because early sapiens and descendants of *Homo erectus* also used them. Just as we cannot assume that the distribution of cultural objects corresponds with the distribution of an associated language, we cannot assume that the distribution of human species corresponds with these objects either. Thus we associate a trove of Mousterian objects with Neanderthals only when contemporaneous corresponding bones are also found there.

A few Central Asian Neanderthal sites provide interesting evidence of their unexpectedly well-developed social relationships. While the 30,000- to 38,000-year-old bones found by Okladnikov attest to an advance of the Neanderthals almost to Mongolia, three sites are known in Uzbekistan: the Obi Rakhmat grotto north of the present capital of Tashkent with 30,000 (!) items about 70,000 years old;[41] the caves of Anghilak, in the south-eastern part of the country, with 40,000-year-old artefacts and the most interesting, that of Teshik Tash. Here in 1938 the Soviet archaeologist A.P. Okladnikov discovered not only many Mousterian tools but also a well-preserved skeleton, including the skull, of an eight- or nine-year-old Neanderthal child who died some 60,000 to 70,000 years ago. Assuming that the identification of this skeleton and the estimate of its age are correct, this refutes the theory sometimes put forth that Neanderthals first entered Central Asia about 35,000 to 40,000 years ago in reaction to the advancing sapiens.[42]

The young deceased Neanderthal was obviously intentionally buried; six pairs of horns of the Siberian mountain goat called 'Capra Sibirica' encircled the corpse, with the horns stuck point-down in the ground and oriented toward the skull.[43] This arrangement surely was not coincidental but rather manifests a burial rite; this represents one of the oldest gravesites in the world.[44] The Soviet archaeologist Vadim Masson interpreted this ritual as the start of totemism and compared it to the bear cult of the European Mousterian.[45] Interestingly, in the Pamir Mountains of Tajikistan the mountain goat is still venerated today; its horns often adorn the enclosure walls around Islamic sanctuaries.

Perhaps the humans of that time were familiar not only with burial rituals but also with cultic sites, as the cave of Ogzi-Kichik in southern Tajikistan suggests. There in 1979 Vadim Ranov discovered, together with about 10,000 artefacts, a 30,000-year-old oval stone arrangement without reference to a burial, with a pair of ibex horns on the end of the oval stuck in the ground.[46] Finally, a Neanderthal skull that is at least 30,000 years old was found south-west of Ogzi-Kichik, near the stone shelter of Dara-i Kur in north-eastern Afghanistan.

Although the cave of Shanidar in northern Iraq lies beyond Central Asia, it must be mentioned on account of its significance for the early settlement of Eurasia. In the 1950s in a back tunnel of the cave Ralph Solecki unearthed nine buried Neanderthals, 60,000 to 80,000 years old, of which skeletons I, III, and IV are the most famous.[47] The individual called Shanidar I was a 40- to 50-year-old man who was crippled by healed injuries suffered earlier and would not have been able to survive without help from others. From this Solecki inferred that these Neanderthals recognised a kind of social responsibility and cared for the sick and the elderly. Shanidar III, by contrast, died of a spear wound to the left lung; whether this was the result of a hunting accident or an intentional act of aggression is unclear.[48] The individual known as Shanidar IV, a 30- to 45-year-old man, was laid in a foetal position on a pallet of branches and twigs and likely covered with flowers that impeded inflammations. This was thus a planned, ritual Neanderthal burial like that at Teshik Tash.[49] The 40-m-wide, 45-m-deep, and 12- to 18-m-high cave was divided by stone walls and provided shelter to some 20 families. Holes bored in the ground in front of the rock face could indicate that the people stretched a kind of tent made of animal skins in front of the cave.

The modern human *Homo sapiens* left their East African homeland twice. They first set out for the Levant some 100,000 to 130,000 years ago, moving into the fertile bands on the eastern shore of the Mediterranean that stretch from Gaza in the south to north-western Syria in the north. This early *Homo sapiens* presumably died out here more than 80,000 years ago or returned from here to Africa. A few millennia later, however, modern humans began their successful settlement of the entire world. The climate was much drier than today and the sea level correspondingly low, which made it possible to cross the then-small Red Sea to reach the south-western Arabian Peninsula.[50] From here sapiens headed east toward India and Indonesia, from where they travelled to Australia about 60,000 to 55,000 years ago. A few millennia earlier, modern humans from India had settled in Southeast Asia and south-eastern China.

Only 10,000 years later did sapiens move from western Asia to the north and west, presumably because the climatic conditions at that time allowed for settlement. About 45,000 years ago modern humans reached Europe. At about the same time sapiens, coming from both Pakistan and East Asia, arrived in Central Asia, from where a few Central Asian sapiens turned west toward Eastern Europe, while others marched on toward Mongolia and eastern Siberia. DNA analyses indicate that the ethnic distinctions between European and Sino-Mongolid modern humans began to develop slowly about 60,000 years ago, and more than 40,000 years later – about 15,000 to 10,000 years ago – the differentiation of the current Asian ethnicities emerged.[51]

It is certainly conceivable that sapiens in the Siberian Altai encountered representatives of the Denisova ancient humans, whose genetic difference from sapiens is twice as great as that between Neanderthals and sapiens. For this reason the evolutionary anthropologist Johannes Krause of the Max Planck Institute has suggested that at one time in the Altai, which is about the size of Texas, three different human species lived simultaneously.[52] Before the end of the last ice age, presumably about 15,000 to 20,000 years ago, sapiens from eastern Siberia crossed the Bering land bridge, at that time dry land, which linked Asia with Alaska.[53]

3. The birth of art

Just before the start of the Upper Palaeolithic, *ca.* 42,500 years ago,[54] a millennia-long cultural revolution began, marking the start of the pictorial, figurative and musical arts. Art blossomed quite suddenly, like a creative big bang, from the Iberian Peninsula in the west to Mongolia in the east. Perhaps it was the ecological conditions – extended cold periods, broad grass steppes, and changing fauna – which forced early humans to adopt a

Rock painting of two mammoths in the cave of Khoit Zenger Agui, Khovd Aimag, western Mongolia, *ca.* 13,000–15,000 BC.

The world's oldest portrayal of a Bactrian camel; rock painting in the cave of Khoit Zenger Agui, Khovd Aimag, western Mongolia, *ca.* 13,000–15,000 BC.

Rock painting of a bear hunt: from left to right, a hunter with a bird's head, a boar and two bears. Shakti, Pamir Mountains, Tajikistan, *ca.* 8000 BC.

mobile way of life. As they lived mainly off the hunt and secondarily from the gathering of edible plants, they had to follow the migration of animals. This led to social relations developing over large distances, which enabled the exchange of goods and pictorial styles. Examples of this are the snails from the Mediterranean used as jewellery and found in Central Europe, cave paintings, and the small, amply proportioned female figurines called 'Venus statues', which are found from Western Europe to Lake Baikal.

Of course, earlier human species such as the Neanderthals also exhibited an aesthetic sense, which may be seen in the symmetrical, superbly crafted hand axes of the Middle Palaeolithic, whose formal perfection far exceeds their functional purpose. An artistic engagement of the human being with himself and his world first began in the Upper Palaeolithic, as the more ancient, *ca.* 77,000-year-old piece of ochre engraved with lines from Blombos, South Africa, is certainly an artefact but hardly a work of art.[55] In the Upper Palaeolithic, however, cognitive abilities arising from interaction with the human environment enabled the creation of works of art in the form of colourful cave and rock paintings; small, portable figures of animals and people; and simple wind instruments.

While in Europe the earliest cave paintings were made in the Chauvet cave (France) 30,000 to 33,000 years ago, the oldest discovery in Central Asia were painted some 15,000 years later.[56]

The earliest rock paintings in Central Asia are in the cave of Khoit Zenger Agui in the province of Khovd in western Mongolia.[57] In the depths of the cave, where semi-darkness prevails, one can recognise on a pinkish-yellow limestone background contour drawings of animals, as well as arrows and dots, drawn in brown and reddish ochre tones. All the animals are shown in profile and consist at most of an outline. They represent wild sheep, ibexes, antelopes, a wild, two-humped camel and giant ostriches, as well as two mammoths or a small elephant of the species *Elephas namadicus*.[58] These last two animals provide evidence of the age of the paintings, since the mammoth and the *Elephas namadicus* died out in Mongolia 15,000 years ago at the latest; this is thus the lower limit of the dating. At that time a warm interim period forced both species to migrate north into colder Siberia. Simultaneously with the mammoth, or shortly thereafter, the ostrich also died out in Mongolia. Petrified ostrich eggshells show that the species was once much more widespread. The portrayal of the camel is also highly significant. In the first place, it is the oldest representation

View from the Shakti cave, located 4,199 m above sea level, on the Pamirs, Murgab District, Gorno-Badakhshan, eastern Tajikistan.

in the world of a two-humped, Bactrian camel. In addition, a slightly curved line drawn under the animal indicates a sand dune and a second line above it shows the horizon, lending the drawing a hint of three-dimensionality.[59]

As on a palimpsest, somewhat later portrayals of Siberian deer heads, snakes and arrows overlay the Palaeolithic paintings; it appears that the original pictures were reinterpreted as a hunting scene. In the Palaeolithic rock paintings of Khoit Zenger the complete absence of human representations also stands out; the animal reigns supreme in art and presumably also in myth.

Of a somewhat later date are the wonderfully well-preserved rock paintings of the abri of Shakti in south-eastern Tajikistan. The figures, drawn in ochre pigments of various shades, date from the early Mesolithic and are about 10,000 years old. They are found in the Pamir Mountains at a height of 4,199 m above sea level in a long dry riverbed, and are the highest Stone Age rock paintings in the world. The rock drawings are the work of people who came from western Tajikistan and were the first to settle in the eastern Pamir Mountains, at the end of the ice age after the retreat of the glaciers. At that time, the start of the Holocene, the climate in the eastern Pamir Mountains was warmer and more humid than today, offering the people a seasonal livelihood. In the summer hunters went up into the mountains, where they hunted red deer and boars. These hunters used the abri of Shakti, where they drew on the rock faces animal and human figures that most likely were related to hunt magic.

Today, however, this part of the Pamirs is a desolate wasteland of rocks and rubble, devoid of vegetation; even nomads can no longer live there. The French naturalist and hunter Vicomte Edmond de Poncins reported the impressions of his 1893 travels there as follows:

> The words at the start of Dante's Inferno came to mind: *'Abandon hope, all you who enter here'*. Regardless of one's ideas of desolation, desert, and aridity, the view of Kyzyl Art [the stone desert surrounding Shakti] will exceed all expectations. One could believe himself to be the only person who had ever seen this endless, accursed land, but the bleached bones that indicate the direction to follow show that others have come before.[60]

The abri of Shakti was discovered by archaeologists by chance in 1958, when they sought refuge from the weather. The cave-like shelter, oriented to the north, has an opening that is about 6.5 m wide and 8 m high. It is less than 4 m deep, but nonetheless offers protection from sun and rain. The drawings on limestone are arranged on a 250-cm-long frieze about 160 to 200 cm above the ground on the southern side of the cave. Of the seven figures, four are clearly recognisable: to the far left a 23-cm-tall man, holding a club, approaches three rather large animals; he resembles a bird and has a bird's head. The figure could represent a hunter wearing a bird mask and a bird-like costume as camouflage, a hunting tactic still used today in Central Asia and Mongolia. To the right stands the 40-cm-long figure of a boar, turned away from the hunter; it has either fallen into a trap or is surrounded by highly stylised hunters. To the right of the boar a 60-cm-long bear is ready to spring to the left, as if to attack the boar; below the bear are stuck in the ground one or two spears, with which it has been injured. To the far right stands an 85-cm-long bear, looking to the right, toward which fly three arrows from different directions; the scene portrays a bear hunt.[61] These rock paintings are part of the **Markansu** culture of the eastern Pamirs, to which the Mesolithic site at Oshkhona also belongs. Appearing in the eastern Pamirs at the same time as the Markansu culture was the Mesolithic culture of **Ishtyk**, whose stone tools displayed similarities to finds made in northern Afghanistan, which, for their part, were influenced by early Mesolithic cultures of south-western Central Asia.[62]

Just 2 km from Shakti is the shelter of Kurteke, 4,020 m above sea level, with traces of Neolithic drawings. Also close to Shakti, near the Naiza Tash pass, 4,137 m above sea level, there is another rock shelter with a few Neolithic paintings, presumably portraying a hunting scene.[63] Dating from the same epoch are the rock paintings in the cave of Ak Cunkur, at a height of 3,151 m above sea level in far north-eastern Kyrgyzstan on the border with China. The 45-m-long cave features hunting and dancing scenes drawn in ochre pigments that, as the author discovered in 2004, are no longer recognisable as they lie under a thick layer of soot.[64]

In contrast to the rock paintings of Khoit Zenger, in those of Tajikistan and Kyrgyzstan human figures clearly appear in the context of a hunt in at least three of the four caves. Thanks to the invention of the bow almost *ca.* 12,000 years ago[65] and the increased organisational abilities of the Mesolithic and Neolithic people, hunts could be more efficiently organised. Among the preparations for a successful hunt were attempts to actively influence elements of the environment. Presumably the rock paintings portraying hunting scenes had a magical relationship to the hunt preparations, whether as a wish that powerful spirits would provide for a successful hunt or that the corresponding animals would increase and remain in their usual habitats.

A somewhat different kind of coloured rock painting is found in the southern Urals in the Palaeolithic caves of Kapova and Ignateva, east of the city of Ufa. More than 50 drawings of mammoths, horses, a rhinoceros and possibly an ox, as well as unidentifiable beings and geometric figures, adorn the limestone walls of the Kapova cave. These drawings are divided into eight groups over the three levels of the cave. Most notable is a 35-cm-tall anthropomorphic figure consisting of a human torso and arms and a horse's legs; the head is no longer discernible. The colours used for the 14,000- to 16,000-year-old drawings were mostly ochre in various shades, ranging from a light red to a dark red-brown and purple-brown, with these different ochre tones being produced by the burning of iron ore or iron concretations. Added to these was the colour black, which was made from charcoal or manganese oxide.[66] On the basis of this discovery archaeologists assume that this complex cave had a cultic purpose and did not serve as a residence.

The humans of that time sheltered from cold, rain and predators not only in the caves or abris. They also built dwellings made of mammoth bones and tusk on terraces above a nearby canyon. Over the top of these makeshift dwellings, which were sunk slightly into the ground, they laid animal skins sewn together with sinew and bone needles. About 40 tusks driven into the ground formed supports for the roof and the entryway; on the ground, between the tusks, lay mammoth thighbones and skulls. Jawbones usually extended between these lower halves of the walls and the roof. The mammoth dwellings had a circular or oval floor plan of about 5 to 7 m in diameter and offered shelter to eight to ten people.[67] In Mezin, Ukraine, archaeologists found the remains of five such dwellings, consisting of 1,350 bones from at least 116 animals. At Mezhirich four such houses were discovered, the largest of which alone used 385 bones from 95 animals. Very similar dwellings made of mammoth bones were likewise found near Malt'a west of Lake Baikal. They usually did not stand alone but rather formed small settlements of three to six dwellings. These dwellings represent not only one of the earliest forms of architecture but also of the artistic embellishment of human habitations. The walls of Dwelling 1 in Mezin were decorated with zigzags, parallel lines and chevrons in reddish yellow pigments obtained from hematite and jarosite.[68]

These settlements show that in the Upper Palaeolithic southern Siberia and neighbouring Ukraine were rather well settled – in

Rock painting in the Kapova cave in the southern Urals, Russia. From left to right, a horse, a mammoth, a rhinoceros or a mammoth, a trapeze-shaped object, *ca.* 12,000–14,000 BC.

the Ukraine alone more than 500 Upper Palaeolithic archaeological sites have been found. They also indicate that the big game hunters of the Eurasian 'mammoth steppe' were semi-sedentary. Based on spear tips made of mammoth bones and the bones of slain bison and mammoths, which were found in the valley of a narrow canyon, the archaeologist Pidoplichko opined that the entire adult population of the settlement, including women, participated in the hunt. A few drove the animals over the ledge of a steep canyon, while others killed them with spears and presumably also spear-throwers as soon as they reached the valley floor. Such two-part spear-throwers had an effective range of about 30 m, and the spears reached a launch speed of more than 100 km/hr.[69]

The people also crafted arrowheads, hammers, needles and scrapers from mammoth bones and sharp awls from the shinbones of hares.[70] As long as sufficient big game lived within a habitat – the mammoth bone settlements stood dozens of kilometers apart – the hunters in it remained sedentary. According to Pidoplichko's estimate, these settlements lasted seven to 20 years, after which hunting communities moved on.[71]

At the 14,000- to 17,000-year-old settlement of Mezhirich, archaeologists also discovered jewellery in the form of carved mammoth bones coloured with ochre, small, flat, stylised female figurines and a rare engraved, flat mammoth bone. The archaeologist Ninelj Kornietz believes that mammoth bone dwellings, trees and a river are recognisable in the engraved forms. This would indicate that the piece was a kind of map. If this is true, it would represent by far the oldest map in the world and would attest to great imaginative abilities of the people at the time. At another mammoth bone settlement at Mezin, about 260 km northeast of Mezhirich, archaeologists found jewellery made from seashells that must have come from the Black Sea over 600 km to the south. This discovery provides evidence that even some 15,000 years ago goods were being exchanged between these hunting communities and people on the Black Sea, perhaps along the Desna and Dnieper rivers.[72]

At the Ignateva cave about 150 km north of the Kapova cave, only the entrance hall served as a place of settlement. The rooms decorated with 13,000- to 14,000-year-old paintings are, however, found deep in the cave's interior where complete darkness and nearly 100 per cent humidity prevail, since the air does not circulate. In this cave images of animals in shades of red and black also predominate; unfortunately, due to vandalism, they are not as well

Illustration according to archaeological data of a settlement made of mammoth bones in the Ukrainian–Russian grass steppe from the Upper Palaeolithic.

Skeleton of a young mammoth which fell into the dripstone cave of Emine Bayir Chosar, central Crimea.

preserved as those at Kapova. Most of the animals portrayed are mammoths, but there are also horses, a rhinoceros, an auroch and a two-humped camel. Other figures depicted include a woman, a kind of stick figure, and a human-animal hybrid made up of a human body and a bird's head and legs, and arrows.[73] The very poorly preserved paintings of Serpievka 2 presumably date from the late Upper Palaeolithic; those of Muradymovka are more recent.[74]

Portrayals of mammoths are also prominent in the cave paintings of Western Europe, which date from *ca.* 10,000 to 17,000 years ago. Mammoths appear in at least 370 pictures in 41 different caves. European cave paintings also feature images of mysterious human-animal hybrids such as painted bull-, bison-, and deer-men or anthropomorphic statuettes like the 32,000-year-old figurine of the 'lion man of Hohenstein Stadel', made of mammoth ivory. In the Neolithic such hybrids also appeared in the petroglyphs of Central Asia. In the absence of written sources we can only guess at their deeper significance. Are they animal spirits and deified animals that appear to us with human attributes, or are they highly unusual humans endowed with animal attributes, who make contact with animal spirits? We do not know; evidence of parallels to shamanistic rituals remains speculative.

In any case, the rock paintings suggest that the people of the time saw the boundary between human and animal as not unbridgeable but rather in flux. It is also striking that the wall paintings of the Urals and Western Europe are found deep in the inaccessible cave interiors, where complete darkness and silence prevail. These were not residences but rather cultic sites, which were presumably open only to selected individuals. Whether they served purposes of hunting magic, were magical places of healing or initiation, or represented a bridge to the supernatural remains unknown. The appearance of rock paintings in the Earth's interior is hardly a coincidence, however; perhaps this development is related to dreams and memory, and it was the recollection of dreams that suggested to early humans the existence of a self-contained dream world and of beings independent of the body. Dreams opened for human beings the door to the unseen. Time spent in a dark cave, which offer hardly any stimuli to the senses, comes close to the conditions of a sleeping dream.

Regardless of their intended purpose, these paintings and drawings should be seen as art, since they express the desire to portray a figure or object according to aesthetic principles such that it is clearly recognisable and its attributes can be identified. Capacity for abstract thought, imagination, and the ability to think in symbols – capabilities that the Upper Palaeolithic human clearly possessed – are all essential preconditions for art, both its creation and its viewing.

In addition to cave paintings, the so-called Venus figurines connected Central Asia with Western and Central Europe in the Upper Palaeolithic. These tiny female figures, rarely more than 10 cm tall, may be made of stone, bones, mammoth ivory and clay. The term 'Venus' is misleading insofar as the statuettes have no relation to any 'goddess of love', but rather it denotes their nakedness. The statue that is presumably the oldest in the world is the 6-cm-tall 'Venus of Hohle Fels'. More than 35,000 years old, it is made of carved ivory and was discovered in Germany in 2008. This and the other 12,000- to 24,000-year-old Venus figurines of Western and Central Europe have pronounced feminine features, such as ample breasts and buttocks as well as abdomens and thighs. They give the impression of being pregnant or overweight; their faces are barely indicated. Their meaning has been interpreted in various ways, as amulets, as symbols of human fertility or an adequate diet, and as portrayals of goddesses.

About 2,000 km farther east similar figures of comparable age have been found in the Russian-Ukrainian lowlands west of the Urals. These include more than 120 statuettes discovered at Kostienki 1, as well as at Avdeevo and Gagarino.[75] Most notable is the 26,000-year-old 'Venus of Dolní Věstonice', discovered in the Czech Republic. This 11-cm-tall ceramic statuette lay near a camp of Upper Palaeolithic mammoth hunters. This female figurine and other terra cotta figures of mammoths and big cats found there show that the practice of hardening clay with heat was known millennia before the start of settled agrarian culture. Analyses of the statues of Dolní Věstonice reveal that they were fired in specialised kilns at temperatures of 500–800 °C.[76]

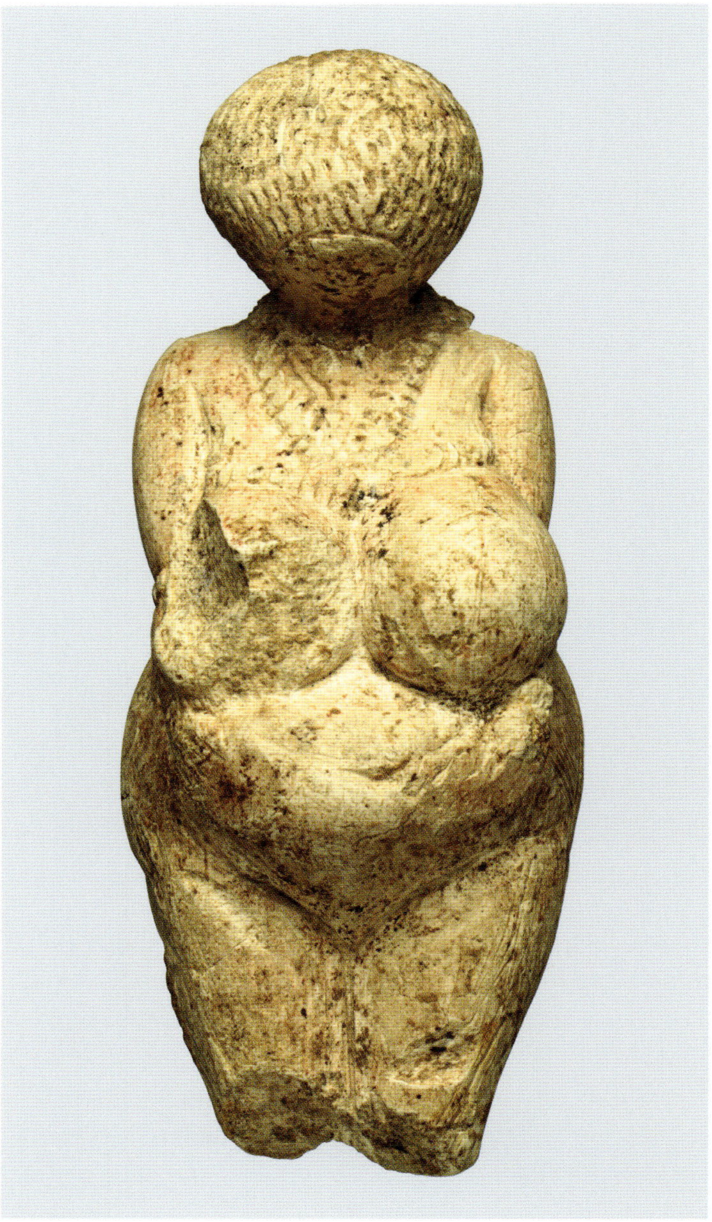

Palaeolithic female statue made of limestone, Kostienki-1, Don River basin, eastern Ukraine, *ca.* 20,000 BC. The State Hermitage Museum, St. Petersburg.

The small ivory figures from Bouret and Malt'a, north of Irkutsk on the western bank of the Angara River, reveal that 20,000 years ago the Upper Palaeolithic cultural zone extended over nearly 7,000 km from Western Europe to Lake Baikal. Here between 1956 and 1958 the archaeologist Gerasimov discovered near the remains of hunters' dwellings made of mammoth and woolly rhinoceros bones the grave of a child whose body had been covered with ochre and who had been given a diadem made from mammoth tusk. At the settlement Gerasimov discovered also dozens of small animal and human figurines, among them 24 Venus statuettes, whose age has been estimated at 20,000 to 23,000 years.[77] They belong to two different types, of which both are also represented in Western and Central Europe. The first are naked and have large breasts and wide hips, similar to most European female statuettes. The others, by contrast, appear to wear a fitted garment with a hood and have a sophisticated hairstyle and a very slender, even unnaturally thin figure, similar to the slim 'Venus of Galgenberg', who stands in a dancing pose.[78]

The culture of Malt'a on Lake Baikal existed at the same time as that of Kostienki-Avdeevo-Gagarino and along with the Western European hunter-gatherer culture of the Gravettian and Epigravettian, perhaps also along the preceding culture of the late Aurignacian. There is little doubt that they all formed a

Palaeolithic female statue made of mammoth bone, Malt'a, Siberia, Russia, 18,000–21,000 BC. The State Hermitage Museum, St. Petersburg.

wide-ranging shared cultural horizon, in which social networks existed – a kind of pan-Eurasian proto-Silk Road of the northern steppe. When a markedly cold period set in about 20,000 years ago, Siberia and the Eastern European plains were depopulated as the hunter-gatherer communities migrated south and west for survival. These regions were slowly resettled only 4,000 years later, as the continental ice shield gradually receded.[79]

4. The bow – a 12,000-year-old success story

A second, somewhat later invention of the Palaeolithic was the bow. This new long-range weapon could be used both for hunting and fighting, and it had several advantages over the spear. Thanks to its greater range, the shooter was less exposed when taking a shot than was the thrower when using the spear. Second, it offered greater accuracy and, third, it was much lighter in weight, so a hunter could take many more arrows with him than spears. Finally, the arrow was faster and more convenient to make and could be shot from almost any body position and in any terrain. The bow revealed its full potential only millennia later in combination with the horse, when in the early first millennium BC on the steppes of Eurasia bands of mounted archers developed into the most feared fighting force of their time. As the rather small recurve bow of the Scythians could be drawn with relatively little effort, it was also an ideal weapon for women, especially as young female riders were the equals of male riders in agility and speed. The bow remained the dominant long-range weapon for *ca.* 12,000 years – gradually superseded by firearms only at the start of the late Middle Ages.

When precisely the bow was invented is disputed, since the oldest indications – *ca.* 20,000-year-old points made of flint – could also have served as the tips of light spears. A bow found near Mannheim in Germany in 1976 or 1978 is thought to be the oldest bow in the world. It is a 40-cm-long worked piece of pine, originally about 110 cm long. This approximately 11,700-year-old bow had a range of 80 m and a draw weight of 11 to 14 kg. The other and indisputable evidence for the bow is the approximately 12,000-year-old intact bows from Stellmoor near Hamburg, northern Germany, as well as two 8,000-year-old bows from Holmgård IV in Denmark.[80] Of roughly comparable age are the portrayals of bow hunters in petroglyphs on the eastern coast of Spain, which date to between 5000 and 2800 BC,[81] as well as those of Tsagaan Salaa in western Mongolia.[82]

The first bows were simple self bows without an arrow rest or a grip; out of this developed the longbow, whose length nearly equalled that of the bowman. More efficient than the self bow was the recurve bow, which features tips that curve backwards, so that it stores significantly more energy. Contrary to popular belief, the recurve bow did not first appear in the Bronze Age. This is shown by images of such bows in petroglyphs on Spain's Mediterranean coast and the almost contemporaneous rock paintings of Alta in Norway, dating from 5,000 to nearly 7,000 years ago.[83] Sixteen

A mounted archer hunts camels. Petroglyph in the Sirven foothills, Ömnögov Aimag, southern Mongolia, *ca.* 1000 BC.

4,500- to 5,000-year-old bows from a burial ground near Pribaikalja, north-west of Lake Baikal, may represent the oldest archaeological discovery of a recurve bow.[84]

The combination of a recurve bow with first bilobite arrowheads and, beginning in the late Bronze Age, three-winged trilobite arrowheads, was a deadly weapon. While arrowheads with bilobite tips could be pulled out of a wound that did not involve any vital organs, a trilobite arrowhead, with added barbs, caused a fatal loss of blood from the many parts of the body it could strike. In the later first millennium BC bands of Scythian riders multiplied the deadly effect of the weapon by dipping the arrow in a mixture of snake venom and blood contaminated with dung; the Greeks called this poison 'scythicon'.[85]

The composite bow, very likely invented on the steppes of Central Asia before or around the middle of the second millennium BC, represents a further refinement of the recurve bow. It was made of at least two materials, which further increased the tension force and draw weight and lessened the bow's length, so that it served as the ideal weapon for horse riders. Composite bows are usually made of a wooden core, over which, during a multi-year process, other materials like bone, horn, metal, or other types of wood are layered and wrapped in sinew and animal skins or tree bark. Depending on the type of arrow used, the later composite bows of the Mongol and Turkish horsemen had a range of more than 500 m. The laminated composite bow also had weaknesses, however, since it is vulnerable to humidity, which causes the layers to separate due to retained water. Thus horsemen from the north who invaded the humid plains of India, such as the Kushan, often discovered that their best weapons literally fell apart. For that reason the Byzantine Emperor Maurikios (*r.* 582–609 AD) who had successfully waged war against horse peoples recommended in his strategy handbook *Strategikon*: 'If the enemy has a very strong force of archers, watch for wet weather, which affects the bow, to launch our attack against them.'[86] With the introduction of the composite bow, bronze arrowheads with sockets of standard size and weight began to be produced, which made it easier to set up a shot and thus improved accuracy.[87]

Since bows were made of organic materials, well-preserved archaeological specimens remain rare in Central Asia. Among the oldest is the broken bow of Arzhan 2, Tuva (southern Siberia), which was unearthed in 2001 from the grave of a Scythian royal couple who lived in the seventh century BC.[88] Somewhat less old but better preserved is the asymmetrical horseman's bow of Olon Kurin Gol, found in Mongolia in 2006.[89] For climatic reasons the two best-preserved ancient composite bows come from the Turfan Basin and the Taklamakan Desert of China, two very arid regions on the eastern edge of Central Asia, where organic matter remains preserved for millennia. Both bows were grave goods; the one from Subexi[90] near Turfan dates from the fifth to the third century BC, and the one from Niya[91] in the interior of the Taklamakan Desert from the first three or four centuries AD.

III

A Global Climatic Warming Ushers in the Mesolithic

The paintings on rocks, they are the earliest dialog of the human being with eternity. With these pictures the human of prehistory recorded his wishes, his dreams, his worldview, his thoughts, and his experiences.

HERBERT KÜHN, FOREWORD TO *A.P. OKLADNIKOW, DER HIRSCH MIT DEM GOLDENEN GEWEIH*, 1972[1]

1. The retreat of the glaciers

The temperature in the northern hemisphere began to rise markedly about 14,700 years ago. This increase was caused by heightened solar activity, a notable increase in carbon dioxide in the atmosphere, and a shift to the north of the warm Gulf Stream ocean current. This warm period ended after two millennia with a return to cold conditions, but 11,700 years ago the current warm period began abruptly, caused by an increased intensity in solar radiation, with a temperature rise of as much as 8 °C in ten years.[2] With the retreat of the great glaciers, the Pleistocene ended and the Holocene began, coinciding with the transition from the Palaeolithic to the Mesolithic.[3]

The Mesolithic is defined by scholars according to two different criteria. Its start is identified according to geochronological considerations and placed at the beginning of the Holocene around 9700 BC; its end, however, is determined by archaeological criteria. The Mesolithic ends with the Neolithic revolution, the beginning of productive economic activity in the form of animal husbandry or farming. Thus the transition from the Mesolithic to the Neolithic occurred at different times in different regions.

The huge increase in temperature, well above our current level, had lasting consequences for flora and fauna. In the northern half of Central Asia large wooded zones expanded, forcing the steppes southward; in the southern half, however, several steppe regions became drier and turned into hostile deserts, so Mesolithic archaeological discoveries occur there much less frequently than do Palaeolithic.[4] Only the technology of artificial irrigation enabled Neolithic people to settle successfully in desert oases, as they did in, for example, south-western Turkmenistan.

The warming of the climate also forced large mammals adapted to the cold, such as the mammoth, to migrate north, where they quickly died out. Among the animals, besides the mammoth, that went extinct at the end of the Pleistocene were the woolly rhinoceros, the steppe bison, the cave lion, the cave hyena and the giant deer. Scientists still do not know, however, whether these large mammals fell victim only to the temperature increase, since they had adapted to earlier climate fluctuations, or if additional factors, such as a decreased rate of reproduction or intensive hunting, also played a role. Particularly in the case of popular meat sources such as the mammoth, the steppe bison and the giant deer, increased hunting may have contributed to their demise. At the same time, the great herds of wild horses and reindeer also disappeared, forcing hunters to change their strategies. They could no longer ambush herds or lure them into a trap, such as a rock pit, but rather had to pursue individual animals, for which the bow, as an accurate weapon, was indispensable.

In north-eastern Central Asia and in the northern steppes, unlike in the south-east, the temperature increase at the start of the Holocene did not cause a drying out of the landscape but rather, thanks to increased precipitation and the melting of permafrost and glaciers, a rise in humidity. In the region of modern western Mongolia, the Altai and southern Siberia, large woodland areas and marshy plains expanded, opening new habitats for other animals such as aurochs, elk, red deer, argalis (mountain sheep), bears and wild pigs. These new arrivals offered humans a rich hunting ground, while simultaneously forcing them to become more mobile.[5] At that time north-eastern Central Asia provided hunters, fishermen and gatherers with a wealth of sustenance. With the retreat of the permafrost and the cold far to the north, human beings and animals adapted to relative warmth advanced into regions that today have a harsh climate.

2. Petroglyphs as information sources

For the Middle Stone Age onwards, scholars of culture and history have access to a new source of knowledge in addition to archaeological, ecological and genetic data. These are petroglyphs, widespread in the eastern half of Central Asia though found mostly in inaccessible locations. These stone engravings not only have a mythical, magical or shamanistic meaning, depending on the interpretation, but also reflect the material reality of the time.[6] Thus they convey irreplaceable information about the fauna, human lifestyles and technologies used, such as the emergence of domesticated cattle herds, the use of tents or four-wheeled wagons and two-wheeled chariots, as well as the adoption of horse riding and various weapons. The relevance of the petroglyphs for history is enhanced by their continuity in a particular place, since they were often carved over the course of several millennia in the same, clearly sacred location. In this way they may be understood as both open-air holy sites and the earliest stone 'history books'. Since such sites with petroglyphs were often used for centuries or even millennia, they must have contributed to a strong sense of social and cultural identity in the community concerned.

Sites with thousands or even tens of thousands of engravings in Mongolia, Xinjiang, Kazakhstan, Kyrgyzstan, Tajikistan and southern Siberia offer graphic information from the Mesolithic into the Middle Ages, provided the climatic conditions permitted human survival. Petroglyphs are an important extension of archaeological data because the latter provide information mostly from burial sites and the corresponding grave goods, while there are no portrayals of funerals in the petroglyphs. Instead, they depict important life events and traditions and the mythical and magical ideas associated with them.[7] In broad terms, archaeological burial sites give insight into a particular funereal culture, social norms, and to some extent material culture; petroglyphs, by contrast, tell us about life in this world and its associated ideals.

However, in the absence of organic material that permits the use of radiocarbon methods, petroglyphs are difficult to date. The organic material that becomes embedded in the fine engravings in the rock often oxidises, so that measurements result in a too recent date. In addition, organic matter can be blown by the wind into a layer of rock. Serving as a starting point for dating are analyses of the patina and the degree of weathering, the palaeoecological environment, and the technology employed. Dating based on stylistic characteristics is still highly inexact.

As surfaces for petroglyphs the artists chose granite-like stones, smoothed and polished by glaciers, or preferred so-called greywacke,[8] a relatively hard sandstone consisting of feldspar, clay shale, quartz, clay minerals, chlorite and mica. The boulders have a smooth surface and a patina whose colours range from dark brown through brick red to dark pink, so that the artists found ideal, naturally occurring 'canvases'. The engraved motifs first appeared white and were visible from greater distances than they are today; after a few centuries a new patina formed, lessening the contrast with the background. In the Mongolian Altai, for instance, it took about 3,000 years for the white colour of the petroglyphs to begin disappearing.[9]

Petroglyphs, which are defined as pictures either directly or indirectly engraved, embossed or scraped into rock, must be distinguished from rock painting, in which pigments are applied to rocks. In petroglyphs rock is removed, but this is not the case

Crater of the Khorgo Uul volcano, 2,285 m above sea level and extinct for the past 8,000 years, Arkhangai Aimag, Central Mongolia.

The petroglyphs of Tsagaan Salaa and Baga Oigor, Mongolia

The archaeological complex of Tsagaan Salaa and Baga Oigor is found in a sparse mountain steppe landscape of western Mongolia and, with its approximately 100,000 stone engravings, resembles a huge open-air museum that runs along the mountain rivers Tsagaan Salaa and Baga Oigor over an area of 15 km^2. The lowest engravings are about 30 m above the valley floor at a height of 2,240 m above sea level; the highest are at 2,630 m above sea level. They are mostly oriented toward the sun to the south, south-west or south-east. A few of the most heavily decorated and interesting complexes are found near areas sheltered from the wind, and presumably served as winter camps.

An exploration here is like a richly illustrated journey through 13,000 to 14,000 years of history. This petroglyph complex, still well preserved today thanks to its remote location, is not only one of the largest in Central Asia but also the most comprehensive with regard to chronological coverage of various cultural epochs. The stone engravings are landmarks of life over the course of climate fluctuations and the attendant development of a hunter-gatherer society into one of nomadic stockbreeders. This stone history book begins in the late Upper Palaeolithic when, toward the end of the last ice age, human beings hunted mammoths, which are portrayed in primitive form in a dozen petroglyphs. In the subsequent warm period of the Mesolithic, thick forests and marshy plains emerged in the Altai, which were inhabited by aurochs, elk and red deer. The petroglyphs of these animals, as well as of argalis and horses, were usually portrayed in the style of a monumental, somewhat static idealised realism; a captivating minority of them feature a lifelike, almost elegant realism, and all appear in profile. Toward the end of the Mesolithic they are joined by pictures of bears and Siberian ibexes; the latter suggest the start of a retreat of the forests.

The first human figures appear in petroglyphs dating from the Neolithic, which began about 6,000 to 6,500 years ago. Before this, stone art was dominated by animals. Now, however, not only the relationship between human and animal was reflected in the petroglyphs but also essential aspects of human existence. Animals no longer stood at the centre of the picture; the human being moved into that space. In Tsagaan Salaa three theme cycles can be seen: the hunt, human reproduction, and perhaps also a first step into the world of the supernatural. Neolithic hunters, usually large figures armed with a club or spear, were mostly portrayed frontally, as were birthing women. The third type of human portrayal is mysterious. It shows a bell-shaped figure with short legs, whose faceless head

▲ (Top) Fight between two men with lances wearing mushroom-shaped headdresses, Tsagaan Salaa II, Bayan Ölgyi Aimag, western Mongolia, Bronze Age.

◥ (Above) Three archers attack a giant, Indian ink drawing of petroglyphs, Eshki Olmes, eastern Kazakhstan, Bronze Age.

◤ (Left) Bell-shaped figure with a mountain goat in its body, Baga Oigor I, Bayan Ölgyi Aimag, western Mongolia, Neolithic.

◀ (Opposite) Aurochs and horse, Tsagaan Salaa/Baga Oigor complex, Bayan Ölgyi Aimag, western Mongolia, Mesolithic.

wears a pair of horns, and inside the body there appears an infant or an animal like an ibex.

Four thousand six hundred years ago a cooling and drying trend that had begun about 800 years earlier in the north-eastern half of Central Asia accelerated, affecting western Mongolia and the Altai in particular and heralding the start of the Bronze Age. As a consequence of the climatic disruption, forests shrank and the landscape that had developed in the once-humid climate disappeared,

▲ Cattle herd, Tsagaan Salaa II, Bayan Ölgyi Aimag, western Mongolia, Bronze Age.

◀ Two-axle wagon with spoked wheels pulled by a camel, Indian ink drawing of petroglyphs, Arpa Uzen in the Karatau Mountains, southern Kazakhstan, Bronze Age.

▶ Light chariot pulled by a deer, Baga Oigor II, Bayan Ölgyi Aimag, western Mongolia, later Bronze Age.

leading to the loss of habitat for aurochs and large woodland animals. With the retreat of the forests, grasslands rapidly expanded. In the petroglyphs aurochs disappear and scenes in which bears, deer, wild yaks, horses and ibexes are hunted with flat bows and spears became common. In other places, such as Ak-Kainar or Tamgaly, southern Kazakhstan, the aurochs remained venerated for a longer time, as seen in petroglyphs of the aurochs with very long horns either strongly curved or directed forward. But in Tsagaan Salaa the animals are no longer portrayed statically but rather dynamically in motion. Sometimes the hunters wear a mushroom-shaped head covering and on the back of their hips something that looks like a ball-shaped tail.[10] This motif appears in the entire eastern half of Central Asia, in Outer and Inner Mongolia, southern Siberia and Kazakhstan, which suggests inter-regional cultural ties. That armed conflicts increased towards the end of the Bronze Age is suggested by battle scenes, such as at Eshki Olmes (eastern Kazakhstan), where two groups of bowmen shoot arrows at each other.[11] Another previously unknown battle scene is the attack of a giant by archers, as found at Eshki Olmes and Langar (Tajikistan).

A surprising, rarely seen motif from the Bronze Age shows a man on skis, pursuing a deer or an elk, which bears a round disc on its antlers.[12] This striking scene recalls a myth of the Evenks, formerly called the Tungus. According to this myth, the giant elk Kheglen stole the sun, impaled it on its horns, and carried it to the north. Eternal night and cold threatened humanity. In order to save it, the divine hero Ma'en pursued the elk and tore the sun away from it, returning it to the people at dawn. The Evenks believed that this cosmic drama played out every night. According to this, the engraved skier would represent Ma'en, who is pursuing Kheglen. In another version, an elk kidnaps the sun and carries it on its horns through the daylight sky until a bear catches it and returns the sun to the underworld. Thus night follows day.[13]

Toward the end of the Bronze Age, about 3,100 years ago, a rapid decrease in wild game forced a gradual transition from an economy based on hunting with little animal husbandry to a system of nomadic livestock-raising with large herds. An increase in precipitation, leading to the emergence of lush grazing lands, encouraged this development. The petroglyphs reflect this shift in lifestyle, with hunting scenes becoming markedly less common and portrayals of domesticated cattle herds correspondingly more widespread. Images of laden oxen and advancing herds led by herders on foot or on horseback and guarded by dogs suggest that stockbreeders varied their grazing areas. But they also had settled winter residences, as depicted in the stone engravings showing outlines of huts and stables with cattle standing inside them. In the petroglyphic world camels now appear as mounts or draught animals.[14] Scenes of

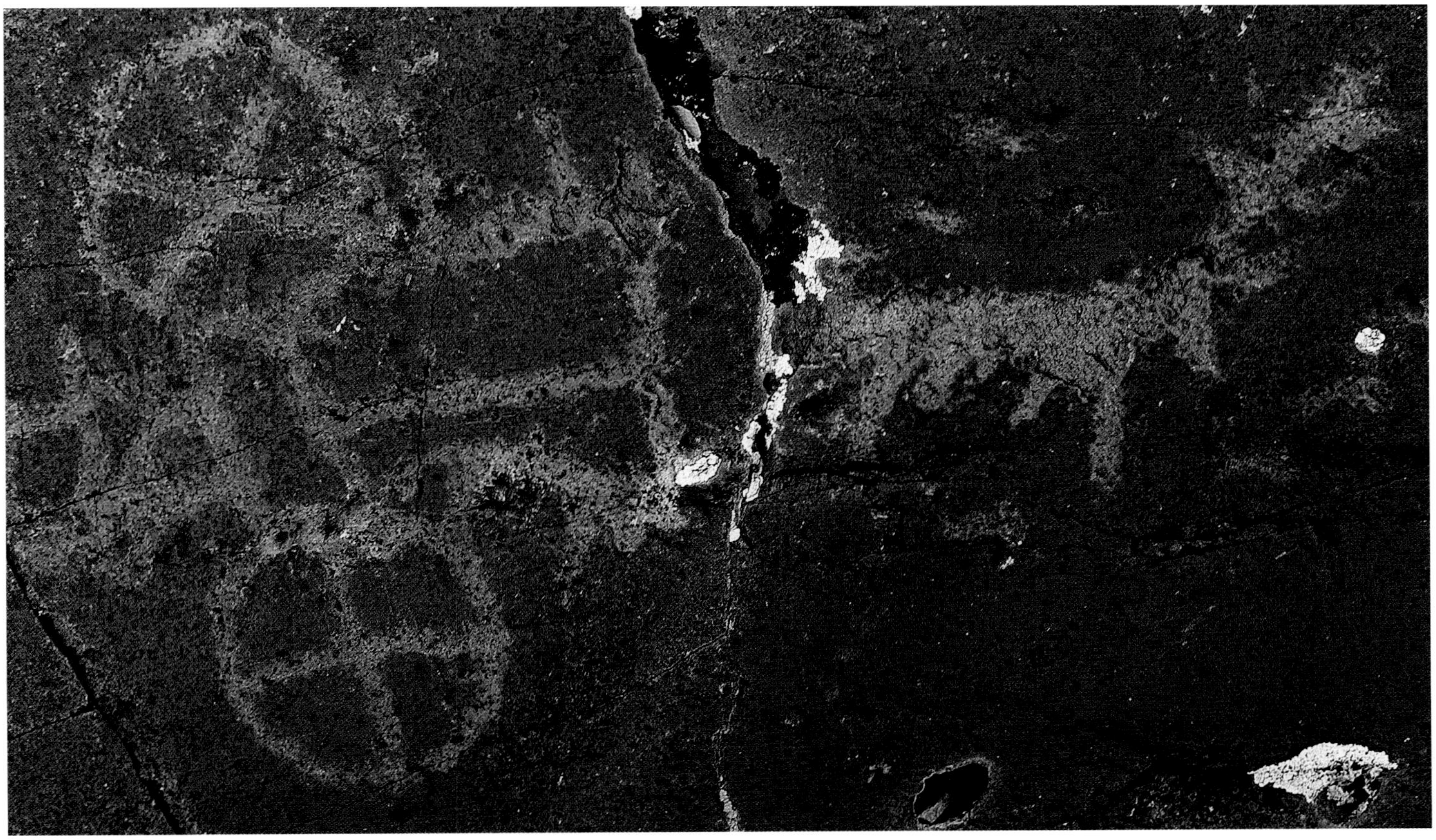

conflict between armed men, bearing lances and longbows, are also depicted. Such images show that fights arose over herds, grazing lands and winter camps, which indicates that the idea of property was well established in the herding society. Among hunter-gatherers, the idea of property was presumably not widespread and was dangerous for the community. Insofar as herder families or groups identified protected winter camps with secure access to water as 'their own' and would regularly return to them, they became owners of a particular territory, which they had to defend. Another new motif is wagons and carts. There are usually two-wheeled carts, pulled by horses, oxen, camels or even deer, but no scenes of conflict, as one finds in northern China. In the mountainous regions of western Mongolia wagons and carts were ineffectual for fighting; they had a ceremonial function only. Occasional engravings of spoked wheels could also represent sun symbols, as found in Tamgaly, Kazakhstan.

Also from the second half of the Bronze Age are elegantly portrayed deer and elk with strongly stylised horns and sometimes elongated noses that resemble birds' beaks. The same deer figures are found on the so-called deer stones of central Mongolia.

The deer steles were one of the forerunners of the animal style widespread among the Saka and Scythians, which extended from the Altai to the Black Sea.[15] In another type of stylised portrayal of deer the antlers assume the form of a tree, becoming a metaphor for the tree of life. In this context the deer with the tree-like antlers also symbolises fertility. Its antlers, shed and regrown each year, stand for the cycle of life and death; they symbolise the reproduction of humans and animals as well as the fertility of nature.

In the next cultural epoch, the Iron Age, which began about 900 BC and coincided with the age of the warrior nomads, battle scenes and hunting scenes with the recurve bow predominate in Tsagaan Salaa. The final significant period of petroglyphic art, that of the Turkic empires, is represented only sparingly in Tsagaan Salaa; outstanding examples of it are found about 40 km south at Tsagaan Gol. Among these are images of heavily armoured horsemen and falcon hunters.

Chronological correlations between climatic and cultural developments in the example of the petroglyphs of Tsaagan Salaa and Baga Oigor, Mongolia

PERIOD	DATE	CLIMATE	FLORA	FAUNA	ECONOMY	IMAGES
Late Upper Palaeolithic	– 9700 BC	Cold, dry	Dry steppe	Mammoth, woolly rhinoceros, ostrich	Hunter-gatherer	Mammoth, woolly rhinoceros, ostrich
Mesolithic	9700–4500 BC	Warm, humid	Forests, marshy plains	Aurochs, elk, argali, bear, horse	Hunter-gatherer	Aurochs, elk, argali, bears, horses, Siberian ibexes
Neolithic	4500–2400 BC	Start of cooling trend	Forests, marshy plains	Bear, deer, yak, ibex, horse	Hunter-gatherer	Hunters with clubs, birthing women, bell-shaped figures
Bronze Age	2400–900 BC	Cold, dry	Forests disappear, steppe	Bear, deer, yak, ibex, horse, camel	Hunter, herder	Hunters with bows, fighting, carts, cattle herds, stables, camels, stylised deer
Iron Age	900 BC–550 AD	Moderately cold, humid	Grass steppe	Bear, deer, yak, ibex, horse, camel	Nomadic herder, warrior horsemen	Recurve bows, battle scenes, cattle herds
Turkic Empires	550–750 AD	Moderately cold and dry	Grass steppe	Bear, deer, yak, ibex, horse, camel	Nomadic herder, warrior horsemen	At Tsagaan Gol: armoured horsemen, mounted falconers

in rock painting. Petroglyphs are carved into rock, with lines engraved with the help of a hard instrument made of stone or metal. Pictures could also be embossed by carving away the rock around a picture, or scraped by grinding. In the direct method, the surface was chipped away with a single hard tool; in the indirect, a stone was hammered by a second hard instrument, enabling much more controlled and precise work. Finally, to be distinguished from these two types of rock art are geoglyphs, also found in Central Asia, enormous pictorial or geometric designs made on the ground itself. Geoglyphs are drawings or geometric designs made by either removing material from a dark upper layer of pebbles or soil to reveal a lighter layer beneath, or by placing dark or light stones on a contrasting background. The geoglyphs of Peru, Chile, Arizona and England belong to the former category; those of Tajikistan and Mongolia to the latter.

Among the oldest petroglyphs of Central Asia are those that include unambiguous portrayals of mammoths, woolly rhinoceroses or ostriches, such as the rock pictures of Oglakhty[16] and Tepsej[17] in southern Siberia, which unfortunately have been flooded by a reservoir, or the two western Mongolian sites at Aral Tolgoi near Khoton Nuur lake[18] and Tsagaan Salaa.[19]

The Tsagaan Salaa site was important, indeed sacred, for hundreds of generations, or else the rocks would not have been used for engraving for so long. A similar, much smaller petroglyph site is Arschaan Khod in the Khentii Mountains in north-eastern Mongolia. In contrast to Tsagaan Salaa, which has been known only since 1994, the region of Khentii played an important role in the consciousness of the Mongols, since Genghis Khan was born here in 1167 and buried in 1227 in a still unknown location. The pan-Mongol diet of 1206, which declared Genghis Khan ruler of all the Mongol peoples, took place just 34 km north of Arschaan Khod.[20] This place remained holy even after prehistoric times, as evidenced by medieval inscriptions in Old Mongolian, Chinese and Arabic, more recent Buddhist epigrams in Tibetan script, and numerous blue offering scarves, which are placed in cracks in the rock as votive offerings. Arschaan Khod is still an open-air sanctuary with the sky as its roof. The oldest petroglyphs date from the early Mesolithic, and portray no living things but rather symbols of indeterminate meaning.[21] They are circles with or without dots in the centre; circles with two legs; triangles, some with legs, which could represent humans; arrows; and many hoof prints. In the Bronze Age petroglyphs of ibexes and yaks were added. (In Mongolia there have been additional archaeological discoveries of hunters, fishermen and gatherers, who left behind their tools such as microliths, but there are no other petroglyphs from the Mesolithic.)[22]

3. Microliths

During the Mesolithic one of the most popular tools was the microlith, which first appeared in Central Asia in the Upper Palaeolithic. In the Mesolithic and subsequent Neolithic it was used in hunting and fishing, as well as for agriculture and woodworking. It was an implement made of flint or obsidian, up to 3 cm long and 1 cm wide, needle- or blade-shaped, which was chipped out of a stone and then finished. Before people recognised the potential uses for these flakes of stone, they were simply thrown away.

Fastened to lightweight projectiles such as spears and harpoons, they increased the piercing force of these weapons during hunting or fishing and acted as barbed hooks that stuck in the flesh of the victim. Affixed to thin wooden rods, pointed microliths became light and effective arrowheads. Somewhat broader microliths shaped like triangles could also be placed like teeth on a bowed shaft made of horn or a handgrip and attached with a resinous substance. Such implements could serve as sickles for cutting grass or grain or saws for cutting wood. Attached to shorter and somewhat thicker wooden rods than were used for arrows, they could be used to make a borer.

Microliths, were a brilliant addition to Stone Age technology that had many advantages. The source of the microliths, that is the stone from which they were cut, was available in nature and did not have to first be produced out of other materials, as did bronze, for instance. Additionally, a skilled stonecutter could produce microliths quickly and efficiently with no waste, and they could be used in a variety of ways. For this reason this 'cheap mass-produced object' was also used during the Bronze Age and even the Iron Age, especially in those regions that had to import the raw materials for the production of metal. There expensive metal arrowheads were used only in war, while hunters were satisfied with the cheaper microlith arrows. For this reason microliths, like flint arrowheads, are poor sources for the dating of archaeological sites.

Hunters and dogs attack a deer, Tsagaan Salaa IV, Bayan Ölgyi Aimag, western Mongolia, Bronze Age.

IV

The Economic Revolution of the Neolithic

The camel is the constant companion of the nomad and often the source of his prosperity. Besides serving as a beast of burden and for riding, the camel supplies wool and milk and the hair is spun into ropes.

LT. COLONEL NICOLAI MICHAILOVITSCH PRZHEVALSKY, MONGOLIA, 1876[1]

1. The primary and secondary Neolithic revolutions

In the quotation above the Russian explorer of Central Asia Przhevalsky summed up the main principle of the two-part Neolithic revolution: in the first revolution, which was really a millennia-long evolution beginning in the tenth millennium BC, plant and animal sustenance was no longer only gathered and hunted but rather farmed and raised.[2] This innovation from the Near East marks the advent of farming and animal husbandry and simultaneously of the Neolithic.[3] Starting in the seventh millennium BC a few of these technologies also appeared in the warmer regions of the southern half of Central Asia, such as southern Turkmenistan. On the fertile western edge of Central Asia, in modern Ukraine, the encounter between hunter-gatherer cultures and agricultural-herding societies took place a millennium later.

The second Neolithic revolution, which began later, in the fifth millennium BC, is related to the use of animals. Instead of just consuming domesticated animals such as cattle, sheep, goats, horses and camels and using the inedible remains such as skins, bones, and sinews, people gradually began to use the animals in varied, combined, and repeatable ways without having to kill them. They were used as pack-animals for people and goods as well as draught animals for sleds, carts and ploughs; they provided hair for wool, felt and knitting, as well as milk and, in the case of horses, blood. For meat it was sufficient to slaughter just a fraction of the herd. Thanks to this varied and sustainable use of animals the people of the northern half of Central Asia now had the means of meeting their basic needs for food, clothing and shelter, as well as transportation for themselves and their goods, with a herding economy. The second Neolithic revolution was the genesis of mobile herding; now it was possible to use as grazing land the grass steppes that could not be used for planting and supported little wild game. The Neolithic revolutions changed the course of history. It enabled increased productivity and trade, giving rise to rapid population growth and the development of social hierarchies, but it also led indirectly to overgrazing and depletion of the soil and forests. However, those who lived in regions lacking the necessary conditions for both agriculture and nomadic herding, and nevertheless did not emigrate, remained part of a hunter-gatherer cultures even in the Neolithic, which we refer to as 'archaic Neolithic'.

As a consequence of the varied topography of Central Asia and its differing climates, all three developments – the transition to farming or to livestock breeding or the continuation of an archaic Neolithic – occurred in parallel. In the eastern half of Central Asia the boundary between the southern cultural sphere with agrarian and proto-urban cultures and the northern sphere of settled or semi-nomadic herders ran at first along the Amu Darya River. The proto-urban culture of Sarazm (fourth–second millennia BC) north of the Amu Darya was an exception. Towards the end of the second millennium BC this cultural boundary shifted north to the Syr Darya. In the geographic centre of eastern Central Asia, however, there existed an oasis of the archaic Neolithic with two noteworthy cultures: Hissar and Kelteminar.

2. Hunters and gatherers in the mountains and along the waterways of inner Central Asia

Toward the end of the seventh millennium BC, between the Amu Darya River on the southern border of Tajikistan and Lake Issyk Kul in north-western Kyrgyzstan, the archaic Neolithic culture of **Hissar** arose, with its geographic centre in south-western Tajikistan. In the then-forested mountains and their foothills communities of hunters, fishermen and gatherers, who used archaic pebble tools and hand axes, lived along the streams and rivers. The absence of microliths and the sparse discoveries of arrowheads underscore the archaic character of Hissar until the fourth millennium BC.[4] Beginning at this time, thanks to influences from the south-west, people on the peripheries and in the more accessible valleys gained knowledge of the domestication of goats and sheep, rudimentary farming and crude ceramics. The hand-crafted vessels, which were decorated with textile prints, did not have flat bases but rather came to a point, as people stuck them in the ground. In remote mountain regions of the upper Vakhsh valley an archaic form of the Hissar culture continued until the end of the second millennium BC, a kind of Stone Age enclave in an established culture of bronze.[5]

North-west of the mountain region of the Hissar culture, east of the Caspian Sea, extends the Turan Depression, in whose central and eastern part the culture of **Kelteminar** (*ca.* 5500–2400 BC) developed south of the Aral Sea. In light of the absence of sickles with flint blades and the many discoveries of arrowheads, as well as harpoons and net sinkers, it may be concluded that the people practised hardly any agriculture and instead lived by hunting and fishing; they also used slingshots as hunting weapons. The hunted

A Mongol captures a young horse with a catching loop, central Mongolia.

game consisted of gazelles, wild donkeys, boars, red deer, and presumably also wild horses. These people lived in the lower catchment area of the Zerafshan, whose name means 'sprayer of gold', and Amu Darya rivers.

At that time, the Amu Darya did not empty into the Aral Sea, as it did until the 1970s, but rather most of the water flowed into the Caspian Sea via the Sarykamysh Lake and formed the erstwhile Uzboy River, whose 700-km-long bed is today dry and in parts covered with sand, apart from a few long, shallow basins that appear in early summer with the snowmelt. Since the end of the last ice age the waters of the Amu Darya have repeatedly chosen this westward-tending riverbed and brought the Uzboy back to life, as shown by archaeological discoveries from times beginning with the Kelteminar culture in the sixth millennium BC. At that time the desolate Kara Kum Desert bordering on the Uzboy changed into a habitable steppe landscape with reeds and small alluvial forests.[6] The name 'Kelteminar' was coined by the Soviet archaeologist Sergei Tolstov (1907–1976), who was the first to explore the region of the Uzboy and that of Choresm, just to the north.[7] After the collapse of the Kelteminar culture in the second half of the third millennium BC the banks of the Uzboy were resettled and the river used as a transportation route in the mid-first millennium BC under the Iranian Achaemenids and the subsequent Parthians.[8] Parallel to these changes in the riverbed, the area of the Aral Sea also oscillated, since with the loss of the Amu Darya it had only the Syr Darya as a significant feeder river. In the sixteenth century, for instance, the Aral Sea contracted particularly significantly, and life along the Uzboy flourished.

When the English explorer Anthony Jenkinson (1529–1610), who travelled to Central Asia on behalf of the Muscovy Company, camped on Sarykamysh Lake in 1558, he noted that the Uzboy was being depleted by irrigation and no longer reached the Caspian Sea. He also predicted that the fertile landscape could soon become desert if water failed to return to the Uzboy: 'The water that serveth all that country is drawn by ditches out of the river Oxus [the Uzboy], unto the great destruction of the said river, for which cause it falleth not into the Caspian Sea as it hath done in times past, and in short time all that land is like to be destroyed, and to become a wilderness for want of water, when the river of Oxus [its western branch, the Uzboy] shall fail.'[9] The fertile Uzboy valley did in fact dry up abruptly at the start of the eighteenth century, when the Amu Darya returned to its northern course, and the Turkmen inhabitants abandoned their land.

A Mongol nomad woman spins yarn out of sheep's wool. She sits in a yurt on a felt carpet with a pattern of highly abstracted heads of horned animals. Nomads' camp near Khar Nuur Lake, Bayan Ölgyi Aimag, western Mongolia.

The people of the Kelteminar culture were mostly sedentary and lived, presumably as extended families, in spacious, oval-shaped huts with an area of 270 to 300 m^2 and covered by a cane roof. The hearths for individual families were found on the edges of the huts, while the one in the middle may have served a fire cult. Near their dwelling the people raised a few cattle, and they had dogs. Their pottery consisted of round-bottomed, hemispheric vessels as well as some that came to a point so they could be stuck in the ground. They were decorated with wavy or zigzag lines as well as triangular or rhomboid patterns, either painted or engraved with a stylus before firing.[10] Towards the end of the Kelteminar culture, around 2500 BC, its representatives came into contact with copper metallurgy and with agriculture, which they used to a limited degree, as can be determined from the small number of copper artefacts and a few stone sickles. They remained, however, largely a Neolithic society. Kelteminar was followed by the culture of Zamanbaba.

South of the Kelteminar culture there was in the sixth and fifth millennia BC a related culture, as can be seen in the archaeological finds in the caves of Jebel and Dam Dam Chasma II south-east of the Caspian Sea. The inhabitants hunted and fished and also raised domesticated sheep and goats. These animals appear not to have descended from the local wild sheep and goats, however, but rather from those of western Asia, Syria, or Mesopotamia – indicating a cultural transfer from the west.[11]

3. Agriculture and early settlements in southern Central Asia

On the Eurasian continent the cradles of stockbreeding and farming lie in the Fertile Crescent, a relatively rainy region in the Near East that extends in a sickle shape north of the Syrian Desert from the Persian Gulf in the east to Gaza in the west.[12] Here about 12,000 to 13,000 years ago people began to keep goats and sheep as domestic animals as well as to cultivate, irrigate, and store crops such as barley, wheat, lentils and peas. Two millennia later the raising of cattle and pigs began. As the next step of the second Neolithic revolution, additional uses were found for animals, such as the production of wool and their use for transportation and traction.

Over the course of millennia the introduction of these new methods of production in the Fertile Crescent yielded consequences of global significance. Settlements with production surpluses arose, as did cities with high population density, division of labour and centralised administration, with hierarchies and the attendant worldviews, as well as prestigious architecture. At the same time the ideas of private and state property emerged, bound up with the need to enforce and defend this property. Thanks to the division of labour, long-distance trade could also expand, and the anonymous and silent communication form of writing arose, presumably from the need to keep records of goods.

Towards the end of the eighth millennium BC the 'Neolithic idea' of the cultivation of wheat and barley as well as the raising of sheep and goats began to spread beyond the Fertile Crescent, first to the south-east and then, presumably in step with local climatic changes, into the Nile Valley, to Anatolia and south-eastern Europe and farther to Central and Western Europe. In the east migrants from western Asia reached the western part of the fertile Indus Valley in Baluchistan in western Pakistan around 7000 BC, where they encountered indigenous hunters and fishermen. From this grew the settlement of **Mehrgarh**, one of the first agrarian settlements of South Asia, which consisted of two dozen four-room mud brick houses and offered shelter to over 100 people. At burials goats were sacrificed and the dead were buried with grave goods such as tools, pendants, necklaces, bracelets and anklets, under houses or in the inner courtyard; seashells and lapis lazuli indicated trade with coastal regions and northern Afghanistan, where agriculture gained a limited foothold at Aq Kupruk around 6250 BC. Farmers not only raised sheep and goats; they also domesticated the local zebu cattle, which they used for ploughing. They kept clay statues of animals and seated people, a custom also found in the earliest agrarian settlement of Central Asia at Jeitun.[13]

In the seventh millennium BC the new technologies reached the south of Central Asia, first the southern coast of the Caspian Sea near the Gorgan valley and then the plains at the northern foot of the Kopet Dag Mountains in southern Turkmenistan. The systematic excavation begun by the Soviet archaeologist Vadim Masson in the 1950s has to date yielded some 20 farming settlements, of which **Jeitun** (6500–4500 BC) was the largest. Insofar as the culture of Jeitun appeared suddenly and without predecessors and no traces of wild wheat or barley have been found, it is likely that it emerged thanks to migrants from western Asia, who also brought with them domesticated sheep and goats. Since a dry desert climate with little precipitation prevailed in the northern foothills of the Kopet Dag Mountains, all the settlements lay in the deltas of rivers flowing out of the mountains. Without simple systems of irrigation no agriculture could be undertaken on the dry land.

An archer hunts an ibex, Tsagaan Salaa/Baga Oigor complex, Bayan Ölgyi Aimag, western Mongolia, Bronze Age.

The oases thus relied on the mountains retaining sufficient water in the form of snow and ice and rivers bringing the spring snowmelt to the plains, where the farmers stored it. In the absence of precipitation in the oases, life there was directly dependent on precipitation in the mountains.

The settlements consisted of 30 to 35 standardised mud brick houses with a single rectangular room of about 25 m^2. In these small, single-family houses, the hearth was found to the right of the entrance. Since the houses were freestanding and the villages had only low surrounding walls, the inhabitants at the time must have felt little threatened, presumably thanks to the very low population density. Noteworthy was the discovery in the centre of the 7,500-year-old settlement of Pessejik Tepe of a house more than twice as large as the others, where no implements of daily life were found.

Godon Go River, Bayan Ölgyi Aimag, western Mongolia. This region witnessed in the 3rd millennium BC the shift from a hunter-gatherer society into one of semi-nomadic stockbreeders.

On one side of the room, whose floor was covered by a thin layer of lime, there was a large fireplace and across from it a leopard was painted on a whitewashed wall in red and black pigment. This is the oldest wall painting of Central Asia, and it shows similarities to the wall paintings of Catal Hüyük in the Anatolian highland.[14] This room presumably served as a public cultic site, perhaps for a fire cult, and was thus one of the earliest cultic sites of Central Asia.

As in Mehrgarh, archaeologists found small clay statues of women and animals, which perhaps served as amulets, as well as ceramics decorated with red linear patters on a yellow background. Finds here included more than 500 sickles made of bone and antlers, which were trimmed with sharp flint blades, and many hand grinding stones. These objects underscore the significance of the cultivation of wheat and barley. In addition, the hunting of gazelles, wild sheep and wild asses with slingshots and spears continued to play an important role. Although the settlements were home to 200 to 350 people each, they were organised decentrally. Each family produced its own tools and made animal skins into clothing for themselves; there was not yet any task-specific division of labour. In Jeitun the dead were buried, as in Mehrgarh, within the villages, after they had been richly sprinkled with ochre – a custom that runs as a leitmotif through the prehistory of Central Asia.[15] In summary, the culture of Jeitun, lasting till 4500 BC, was a Central Asian outpost of the Near Eastern Neolithic, which laid the foundation for the coming cultures in southern Central Asia.[16] Although the settlements showed a standardised and thus planned architecture, which included public cultic sites or gathering spaces, the culture of Jeitun can still not be described as proto-urban, since the criteria of high population density, production surplus enabling trade, and an administrative structure remained unmet.

4. The northern steppes of Central Asia – meeting point of hunters and herders with farmers

In Mongolia economies developed differently according to the prevailing climate type. About 7000 years ago, in the humid half of the land east of the modern capital Ulaan Baatar arose settlements of farmers who grew millet, having adopted the art of farming from China.[17] The dead, buried with their feet bound together, were sprinkled with ochre and buried in a crouching position with bull skulls including horns buried in adjacent pits, which could indicate veneration of the bull as a fertility symbol. The settlements had stationary shelters, which were half-sunk into the ground and whose entrance was found in a roof that reached to the ground. By contrast, in the drier, western half of the region only seasonal shelters of hunters, fishermen, and gatherers have been found. The people living in these seasonal shelters also buried their dead in a crouching position, but covered the grave with a roughly cone-shaped, low pile of stones, so that these late Neolithic or early Chalcolithic (Copper Stone Age) kurgans[18] of western Mongolia are among the earliest burial mounds of Eurasia. A further difference between the two halves of the region concerns ethnicity, since the farmers in the east were Palaeo-Mongols, while the hunters and fishermen in the west were Europids.[19] This ethnic boundary between the Europid and Mongolid peoples began to shift slowly to the west only in the second half of the third millennium BC.

In the forest steppes of southern Siberia west of Lake Baikal lived other hunters and fishermen who sprinkled their dead with ochre.[20] Here followed various cultures with very similar burial practices, which often overlapped in time: the group called **Kitoi**, which began around 5500 BC was superseded in 4250 BC by the **Isakovo** and **Serovo**, who were followed around 3250 by the **Glazkovo**, who also erected burial mounds and lasted till 2100 BC. As artworks these people left behind bone carvings and petroglyphs portraying elk and deer as well as anthropomorphic figures.[21] South-west of the Baikal region, in northern Kazakhstan there were also hunting and fishing communities of the **Atbasar** and **Makhandzhar** cultures (5500–3000 BC). These people had highly developed stone tools and hunted wild horses and goats, though they raised neither animal.[22] That the economic systems of the time were similar from western Mongolia almost to the Urals can be explained by the fact that the same climatic conditions prevailed across the area and no technological influences infiltrated from outside.

Things unfolded differently in western Central Asia. While in south-eastern Central Asia a relatively linear development from a hunter-gatherer economy to an agrarian one may be observed, in the north-west economic and cultural change occurred in a variable way as the boundary between hunters and herders shifted back and forth with the rhythm of climate fluctuations and human-caused changes in regional ecosystems. About 8,500 years ago knowledge of farming and animal husbandry expanded from western Anatolia to Greece and Macedonia, after which, around 6200 BC, pioneers began to spread this knowledge northward, both along the western coast of the Black Sea and into the Pannonian Plain. These emigrants did not speak Indo-European languages but rather an idiom derived from a very ancient Anatolian language.[23] From this arose the Körös-Criä Culture in Hungary and Romania, whose farmers cultivated millet, barley and peas and raised cattle, pigs and sheep. The farmers who moved farther north-east encountered around 5700 BC in the south-western part of today's Ukraine the **Bug-Dniester Culture** (6500–5200 BC) from the earliest Neolithic.[24] After an earlier, pre-ceramic period, these hunters and fishermen adopted the pottery of the **Elshanka Culture** (7000–6000 BC) of north-western Central Asia. The very early Neolithic community of Elshanka lived in the middle Volga region in the area around the modern city of Samara and had mastered the art of pottery as early as 6700 BC.[25] Representatives of the Bug-Dniester culture presumably spoke an idiom derived from the large language family out of which proto-Indo-European, called PIE, crystallised around 4500 BC.[26]

For half a millennium the Dniester River formed the boundary between two different economic structures: sedentary farmers in the west and hunters and fishermen in the east, with the latter, in a process of 'Neolithicising', adopting over time the raising of pigs and cattle, as well as some cultivation of wheat, millet and barley.[27] After 5200 BC the Neolithic and later the Chalcolithic Age culture of Cucuteni–Tripolye,[28] whose origin lay west of the Dniester, advanced eastward and expanded to the Dnieper River near the modern city of Kiev. With this the boundary between agrarian and hunting economies shifted about 300 km to the north-east.[29]

East of the Dnieper lived hunters, fishermen and gatherers of the very early Neolithic **Dnieper–Donets Culture I** (5700–5200 BC), who still used rough-hewn stone axes and were not familiar with the finely polished axes of the contemporaneous Bug–Dniester Culture. They buried their dead in a supine position and sprinkled them with red ochre. Around 5200 BC the people east of the Dnieper began to domesticate cattle, sheep and goats, as well as to use polished axes, thus founding the Neolithic **Dnieper–Donets Culture II** (5200–4200 BC).[30] They lived in simple huts with roofs made of birch bark but carried out complex burial rites. Analyses of skulls and skeletons indicate that members of the Dnieper–Donets Culture II were strong, broad-faced Europids, in contrast to the farmers of the Cucuteni–Tripolye Culture, who corresponded to a gracile, Mediterranean type.[31]

The dead of the Dnieper–Donets Culture II were often laid first in an open charnel-house, after which the bones were stripped of their remaining flesh, covered with ochre, and placed in communal graves. As can be inferred from various rich grave furnishings, this society of early Central Asian stockbreeders was hierarchical, with a chief at the top of the hierarchy. Chiefs were buried with thousands of pearls, crystal, copper and gold jewellery, carved boars' teeth and stone maces. While the copper ornaments were imported from the Balkans, the polished maces, whose heads were sometimes formed into the shape of a horse's head, were local symbols of authority. They spread quickly east as far as the Urals and west as far as the Danube, where they found acceptance in farming cultures. The symbol of the horse clearly served as a powerful status symbol in the herding societies of the fifth millennium, elevating the chief above the rest of the people. The opulent burials were accompanied by sacrifices of cattle, horses, sheep and goats, whose meat was distributed to the participants. Thus more than 6000 years ago there emerged a burial culture which became, with modifications, the norm for the highest classes on the steppes of Central Asia into the Middle Ages.[32]

In summary we can see that the Neolithic revolution led to an agrarian economy beyond the western boundary of Central Asia, while in western Central Asia itself it took the form of adoption of technologies of animal husbandry. In the grass steppe regions this had the unrivalled advantage that cattle and sheep were able to use grass that was inedible for humans, and thus opened to them the possibility of surviving on the grass steppe without having to hunt. However, livestock are vulnerable to bad weather and can easily be stolen, which led to conflicts with thieves or foreign, predatory groups. The volatility inherent in the raising of livestock, which increased with growing mobility, forced herders to stand in constant readiness to fight, and clans to cooperate more closely.

Hence, west of the Dnieper people mostly engaged in farming; to the east, livestock-raising was supplemented by hunting, often connected with particular burial rites. This contrast marked the history of Eurasia until the end of the Middle Ages. Within the Central Asian steppe there was likewise an economic boundary, with stockbreeding well established west of the Urals and ignored for more than a millennium east of them.

V

The Chalcolithic and the Early Bronze Age

The only god they [the Massagetae] worship is the sun, to which they sacrifice horses: the idea behind this is to offer the swiftest of mortal creatures to the swiftest of the gods.

HERODOTUS, *THE HISTORIES*[1]

1. The division of early history and the beginnings of metallurgy

The basic division of prehistoric cultural history according to the raw material used to make tools and weapons traces back to the French scholar Nicholas Mahudel (1704–1747), who in 1734 published *The Three Successive Ages of Stone, Bronze, and Iron*. More than 80 years later the Danish museum curator Christian Jürgensen Thomsen (1788–1865) implemented this concretely when he reclassified the collections of the future National Museum of Denmark. In the exhibition, which opened in 1819, he combined the objects in three large halls: in the first hall of the Stone Age, all stone objects came from a grave or an environment completely lacking metal objects. The second hall, of the Bronze Age, featured exclusively bronze objects from archaeological sites where there were no iron objects, and the Iron Age hall had only iron objects. The exhibition was a tremendous success and the underlying principle was put into place in other museums and collections.[2] Thomsen's classification was based on the belief that earlier humans had undergone a technological development that was reflected in their tools and weapons. In this the new, more powerful tools in each case superseded the older ones, and human prehistory proceeded in steps from simpler to more advanced technologies and products. Thus Thomsen's classification by technologies of production gave archaeology a way to work according to the principles of stratigraphy and wrested human prehistory away from the authority of mythology and religion by offering it a scientific foundation.

Later Thomsen's schema was expanded to include the Chalcolithic, the Copper Stone Age, as a fourth age, and the Stone Age was divided into three parts, so that the chronology consisted of Palaeolithic, Mesolithic, Neolithic, Chalcolithic, Bronze Age and Iron Age. Such a model is, of course, subject to certain limitations. In practice it was quickly shown that the transition from one period to the next was not abrupt but rather took place over centuries or even millennia. As has already been discussed, in certain steppe cultures simple tools and arrowheads made of stone remained in use long after the introduction of bronze or even iron. Such a division according to the raw materials of tools and weapons is also not automatically meaningful for the entire developmental process of a culture, as shown by, for instance, the classical epoch of the Maya of Central America (200–900 AD), who lived in the Stone Age but had a sophisticated and precise astronomical calendar. Finally, the model cannot be applied worldwide, as certain cultures outside the Eurasian continent had no access to particular raw materials, such as copper. Nevertheless, for the history of Central Asia this scheme remains a generally recognised aid to orientation.[3]

In Central Asia the Chalcolithic followed the Late Stone Age. The name, derived from the Greek, means *khalkos*, 'copper', and *lithos*, 'stone', thus 'Copper Stone Age', which preceded the Bronze Age. In this period there appeared beside the dominant stone tools the first copper objects, such as first ornamental plates and soon thereafter simple tools.[4] The Copper Stone Age is sometimes hard to distinguish from the early Bronze Age, however, because at an early stage people began to blend additional arsenic with the small amount of naturally occurring arsenic in copper ore to harden it. The earliest copper ornaments appeared sporadically in Neolithic contexts of western Asia and Anatolia in the eighth and seventh millennia BC; true production, which included the forging and casting of everyday objects, began first in the fifth millennium BC, centred in south-eastern Europe, the southern Caucasus and southern Turkmenistan. In south-eastern Europe there arose the **Balkano–Carpathian Metallurgical Province** (*ca.* 4800–3700 BC), producing mostly pure copper objects, which extended from Serbia and Romania to the western part of the Ukraine and corresponded more or less to the region of the agrarian culture of Cucuteni–Tripolye.[5] The new material was not particularly suitable for the production of everyday objects, however, as copper bends even when cold and copper blades rapidly become dull. Thus attempts were soon made to improve the metal by alloying. This transitional period to the Bronze Age, in which artificial alloying played an important role, lasted several centuries. Following on the Balkano–Carpathian Metallurgical Province was the **Circumpontic Metallurgical Province**[6] (3300–1900 BC), which encompassed the Balkans, the Carpathians, the Caucasus, Asia Minor, the northern coast of the Black Sea and the western Central Asian steppes as far as the Urals. This 'province', which really represented a network of bronze-producing centres, played a leading role in the transmission of knowledge about metallurgy to the east as far as China.[7] A few of the richest copper mines were found in the Urals at the junction between western and eastern Central Asia, including the unique 500-km^2 Kargaly complex. The shafts, which ran as deep as 42 m under the surface of the earth, were hundreds of kilometres long, and it has been estimated that about 120 million m^3 of rock and marl were dug out with pickaxes and shovels, yielding 2 to 5 million tons of copper ore.[8] At the time the Urals formed a kind of export boundary to the east, as for a thousand years copper ore went only westwards, to the workshops on the Volga and the Don.

A hunter in the Russian Altai.

The first bronze alloy was presumably invented between 3750 and 3500 BC by the stockbreeding culture of Maikop on the south-western border of Central Asia.[9] This culture, which existed from 3750 to 3000 BC, extended into the northern Caucasus and had its centre in the valley of the Kuban River. Although the Kuban region lies just outside the geographic borders of Central Asia, its culture belongs to the cultural sphere of the Central Asian steppe. The Caucasus and especially the Kuban region met the requirements for early production of bronze, as they were rich in metal ores like copper, lead, silver and gold. Because tin was not available in the Caucasus, however, the early, high-quality bronze of Maikop consisted of a copper-arsenic alloy and later of copper and lead. Arsenic bronze is harder in a cold state than pure copper, easier to cast, and has a lighter colour. Because of its geographic location, the Caucasus formed a bridge between Mesopotamia in the south and the Central Asian steppe in the north, so the Maikop Culture exported its bronze in both directions as finished products or as bars. Soon the specialised forges of Maikop became the chief bronze producers for north-western Central Asia up to the Urals and had a decided influence on local workshops. Arsenic bronze also spread quickly west around 3250 BC as far as the Danube delta, but it only reached Central and Western Europe a millennium later.[10] Maikop also played a leading role with regard to another very significant invention: its people were the first in Central Asia to use heavy, four-wheeled wagons pulled by oxen.[11]

The superior tin bronze was developed not in the south-west of Central Asia like arsenic bronze, but rather in the north-east, in the forest steppes of the Urals and the Altai. Here lived bellicose, semi-nomadic herders, who began around 2000 BC to produce outstanding and superior weapons out of tin bronze, whose development is described as the phenomenon of Seima-Turbino.[12] This bronze was not only significantly harder and stronger than copper; it also had a bright gloss. The new technology was based on the enormous supply of tin in eastern Kazakhstan and the nearly inexhaustible reserves of wood for processing.[13] Thus these nomadic herders from the Altai broke the monopoly of the Caucasian arsenic bronze and began exporting new products and technologies to the west. Two millennia before the Silk Roads the tin and tin bronze roads emerged, stretching from the Russian–Mongolian Altai and eastern Kazakhstan to Eastern Europe. The early bronze technology based on arsenic or lead had spread from west to east, but the superior type of bronze using tin – whether in finished products or in bars – moved from east to west.

Tin bronze was also superior to unalloyed iron. In Iraq as early as the third millennium BC iron blades were fashioned out of meteorites, but because of their lack of purity they were often softer than comparable bronze blades.[14] Only when it became possible to produce iron alloys with small amounts of carbon – that is, steel – did iron become useful in weapons and tools. The blacksmith had to be aware that the red-hot steel needed to be plunged into cold water, in contrast to molten bronze, which requires slow cooling. The increasingly acute shortage of tin certainly also contributed to the triumph of iron.[15]

2. An initial proto-urban development

Towards the end of the sixth or beginning of the fifth millennium BC, the people of the Neolithic Jeitun Culture began to spread to the south-east, presumably under pressure from a rapidly growing population. They settled in the narrow, 350-km-long fertile band in the northern foothills of the Kopet Dag Mountains, where the many rivers that flow north from the Kopet Dag into the Kara Kum Desert enabled farming and the creation of new settlements.

In the early twentieth century Raphael Pumpelly conducted pioneering excavations at **Anau** in southern Turkmenistan; later excavations confirmed most of his observations and many of his conclusions. At the northern Tepe of Anau it is possible to observe the transition from small, single-room dwellings to multi-room structures, with the organisation of the buildings corresponding to a typical agrarian settlement of the Chalcolithic. It consisted of several groups of closely standing building complexes with ten to 15 rooms, which had their own hearths. Each complex had a shared inner courtyard with children's graves beneath it and a large storehouse for agricultural products. The multi-family complex with communal facilities replaced the earlier single-family house of Jeitun. Presumably the families were related and formed a clan. Between these groups of buildings, narrow streets ran through the settlement, which also had an especially grand building with plaster walls and floors. This building presumably served the entire population for common ritual purposes.

Particularly striking in Anau North are the buildings with a circular floor plan, since these not only served as storerooms but were also in some cases clearly inhabited and may have been used as observation towers. They seem to anticipate the somewhat later defence towers of the settlements of Yalangach and Mullali Tepe 200 km to the east (after 3500 BC), where mud brick walls connected the towers to one another and thus fortified the site.

The pioneer Raphael Pumpelly in Anau

The honour of discovering this proto-urban culture went to the American Raphael Pumpelly (1837–1923). Pumpelly was a geologist and mineralogist who undertook large surveys in Japan, China, and, in 1864–65, the Gobi Desert, after which he was named the first professor of mining science at Harvard University. After his retirement Pumpelly decided to work as an archaeologist in Central Asia, with a goal of making a scientific study of the connections between geological conditions, climatic fluctuations and the development of early civilisations. He wanted to test the hypothesis that climatic changes represented a decisive factor in geographic shifts of entire settlements and migrations. Thanks to his multidisciplinary approach Pumpelly was a revolutionary who not only assembled an interdisciplinary team but also, because of his geological expertise, understood the great importance of carefully documenting each stratigraphic layer. He was one of the first archaeologists to use stratigraphic surveys to determine the age of finds and to establish complex relationships.

At age 65 Pumpelly travelled to the site of Anau in the northern Kopet Dag region of Turkmenistan, 8 km south-east of the modern capital Ashgabat. During an earlier trip he had been intrigued by two free-standing mounds (known as 'Tepe' in Central Asia) here. One was 12 m tall and the other 15 m; to the east stood a third mound, inhabited until about 1850. When he investigated a deep test trench in the northern Tepe, which had been excavated by the Russian general Komarov and his soldiers in a quest for treasure in 1886, Pumpelly counted 20 layers of settlement lying one atop the other. He recognised that this was a very old settlement that, over the course of time, had been rebuilt again and again over the naturally eroded ruins of an earlier layer. In 1904 he returned to Anau in the company of his wife Eliza, the economic geographer Ellsworth Huntington and the archaeologists Langdon Warner and Hubert Schmidt and began excavations.[16]

Based on his discoveries Pumpelly concluded that the northern Tepe represented the older of the two settlements. He found simple, rectangular mud brick houses, made out of air-dried bricks of a standard size. Under their floors were buried children in the foetal position, a custom that can be seen in many later settlements of southern Turkmenistan. In the lowest, earliest layer of the northern mound graves of adults were also found under the floors of some residences, and in these cases the room above the graves was no longer used.[17] Pumpelly also found pottery made by hand and painted with geometric patterns, spindle whorls and a few copper needles. There were no metal weapons, only stone maces and slingshots. Clearly the people were farmers who cultivated barley and wheat and also raised sheep, goats, pigs and dogs. Pumpelly believed the climate at that time was considerably more humid than today.

This northern settlement, attributed to the early Chalcolithic, was gradually abandoned after more than 1000 years, and a new settlement was built about 800 m to the south, where public and ritual spaces played a more important role than they had in the northern mound. Here Pumpelly also uncovered children's graves under the floors of the houses, from which he concluded that the inhabitants of the southern, Chalcolithic settlement belonged to the same people as those of the north. New, however, were vessels crafted on a potter's wheel, bronze sickles, daggers, spear points and arrowheads, as well as the occasional weapon made of arsenic bronze. In the lower layers there were also many small terra cotta figurines of bulls and women with broad thighs, the latter often near the children's graves. Finally there came to light a cube-shaped seal, on whose sides were carved a lion, a man and a griffin in the form of a winged lion with the head of a bird. The upper 12 layers, however, belonged to another, Iron Age culture, whose representatives resettled the southern mound after it had been abandoned for a couple of centuries. When the nearby meandering river shifted its course to the east, the people followed and established a new settlement at the eastern mound.[18]

Pumpelly divided the two excavated mounds into four cultural periods, which were later, omitting the post-Bronze Age layers, organised into Anau I A, I B, II A, and II B. His original dating of Anau I as about 10,000 years old proved to be too early, but his second, of 6,500 years, was correct and has been confirmed by carbon-14 dating.

In this sense the *ca.* 6,000-year-old round towers of Anau North could represent prototypes of the typical fortified desert oasis architecture of the Bronze Age in south-eastern Central Asia.

The air-dried bricks used for house-building in Anau North were vulnerable to the rare rainfall and had a limited maximum life of 30 to 35 years. If a building fell into disrepair, the inhabitants did not patch it up but rather tore down the entire house or even a whole complex and rebuilt on the 30- to 40-cm layer of rubble. Since houses and building complexes were built and rebuilt over generations on the same site, long-term land tenure can be hypothesised. Even after large-scale destruction, for example by conflicts or earthquakes, and short-term abandonment of the mound, the farmers did not leave the site of their settlement but rather razed the ruins and rebuilt the village. This meant that no fewer than 20 different architectural layers were found on top of each other at Anau North.[19] Presumably the large cultic space, which was rebuilt many times, formed a geographic anchor for the location of the settlement.

In contrast to the farmers of Jeitun, who depended on the collection of rainwater, those of Anau were familiar with the principle of tiered irrigation. They did not disperse the water that flowed out of the mountains when it reached the river delta but rather captured it upstream and directed it by means of clay and wooden canals, as well as low dams, over artificially built terraces, stepwise into the lower delta. In addition to farming, they raised sheep, goats, cattle, pigs and camels and hunted antelope and, in the mountains, ibexes. The discovery of the bones of Bactrian or two-humped camels in Anau as well as in settlements further south-east such as Altyn Tepe and Geoksyur from the time of Anau II B/Namazga III and IV suggests that in southern Turkmenistan the camel was for the first time not only hunted or raised for meat but also domesticated for transportation purposes as a pack or draught animal. Small, four-wheeled terra cotta wagon figurines from Altyn Tepe, approximately 4,500 years old, with a Bactrian camel as draught animal provide evidence of this. Their discoverer, Soviet archaeologist Vadim Masson, believed that the high population density of the small oasis at that time meant that food had to be acquired from far away, which encouraged the domestication of the camel and the development of four-wheeled wagons. At the same time the scarcity of resources forced people to construct complex organisations and societal structures.[20]

The original habitat of the two-humped camel extended from Inner Mongolia over the Mongol Republic as far as Kazakhstan, so that the name 'Bactrian' camel, given by Aristotle, refers not to its origin but rather to the approximate location of its earliest domestication.[21] The life expectancy of the camel is 35 to 40 years, of which it can work for 20 to 25 years. A well-fed animal can carry 200 kg for eight days without water if travelling on solid ground; in soft sand, however, it can go only five days carrying 120 kg without water. In the winter it can withstand temperatures as cold as -25 °C without problems, as well as heights up to 4,000 m above sea level, but extended periods of heat are intolerable, so caravans crossing the Gobi or Taklamakan desert traditionally avoided the summer months and travelled by night. In southern Central Asia people raised not only two-humped Bactrians but also, for cross-breeding purposes, single-humped

Chronology of the early settlements of Kopet Dag

CENTRAL KOPET DAG	EASTERN KOPET DAG: ETEK PERIODS	EASTERN KOPET DAG: GEOKSYUR PERIODS	MURGAB & BACTRIA: BMAC PERIODS	TIME (BC)
Jeitun				6500–4500
Anau I A (Anau northern mound)	Anau I A			4800–4000
Anau I B (Anau northern mound)	Namazga I	Dashli		4000–3500
Anau II A (Anau southern mound)	Namazga II	Yalangach		3500–3100
Anau II B (Anau southern mound)	Namazga III	Geoksyur		3100–2500
	Namazga IV	Altyn Tepe		2500–2200
	Namazga V	Khapuz Tepe	Kelleli	2300/2200–1900
Anau III	Namazga VI		Gonur, Togolok	2000/1900–1500
			Sapalli, Jarkutan	1700–1350

In 1952 Pumpelly's four-period chronology of Anau was superseded by Kuftin's 'Namazga' classification in six periods, which is used today for dating prehistoric archaeological finds in flat regions of south-eastern Central Asia up to the Iron Age. At the prehistoric site of Namazga, which lies 90 km south-east of Anau and consists of a 34 m settlement layer, B.A. Kuftin identified six cultural periods.[22]

Palimpsest of two male camels; the larger of which is more than 1 m high. Petroglyph complex of Arpa Uzen in the Karatau Mountains, southern Kazakhstan, Bronze Age.

dromedaries. The single-humped hybrid resulting from a male Bactrian and a female dromedary was significantly stronger than its parents. The 650- to 900-kg beasts were able to carry up to 450 kg, more than twice as much as a Bactrian. The descendants of hybrids proved to be ill-tempered and dangerous, however, so the male hybrids were castrated.[23]

Before camels were used to pull wagons in Kopet Dag, beginning at the end of the fourth millennium or start of the third millennium BC oxen had been yoked to single-axle carts, as depicted in miniature clay figurines. Because of the worsening drought, however, the more efficient camel replaced the ox as the preferred draught animal in the second half of the third millennium BC.[24]

In conclusion it seems likely the American archaeologist Frederick Hiebert is correct in saying that in Anau a local development from loosely organised farming villages of the Jeitun Culture to the proto-urban settlement of the southern mound took place, after which this type of settlement spread as far the Geoksyur oasis. These settlements had contact with northern Iranian cultures, although the migration of Iranian farmers to the northern Kopet Dag plain at the start of the fifth millennium BC that was postulated by the archaeologists Vadim Masson and Viktor Sarianidi is highly improbable.[25]

Chalcolithic and Early Bronze Age sites of south-eastern Central Asia and the Kopet Dag sites

List of Geoksyur sites (opposite)

1. Dashli Tepe
2. Aksha Tepe
3. Geoksyur 1 Tepe
4. Yalangach Tepe
5. Mullali Tepe
6. Khong Tepe
7. Khapuz Tepe

● Ruins | ancient sites

○ Modern cities and towns

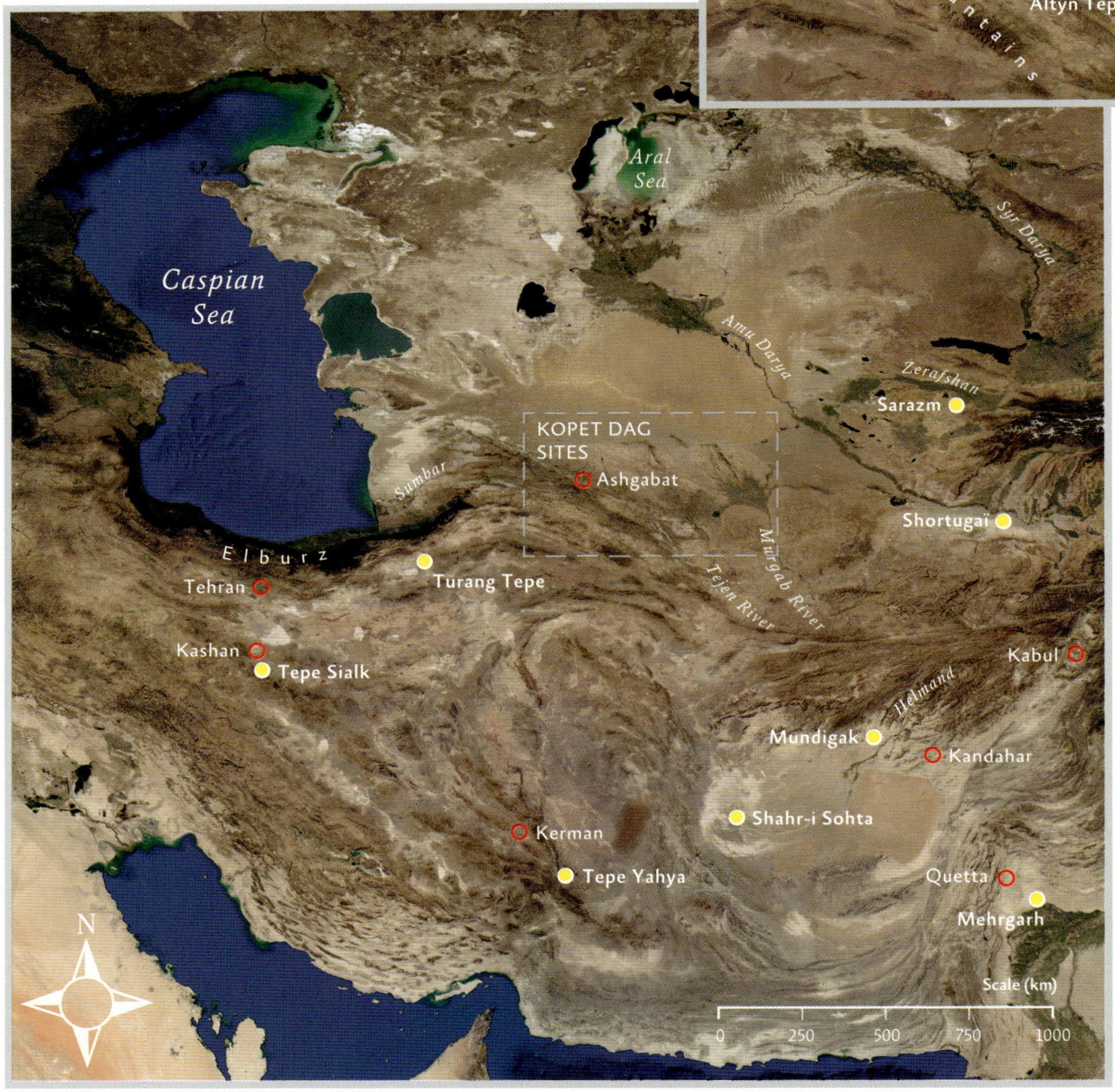

3. The first cities of Central Asia in southern Turkmenistan

In the second half of the fourth millennium BC there was a first wave of urbanisation in southern Turkmenistan, when farmers from the Anau region spread to the south-east and founded the settlements of Namazga, Ulug Tepe and Altyn Tepe.[26] After travelling about 200 km they reached the Tejen River, in whose delta they established, over the course of time, the nine settlements of the **Geoksyur oases**, which belong to the time periods of Namazga II and III. These stood on small, naturally occurring alluvial rises, which emerged like islands out of the swampy surrounding waters and whose banks were overgrown with thickets of reeds and riparian forests. The farmers of these small settlements began, with the help of clay spindle whorls, to turn the wool of domesticated sheep into yarn, so that the new materials replaced the earlier animal skin clothing.[27] The sheep *ovis orientalis* was first domesticated around 8000 BC in Mesopotamia as a source of meat, but its wool was first worked into yarn only 4000 years later. Now the sheep was valuable not only once as food but also daily as a source of milk, and annually or semi-annually for wool for textiles.

The earliest villages, established in the northern part of the river delta, such as Dashli Tepe, Yalangach Tepe and Aksha Tepe, were short-lived. The dramatically shifting Tejen River, which drifted westward, began, as a consequence of climate changes, to carry less water and no longer reached the mound settlements. The land dried up, forcing wild game to move to the south and making the cultivation of barley and wheat impossible. The farmers had to follow the water and built their dwelling farther south, but soon the steady disappearance of water forced the abandonment of Mullali Tepe and Geoksyur Tepe 9 as well. Geoksyur 1 was abandoned shortly after so that only the settlement of Khong Tepe in the south remained. The drying up of the delta continued unabated, however, and despite the construction of long irrigation canals the farmers had to leave Khong Tepe, too, after which they moved 18 km farther south to Khapuz Tepe (Namazga IV/V period).[28] This phenomenon, in which oasis settlements had to be abandoned as a consequence of dwindling water supply, was repeated many times in other agricultural oases, such as in the delta of the Murgab River east of the Geoksyur oases

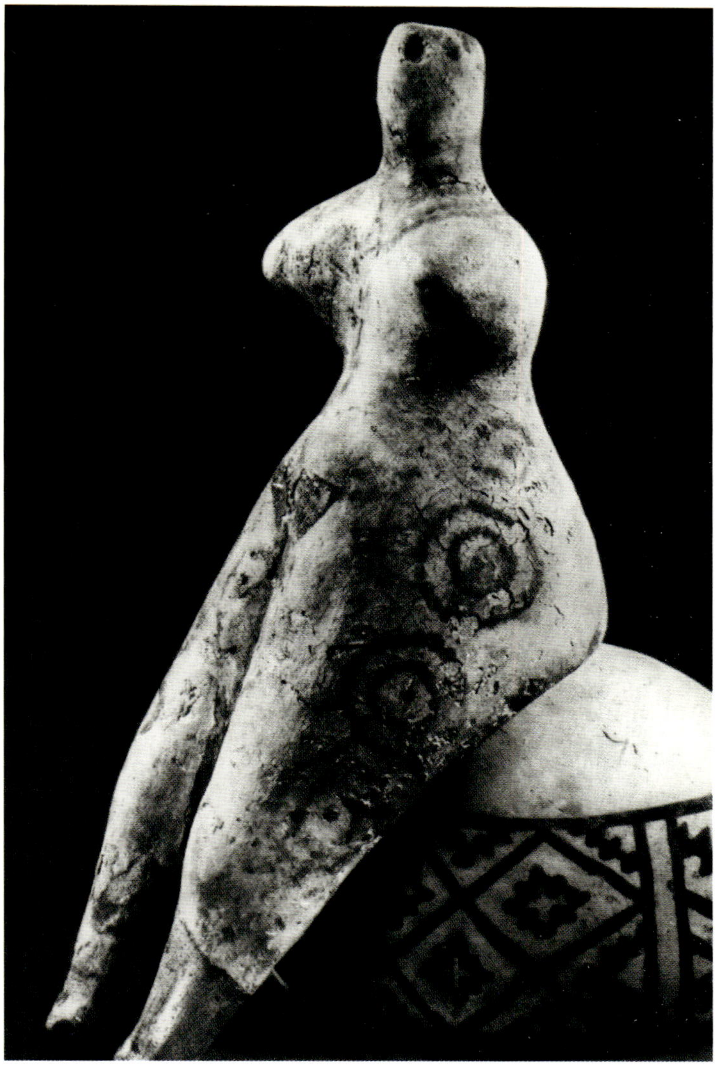

Painted terra cotta statue of a seated woman, presumably portraying a fertility goddess, Yalangach Tepe, Turkmenistan, *ca.* 3500–3100 BC. National Museum of Turkmenistan, Ashgabat.

Four-wheeled clay model of a wagon with painted side walls and a camel as draught animal, Altyn Tepe, Turkmenistan, *ca.* 2500 BC. The State Hermitage Museum, St. Petersburg.

Flat female statues made of terra cotta, which were part of a private domestic cult, Altyn Tepe, Turkmenistan, *ca.* 2600–2100 BC. National Museum of Turkmenistan, Ashgabat.

Gold bull's head with turquoise inlays found in a tomb close to the step pyramid of Altyn Tepe, Turkmenistan, *ca.* 2600–2100 BC. National Museum of Turkmenistan, Ashgabat.

or in the Taklamakan Desert in north-western China, in the deltas of the Keriya, Niya and Andier Rivers, as well as the Tarim.[29]

As at Anau the Geokysur oases had circular buildings fortified with thick walls, which may have been used as granaries or defensive towers. Even if they served primarily as storerooms, they had a defensive function, since they were, as at Yalangach and Mullali, connected to one another by a wall around the settlement.[30] The houses of the earliest settlement at Dashli Tepe appear to have taken up the old idea, familiar from the Jeitun Culture, of one-room, single-family structures, although at Yalangach Tepe multi-room buildings also appeared. Clay statuettes found beside some ovens there depict rams and large-bodied, seated women, often painted with geometric patterns. These figures suggest that these hearths served profane as well as cultic purposes.[31] The female figurines, whose thighs were sometimes also decorated with the profile of a goat, and the ram statues, can be interpreted as typical fertility symbols of a Chalcolithic agrarian society in then-fertile southern Central Asia. Other, somewhat older female figurines, such as those from Kara Tepe, have strange, birdlike faces with almond-shaped eyes.[32]

About 600 years after the founding of the settlement of **Altyn Tepe** around 3200 BC the site developed into a city with all the attributes of an early Bronze Age urban culture in southern Central Asia. The urban characteristics consist of high population density, compact architecture, monumental buildings, centralised administration, coordinated provision of food, specialised types of work and commercial activities and a means of security, in the form of a city wall or defensive troops. The 25-ha city stood on a natural rise with steep sides, and in its heyday from about 2600 to 2200/2100 BC (Namazga IV and early V) the 4- to 4.5-m-high city walls made of mud bricks protected a population of 6,000 to 7,000 inhabitants. On a wide road through the 7- to 8-m-high monumental gate, which resembles the imposing entrance gates of Mesopotamian cities, carts pulled by camels travelled into the inner city, where perpendicular streets connected the individual quarters to each other.

As can be seen from the various types of private homes, Altyn Tepe was divided into four social strata. The lowest class was made up of servants or household slaves, who did not have houses of their own but rather lived with their masters. The next level

▶ Illustration according to archaeological data of the Bronze Age fortified settlement of Altyn Tepe, Turkmenistan, *ca.* 2600–2100 BC. The camel drivers in the foreground wear a kaunakes, a cloak made of either sheep- or goatskin or sheep's wool, which was popular in the Bronze Age from Mesopotamian Sumer to southern Turkmenistan; in the background are the city gate and the step pyramid.

One of the five excavations of Sarazm, protected by a metal roof, north-western Tajikistan, period of Sarazm II, *ca.* 3200–2900 BC.

consisted of free artisans, who lived in their own quarters in large, multi-family complexes with living and work areas. Belonging to this class were potters who worked with potters' wheels; producers of the many small clay figurines of women; and blacksmiths, who worked with both arsenic-copper and tin-copper alloys. They most likely procured the necessary ores from the agrarian settlement of Sarazm in far north-western Tajikistan. Sarazm, whose founders came from the Kopet Dag oases, was one of the most important centres of metallurgy in south-eastern Central Asia and had, along with the nearby Fergana valley, rich sources of copper, lead, tin, arsenic, gold and silver.[33]

The affluent citizens had their own residential quarter made up of single-family houses, while the carefully constructed, spacious homes of the elite were concentrated along perpendicularly arranged streets around the cultic centre. As the graves with the richest inventory of grave goods were found in the cultic complex, the elite who lived and were buried here must also have served a cultic purpose. The cultic centre consisted of a 12-m-high, multi-storey pyramid with a rectangular base, which was topped with a tower made of mud brick. One side of the pyramid abutted a natural mound. This step pyramid, unusual for Central Asia, which could also be described as step terraces with an attached tower, strongly recalls the early ziggurats of Mesopotamia. This led the excavating archaeologist Vadim Masson to conjecture that this particular idea of sacred architecture was influenced by Mesopotamia and Iran.[34] Aside from the lack of ascending ramps, the similarities between the step pyramid of Altyn Tepe and the proto-Elamite step pyramid of Tepe Sialk, Iran, are indeed astonishing. The step pyramid of Tepe Sialk was built around 2900 BC on the ruins of a still older terrace shrine. Like Altyn Tepe, it had four increasingly smaller platforms one on top of the other. Right at the top was a small, tower-like structure, the symbolic home of the deity to which the pyramid was consecrated.[35] Another point of reference for the proto-Elamite culture may lie at the site of Tepe Yahya in south-eastern Iran. Here the massive step-style construction of Konar Sandal I from the mid-third millennium BC has been excavated. Individual chlorite vessels of a similar age from the neighbouring archaeological site of Jiroft are also decorated with schematic portrayals of ziggurats, so it is conceivable that Tepe Yahya and Jiroft provided inspiration for the step pyramid at Altyn Tepe.[36] Similar step pyramids are also found in the contemporaneous cities of Tureng Tepe south-east of the Caspian Sea, Mundigak north-west of the Afghan city of Kandahar, and Shahr-i Sokhta in south-eastern Iran.[37]

In Altyn Tepe there were two different cultic forms; an institutional one of the city and a private one of the households. In each house, in granaries and in some collective graves, there were schematically portrayed female terra cotta figurines with broad but flat hips, a flat torso with prominent breasts, a long neck, affixed eyes of a rhomboid shape, a hooked nose and snake-like braids falling on both sides of the face. The lower part of the body ended in a triangle instead of legs, since it would be stuck in the ground or in a recess beside an altar, analogous to the female statuettes of the contemporaneous agrarian culture of Tripolye in far western Central Asia and those of the Indus Valley Civilisation.[38] In other statues the lower part is bent forward at a right angle, representing a seated position.[39] These flat statuettes from the transition period from the Copper Stone Age to the early Bronze Age are fundamentally different from the voluptuous matrons of the mid-Chalcolithic, such as those from Yalangach Tepe.[40] In addition, many of the statuettes of Altyn Tepe have engraved symbols consisting of combinations of lines, which had a hidden meaning. Their unknown message is all the more intriguing because the symbols can be grouped and often appeared in identical form. Vadim Masson has compared these statuettes with the proto-Elamite marks of Mesopotamia and those of the Indus Valley Civilisation (*ca.* 2800–1800 BC), and found a few remarkable similarities.[41] The birdlike faces also indicate clear relations to Mesopotamia, as the snake-like braids do to the Indus Valley Civilisation, which may reflect an orientation toward Mesopotamia and particularly to the Indus delta.[42] These figurines of women presumably portray female deities, which were venerated in the context of private households.

Unlike in the profane dwellings, no female figurines were found in the civic cultic complex. In the grave of a man near the step pyramid archaeologists discovered rich grave goods that presumably had a cultic purpose. Among them was the 7.5-cm-high head of a bull made of pure gold, with horns made of silver covered in gold leaf. The eyes are made of turquoise and a third, crescent-shaped turquoise adorns the forehead. This golden bull's head recalls Sumerian toreutics,[43] especially the bulls' heads on the resonators of the lyres from the royal tombs of Ur.[44] Moreover, the Sumerian moon god Nanna-Sin, who could appear in the form of a bull, was the patron deity of Ur and the large, three-story ziggurat of Ur was dedicated to him. Thus Masson surmised that 'the cultic centre of Altyn Tepe was apparently dedicated to a male god, a local variant of Nanna-Sin, whose multi-story tower so obviously followed the prototype of the ziggurat of ancient Sumer'.[45] This means that in Altyn Tepe a private cult of mostly female fertility goddesses, which also protected the hearth and family, coexisted with a public cult of a patron god with roots in Mesopotamia. It is the moment at which male deities began to replace female deities at the top of the pantheon of south-eastern Central Asia. There was, in broad terms, a 'twilight of the goddesses', which heralded the transition from a purely sedentary agrarian society to nomadic trading societies and, before long, to bellicose stockbreeding societies.

The significance of the metal seals found here is still unknown. They are made of an alloy of bronze and low-grade silver with geometric or zoomorphic motifs, and they may have served as amulets. The most striking seal is in the form of a three-headed beast with the body of a big cat, two snake heads, and one head of a bird of prey, which was discovered in the grave of a woman in the temple district.[46] This fantastical creature seems to anticipate the three-headed demon Aži Dahāka from the Zoroastrian

With their decorative patterns of Maltese crosses and three-step pyramids, the ceramics of Sarazm II and III (3200–2500 BC) show close ties to those of the Geoksyur oasis of Turkmenistan. Local museum of Sarazm, north-western Tajikistan.

The late medieval fortress of Derawar Fort in the Cholistan Desert guarded an ancient trade route that linked the cities of the Indus Valley Civilisation with trade partners in Central Asia 4,500 years ago; Punjab Province, central Pakistan.

Avesta – one of the most feared servants of Ahriman, the destructive spirit.[47]

The inhabitants of Altyn Tepe continued the practice, begun in Anau, of 'intra muros' burial of infants. They were buried within houses, primarily in corners under the floor or beneath the threshold, rarely in containers. Adults, however, were buried in communal graves, which were either close to inhabited house complexes or in uninhabited, abandoned sections of the city.[48]

The domestication of the camel and the adoption of four-wheeled wagons made the transportation of goods much easier, enabling the oasis cities of Kopet Dag to engage in trade. They were part of a large trade network that stretched from Mesopotamia in the west to Sarazm (Tajikistan) in the north-east, Shortugaï (Afghanistan) in the east, and the Indus Valley Civilisation (Pakistan) in the south-east. Geographically speaking the oasis cities of Kopet Dag lay in the centre of this network. The distances from here, as the crow flies, to the Mesopotamian cities such as Ur was about 1,300 km; to Sarazm, 800 km; to Shortugaï, likewise 800 km; and to the Indus cities of Harappa or Mohenjo-daro, 1,400 to 1,700 km. The impulse behind this transcontinental trade was the insatiable hunger of the cities of Mesopotamia for ores and gemstones from eastern Central Asia.[49] These land routes supplemented the sea routes between the cities of the Indus Valley Civilisation and Mesopotamia. It is possible that merchants at that time were able to communicate directly with each other thanks to a common language, since similarities between the Dravidian languages of India and Elamite, which is now extinct, have led to the hypothesis of a shared precursor language. This proto-Elamite-Dravidian language would then have been the lingua franca between Elam and the Indus Valley Civilisation with its branches in the oases of Central Asia.[50]

One of the most sought-after commodities was tin, which was less widely available in Eurasia than copper or iron. One of the oldest and richest tin mines of the prehistoric world was found in the valley of Zerafshan near **Sarazm**, whose Tajik name Sar-i zamin means roughly 'beginning of the land'.[51] The proto-urban settlement of Sarazm lies near the city of Panjikent in north-western Tajikistan and was for a long time the most northerly settled agricultural centre in eastern Central Asia. Although only 5 ha of the 100-ha settlement have been excavated – the site is mostly covered by a farming village – four stratigraphic layers have been identified. Sarazm I (3500–3200 BC) was founded as a kind of colony of earlier oasis cities of Kopet Dag from the transition period from Namazga I to II in the fertile valley of the middle Zarafshan on a site settled since the Neolithic, as demonstrated by the discovery of pottery of the Kelteminar Culture. It was probably established for economic reasons, as the area around Sarazm is rich in ore and semiprecious gems such as turquoise.

That Sarazm developed from the blueprints of the immigrants, so to speak, can be deduced from the city plan of the well-preserved layer of Sarazm II (3200–2900 BC). The two- and three-room residences stood along straight streets, with public plazas with workshops and storehouses following sets of three to six houses. As in Altyn Tepe, monumental architecture enriched the

The 20-year-old Europid woman buried in Sarazm with a man and a girl was clothed in garments adorned with lapis lazuli, turquoise and carnelian, *ca.* 3000 BC. National Museum of Antiquities of Tajikistan, Dushanbe.

cityscape of Sarazm. One building, 7 m high and with a square floor plan of 15 x 15 m, was interpreted by the first excavator, Isakov, as the administrative centre, and a second as a temple, where first the sun was worshipped and later bulls were sacrificed. At the same time, small cultic niches stood in private homes, with a hearth for the sacred fire.[52] The close connection of Sarazm II and Sarazm III (2900–2500 BC) to Altyn Tepe and the Geoksyur oases can be seen in the nearly identically painted ceramic objects. Among the most striking patterns are white or red Maltese crosses on black or white backgrounds, as well as red three-level pyramids on a black background.[53]

The triple burial of a 20-year-old couple with a girl gives a sense of the prosperity of Sarazm at that time. The woman was buried in rich clothing adorned with beads made of lapis lazuli, turquoise and carnelian, and her head and arms were covered with dozens of gold and silver beads. Two bracelets made of seashells underscore her high social standing and indicate trade with the Indus Valley Civilisation. Craniological studies showed that both the adults were dolichocephalic – that is, they had long, relatively narrow skulls and a gracile build. Like the inhabitants of the northern foothills of the Kopet Dag and the Geoksyur oases, these people were Europids of the Mediterranean type.[54]

The final period, Sarazm IV (2500–1500 BC), flourished again for about 500 years, until the start of a widespread drought in Central Asia around 2000 BC, which also constrained life in the Kopet Dag and Geoksyur oases. Then, in the nineteenth/eighteenth centuries BC, stockbreeders from the Andronovo cultural horizon advanced from the north. They used the valley floor as grazing land and took over the mining of tin. At this time the last farmers of the Geoksyur–Sarazm Culture left the area.[55]

The trading cities of southern Turkmenistan were not satisfied with merely securing raw materials from the east; they also ensured their trade channels to the cities of the Indus Valley by founding the urban settlement of **Shahr-i Sokhta** in south-eastern Iran. This city was founded around 3200 BC and grew as large as 80 ha in area. Like Altyn Tepe, it had a monumental step pyramid. Shahr-i Sokhta lay halfway along the southern trade route, since it was 750 km from Altyn Tepe and 800 km from Mohenjo-daro. The distance to Ur in south-eastern Mesopotamia was 1,300 km. The city was not just a way station for trade caravans, however, but also a centre of artisanal production, where lapis lazuli, turquoise, carnelian, chlorite and seashells were crafted into objects that were usually exported to the city-states of Mesopotamia. At the same time as the collapse of Sarazm, at the start of the second millennium BC, this city fell and burned to the ground.[56]

The lapis lazuli and seashells discovered in the grave of the 'princess of Sarazm', as well as other finds, such as square clay seals, indicate that Sarazm conducted trade not only with the Altyn Tepe and Kopet Dag oases but also with Afghanistan and the cities of the Indus Valley Civilisation. Clay seals discovered in Altyn Tepe, as well as imported objects made of elephant ivory, underscore the trading relationships with the Indus Valley Civilisation, which had a trading post at **Shortugaï** in northern Afghanistan. This settlement in south-eastern Central Asia lies not far from the confluence of the Amu Darya and the Kokcha, close to Aï Khanum, where later Seleucus I (r. 305–281 BC) had a Persian settlement rebuilt as a Greek city. In the vicinity of Shortugaï there were also exceptionally rich reserves of lapis lazuli and turquoise.

Many objects found here were undoubtedly imports from the then-flourishing cities of the Indus Valley Civilisation. These include carnelian beads, worked agates, soapstone seals with carved images of rhinoceroses and ideograms typical of the Indus Valley Civilisation. Also other finds including bracelets made of seashells and game pieces made of clay, among them miniature zebus, camels and carts, as well as specially painted vessels were imports from the Indus Valley Civilisation. The gold, turquoise and faience objects were, however, fashioned by local artisans according to the techniques and taste of the Indus Valley Civilisation.[57] Shortugaï was a branch of one of the leading merchant cities of the Indus Civilisation, Harappa. Mohenjo-daro, like Sarazm, was a trading outpost of the Kopet Dag and Geoksyur oases of southern Turkmenistan.

In the first, urban period (2500–2100 BC), Shortugaï was a trading colony of the Indus cities with an outstanding production of pottery and brick buildings. Parallel to the collapse of the oasis culture of southern Turkmenistan, the post-urban period began in Shortugaï (2100–1700 BC) when a rustic tribal culture with traditional mud brick buildings replaced the urban trading culture. Contact with the Indus Valley Civilisation soon broke down, as that civilisation also reached its end. Trade dwindled and was conducted only with Bactria in the north. In the eighteenth century BC crude steppe pottery appeared – a clear indication that the nomadic stockbreeders who had earlier overrun Sarazm had now crossed the Amu Darya and advanced into northern Afghanistan.[58] Only 14 centuries later did Shortugaï experience a limited rebirth under Greek colonists.[59]

Although smaller cities with broad trade networks developed between Altyn Tepe and Geoksyur, the relatively large distances between the individual cities, as well as their limited militarisation, hampered the establishment of supra-regional entities like

Ruins of the city of Mohenjo-daro from the Indus Valley Civilisation, central Pakistan, *ca*. 2800–1800 BC. To the right in the background a Buddhist stupa from the second century AD rises above the ancient citadel.

The Indus Valley Civilisation, trade partner of Central Asia in the early Bronze Age

The cities of the Indus Valley Civilisation (*ca.* 2800–1800 BC), in today's Pakistan and north-western India, were the most important trade partners of the trading cities of southern Turkmenistan. The Indus Valley Civilisation was a unique urban culture that arose from the agrarian culture of Mehrgarh. It had highly productive agriculture and followed a revolutionary strategy of urbanisation. Over an area of 680,000 square kilometres traces of about 1,500 settlements[60] have been discovered. The most important cities, such as Mohenjo-daro, Kalibangan and Harappa, were constructed in a uniform manner according to a geometric master plan, whether this meant completely rebuilding older settlements or undertaking new construction from the ground up. The small upper city always stood in the west and was slightly elevated, and in the east lay the rectangular or parallelogram-shaped, much larger lower city with housing, workshops and storage facilities. The two- or three-storey houses were built of standard-sized clay bricks, 28 x 14 x 7 cm in size, which further increased the homogeneity of the architecture. Streets ran along the north–south axis of the cities, which had a secure water supply and a sophisticated system of waste water canals. In Mohenjo-daro, for instance, almost 700 wells provided fresh water for the 50,000 to 80,000 inhabitants, and from each house covered canals carried waste water to a communal canal that led to the nearby Indus.[61] In Mohenjo-daro there are no signs of monumental architecture, whether secular or sacred, which, considering the size of the city and its well-thought-out plan, is surprising.

The most important trading partners of the Indus Valley Civilisation were the cities of Mesopotamia, which were reached either by land through Iran or by sea. Trade between these parties was simplified by the introduction of standardised weights and measures. The second pillar of the domestic economy was agriculture, with crops transported to the cities by oxcart and barges. The Indus Valley Civilisation also developed its own script, which is preserved on small soapstone seals. To this day it has resisted all attempts to decipher it, since no multilingual documents like the famous Egyptian Rosetta Stone have been preserved. Making it yet more difficult is the fact that the inscriptions are very short; the longest consists of only 26 symbols or phonemes, and many of the more than 400 different symbols appear only rarely.[62] The script is presumably related to proto-Elamite, but the language affiliation remains unknown.

Another innovation of this culture is an early form of woven silk. The earliest evidence of silk worldwide comes from the Neolithic site of Qianshanyang in the Chinese province of Zhejiang, where silk threads about 4,570 years old were discovered. However, the most recent excavations at Harappa have brought to light silk fibres of almost the same age, dating to 2200–2450 BC.[63] The silk threads of China and of the Indus Valley Civilisation come from different moths, however: the Chinese from *Bombyx mandarina*, which was later domesticated as *Bombyx mori*, and those of Harappa from *Antheraea assamensis* and *Antheraea mylitta*. Interestingly, the threads of Harappa were spun in two different ways, which suggests the use of two different production techniques.[64] This most recent discovery has far-reaching consequences, because up until now early, pre-Christian discoveries of silk in Central Asia, Egypt or Europe were seen as indications of contact with China. In light of the long-standing isolation of China into the second century BC and, on the other hand, the transcontinental trade network already established in the third millennium BC of the Indus Valley Civilisation, exports from the northern Indian subcontinent now seem more likely.

The reason for the collapse of the Indus Valley Civilisation remains just as puzzling as its script. Presumably a variety of factors contributed, with both natural and human-caused ecological changes proving decisive. For one thing, at the start of the second millennium BC a pronounced drying of the climate in eastern Central Asia sped up, coupled with a weakening and a shift to the east of the monsoon rains. More dramatic effects were produced by tectonic shifts, most likely earthquakes, which led to the waters of the Sarasvati and Drishadvati rivers no longer reaching the Indus river system but rather moving eastward into the hydrological system of the Ganges. Thus the fertile, arable land also moved east, and the cities of the Indus began to suffer water shortages.[65] Furthermore, it may be assumed that the centuries-long intensive cultivation of the soil depleted it and that an irrigation system that paid little heed to drainage made the farmland too salty. In addition it is conceivable that overgrazing by goats and sheep – a phenomenon still seen in Central Asia and Mongolia today – also destroyed the vegetation that held the soil in place.

Finally, the enormous construction activity took its toll, as the production of bricks required vast amounts of wood. This led to radical deforestation of the surrounding environment with corresponding climatic consequences, as can also be seen in the fall of the cities of Mesopotamia.[66] External causes included the simultaneous collapse of trading partners in Mesopotamia and in southern Turkmenistan, as well as raids from the north. Although most scholars today believe that an attack by nomadic horsemen from the north did not take place, it is a fact that mass graves from the final period of Mohenjo-daro betray hasty and disorganised care for the dead. In addition, skeletons have been discovered lying in the streets, on thresholds and inside houses, indicating a violent end to a presumably already weakened city.[67] In any event, after the eighteenth century BC the agrarian-mercantile Indus Valley Civilisation disappeared, leaving behind no further trace.

Traditional single-axle cart in Punjab, Pakistan.

principalities or kingdoms. This markedly local character of the municipal government remained a hallmark of later cultures in the region of Bactria and Margiana until the Kushan era in the first centuries AD.

At the turn of the third to the second millennium BC Altyn Tepe and the last settlements of the Geoksyur oasis broke down, for a number of reasons. Climatic and tectonic factors played their part, as did the action of humans, although no effects from hostile enemies can be seen. As already mentioned, in the second half of the third millennium BC a weakening of solar radiation in the northern hemisphere ended the ideal climate of the early and middle Holocene, which caused both temperatures and precipitation to drop. Steppes dried out and deserts advanced not only in Central Asia but also in the Arabian Peninsula and North Africa.[68] In addition, the rivers that wound through the flat landscape tended to change their course as they silted up with sand. Thus the Tejen River shifted its delta to the west as early as the second half of the third millennium BC, forcing the people of the ancient Geoksyur oasis to abandon their settlement and relocate to Khapuz Tepe in the south-west.[69]

Human beings helped bring about the impending catastrophe, although the causes and effects involved were still unknown to them. The population growth in Altyn Tepe led to increased deforestation, salinisation of the soil resulting from excessive irrigation without adequate drainage, and overgrazing by herds of goats. All of these factors reduced the amount of land available for life-sustaining agriculture, and Altyn Tepe began to shrink. First the cultic centre and the residential quarter of the elite were abandoned and a gradual decline set in. As living conditions worsened people began emigrating eastwards out of the Kopet Dag–Tejen oasis system towards the neighbouring delta of the Murgab River north of the modern city of Merv (Mary) in south-eastern Turkmenistan. This theme, of natural and man-made factors forcing people to abandon their oasis settlements for a more favourable environment, would recur frequently in Central Asia until modern times.

Clay vessel from the Tripolye Culture in the shape of cattle, Shushkivka, Ukraine, *ca.* 3500 BC. National Museum of the History of Ukraine, Kiev.

Clay jar with dynamic decoration typical of the Tripolye Culture, Konivka, Ukraine, 4000–3500 BC. Museum of Archaeology, National Museum of Sciences of the Ukraine.

4. Agrarian and stockbreeding cultures in northern Central Asia

4.1 The cultures of Cucuteni–Tripolye and Usatovo

As in the Neolithic, Chalcolithic and early Bronze Age, this period in the history of northern Central Asia was marked by encounters between agrarian and stockbreeding societies. On the other side of the western border of Central Asia, in the second half of the sixth millennium BC during a Climate Optimum, there arose west of the Dnjestr River the sedentary agrarian culture of **Cucuteni–Tripolye** (*ca.* 5200–2800 BC), which also raised livestock.[70] In contrast to the steppe cultures, which are reconstructed largely on the basis of grave furnishings and classified by burial type, the Cucuteni–Tripolye Culture can be studied only by examining the architecture of its settlements and domestic finds. In the first period the small settlements consisted of either rough dug-out huts, which were easily flooded and needed regular repairs, or ground-level buildings made of stamped clay and used by nuclear families.[71]

Beginning in 4000 BC in the Ukraine, the second, middle period saw a population explosion, which led to the construction of gigantic settlements. They consisted of two or three – or, in extreme cases, even five – concentric circular or oval rings of two-storey houses, about 20–30 m long and 6–10 m wide, which were connected along their long sides into groups of four or five. The largest settlements reached an area of 450 ha and numbered 2,700 dwellings, which corresponded to a population of approximately 25,000 to 30,000 people.[72] These mega-settlements were earlier and larger than the first Sumerian cities, but they show no signs of a division of labour or of social stratification, and they had no public buildings, so they are seen not as cities but rather as gigantic settlements. As the self-sustaining farmers practised slash-and-burn agriculture, and the soil was quickly depleted, they were forced periodically to move eastward to seek new, virgin land, so the culture spread as far as the Dnieper. They ritually burned the abandoned settlements.[73] The Tripolye farmers obtained copper bars from what is today Bulgaria, working the metal into jewellery and also selling it to the nomadic stockbreeders north-east of the Dnieper.

Female deities played an important role in the Tripolye Culture, as can be seen in the approximately 2,000 clay figures depicting either small, standing women or seated women with outstretched legs, broad thighs and backward-leaning torsos. Occasionally they sit on stools in a circle of as many as a dozen women. Such clay statuettes stood in houses near the hearth and presumably served a protective purpose. As the clay was often mixed with wheat and barley grains, they also symbolised fertility. In addition to the female powers, spirits associated with horned cattle also played an important apotropaic[74] role in the domestic cult, since in a few settlements the skull of a bull or a cow was found buried beneath each house.[75]

The Tripolye farmers were innovative not only in the way they built settlements but also in their means of transportation. Clay figurines of oxen pulling sleds and of oxen standing on two axles with four wheels indicate that in the winter these farmers used sleds on snow and frozen waterbodies, and knew that heavy loads could easily be moved by means of wheels and axles.[76]

Around 3300 BC Tripolye was overtaken by a severe, mostly self-inflicted crisis. A climatic cooling that had begun there around 3500 BC hampered farming, but the slash-and-burn agriculture that had been practised for centuries and the increasing depletion of the soil were more serious. Worse still, the slash-and-burn approach and massive deforestation for building and heating purposes reduced the forested part of Tripolye's area from 50 percent to about 9 percent.[77] In this way the Tripolye farmers destroyed their own natural barrier against the slowly advancing steppe nomads in the north-east, who at first could not cross this wall of forest with their herds. The stockbreeders in western Central Asia, who sought to escape the cooling climate by migrating to the south, began to infiltrate the cultural realm of the Tripolye. The new steppe landscapes exercised a pull on the herders to the north. They travelled on foot, as the use of the horse as a mount to overcome long distances began only about a millennium later.

Astonishingly, the Tripolye Culture did not collapse as a result of this migration but instead experienced a revival. In the third and final period of Tripolye the mega-settlements disappeared and smaller, better defended communities emerged. The farmers adopted the technologies of the advancing herders and used their land, which had been transformed into steppe, for grazing cattle, sheep and goats. It appears that the expansion of the steppe nomads' lifestyle to the west came about not so much through military attacks as by the adoption of technologies of animal husbandry appropriate to the changed climatic and ecological conditions.[78]

The steppe herders who advanced slowly into the territory of the Tripolye farmers, who now practised stockbreeding, belonged to the proto-Indo-European (PIE) language family and contributed essentially to its westward expansion.[79] Its culture can be seen as one of the precursors of the vast Yamnaya Culture. Most notably the two peoples who lived side-by-side, the local Tripolye farmers and the nomadic steppe herders, both maintained their own ancient cultural elements, which blended along the Dnieper and Dniester rivers into the hybrid **Usatovo Culture** (3300–2800 BC). In the flat graves near the settlements small female figurines were laid beside the dead. Such figurines are, however, not found in the kurgan graves, where the leaders of the steppe herders were buried. Instead of statuettes of women, their grave goods consisted of a pair of bronze weapons made of arsenic copper. The tumulus was surrounded

A 120-cm-tall stone statue portraying an older warrior from Kernosovka, Usatovo Culture, Ukraine, *ca.* 3300–2800 BC. Historical Museum of Dnepropetrovsk.

by a cromlech, a circular arrangement of megaliths (a custom that was also known to the culture of Mikhailovska that preceded the Usatovo Culture).[80] A few Tripolye graves also contained ceremonial stone maces with horse heads.[81] Presumably the newcomers, who helped spread the practice of using domesticated horses for meat, appointed themselves patrons of the local populace, but left their social structures and culture untouched. Metaphorically speaking, the subjected agrarian communities were like the goose that laid the golden egg, which only had value as long as it lived.

The burial sites also included stone steles, some simple and some anthropomorphic, made of granite, lime or sandstone and standing as tall as 270 cm, which were located south-west of the mounds.[82] The best-preserved anthropomorphic stele of Kernosovka portrays an older warrior with a drooping moustache, his hands folded on his chest. On the front are engraved weapons such as a battle axe and a pickaxe, as well as a lance, and under these are two horses. On the sides are a copulating pair, an ox, and geometric patterns; on the rear, two footprints and schematically drawn ribs and a spine.[83] The meaning of these steles is not known; perhaps they represent an idealised image of the deceased leader and his world in a coded form, which could indicate a marked social stratification and the elevated position of the leader. Alternatively, the steles may be an expression of ancestor worship, in which the dead do not disappear from the world but rather take on a new societal function in a changed form. With the demise of the honoured man, his 'afterlife' as an ancestor begins. In the subsequent Yamnaya period these steles were reused, whether for the building of stone circles or as tomb slabs inside kurgans.

Dimitri Telegin has suggested that the anthropomorphic steles had their origin in the related, settled stockbreeding cultures of Mikhailovska and Kemi Oba on the northern coast of the Black Sea and in the Crimea. The surprising similarities to contemporaneous steles of southern France and northern Italy are generic and coincidental, however, as there was little cultural contact between the Black Sea region and the western Alps.[84] The custom of erecting stone statues of the dead, usually armed, at the gravesite or on a cultic site dedicated to the deceased, found its way into the entire northern half of Central Asia as far as Mongolia, where the so-called deer stones represented a particularly stylised and symbolically rich variant.[85] It was widely practised for over four millennia into the fourteenth century AD, and in Mongolia and southern Siberia the ancient stone figures are still venerated.

◀ A Mongol rider captures a horse from a herd, central Mongolia.

The Usatovo Culture and its mixed economy of primarily stockbreeding and secondarily crop farming influenced the economic forms of the eastern Funnelbeaker Culture of north-eastern and central Europe, from which the Globular Amphora Culture (3400–2700 BC) emerged. These people were not semi-nomadic herders but rather settled farmers who also devoted themselves to stockbreeding. Out of the Globular Amphora Culture emerged later the settled, socially hierarchical Corded Ware Culture (2800–2200 BC), which bordered the Yamnaya steppe culture to the east. This influence of the Usatovo Culture to the west has been associated by some scholars with the spread of Indo-European dialects, such as the proto-Germanic, proto-Slavic and proto-Baltic languages.[86] In any case, this development proceeded peacefully and gradually; an Indo-European invasion of Europe from the east never took place.

4.2 Early stockbreeding cultures

North-east of the Chalcolithic Dnieper–Donets Culture II, in the steppe forests of the middle Volga, two cultures with similar burial rites arose. The **Samara Culture** (*ca.* 5000–4500 BC) is the older of the two. These people used horses, as well as sheep and goats, for meat. Ochre was spread over the shallow burial chambers of male leaders, and the skulls, hooves and jaws of horses, sheep and goats sacrificed by the grave were laid in flat bowls. Additional grave goods were horse figurines carved from bone as well as sharp flint

A rider shoots a lion with a 'Parthian shot', shooting behind him while riding at a gallop. Silk weaving from Astana, Xinjiang, north-western China, Tang Dynasty (618–907 AD). Xinjiang Uyghurs Autonomous Region Museum, Urumqi.

Mummy of a Europid man wrapped in a crimson cloak, wearing wool trousers and felt boots, necropolis of Zaghunluq near Qiemo, grave M 2, Xinjiang, north-western China, *ca.* 800 BC. The man was a rider; a leather saddle was placed near him. Xinjiang Uyghurs Autonomous Region Museum, Urumqi.

daggers. A few graves were covered with low mounds of earth or stone.[87] The **Khvalinsk Culture** (4700–3800 BC), found south of the Samara Culture, extended from Saratov on the Volga to the northern Caucasus in the south and the Urals in the east.[88] This culture overlapped in parts with the Samara Culture and also made reference to the culture of Dnieper–Donets II, as can be seen in the burials of adult men from ages 30 to 50. After death they were first laid in a communal ossuary, where their bones were cleaned and covered with ochre then placed in individual or communal graves. The grave goods were skulls, skins and hooves of sacrificed horses, copper jewellery, flint daggers and maces made of serpentine and soapstone, whose zoomorphic heads resembled that of a horse. Presumably these maces were status symbols.[89] A few of the graves were covered with a low stone mound.

These graves of the Samara and Khvalinsk cultures displayed several hallmarks of the burial practices of the subsequent stock-breeding cultures of the Central Asian steppe, which remained dominant for the warrior elite into the first centuries AD. The essential criteria were grave goods, varying in quality according to social status, weapons, status symbols associated with the horse, jewellery, and animal sacrifices, as well as the practice of covering the corpse with ochre and the erecting of a stone or earth mound. Later, at the great kurgan of Maikop or, above all, in the Scythian period, the burial of chiefs also included rituals of human sacrifice, in which a young woman, fellow warriors and servants of the deceased had to accompany the dead into the afterlife. The subsequent **Late Khvalinsk Culture** (3800–3300 BC) laid the foundation for the establishment of the important Yamnaya Culture on the lower reaches of the Volga and Don around 3300 BC.[90]

Contemporaneous with the Khvalinsk Culture, the **Srednyi-Stog Culture** (4500–3500 BC) flourished between the Dnieper and the Don, serving as the western counterpart of Khvalinsk and likewise playing an important role in the establishment of the Yamnaya Culture.[91] The farmers raised sheep, goats, horses and pigs, and they also fished. They lived in small, semi-nomadic communities and buried their ochre-covered dead on their backs with bent knees; a small, low mound of stone or earth was placed over the grave. The scholars David Anthony and, with a few reservations, J.P. Mallory, believe that this contiguous cultural area of Srednyi Stog and Khvalinsk, between the Dnieper and the Volga in the Ukraine and southern Russia, is the homeland of the proto-Indo–European language (PIE), which arose between the Dnieper, northern Caucasus, and western Urals between about 4500 and 3000 BC.[92] Anthony's hypothesis also states that toward the end of the Srednyi Stog Culture an Indo–European language group branched off from archaic proto-Indo–European, as successive groups of people moved south-west as far as Anatolia. This language group was proto-Anatolian, from which developed the languages of Hittite, Luvian and Palaic. Other authors, such as Kristian Kristiansen, relate this first expansion of an Indo–European language to the culture of Maikop (3750–3000 BC).[93]

It is not known precisely which culture began to use horses for transportation as well as for meat. Most authors presume that the horse was first domesticated as a food source in the fifth millennium BC on the steppes north of the Caspian and Black seas – that is, in the region between the Urals and the Dnieper.[94] These horses would not have been used as mounts, however. The bones of a buried stallion from the Srednyi Stog Culture found in Dereivka were cited by Marija Gimbutas as evidence for her theory of a 6,000-year-old invasion of 'Old Europe' by nomadic horsemen. However, this theory fell apart when it emerged that the horse burial dated to the period of the Scythians (*ca.* 800–200 BC).[95] In Dereivka domesticated horses were used not for riding, but rather as a source of meat.[96]

About a millennium later, also east of the Urals, the horse was not only hunted but also domesticated. In the 1980s the Kazakh archaeologist Victor Zaibert explored the site of **Botai** in northern Kazakhstan. Here he discovered a Chalcolithic hunter-gatherer culture dating from about 3700–3000 BC. The site held a settlement of 150 round or oval pit-houses, of which the dome-shaped roofs were covered with sod, as well as the bones of no fewer than 70,000 horses. At that time a more humid climate than today prevailed in northern Kazakhstan, and the steppe fed millions of wild horses. The people of the Botai Tersek Culture, who lived in settlements more than 150 km apart, hunted horses for their meat and also began to domesticate and breed them. Traces of simple cheek pieces from harnesses and signs of wear on teeth have led a few scholars to propose that primitive forms of bridles were in use beginning around 3500 BC, which suggests the use of horses for riding.[97] Presumably hunters used their horses during the hunt and while guarding their herds, certainly not for military purposes.[98] In any event, around the mid-fourth millennium BC there were two epicentres of horse husbandry, one east of the Urals in northern Kazakhstan and the other west of the Urals between the Don and the Dnieper. Both stockbreeding communities were not nomads but rather practised transhumance, moving their herds to different grazing areas according to the season.

Grave M 1100 in the necropolis of the Yan state with buried light chariots and harnessed horses. Liulihe, south-west of Beijing, dynasty of the Early Western Zhou, *ca.* eleventh century BC.

The first clear-cut example of the use of horses for riding that can be confidently dated is more than a millennium younger than Botai, however, and comes from Mesopotamia. It is a cylinder seal of Abbakalla of Ur, a scribe of King Shu Sin, who ruled from 2037 to 2029 BC.[99]

4.3 The emergence of horse riding

Besides the further development of metallurgy, the domestication of the horse and its use for riding was one of the most important innovations of Central Asia. Getting on horseback enabled the people to shift from largely stationary stockbreeding to an economy that was truly mobile. It also helped them take full advantage of the economic potential of the endless grass steppes of Central Asia. The combination of horse riding and the composite bow, invented before or around the middle of the second millennium BC, gave the steppe peoples unprecedented military might, against which the settled agrarian cultures could offer little resistance.

While innumerable wild horses grazed the steppes of Eurasia and North America during the Palaeolithic, in the Mesolithic they died out in North America and dwindled rapidly in Eurasia. Their last refuge was in the northern steppes between the Carpathians and western Mongolia, since in the dry and treeless steppes they were second to only the wild camel in their ability to survive. Thanks to their large, wide-set eyes, horses have a range of vision of about 300 degrees and are able to quickly spot almost any predator in an open landscape.

The further development and refinement of horse riding was a slow process. In the steppes bridle bits were originally made of organic material, such as wood or bone. In about 1200 BC, however, single-piece bronze bits started to be used. These enabled the rider

Two horses pull a light chariot; petroglyphs from Baga Oigor III, western Mongolia, late Bronze Age.

to steer the horse accurately and stop it in its tracks. Thanks to this newly gained control, he could enter battle on horseback. Like the solid bronze bit, the split, two-part bit was presumably invented in Egypt around the mid-second millennium BC; it was first introduced in the steppes beyond the northern Caucasus in the ninth century BC and from there it spread rapidly as far as Mongolia.[100] With it the rider could control his horse so well that he could simultaneously use the short recurve bow, whether riding forward into the wind or fleeing at a gallop, aiming the bow backwards at a pursuer and shooting with the wind. This tactic, called the Parthian shot, was mastered to perfection by the mounted archers of the Central Asian steppes.

At about the same time or somewhat earlier than the two-part bit the soft saddle made of cloth and leather appeared in eastern Central Asia, which Assyrian horsemen likewise used beginning in the ninth century BC. The horsemanship of the early mounted archers of Assyria appears to have been limited, however, as each bowman had to be accompanied by another rider, who held the reins of both horses. In this way they were inferior to the attacking steppe peoples of the Cimmerians and the Scythians, who were able to control their horses with their bodies and voices.[101] Another variant of 'two-man archery' was practised by Near Eastern warriors, who rode a camel in pairs, with the front man directing the animal and the rear man shooting.[102]

The oldest preserved riding saddle came from the south-eastern part of the Tarim Basin in north-western China. Here in 1985 in the cemetery of Zaghunluq near Qiemo Chinese archaeologists discovered the grave of a Europid man, approximately 50 years old, wearing wool trousers and felt boots. A leather saddle, as well as the skull and a hoof of a horse, had been laid beside him in the grave. The deceased was undoubtedly a horseman, who died around 800 BC and was accompanied into the afterlife by three women and an infant.[103]

Finally, the stirrup, combined with a solid saddle, was invented at the beginning of the fourth century AD in northern China, when Turko–Mongol steppe peoples began to conquer the area. The earliest representation of stirrups comes from a Chinese grave from 302 AD but this was in the form of a single short stirrup used as an aid for mounting. The first depiction of a complete stirrup pair comes from another grave, from 322 AD, and the oldest bronze stirrup was found in a grave of similar age containing the remains of a warrior of Xianbei, one of the nomadic federations of eastern Mongolia.[104] Such pairs of stirrups attached to saddles not only enabled riding in a squatting or almost standing position, which improved the rider's mobility, but also increased the impact of an attacking cavalry. They enabled armoured horsemen, sitting on likewise armoured horses, to attack with lances raised and support themselves with stretched legs against their saddles. It was the Xianbei tribe of the Toba that made a heavy, armoured cavalry the foundation of their army before the conquest of Northern China starting in 386 AD. The iron stirrup came to Europe only with the invading Avars in the second half of the sixth century.[105] The stirrup was not a requirement for the development of heavy cavalry, however, as the Scythians had begun protecting themselves with iron scale armour and lamellar shields beginning in the sixth/fifth century BC. At the same time, according to Herodotus, the horsemen of the Massagetae also covered the chests of their horses with bronze armour.[106] In combat the Saka and Massagetae first advanced with light cavalry or attacked repeatedly with lightning speed and released a hail of arrows at the enemy. This attacking force melted away as rapidly as it had struck, and moments later the heavy cavalry dealt the bewildered opponent the deathblow. The stirrup was also not a necessary condition for the introduction of long lances into cavalry, as can been seen in the armoured mounted warriors of the Sarmatians. The rider elite of the Sarmatians, who besieged the Scythians of the northern Pontic region as of the late fourth century BC, fought mainly with a lance of up to 5 m in length that they held in both hands.[107]

In most steppe nomadic cultures both girls and boys began to learn to ride at the age of three, growing into outstanding riders who constantly practised and refined their art in their everyday work of herding and hunting. 'Nature cannot bind the centaur more closely to his rear than the Hun sitting upon his horse', noted the Roman historian Claudianus (*ca.* 370– after 405 AD). In extreme cases every nomad, male and female, was a warrior from ages 15 to 30. The Chinese historian Sima Qian (*ca.* 145–*ca.* 87 BC) explained: 'The little boys start out by learning to ride sheep and shoot birds and rats with a bow and arrow, and when they get a little older they shoot foxes and hares, which are used for food. Thus all the young men are able to use a bow and act as armed cavalry in time of war.'[108] In the stockbreeding cultures of the Central Asian steppes women learned most of the skills that men did and sharing labour was necessary for survival, so that among the nomads social inequality between the sexes was much less pronounced than in agrarian or urban societies. To the nomad the idea of isolating his wife or wives in a house, as in urban civilisations, would be incomprehensible.

The riding and fighting abilities of the nomadic herders were necessary for survival as enemies often threatened to steal their herds. Besides, any increase in the size of the herd created a need for more grazing land and secure access to water, which extended the territory of a clan and increased the potential for conflict with other clans. For the nomads, everyday life was ideal training for warfare; because the handling of large, strong animals is more strenuous and dangerous than looking after plants, nomadic life prepared one much better for combat than did the settled life of the farmer. These skills were further developed by organised hunts. Leading large herds over sometimes unfamiliar territory also sharpened abilities in planning, coordination, and navigation. Now the horse changed from a hunted source of meat and milk to the vehicle of the steppe peoples. Nonetheless, during migrations and war horses were still used as food, whether a rider resorted to the emergency supply of dried horse meat that he carried in a saddlebag or opened the neck vein of a living animal and drank its blood.

The weapon system of the efficient cavalry emerged in the second half of the first millennium BC when horsemen no longer performed as heroic individual warriors but rather placed themselves under the command of a leader. He divided his riders into several disciplined bands, whose deployment he planned, coordinated and oversaw. Scythian, Sarmatian and later Hunnic bands of horsemen were able to maintain their cohesion during a battle and carry out tight shifts in direction on command. Combat was no free-for-all but rather a planned, corporate matter. During a campaign each mounted warrior had two or three horses, which he could ride in turn, so that such bands could move with extraordinary mobility and speed. This made them experts at surprise manoeuvres. The horsemen of the steppe were also masters of the feigned retreat from close combat. They would lead their pursuers on for days, so that they could stop and defeat the by-now disorganised enemy in a location of their choosing. The mounted warriors used the wide landscape as a tactical and strategic instrument; the armies of settled peoples usually found themselves completely at their mercy. It was this combination of skills with new technologies, honed in everyday life, and strategic leadership structures that made the bands of nomadic horsemen practically invincible for more than two millennia, except in the Mediterranean region.

The horsemen met their match in the disciplined and flexible Macedonian phalanx of armoured hoplites fighting with lances up to 6 m long, and against the Roman refinement of a phalanx divided into cohorts and thus even more flexible. As long as the phalanx maintained its fighting line and formation the horsemen made no headway and suffered severe losses. If the horsemen attacked with bows, the phalanx formed a dispersed and shallow line in an attempt to surround the horsemen or the Roman phalanx would alternatively take the tortoise formation. In this very tight formation the front and both side rows of soldiers held their long shields vertically up to their eyes in order to fully cover the front and sides and the soldiers further back would place their shields horizontally on the helmets of the front men. If the horsemen tried to advance on the infantry with drawn swords and battle axes in a shock attack, the soldiers immediately formed themselves into a dense phalanx with lances held forward that no riders could break through, or waited in the tortoise formation till the attack passed and then attacked themselves.[109] Alexander the Great's cavalry victories against Greek and Persian infantry formations stand as exceptions to this rule, attributed to his tactical genius and bravado. Alexander's extraordinary military skill also showed itself in the victories of the cavalry under his command over Bactrian, Sogdian and Saka cavalry units – victories in which the Greek spears played an important role.[110] Finally, as already mentioned, the humid climate with heavy rains that damaged or destroyed composite bows, and the dependence on grazing land for the horses, as well as on flat or rolling landscapes for the deployment of the mounted bands, remained their inherent weaknesses.

4.4 The invention of wheel and wagon

Two additional inventions not only encouraged the development of nomadic stockbreeding but also literally gave drive to human history. These are the wheel and the wagon, which required the interplay of three fundamental technological principles. These technologies developed independently of one another for uses other than the wagon. The first uses the principle of rotation of an axle and wheel, the basis of which was the potter's wheel. The second consisted of a flat bed resting on axles. A sled outfitted with skids,

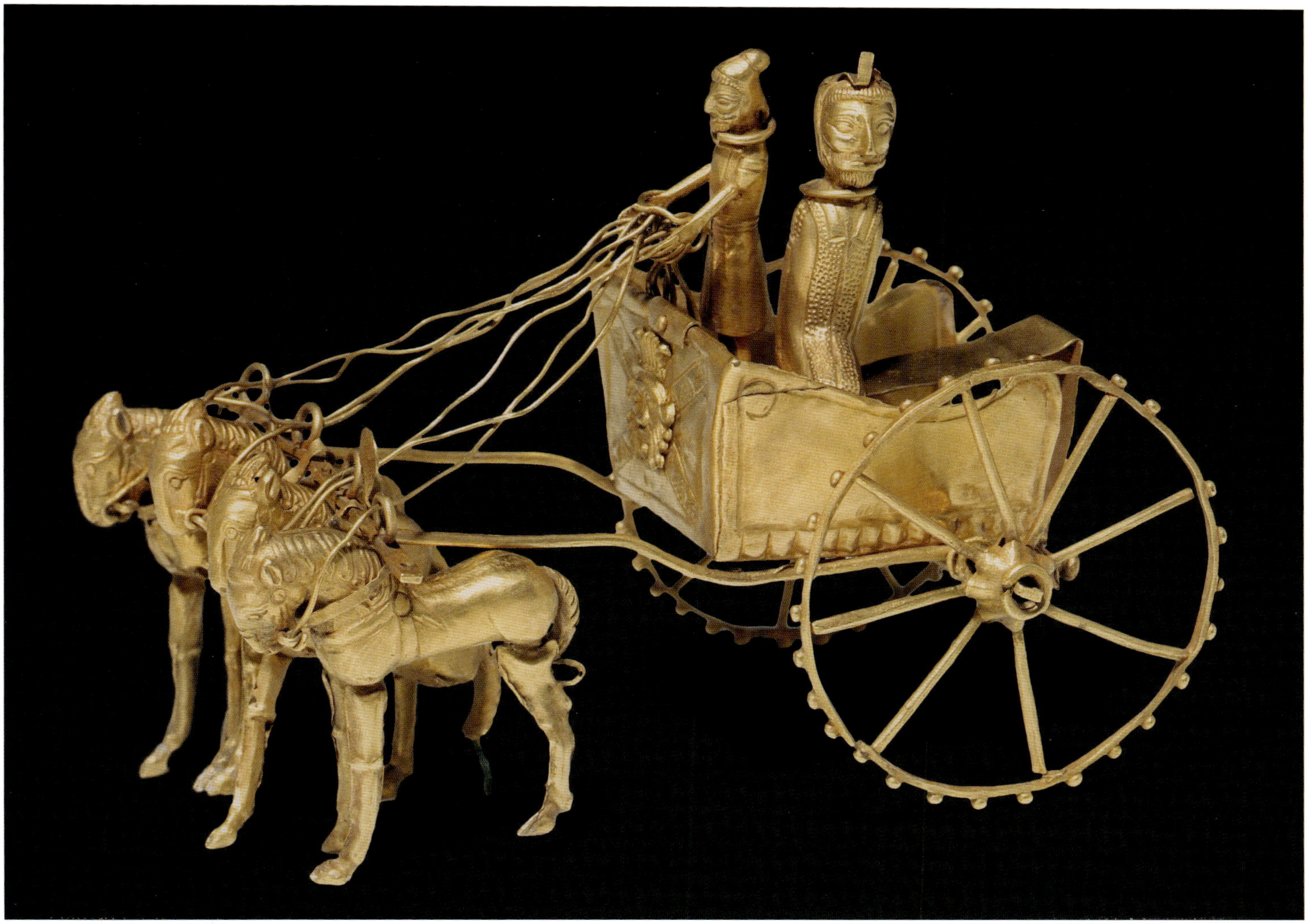

Achaemenid gold model of a light chariot with a driver and seated passenger, Oxus Treasure, fifth–fourth century BC. The British Museum, London.

Two Mongol nomad families on the way to their winter camp on the northern shore of lake Terkhin Tsagaan Nuur, Arkhangai Aimag, central Mongolia.

of the type used in both Mesopotamia and the far north, could have been the forerunner of this invention. The third piece of knowledge was the use of animals for pulling.

It is not known where or by whom the wagon was invented, as the use of wheeled transport appears to have begun simultaneously around 3500 BC in connected regions within a vast territory stretching from Central Europe as far as Mesopotamia. This revolutionary technology must have spread very rapidly. Among the oldest certain discoveries are the clay cups in the form of a four-wheeled wagon from about 3500 BC from the Baden culture;[111] a depiction of a wagon on a funnel beaker from about 3500 BC from Bronocice, southern Poland;[112] wooden disc wheels from the Alps from the mid- to late fourth millennium BC;[113] and discoveries in peat bogs in Northern Europe from the end of the fourth millennium BC.[114] Further to the east, terra cotta vessels from the Tripolye Culture in the form of animals standing on two axles with four wheels, which date to the first half of the fourth millennium, testify if not directly to the use of wagons for transportation then certainly to the knowledge that objects could be pulled with axles and wheels.[115]

The importance of the wagon was shown by the discovery of a wagon grave of the Maikop Culture in the region of Kuban north-east of the Black Sea, presumably the oldest of its kind. In wagon graves a usually disassembled wagon was placed in the grave with the corpse, which had been brought to the burial on it. Presumably the wagon was an important status symbol and enabled the deceased to make the journey into the afterlife in a manner befitting his rank. The two solid wooden wheels from the kurgan of Starokorsunskaya in the Kuban region have been dated to the second half of the fourth millennium.[116] Soon thereafter the number of wagon burials in the Kuban region multiplied; of the nearly 200 wagon burials, with a total of 270 wagons, of the subsequent Novotitarovskaya Culture and the related Yamnaya Culture known today about half come from the Kuban region.[117]

Gold bull figurine that decorated a baldachin pole in the kurgan of Maikop, Kuban region, southern Russia, 3700–3400 BC. The State Hermitage Museum, St. Petersburg.

About two millennia after the first wagon grave of Starokorsunskaya, the Chinese royal dynasties of the Shang (*ca.* sixteenth–eleventh century BC) and the Western Zhou (*ca.* eleventh century–771 BC) adopted this custom from the steppe peoples, as can be seen in the 41 wagon graves of the Shang. Thirty-seven of these graves appeared in the thirteenth to the eleventh centuries BC in the then imperial capital Anyang (today's Henan Province); in them single-axle chariots with spoked wheels, along with harnessed horses and charioteers, accompanied chiefs into the afterlife.[118] Three of the innovations of central China discovered in Anyang – wheeled transport, horse husbandry, and metallurgy – appeared all of a sudden in a highly developed form, which suggests that these skills were borrowed from the steppe cultures of Central Asia.[119] As in China, wagon graves also appeared in the Alpine regions of Central Europe in the thirteenth and twelfth centuries BC and, after an interruption, again in the eighth century and in the Hallstatt period.[120]

Regarding the much-cited evidence from the late fourth millennium BC for the invention of the wheel in Mesopotamia, these are either simply depictions of sleds on stone insignias and cylindrical seals or clay tablet pictograms of a sled that rests on wooden rollers or wheels. The earliest discoveries of actual wheels in Mesopotamia come from the first half of the third millennium BC – more than half a millennium later than the first finds from the Kuban region.[121] It appears that the technology of the wagon emerged in the north-western and eastern Pontic territory of the Tripolye and Maikop cultures and from there spread rapidly to central and southern Europe and Mesopotamia. The close trade relations between Maikop and Mesopotamia certainly contributed to the rapid transfer of technology to the south.[122]

In about 3200 BC[123] northern Central Asia began to experience drought and a climatic cooling. The wagon helped the stockbreeders, who until then were not fully mobile, to adapt successfully to the new ecological conditions. As drier grazing lands are more quickly threatened by overuse, the herders had to move their animals more

Anthropomorphic and theriomorphic figures with headdresses of circularly arranged feathers or sunrays, painted on a stone slab from a cist grave. Karakol, Altai, southern Siberia, *ca.* 2400 BC.

frequently. Thanks to wagons pulled usually by oxen but sometimes, beginning in the late third millennium BC, by harnessed camels, herders could take with them their modest possessions, supplies and simple tents. At the start of the first millennium BC at the latest the Scythians and their eastern forerunners perfected this kind of 'mobile home nomadism'. With their two- or three-axle wagons, pulled by oxen, they were able to carry with them their domed, yurt-like dwellings, made of felt and attached securely to the wagons, as well as their possessions and supplies, and to make wide-ranging use of the grass steppes.[124] On other wagons, the upper part of the wagon, covered with a barrel-shaped piece of felt tarpaulin, could be removed and reconstructed quickly on the ground.[125] The wagon and the riding horse allowed herders not only to manage large herds and retrieve straying animals but also to seek lush grazing lands and water sources over large distances. The wagon had an additional advantage, in that it did not have to be unloaded every night like a pack animal and goods stayed dry during rain without the need to set up special protection. As the increasing relative cooling, which was more pronounced in the east than in the west, forced the herders to seek warmer latitudes at least in the winter, there emerged a pattern of cyclical north–south migration. One result of this was that nomadic herders began to encroach on the territory of settled farmers.

Soon after the introduction of the wooden solid wheel and the three-part disc wheel, people sought to reduce its weight by hollowing out the discs and reducing the axles from two to just one. The breakthrough came with the introduction of the spoked wheel. This was not, as often assumed, invented in Mesopotamia, but rather in the Central Asia steppes east of the Urals. In wagon graves of the cultures of **Sintashta**, between the Rivers Ural and Tobol, and **Petrovka**, farther east in northern Kazakhstan, archaeologists discovered clear traces of spoked wheels as old as 4,100 years with eight to twelve spokes. They are about 200 years older than Anatolia's earliest seal impressions showing light chariots,[126] and 300 years older than the earliest evidence from Mesopotamia.[127] These funeral wagons of the Sintashta–Petrovka Culture are precursors of the light chariot, which is defined by two spoked wheels; a lightweight wagon body, open to the rear, which could carry at least a spear-throwing combatant; and a yoked harness for a team of horses controlled by bits. Both the light chariot on spoked wheels and the control by means of combined reins and bit, were inventions of the Eurasian steppe. Only with the invention of the light chariot with spoked wheels did the horse take on military significance.[128]

The chariot spread quickly from the steppe and reached a peak of its development in the Near East. From the eighteenth/seventeenth century BC in Egypt, the Hittite Kingdom and, to a lesser degree, in Assyria the chariot was one of the most prestigious and important implements of war. If the body of the chariot was small it carried only a single warrior, who either held the reins with one hand and threw spears with the other or wrapped the reins around his body and fought with a bow. Larger chariots normally carried two men; a driver and an archer. Because the wheels were attached to the axle independently of one another, they could move at different speeds when going around curves, enabling sharp turns. Chariots had the advantage over infantry of speed and surprise, as they could easily attack on the flanks or from the rear and could retreat just as quickly. They were suitable for carrying into battle a large quantity of 'one-way weapons' such as spears and arrows. On the other hand, chariots were highly vulnerable to salvos of enemy arrows and dependent on flat, dry land. Thus it should not be assumed that chariot battles took place on the grass steppes of Central Asia as they did in the Near East. In the grass steppes the chariot remained a means of transportation, also appropriate for raids and skirmishes, as well as an exclusive status symbol. When, in the ninth century BC, bands of mounted archers emerged in the Near East, they quickly superseded the chariot formations, since they were less vulnerable and more capable on rough terrain, as well as much more flexible.

The horse-drawn chariot was at the same time a fast means of transport, a dangerous weapon and an outstanding status symbol. It also had cultic functions, which is why it found a prominent place in art, even in impassable mountains at a height of 3,500 m above sea level, as in petroglyphs in the Pamirs or at Saimaly Tash in Kyrgyzstan. Interestingly, in the Near East chariots were usually portrayed in profile, while in the petroglyphs of Central Asia they are mostly shown in top view. This perspective resembled the view from above into an open grave, in which a chariot had been laid along with the sacrificed charioteer and horses in harness. In the petroglyphs of Central Asia all other depictions of people and animals are shown in profile, so such images of chariots can hardly be a coincidence. The chariot had symbolic significance as a grave good, presumably as a vehicle into the afterlife befitting the status of the deceased. In this way it was transformed into a cultic vehicle, which, depending on cultural emphases, took on different shadings of a common motif. In the steppes of Central Asia and in China it became a select vehicle for the dead; in northern Europe, the sun chariot, as in the sun chariot of Trundholm, Denmark; and in the Hellenistic territories of south-eastern Europe, as well as in the later Greco-Buddhist cosmology of Central Asia, it was the vehicle of the sun god.
In countless petroglyphs of Central Asia the spoked wheel also symbolised the sun, which was also the focus of a cult in Iron Age steppe cultures, such as the Massagetae, who sacrificed horses to the sun.[129]

Finally, in the hymns of the Indian Rig Veda, composed in the late Bronze Age by speakers of an early Indo-European language, there resonates a bygone age of heroic charioteers and rich wagon burials, whose original homeland may have been in the cultural sphere of Sintashta–Petrovka.[130] In the Rig Veda not only do the most noble warriors fight in chariots, but the gods also ride them through the heavens; the sun god Surya, for instance, drives a wagon pulled by seven horses. In the Rig Veda the light chariot also serves as the metaphor par excellence for the nobility, as a hymn to the fire god Agni reveals: 'Him [Agni] have the Gods established at the region's base, doer of wondrous deeds, Herald of heaven and earth; Like a most famous chariot, Agni the purely bright, like Mithra to be glorified among the folk.'[131]

4.5 The culture of Maikop

The northern Caucasian **Maikop Culture** (3750–3000 BC), which superseded the settled agrarian culture of Svobodnoe and preceded the Yamnaya Culture, was in many regards groundbreaking. They probably invented bronze in a process of alloying arsenic and copper, were among the first to use two-axle, ox-drawn wagons, and introduced into the western steppes of Central Asia the large burial monuments called kurgans, reserved primarily for the elite and for warriors, along with certain rituals of sacrifice and grave goods. The Maikop Kurgan on the Belaya River was made between 3700 and 3400 BC and originally stood 11 m high with a diameter of 100 m. It was explored in 1897 by the archaeologist Vesolovskji, who discovered the mortal remains of an adult man in a grave

A man with a sun-like head drives a light chariot. Indian ink drawing of a petroglyph from Eshki Olmes, eastern Kazakhstan, Bronze Age.

Two sun figures stand above and 12 people dance below, petroglyphs from Tamgaly, southern Kazakhstan, Bronze Age.

The Iranian god Mithra, with a crown of sunrays, holds a barsom bundle and sanctifies the investiture of the Sassanian king of kings Ardeshir II (r. 379–383; not pictured). Taq-e Bostan, Kermanshah, Iran.

covered with red ochre. He was clearly a high-ranking chief, as two women, presumably concubines, had been made to follow him into the grave. The site held rich grave goods. The deceased was laid under a baldachin supported by six or eight narrow poles, four of which were decorated with figurines of bulls with long horns. Two of these were made of solid gold and two of solid silver, crafted using a lost wax process. It is notable that the Russian scholar Rostovtzeff recognised as early as 1913 that the burial style of a 'grave tent', widespread among the Iron Age Scythians and described by Herodotus, traced back to the great kurgan of Maikop.[132] In a few of the burial chambers the walls and floor were plastered, perhaps to create a sacral reproduction of a house.[133]

The head of the deceased was adorned with a diadem of golden rosettes, most likely an import from the culture of Uruk in Mesopotamia. There were also decorated silver vessels and vases imported from Mesopotamia; small gold discs in the form of lions and bulls sewn onto clothing; weapons made of arsenic bronze; and necklaces with turquoise from north-eastern Iran and Tajikistan, red carnelian beads from western Pakistan, or lapis lazuli perhaps from Badakhshan in northern Afghanistan.[134] All of these discoveries attest to the wide-ranging trade relations of Maikop, which also served as the contact zone between the Tripolye Culture and the dynamic urban culture of Uruk.[135] The burial ritual of the Central Asian stockbreeding elite, fully in evidence for the first time at Maikop, consisted of a grand burial with the sacrifice of associated persons and horses, as well as the deposit of grave goods. These included weapons, jewellery, and, until some time in the middle of the second millennium BC, light chariots, over which an earth or stone mound was erected. In the cultures of Yamnaya and Sintashta–Petrovka, which followed Maikop, this burial practice and the worldview associated with it spread throughout northern Central Asia.

Interestingly, similar but still more spectacular grand burials took place in Ur, Mesopotamia, at the time of the Early Dynastic IIIA period (*ca.* 2600–2500 BC), in which concubines, musicians, soldiers and ox- and donkey-drawn wagons accompanied the king into the afterlife. The burials of Mesopotamia were embedded in a different worldview, however, founded on cyclically recurring agricultural events. Just as the plants die each autumn and sprout anew the following spring, Dumuzi, lover of the fertility and war goddess Inana, dies at the end of the year and is reborn in the spring. Presumably the royal burials of Ur are to be understood as representations of such myths.[136]

The heyday of Maikop coincided with that of Uruk from 3700 to 3100 BC. Regular trade occurred between the two cultures, driven by Uruk's insatiable appetite for ore, bronze bars and gemstones. In exchange the elite of Maikop obtained finished gold and silver jewellery from Uruk. Maikop was not only an important hub on the trade routes of Mesopotamia to the east and west; a fascinating mixed culture also developed there, as semi-nomadic stockbreeders took over the legacy of a settled agrarian culture. Maikop society was based on the raising of cattle, pigs, sheep, a few horses, and some cultivation of the land; the dead of the elite were buried in sites that were periodically visited. Evidence of this life style is gleaned from the fact that in the cultural sphere of Maikop about 150 necropolises have been discovered, but only 30 small settlements of sunken and round houses.[137]

The culture of Maikop also took part in the 'fibre revolution' of the second half of the fourth millennium BC, when in Mesopotamia wool from sheep began to replace flax in the production of textiles. This change had the great advantage of freeing high-quality soil from the cultivation of flax in favour of crops. It also meant that otherwise unusable land could be used for the rapidly growing herds of sheep. This gave rise to the new job of shepherd, often taken by women or children. Archaeological finds alone cannot tell us whether sheep were first raised for wool in Mesopotamia or the northern Caucasus, partly because this new technology spread very quickly. In any case, robust wool sheep were bred at the same time in Maikop and Mesopotamia, and in the kurgan of Novosvobodnaya 2 archaeologists discovered the earliest wool fragment.[138] The culture of **Kura–Araxes** (3500–1900 BC), originally located in the north-eastern and central Caucasus, served as intermediary between Maikop and Mesopotamia. Discoveries on the western coast of the Caspian Sea show that the Kura–Araxes people were influenced by the steppe culture of Maikop, constructing kurgans as well as flat graves.

4.6 The Yamnaya–Afanasievo Cultural Complex

At about the time the Maikop Culture was at its peak the **Yamnaya Culture** (*ca.* 3300–2250 BC) emerged on the Don and the Volga. The Russian word 'yama' means 'pit' and refers to the typical burial style, in which the dead rested in a pit-like grave. Hence this culture is also called the 'pit grave culture'.[139] It developed out of the horse- and stockbreeding culture of **Repin** on the middle Don (3600–2900 BC)[140] and the neighbouring culture of **Late Khvalinsk** (3800–3300 BC). In terms of lifestyle the Don represented a boundary within the Yamnaya Culture, since west of the river archaeological remains of partially fortified settlements indicate a sedentary community, while east of the Don the signs of settlement disappear, suggesting a semi-nomadic stockbreeding economy. The Yamnaya culture and its semi-nomadic form of economy represents an adaptation to an ecological crisis around 3500–3300 BC, when a change to a significantly cooler and drier climate led to a loss of agricultural production west of the Don and to sparser steppes east of the Don. These new baseline conditions forced the mostly settled livestock- and horse-breeders between the Don and the Volga to change the grazing lands for the herds more often; they had to shift to a semi-nomadic herding lifestyle. They transported their dwellings, possessions and supplies on two-axle wagons drawn by oxen and, perhaps starting early in the third millennium BC, they began to watch over their herds on horseback. In isolated, more humid forest regions, however, the cultivation of crops still took place.[141]

This semi-nomadic economy of the fourth to second millennium BC, in which the herders returned each winter to their grazing lands on a valley floor, is fundamentally different from the Iron Age nomadism of the first millennium BC, when Scythian and Sarmatian nomadic horsemen swept across the Eurasian steppes with their herds and wagons and often without a fixed home.

As a consequence of the absence of clear signs of settlements, the Yamnaya Culture is defined by its thousands of burial sites. The great necropolises lie in the open steppe near lush grazing lands, where the herders regularly brought their herds in particular seasons. The concentration of final resting spots in certain places indicates that the semi-nomadic herders organised their lives according to a defined system, coordinated with other clans and groups, and changed their grazing lands along established routes, following the rhythm of the seasons. The dead were buried on their backs with knees bent. Both the body and the ground were covered with ochre, which is why the Yamnaya Culture is also called the ochre grave culture.[142] Laid beside the dead were elongated, egg-shaped ceramic vessels of a yellowish colour, bone needles, and daggers and axes made of flint or bronze, as well as the skulls and bones of sacrificed sheep, cattle, and dogs. For chiefs or warriors, a wagon and a horse were sometimes also placed in the grave. In some cases anthropomorphic stone steles from earlier cultures were reused to close the burial chamber. Finally a kurgan of stone and earth was built over primary burials. This was not the case for secondary burials when additional dead were buried in the same kurgan, as many kurgans were used over decades or even centuries.

Around 3100 BC representatives of the Yamnaya Culture began to spread to the west and south-west, infiltrating the Circumpontic Region of the erstwhile culture of Srednyi Stog and the territory of Usatovo, until they reached the Carpathians and the lower Danube valley. The lack of archaeological evidence of destruction suggests that this migration of Yamnaya herders happened without significant warfare, and moreover, that the local settled populations adopted the economy of the newcomers.[143] The archaeologist and anthropologist David Anthony believes that this migration of Yamnaya people, whose homeland is identical to that of the proto-Indo-European language, was the vehicle for the rapid expansion of archaic western Indo-European dialects, out of which developed proto-Germanic, proto-Italic and proto-Celtic.[144] Anthony also believes that the migrants also took up elements of settled agrarian cultures, as can be seen from their burial rituals. In the west they encountered cultures that had female deities and buried statuettes of women beside the dead. This may explain why there are considerably more burials of women in the western part of the Yamnaya culture than in the east, where almost exclusively men and children were buried in the kurgans. This inequality changed, however, in the second half of the first millennium BC, the time of the Scythians, Sauromatians and Sarmatians – whose highest deity, Tabiti, was female. For example, some 20 percent of the Sauromatian kurgans with weapons as grave goods dating from this time held female 'Amazons', who, like male warriors, were buried armed and ready for battle.[145]

More than 3,300 km east of the origin of the Yamnaya Culture and at about the same time the **Afanasievo Culture** (*ca.* 3300–2350 BC) flourished in the Minusinsk Basin of southern Siberia. Its name is derived from Afanasyeva Gora in Khakassia, where the first three graves of this culture were excavated in 1920.[146] Although it is often considered a distant branch of the Yamnaya Culture, new carbon-14 analyses suggest that Afanasievo emerged at least contemporaneously if not somewhat earlier than the pit grave culture.[147] Anthony proposes that a group from the Repin Culture broke off and turned east before the establishment of the Yamnaya Culture, perhaps in a quest for new grazing lands or ore mines, which they found in abundance in the Minusinsk Basin and in the Altai. They settled here and brought to the local hunters and fishermen the skills of raising horned cattle and horses, as well as metallurgy and the construction of wagons. Out of this arose the culture of Afanasievo, which is considered by most Russian scholars to be the first real metal steppe culture east of the Urals.[148] Since these migrants came into contact with the Botai Culture while crossing the northern Kazakh steppe, it is not surprising that a few elements of this horse-hunting and -breeding culture found their way into the Afanasievo culture.[149]

The burial customs of the Afanasievo and Yamnaya cultures are so similar that one can speak of a widespread cultural complex. The dead were laid on their backs with knees bent in a rectangular pit, which was covered by a very low earth or stone kurgan; this was encircled by a cromlech or a rectangular stone fence. The dead and the floor of the burial chamber were sprinkled with ochre. Small vessels for smoke offerings in the form of footed bowls, clay vessels with pointed bases, metal items, the occasional wagon, and the bones of sheep, cattle and horses served as grave goods. The bones have been interpreted as the remains of a funeral feast that took place as part of the burial.[150]

The far-reaching correspondence between the material discoveries of the Afanasievo Culture and that of the Yamnaya suggests that its representatives were also Europids, and this has been confirmed by mitochondrial DNA and craniological analyses.[151] As in the case of the Yamnaya peoples who advanced to the west, those that moved east brought with them not only their economic and cultural forms but also their proto-Indo–European dialects. The splitting off of the proto-Tocharian language from proto-Indo–European followed after 3500 or 3400 BC, and it spread toward the end of the third millennium BC as far as the Tarim Basin in Xinjiang in north-western China. The early expansion of the Indo–Europeans far to the east explains why the Tocharian language did not implement many linguistic innovations of the Indo-Iranian language family, which was close to Tocharian in a geographical sense. In linguistic terms the proto-Tocharians were separate from all other Indo–Europeans from the second half of the fourth millennium BC onward.[152]

Early in the second half of the third millennium BC the pendulum of ethnic migrations swung back for the first time. After the spread of the Europids from the Volga as far as the Yenissei on the border of western Mongolia, Mongolid groups of the northern Siberian type advanced slowly to the west and began to exert pressure on the Europids in the Minusinsk Basin, where they developed the Okunev Culture (2400–1750 BC). Perhaps this migration of foreign groups provoked the ancestors of the proto-Tocharians to move southwards and settle towards the end of the third millennium BC in the Tarim Basin.

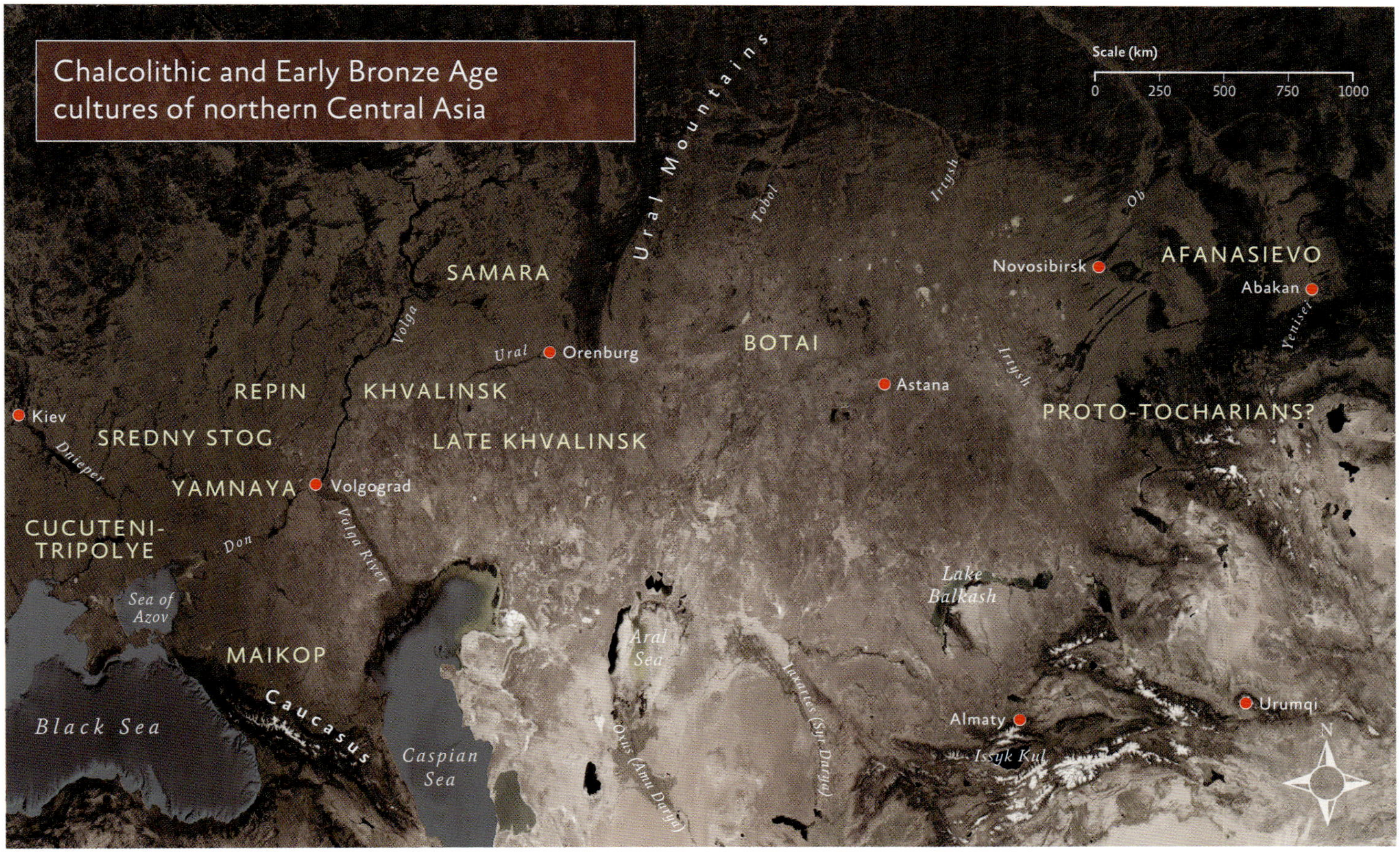

4.7 Sun deities and horse sacrifices

As a consequence of the lack of written sources we know little about the religious ideas of the Afanasievo Culture and its successors, apart from the fact that its representatives presumably worshipped the sun. The stone slabs of the cists[153] of Karakol in the Altai, which date to around 2400 BC and thus belong to the transition period from Afanasievo to Okunev (2400–1750 BC) provide one clue. These slabs were reused in the graves of the Okunev Culture and in earlier times stood as free-standing steles. Painted on them in red ochre, soot and black and white minerals are coloured portrayals of anthropomorphic and theriomorphic (in animal form) standing figures, whose heads are decorated with sunbeams and feathers and who can be interpreted as sun deities.[154]

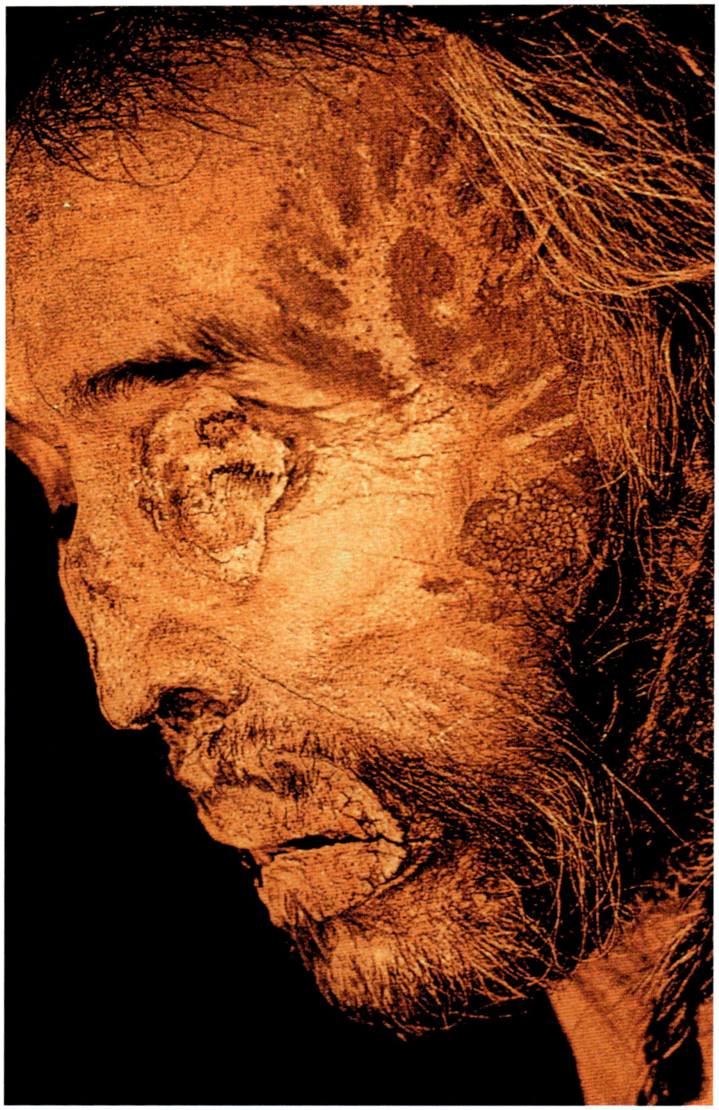

Sun symbols painted with ochre decorate the temples of a naturally mummified Europid corpse. Necropolis of Zaghunluq, grave M 2, Xinjiang, north-western China, *ca.* 800 BC. Xinjiang Uyghurs Autonomous Region Museum, Urumqi.

As the paintings were found on the inside of the cists, they were turned towards the dead and also had a ritual purpose.

The motif of an anthropomorphic figure with a sun-like head was widespread not only on the steles of the Okunev Culture based in the Basin of Minusinsk[155] but also in the petroglyphs of the subsequent cultural complex of Andronovo (widely defined *ca.* 2200–1250 BC), which extended from the Urals to the Altai and was related to the proto-Indo-Iranian language and the Indo-Aryans. Such stone engravings are found in Kazakhstan and in the Altai, for example in Eshki Olmes[156] (eastern Kazakhstan) and in Elangash[157] (Russian Altai), where in each case a 'sun figure' drives a chariot, calling up associations with the Indian sun god Surya. In Saimaly Tash (Kyrgyzstan) and in the open-air shrines of Tamgaly in southern Kazakhstan sun figures are chiselled into the rock in several places, whether alone or as part of a lively scene in which twelve armed, Lilliputian people dance before two large sun figures.[158] It was not only humans who were portrayed with sun-like heads, however, but also such animals as deer, mountain goats, and perhaps oxen, with the sun disc placed either over the animal's head or at the end of its horns.[159]

A few scholars have linked these apparent sun deities with the ancient Indo-Iranian god Mithra.[160] In the Vedas the god of fairness and contracts, Mithra, brings forth the morning light and is correspondingly invoked at dawn in the Rig Veda.[161] In the Zoroastrian scriptures Mithra is not identified with the sun god but rather venerated as the god of truth and contracts. Later, at the time of the Iranian Parthians (247 BC–224 AD) and the Sassanids (224–651 AD), he was also worshipped as the sun god. In images he drives a chariot pulled by white horses or wears a crown of sunbeams. In the Avesta he is glorified as the 'lord of wide pastures', who drives 'a high-wheeled chariot ... drawn by fiery horses', which indicates an origin in a stockbreeding culture that used horse-drawn transport.[162] Finally, Mithra enjoyed great popularity in the Roman Empire, especially in the army, where he was worshipped as Sol invictus Mithras, 'invincible sun god Mithra'. It is quite possible that the idea of a male sun and light deity had its origin in the Central Asian cultural spheres of Afanasievo, Okunev and Andronovo.

Further traces of a sun cult practised by the Indo-Europeans can be found in the eastern Tarim Basin in north-western China, such as in the 3,600- to 3,800-year-old necropolis of Gumugou. Here there are six burial chambers in each case located below a ring of wooden poles tightly placed next to each other and four to seven deep. Around this 'hub' stand seven to nine additional concentric circles of thicker wooden poles, placed further apart. Seen from above, they look like rays streaming outwards from the ring-shaped

In the centre, an anthropomorphic figure uses a Bronze Age axe to kill a stallion with large horns, Bronze Age. The small rider figure on the sacrificed stallion was engraved later. Petroglyphs from Tamgaly, southern Kazakhstan.

centre – the sun symbolism is obvious. As in Gumugou, *ca.* 2,800-year-old Europids were buried in Zaghunluq. A sun symbol is drawn with ochre on the temples of the naturally mummified rider buried with his saddle, mentioned above.[163]

The petroglyphs of Tamgaly also show a burial ritual widespread in the steppes of Central Asia, which played an important role in the religious ideas of the Indo-Europeans. In at least two scenes an anthropomorphic figure kills a horned horse with a typical Bronze Age axe.[164] Horse sacrifices on the occasion of the burial of members of the upper class have been found over a span of nearly 6,000 years, from the steppe cultures of Khvalinsk and Maikop to the Mongol peoples of the late Middle Ages. Besides archaeological discoveries, written sources from Herodotus (*ca.* 484–424 BC) to Rubruk (*ca.* 1215–1270) report the sacrifice of horses at such burials. Particularly informative are the descriptions by Herodotus of horse sacrifices among the Iron Age Scythians and the Massagetae, who lived east of the Caspian Sea. Archaeological finds in dozens of kurgans between the Altai and the Black Sea have confirmed Herodotus' detailed accounts of the burial rites of Scythian kings, but with regard to the Massagetae he directly describes the sun cult and the horse sacrifices: 'The only god they worship is the sun, to which they sacrifice horses: the idea behind this is to offer the swiftest of mortal creatures to the swiftest of the gods.'[165]

The ritual of horse sacrifice, including corresponding grave goods, was fully developed at the latest in the culture of Sintashta (2200–1700 BC), the early form of the Andronovo Culture, east of the Urals.[166] These burial rituals form a surprising link to the Rig Veda. The horse sacrifice described in the Rig Veda, which was performed not at a royal burial but rather by a living ruler to acquire power and glory, recalls the archaeological discoveries made in the elite graves of Sintashta, so that one may surmise a common proto-Indo-Iranian ritual heritage.[167]

Late Bronze Age petroglyphs of ibexes, ordinary horses and horned horses. Tamgaly, southern Kazakhstan.

VI

The Middle and Late Bronze Age

A talent for following the ways of yesterday is not sufficient to improve the world of today.

KING WULING OF ZHAO, when in 307 BC he introduced mounted archers to replace war chariots[1]

1. The Bactria–Margiana Archaeological Complex BMAC

The concept of a Bactria–Margiana Archaeological Complex, abbreviated BMAC, from the Middle and Late Bronze Age, is attributed to the Russian archaeologist of Greek descent Viktor Sarianidi (b. 1929), who has since 1972 led groundbreaking excavations in the ancient delta of the Murgab River in the Kara Kum Desert of Turkmenistan. This complex was an oasis culture that flourished from about 2300/2200 to 1500 BC along rivers in the mostly arid regions of Turkmenistan, southern Uzbekistan, western Tajikistan and northern Afghanistan. The last three areas are subsumed under the term 'Bactria' and the first, farthest west region is called 'Margiana'. The cultural region of the third and second millennia BC known as Bactria extended along both sides of the ancient Oxus.[2]

The heart of Margiana was the broad ancient Murgab delta, north of the medieval city of Merv. 'Margiana' is the Greek version of the Persian name Margush, which is mentioned in the famous trilingual inscription of Bisotun, Iran, dating from about 516 BC. In the Old Persian, Elamite and Babylonian text, King Darius I (r. 522–486 BC) glories in his victory over the princes and provinces that had rebelled against his elevation to the throne: 'I'm Darius, the king: the country of Margush became rebellious. They chose one man, a Margushian, with the name of Frada to be their chief. Later I sent for a Persian, Dadarshish by name, my slave and satrap of Bactria, and told him: "Go and defeat that army." [...] By the grace of Ahura Mazda, my army smashed the rebellious army.'[3] The extent to which the Achaemenid Margush corresponds to the Bronze Age Margiana is unclear.[4]

This culture of Bactria–Margiana arose between 2300 and 2200 BC when migrants from the Kopet Dag–Tejen oasis system, who brought with them their irrigation techniques and elements of the material culture of Namazga IV and V, mingled peacefully with the local inhabitants, who lived in the early Chalcolithic stage of Namazga III.[5] The corresponding discoveries of ceramics in the style typical of the early Namazga V stage contradict the proposal put forward by Sarianidi that these immigrants came from Iran or even northern Mesopotamia. The similarities that do exist between discoveries from the BMAC culture and some from the Mesopotamian cultural sphere are explained by intensive trade contact, without the necessity to resort to unsubstantiated theories of migration.[6] In the oases of Margiana the migrants from southern Turkmenistan found fertile soil, which allowed both the cultivation of millet and various types of wheat and the raising of sheep, goats, horned cattle and camels. Most oases also offered inexhaustible sources of free building material in the form of alluvial clay, which they mixed with water and ashes as a degreaser and, using a wooden mould, produced standardised, air-dried bricks. In Margiana no expensive, water-resistant, fired bricks were produced, unlike in Mesopotamia where they were used to build irrigation canals. Another material basis for this culture was the rich mineral lodes in the east, where certain settlements, such as Sapalli in southern

The most important settlements of the Bactria–Margiana Archaeological Complex and of the Early Iron Age[7]

PERIOD	TIME HORIZON	SETTLEMENTS IN MARGIANA	SETTLEMENTS IN BACTRIA, TYPOLOGY OF SAPALLI
I. Kelleli (Namazga V)	2300/2200–1900 BC	Kelleli	
II. Gonur (Namazga VI)	2000/1900–1650 BC	Gonur, Auchin, Adji Kui, Taip, Adam Basan	
III. Togolok (Namazga VI)	1800–1500 BC	Togolok, Takhirbai	I. Sapalli (1700–1500) II. Jarkutan (1500–1350)
IV. Jaz I	1500/1400–1000 BC	Jaz Tepe	III. Kuzali (1350–1100)
V. Jaz II	1000–800 BC		IV. Molali/Bustan (1100–900)
V. Jaz III	800–329 BC		

◀ The fortified settlement of Gonur Tepe North, Turkmenistan, *ca.* 2000–1650 BC.

The main sites of the Bactria–Margiana Archaeological Complex and of the Early Iron Age

- Ruins | ancient sites
- Modern cities and towns

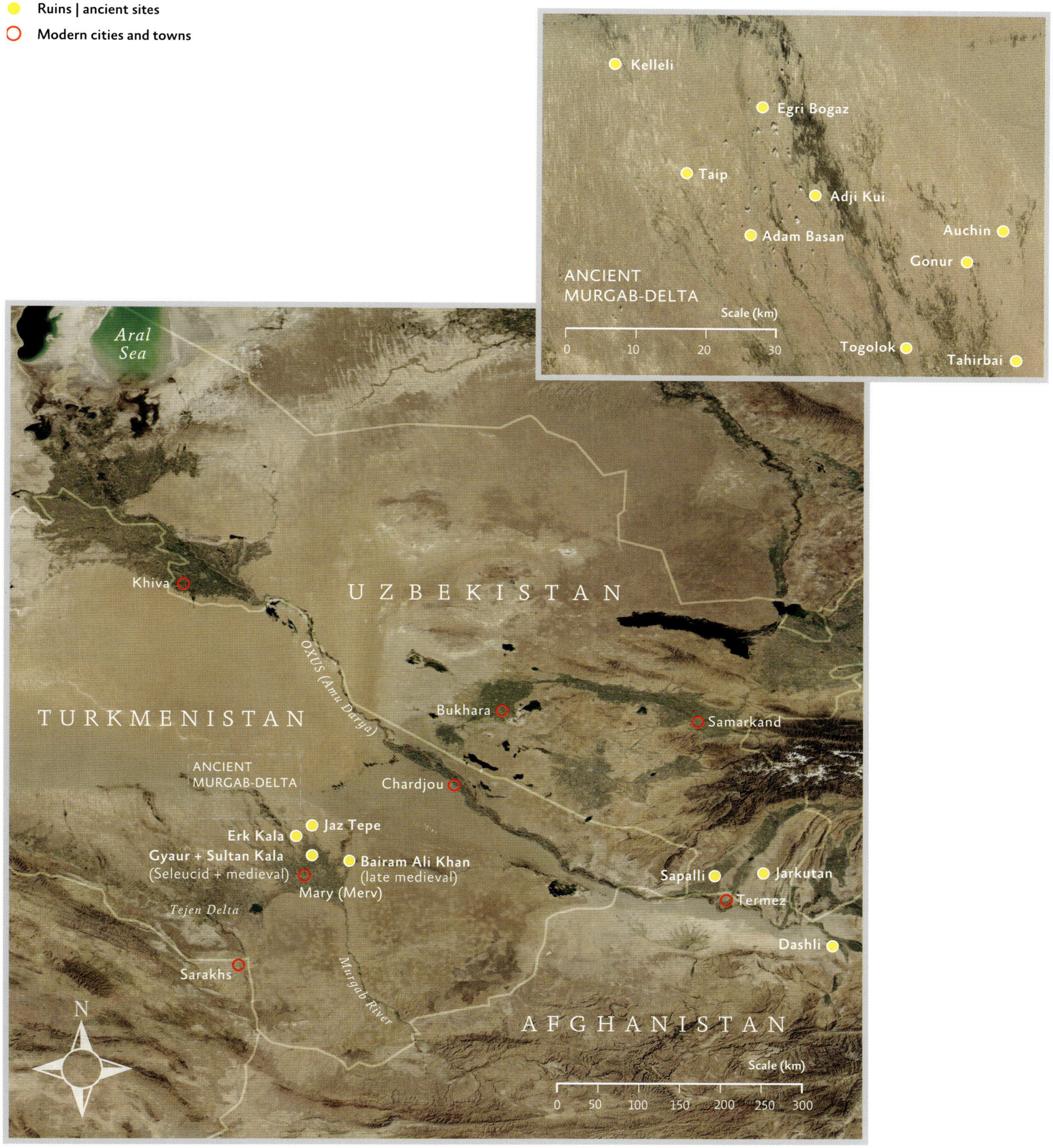

Uzbekistan and Dashli in northern Afghanistan, were located. Great stores of gold, silver, tin, copper, lead, and gemstones like lapis lazuli and turquoise were found here, enabling a profitable and enduring trade with Iran and Mesopotamia, as well as the Indus Valley.

1.1 The BMAC Culture of Margiana

Because of comparable hydrological and tectonic conditions in the Murgab delta and the region of Geoksyur, the settlement history of Margiana followed a course similar to that of Geoksyur 1,500 years earlier. Over the course of the last 4,000 years, small tectonic disturbances and dramatic changes in the River Murgab's course as a consequence of sedimentation, combined with increasing aridity in the region where the river rises, have caused it to shift about 40 to 45 km to the south and the desert to advance accordingly.[8] Thus the settlements followed the water and likewise moved south.

The urban Margiana Culture can be divided into three Bronze Age periods, followed by the three Jaz-Periods, of which the last two extend far into the Iron Age:[9]

I. Period of Kelleli

The earliest, initially unfortified settlement of the BMAC is that of **Kelleli**, the farthest north in the delta. The ceramic objects found here represent transition forms from the classical Namazga V period of the Kopet Dag-Tejen oasis culture and the later ceramics of Gonur. In addition to finely crafted vessels made on the potter's wheel, Sarianidi discovered terra cotta female figurines, as well as statuettes of rams, goats and cattle, that all accorded with finds from the Kopet Dag-Tejen oasis culture. Since ceramics from the late phase of this first period have been found spread over the entire delta, from rich finds in Kelleli in the north to the occasional piece in the lowest level of Togolok 1 in the south, it may be conjectured

Female composite figurine from Gonur Tepe, Turkmenistan, *ca.* 2000–1650 BC. The body consists of soapstone; head and forearms are of limestone. National Museum of Turkmenistan, Ashgabat.

that towards the end of the Kelleli period the whole delta was settled by representatives of the same cultural form.[10]

II. The period of Gonur

At the turn of the third and second millennium BC the fortified settlements of **Gonur**, about 30 ha in size, arose 50 km south-east of Kelleli. Gonur was divided into a large northern and a smaller southern mound. In the centre of **Gonur North** rose a mighty fortress made of clay bricks, 120 x 115 m in extent. Its walls were reinforced by 20 rectangular towers. Inside the citadel archaeologists discovered along the inner walls small buildings with relatively few hearths, which presumably served as housing for members of a particular profession, such as administrators or civil servants, and were also used for storage. They also found a regularly laid out, clearly planned complex of monumental architecture and smaller spaces. The elite of the oasis probably lived here, along with its ruler, so Sarianidi interpreted this complex as the palace of the prince, whose authority may have extended to the entire delta.[11] In any case, such monumental architecture within a citadel indicates a hierarchically ordered societal structure. Residential quarters were found along the outer walls of the citadel. Here each house had its own hearth. This quarter was protected by another defensive wall 180 m by 170 m, with rectangular towers. Gonur North represents a forerunner of the classical structure of medieval urban architecture in eastern Central Asia, which consisted of a residential quarter, called *shahristan*, within a city wall, and a more fortified citadel, called *kala* or *ark*. The widely scattered buildings lying outside the second wall are comparable to the outer quarters called *rabat*.

The complex of **Gonur South** was built somewhat later than Gonur North and consists of a walled parallelogram with sides of 115 m, with the outer wall fortified with 12 round towers. In the centre rose a square citadel, 65 x 65 m in area. The outer wall of this citadel had round towers at the corners and a projecting entrance bulwark on each side, also guarded by two round towers.[12] Rectangular towers are easier to build than round ones but have a more limited firing line and can be undermined and destroyed more easily than round towers. As in the earlier Kopet Dag-Tejen oasis culture, in the early layers of Gonur South graves and cenotaphs – grave-like structures that honour dead not buried there – were found under the buildings. Sarianidi interpreted Gonur South as a temple site, but today the complex is understood as a mature settlement that included both residential areas and workshops.[13]

Both settlements of Gonur came to a sudden end: the northern part burned down between 1700 and 1600 BC,[14] and the southern site was abruptly abandoned during the same time period. Discoveries of storehouses with full clay vessels, valuable stone mortars, and unfired pottery beside kilns indicate that the people fled in great haste.[15] The simultaneous increase in crude, hand-crafted ceramics, of the kind common in the steppe culture of Andronovo – and especially its variant, the culture of Tazabagyab south of the Aral Sea – suggests that the demise of the BMAC Culture in Gonur was connected to the invasion of semi-nomadic representatives of the Andronovo Culture. These people spoke an Indo-Iranian or Indo-Aryan dialect.[16] This rough pottery of the Andronovo steppe culture had already begun to spread to Gonur a century before the settlement's fall, however, so Vadim Masson is probably right to suggest that there was a 'mutual interaction of two cultural worlds – the sedentary civilisation of the Bronze Age and the steppe tribes of herdsmen/farmers'.[17] The attacks from the steppes and the likely change in the course of the Murgab left the once-fertile land of Gonur desolate.

Female composite figurine, Bactria–Margiana, *ca.* 2000–1650 BC. The body and the hat consist of soapstone; the head is made from limestone. The Metropolitan Museum of Art, New York.

The construction of strong defensive walls is likewise an indication of an early threat from the north. About a millennium later, when the Murgab delta and with it the centre of an agro-urban culture had shifted about 50 km south to Merv,

Silver seal from Gonur Tepe, Turkmenistan, *ca.* 2000–1650 BC. A winged deity wearing a kaunakes, perhaps the Sumerian fertility goddess Inana or the war goddess Ishtar, rides a hybrid creature, part panther and part snake. National Museum of Turkmenistan, Ashgabat.

Gold seal of the winged war goddess Ishtar as 'mistress of animals', flanked by two lions, presumably from Turkmenistan, *ca.* 2000 BC. Museum zu Allerheiligen, Schaffhausen, Ebnöther Collection.

oasis dwellers used walls not only to protect their cities from marauding steppe horsemen but also to guard their most important agricultural lands. Strabo reports that the Seleucid King Antiochus Soter (r. 281–261 BC) had the expanded city and its fertile surroundings enclosed by a wall measuring 1,500 Roman stadia, equivalent to 278 km.[18] Such walls also served as a dam against advancing sand and prevented encroachment by the surrounding desert. The archaeologist Frederik Hiebert assumed that the central citadel of Gonur South had been built or rebuilt on the ruins of the settlement after its abandonment, so he assigned the building to the post-BMAC culture. Such citadels, like the neighbouring one of Togolok 21, were later converted into storehouses and hostels, becoming the caravanserais of the Silk Roads of Central Asia.[19]

Both complexes, Gonur North and Gonur South, stood, like nearly all other settlements in the delta, on natural rises not suitable for agriculture. A system that paid attention to maximising the use of arable land, oversaw the construction and operation of a capillary-like irrigation system, and carried on a wide-ranging trade network required governmental structures with a single ruler at the head. The irrigation system was complex; it consisted of a 50-km main channel, from which side channels extended to water a cultivated area of approximately 45 x 20 km. The basic requirement for the existence of a state is a controlled social organisation that holds power for an extended time, whether legitimately or by means of force, and can prevent splits along tribal lines. Social development in Gonur also showed signs of later economic shifts, so that the source of prosperity and wealth was no longer agriculture but rather trade.

In Gonur Sarianidi discovered two cemeteries, a large one with thousands of graves, where the common people found their final resting place, and, in 2004, a much smaller one for the elite. In both necropolises the tombs mimicked the houses of the living, with a table in the centre of the room, a bench along one wall, shelves holding pottery, and a hearth. At both sites the graves served as family crypts that could be opened and closed as needed. A dromos or entrance corridor led to the seven excavated elite graves, which were 30 x 40 m in size and sometimes had several chambers. Although nearly all the graves of both cemeteries had already been plundered in ancient times, the elite graves still show signs of the coloured mosaics that decorated the walls and clay coffers. An Egyptian makeup pencil made of ivory discovered here and a seal from Harappa, engraved with an elephant and an inscription that was found in the residential district of Gonur, offer evidence of the international trade network.

Four elite graves contain extraordinary treasures, including two complete two-axle wagons in two graves and a single-axle cart in each of the other two. A camel was harnessed to one of the wagons, two camels to another one. All of the vehicles had large wooden disc wheels, reinforced by bronze fittings. Whether the practice of wagon burial was adopted from the steppe peoples to their north or from trading partners in Mesopotamia is not clear from the evidence, but the solid disc wheels and the absence of horse bones, with the exception of a sacrificed foal, points to Mesopotamia.[20] In one of the wagon graves the skeletons of ten young men lay beside the wagon; in a second the bones of 15 adults were mixed in with those of various animals such as camels, oxen, and dogs, and in the third grave – no. 3900, excavated in spring 2009, seven men and seven dogs were buried. Since neither grave appears to contain a primary person, they must either be cenotaphs or, as Sarianidi proposes, the remains of a ritual sacrifice, in which the still-living prince was only symbolically represented.[21]

As in the earlier period of Kelleli, in Gonur and the neighbouring oasis of Adji Kui fine polychrome ceramics, fashioned on the potter's wheel, were discovered, as were zoomorphic and anthropomorphic figurines. Among the latter were flat female statuettes, of the type familiar from Kelleli and Altyn Tepe. Many of them display a bird-shaped head with eyes slit sideways and a beak-like nose. The female figurines had a purely domestic protective function, as they were found in practically every house but in only three of nearly 4,000 excavated graves.[22] In the late phase of Gonur there appeared for the first time flat male figurines with similarly birdlike faces, which may signal a religious paradigm shift.[23]

The polar opposites of the flat female statuettes were the 8- to 15-cm-tall seated composite figures of matronly, full-figured women, whose bodies and head coverings were made of green steatite or chlorite, with heads and lower arms of chalk or marble and eyes of lapis lazuli. The women wear a so-called kaunakes, a typical Sumerian cloak of Mesopotamia, made of either sheep- or goatskin or sheep's wool, which was woven into a feather- or leaf-like pattern. The kaunakes was worn not only in Mesopotamian Sumer (*ca.* 2800–2000 BC) but also in neighbouring Elam in south-western Iran. About 40 such stone female figurines from Margiana and Bactria are known, of which 11 came from excavations and the remainder from the antiquities market.[24] The only complete figurine was found in 2001; it lay in an unplundered grave in Gonur, immediately behind the head of a 30- to 35-year-old woman.[25]

While the source of inspiration for such composite figures is to be found far to the west, where they had spread as far as Ebla,

Silver ceremonial axe with a shaft hole, decorated with gold inlays, Bactria–Margiana, twenty-first to twentieth century BC. A winged man with talons and two raptors' heads tames a winged lion and a boar. The Metropolitan Museum of Art, New York.

Lord and Mistress of animals

The motif of an anthropomorphic being standing between two or, rarely, among four or six animals represents an archetype that was known in pre-Christian times throughout Eurasia, from southern Italy to Mongolia, and presumably arose in Mesopotamia. Among the earliest portrayals is a 5,000-year-old cylinder seal from Uruk, on which a ruler stands between two goats, a tree of life sprouting from his shoulders.[26] Around the middle of the third millennium BC the motif took on a mythological dimension, as the semi-divine and semi-legendary king of Uruk, Gilgamesh, was depicted as the sovereign and invincible lord of animals. On the great lyre from the royal grave of Ur he holds two bulls with human heads, standing on their hind legs, and the bearded, anthropomorphic heads of the animals display the same features as Gilgamesh's face, indicating the closeness between the demigod and the two animals.[27] Additional images on the lyre likewise make reference to the BMAC Culture, since they show animals performing human religious activities. Similar scenes are found on cylinder seals from Margiana.[28]

On a Sumerian cylinder seal from the second half of the third millennium BC, however, Gilgamesh stands on two winged lions with crowned, bearded human heads and with each outstretched arm he holds a living lion by the hind leg.[29] In south-eastern Iran at the time unique vessels and weights were made of engraved green chlorite; their particular decoration is referred to as Intercultural Style.[30] The lord of the animals is portrayed in many variations on several vessels. For instance, he is standing on two lions and holding two snakes or standing on the ground while holding two panthers, snakes, or humped oxen.[31] The lord of animals can also himself appear in animal form, however, for example as an eagle subduing two snakes.[32] Portrayals of the lord of the animals were also quite popular in the first half of the first millennium BC in western Iranian Luristan, a centre for the production of metal snaffle bits.[33]

In the Near East in the second half of the second millennium BC a spectacular form of the mistress of the animals appeared.[34] This was the goddess Asherah, who was glorified in inscriptions from the ninth–eighth century BC as the wife of the Israelite god Yahweh.[35] On a gold disc from Ugarit she stands on a lion and holds two ibexes firmly in hand, while two snakes appear behind her hips. On a pyxis lid from Ugarit dating to the thirteenth century BC, she takes the form of the fertility goddess Astarte with a naked upper body and feeds two ibexes.[36] We find a similar composition on the famous 'Grächwil hydria' (570 BC), a bronze water jar from southern Italy. Here the mistress of the animals tames four lions, two rabbits, two snakes and an eagle. The animals symbolise the three spheres of life: the bird of prey, air; the lions and rabbits, earth; and the snakes, the connection to the underworld.[37] Familiar goddesses of antiquity that included aspects of the 'mistress of animals' were Artemis and Cybele.[38]

In the east this motif appeared in Bronze Age petroglyphs from Oglakhty,[39] Minusinsk and Tsagaan Salaa as well as in the Sirven Mountains of the southern Mongolian Gobi Desert, where the lord of the animals stood between two powerful yaks. These portrayals were presumably related to hunting rituals. In the context of these hunting cultures, the human being stands *in* nature, not *over* nature. Animals have souls and deserve respect; they may be killed only for food or clothing. Purposeless hunting is forbidden and could lead to the disappearance of wild game because the souls of animals that had been killed but not used could refuse to be reincarnated in the same area. In the same way the bones of slain animals were to be handled with reverence. Finally, the motif of a man taming two birds of prey can also be found on clay and soapstone seals of the Indus Valley Culture.[40] These seals were produced locally, but the motif originated in Mesopotamia, which did brisk trade with the cities of the Indus.

The motif later enjoyed popularity, in both its male and female forms, among the horse-riding peoples of the Saka and the Scythians, as several gravesites show. Among these is the famous silver mirror of Kelermes, decorated on the back with electrum – an alloy of gold and silver. It was uncovered in 1903 in the burial site 'Kurgan 4', of a Scythian prince north of Maikop. One of the eight triangular electrum sections, which form a universal cosmogram, shows a winged mistress of animals holding two big cats. The mirror was produced between 650 and 620 BC by a Greek-Ionian or Lydian workshop for the Scythian market.[41] Also spectacular are two finds from a small cemetery on the south-eastern edge of Central Asia in Tillya Tepe in northern Afghanistan. Here Sarianidi discovered the graves of an Alan prince of the Kangju tribal group and his five sacrificed wives. The graves contained two pairs of gold pendants with turquoise, lapis lazuli and garnet inlays from the first century AD. One pair portrays a mistress of animals with two wolves, and the other a lord of the animals with two dragons.[42] In Christianity, finally, the motif acquired new symbolic meaning in the depiction of Daniel in the lion's den. The Christianised archetype symbolised the victory of the righteous man over the powers of death – in a certain sense, the resurrection of the individual.[43]

The reverse of the silver mirror of Kelermes, decorated with sheets made of electrum, a gold-silver alloy, which was manufactured in Greek Ionia or Lydia. Kuban region, south-western Russia, around 650–620 BC. In the eight triangular segments, moving clockwise from the upper left, the following scenes are portrayed: the winged mistress of animals holds two panthers; a lion attacks a bull standing on the back of a boar; two winged hybrid creatures made up of predatory cats and women's heads turned backwards flank an Ionic column, while a small panther crouches beneath them; a powerful leopard stands on a crouching ram; two bearded men with thick hair or dressed in pelts attack a griffin. The scene presumably illustrates a story referred to by Herodotus in which the Arimaspi in the far east tried to steal gold guarded by griffins. In the next segment a bird of prey flies over a large bear, which stands over a small dog; two sitting sphinxes face each other above a winged griffin and two lions standing on their hind legs confront each other over an ibex. The State Hermitage Museum, St. Petersburg.

Weight or amulet made of dark green chlorite in the 'Intercultural Style', Soch, Fergana region, eastern Uzbekistan, second half of the third millennium BC. On each side the handle is formed by a snake with a wide-open mouth. Historical Museum of Uzbekistan, Tashkent.

Syria, as early as 2400 to 2300 BC,[44] similar seated or standing female figures were depicted on Elamite silver vases of the same time. R. Ghirsman identified a slender standing female figure, clad in a kaunakes, as the Elamite goddess of war and victory, Narunde, and a crouching, voluptuous figure, by contrast, as the fertility and mother goddess Pinikir.[45] Presumably the composite figurines of Margiana and Bactria were examples of the latter.

Another female deity with Near Eastern roots can be seen on a silver seal found in a grave of Gonur in 1998.[46] On it a winged woman, wearing a kaunakes, sits backwards on a kind of dragon, consisting of a panther's body and a snake's head with an open mouth. She could be the Sumerian fertility goddess Inana or the related war goddess Ishtar, whose symbol was the lion and who was often portrayed with outstretched wings.[47] On another, gold seal – made, like the silver example, using the lost-wax process – two lions flank the winged, standing goddess Ishtar. In the mid-first millennium AD Inana/Ishtar became the Sogdian goddess Nana, who rode a lion and played an important role in the territory of northern Bactria.[48]

The pantheon of Margiana and Bactria also included male deities who tamed wild animals and had one or even two bird heads. One such hybrid is portrayed on both sides of a silver-gilt shaft-hole axe from the twenty-first or twentieth century BC. In the centre stands a winged man with two raptor heads and bird talons, wearing only a loincloth. With one arm, which ends not in a human hand but in three claws of a bird of prey, he manhandles a boar, which forms the cheek of the axe; with the other, he holds at bay a winged lion with bared teeth.[49] This man-animal hybrid is complex. He surely belongs among the various portrayals of the 'lord of animals', the archetypal image of a dominant human asserting power over animals and nature. Since here, as also in the vast majority of depictions of the 'lord' or 'mistress of animals', the tamed animals are living rather than dead. This archetype does not symbolise final victory of good over evil, as with St George slaying the dragon, but rather is related to the lifecycle of plants over the course of the seasons and with the royal responsibility to maintain order within cosmic chaos. By subduing instead of killing these two dangerous animals, the 'lord of animals' forces them to become his helpers. The owners of such ceremonial axes may have believed that they could partake in the extraordinary powers of the 'lord of animals'.

Similar ceremonial axes appeared in Elam and Mesopotamia and have been interpreted by H.-P. Francfort as symbols of power.[50] The winged hybrid of a human with the head of a raptor, which is also found in Bactrian metal and clay seals,[51] resembles the winged genies with eagles' heads of the Syrian-Anatolian world.[52] Such figures also appeared in the significantly later Neo-Assyrian Empire.[53] Another possible interpretation suggests the mythical first king of Sumer, Etana. He rode on the back of an eagle searching for a magical fertility plant to enable his childless queen to bear him a son. The myth of Etana developed around 2300 BC, at the same time as the epic of Gilgamesh, who in turn was figuratively depicted as the sovereign lord of the animals. On the basis of the selected examples it is clear that Bactria and Margiana were in close cultural contact with Elam and Mesopotamia, some 1,500 km away, and figuratively expressed religious and mythical content from them independently.

In 1974 and 1975, 16 km north-west of Gonur, at **Adji Kui**, I.S. Masimov discovered the ruins of nine settlements, four of which had vanished without a trace at the start of the joint Turkmen–Italian excavation project of 2003–2006 because these four sites had been used meanwhile for farming.[54] Of the remaining five ruins, which flourished in the second period of Gonur, the excavations of AK-1 and AK-9 are especially interesting. While the smaller structure of AK-1 was presumably a kind of caravanserai with particular administrative tasks, AK-9 had various functions over the course of its 1,500-year history. As early as the time of Namazga III around 3000 BC, long before the start of the BMAC Culture, the first simple houses were built. In their ruins archaeologists found not only flat clay figures of schematically rendered women but also so-called 'foundation pegs', made of fired clay. In Mesopotamia at the time it was common practice when building a temple to embed such foundation pegs at the corners. They took the form of a standing deity or an animal dedicated to him. This deity was often the personal patron deity of the ruler sponsoring the temple's construction and was his advocate to the patron god of the city, to whom the temple was dedicated. Since these objects were often inscribed, they convey valuable information about the context of the temple's construction.[55] The fact that this ritual was also known in Margiana underscores the intensive contact between the two regions.

In the Namazga V period around 2100 BC AK-9 experienced an appreciable consolidation of housing and erected a defensive wall in the shape of an irregular parallelogram, 4,932 m^2 in area, which was reinforced with at least 14 rectangular towers. Between 1600 and 1500 BC the 600 to 700 inhabitants had to abandon their settlement and make room for advancing migrants from Andronovo. The site remained inhabited sporadically until the fourteenth century AD.[56]

III. The period of Togolok

Togolok is the most important oasis of the third BMAC-period and lies 17 km south of Gonur. The oasis consisted of 30 smaller settlements, the fortified main site of Togolok 1 and the large, triply defended citadel of Togolok 21. The construction of strongly defended settlements and citadels at the start of the second millennium BC in Togolok, as in Gonur South, suggests the presence of external threats. **Togolok 1** was excavated by Sarianidi. Standing on a slightly elevated hexagonal site just 4,600 m^2 in extent, it was surrounded by a defensive wall fortified by round towers. A 30 x 30 m citadel stood in the northern part, integrated into the settlement.[57]

Togolok 21 was originally an impressive structure. In the centre stood a defiant 60 x 50 m citadel, with 8-m-tall walls outfitted with battlements and strengthened by six round towers. Two additional defensive walls surrounded the citadel, with the outer wall being 130 x 120 m. There were many buildings within the citadel and the inner wall, but the area between the two walls to the south and the west remained clear of buildings. Since there were only a few domestic hearths in the outbuildings of Togolok-21, it may be assumed that the well-fortified complex provided protection to the elite and selected workshops.[58] After the BMAC Culture, which

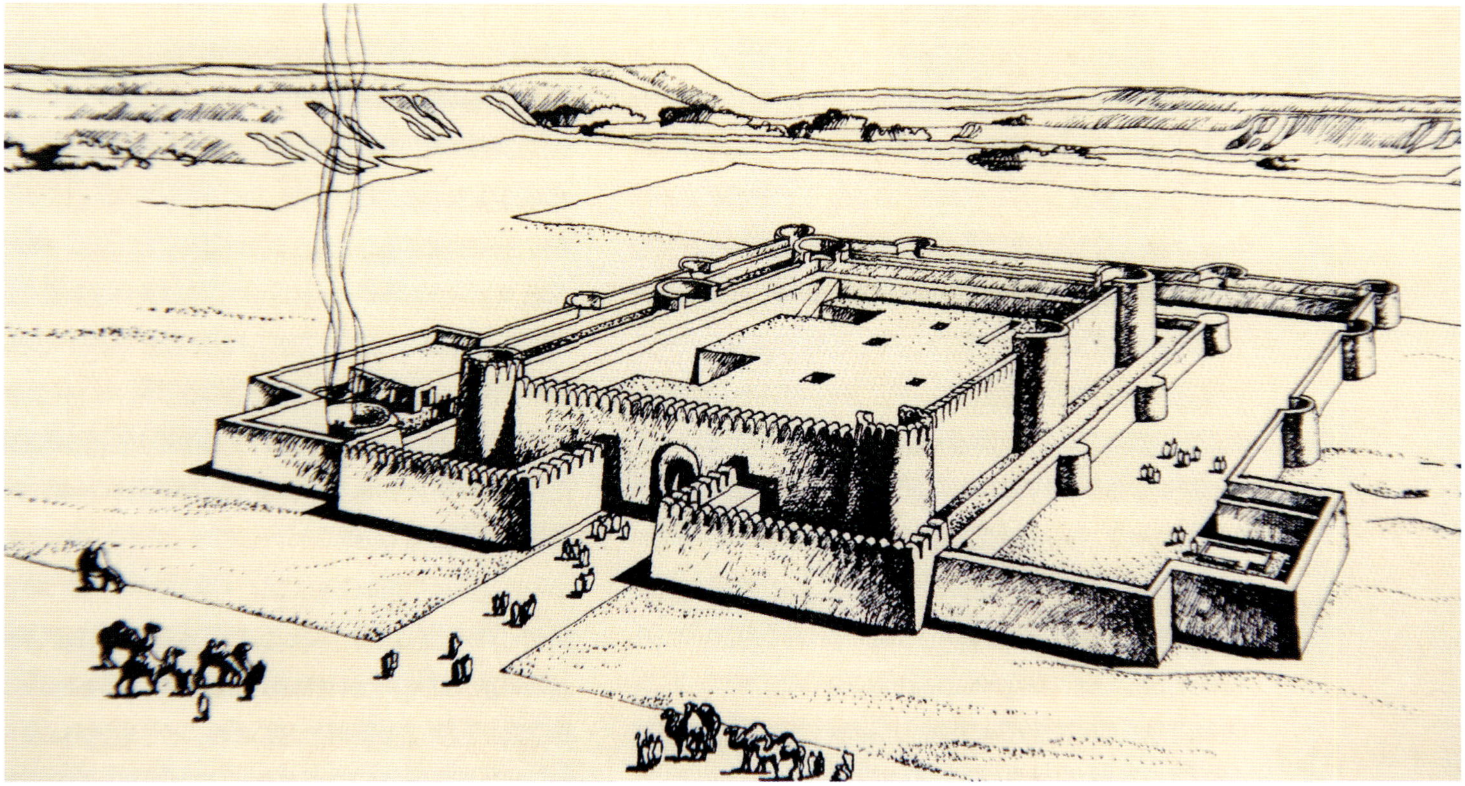

Sketched reconstruction of the fortress of Togolok 21 south of Gonur, Turkmenistan, early second millennium BC. According to Viktor Sarianidi, *Margush*, 2002, p. 172.

died out around 1500 BC, the culture of Jaz followed, marking the transition from the late Bronze Age to the Iron Age.

1.2 The BMAC Culture of Bactria

The agro-urban BMAC Culture expanded into Bactria somewhat later than it did to Margiana. In Bactria fortified settlements like Sapalli and Jarkutan emerged in southern Uzbekistan, as well as **Dashli** in northern Afghanistan, which displayed architectonic similarities with the two most important settlements of Togolok, as well as Gonur. According to Askarov and Ionesov this eastern cultural realm can be divided into four periods named after major archaeological sites: I. Sapalli (1700–1500), II. Jarkutan (1500–1350), III. Kuzali (1350–1100), IV. Molali/Bustan (1100–900).[59]

However, the fortuitous find of the '**Tepe Fullol** treasure' in 1966 south-east of Dashli in northern Afghanistan, which is tentatively dated between 2200 and 1900 BC, suggests that an outpost of the BMAC culture may have existed in Bactria a couple of centuries earlier than Sapalli. The hoard consisted of locally made gold and silver vessels which were hacked to pieces with an axe by the finders and later recovered by government officials. Later excavations unfortunately revealed no further artefacts. The procession of bearded bulls on a gold bowl is likely of Mesopotamian inspiration from the end of the third or the start of the second millennium BC, but the cruciform or stepped decorations on two other vessels are reminiscent of similar motifs at least five centuries older that were found at Sarazm II and III as well as Altyn Tepe, and which correspond to Namazga III. The classification of Tepe Fullol in relation to neighbouring cultures has not yet been settled.[60]

In **Dashli** two monumental structures from the beginning of the first Sapalli period have been discovered. The citadel Dashli-1 dominated the city, it had a square groundplan and was fortified with round towers. Dashli-3 was originally built as a palace, 88 x 84 m in size, with a double wall. After its destruction it was replaced by a fortress with a round defensive wall, which was reinforced by nine square towers.[61] **Sapalli Tepe**, for its part, consisted of eight symmetrically laid out residential quarters, which were arranged around a central plaza and separated from each other by straight streets; a square wall, 82 m long on each side and with no apparent military purpose, surrounded the settlement.[62] In the necropolis archaeologists discovered fragments of silk, approximately 3,700 years old, but it is unclear whether these came from China or the Indus Valley.[63]

The city of **Jarkutan**, founded around 1500 BC and located north of the Oxus River was, in comparison to Dashli and Sapalli, a metropolis, with about 20,000 inhabitants. It lay 60 km north of the modern city of Termez. Jarkutan was made up of residential and workshop quarters, a fire temple, and a palace that stood within the citadel. While the citadel was surrounded by a wall reinforced with 13 square towers, the city did not have a defensive wall. In contrast to Sapalli, where each household had a kiln, the residential quarters in Jarkutan were divided up according to type of handcraft.[64]

The fire temple of Jarkutan, surrounded by a thick wall, dates from the mid-fourteenth century BC and is one of the oldest of its kind, centuries older than the earliest fire temple of Iran. The temple had no fewer than seven fire altars called *atashgah* and basins to collect the sacred ashes, but also three cultic fountains.[65] In this temple the two opposing elements of fire and water were worshipped together. This cult of two contrary elements recalls a myth of the Rig Veda that says that the fire god Agni was born in water in the form of Apam Napat.[66] The pre-Zoroastrian combined fire and water temple of Jarkutan anticipates two developments: first, its architecture looks forward to the early fire temples of Iran, such as those of Bard-i Nishanda and Masjid-Suleiman in Khusistan[67] or of Mele Hairam at Sarakhs[68] on the border of Iran and Turkmenistan, where fire was worshipped as a symbol of vitality and purity. Secondly, it foreshadows the Oxus Temple, dating to 1,000 years later, which was dedicated to both the cult of fire and the river god Oxus.[69] Both cults must have been active in Jarkutan until the abandonment of the temple toward the end of the Molali/Bustan period in the tenth century BC. This is apparent because the sacred fountains were filled up and the entire complex was 'buried' under a 20-cm-thick layer of clay. Soon thereafter the city was plundered and destroyed.[70]

In the graves and necropolises of Dashli, Sapalli, and especially Jarkutan a notable development in burial practices and the corresponding religious ideas can be seen. In the first period of Sapalli the dead were buried intra muros, under the thresholds, walls, and floors of houses, continuing the custom of the early Bronze Age Kopet Dag-Tejen oasis culture. In contrast to Altyn Tepe, where only infants found their last resting place inside houses, in the first period of Sapalli all people were buried intra muros. They then existed no longer as living people but rather as guardian ancestors within the home. With the second period of Jarkutan the burial rites began to change. The dead were now buried in cemeteries outside the city, or cenotaphs were erected and anthropomorphic clay figurines and sacrificed sheep were placed in them. In Jarkutan a river separated the city from the necropolis, a symbolic boundary between the world of the living and that of the dead.

With the construction of the fire–water temple at the start of the third period of Kuzali the rituals developed further. Production and sale of anthropomorphic clay figurines and the newly appearing votive gifts in the form of miniature bronze weapons and tools became monopolies of the new temple, which presumably also had a herd of sheep exclusively for sacrifice. In this regard the temple of Jarkutan also anticipated the one on the Oxus. At the same time the construction of cenotaphs with accompanying sheep sacrifices and anthropomorphic statuettes increased, though it is unclear if this increase is attributable to wars and the lack of remains from fallen soldiers or to the beginning of cremation. Presumably both were factors because, on the one hand, at the start of the Kuzali period Jarkutan experienced serious attacks, as can be seen in the traces of conflagrations, and, on the other hand, several graves show marks of fire, indicating ritual burning. In the fourth period of Molali/Bustan cremation emerged, as did burial after maceration, the removal of the corpse's soft tissue. Another innovation was the placing in cenotaphs of cylindrical ceramic vessels with roof-like covers, which recall yurts and anticipate later Zoroastrian ossuaries.[71] Burying the dead with dogs, intermediaries between the worlds of the living and the dead, was also a new phenomenon.[72]

Towards the end of the second millennium BC an expansion of the late Bronze Age form of the BMAC Culture of Bactria spread to Tajikistan, where the local culture of **Beshkent-Vakhsh** (1100–900 BC) arose, showing characteristics of both sedentary farmers and nomadic herders. Their pottery consisted of crude, handmade wares, and their dead were buried in so-called catacomb graves, in which the dead lay side-by-side in niches and the main chamber held the grave goods. The treatment of the dead was not uniform, however, because cremation was practised as well as burial. Clear testimonials of the urbanisation process triggered by the BMAC Culture in south-western Tajikistan were found in the necropolis of Gelot near the present city of Kuljab.[73]

Petroglyphs of horsemen at Vibist in the Pamirs, Gorno-Badakhshan, south-eastern Tajikistan, late Bronze Age and Iron Age.

Certain burials of the Beshkent-Vakhsh Culture also included standardised fire rituals, as the burial chambers had small fireplaces, as well as charcoal and ashes that came from a pyre burned outside the chamber or from a fire ring. At the necropolis of Tigrovaia Balka in southern Tajikistan signs of burning were found under the largest kurgans, which are surrounded by stone circles. During the funeral a circular fire was lit above the burial chamber and then earth was thrown on it to put the fire out.[74] A similar ritual was also performed from the early Iron Age at the Scythian burial and cultic site of Arzhan-2 in Tuva. The kurgan was surrounded by a huge fourfold ring made up of a total of 336, 352 or 368 small stone rings. Calcined animal bones and ashes were found beneath each one, indicating a corresponding burnt offering. It is not known whether all these sacrifices were performed at the same time or stepwise.[75] Another variation of this widespread fire ritual is found in the contemporaneous or slightly later kurgans of Tagisken South and Ujgarak east of the Aral Sea, Barsučij Log in the Minusinsk Basin, and Kostromskaja in northern Caucasian Kuban, where, at the conclusion of the burial ceremony, the wooden structure built over the dead person was ritually set on fire.[76] This custom, widespread among the Saka and Scythians, was also found among the Sarmatians, as can be seen at the Nogajčik kurgan in the Crimea. At the burial of a prominent Sarmatian from the first century AD the 6-m-tall kurgan was covered with petroleum (naturally occurring crude oil) and set ablaze.[77] Presumably this ritual was thought to anticipate the universal fire that would purify all things at the end of time.

The so-called 'Beauty of Loulan', a naturally mummified Europid woman from the early Bronze Age, Töwän, Lop Nor Desert, Xinjiang, north-western China, *ca.* 2000–1800 BC. Xinjiang Uyghurs Autonomous Region Museum, Urumqi.

In summary, the radically changed burial rituals of Jarkutan reflect several significant innovations in the religious thought of Bactria, which can serve as a herald of Zoroastrianism. Among these proto-Zoroastrian aspects are the worship of fire and the construction of fire temples, maceration and the subsequent interment of the bones and the placement of these bones in ossuaries. Finally, dogs played an important role in Zoroastrian burial rites and served as guardians of the dead in the afterlife.[78] The practice of giving the deceased a dog as a companion can be seen not only in the late phase of the Sapalli Culture but also about a millennium later among the Sarmatians, nomadic horsemen who spoke an Iranian dialect. Zoroastrianism forbade cremation, however, as the practice contaminated the fire.

This change of belief in Bactria, which, like eastern Iran and Sistan, is associated with Zarathustra's earliest alleged areas of activity, could be related in part to the migration of Indo-Iranian stockbreeding tribes from the Andronovo Culture. In this regard one of the sources of Zoroastrianism would lie in the synthesis of the Indo-Iranian steppe culture of Andronovo and the agro-urban Sapalli-Jarkutan Culture of Bactria, which had intensive contact with Mesopotamia and, to a lesser degree, the Indus Valley. Further evidence of the advance of steppe nomads from the north is provided by changes in the material culture of Bactria, such as the decline of cultivation of the land in favour of increased stockbreeding, the ebbing of international trade, and the replacement of fine pottery crafted on the potter's wheel by crude, handmade wares. In the eighth century BC, however, the trend reversed, as trade and agricultural production began to increase rapidly. At the

One of the six graves laid out in a sun shape at Qäwrighul (Gumugou), Lop Nor Desert, Xinjiang, north-western China, eighteenth century BC.

start of the period of Jaz III brisk construction work began with the erection or founding of cities guarded by strong defensive walls reinforced with towers.[79]

Margiana offers a similar picture to that of Bactria. With the start of the first period of **Jaz** around 1500/1400 BC the large cities were depopulated; cultivation of the land declined in favour of the raising of cattle and, in a new development, horses; international trade ground to a halt; and crude pottery replaced sophisticated ceramics, with the first weapons and tools made of iron emerging soon thereafter. This change is the result of the expansion of a steppe culture from the north to the south. It first reached Choresmia, north of the Kara Kum Desert, where it encountered the late phase of the **Zamanbaba Culture** (2400–1500 BC), which had expanded along the lower Zerafshan River west of Buchara. Their ceramics were 90 percent handmade and undecorated.[80] Forms of the Andronovo Culture then moved in a second step into Margiana.[81] From here they spread the production of iron to the east into the Fergana Valley, where they absorbed the settled, late Bronze Age culture of **Chust** (1400–900 BC), which was characterised by the production of thin ceramic tableware. Influences of this culture spread rapidly farther east into the Tarim Basin, as can be seen in new forms of bronze and the start of iron production.[82]

As in Bactria, starting in the third Jaz period the people began constructing strongly fortified settlements with well-defended citadels, such as Jaz Tepe, Ulug Tepe and Elken Tepe. There was also a rebirth of agriculture.[83] Burial rituals also changed radically in the transition from Bronze Age to Iron Age. It was no longer corpses that were buried, but instead containers holding macerated bones. Sometimes the dead were exposed to corpse-eating animals. Both these new rituals foreshadow later Zoroastrian commandments, according to which the elements of earth, fire and water must not be defiled by impure corpses.

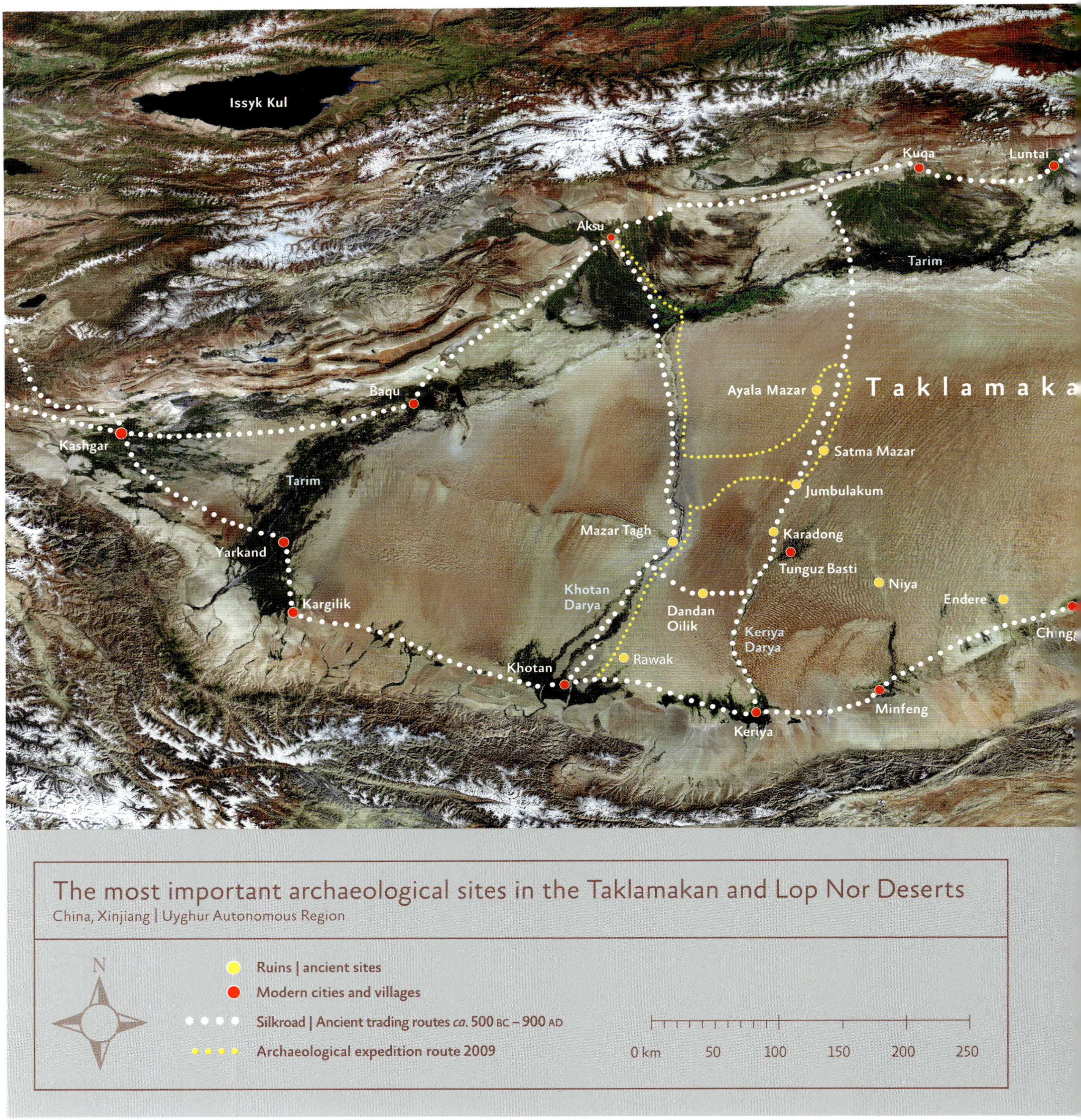

The most important archaeological sites in the Taklamakan and Lop Nor Deserts

China, Xinjiang | Uyghur Autonomous Region

N

- Ruins | ancient sites
- Modern cities and villages
- Silkroad | Ancient trading routes *ca.* 500 BC – 900 AD
- Archaeological expedition route 2009

0 km 50 100 150 200 250

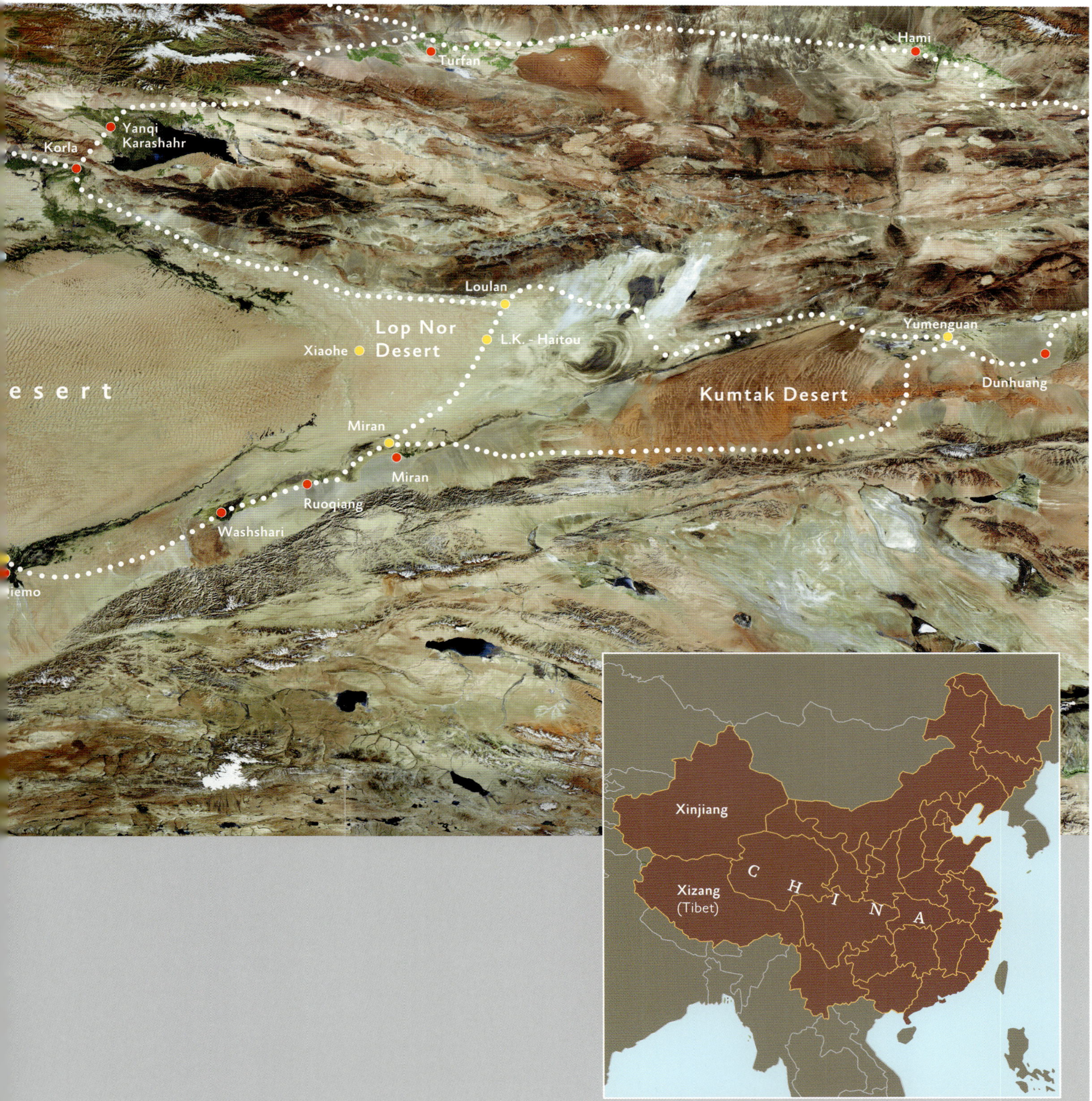
Turfan
Hami
Yanqi
Karashahr
Korla
Loulan
Lop Nor
Desert
Xiaohe
L.K. - Haitou
Yumenguan
Dunhuang
esert
Kumtak Desert
Miran
Miran
Ruoqiang
Washshari
iemo
Xinjiang
C H I N A
Xizang
(Tibet)

The conclusion must finally be made that the infiltration of stockbreeding steppe nomads from the cultural sphere of Andronovo brought an end to the material agro-urban BMAC Culture, but the immigrants gave up their own burial rites, which included building a kurgan over a wooden pit-tomb. The absence of earth burials in Margiana and Bactria from the end of the Bronze Age to the invasion of the Greeks some 1,000 years later supports this conclusion.[84] The proto-Zoroastrian innovations can be explained not only by the infiltration of the steppe nomads; they also arose out of changes in belief within Bactria and Margiana. Thus the mixed economic zones of a mostly settled population in Bactria and Margiana mark the boundary with the world of the steppe nomads in the north, with their bodily burials, until the invasion of Saka, Yuezhi and Alans into Afghanistan in the late second century BC.[85]

In this context, one should note that the migrations from the north were not movements of entire tribes, carrying their material culture with them en bloc, but were rather presumably an incursion of young warriors, who succeeded thanks to superior weapons and mobility. After seizing power they mixed with the local populace, analogous to the founding of the kingdom of Mitanni in northern Syria around 1500 BC, when immigrants or mercenaries, who spoke the ancient Indic language of the Rig Veda, seized power over the non-Indo–European Hurrians.[86]

▲ **Aerial photograph of the graveyard of Xiaohe during excavations. The torpedo- and paddle-shaped wooden stakes standing before the canoe-shaped coffins can be clearly seen. Top layer of graves, *ca.* 1650–1450 BC. Lop Nor Desert, Xinjiang, north-western China.**

◀ **Centre of the early Bronze Age necropolis of Xiaohe, before the start of the excavations, Lop Nor Desert, Xinjiang, north-western China, 2000–1450 BC. The mummy stretched out in the sand and the mummified head behind it were presumably left behind by grave robbers. The wooden palisade to the left divides the graveyard into two halves.**

2. Indo–European mummies in north-western China

For more than a century China has been a rich source of sensational archaeological finds. Among these are not only *Sinanthropus pekinensis* and the royal graves of Anyang, but also the Indo–European mummies of Xinjiang. The question of the origin of metallurgy in China was long debated. Chinese scholars believe that there was an autochthonous development of metallurgy in central China. This view does not take into account the fact that the forging and casting of metal began in the fifth millennium BC in south-eastern Europe and the Caucasus, spreading on the one hand via the Circumpontic Metallurgical Province and on the other across the Near East and southern Turkmenistan to the east. In China, however, metallurgy began immediately in the form of alloying on the north-western edge of the region, in the late phase of the culture of **Qijia** in Gansu (2500–1900 BC). Here horses and wheat also appeared for the first time in China, just before the rise of the Bronze Age culture of **Erlitou** (2000/1900–1600 BC), widespread in northern central China. In 1927 the highly developed Bronze Age culture of **Shang-Anyang** (thirteenth–eleventh century BC) was discovered in Anyang, Henan. This culture saw the emergence of several fully developed technological innovations, but the question of its origin remained open.[87]

In 1979–80 Chinese archaeologists around Wang Binghua made important discoveries in the Lop Nor Desert, Xinjiang, which were also political dynamite: they uncovered dozens of well-preserved mummies, about 4,000 years old, of obviously Europid people! Since these Europids must have come from the west or north-west, hypotheses emerged that the bronze discoveries of Anyang could be related to these mysterious people, their predecessors or their descendants.

Clay capsule grave of a woman, covered with an ox hide from the top layer of graves at Xiaohe, *ca.* 1650–1450 BC. Lop Nor Desert, Xinjiang, north-western China.

2.1 The origins of metallurgy in China

The excavation of the royal graves of Anyang brought to light single-axle light chariots with horses in harness and their charioteer, as well as sophisticated bronze objects, which show that northern central China suddenly mastered innovations in metallurgy, horse husbandry, the use of draught animals, wagons and carts in a highly developed form, which undoubtedly accelerated the cultural-technological development of China at that time.[88] Since these technologies appeared in northern and north-western China without any preceding developmental steps, it may be assumed that they were provided by neighbouring steppe peoples, most likely from the sphere of the late Afanasievo and early Andronovo cultures. Interfaces for this cultural transfer may have been the Bronze Age cultures of Xinjiang and Gansu or the steppe peoples of Inner Mongolia. The simultaneous arrival in central China of wheat and barley, horses and sheep, which could not have been domesticated within China due to a lack of wild ancestors, supports the hypothesis of a mediating role for Afanasievo and Andronovo.

In fact, bronze objects in Xinjiang appeared at the same time as in the neighbouring culture of Qijia in Gansu and at least a century before Erlitou.[89] Evidence that the royal dynasty of Shang-Anyang had trade contact with Xinjiang at that time is provided by the grave of the military leader and royal wife Fu Hao (d. *ca.* 1200 BC), discovered unplundered in 1976, since all 755 jade objects found in her grave were verified to have come from the region of Khotan, south of Xinjiang and over 3,000 km away.[90] Further evidence for contact between Shang-Anyang and Xinjiang is offered by the fact that many ancient Chinese words relating to the wheel, the chariot and the horse have their etymological roots in Tocharian, whose early form, proto-Tocharian, was probably the language of the Europid mummies of Xinjiang.[91] All indications suggest that in the thirteenth century BC central China adopted from the proto-Tocharian-speaking Indo-Europeans – who had been in close contact with the Central Asian Andronovo cultures – not only the technological cluster of horse, wheel and chariot but also the corresponding terminology.

Iron was also adopted toward the end of the sixth century BC from Xinjiang or Gansu, where it had spread as early as the end of the tenth century BC.[92] About two centuries after the introduction of iron King Wuling of Zhao (r. 325–299 BC) adopted from the horse riding tribes on the northern border the concept of mounted archery, including riding apparel, which initiated two millennia of active trade with Mongolia and Tibet for the acquisition of horses.[93] Thanks not least to the introduction of cavalry, the Early Han Dynasty (202 BC–9 AD) was able to force the powerful tribal confederation of Xiongnu back to the north and to wrest from them control of the Silk Roads through Gansu and Xinjiang.[94]

Two wooden dolls buried with all the traditional grave goods, Xiaohe, Lop Nor Desert, Xinjiang, north-western China, *ca.* 1650–1450 BC. In the centre lies a small vessel plaited out of tiny willowy branches, fine roots and stems of grasses; it was filled with grains of millet and wheat.

In summary, the Bronze and Iron Age cultures in eastern Central Asia contributed to the cultures of central China bronze and iron metallurgy, wheat and millet, the use of sheep for wool, the light chariot, the composite bow, the horse and its use as a draught animal and the light cavalry.

2.2 The Ayala Mazar-Xiaohe Culture

As early as 1914 the British archaeologist Sir Aurel Stein (1862–1943) was struck during excavations in the northern Lop Nor Desert by the non-Chinese but rather Europid appearance of the perfectly preserved, naturally mummified man from grave L.F.1, especially his dolichocephalic face, the deep eye sockets, the prominent nose, the moustache and the thick beard. He therefore classified him as the Europid 'Homo Alpinus'. A year later he discovered farther west, at the graveyard L.S., less well-preserved mummies of the 'local herding and hunting populace'.[95] The adjacent deserts of Lop Nor and Taklamakan offer the ideal conditions for natural mummification of buried corpses. First the climate, with annual precipitation of 16.8 mm and a 170 times greater potential evaporation of 2,885 mm, is hyper-arid,[96] and, second, the saline ground absorbs all moisture, which deprives bacteria of nourishment. Third, the wooden caskets were not completely sealed, which would have preserved the moisture in the corpses, and they had no bottoms, so the dead, wrapped in woollen cloths, lay directly on the saline ground. Fourth, during winter burials the extreme cold temperatures, as low as -45 °C, contributed to the killing off of decomposing bacteria.

In the last 30 years archaeologists have discovered about 500 more or less well preserved mummies in the two deserts.[97] The craniological and genetic investigations of Han Kangxin have yielded surprising results. In an extensive study of 302 skulls from nine different cemeteries of southern Xinjiang, dating from 1850 BC to 300 AD, 89 percent displayed a clearly Europid morphology and only 11 percent Sino–Mongolid features, and the 18 skulls from the oldest cemetery, Gumugou, are exclusively Europid.[98] Later studies have confirmed Han Kangxin's results, in particular that the older the mummies and skulls are, the more likely that they are

Two of the eight wooden figures found at Ayala Mazar, Taklamakan Desert, Xinjiang, north-western China, *ca.* 1890–1660 BC. China.

Europid and, conversely, the more recent the sample, the more likely they are of Sino–Mongolid heritage. From this it can be inferred that Europids settled in Xinjiang around 2000 BC at the latest, that Mongolids first appeared in small numbers in eastern Xinjiang around 1300 BC, and that a mass migration of Mongol and Chinese people occurred shortly before the start of the Common Era.[99] Since the necropolises of Tianshan Beilu, Wupu and Yanbulake in Hami in eastern Xinjiang revealed the Europid mummies found farthest east, and no Europids were found in the adjacent province of Gansu, eastern Xinjiang marked the boundary of the spread of Europid people to the east in pre-Christian times.[100] To summarise, there was 'a fault-line between Western Eurasian and East Asian population groups that runs from the territory around the Baikal lake through the Altai region in Western Mongolia, down to the [Xinjiang]-Gansu region' in China.[101] The present inhabitants of Xinjiang, the Uyghurs, first settled in the region in large numbers after 840 AD.[102] Whether the Tarim Basin had been settled by another group before the Europids is not known.[103]

Assuming the ancestors of the mummies from the necropolises of Gumugou, Töwän, Xiaohe and Ayala Mazar came from a neighbouring cultural sphere of Afanasievo, it may be posited that they spoke proto-Tocharian, part of the PIE family. In the second half of the third millennium BC these forerunners presumably yielded to the pressure from the bearers of the Mongol culture of Okunev by advancing to the south-east into the Tarim Basin. The initial, earlier migration of the proto-Tocharians to southern Siberia had isolated them linguistically from the rest of the PIE-speakers, so they did not practise the linguistic innovations of their distant Indo–Iranian relatives. Tocharian is most closely related to Celtic and Italic.[104] The later Europid immigrants of the first millennium BC, however, spoke Iranian dialects. The proto-Tocharian language is extinct but can be reconstructed from the three Tocharian languages of the Tarim Basin, which are known from written documents of the sixth to ninth centuries AD. Tocharian A, also called Turfanian, was used at that time primarily for religious purposes; Tocharian B, Kuchean, was a local vernacular; and Tocharian C, Krorainan, was an older language in Lop Nor that died out around the fourth century AD.[105]

The most important necropolises of the Bronze Age in southern Xinjiang are Qäwrighul and Töwän, Xiaohe, Ayala Mazar and Wupu/Hami.[106]

Töwän (Chinese **Tieban**): One of the oldest Europid mummies of Xinjiang is the 'Beauty of Loulan', discovered in 1980 on the lower reaches of the one-time river Konqi He near Töwän on the northern edge of the Lop Nor desert. The mummy, which has been dated to between 2000 and 1800 BC, is of a 45-year-old woman. She had light brown hair, wore short boots made of leather, and a pointed felt cap made of sheep's wool with a feather stuck in it, and was wrapped in a woven wool blanket. Beside her lay a carefully braided basket made of grass and tamarisk twigs, filled with grains of wheat. On her breast lay ephedra twigs, whose alkaloid ephedrine has both anti-inflammatory and stimulant effects. This discovery shows not only that nearly 4,000 years ago Europid people lived along the river but also that they raised livestock, including sheep for wool, had mastered the weaving of wool and felt, practised agriculture, and knew of the pharmaceutical properties of ephedrine.[107]

Qäwrighul (Chinese **Gumugou**): The necropolis of Gumugou, discovered in 1979 on the northern bank of the 'peacock river', Konqi He, dates from the same time as Töwän. Its Chinese name means old (gu) grave (mu) [in the] small valley (gou). The excavations revealed 42 graves, which could be divided into two groups. The first group consists of 36 shaft graves sunk into the sand, with the graves marked by pillars rising out of the sand to the east by the head and to the west by the feet. The caskets, shaped like canoes, consisted of two slightly concave poplar planks, facing each other on their long sides. Slats placed crosswise closed the casket, which was open on the bottom, and sheep- or goatskins were laid over them. As these dried, they shrank and sealed the top of the casket. The dead lay in the position typical of the Yamnaya-Afanasievo Culture, on their backs with knees drawn up. They were bedded in a wool blanket closed by wooden or bone needles and dressed only in leather boots and a felt cap. Grave goods were braided baskets with ephedra twigs and wheat, jewellery made of bones and deer antlers, jade beads, unidentified bronze objects, wooden vessels and anthropomorphic figurines made of wood and stone, but no pottery.

The interior of the graves of the second group was identical to that of the others, but the six men's graves are distinguished by their sophisticated construction. Over the chamber stood as many as seven very narrowly laid out circles of pillars made of poplar wood, which were surrounded by seven to nine ray-like and more widely arranged rings of pillars. Stein had noticed a similar construction in 1915 east of Gumugou at grave L.S. 1: 'Of these

Naturally mummified skulls of a Europid man and a Europid woman in Ayala Mazar, Taklamakan Desert, Xinjiang, north-western China. Presumably the two were not originally buried together. Accelerator Mass Spectrometry (AMS) carbon 14 dating of the woman's hair gave a calibrated date of 1890–1660 BC, with a 95.4% probability.

The author's camel caravan on the way to Ayala Mazar, Taklamakan Desert, Xinjiang, north-western China, October 2009.

Wooden mask, 10 cm tall, with an apotropaic function, Ayala Mazar, Taklamakan Desert, Xinjiang, north-western China.

Wooden phalli, 9–10 cm long, placed in the graves of women, Ayala Mazar, Taklamakan Desert, Xinjiang, north-western China.

[half a dozen graves] the central grave [L.S. 1] attracted special attention by its sevenfold stockade of wooden posts neatly fixed in the ground to form an oval, 14 feet long from east to west and 10 feet across.'[108] The spectacular arrangement at Gumugou, with a diameter of up to 15 m, recalls the stone cromlechs encircling kurgans or flat graves in the steppe of Afanasievo and Andronovo. Most likely such stone and wooden cromlechs had solar symbolism, like the sun symbol painted with ochre on the mounted mummy of Zaghunluq, which is why the cemetery of Gumugou is also called Täyamu, 'sun grave'. For each of these graves, some 600 trees had to be felled, which strained the already fragile ecological conditions.

While Han Kangxin's analysis of 18 skulls from Gumugou resulted in their classification in the group of Nordic proto-Europids, on the basis of their 'definitely Western racial characteristics,'[109] carbon-14 measurements led to a dating of Group I to 1880 (+/-95) BC and of Group II to about 100 years later. Thus Wang Binghua associated the older graves with Afanasievo and the second with the 'sun graves' of Andronovo.'[110]

Xiaohe: Near the 'Little River' of Xiaohe, a feeder of the Konqi He in the north-western part of the Lop Nor Desert, Folke Bergman first briefly explored the necropolis, which lies 50 km south-west of Gumugou, in 1934. It quickly returned to obscurity, however, and was rediscovered only in 2000 and excavated between 2002 and 2005, although it was unfortunately beset by grave robbers in 2003. The necropolis, which stands on a 7-m rise, consists of 330 graves, placed over one another in as many as five layers, of which 167 have been excavated from the two upper layers, bringing to light more than 30 well-preserved mummies of Europids. Carbon-14 analyses of all five layers yielded dates between 2000 and 1450 BC, with the two upper layers, the most recent, dating to between 1650 and 1450 BC.[111]

The excavations revealed the fertility cult of a society of herders, who also practised some farming. In front of the women's graves stood polygonal, torpedo-shaped wooden posts, painted red on top, presumably phallic symbols, and in front of men's graves were paddle-shaped pillars, interpreted as vulva symbols. As at Gumugou, the dead wore red-painted leather boots and a felt cap; they were wrapped in wool blankets and laid in canoe-shaped caskets, which were covered with the skins of cattle and sheep, presumably sacrificed at the site. Since Xiaohe and Gumugou lay close to rivers, which were used for transportation, the 'ship burials' could also symbolise crossing a river into the afterlife. In the four largest clay capsule graves women lay with the richest grave goods of the necropolis, which could indicate preferential treatment for women.

The various types of wooden statues are striking. The five nearly life-size statues, once painted red, originally stood before a grave and may have represented a guardian deity or an ancestor.[112] They are distinctly different from the six simpler and crudely carved male figures, made of wood and wearing leather boots and felt caps, which were buried in Xiaohe with a full set of grave goods, presumably as stand-ins for absent corpses. As in Gumugou the dead were given small portions of wheat and *Ephedra sinica*, whether in braided baskets or in small pouches, which were tucked into corners and edges of the shroud. Very surprising for archaeologists were two additional discoveries, as in almost all the burial

Comparison of finds at the Bronze Age graveyards of Xiaohe (Lop Nor) and Ayala Mazar (Lower Keriya Delta)[113]

ITEM	CHARACTERISTIC	XIAOHE	AYALA MAZAR	COMMENTS REFERRING TO AYALA MAZAR
1	Coffins stacked on top of each other	x	x	
2*	Canoe-shaped coffins	x	x	
3*	Coffins covered by ox-hides	x	x	
4	Mud-covered outer coffins	x	Not found	Destroyed by looters?
5	Sacrificial altars	x	Not found	Destroyed by looters?
6	Paddle-shaped wooden posts standing in front of male burials	x	x	Paddles lying on the ground
7	Torpedo-shaped wooden poles standing in front of female burials	x	x	Poles lying on the ground
8*	Small wooden figurines	x	Not found	
9*	Standing wooden figures	x	x	Lying on the ground
10	Wooden figures as mock-corpses	x	x	Differentiation between both types difficult
11*	Indo-European looking mummies	x	x	
12*	Faces painted red	x	x	
13	Ox skull with red paint	x	Not found	Only isolated ox horns
14*	Felt caps with red strings and feathers	x	x	
15	Short leather boots with red painting and feathers	x	x	
16*	Wooden phalli in female burials	x	x	
17	Wooden masks with huge noses	x	x	
18*	Miniature bows and arrows decorated with triangular shaped incisions on the shafts	x	x	
19*	Ephedra twigs placed in coffin	x	x	
20*	Small bags tied in shrouds	x	x	
21*	Straw vessels	x	x	
22*	Amulet made from white-grey soapstone	x	x	
23	Wooden staff with an inlaid design of a human face	x	?	
24*	String of small jade beads	x	x	
25*	No pottery in burials	x	x	

Characteristics marked with an asterisk (*) are occasionally also shared with other Bronze Age burials of northern Lop Nor such as Gumugou, Töwän or single sites on the Konqi He.

sites they found small wooden masks with over-sized noses,[114] which presumably served as protection from evil spirits, and many women's graves also held small wooden phalli, consisting of two halves bound together with red-brown wool. Some of the male corpses had been given miniature bows and arrows, and women wore bracelets with one to three jade beads. A few skulls had been painted with red stripes, as had a few cattle skulls.[115]

A study published in 2010 of mitochondrial and Y-chromosome DNA from 20 mummies from the lowest layer at Xiaohe, which date, according to carbon-14 analysis, to 1980 (+/-40) BC, yielded results largely supporting current hypotheses. All the male genetic lines came from a genetically European population; the females were mixtures of European and Asiatic, most likely southern Siberian, populations. The results were interpreted by the authors to mean that early Europids migrated to southern Siberia long before 2000 BC and interbred with local women there. Toward the end of the Afanasievo Culture they left their homeland and settled in the Tarim Basin.[116] Until 2009, however, Xiaohe was puzzling in two regards. First, the search for neighbouring settlements remained fruitless, and second, Xiaohe appeared to represent a culturally isolated case in that it was only here that a prominent cult of human reproduction was discovered.

Ayala Mazar: Until late 2009 it was believed that there were virtually no signs of the Bronze Age (*ca.* 2000–900 BC) in the interior of the Taklamakan Desert, as the oldest finds dated to the Iron Age (900–202 BC). These came from the fortified city of Jumbulakum (Yuan Sha), on the one-time lower reaches of the Keriya Darya River.[117] But in autumn of 2009, 80 km north of Jumbulakum, the author discovered the Bronze Age necropolis of Ayala Mazar, located on a 5-m rise west of the former riverbed of the Keriya Darya.[118] Although the necropolis had been plundered once or twice and badly damaged before the author's visit, discoveries on the surface revealed clear evidence that it was very similar to that of Xiaohe, 594 km farther east. The graveyard, 1,200 m^2 in size, was half as large as Xiaohe and originally held 80 to 100 coffins. Of the 45 skulls lying on the ground, two-thirds were presumably female, which is why the site was named Ayala Mazar, 'cemetery of women'. An AMS (accelerator mass spectrometry) ^{14}C measurement of human hair sampled at the cemetery confirmed a calibrated date between 1890 BC and 1660 BC at a 95.4% probability.[119]

A direct comparison of the objects found shows that of the 25 archaeological characteristics of Xiaohe, at least 20 are attested to in Ayala Mazar. As in Xiaohe, the dead wore only red-painted, short leather boots and a felt cap. They were wrapped in a wool blanket and buried in canoe-shaped coffins, which were placed

Interior side of the eastern wall of the Bronze Age settlement of Sebier, Taklamakan Desert, Xinjiang, north-western China, *ca.* 1500–1200 BC.

on top of one another in at least two layers and covered with cowhides and sheepskins. There were also torpedo- and paddle-shaped wooden posts, eight standing wooden statues, at least one wooden mock-corpse, tiny wooden masks with over-proportioned noses,[120] and red-painted, two-part wooden phalli. The objects included miniature bows and arrows with a notched triangular pattern, cattle horns, braided baskets holding wheat and ephedra twigs, amulets made of white-grey soapstone, as well as jade beads. Finally, all the completely preserved skulls of adults displayed dolichocephalic facial features, and one man and six women still had their hair.

The apparent celebration of human reproduction was presumably a reaction to the difficult living conditions and high infant mortality rate – several mummified infant skulls were found, as well as 60- to 80-cm coffin planks – so that the community of that time was aware that they needed to maintain a stable population by means of frequent births.

◀ Four re-erected wooden figures and coffin planks placed atop one another at the early Bronze Age necropolis of Ayala Mazar, Taklamakan Desert, Xinjiang, north-western China.

In contrast to Xiaohe, near Ayala Mazar at least two Bronze Age settlements, were found.[121] **'House 18'** stood 14 km north-east of Ayala Mazar and consisted of a complex of living spaces and stables that was wilfully destroyed in very recent times. The other settlement lay 14 km south-east of the necropolis and was a fortified community at least 3,350 m^2 in extent called **Sebier**. Its defensive wall, originally 4 m high, consisted of seven layers of crude mud bricks, reinforced with horizontally laid tamarisk branches, over which stood dense rows of clay-plastered poplar posts. South-west of the settlement ran a 90-cm-wide irrigation channel. Red cylindrical or spherical ceramic vessels with flat bottoms and carved fishbone patterns show characteristics of the pottery of the Xintala Culture (1700–1300 BC), a complex near Kuqa on the northern edge of the desert, which was influenced by the Andronovo Culture and produced bronze objects.[122] A few kilometres south of Sebier a small hoard of bronze objects was found on the surface. The hoard consists of two tanged flat small lance- or spearheads, two possibly ritual knives or knot openers, a shaft-hole axe-head, a flanged adze and a chisel. It indicates connections to both Andronovo and Aga'ersen in north-western Xinjiang, as well as Tianshan Beilu near Hami.[123]

With the finds at Ayala Mazar it is evident that in the first half of the second millennium BC a unified cultural sphere extended over a distance of more than 600 km; we call this the **Ayala Mazar-Xiaohe Culture** (*ca.* 2000–1400 BC), and it stretched from Ayala Mazar in the west to Xiaohe and farther east to as far as Gumugou, L.S., and Töwän.[124] The respective ^{14}C measurements at Ayala Mazar and Xiaohe suggest that this culture started in the Keriya Delta around Ayala Mazar and subsequently spread eastward to Xiaohe in Lop Nor. Their representatives were Europids who practised a fertility cult and had a mixed economy of artificially irrigated farming and the raising of cattle, sheep, and goats. They were in contact with both the jade-producing centres in the south and with Andronovo-affiliated cultures in the north. When the Keriya Darya began to carry less water towards the end of the second millennium, however, the Bronze Age settlements were abandoned in favour of oases farther south. The change from red to grey pottery, from bilobite bronze arrowheads to socketed trilobite arrowheads with barbs, as well as the appearance of iron objects and slag, supports a geographic transition from the Bronze Age to the Iron Age at between 39° and 39° 15' northern latitude. A millennium later the Iron Age settlements like Gäze and Jumbulakum – the latter of which had a clever system of irrigation channels – also had to be abandoned on account of water shortages, and life moved about 40 km further south to the fortified caravanserai of Karadong (*ca.* first century BC–fourth century AD).

Assuming that 3,000 to 4,000 years ago in the terminal inland delta of the Keriya, along creeks and in small oases like Sebier, a subsistence economy flourished, practising artificially irrigated farming and raising livestock, we can speak of a Bronze Age oasis culture. Withered tree trunks recall the lowland forests that once grew here, providing the settlements with necessary wood. Since the most important elements of this economy, such as wheat, barley, wool sheep, goats and metallurgy, came from the west, the question of their origin arises. The notable similarities in the ecological conditions and the corresponding economic forms between the oases of Bactria and Margiana and those of the Tarim Basin allow us to presume that the origin of this economy was the BMAC Culture.[125] In light of the results of the craniological and genetic research mentioned above, we can proceed from the hypothesis of a first social stratum of Europid, livestock-raising immigrants, who soon came into contact with representatives of the BMAC Culture and adopted from them irrigated farming. Thanks to sustained relations with steppe peoples of Andronovo, their advanced bronze metallurgy, the horse and the wagon soon spread throughout the Tarim Basin, as did gorgeous weavings in the tenth century BC and iron, presumably via Fergana's Chust Culture (1400–900 BC).

Chance discovery south of Sebier, from left to right, a bronze chisel, an adze, a shaft hole axe, two (ceremonial?) knives or joint openers decorated with rhombic patterns and two small lance heads with shafts. Taklamakan Desert, Xinjiang, north-western China, *ca.* 1500–1200 BC.

The petroglyphs of Kangjia Shimenzi near Quergou, dating largely from the late Bronze Age, are found at the foot of a 100-m-high rock wall, Xinjiang, north-western China.

2.3 The wheel, the horse and fertility rites

Toward the end of the Bronze Age the influence of the steppe on the Tarim Basin increased, as can be seen in the introduction of the wagon and horse riding. At the same time, a unique fertility cult flourished at the northern foot of the Tian Shan Mountains.

Wupu: In the cemetery of Wupu, 60 km south-west of Hami in eastern Xinjiang, archaeologists discovered more than 100 shaft-pit graves from the late Bronze Age (1300–900 BC), in which the majority of the dead were Europids with tattoos on their arms and hands. Notable among the discoveries were textiles with diagonal weave and embroidery made of wool, trousers like those worn by riders, and a three-part disc wheel from a wagon burial dating to about 1200 BC. Trousers, the wheel and the wagon burial, as well as the tattoos, which are known from later graves of the Altai, indicate a close connection to the northern steppe cultures.[126] The discovery in Zaghunluq near Qiemo of a man wearing riding trousers with a gusset, along with his saddle, shows that in the ninth century BC horse riding had spread as far as the southern rim of the Tarim Basin.[127]

Quergou: The petroglyphs of Kangjia Shimenzi near Quergou, Hutubi District, are found 150 km south-west of Urumqi on the northern side of the Tian Shan, the celestial mountains. The little-studied petroglyphs are unique in Central Asia in both design and content, since they celebrate an obvious fertility cult that recalls the older cult of the Ayala Mazar-Xiaohe Culture. Some 300 almost exclusively anthropomorphic figures are spread over a 14-m-long shelf 5 m above the ground that nestles against a natural protrusion in a 100-m-high rock wall. The figures range in size from a few centimetres to more than 2 m, and they come from different periods. The foot of the rock face, beneath the shelf, is decorated with archaic hunting scenes, ibexes and wave patterns from the late Neolithic.

The large composition, stylistically unified and consisting of seven or eight scenes, exudes a palpable vitality and eroticism. Dance scenes predominate, sprinkled with depictions of sex acts, men with giant erect penises, masks, and two-headed women or hermaphrodites. Most of the figures have a triangular upper body with broad shoulders and a narrow waist, and oval heads; a few of them wear a kind of mask with two antenna-like attachments.

The narrow, small faces with prominent noses and brow ridges suggest Europid people. Between the figures are engraved dozens of masks, a few even on the upper bodies of the dancers. In the uppermost scene only women dance beside a prone ithyphallic man; in two lower registers small figures, each a few centimetres tall, dance in front of a standing ithyphallic man. The large figures are deeply chiselled and polished to a shine; a few retain traces of their paint. The sight of this composition, originally painted red and white, must have made an overwhelming impression; perhaps corresponding fertility rites once took place here.

Without comparable examples, these petroglyphs are hard to date, but a few later chiselled pairs of figures provide clues. There are two pairs of horses, presumably heraldic, standing on their hind legs across from each other, from the middle of the first millennium BC, as well as two tigers, depicted in the Scythian animal-style, from the sixth–seventh century BC. Thus we can date the large composition, which was produced in at least two or three layers, one over the other, presumably over the course of centuries, toward the end of the Bronze Age in the last quarter of the second millennium BC. The latest petroglyphs of a few riders and camels come from the thirteenth century AD.[128]

3. The steppes of Central Asia: 'origin' of the Indo–European languages?

The history and development of at least three large language families are closely tied to the steppes of Eurasia. The first is the Altaic family with the Turkic, Mongol, and Tungusic subfamilies, with 160 million native speakers. The second group is the Uralic with the Finno-Ugric and Samoyedic subfamilies, which count 25 million native speakers. The third is the Indo–European, and, with more than 3 billion native speakers worldwide, it is the most widespread. The British official Sir William Jones was the first to hypothesise a common birthplace for different languages such as Sanskrit, Persian, Greek, Latin, Germanic and Celtic – which was later shown to be correct – though he also added Egyptian, Chinese, Japanese and Peruvian, which was clearly wrong.[129] The term 'Indo–European', which is supposed to encompass the geographic expanse of this language family, was coined by Thomas Young in 1813, and outside of Germany it replaced the description 'Indo–Germanic', introduced by Conrad Malte-Brun in 1810.[130] Since Tocharian was deciphered in 1908, the term 'Tocharo–Celtic language family'

Erotic dance scene in the petroglyphs of Kangjia Shimenzi, Xinjiang, north-western China, *ca.* 1250–1000 BC. The central figure has two heads.

might really be more appropriate, because the languages farthest apart geographically are no longer Germanic and Indic but rather Celtic and Tocharian.

Otto Schrader (1855–1919) was the first to state the hypothesis in 1890 that the original homeland of Indo-European should be sought among the steppe nomads between the Black Sea and the Aral Sea.[131] Since the oldest well-documented languages, such as Hittite, Mycenaean Greek or Old Indic, represent independent languages, the hypothetical Indo-European ur-language, called Proto-Indo-European, PIE, had to be reconstructed. In a second step linguists attempted to reconstruct a corresponding proto-lexicon. This revealed that PIE-speakers used the wheel and wagons, raised horses, cattle and sheep, planted corn, wove wool fabrics, collected honey, and sacrificed horses, sheep and cattle to the gods. They lived as farmers who practised stockbreeding and planting. On the basis of the common vocabulary of the descendant languages, supporters of the 'steppe theory' were able to locate PIE chronologically by means of dating the skills listed above. Since the wheel and the weaving of wool were introduced around 3500 BC and are thus the most recent innovations, no descendant languages could have branched off before this time. Soon after 3500 BC proto-Anatolian split off from PIE, followed by proto-Tocharian, then proto-Italic and proto-Celtic some time before 2500 BC, proto-Greek after 2500 BC, and proto-Indo-Iranian around 2200 BC. Proto-Indo-European, which emerged around 4500 BC, had disappeared by shortly after 3000 BC. It is assumed that the Indo-Iranian language family, which appeared around 2200 BC, was related to the cultural complex of Andronovo in eastern Central Asia. Around 1800 BC or earlier it began to split into three subgroups: Iranian, Indo-Aryan and Nuristani.[132]

Monumental stele of the Okunev Culture with an anthropomorphic face, Khakassia, southern Russia, 2400–1750 BC. Photograph from the early twentieth century.

In any case, the linguistic similarities between the Vedic Sanskrit, the language of the oldest part of the Rig Veda, which appeared around 1500 BC, and the older Avestan of the Gathas, the language of the earliest sections of the Zoroastrian Avesta, composed around 1200 BC, are so striking that a few scholars claim that 'Avestan looks less like an Iranian language than like a phonologically Iranised Indic language'.[133] The two language groups, the Iranian and the Indo-Aryan, separated around 1800 BC, presumably as individual groups from the Andronovo cultural complex began to leave their homeland between the Volga and the Yenisei. The factors that provoked the emigration of small groups of young men remain unknown. Probably not only overpopulation and overgrazing, as well as regional drought, but also the superior weapons of the emigrants played a role. One group set out to the south, toward Bactria and the Pamir Mountains, where the mythical homeland of the Aryans, called Aryana Vaeja, is presumed to have been;[134] the other headed south-west to the Iranian high plateau. In the second half of the second millennium BC in north-western Iran the sudden appearance of innovations like polished grey ceramics and horse burials, as in Hasanlu and Marlik, has been associated with the arrival of Indo-Europeans from regions east of the Caspian Sea such as Gorgan. These distant ancestors of the Medes and the Persians, who are mentioned for the first time in the inscriptions of the Assyrian king Shalmaneser III (858–824 BC), may have settled in Hasanlu, south-west of Lake Urmia, where most of the grey pottery was found. Around 800 BC Assyrians or Urartians burned the city to the ground, and towards the end of the eighth century BC the Persians moved south-east.[135]

The sacred books of the Hindus and the Zoroastrians present a rural world of primarily stockbreeders and secondarily farmers, not an urban world.[136] How close the two language groups were to each other at the time their scriptures were composed is shown by two shared terms with opposite meanings. The Indo-Iranian word *daiva* maintained in the Vedas as *deva* its original sense of 'deity'; in the Avesta, however, *daeva* are demons, false gods. In the Vedas the term *asura* describes sinister and even demonic beings; they are the adversaries of devas.[137] In Zoroastrianism, by contrast, *Ahura Mazda* is the one true god.[138]

Regarding the question of the geographical homeland of the PIE speakers, two contrary views exist: the 'Anatolia hypothesis' of Colin Renfrew[139] and the 'steppe hypothesis', outlined above, of James P. Mallory[140] and E. Kuzmina.[141] For Renfrew Indo-European, or Indo-Hittite, emerged around 7000 BC among the Neolithic farmers and stockbreeders of Anatolia. In around 6700–6500 BC, when they began to spread the technologies of planting and husbandry to Greece and farther west and north, Proto-Indo-European branched off from Indo-Hittite.

The Indo-Hittite hypothesis elegantly combines the spread of Indo-European with that of the Neolithic revolution, but also reveals an indissoluble problem: how can the vocabulary of the wagon and woven wool have emerged within Proto-Indo-Hittite as early as 6500 BC, 3,000 years before their invention? Is derivation of the Chalcolithic steppe cultures from agrarian cultures conceivable? Is it imaginable that settled farmers spread their language over the entire Eurasian continent? The appearance of proto-Greek within Greece as early as the seventh millennium BC is improbable. Why did Anatolian adopt in its original homeland so many non-Indo-European loan words? Most linguists believe speakers of proto-Hittite were immigrants into an agriculturally advanced but non-Indo-European environment of Hattic, Hurrian and Semitic languages.[142]

The steppe theory, which proceeds from a combination of linguistic palaeontology and archaeology, locates the nucleus of a common linguistic and cultural sphere, i.e., the homeland of PIE, in the eastern Ukrainian and Russian steppes between the Dnieper, northern Caucasus and the Urals. In tandem with the largely peaceful migration of groups of stockbreeders and farmers who also practised some agriculture, individual language families began, in about 3500 BC, to spread to the east and to the west. Although the steppe hypothesis is coherent and does not conflict with archaeological dating, it remains unclear *why* the older populations, who spoke non-Indo-European languages, adopted the languages of these immigrants. Was it because of the greater prestige of the bearers of new technologies, as well as their more significant economic power and more effective social organisation?[143]

4. Mysterious stone steles of the Okunev Culture in Khakassia

Around 2400 BC an ethnic and cultural rupture took place between the Irtysh and Ob rivers in the west and Khakassia and the Altai in the east. For the first time Mongolids of the Siberian type began to spread west and curb the expansion of the Europids, resulting in the emergence of an ethnically heterogeneous population. At the

Monumental steles of the Okunev Culture with an anthropomorphic face, Khakassia, southern Russia, 2400–1750 BC. Museum of local History, Abakan.

Rock figure of Chortcha Kho near Kazanovka, Okunev Culture, Khakassia, southern Russia, 2400–1750 BC. The figure is brought offerings of food and drink to this day.

same time new burial practices appeared in the **Okunev Culture** (2400–1750 BC) of Khakassia, the Minusinsk Basin and northern Tuva. Rectangular and square stone enclosures made of upright slabs, 100 to 200 m^2 in size and sunk into the ground, replaced the stone circles of the earlier Afanasievo Culture. Inside the Okunev stone fences there were as many as two dozen small stone casket graves, used several times over an extended period, with the bones of those buried earlier pushed into a corner to make room for a new burial. Although the economy of the Okunev Culture was simple and based on hunting and fishing, supplemented by the raising of sheep, cattle and horses, they made notable advances in the development of metallurgy. Metal objects not only appeared much more often than during the Afanasievo Culture; simple copper objects were also superseded by tin alloys. Thus the Okunev Culture and the neighbouring, contemporaneous **Samus Culture** on the Ob and the Irtysh produced the first tin bronze in north-eastern Central Asia. The type of settlement found in the Okunev Culture is unknown, however, except for traces of a few high fortresses.[144] Their economy was complex, as the people practised not only stock-breeding and hunting but also some farming, which suggests a settled lifestyle for at least part of the society.[145]

In contrast to the simple decoration of the pottery, the Okunev and Samus cultures left behind three groups of extraordinary, canonical examples of representative art: small amulets, stone steles up to 4 m tall, and petroglyphs. Among the amulets are 3- to 7-cm-long, schematic human figurines made of white-yellow soapstone, bone or horn, that were laid in graves with the dead; presumably they had an apotropaic function.[146] The bear figurines of the Samus culture, which were of about the same size, had a similar purpose; they were either worn as bronze pendants or placed in graves in the form of clay statuettes.[147]

The impressive stone steles of the Okunev Culture were originally erected at gravesites and were subsequently reused more than a millennium later in the Scythian-era kurgans of the Tagar Culture.[148] Anthropomorphic and zoomorphic faces or masks with geometric patterns are carved into these monumental steles, often many on the same stele. Such abstract masks also adorn ceramic vessels of the Samus Culture. Some Okunev steles end in a human

Indian ink drawing of a hybrid creature with an anthropomorphic body and the head of a bear, surrounded by a wreath of feathers or sunrays, petroglyph of Karakol, Altai, southern Siberia, *ca.* 2400 BC.

head, bent slightly forward; others have a ram's head. In other stone statues breasts and a swollen belly indicate the portrayal of a pregnant woman. On other steles the lowest face wears a conical head covering that extends the length of the stele, in which other masks are engraved. On still other steles, sun-headed faces are carved, which are very similar to the painted grave slabs of the contemporaneous **Karakol Culture** (2400–1750 BC) in the neighbouring Altai. Solar symbols are also discernible on the front and both sides, as are bears with their teeth bared. All the steles were oriented to the east-southeast and often stood immediately beside a cultic site where animal sacrifices were performed, allowing one to presume that they were related to cyclically celebrated rituals of a fertility and sun cult. Finally, the same motifs as on the steles are found in petroglyphs and on stone slabs: sun people and solar symbols; figures with very tall, conical headdresses; ithyphallic men; open-mouthed bears pursuing elk; masks; two-axle wagons pulled by oxen; horses; ibexes; snakes; cattle; elk and red deer.[149]

On the stone slabs of Karakol, which were originally free-standing steles with animal carvings and were repurposed as grave slabs, the standing anthropomorphic and theriomorphic figures are striking; their heads are encircled by sunrays or a wreath of feathers or they wear horned masks or take the form of a snare. These are joined by hybrid creatures with human bodies and bears' heads adorned with feathers, holding a branch in each hand, or a human figure with elk antlers or a bird's head.[150] Perhaps the numerous depictions from Okunev and Karakol of a bear pursuing an elk are related to the ancient myth in which an elk carries the sun through the heavens on his antlers. The bear chases the elk and abducts the sun into the underworld, so that day is followed by dark night.[151]

The approximately 300 Okunev steles are connected to particular rituals and were created with standard requirements for content and form, yet their religious significance eludes us. In any case, they anticipate both the later Scytho-Siberian animal style and the deer stones found in Mongolia, Tuva and the Altai.[152]

5. From the Volga to the Yenisei: homeland of the Indo-Iranians?

The broad region between the Volga and the Yenisei serves as the nucleus of the early Indo-Iranians before the language family split into Iranian and Indo-Aryan. Although most representatives of this culture lived east of the Urals and are included in the general term of the cultural complex of Andronovo, the Urals were not an insurmountable barrier, since isolated cultures west of the

Cultures of the Bronze Age and the Iron Age in the Minusinsk Basin

Thanks to the systematic excavation of the multi-period graveyards of Suchanicha near Minusinsk between 1995 and 2003 and the subsequent carbon-14 dating of the discoveries, calibrated to their corresponding layers, archaeology has a new dating scheme, supported by modern methods, for a nearly 4,000-year-old epoch.[153] Although the dating presented here refers to the Minusinsk Basin only, it provides important clues about chronological divisions outside of the basin as well.

CULTURE	TIME SPAN	NOTES
Afanasievo	3300–2350 BC	Related to Yamnaya and Botai
Okunev	2400–1750 BC	
Andronovo	1750–1400 BC	In a narrower sense, since Okunev is not counted as part of it
Karasuk	1450–1000 BC	Coincides with the culture of Kamennyi Log
Tagar Bainov Podgornovo Saragash	1000–200 BC 1000–800 BC 800–450 BC 450–200 BC	Start of the Iron Age Transitional stage
Tes'	200 BC–50 AD	Migration of the Huns
Tashtyk	50–500 AD	

mountain range appear also to have belonged to the homeland of the Indo-Iranians. They stood in the tradition of the Yamnaya Culture and shared a few essential hallmarks of the cultures east of the Urals.

5.1 Cultures west of the Urals

The **Abashevo Culture** (2200–1900 BC) extended west of the Urals as far as the Don in a forest steppe zone.[154] It continued the burial customs of the Yamnaya Culture; most of the cemeteries consisted of about a dozen small kurgans with individual interments, a few animal sacrifices and comparatively poor grave gifts, including shaft-hole axes made of arsenic bronze. An exception is found in the kurgan of Peplino, which contained 28 young men, who probably fell in combat: 18 had been beheaded and the remainder bore severe injuries caused by the blows of an axe.[155] Representatives of this culture raised cattle, sheep and pigs, but few horses, which suggests a semi-sedentary lifestyle.

Like the Abashevo Culture, the Katakombnaya Culture in the south-west and the Poltavka Culture to the south-east stood in the tradition of Yamnaya. The distinctive feature of the **Katakombnaya Culture** (2450–1950 BC), which extended from the Dnieper to the Volga, was that they placed the dead in niches or catacombs.[156] Grave goods included bronze weapons and tools, ceramic vessels with funnel-shaped or cylindrical necks and sometimes decorated with spiral patterns, smoking bowls and, for members of the elite, animal sacrifices and one- or two-axle wagons.[157] Another hallmark of the elite was the shaping of a clay mask over the skull of the deceased.[158] Such masks appear again in the much later culture of Tashtyk (first–fifth centuries AD) in the Minusinsk Basin. In the second half of the third millennium BC the drying of the climate between the Dnieper and the Don gathered pace and the forests in the river valleys receded further. For this reason the economy of the Katakombnaya Culture was based primarily on semi-nomadic herding and secondarily on the raising of pigs, as well as cultivation of the land surrounding the permanent settlements, which also served as winter camps and were partially fortified.

The culture of **Poltavka** (*ca.* 2700–2100 BC) was likewise a successor culture to Yamnaya and extended from the Volga to

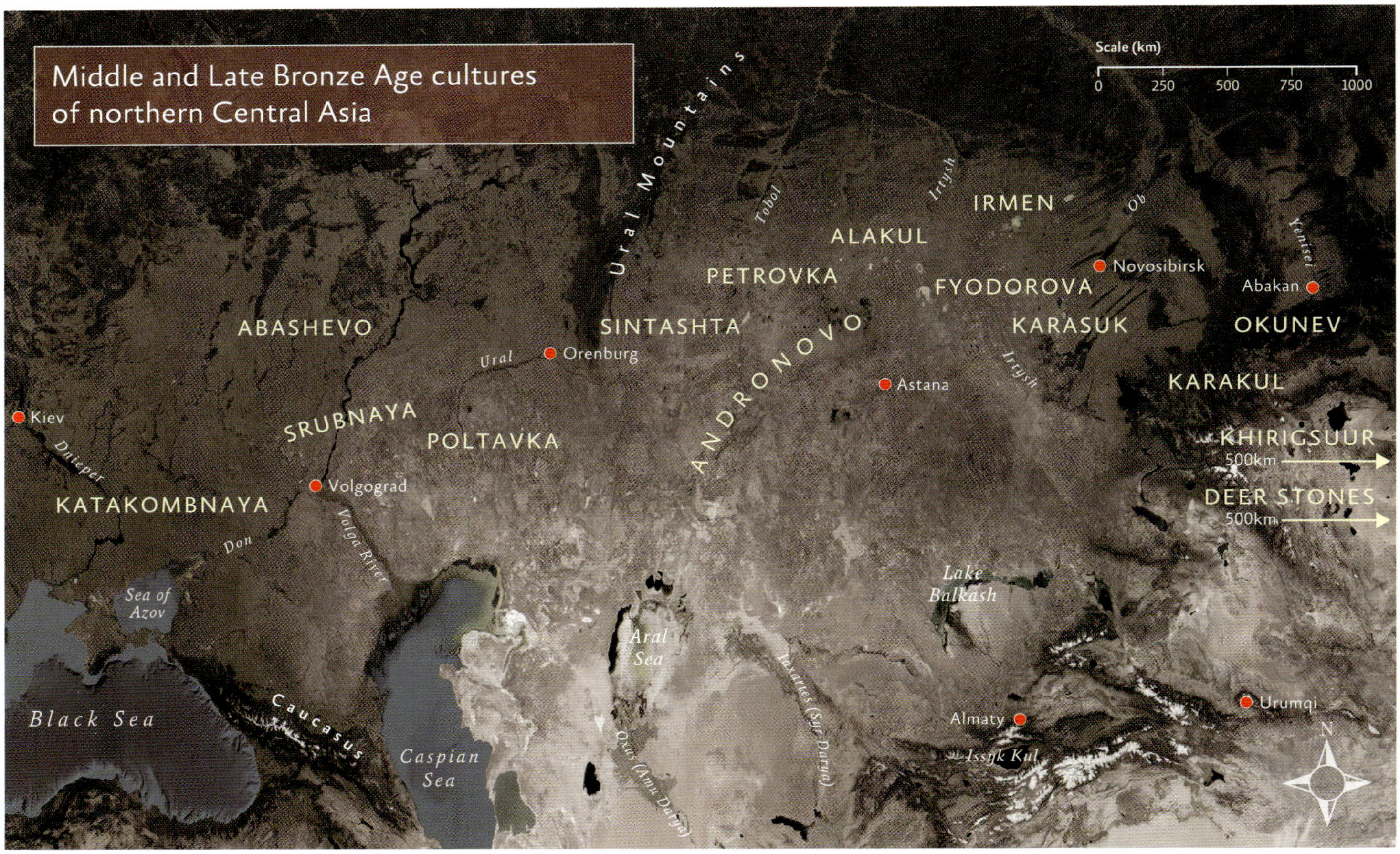

north-western Kazakhstan.[159] Its pottery was differentiated from that of Yamnaya in that its vessels were no longer pointed at the bottom but rather flat. Wooden arbours covered some of the gravesites, so in this regard it anticipated the timber-grave culture of Srubnaya. Like the culture of Sintashta, that of Poltavka belonged to the circle of early Indo-Iranian cultures.

The **Srubnaya Culture** (*ca.* 1950–1200 BC)[160] was a successor culture of Poltavka, Abashevo and Katakombnaya, and is closely related to the neighbouring complex of Andronovo, with the Ural River, which flows into the Caspian Sea, forming the border between the two cultures. Offshoots of each culture were found on each river-bank, however. It extended from the Urals across the Volga as far as central Ukraine, and its name, Timber-Grave Culture, refers to its log-cabin-like grave structures, found under kurgans; in Russian *srub* means essentially 'timber framework'. These wooden burial chambers resembled underground replicas of the above-ground winter quarters. Such timber graves, which were presumably thought of as subterranean houses of the dead, were the exception, however, since they appear in fewer than 5 percent of all Srubnaya graves.[161] Most of the dead lay in ordinary earthen graves, sometimes covered by horizontal wooden poles. In one regard the Urals formed a clear boundary, since in the Andronovo tombs grave goods made of tin bronze predominate, while in those of Srubnaya arsenic bronze ones do. The subsistence economy of the Timber-Grave Culture was based primarily on settled stockbreeding and, in the regions west of the Don, it used the moister climate to practise modest farming.

5.2 Cultures east of the Urals: The Andronovo complex

The term **Andronovo** (*ca.* 2200–1250 BC) refers in general to an enormously widespread archaeological complex of the Bronze Age. It extended from the Urals in the West to the Yenisei in the east and from Margiana in the south-west to the Tian Shan of Xinjiang in the south-east. Despite the variety of elements of material culture, essential common features are identifiable: whether as bodies or cremated remains, the dead were buried in timber chambers covered with a low kurgan; the economy was oriented toward semi-nomadic herding and limited farming; and people lived in sunken log cabin dwellings. Representatives of the Andronovo Culture are classified as members of the early Indo-Iranian language family, and they serve as inventors of the light chariot with spoked wheels and further refiners of tin bronze east of the Urals. At burials of the warrior elite horses and cattle were sacrificed and a chariot was sometimes placed beside the deceased in the grave. Early forms of the Andronovo Culture include the cultures of **Sintashta** and **Petrovka** (2200–1700 BC) between the Urals and northern Kazakhstan. The cultures of **Alakul** (2100–1400 BC), which stretched from the Tobol River almost as far as the Ob, and **Fyodorovo** (1850–1250 BC), which extended from the Irtysh to beyond the Yenisei, belonged to its heyday.[162] Later representatives of Andronovo included cultures south of the 47th parallel, such as Tazabagyab (mid-second millennium BC)[163] south of the Aral Sea, and the post-BMAC cultures.

5.2.1 The culture of Sintashta – fortified circular settlements and chariot burials

Shielded by the Urals from the moist air masses from the west, the distinctive continental climate between the Urals and northern Kazakhstan experienced a period of increasing drying beginning around 2300 BC. The southern forest line shifted northwards and the steppe expanded correspondingly, creating ideal conditions for the raising of livestock. Semi-nomadic herders from the region between the Volga and the Urals took advantage of this opportunity towards the end of the Yamnaya Culture, which was likewise exposed to an increased climatic drying.[164] They turned to the east, went around the southern foothills of the Urals, and founded the culture of **Sintashta** (*ca.* 2200–1700 BC) in the region south-east of the modern Russian city of Magnitogorsk between the Ural, Tobol and Ishim rivers.[165] The wealth of copper ore and gold increased the attraction of the region. The Sintashta Culture is characterised by two spectacular features: light chariots, with spoked wheels and very compact wooden settlements, built according to a master plan, with double protective walls, which could reach a size of 35,000 m^2. The 21 known fortified settlements were distributed over an area of 30,000 km^2 and surrounded by numerous unfortified villages. They lay along rivers and were each constructed in a short time according to a previously defined plan. Six of them have a circular layout; six more an oval one; and the remainder, a rectangular layout. During the annual snowmelt in early summer they emerged like islands out of the flooded landscape.

The approximately 4,000-year-old settlement of Arkaim, first discovered in 1987, is similar to that of Sintashta, in whose cemetery the first light chariots dated 2100 BC, were excavated,

▶ **Illustration according to archaeological data of the circular settlement of Arkaim, south-eastern Ural steppe, southern Russia, *ca.* 2000–1700 BC. The defenders of the city face hostile charioteers with their own light war chariots and foot soldiers armed with bows and spears. The chariots carry two men; a driver and an archer having also javelins.**

Traditional turning over of cut grass near Issyk, Almaty Oblast, southern Kazakhstan.

but it is considerably better preserved. The circular settlement with a diameter of 145 m is enclosed by an outer stone wall, 2.5 m high, which included an open walkway, as well as an equally deep moat 4 to 6.5 m wide. Beyond this was a 5- to 6-m-thick defensive wall, up to 6 m high, which was topped by a walkway covered by a roof sloping outward. The wall was built from large mud bricks, in parts reinforced by stones stacked on top of each other. The interior side of the compact outer wall was attached to the first, outer ring of buildings, which consisted of 39 narrow, trapezoidal houses, built against one another along the long sides. The rear, short sides of the houses, about 7.5 m wide and without entrances, formed the exterior of the settlement, reinforced by the defensive wall. The single-storey houses had common long sides 19 to 22 m long. The front short sides of the houses were up to 6 m wide and their entrances faced the 4-m wide circular street in the interior of the settlement. After this circular street came a second ring of buildings, consisting of about 23 somewhat smaller houses 16 to 18 m long with shared long sides. The entrances of these houses also stood on the inward-facing short side and opened onto a plaza with a diameter of 30 m. The rear side of this inner ring of buildings was, at over 7 m high, taller than the outer ring. The houses were built out of mud bricks, the roofs out of wood. No building displayed a size or shape that departed from the norm.[166]

The settlement, which once numbered about 1,200 to 1,600 inhabitants, had an approximately 12 m-wide main entrance to the south-west and three small, labyrinthine side entrances. Since the only entrance to the inner circle of houses was also found on the south-west side but was a few degrees farther to the south and separated from the main entrance by a wall, anyone who wanted to reach the interior of the settlement had to walk clockwise along the ring street, which was paved with timber. From above the settlement looked like a giant wheel with two concentric spoked rings.

The houses, sunk about 30 cm into the ground, displayed standardised interior arrangements and furnishings. Each consisted of a living and a working area, as well as an antechamber, and had a hearth in the centre or the back. Each house also had its own well with a domed oven beside it, as well as a covered drain that carried wastewater to the sewer that ran beneath the ring street. Such sewerage systems became widespread in Europe only at the beginning of the nineteenth century AD. Dross that still remains in the ovens indicates the production of copper and arsenic copper objects.[167] The necessary ore was found in the many nearby copper mines, such as that of Vorovskaïa, 40 km north of Arkaim.[168]

The rectangular cities, such as Olginskoe, also featured standardised structures. The settlement had a ring of fortifications with two gates strengthened by towers, which protected four rows of 20-m-long buildings, compactly arranged against one another along their long sides. Each of the two middle rows numbered seven buildings and each outer row had six. As in Arkaim each house had a well, an oven and a wastewater drain. Just under half of the area remained unbuilt, and here archaeologists discovered not only slag from copper smelting but also a small mine with gold ore. This indicates that Olginskoe was a small centre of metallurgy, where gold and copper ore were processed.[169] The economy of Sintashta was based on metalworking, the export of copper objects and bars to the BMAC cultural sphere,[170] stockbreeding, and some farming of millet and barley.

Such reinforced settlements were an innovation in this steppe region of Central Asia and suggest a need for security in a conflict-ridden environment.[171] The many weapons found in graves of the elite support the impression of an age marked by raids and skirmishes. In graves of the Sintashta Culture there are not only many more weapons than in earlier periods but also new types of weapons, which were particularly suited for battles with light chariots, such as light spears with long flint blades and spears with heavy copper or bronze spearheads. Added to these were traditional weapons such as daggers, battle axes and arrowheads as well as tools like adzes, barbed harpoon heads and fishing hooks. The discovery of numerous bone reinforcements for bows suggests that forerunners of the composite bow were also developed here.[172]

The burials of the Sintashta culture are concentrated in 12 necropolises, which correspond to the lifestyle of settled populations. The importance of stockbreeding is reflected in the elaborate

Kirghiz nomads build their yurts beside Karakul Lake, 3,610 m above sea level; in the background stands Muztagata, a mountain rising 7,546 m above sea level, Xinjiang, north-western China.

animal sacrifices, and the importance of readiness for combat in the rich grave goods of weapons, harnesses and even light chariots along with entire horses. The graves also reflect the social stratification of the society of Sintashta. Only a third of the dead were posthumously honoured with the construction of a kurgan and only 14 percent of the men's graves were distinguished by the privilege of a chariot buried in them. These were presumably the graves of the warrior elite. With the exception of daggers and knives, which also served as tools, only men had weapons laid in their graves; women received jewellery as grave goods. These were bracelets and frontlets, from the side of which a light chain made of bronze discs and glass beads hung to the chin, framing the entire face. From the back of the frontlet hung a long leather band, covering the neck and back and decorated with bronze ornaments and glass beads. The average life expectancy at the time of the Sintashta Culture was, at 28 years, quite low.[173]

Animal sacrifices also accorded with social considerations: horses were sacrificed only at the burials of men; sheep and goats mostly at those of women. A kurgan at Arkaim, where 115 animals – among them 22 horses, 29 cattle, 48 sheep and 11 goats – were sacrificed for the burial of 24 or 28 dead, was unusual.[174] With the exception of horses killed right beside the chariots, the meat from the sacrificed animals was used to feed the many mourners. In Sintashta animal sacrifices were an indispensable part of a burial, since more than 90 percent of Sintashta graves show evidence of animal sacrifices. In comparison, only 15 percent of Yamnaya graves of the lower Volga indicate animal sacrifices, 16 percent in the Timber-Grave Culture, and 17 percent at Alakul in the region of Chelyabinsk.[175]

A few graves of the military aristocracy were arranged like a three-storied house. In the lowest wooden chamber was the chariot with its harness and its charioteer. In the middle, somewhat smaller wooden chamber, the clothed corpse lay on his back with knees bent beside his weapons and with containers filled with symbolic food for the afterlife. In the upper chamber sacrificed horses, cattle, sheep and dogs lay beside a small hearth. After the sealing of the upper chamber a ritual fire was lit and an earthen tumulus mounded up.[176] In light of the complexity of the burial rites and the organisation necessary for the construction of the large settlements, one can posit the existence of hierarchical social structures; presumably large settlements were a kind of chiefdom.

The distinctive features of the burial rituals and grave goods in Sintashta suggest distant resonances with the world of the Rig Veda. Archaeological investigations have brought to light that members of the warrior elite were honoured with lavish burials,

The motorcycle fits seamlessly into the traditional life of Mongolian nomads.

which included the sacrifice of horses, cattle, sheep and dogs, as well as light chariots with eight, ten or 12 spokes, weapons and horse harnesses as grave goods. Towards the end of the ceremony a ritual fire was lit over the grave, and the kurgan was erected. In the Rig Veda warriors were praised as charioteers[177] who proved themselves in chariot battles[178] and races.[179] The lordly chariot also serves as the vehicle of the gods[180] and the sun.[181] The hierarchy of sacrifices of horse, ox, and ram/sheep[182] also corresponds to the findings in Sintashta. Although in the Rig Veda the dog is not a special kind of sacrificial animal, in a funeral oration the deceased is called upon as Yama, 'And those two dogs of thine, Yama, the watchers, four-eyed, who look on men and guard the pathway ...'[183] The dog is a guardian of the deceased and shows him the way. Then the fire god Agni is invoked to purify the deceased with fire but not to burn him up or consume him.[184] After this the earth is called upon to create a tumulus for the deceased as a final resting place: 'Heave thyself, Earth, nor press thee downward heavily: afford him easy access, gently tending him. Cover him, as a mother wraps her skirt about her child, O Earth. Now let the heaving earth be free from motion: yea, – let a thousand clods remain above him. Be they to him a home distilling fatness [richly furnished], here let them ever be his place of refuge.'[185]

The six towns of Sintashta with a circular plan show some similarities to the triple-walled circular complex of Dashli-3, dating to a millennium later, and Kutlug Tepe in northern Afghanistan, as well as the doubly fortified cultic site of Koi Krylgan Kala in western Uzbekistan on the one hand and the mythical circular city of Var from the Avesta on the other.[186] Although composed later, both the Rig Veda and the Avesta are rooted in an originally shared tradition some 3,800 to 3,900 years old.[187] The first ruler of the world and livestock, Yima, built the mythical, circular city of Var at the behest of Ahura Mazda to protect the healthy and pure living beings from the deadly winter Ahura Mazda will conjure.[188] The radial architecture of the circular settlements of Sintashta could also be a distant forerunner of kurgan 1 at Anchil Chon from the Karasuk period (1450–1000 BC), the Tuvan kurgan of Ulug Chorum, and the radial wooden construction of the early Scythian royal kurgan of Arzhan 1 in Tuva.[189] In this last case the radial tomb architecture could symbolise an underground form of the mythical city of Var and the interred prince would be symbolically associated with Yima, who saved pure beings from death.

The factors that led to the end of the Sintashta Culture are debated. A drying climate and increasing deforestation may have led to renewed migration, with the departing people ritually burning down their towns, such as Sintashta, which bears traces of fire,

Nomad woman in front of the wooden door of her yurt, central Mongolia.

analogous to the settlements of Tripolye, 2,000 years older.[190] The unfortified and circular hamlets on the Tobol River of the forest-steppe **Tashkovo** Culture, which lay about 200 km farther north-east and existed contemporaneously with Sintashta, were also ritually burned down without being affected by conflict.[191]

East of the Sintashta Culture the culture of **Petrovka** (2200–1700 BC) flourished at the same time in northern Kazakhstan. It is so similar to Sintashta that a common Sintashta–Petrovka Culture is also spoken of.[192] Certain differences can be seen, however. The compact settlements of Petrovka were smaller and less strongly fortified. They did not have a circular or oval layout but were always rectangular. Although the houses also had a well and an oven for metalworking, the discovery of infant burials beneath the floors was surprising.[193] As the Petrovka Culture expanded over time toward western and central Kazakhstan, the burials became less complex; the number of animal sacrifices and weapons provided as grave goods decreased and wagon burials ceased. These changes indicate less social stratification and a decline in the militarisation of society.

While the forges of Sintashta almost exclusively produced copper, arsenic bronze and slightly ferrous arsenic copper,[194] around 2000 BC in the forest steppes between the western foreland of the Urals and the Altai, as well as in the Sayan Mountains, high-quality weapons made of tin bronze appeared. In the absence of common burial rituals,[195] settlement types and pottery, these discoveries do not provide the basis for a culture, but they are described as the phenomenon of **Seima Turbino**, named for two of the five most important discovery sites.[196] The term really defines a group of outstanding weapons crafted of tin bronze in a certain style. In particular, the tin bronze spear points with a cast, closed socket, daggers, axes and arrowheads with sockets were, thanks to their superior hardness and better quality, superior to similar weapons made of arsenic bronze. The numerically small warrior elite who used such weapons also increased their advantage in close combat by wearing breastplates made of long discs of horn, sewn together in an overlapping pattern.[197] The weapon-makers of the Seima Turbino bronze industry were also artists, as they produced single-edged knives and double-edged daggers whose hilts end in an animal protome, or where an animal standing on the flat end replaces the knob.[198] These skilfully produced knives anticipate not only similar bronze knives of the Karasuk Culture but also to a certain degree the animal style that spread throughout Central Asia in the first millennium BC.[199]

This advanced production of bronze weapons was presumably developed by blacksmiths in the area around the Altai, who made use of the rich local sources of tin and supplied the warrior

Single-axle ox carts with heavy wooden wheels at a nomad camp near Khanuy Gol River, Arkhangai Aimag, central Mongolia.

elite with superior weapons. Koryakova argues that the blacksmiths of Seima Turbino were organised as clans and spread to the north-west, following the flow of their goods, so to speak.[200] The technology of Seima Turbino, which bore fruit in the emergent cultural complex of Andronovo, changed trading patterns as the earlier export of Caucasian arsenic bronze from west to east was superseded by the export of tin bronze from the Urals in the opposite direction.

5.2.2 Alakul and Fyodorovo

Around the turn of the third to the second millennium BC four related and partially overlapping cultures belonging to the Andronovo cultural complex flourished or arose east of the Urals. They were, from west to east: Sintashta and Petrovka (2200–1700 BC) between the Urals and the Irtysh, **Alakul** (2100–1400 BC) between the Tobol and nearly to the Ob, and **Fyodorovo** (1850–1250 BC) from the Ob to beyond the Yenisei.[201] Seeing that the earliest culture lay in the west and the most recent in the east, one can assume not only further development of the local cultures but also a migration out of the region between the Volga and the Urals. Together with the cultures west of the Urals, there arose a chain of similar steppe cultures that stretched over an expanse of 4,000 km from the Dnieper to beyond the Yenisei and was in contact with settled civilisations at both ends. Not only were goods exchanged along this steppe corridor; innovations were also spread, as can be seen in the appearance of battle chariots simultaneously in central China and Greek Mycenae.

The bearers of the Andronovo Culture were Europids and belonged to the Indo-Iranian language family.[202] Thanks to a more humid climate the pastures between the Ob and the Yenisei

Staging of the fire ritual at the conclusion of a late Bronze Age burial near Ulken Kuduk, Mangyshlak Peninsula, western Kazakhstan, *ca.* 1350–1250 BC. The egg-shaped stone dome over the grave corresponds to the contours of the egg-shaped cist grave beneath.

were lush, and the people of Alakul and Fyodorovo lived as settled stockbreeders. They had smaller, permanently inhabited settlements along the riverbanks, which also served as winter camps for the herders who moved around over short distances during the summer, and their livestock. Discoveries of bronze sickles and corn grinders suggest that farming was probable. The small villages included grazing lands and a necropolis. Each village had one or two dozen sunken houses, initially with an area of 25 to 100 m^2 and later up to 300 m^2 in extent. Presumably extended families lived in the houses and the village consisted of a single clan. As the fields were soon consumed and trampled by the larger herds, the inhabitants of the settlement had to change its location every 20 years or so.

In the first half of the second millennium BC walls and moats protected many settlements, but from about 1500 BC unfortified settlements became more common. This suggests either peaceful times or, more probably, increasing mobility.[203] At that time many herding families lived in an early type of yurt, which they either dismantled when changing camps and transported on pack animals such as camels or kept them mounted on a two-axle wagon pulled by camels or oxen. In this way emerged the new style of settlement that marked the steppes for more than three millennia: mobile yurt cities and villages. The fact that in the last quarter of the second millennium BC the unfortified settlements were also depopulated provides clear evidence for the transition of a largely settled stock-breeding economy to a semi-mobile and soon thereafter nomadic one. Petroglyphs of quadrigas, two-axle chariots drawn by four horses, from the epoch of Karasuk (1450–1000 BC) show that the people of that time possessed the necessary draught power.[204]

Graves and kurgans were grouped into cemeteries near rivers, unlike the later Iron Age kurgans that stood on elevated sites visible from afar and a certain distance from rivers. The graves were surrounded by either a circular or a rectangular fence made of stone and they were covered by a usually low mound of earth or stones, of which the outer edge was held in place by a ring of stones. The fence marked the physical boundary of the grave complex – the transition from profane to sacred space. Such a boundary fence was meant to protect the dead from hostile people or spirits and also to prevent the dead from infiltrating and troubling the land of the living. This symbolic function of the kurgan is expressed in the Rig Veda: 'Here I erect this rampart for the living; let none of these, none other, reach this limit. May they survive a hundred lengthened autumns, and may they bury Death beneath this mountain [kurgan].'[205] In the eastern part of the Andronovo cultural realm, the graves consisted of a cist made of large slabs; in the west, they were timber chambers.[206]

Regarding the handling of dead bodies, a significant innovation arose in the Fyodorovo Culture. While the Alakul Culture carried out only bodily burials and placed entire grave complexes under a single kurgan, in the southern Siberian regions Fyodorovo practised mostly cremation and individual graves. Cremation took place outside the graves, and, in a second step, urns containing the ashes and remains of bones were laid in the grave. In some cases entire kurgans were set on fire.[207] In northern Kazakhstan, however, the burial of corpses remained the norm even at the time of Fyodorovo, but on the Mangyshlak Peninsula in western Kazakhstan cremation was also practised and the barrows were often put on fire.[208] Only certain tribes introduced the innovation of cremation; the others maintained traditional burial rites. A distinctive feature of the Alakul Culture was the occasional burial of infants within the settlements, surely a continuation of an archaic custom from the Petrovka Culture. Finally, one other innovation appeared in the Fyodorovo Culture, which later spread to the elite graves of the Scythians, since in a quarter of the graves in the Minusinsk Basin two corpses, a man and a woman, lie in the cist. In some cases, the woman, who died a natural death, had been buried a few years later than the man; in others, however, both were laid in the grave at the same time. This means that at the burial of the man the chief wife or one of his other wives was killed in order to follow the man into the grave.[209]

Burial of an approximately 45-year-old woman in the foetal position in an egg-shaped cist grave, near Ulken Kuduk, Mangyshlak Peninsula, western Kazakhstan, *ca.* 1350–1250 BC.

As in the other Andronovo cultures, at burials a funeral feast was held and animal sacrifices were performed. The sacrifice of dogs increasing rapidly from about 1500 BC, while the sacrifice of horses and the use of horse gear for grave gifts declined just as rapidly. This probably attests to the disappearance of the chariot.[210] Practically all the dead were given pottery, but of two different qualities. More than 90 percent was of a crude type with simple forms and ornaments; the remainder was elegantly shaped and decorated with complex geometric patterns such as bands of zigzag lines, fishbone patterns, hatched rows of triangles, meanders and swastikas.

6. Karasuk and the cultures of Khirigsuurs and Slab Graves during the transition to the Iron Age

In the late Bronze Age, after 1400 BC, the culture complex of Andronovo began to collapse and regional cultures[211] emerged again, of which the most important in the northern steppe were that of Karasuk in the Minusinsk Basin and the Khirigsuur and the Slab Grave cultures farther east. North of the Andronovo cultural realm, in the forest steppe belt between the Irtysh and the Ob, the **Irmen Culture** (1450–800 BC) followed, with its people living in small settlements of pit-houses and practising stockbreeding.[212] The previously mentioned regional cultures of Jaz, Tazabagyab and Beshkent-Vakhsh emerged south of Andronovo.

In the northern steppe climatic and economic factors brought about the end of the settled or moderately mobile Bronze Age and led to the Iron Age of nomadic steppe horsemen. In southern Siberia the transition period shaped the culture of **Karasuk** (1450–1000 BC). Migration out of Mongolia and northern China, as well as mixing with the local Fyodorovo population, played a role.[213] The representatives of the Karasuk Culture practised nomadic herding, concentrating on sheep, goats and some cattle. A few groups maintained permanent winter settlements, such as that of Kamennyi Log on the Yenisei, which consisted of spacious sunken houses. 'The houses in these winter settlements looked from the outside like earthen mounds; but under the mounds were spacious rectangular structures with an area of 100 or 200 square m, sunk into the ground to a depth of 1½ metres or so.' A 'ladder in the form of a tree trunk with notches cut into it' allowed the chimney, 'an aperture to admit light and let out smoke from the fire', to be used as an entrance.[214]

The metallurgy of Karasuk was distinguished by its outstanding quality, which continued the tradition of Seima Turbino, and by special forms of knives and daggers. The bronze ring-pommel knives were either slightly concave or flexed at the transition point between hilt and blade; they may have been the inspiration for the knife coins with ring hilts that were widespread in China in the first millennium BC.[215] Other Karasuk knives and daggers either had animal protomes as the knob or a standing animal on the flat end. These daggers enjoyed great popularity and were found from the Urals over the Ordos as far as northern and central China; it is conceivable that they may for a time have served as a form of currency. The graves of the Anyang Dynasty, such as the one of Fu Hao, have yielded not only such bronze daggers with animal protomes, but also some daggers made of jade. The question of where this special type of dagger originated is unknown. This point is significant because these daggers and knives are among the forerunners of the Scythian animal style. The Minusinsk Basin, Anyang, the Ordos, or even Iran have been named as their birthplace.[216] The last two may be ruled out, and China is improbable for two reasons. The finds in the grave of Fu Hao (d. *ca.* 1200 BC) are later than the earliest exemplars from Khakassia, and the zoomorphic dagger knobs appear foreign to the Chinese aesthetic tradition of the time, which usually decorated bronze vessels with dragons, tigers and snakes. Thus the culture of Karasuk is not only the origin of the daggers with animal protomes but also an essential source for the animal style that spread to all the steppe peoples of the Scythian period. Discoveries of cowry shells in Karasuk graves suggest that it engaged in trade with China.

In contrast to the smaller cemeteries of Andronovo, in Karasuk the burials were concentrated in huge necropolises with thousands of graves. The dead lay in narrow cists, which were sometimes sealed by one or two stone slabs. Rectangular or circular stone enclosures surrounded the graves. As food for the afterlife they placed one or two jars containing beverages by the head and pieces of mutton, from the shoulder, breast and both haunches, beside the feet.[217]

Chinese jade pendant, 35.6 cm in length, in the form of a dagger with an animal protome in the style of Karasuk, central China, late Shang to early Western Zhou Dynasties, *ca.* 1300–1000 BC. Throckmorton Fine Art, New York.

One of the most interesting kurgans of Karasuk is the above-mentioned kurgan 1 of Anchil Chon near Kazanovka, Khakassia. The central cist is surrounded by a circular enclosure made of standing slabs, which were themselves surrounded by ten radially arranged stone settings. Not only was the neighbouring kurgan 5 also laid out 'like sunrays' but both kurgans were oriented to the rising and setting sun, as well as to the North Star. 'Graves 1, 2 and 6 of kurgan 1 lie in a line. On the day of the autumnal equinox (September 22/23), the final rays of light before the sun disappears behind the mountains strike the centre of these graves.'[218] Since the graves are laid out according to astronomical criteria it is conceivable that they also had an astronomical function, provided they remained marked after the sealing of the kurgan. Kurgans 1 and 5 of Anchil Chon share their architectonic principle of a ring-shaped central structure around which other enclosures or structures are arranged radially with not only the 'sun graves' of Gumugou, the circular cities of the Sintashta Culture, and the fortress of Dashli 3, but also the 'sunray-like' layout of the great kurgans of Arzhan 1 and Ulug Chorum. Thus Nikolaj Bokovenko classifies the two kurgans of Anchil Chon as 'an important link between Arkaim and Arzhan'.[219]

In Khakassia the graves of **Lugavskoe** from the tenth/ninth century BC mark the transition from the late Bronze Age to the Iron Age, which is characterised by a different burial topography. The people of Lugavskoe belonged to the early warrior horsemen of southern Siberia, who, as a consequence of their increased mobility, no longer constructed large necropolises but rather erected considerably smaller and isolated kurgans. The numerous discoveries of weapons and horse gear underscore the martial character of this new culture of nomadic horsemen.[220]

During the transition period from the Bronze Age to the Iron Age two cultures emerged east and south-east of the Minusinsk Basin that were characterised not only by different types of burial but also by differing ethnic affiliations. The shared geographic borders divided two ethno-cultural complexes from each other. They had in common, however, the integration of the so-called deer stones into their gravesites. In the region of Baikal east of Khakassia and in the eastern half of Mongolia the **Slab Grave Culture** (*ca.* 1250–100 BC) predominated. The gravesites consisted generally of rectangular, sometimes square or oval enclosures made of large, flat or cigar-shaped stone slabs sunk into the ground; occasionally steles marked the corners of the enclosures. Sometimes older deer stones, which originally fulfilled other purposes, were

Kurgan 1 of Anchil Chon near Kazanovka, Khakassia, southern Russia, Karasuk Period, 1450–1000 BC.

Deer stones and one of the Khirigsuurs of the burial and sacrifice site of Tsagaan Asgat, Bayan Ölgyi Aimag, western Mongolia, Khirigsuur Culture, 1400–300 BC.

At the burial and sacrifice complex of Jargalant (*ca.* 1250–100 BC), older deer stones were repurposed to create an enclosure for Slab Graves, Arkhangai Aimag, central Mongolia.

reused, whether standing as corner steles or lying down as part of the enclosure fence. The interior of the enclosure was filled with stone paving, under which the deceased was laid on his back in a cist or a simple pit, with his head always oriented toward the east. On the one hand the dead were given as grave goods animal skulls, especially horse skulls, a custom continued by the Xiongnu, and on the other, bronze objects in the Karasuk style such as ring hilt knives, daggers with animal-shaped knobs, and small decorative platters with pictures of animals.[221] Two discoveries of heavy bronze helmets, like those used in China at the time of the Western Zhou (*ca.* eleventh century–771 BC), indicate contact with their southern neighbours.[222] Examination of the skeletons suggests that they came from a Mongolid population.[223] These people lived mostly by herding; signs of settlement have not been found.

South-west of the Slab Grave Culture, in western Mongolia and the Altai, Slab Graves are very rarely found; there are instead stone kurgans, called Khirigsuurs. Both types of burial are found in central Mongolia and Khirigsuurs are occasionally found in eastern Mongolia, too. In the **Khirigsuur Culture** (*ca.* 1400–300 BC) the dead lay in shallow pits or stone caskets or in a wooden chamber, always with the head oriented toward the west. A stone tumulus stood over them, and it was surrounded by a round, square, or rectangular stone enclosure with a diameter of 25–30 m. The kurgan and the circular fence were sometimes connected by four or eight ray-like rows of stones, oriented to the four cardinal directions and the intermediate directions, which gave the site a sun symbolism and strongly recalls the radial wooden architecture of Arzhan 1.[224] The Khirigsuurs, which lay along rivers, did not contain Mongolids, as the Slab Graves did, but rather Europids.[225] One such burial ground was that of Ulangom (second half of the first millennium BC) on the border with Tuva. In the 22 timber graves and 20 stone casket graves a total of 143 people of the Europid type were buried, with 17 percent of the men having died a violent death.[226]

There are also many Khirigsuurs, however, that were not gravesites but rather places of sacrifice. During the transition from the Bronze Age to the Iron Age there were in Mongolia two realms, differentiated along ethno-cultural lines: in the east the world of Mongolids and Slab Graves, and in the west the world of Europids and Khirigsuurs. Central Mongolia formed a contact zone where the two spheres intermingled. Despite these clear differences, the deer stones were a common denominator, as they are found by both Slab Graves and Khirigsuurs, so one can almost speak of a '**deer stone culture**' (*ca.* 1400–500 BC), with representatives among both Europids and Mongolids.

Rubbing traced with Indian ink of the anthropomorphic deer stone of Ushkin Uver, Khövsgöl Aimag, northern Mongolia, *ca.* 1400–850 BC. (The lowest part is not in the picture.) Twenty-seven images of deer cavort on the stele; late Bronze Age weapons hang from the belt that divides the middle part of the stele from the lower. The statue has a five-pointed shield on its back.

6.1 Deer stones: flying deer as companions in the afterlife?

Western and central Mongolia is a land not only of petroglyphs but also of deer stones. The latter are free-standing stone steles, up to 4 m tall, with low relief carvings, in which deer and weapons are the dominant motifs, followed by horses, big cats and boars. Of the approximately 700 known deer stones, 90 percent are found in Mongolia, with the remainder in the Altai, Tuva and Xinjiang.[227] They continue the tradition of cultic stone steles of earlier steppe cultures, such as those of the Usatovo Culture (3300–2800 BC) in the northern Pontic region and the Okunev Culture (2400–1750) in the Minusinsk Basin and Khakassia. This tradition was further developed in the second half of the first millennium BC in the anthropomorphic stone sculptures of the northern Pontic Scythians[228] and the Sarmatians on the Mangyshlak Peninsula.[229] A few centuries later the stone statues of the Turkish khanate[230] began to appear in the regions to which the deer stones had spread. Later came the stone portrayals of both warriors and women by the Polovtsi (Cuman) people,[231] who ruled over a band of steppe stretching from the Ukraine to central Kazakhstan from the eleventh to the thirteenth century. Such statues still enjoy veneration today from Mongolians and Tuvinians; they tie blue bands around their necks, rub fat into their hands and bellies, and bring them flasks of vodka as offerings, after which they ask for the blessing of their ancestors. This veneration impressed the German explorer of Siberia Daniel Gottlieb Messerschmidt (1685–1735) in the Minusinsk Basin. In 1722 he wrote, 'The heathen Tatars [of Abakan] showed much reverence for these [statues] and rode three times around each one, after which ceremonies they offered them some of their own provisions or placed these on the pedestal under the grass so they [the statues] could eat from it according to their appetite.'[232]

A long block of granite or, more rarely, sandstone or marble, served as material for the deer stones. The artists first carefully polished the surface, before they carved figures on all four or at least on both wide sides, according to a defined iconographic canon. All the stones were divided into three parts. The top represented the head, which was portrayed three-dimensionally only in very rare cases[233] and was usually represented simply by a necklace, a pair of curved lines, and earrings. The 318-cm-tall, well-preserved stele 14 from the cultic site of Ushkin Uver in northern Mongolia makes clear with its human face, oriented

▶ The 318-cm tall anthropomorphic deer stone at the burial and sacrifice site of Ushkin Uver, Khövsgöl Aimag, northern Mongolia, *ca.* 1400–850 BC. The rubbing with mulberry paper makes the engraved figures stand out.

toward the east, that the deer stones were anthropomorphic representations, even though, unlike the Old Turkic statues, they have no arms. The weapon belt that divides the upper from the lower section supports this interpretation. On this belt are found the typical weaponry of steppe horsemen of the time, such as a sheathed bow, an axe, a decorated dagger, a knife and a whetstone, so that the deer stone may be seen as a codified portrayal of an armed warrior from the late Bronze Age and early Iron Age. In addition to the weapons, five-pointed shields, which were also widespread in China, adorned the lower third, as did small deer. In the centre section stylised deer frolic, some bearing disproportionately large, broadly branching and upright-standing antlers. Others have a long, bird-like snout and antlers that cover their entire backs, and are flying heavenward at full gallop. On a few cigar-shaped steles, the deer circle around all sides, moving dynamically upward. On other steles are carved horses, gazelles, boars or hunting scenes, in which predatory cats eat a horse or a kulan. Sometimes on the narrow sides obvious sun symbols replace the earrings, and a sun symbol occasionally tops the upper section of the front side. That the deer stones were anthropomorphic representations of a warrior is further suggested by the fact that the elongated trunks of the stylised deer have exactly the same shape as a typical Karasuk dagger, as highlighted recently by Anatoli Nagler.[234]

The deer stones may be divided into three chronologically sequential groups:[235]

Petroglyphs of stylised deer at Eltsin Bulak, *ca.* 900–700 BC, Arkhangai Aimag, central Mongolia.

First group (1400–850 BC): In the earliest group stylised deer and knives and daggers with animal protomes, typical of the Karasuk Culture, predominate, suggesting a dating in the late Bronze Age. The 15 steles of the cultic site at Ushkin Uver come from this early time, as typical Karasuk weapons are engraved on several of them. The motif of deer flying heavenward is also found on contemporaneous petroglyphs and on later tattoos of Scythian warriors of the Altai.[236] Together with the Okunev stone steles, Seima Turbino bronze objects, and the decoration on the knobs of Karasuk daggers, this first group of deer stones represents the most important element of the Scytho-Siberian animal style of the Iron Age.

Second group (900–700 BC): In this group both the dynamism of movement and the stylised deer have disappeared and the weapons lack any decoration. Now deer standing on tiptoe, boars, leopards, horses and kulans are depicted realistically, and they are joined by coiled up predatory cats. Petroglyphs of deer and boars standing on tiptoe are also widespread in Tuva, in north-eastern Xinjiang and in southern Kazakhstan, for example at Usek, Ur-Maral and Arpa Uzen.[237]

Third group (700–500 BC): On the stones of this final, numerically small group the tendency toward simplification reached its austere highpoint. Animals have practically disappeared, while simply sketched weapons in the lower section and slashes and circles in the upper remain.

The primary function of the deer stones is not easy to determine. While it appears that they were later reused as building

Deer stone at the sacrifice and burial site of Ushkin Uver, Khövsgöl Aimag, northern Mongolia, *ca.* 1400–850 BC. In the upper section stylised deer with bird-like noses and oversized antlers 'fly' heavenward; below are engraved weapons such as a bow and a quiver, a battle axe and daggers.

material in the Slab Graves and Scythian graves such as Arzhan 1 (late ninth century BC) and Arzhan 2 (last quarter of the seventh century BC), they are also part of large khirigsuur complexes, as in Ushkin Uver, and of slab grave sites, as in Jargalant and Altan Sandal, both found in Arkhangai Aimag (province). The complex of Ushkin Uver lies in Hövsköl Aimag, central Mongolia, on the Delger Saikhan River, and measures about 950 x 400 m. It is part of an approximately 25-km^2 sacred site with more than 200 stone structures. In the northern half of the complex a slab grave, a stone platform and 15 Khirigsuurs are found in an enclosure, alongside small piles of gravel. In the southern half 15 deer stones made of granite are arranged in two rows and oriented with their front sides facing east.[238] Small stone circles lie between the steles. Since many of the steles, which are mostly carved on all four sides, lay beneath the ground until the 1970s, they are very well preserved. Stele 14, with its peak shaped into a human face of uncertain gender, is especially outstanding.[239] In the centre and lower sections at least 27 deer romp, crowding against one another. On the front of the weapon belt is a yoke-shaped fastener; on the right side, an axe and a whetstone; and on the left a dagger with an animal knob in the classical style of Karasuk. The figure has a pentagonal shield on the back at shoulder height.

Partial excavations carried out in 2003 brought to light human burials in only two of the 15 Khirigsuurs, although five horse burials were found at each group of the Khirigsuurs and the deer stones. The sacrificed horses were buried in the same way in both places: the skulls were laid with noses pointed east and accompanied by neck vertebrae and hooves.[240] This common burial practice suggests that the Khirigsuurs and deer stones were erected at the same time. Ushkin Uver was primarily a sacrifice site, where horse sacrifices were performed in the context of an ancestor cult. It is conceivable, however, that Khirigsuurs with empty cists beneath them served as cenotaphs.

Similar sacrifice sites were originally also found at the slab grave complexes of Jargalant and Altan Sandal in the Arkhangai Aimag in central Mongolia, where most of the deer stones were repurposed for the construction of slab grave enclosures. Similar to Altan Sandal, at Jargalant 1, on the Khanuy Gol River, one deer stone of the first type stands in the eastern part of the site; two others have been overturned. A field 50 x 250 m in extent lies just to the west of the three steles. It contains more than 100 round gravel mounds and three large Slab Graves. In these graves nine, eight and five earlier deer stones respectively are reused. Bones of horses, rams, sheep and goats are found beneath the miniature kurgans.[241] An analogous arrangement is found at Altan Sandal, where three horses

Deer Stele at Altan Sandal with three engraved horses, *ca.* 900–700 BC, Arkhangai Aimag, central Mongolia.

are carved into one of the two steles still standing. Near the Slab Graves at Altan Sandal, also built of deer stones, there are also two ancient Turkic stone men from the mid-first millennium AD, giving evidence of over a thousand years of use for the site. Like Ushkin Uver, Jargalant I and Altan Sandal served primarily as cultic places for ancestor worship and were later used as cemeteries.

In attempting to divine the deeper meaning of the stylised deer, comparisons to petroglyphs, animal-style objects and Iron Age burials of the Altai are worth considering. The motif of a standing, unmoving deer with tall, many-branched antlers is first found in petroglyphs, such as those of Tsagaan Salaa in western Mongolia, Tamgaly in southern Kazakhstan[242] and Kara Oy in northern Kyrgyzstan. The motif was also popular for gold grave goods, such as the 26 50-cm-tall wooden statues overlaid with gold foil from the Sarmatian grave of Filippovka in the southern Urals (fifth/fourth century BC),[243] the gold decorative plaque with two small deer figures shown in mirror image with their antlers growing together at the tips from Zhalauly and Čilikty in southern Kazakhstan (fifth–third centuries BC),[244] and on a gold plaque from Arzhan 2 (end of the seventh century BC).[245] Since antlers, which are shed after mating season in late autumn, grow back annually, deer antlers serve as a symbol of fertility and cyclical renewal, analogous to the tree of life. Thus an archaic myth of the Evenks, who lived in Siberia and northern Mongolia, said that the tree of life grew out of the head of a deer lying on the ground.[246] Perhaps the fusion of deer and raptor, in which the heads of the birds grow from the antlers, symbolises the same idea of a spring-like burst of new life.[247]

Excavations also provide evidence that deer, together with the ibex, accompanied the dead into the afterlife. Among these were discoveries from the graves of Pazyryk and Tuekta in the Russian Altai and from Berel in the Kazakh Altai from the sixth–fourth century BC. Here archaeologists discovered sacrificed horses wearing masks made of felt, leather and wood and depicting deer, elk or ibexes. In some cases gold leaf covered the antlers and horns.[248] The small winged horse figurines, covered in gold leaf and bearing ibex horns or deer antlers, which adorned the felt caps of the dead, belong in the same context.[249] Thanks to these grave gifts, the horse acquired the attributes of the deer and its regenerative power, or that of the ibex, which was venerated as an 'inhabitant of heaven'[250] and a symbol of fertility. It appears that the horse, symbolically transformed into a deer or ibex, served as guide and mount for the deceased in entering the afterlife. This idea was present in south-western Eurasia in the Caucasus earlier as well. In 1941 Soviet archaeologists discovered near Hanlar in Azerbaijan a grave from the fifteenth/fourteenth century BC, in which the mortal remains of the deceased had been placed on a sled to which two deer were harnessed; a horse had also been sacrificed.[251] This burial recalls a petroglyph from Baga Oigor in western Mongolia, in which a deer is harnessed to a chariot. It is thus conceivable that on the deer stones the deer with bird-like noses galloping toward heaven are symbolically accompanying into the afterlife the deceased person to whom the stele is dedicated.

▶ Thracian silver vessel with images of deer, which have raptors' heads growing out of the tips of their antlers, lower Danube plain, fourth century BC. The Metropolitan Museum of Art, New York.

VII

The Iron Age

The horseman lives day and night on his horse, which is not only his seat but also his dining table, his divan and his bed, and such a horse herdsman has the remarkable ability to carry out all activities, for which we need all kinds of equipment, upon his horse, from whose four legs he may be no more easily separated that a centaur from his.

JOHANNES GEORG KOHL, *TRAVELS IN SOUTHERN RUSSIA*, 1841[1]

Canyon of Sharyn, south-eastern Kazakhstan.

The end of the culture of Karasuk around 1000 BC marked the start both of the Iron Age and of genuine nomadism. Iron was already known but until then had been used only for ritual purposes. A drastic shortage of tin around the mid-second millennium BC led first to a significant reduction in bronze production and then, in the region between the Don and the Urals, a return to archaic stone and bone tools. Iron soon offered an alternative. The Greek historian Hellanikos of Lesbos (490/480–*ca.* 400 BC), a contemporary of Herodotus, attributed the invention of iron to the Scythians, who came from Central Asia.[2] Whatever the truth of this, in the early centuries of the first millennium BC, with the development of early types of smelting furnaces, blacksmiths west and east of the Urals began to produce iron with low carbon content, which was suitable for the manufacture of weapons and heavy tools.[3]

At the same time climatic changes in the north-eastern part of the steppes of Central Asia encouraged the transition from a largely settled grazing economy to one based on nomadic stockbreeding. In a few regions, such as the Minusinsk Basin and, beginning in the ninth century BC, in Tuva, reduced solar activity produced a more humid climate, so that steppe-like landscapes blossomed into lush grazing lands. This led to a rise in population.[4] Indications are that the subsequent expansion of the moister climate to the west and the corresponding spread of rich pastureland encouraged the migration of Scythian and later Sarmatian nomadic horsemen westward to the Dnieper and Crimea.[5] The Iron Age in the northern half of Central Asia shows that stockbreeding practised by nomadic horsemen was not an archaic economic form but rather an appropriate and intelligent adaptation to new ecological conditions.

Their skills as horsemen and possession of the horse-drawn wagon facilitated the transition of these people to the nomadic lifestyle. Increased mobility meant they could move on more quickly to new grazing lands and maintain larger herds. Despite this increased mobility, the nomadic horsemen of the Iron Age had fixed sacred points in the arrangement of their royal necropolises. In 513/512 BC the Achaemenid 'king of kings' Darius I accused the northern Pontic Scythian king Idanthyrsos of avoiding a decisive battle out of fear and pursuing a strategy of scorched earth and poisoned wells. Idanthyrsos angrily responded: 'In our country there are no towns and no cultivated land; fear of losing which, or seeing it ravaged, might indeed provoke us to hasty battle. If, however, you are determined about bloodshed with the

Kurgan at Kuten Buluq, Khakassia, southern Russia, fourth century BC.

Kyrgyz eagle hunter. 1874 photograph of a painting by W.W. Wereshhagin (1842–1904).

least possible delay, one thing there is for which we will fight – the tombs of our forefathers. Find those tombs, and try to wreck them, and you will soon know whether or not we are willing to stand up to you.'[6] The guerrilla strategy of the Scythians was successful and Darius was able to save himself and his decimated army only because the Scythians had failed to destroy his pontoon bridge over the Istros (Danube) River.[7]

With the growth of herds and their increasing mobility the nomadic societies also became more militarised, as water sources, grazing lands and winter camp sites had to be defended against both other stockbreeding groups and settled tribes. Winter pastures in particular had to be guarded throughout the year and defended by force when necessary, to ensure that the herds returning in late autumn would not find their pastures had been devoured by foreign herds. The remaining farmers, who represented tempting targets for plunder, had to either subordinate themselves or adopt the nomadic lifestyle of their belligerent neighbours. Only centrally controlled states such as the Achaemenids or the kingdoms of northern China were able to defend their borders by making massive investments in defensive measures. In the steppes the militarisation of society led to the creation of clear hierarchies, which were reflected in burial rituals. As Michail Grjaznov notes, 'War now became, therefore, almost a permanent occupation. Military leaders at different levels gained enhanced importance in the social structure and grew rich on the spoils of war. It became necessary to evolve a new and more efficient organization of the whole life of the community on a military footing.'[8]

1. Nomadic horsemen in north-eastern Central Asia

1.1 The kurgan steppe of Minusinsk

During the Iron Age the southern Siberian Minusinsk Basin in the modern Russian republic of Khakassia had lush grazing lands and rich ore sources, which drew nomadic stockbreeders like a magnet. Today an impressive concentration of grave markers testifies to the population at that time: Khakassia has more than 30,000 kurgans and cist tombs! The burial sites, marked by earthen mounds, stone slabs or pillars, soon attracted grave robbers. They usually melted down the objects made from precious metals, especially gold, or, beginning in the early eighteenth century, sold them to European collectors. Thus the first scientific excavation in Russia, undertaken in 1722 by the German physician and scientist D.G. Messerschmidt (1685–1735) a few kilometres west of the city of Abakan, discovered only an empty tomb. Equally fruitless were the excavations of kurgans in the Minusinsk Basin made by the pioneers J.G. Gmelin (1739), P.S. Pallas (1772) and V.V. Radlov (1865).[9]

In the Minusinsk Basin the Iron Age may be divided into two cultures, Tagar (1000–200 BC) and Tashtyk (50–500 AD), between which lies the transition period of the Tes' phase (200 BC–50 AD).[10] The common hallmark of all kurgan graves of the **Tagar Culture** is their four-cornered enclosures made of thick stone slabs and the four elevated cornerstones that act as steles. Today the slabs are often missing and only the stone pillars remain. The division of the nearly thousand-year culture was developed by the archaeologist Grjaznov.[11] In the **Bainov phase** (1000–800 BC) small enclosures, of an area of *ca.* 4 x 5 m and made of stone slabs, with cornerstones standing up to 2 m high, were built over cists with individual burials, while in the **Podgornovo phase** (800–450 BC) timber graves often replaced the stone cists, the cornerstones usually rose just 20–30 cm above the ground and the enclosure surrounded one to four burials. Flat earthen mounds now also appeared over the graves. Clay vessels adorned with simple linear patterns, objects decorated in the early animal style and bronze weapons predominated as grave goods. Iron weapons were either too valuable to be buried or they still played a lesser role. Decorations included sword chapes in the form of coiled animals, buckles in the shape of recumbent deer with tucked in legs and stylised birds' beaks on the sockets of knives.[12]

During the **Saragash phase** (450–200 BC) the individual graves were replaced by collective graves, family and clan crypts with as many as 100 corpses. Among the grave goods, symbolic miniature weapons stand out. At the same time individual cornerstone kurgans grew to monumental, indeed Cyclopean dimensions, such as in the necropolis of Salbyk with its 14 great kurgans. The largest kurgan, from the fourth century BC, was originally 11 m tall and covered an area of 70 x 70 m. It was encircled by 23 gigantic dressed stones up to 5.4 m in height and 40 metric tons in weight, which must have been transported from a quarry 60 km away. As revealed by the excavations of 1954 to 1956, adult and child burials were found under the cornerstones, attesting to building sacrifices. Unfortunately in the excavated central timber grave the archaeologist S.V. Kiselev found only the Europid skeletons of a man and a woman, as well as three additional male skeletons in the dromos; the dead were presumably a tribal royal couple with selected servants.[13]

Thirty kilometres north-east of Salbyk is the kurgan of Barsučij Log, dating from the early Saragash-phase towards the end of the fifth century BC. In the kurgan, which was originally 11 to 12 m tall, archaeologists discovered traces of a fire ritual. As in the kurgans of the Saka in Tagisken South and in Ujgarak, the dead were buried in a 7 x 7 m grave, over which was erected a wooden chamber covered in birch bark. After a certain length of time the whole wooden structure was set on fire and destroyed. The grave was then filled in and the kurgan built of thickly layered sod. To ensure the stability of the kurgan, clay mortar bound together the individual layers of sod. An elaborate, 54 x 54 m enclosure wall surrounded the kurgan and prevented the mound from sliding. This wall was made of layered stone slabs, reinforced with orthostats and upright steles. Twenty-eight of these orthostats and steles featured petroglyphs. Some of these were obviously older than the kurgan and had been deliberately taken from older sacral monuments. Among them figure Bronze Age hunters wearing mushroom-shaped hats and animals standing on tiptoes in the early Scythian style.[14] It seems that the builders of Barsučij Log wanted to sanctify the burial with venerated relics from bygone cultures.

Finally the kurgan got its unique pyramidal shape, with the gently sloping southern side and the three other steep sides covered with orange-red clay blocks and a flat top.[15] Glowing like a fiery crystal, the kurgan must have been a spectacular landmark in the grass-green steppe. Like other great kurgans of the Iron Age, Barsučij Log was not only a huge mound of earth over a grave but also a planned work of architecture, which was embedded in particular rituals. At the beginning of the following phase of Tes' (200 BC–50 AD) the burial chamber was not only plundered but also wantonly vandalised and the four skeletons of the main burial 1 widely scattered. The intruders left the head of a dog in the tomb. The leading excavator of Barsučij Log, Anatoli Nagler, believes, that representatives of the new rulers of Tes' desecrated this und other princely burials form the previous Saragash rulers in order to end a

Great kurgan of Salbyk, Khakassia, southern Russia, fourth century BC. Photograph from 1910, M.W. Fjodorowa.

likely ancestor cult and to erase the glory of the former sovereigns from memory, a kind of 'damnatio memoriae'.[16]

The representatives of the Tagar Culture were Europids, who presumably spoke an Iranian dialect and were related to the Scythians of the northern Pontic region. They were semi-nomadic stockbreeders, and it is not known what form their shelters took. Although a few spur fortresses have been discovered, their purpose remains unknown; were they refuges, protected cultic sites or places used over a long period? In the subsequent transition phase of **Tes'** (200 BC–50 AD) the people lived in tomb-like block houses and in yurt-like residences, consisting of a round wooden frame covered with felt, as can be seen in the petroglyphs of Bojarskie pisanicy.[17] In forested regions birch bark may also have covered the yurts. At this time weapons made of iron, as used by the Xiongnu of the Transbaikal region, prevailed; only miniature weapons without practical value used as grave goods were made of bronze. At the same time Hunnic bands began migrating to Khakassia, so the proportion of Mongolid people in the total population grew rapidly. Dating from this time are branding irons for cattle, evidence of the need to recognise private property in the relatively densely populated Minusinsk Basin. The Tes' Culture continued the practice of collective burials in monumental kurgans but also had cemeteries with stone cist graves laid close together without earthen tumuli.

In the Tes' phase and the subsequent **Tashtyk Culture** (50–500 AD) a new burial custom arose. Skulls were trepanned and the brain and soft tissue removed, after which a silk cloth was laid over the face and covered with a clay mask, which usually had Mongolid, rarely Europid, features. These clay heads were partially covered with a thin layer of plaster and painted red. Although there is no reason to believe they have a cultural connection, they resemble the famous mummy of Yingpan from the fourth/fifth century AD, discovered in 1995 in the north-western Lop Nor Desert. The face of the dead person was covered by a mask made of hemp, and fine black lines on a white background indicate a Europid face. The deceased was presumably a Sogdian merchant.[18] In the Tashtyk epoch other new tribes migrated from the east, presumably ancestors of Yenisei Kirghiz, who spoke a Turkic language. At the same time other innovations appeared in burial rituals, since now corpses were mummified and embalmed or cremated. In the latter case they buried a clothed leather figure stuffed with grass, with a painted face sculpted out of clay, in whose belly were placed pouches containing the burnt bones of the deceased. The dolls wore silk clothing or fur coats, trousers, lined boots and mittens.[19] As part of the cult of the dead, animal and human sacrifices were performed at neighbouring stone steles.[20]

Ochre-painted plaster death mask over the trepanned and mummified head of a woman. Tashtyk Culture (50–500 AD), Minusinsk steppe, southern Russia. The State Hermitage Museum, St. Petersburg.

The complex burial rituals of the Tes' phases and the Tashtyk Culture show us how widespread was the fundamental need to ensure a more or less symbolic but still physically perceptible afterlife. Such desires found consummate expression not only in pharaonic Egypt but also in the steppes of the Urals. During the Catacomb Culture (2450–1950 BC) the head was sometimes separated from the body of the deceased and trepanned, with the brain and soft tissues removed, after which it was covered with clay and the facial features sculpted and painted in colour. The prepared head was then returned to the body in the grave. More rarely, the entire body was stripped of soft tissue and the skeleton served as the basis for the creation of a doll.[21] That this desire lives on in the twenty-first century is shown in the costly attempts to cryogenically preserve corpses for the future.

1.2 Herodotus's geography of Central Asian peoples

'The nomadic tribes of Scythians [...] lived in Asia',[22] reported the Greek historian and geographer Herodotus of Halicarnassus (490/480–*ca.* 424/420 BC). Thanks to him, we have access for the first time to a written source for the cultural history of Central Asia.[23] He devotes sections of the first and fourth books of his *Histories* to the nomadic horsemen of Central Asia. The value of Herodotus's nine-part history consists in his extensive travels, which led him from southern Italy to Babylon and from Egypt to the northern coast of the Black Sea. Here he stayed in the Miletian colony and trading city of Olbia, in the delta of the Dnieper (Greek Borysthenes) and the Bug (Hypanis), east of the present-day city of Odessa. There Herodotus is said to have spoken before 460 BC with the agent (epitropos) of the Scythian king Ariapeithes, Thymnes.[24] Regarding the Scythians of the northern Black Sea region, Herodotus concentrated on their wars against the Persians, their geography and their myths and customs. Since the nineteenth century Herodotus's history has served as a source not only for historians but also for archaeologists. Three significant questions come to the fore: Where was the nucleus of the Scythians? Where was the royal necropolis of Gerrhos? Did the descriptions of spectacular burial rituals correspond to reality? Despite doubts, archaeology has confirmed the third question practically in its entirety, revealed a kernel of truth in the partially fantastical geographic descriptions and developed a plausible hypothesis in response to the second question.[25]

Herodotus refers to four traditions about the origins of the Scythians, who lived in the northern Pontic region between the Dnieper (Borysthenes) and the Don (Tanaïs) and who called themselves the Scolotoi.[26] The Scolotoi believed they were a native

The archaeologist Dr. Valery Balachtchin, Abakan, beside an engraved megalithic stone belonging to one of the 13 kurgans of Safronovo near Poltakovo, Tes' Phase of the Tagar Culture (200 BC–50 AD), Khakassia, southern Russia.

The petroglyphs of 'Bojarskie pisanicy' on the Yenisei River show that the Khakassian stockbreeders of the Tes' Phase (200 BC–50 AD) lived in yurt-like dwellings. Indian ink drawing, Khakassia, southern Russia.

people and were descended from Targitaos, a son of Zeus (Papaios) and a daughter of the river god Borysthenes. In this mythical system three spheres are represented: as son of the sky god Zeus, Targitaos represents the upper world; the daughter of the river god, the underworld; and the ancestors of the Scythians, the earthly middle world. Targitaos had three sons, each of whom presided over a tribe: Lipoxaïs, Arpoxaïs and the youngest, Scolaxaïs.[27] When they were grown, 'there fell from the sky a golden plough, a golden yoke, a golden battleaxe, and a golden cup.' The two older brothers both tried to pick up the objects, but 'the gold caught fire' as they approached them. The youngest, however, picked them up and carried them home and was declared king of all the Scythians.[28] From then on the various Scythian tribes called themselves 'Scolotoi' after the name of their first ruler. Scolaxaïs established three lordships for his sons.[29] From this myth a few conclusions may be drawn about the governing structure. Succession passed from the father to the youngest son, but the son could only receive his inheritance after passing a test. His position as king of all Scythians was not absolute, however, since he could be deposed on account of dishonourable behaviour and replaced by one of his brothers, as illustrated by the example of the unfortunate King Scylas. When Scylas began around 440 BC to adopt Hellenistic customs, worshipping Greek gods and participating in Dionysian mysteries, the assembly of the people and the army deposed him. They named as king his half-brother Octamasadas, who wasted no time in beheading Scylas with his own hand.[30]

The myth also suggests a tripartite division of power, which Herodotus confirmed in another place. When the Persian kings of kings Darius attacked the northern Pontic Scythians in 513/12 BC, the Scythian supreme king and commander of the Scythian Idanthyrsos determined the defensive strategy and gave his subordinate rulers Scopasis and Taxakis corresponding tactical instructions.[31] On account of the nomadic lifestyle, during peacetime there was no need for a strong central government, but one was certainly required in times of war. Thanks to the existing political structure of the Pontic Scythians of a chief king, two lower kings, and a number of subordinate nomarchs (prefects), the Scythians could very quickly mount a large army, which the chief king commanded as general.[32] The Xiongnu later adopted a similar three-part power structure with a central chief king, the *shanyu*, and two viceroys, one on each flank.[33] In contrast to the Xiongnu, the Scythian kings who ruled in the northern Pontic region appear not to have created a stable state structure.

The Greeks who lived on the Black Sea believed, however, that the ancestor of the Scythians was Scythes, whose parents were Hercules and a creature that was half woman, half snake. This tradition is similar to the first insofar as the youngest of the three brothers was made the first king of the Scythians after proving himself in a test. When Hercules rested his horses and fell asleep in Scythia, a snake-woman stole them. She agreed to return the horses only after Hercules had fathered three sons with her. In order later to select the most capable of his three sons, Hercules left behind his second bow and his war belt. Only the youngest, Scythes, was able to put on the belt and bend the bow of his father, and thus he bested his older brothers.[34] The test of bending the bow recalls the story of Odysseus's bow. When Odysseus returned to Ithaca tests of strength were being held for the suitors of his wife Penelope. However, the great man's bow could be bent by no one other than himself.[35] A gilded silver vessel from the necropolis of Častye near Voronezh in southern Russia illustrates a transfer of power in which an older warrior hands a drawn recurve bow to a young man.[36]

Gold clothing plaque, Kul Oba Kurgan, eastern Crimea, Ukraine, *ca.* 350 BC. The plaque shows a female creature with snake-like legs, who holds in her left hand the decapitated head of a bearded man. Two horned birds of prey grow from her shoulders and two more raptors' heads emerge from her waist. The figure is ambiguous and could represent both the ancestress of the Scythians who was impregnated by Hercules and a mistress of animals. She also displays characteristics of the tendril-limbed woman popular among the Scythians and in the Mediterranean region, whose limbs took on plant-like forms and who symbolised fertility and the annual rebirth of nature. The State Hermitage Museum, St. Petersburg.

Herodotus himself described a third tradition, according to which Scythians living east of the Caspian Sea were driven out of Central Asia, after which they chased the Cimmerians out of the Black Sea region.[37] From a geographic standpoint, however, the fourth version, which reports a domino-like migration of peoples from north-eastern Central Asia, is the most interesting. To elucidate the tradition, known to both 'Hellenes and non-Hellenes', Herodotus turned for help to the fantastic-sounding geography of the Greek poet Aristeas of Prokonnesos from the seventh century BC. According to him, east of the northern Pontic Royal and Nomadic Scythians lived the related Sauromatians; south-east of the Sauromatians were the warlike Massagetae; and east of them the Issedonians. At the burials of patriarchs, the Issedonians are said to have mixed the flesh of the corpse with that of slaughtered cattle and eaten it at a funeral meal. They were also reputed to gild the skulls of the highly regarded dead and to venerate them. North-east of the Sauromatians lived the bald-headed and snub-nosed Argippaoi in white felt yurts, to whom Scythian and Greek merchants travelled. North-east of the Issedonians lived the 'one-eyed' Arimaspians, and still farther north-east their enemies the 'gold protecting griffins', as well as the Hyperboreans, whose land bordered on the hyperborean ocean, the Arctic Sea. The Arimaspians once forced the Issedonians from their homeland, after which the Issedonians drove out their western neighbours, the Scythians, who subsequently chased the Cimmerians from the northern Caucasus and the Black Sea region.[38]

Partially gilded silver cultic vessel from kurgan 3 of the necropolis of Častye, Voronez Oblast, central Russia, fourth century BC. The vessel shows three scenes from Scythian mythology; shown here, the ancestor of the Scythians, Hercules, gives his youngest son, Scythes, his bow as a sign of handing power over to him, since only he was able to bend it. The State Hermitage Museum, St. Petersburg.

The story describes how a single migration can lead to further migrations, much like falling dominoes. The background is formed by the historical military campaigns of the Cimmerian and Scythian tribes from Central Asia, which advanced as far as the Ionian cities of Asia Minor and on to Egypt. Such interconnected waves of migration are also found historically in later migrations of peoples, such as those of the Sarmatians, Alans and Huns. With regard to the peoples described by Herodotus and Aristeas, the historical peoples of the Cimmerians were originally found in the Pontic region and the northern Caucasus; the Sauromatians between the lower reaches of the Don and the Volga or the Ural; and the Massagetae between the Caspian Sea, the Aral Sea and the Syr Darya. The snub-nosed Argippaoi were probably of Mongolid heritage and had migrated from the east; they also spoke a non-Iranian language, since Herodotus says that the Scythians visiting them needed interpreters to understand them.[39] Presumably these nomadic horsemen lived in the central or eastern Kazakh steppe.[40] Their elusive Issedonian neighbours may have lived on their southern border on the Syr Darya, north of the Saka, relatives of the Scythians, who also lived as cattle-raising nomadic horsemen.[41] The Arimaspians were probably found in north-eastern Kazakhstan or south-western Siberia. Herodotus was, however, misleading in stating that their ostensibly Scythian name refers to one-eyed people, because *arima* means 'one' and *spu* means 'eye'.[42] In fact, the Iranian name contains the word *aspa*, meaning 'horse', so the name may be understood to mean 'owner' or 'friend of horses', implying nomadic horsemen.[43]

The homeland of the gold protecting griffins may have been in the Altai, whose Turkish name means roughly 'golden mountain' and which has rich deposits of gold. Their conflicts over gold with the neighbouring Arimaspians are alluded to on the famous Kelermes mirror, in which two men who are either very hairy or wearing animal skins attack a griffin.[44] The assumption that gold-prospecting tribes who took as their totem the griffin, a mythical animal with the head of a bird of prey, lived in the Altai, is supported by the fact that griffins played a prominent role in the Scytho-Siberian animal style in general and in the Altai in particular. As the northern Pontic Scythians had no sources of gold themselves, they had to import it, presumably from the north-western Caucasus, as well as from Kazakhstan and the Altai.

Gold aigrette from the Siberian collection of Tsar Peter I (unknown provenance), fifth–fourth centuries BC, depicting a bird of prey attacking an ibex with its talons. The State Hermitage Museum, St. Petersburg.

The trade contact between the Scythians and the Argippaoi, referred to by Herodotus, suggests the existence of a trade route for gold between the southern Ukraine and the Altai. This is all the more likely as toreutics made in the Scytho–Siberian animal style, whose roots lay in the southern Siberian of Tuva bordering the Altai, developed works of art similar in content and style throughout the Scytho–Eurasian steppe.

1.3 Tuva, nucleus of the Scythian peoples and the Scytho–Siberian animal style

Was Herodotus correct when he located the kernel of the Scythian homeland in distant north-eastern Central Asia? Or were the Scythians the descendants of representatives of the Srubnaya Culture between the Volga and the Urals?[45] And where did the Scytho–Siberian animal style, characterised by a very lively depiction of individual features of certain animals, arise? In Central Asia under possible northern Chinese influence or in the Pontic–Caucasus region under strong Near Eastern influence?

The Russian Republic of Tuva is separated from the Minusinsk Basin by the Sayan Mountains, where the popular general and governor of Krasnoyarsk, Alexander Lebed, died in a helicopter crash on 28 April 2002. The valley of Ujuk on the south-western edge of the Sayans has lush, green pastures, and at Arzhan there is a necropolis stretching over kilometres with hundreds of Iron Age and Old Turkish kurgans, including monumental great kurgans. These give this part of the valley the Russian name *dolina zarej*, 'valley of the kings'. During the second millennium BC the climate in Tuva was quite arid and led to a depopulating of the region during the Andronovo period. At the start of the first millennium, however, it became considerably more humid, allowing for the development of fertile grazing lands and the arrival of nomadic herders from the surrounding area. The proximity to the immeasurable ore deposits in the Minusinsk Basin further increased the attractiveness of the Ujuk valley. Even today strong winds prevent snow from accumulating in the winter on the hills around the Ujuk valley, making the area an ideal winter camp.[46] It thus appeared that the ruling families of Tuva chose the valley as their dynastic necropolis, a kind of Tuvan Gerrhos.

It was here in 1971–74 that Michail Grjaznov set his spade on the largest kurgan, called Arzhan 1, which was no earthen tumulus made of sod but rather a 3–4-m-high stone platform with a diameter of over 100 m, which was surrounded by another stone wall, a krepis, 2.5 m in height. A deer stone once stood on the kurgan, and on it were engraved deer and wild pigs standing on tiptoe and a belt with weapons hanging off it.[47] In the kurgan, which had unfortunately been completely robbed of its contents, Grjaznov discovered a wooden structure that remains unique to this day. Over 70 rectangular and slightly trapezoidal wooden chambers made of century-old larch surrounded in the shape of six concentric circular rings the almost square central wooden chamber, forming a wheel- or sunray-like design. In the plundered central chamber lay the mortal remains of a once magnificently buried royal couple, surrounded by six sacrificed horses and eight trough-shaped wooden caskets. These were the coffins of eight sacrificed henchmen. In 13 of the over 70 trapezoidal chambers lay seven additional men and more than 160 bridled, saddled and decorated horses. Thus a total of 15 attendants had to accompany the royal couple into the afterlife; all 17 of the dead were dolichocephalic Europids.[48] As the sacrificed horses were adult stallions and geldings, they did not represent a herd but had rather been selected from various herds of the tribes subjugated by the defunct chieftain and sacrificed as a final tribute to him. A typological study of the horse-gear showed that not only were neighbouring tribes from

Moscow
Minsk
Warsaw
BUDINI
THYSSAGETAE
IRKY
ANDROPHAGI
MELANCHLAENI
Orenburg
NEURI
Volga
Kiev
GELONI
PLOUGHING SCYTHIANS
AGATHYRSI
ALAZONES
FARMER SCYTHIANS
Volgograd
NOMADIC SCYTHIANS
Volga River
CALLIPIDAE
ROYAL SCYTHIANS
SAUROMATIANS
Olbia
Sea of Azov
MAETOTAE
TAURI
SINDI
THRACIANS
Chersonesos
Caucasus
Danube
Black Sea
MASSAGE
Caspian Sea
CHOLCHIANS
Istanbul
Tbilisi
Baku
ARMENIANS
CIMMERIANS
Ankara
LYDIANS
DA
PHRYGIANS
SASPIRI
URARTU
MEDIANS
PARTH
ASSYRIANS
Tehran
Baghdad
PERSIANS

Mountains
Ob' River
HYPERBOREANS
Jekaterinburg
Novosibirsk
Yenisei
Irtysh
Abakan
GOLD PROTECTING GRIFFINS
Kyzyl
Astana
ARIMASPIANS
Altai
ARGIPPAOI
ISSEDONIANS
Lake Balkash
ral
ea
SAKA TIGRAXAUDA
Iaxartes (Syr Darya)
Almaty
Urumqi
ORESMIANS
Issyk Kul
Tian Shan
Tashkent
A TIGRAXAUDA
SAKA HAUMAVARGA
Oxus (Amu Darya)
SOGDIANS
Taklamakan Desert
gabat
Pamirs
BACTRIANS
Hindu Kush
Kabul
The peoples of the fifth century BC mentioned by Herodotus
Modern cities and towns
SCYTHIANS AND RELATED PEOPLES
OTHER PEOPLES
PEOPLES MENTIONED BY OTHER AUTHORS OF ANTIQUITY
N
Scale (km)
0
250
500
750

Tuva, the Minusinsk Basin and the Altai represented at the burial but also more distant tribes from Kazakhstan and Mongolia.[49] At the foot of the kurgan about 300 stone mounds, 2–3 m in diameter, were laid in a semicircle, under which lay the remains of an enormous funeral feast, such as choice bones of cattle, sheep, goats and especially horses. The skins of the slaughtered animals were ceremoniously hung. Grjaznov estimated that around 300 horses were slaughtered on the occasion of this commemoration.[50] It is unknown how long such memorial ceremonies lasted. Within the bounds of the funeral events a total of approximately 460 horses were killed.[51]

Despite the grave robbing, the picture emerges of a magnificent burial. There were remains of splendid sable robes, gold beads and appliqués, gold earrings with turquoise inlays, a gold choker, gold clothing plaques and many turquoise inlays. The last were typical inlays for large gold objects, as are familiar from Tsar Peter I's

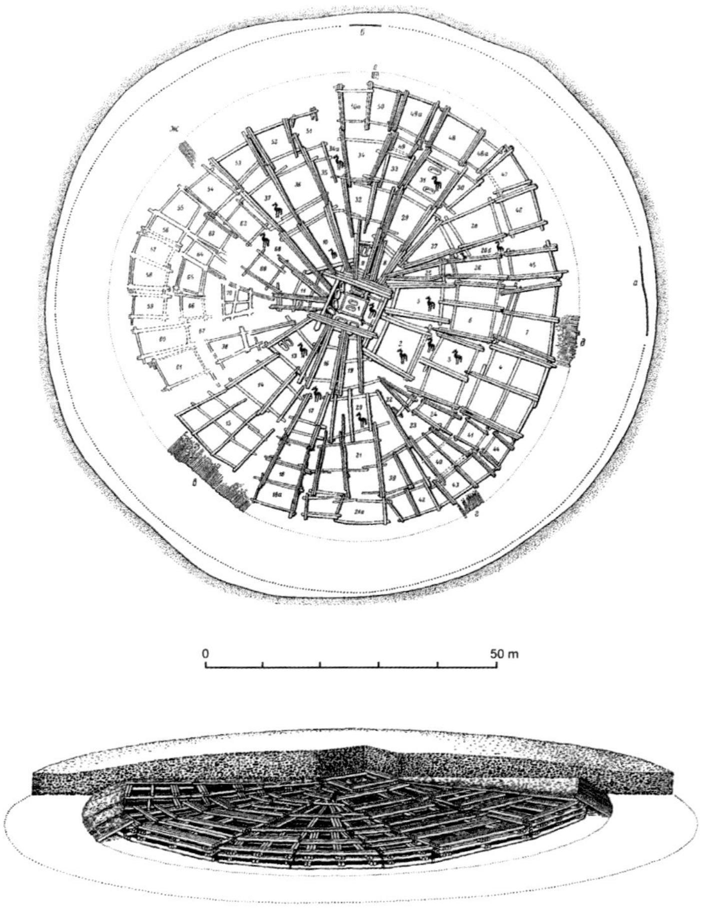

Elevation and plan of the kurgan of Arzhan 1, Tuva, southern Russia, around 800 BC. The kurgan has more than 70 compartments, and the drawings of a horse indicate those compartments with horse burials. According to Michail Grjaznov, *Der Großkurgan von Arzhan in Tuva, Südsibirien*, 1984, p. 18.

Siberian collection in the Hermitage. The comparable gold objects stolen from Arzhan 1 were most likely completely melted down. To these were added discoveries of early Scythian bronze daggers, a battle pick, bilobite bronze arrowheads and a dagger with a boar on tiptoe at the end of the hilt. Other early Scythian objects included the harness with its complete bronze bridle, decorated with stirrup-shaped cheek pieces (psalia), three-holed knobs and pendants made of pierced boar's teeth. There was also a bronze plate with a diameter of 25 cm in the form of a coiled big cat, presumably from the breastplate of a horse. Such coiled animals belonged to the code of the early Scytho-Siberian animal style; the wide-open mouth with bared teeth in the coiled panther from Arzhan 1 recalls portrayals from the late Bronze Age.[52]

A pair of bronze finials topped with figures of mountain rams also belongs to the early Scytho-Siberian animal style.[53] The first known pole-tops were found in the great kurgan of Maikop (3700–3400 BC), where rods held up the baldachin over the deceased prince. Such bronze supports with depictions of animals and deities were also widespread in the Pontic region.[54] As Schiltz surmises, the rods topped with animals served not only to support the baldachin above the dead but also to mark off a sacred space.[55] While sedentary peoples enclosed 'sacred' cultic sites with walls, steppe nomads indicated their cultic places with portable standards topped with animal figures; the symbolic appearance of animals or a deity like Papaios, founder of the Scythian royal dynasty, defined the cultic space. Just how magnificent the royal tomb of Arzhan 1 must have been can be seen in the stunning discoveries made at the nearby undisturbed kurgan of Arzhan 2 from the late seventh century BC.

On the basis of dendrologically calibrated radiocarbon dating, **Arzhan 1** has been dated to the late ninth/early eighth centuries BC and is the oldest known kurgan of the Scythians.[56] This **Arzhan 1 phase** of Tuva (850–700 BC) can be synchronised with the Tagar-Bainov phase in the Minusinsk Basin. From this dating and the discoveries made, despite the extensive plundering, highly significant conclusions can be drawn regarding the early Iron Age of Central Asia:

1. The kurgan of Arzhan 1 reveals a mature form of nomadic Scythian culture more than a century before the earliest Scythian kurgans of the Eastern European Black Sea region, such as the kurgans of Kelermes in the Kuban region from the mid-seventh century BC.[57] Herodotus was right: the Scythians and their culture originated in Central Asia.
2. Both the Scythians and the Saka belonged mainly to Europid peoples, descendants of representatives of the cultures of Andronovo and Karasuk. Neither the Scythians nor the Saka

Bronze bridle decoration in the form of a coiled carnivore, Arzhan 1, Tuva, southern Russia, around 800 BC. National Museum of Tuva, Kyzyl.

Gold bridle decoration in the form of a coiled panther, unknown provenance, Siberian collection of Tsar Peter I, sixth–seventh centuries BC. The State Hermitage Museum, St. Petersburg.

were homogeneous peoples, however, but rather a cultural community of mostly Europid nomadic horsemen who spoke Iranian dialects. From the perspective of the Pontic Scythians, one may concur with Parzinger that 'farther to the east of the Eurasian steppe belt there lived similarly structured bands of nomadic horsemen, who were progressively less ethnically related to the Scythians of the northern Black Sea region but remained culturally connected to them'.[58]

3. The early Iron Age horse-based nomadism of the steppe belt of Central Asia arose in Tuva in the tenth/ninth centuries BC. In the following centuries, the early Scythian material culture as well as their customs and rituals, spread through migrations from the Tuvan epicentre westward as far as Crimea.[59] In the Pontic region Scythian material culture was influenced by the Near East and Greece.
4. Between the Altai and the Pontic region there was intense trade contact, something like a transcontinental steppe road for gold.
5. The common thread that drew together all the Scythian groups of the Central Asian steppe belt, the so-called 'Scythian triad', had its start in Tuva, as can already be seen in Arzhan 1. This encompassed a particular composition of grave goods, consisting of three elements: first, Scythian weapons such as double-edged, straight daggers, arrowheads and a gorytos (a combined case for a bow and arrows); second, parts of the horse-gear such as bronze bits with stirrup-shaped psalias and pierced bid rods, and third, animal-style artwork.[60]
6. The unique motif of a coiled predatory animal, first a panther and later, during the Sarmatian period, a wolf, arose in north-eastern Central Asia, with the earliest influences perhaps originating in northern and north-eastern China. There, depictions of coiled animals were common not only during the contemporaneous epoch of the Western Zhou (*ca.* eleventh century–771 BC) on cheek pieces for draught horses but also in the C-shaped jade dragons of the Neolithic Hongshan Culture (fourth millennium BC).[61]
7. The third element of the Scythian triad, the Scytho–Siberian animal style, also began in north-eastern Central Asia. These animal images, portrayed according to a strict code, emphasise certain features of the animal that had particular symbolic content in the Scythians' hierarchy of values. In the animal style there is the representation in animal form of elements of a worldview that is difficult for us to decipher today.[62] The animal-style discoveries at Arzhan 1 refute hypotheses that the animal style developed first out of decisive influences from Assyria and Urartu, Anatolia or the Maeotian Kuban region.[63] The inspirations for the animal style should be sought in the

east; in southern Siberia, in the petroglyphs and deer stones of Mongolia and, as the Russian historian Rostovtzeff (1870–1952) surmised as long ago as 1929,[64] in northern China, especially in the hunting and stockbreeding cultures in north-eastern Inner Mongolia.[65] Even before Rostovtzeff, in 1913, the archaeologist Ellis Minns (1874–1953) had emphasised the tight relations between the Scytho-Pontic animal style and the Siberian animal style and spoken of 'Scytho-Siberian art'.[66] Beginning in the seventh century BC the Scythian animal style began to adopt iconographic elements from Urartu, Assyria and later Iran.

8. A few of the most striking burial rituals described by Herodotus are confirmed by Arzhan 1. After the deceased ruler assumed his final resting place in the grave, 'various members of the king's household are buried beside him: one of his concubines, his butler, his cook, his groom, his steward and his chamberlain [messenger] – all of them strangled. Horses are buried too and gold cups. [...] This ceremony over, everybody with great enthusiasm sets about raising a mound of earth.'[67] The younger woman buried at Arzhan 1, the eight attendants in the central chamber and the approximately 160 sacrificed, uneaten horses correspond with Herodotus's account. By comparison, the 38 largest kurgans of the fourth century BC in the northern Pontic region contained between three and ten additional corpses.[68] In the Kuban region the contemporaneous Elisavetinskaja Kurgan held 200 sacrificed horses and kurgan 1 at Ul'skji contained 360 horses.[69]

The discovery in 2001 by a German–Russian archaeological team of the undisturbed tomb of a Scythian prince in the kurgan of **Arzhan 2** marked a breakthrough in the archaeology of Siberia.[70] For the first time it could be shown that the Siberian Scythian kurgans were not only as magnificently appointed as those of the Pontic region but also that they predated the latter. Like Arzhan 1, Arzhan 2 consisted not of an earthen tumulus but rather of a 2- to 2.5-m-high stone platform, in the centre of which stood a deer stone. Inside the kurgan there were two additional deer stones, as well as pre-Scythian and Scythian stone slabs with engravings of deer, elk and boars walking on tiptoe in the then-common style. Arzhan 2 had no interior wooden structure, however. The excavations, which took place from 2002 to 2004, showed that the complex had been built over an older settlement layer from the Okunev period. The main grave resisted multiple attempts at plunder thanks to a ruse, as the two central pits were mock graves and a peripheral side grave was the main burial. The archaeologists

The Siberian collection of Tsar Peter the Great

The first scientific collection of Scytho–Siberian objects was initiated by Tsar Peter the Great (r. 1682–1725), who met the scholar and mayor of Amsterdam N.K. Witsen (1641–1717) during his stay in Amsterdam in 1697/98, where he studied shipbuilding in the dockyards. Witsen came from a family who engaged in trade with the Moscow principality and spent 1664/65 in Moscow. There he saw Scytho–Siberian gold and bronze objects that had come from grave robbing. At that time the governors of Tomsk and Krasnojarsk – the latter government also included the Minusinsk Basin, Tuva and the Altai – organised expeditions to find natural deposits of gold and plunder Scythian kurgans, called 'Tatar graves'. The gold objects were usually melted down or sold to collectors like Witsen. Presumably Witsen made his illustrious Russian guest aware of the gold artefacts. The core of Tsar Peter's collection was made up of shipments from Prince Gagarin, the first governor of Siberia, who between 1711 and 1719 sent the tsar many objects from the burial mounds of Siberia. Peter ordered the collection of objects made not only of gold but also of other metals and especially 'everything that appears very old and unusual'.[71] A few of the most spectacular pieces in the collection were donated to the tsar and his wife, Katharina, by the industrialist Akinfiy Demidov (1678–1745) in 1715 on the occasion of the birth of their son Peter. After Witsen's death the tsar tried in vain to acquire his collection. It was sold at auction in 1728 and the art objects vanished without a trace; only Witsen's book *Noord en Oost Tartarije*, which appeared in 1705, bears witness to them.[72]

Tsar Peter collected gold objects not to melt them down but rather because of their scientific value in explaining ancient history. For this reason he ordered that all discoveries be documented by sketches. His second decree, that apprehended grave robbers be put to death, yielded the opposite result from that intended, since now illegal finds of gold were melted down immediately, in order to destroy all possible evidence. D.G. Messerschmidt believed that even in the 1720s the richest burial mounds had long since been plundered.[73] In fact archaeologists succeeded in discovering in southern Siberia an undisturbed Scythian kurgan with rich gold finds only in 2001 at Arzhan 2. Stylistic similarities between the collection of Tsar Peter, numbering 240 gold objects, which can be admired in the Hermitage in St Petersburg, and the discoveries in controlled excavations suggest that the Siberian collection comes largely from the steppe region between the Ob and Irtysch rivers but also from the forest steppes east of the Urals.[74]

A golden deer figure crowned the headdress of the prince of Arzhan 2, Tuva, southern Russia, last quarter of the seventh century BC. National Museum of Tuva, Kyzyl.

Fourteen sacrificed horses were buried in grave 16 of Arzhan 2, Tuva, southern Russia, last quarter of the seventh century BC.

discovered a total of 41 human skeletons, including the royal couple, a retinue of 16 violently killed men and women, as well as 23 later burials, with the most recent dating from the Mongol period. To these were added a grave laid shortly after the main burial with the skeletons of 14 sacrificed horses in harness, a ritual complex that archaeologists call a 'symbolic horse grave', as well as a few hoards of ornaments for horses.

As at Arzhan 1, the main tomb consists of two block structures made of larch and placed one inside the other, with the interior chamber having originally been covered with coloured felt. Here the archaeologists discovered the skeleton of a 50–55-year-old man, who had died of prostate cancer, and a woman, 20 years younger, as well as 9,300 objects, 5,700 of which were made of gold. The man wore a 1.8 kg gold torque with animals depicted all around it; a leather or felt cap with five disc-shaped animal ornaments; a red jacket decorated with more than 2,500 small panther figurines cast in gold; trousers adorned with thousands of tiny gold beads; and boots with gold cuffs. An iron dagger with gold encrustations and two knives with golden knobs, an iron battle pick with gold encrustations, a riding crop decorated with gold and a gorytos, whose long side was made of a thick sheet of gold with a fish scale pattern, hung from two belts decorated with gold ornaments. The remains of a composite bow and arrows with three-winged iron arrowheads were found in the gorytos, which protected the delicate weapon from the weather.

The straight, double-edged iron dagger represents one of the earliest forms of the *akinakes*, common among the Scythians, Saka, Medes and Persians. The akinakes was a hybrid of a dagger and a short sword with a straight, double-edged blade 30 to 35 cm in length. It was a thrusting weapon and, because of its light weight, an ideal secondary weapon for both fallen riders in close combat and spear bearers. The akinakes was often made from two metals and consisted of an iron blade and a bronze or gold-encrusted hilt,

▶ **Illustration after archaeological objects of the princely couple buried at Arzhan 2, Tuva, southern Russia.**

which had a butterfly-like form or ended in two symmetrically arranged animal protomes. Among nobles the akinakes was carried in an elaborately decorated sheath made up of a wooden scabbard with a golden casing, which among the Saka and Sarmatians was sometimes adorned with colourful semiprecious gems. The sheath was fastened to a belt to the front or right side of a warrior. Whether the origin of the akinakes is to be found in the northern Caucasus or, as the author believes, among the daggers of the Karasuk Culture, remains uncertain.[75]

The woman was just as sumptuously clothed as the man. She wore a gold pectoral decorated in the animal style with gold and silver incrustations; a red cloak, on which were sewn 2,500 panther figurines made from sheets of gold; a knee-length dress; and boots decorated with miniature gold beads. She had an iron dagger with a gilded hilt; a miniature kettle decorated in the animal style; a gold comb; and a wooden ladle with a gold handle in the shape of a hoof. Her headdress was a tall, pointed cap, adorned with gold figures of two horses, a panther and the head of a bird of prey, as well as two long gold needles. This tall headdress shows similarities to those of Ak-Alacha[76] and Olon Kurin Gol[77] from the subsequent Pazyryk Culture (fifth–third centuries BC) and that of the 'Golden Warrior' of Issyk[78] in southern Kazakhstan. Similarly tall but undecorated conical headpieces were discovered in Subexi near Turfan, Xinjiang (fifth–third centuries BC);[79] they were also found on significantly older petroglyphs of the Okunev Culture.[80] Tall hats were also common among the Scythians who lived farther to the west, as can be seen in the Achaemenid inscription of Bisotun (also Behistun) from *ca.* 516 BC. In it Darius I (r. 522–486 BC) proclaims, among other things, the quelling of a revolt of the *Saka tigraxauda*, the 'pointed-cap Saka', and boasts of his victory over Skunkha, chief of the neighbouring Dahae. Beside the inscription a relief shows the captured Skunkha, wearing a tall, pointed hat.[81] The gold objects found in the kurgan were locally produced in Tuva, as the necessary tools were easy to transport; the high quality suggests a longer development of the Scytho-Tuvan gold-working art.

The 14 sacrificed horses were male animals belonging to ten different haplotypes or genetic variants. This large variability indicates that, as in the sacrifices at Arzhan 1, the sacrificed horses came from different herds. Surprisingly, additional analyses of the horses from both kurgans showed a considerable genetic distance

On the rock relief of Bisotun, carved around 516 BC, the king of kings Darius I (r. 522–486 BC) proclaims his victory over the nine rebellious kings, who appear before him with their hands bound behind their backs and chained together by the neck. The last king in the line, with the tall, pointed cap, to the right in the picture, is Skunkha, king of the Sakan Dahae.

between them and the Przewalski's horse, and thus that it was not part of the development of the Scythian horses. Likewise striking was the discovery of a small pile of human finger bones; a similar find of six fingers from a minimum of three or four individuals had previously been seen only in the great kurgan of Čertomlyk (fourth century BC) on the lower reaches of the Dnieper.[82] This evidence of presumable self-mutilation recalls Herodotus's description of mourning rituals at the death of a king: 'The Royal Scythians cut a piece from their ears, shave their hair, make circular incisions on their arms, gash their foreheads and noses, and thrust arrows through their left hands.'[83] Such self-mutilation at the death of the ruler was also common among Huns and Central Asian Turks.[84]

Like Arzhan 1, Arzhan 2 represented no mere tomb, but rather a sophisticated ritual complex with a planned layout. If one draws a line through the kurgan from the north-west to the south-east, it becomes apparent that all the burials of women lie to the west of this line and all burials of men and horses, as well as all four hoards of horse ornaments, lie to the east. This division into a female half, oriented toward the setting sun, and a male half, oriented toward the rising sun, is also found in the main tomb. The line runs through the grave, and the woman lies to the west, the chief to the east. To this day in their yurts Mongolian nomads follow a strict arrangement of rooms according to sex, although reversed. The entrance points to the south and the left, western side belongs to the men; the right, eastern side, to the women and young children. As mentioned above, four parallel circular and concentric rows of small stone rings border the outer edge of the kurgan, totalling 336, 352 or 368 stone settings, which served as sites for burnt offerings.[85] The cultural proximity to the great kurgans of Tagisken South (eighth–early fifth centuries BC) and Ujgarak (seventh–early fifth centuries BC) east of the Aral Sea is revealed not only in the analogous fire rituals but also in the practically identical horse-gear, which can also be found in part in the Central Kazakh Tasmola Culture. Thus Hermann Parzinger speaks of a 'Eurasian-Central Asian interaction zone'.[86]

Carbon-14 measurements and dendrological analyses date the main grave to the last quarter of the seventh century BC, so Arzhan 2 belonged to the **Aldy Bel' Culture** of Tuva (700–500 BC), which corresponded to the middle Podgornovo phase of the Tagar Culture. Arzhan 2 is roughly contemporaneous with the western Scythian kurgans in the Kuban region such as Kelermes. The royal couple and their sacrificed attendants were without exception Europids of the southern Eurasian type, who also had some Mongolid heritage. A century later Europid tribes advanced again from the south-west into Tuva, initiating the **Sagly Bazy cultural phase** (500–200 BC) and ending the use of the royal necropolis of Ujuk Valley. In summary it can be concluded that the kurgans of Arzhan 1 and Arzhan 2 illustrate the establishment of a new aristocracy of nomadic horsemen, in which the accumulation of wealth provided the basis from which to use rich gifts to help one's own clients appease foreign tribes and clans. The rider elite consolidated its power through the redistribution of levied tribute to loyal tribal chiefs. In a nomadic society no feudal rule could develop on the basis of the possession of real property, so the elite had to accumulate material possessions in the form of herds and precious metals. Thus burials provided the backdrop for demonstrating the wealth of a ruling family, entertaining followers at a funeral meal and, through the memorial cult, ensuring the legitimacy of the successor.

Petroglyphs of two 1-m-tall deer with upright antlers, Kara Oy near Ornok, northern shore of Lake Issyk Kul, Kyrgyzstan, fifth–third centuries BC.

Open grave of a rider with a horse on the upper reaches of the Katun River, Altai, southern Russia, fifth–fourth centuries BC.

1.4 The ice kurgans of the Altai

In the very cold valleys of the Altai, between 1,600 and 2,500 m above sea level, the particular climatic conditions result in the natural conservation of mummified corpses with their tattoos, clothing and organic grave goods. When water flowed into the burial chamber after interment and froze to ice, it formed a compact lens of ice, which surrounded all the organic material and protected it from decay. The stone mound placed over the grave, through which the warmth of the sun barely penetrated, prevented the thawing of the ice lens until the moment the grave was opened. The current warming of the climate threatens the ice kurgans acutely, however. In 1865 Radlov was the first to explore ice kurgans, using brute force, near Berel in northern Kazakhstan. 'The earth was frozen solid. I gathered dry tinder, stacked it on the floor of the grave and lit it, then removed the upper, thawed layer of soil.'[87] The first, sensational discoveries were made by Michail Grjaznov in 1929 and Sergei Rudenko in 1947–49 at Pazyryk in the Russian Altai. The dating of the **Pazyryk Culture** proposed by Grjaznov and Rudenko to between the fifth and the early third centuries BC is still considered valid today. However, the most recent carbon-14 measurements, combined with dendrological analyses called 'wiggle matching', pinpoint the time frame of the five most important kurgans of Pazyryk more precisely. The earliest burial of kurgan 2 dates from 300 (+25/-28) BC; the most recent from kurgan 5 with the two famous carpets from 241 (+/-5) BC.[88]

As in Arzhan 1 and 2, the burial chambers of the largest kurgans of Pazyryk consisted of two log cabins made of larch, one inside the other, and the deceased rested in timber coffins.[89] This feature of a double wooden burial chamber decorated inside with felt or silk fabrics was later also applied at elite tombs of the Xiongnu (early first century AD) and of the Tashtyk Culture (50–500 AD).[90] The Europid or Europid–Mongolid corpses of Pazyryk were, in contrast to the mummies of the Tarim Basin, artificially mummified. The brain, viscera and muscles were removed from the deceased and the cavities filled with grass and shredded twigs, after which the openings were sewn shut with horsehair. Mercury was also used for embalming. The skull of a warrior who had been killed and scalped in battle was first covered with another piece of human skin. This discovery confirms Herodotus's accounts on two further points, since he reports that the Scythians removed the scalps from conquered enemies, tanned them and tied them to the reins of their horses as trophies.[91] Regarding the mummification of kings he stated, 'the corpse [...] has been prepared in the following way: the belly is slit open, cleaned out, and filled with various aromatic substances, crushed galingale, parsley-seed, and anise; it is then sewn up again and the whole body coated over with wax.'[92] The bodies of the dead men buried in the Pazyrk kurgans 2 and 5 were decorated with tattoos in the animal style of deer, ibexes, winged predatory animals and panthers; in some animals the haunches are turned 180 degrees relative to the head. A fish hanging downward adorned the right lower leg of the dead warrior in barrow 2.[93] In this regard the Siberian Scythians differentiated themselves from their Eastern European relatives, since the latter were not tattooed.

The men wore leather caps with earflaps, which were decorated with deer figures covered in gold foil; the women wore felt caps as tall as 90 cm (!) with built-in wooden rods, which were similar to the contemporaneous woollen headdresses of Subexi near Turfan. Another connection to the burials of Xinjiang is presented by two women's skirts, consisting of several colourful pieces of wool sewn together horizontally. At the time wrap-around skirts predominated in the Pazyryk Culture and stitched skirts, found in several necropolises of Xinjiang such as Satma Mazar and Shanpula, were exceptions. The nomadic riders of Pazyryk were thus in contact with the stockbreeders of the Tarim Basin. Other indications of trade relations to the south were a shirt made of Indian cotton and the handle of a mirror made of Indian ox horn. Bronze mirrors were given to both women and men, since they warded off evil spirits and also served as the seat of the soul. A few of these mirrors

Illustration based on the excavation of a horse prepared for sacrifice. The State Hermitage Museum, St. Petersburg.

Leather and felt mask covered with gold leaf with attached horns for a sacrificed horse, kurgan 1 of Pazyryk, Altai, southern Russia, around 300 BC. The State Hermitage Museum, St. Petersburg.

display Chinese decoration and were produced in China. They were often intentionally broken during burials, so that the soul would follow the dead person, or to prevent it from staying at the grave, close to the world of the living.[94]

Unique to the Pazyryk Culture are the elaborate masks, made of leather, felt, cloth and wood and covered with gold leaf, which covered the heads of a few sacrificed horses. These masks had deer antlers or ibex horns, which were often gilded with gold leaf. In a few cases a tiny wooden figure of a bird of prey or a griffin sat between the ears of the mask. On other masks a griffin fought with a tiger, or a griffin with the head of a devoured deer in its sharp beak wore leather deer antlers, whose tips ended in heads of birds. In a magical sense the horses that pulled the funeral cart also had the attributes of other animals, which played an important role in the theriomorphic – relating to the animal world – worldview of the Scythians.

Belief in the mutability of animals or the transferability of their characteristic qualities is also expressed in works of art, whether in bronze depictions of hybrid animals or the small wooden horse figurines covered in gold foil that decorated the felt caps of warriors and had gilded deer antlers or ibex horns. Such deer-horses and ibex-horses were found in the Pazyryk Culture graves of Pazyryk itself, of Tuekta[95] and Ak-Alacha[96] (Russian Altai), Olon-Kurin-Gol[97]

(Mongolian Altai) and Berel[98] (northern Kazakhstan). In Tuekta archaeologists even discovered a depiction of a tiger with deer antlers.[99] As already indicated at the petroglyphs of Tamgaly and the deer stones, the horse accompanying the deceased into the afterlife possessed the regenerative power of the deer, the ability of the ibex to advance to heaven and the conquering strength of the griffin. In the holistic thought of the Scythians these animal qualities were transferred to human beings through tattoos.[100] The most sacred animals of the Scythians of the Pazyryk Culture, such as the eagle that ruled the skies, the powerful leopard, the sure-footed ibex and the deer with its antlers that grew again each year, were all native to the Altai.

The horse harnesses in Pazyryk were adorned with gilded wooden figurines and protomes of griffins, ibexes, wolves and birds of prey, which held in their mouths or beaks the head of a deer or an ibex. To these were added leopards, horned predatory cats and bearded men's heads with ears positioned high.[101] The last images strongly recall the Egyptian patron deity Bes, who enjoyed great popularity in amulets in the Persian Achaemenid Empire (550–330 BC). In the contemporaneous necropolis of Berel, south of Pazyryk, statuettes of winged or horned griffins and sphinxes were also discovered; the latter indicate an Egyptian influence mediated by Iran. The griffins, ubiquitous in the art of the Pazyryk Culture, not only recall Herodotus's gold-protecting griffins, which may be identified with the Altai Scythians, but their figures awaken associations with the contemporaneous griffin protomes of the Achaemenid capitals of Persepolis, who for their part had forerunners in the Babylonian and Neo-Assyrian portrayals of griffins. The griffin motif was also prominent in Scythian jewellery, as in the griffin-shaped ends of torques (smooth and twisted neckrings) and rhytons (drinking horns), whose mouths took the form of animal heads.[102]

Related to the choker are the bracelets that ended in griffin protomes, the most spectacular example of which is the pair of massive golden bracelets from the Oxus treasure of the fifth/fourth centuries BC.[103] As can be seen in the relief of the tribute-bringers on the stairway of the Apadana audience hall of Persepolis, built by Xerxes (r. 486–465 BC), such bracelets served as tribute gifts for the king of kings. The relief shows not only Scythians but also Syrians, Medes, Sogdians or Lydians presenting bracelets as tribute.[104] Griffins were also prominent in the decoration of gold diadems,[105] pectorals,[106] scabbards[107] and brooches.[108] This mythical

Leather appliqué of a tiger with deer antlers, Tuekta, kurgan 1, Altai, southern Russia, fifth century BC. The State Hermitage Museum, St. Petersburg. The depiction of the tiger's shoulders and haunches in the form of a spiral belongs to the vocabulary of the Scythian animal style.

creature made up of a winged lion's body and the head of a bird of prey united the strongest and most dangerous animals of the earth and sky, so the griffin presumably symbolised rule over heaven and earth. At the same time it could have served as guardian not only of gold but also of the sun. Both the Persian capitals and the chokers and bracelets had an apotropaic function.[109]

In kurgans 1 through 4 of Pazyryk there were simple carts for the dead with disc wheels, but kurgan 5 had an extraordinarily well-preserved wooden wagon with four spoked wheels. Since Rudenko also found Chinese silk in the same grave, he posed the question of whether this tall, two-axle ceremonial wagon could be a traditional dowry of a Chinese princess, of the type seen during the time of the Chinese Han Dynasties (202 BC–220 AD) when Chinese ruling families were related by marriage with the Xiongnu.[110] A baldachin decorated with colourful felt figures of swans and supported by thin wooden rods stood over the simpler carts. The grave also held modern-looking wooden tables. Their four wooden legs, carved in the shape of standing predatory beasts, could easily be removed and then reattached to the tabletop when required.[111]

Rudenko also came upon another confirmation of Herodotus's descriptions; he found copper kettles and stone vessels with charred hempseed (*Cannabis sativa*) and seeds from sweet clover (*Melilotus*), another intoxicant.[112] Next to them lay leather pouches filled with hempseed and wooden frames made up of six or seven wooden rods bound together that could be set up very quickly. Decorated felt or leather coverings were placed over the 120-cm-tall frames. Herodotus reported that after burials the Scythians take 'a framework of three sticks, meeting at the top, [on which] they stretch pieces of woollen cloth, taking care to get the joins as perfect as they can, and inside this little tent they put a dish with red-hot stones in it.' Then 'they take some hemp seed, creep into the tent, and throw the seed on to the hot stones. At once it begins to smoke, giving off a vapour unsurpassed by any vapour-bath one could find in Greece. The Scythians enjoy it so much that they howl with pleasure.'[113] Rudenko had undoubtedly found the equipment used to create intoxicating smoke, as described by Herodotus. Use of cannabis among the eastern Scythians was presumably not limited to burial rituals, as can be inferred from another proclamation of the Persian king of kings Darius. The inscription of Naqsh-e Rostam, found close to Persepolis, mentions the *Saka haumavarga* – 'the haoma (intoxicant drink)-worshiping Saka', which scholars have tentatively located in the Fergana valley or the Pamirs.[114]

Pazyryk was also known for its distinctive saddles with their decoratively carved wooden frames, over which fabrics were stretched. In the case of the kurgan of Bashadar in the Russian Altai[115] a powerful eagle adorned the frame. The saddlecloths used to cover the frames were often richly ornamented, perhaps with felt appliqués of attacking griffins and galloping elks, or blankets decorated with Chinese silk embroidery depicting pheasants or phoenixes. On another pelmet, made of Iranian fabric, women are portrayed praying before a fire altar. Two unique and exceptionally well-preserved carpets were found in kurgan 5. The first

Tattoed skin from the arm of the man buried in kurgan 2 of Pazyryk, Altai, southern Russia, around 300 BC. The tattoos show mythological animals. The warrior was tattooed on both arms and shoulders as well as on the lower right leg and looked like a living work of art. The State Hermitage Museum, St. Petersburg.

Two Kazakh eagle hunters at the foot of Tsengel Khairkhan, which rises 3,943 m above sea level, Ölgyi Aimag, western Mongolia. Golden eagles used for hunting are traditionally released into the wild between ages 15 and 18 and can live to be 30 years old.

was a densely knotted wool carpet, 183 x 200 cm in size, with silk embroidery, one of the oldest examples of its kind in the world.[116] The borders depict griffins, pacing fallow deer and riders, in a procession recalling the parade of tribute-bringers in Persepolis. Presumably the carpet was made in an eastern Persian satrapy (a regional governing unit), using crimson pigments from the steppe.

The second carpet or wall-hanging, 29.3 m^2 in size, was made of felt with sewn-on appliqués. One motif shows a winged hybrid animal with a human upper body, a bearded head and deer antlers, as well as a winged lion's lower body and a long tail. The creature, which resembles Achaemenid monsters, does battle with a phoenix, which also has antlers.[117] The second, dominant motif, often repeated, shows a rider with a billowing cape and a gorytos, high on a horse, who rides proudly but respectfully toward a presumably female person sitting on a throne. She wears on her bald head a headpiece reminiscent of a Persian crown and, analogous to an enthroned Persian king who holds in his hand a lotus bud, an Egyptian symbol, she holds out a large plant to the rider.[118]

The symbolic content of this striking scene is unclear. Does the rider represent a chief approaching the highest deity of the western Scythians, Tabiti, goddess of the hearth and domestic life, who holds in her hand the tree of life and validates the ruler in his role? Is the goddess receiving a deceased person?[119] Or does the scene show the ritual marriage of the chief with Tabiti, who, according to Herodotus,[120] was venerated as 'queen of the Scythians'? Or perhaps the rider has come before the ancient Iranian judge Mithra to receive the drink of immortality, *haoma*?[121] Many golden decorative clothing or strap plaques have been found in the western Scythian territory depicting a man drinking from a rhyton and standing in front of a seated woman who is looking into a mirror. This scene may be interpreted as a symbolic transfer of power by Tabiti to the new ruler.[122] In this sense the picture on the felt wall-hanging of Pazyryk may symbolise the investiture of a deceased chief in the afterlife. However, in the world of the Pontic Scythians, influenced by Hellenism, the seated woman could also represent the goddess of destiny Tyche, who hands the chief a cornucopia or, as in the carpet,

Two griffins attack two ibexes on a saddle blanket made of felt, horsehair and leather, Pazyryk, kurgan 1, Altai, southern Russia, around 300 BC. The State Hermitage Museum, St. Petersburg.

A Median ceremonial attendant with a ball-shaped felt hat leads the delegation of the Saka, which brings as tribute a stallion and heavy armlets, to the Achaemenid king of kings. Both the Median leader and the Saka carry akinakes short swords on their right sides, and the Saka leader carries a gorytos on his left. The tall, pointed cap of the Saka recalls the cap of the defeated ruler of the Dahae, Skunkha, on the Bisotun relief, so the delegation may be identified as Dahae or as the neighbouring Saka tigraxauda, the 'pointed-cap Saka'. Tribute procession on the Apadana steps to the hypostyle hall of Persepolis, first half of the fifth century BC.

a tree of life. The archetypal motif is also found on considerably older silver seals from Gonur Tepe in southern Turkmenistan,[123] among the Iron Age Thracians,[124] and also on anthropomorphic stone stelae of the Viking age from the eighth/ninth centuries.[125]

Compared with the Tuvan phase of Arzhan 1 and Aldy Bel', the animal style developed dramatically around the mid-first millennium BC as a consequence of trade contact with China and especially with Iran. In terms of content, new mythical creatures appeared, as well as fight scenes between a victorious carnivore and a defeated herbivore. Such scenes were adopted by the Xiongnu and the Saka of the southern Tarim Basin towards the end of the first millennium BC, as can be seen in the embroidery on the felt carpets of Noin Ula[126] in northern Mongolia and the wool tapestry bands of Shanpula[127] in southern Xinjiang.

Formal innovations also appeared in Pazyryk. Muscles and body parts that were to be emphasised were highlighted by special marks like commas and periods, whether through the use of colourful felt or leather appliqués or the implementation of a cloisonné gold working technique, in which first blue and green and later also red gemstones were incorporated into gold objects. The earliest gold inlaid objects had appeared in the seventh century BC, however, as discoveries from kurgan 5 of Čilikty show. Here green semiprecious gems accentuate the eyes, ears, mouths, beaks and hoofs of small gold animal statues. They are evidence that the toreutic technique of coloured inlays developed not in the Achaemenid Empire but rather among the Scythians of the Kazakh Altai.[128] Polychrome gold working developed several centuries later, however, and was perfected shortly before the start of the first millennium AD by the Saka of Bactria and the Sarmatians of the Black Sea region. As Ellis Minns determined in 1913 and Rostovtzeff in 1922, first the Sarmatians and then migrating tribal bands such as the Goths, Lombards, Vandals, Franks and Merovingians took the Sarmatian art of polychrome gold working to all of Western Europe as far as the British Isles.[129] Not only were products and raw materials transported on the Iron Age trade routes of the steppes but representatives of cultures with specific worldviews and corresponding practices travelled along them – an early and impressive example of transcontinental globalisation.[130]

Around 200 km south of Pazyryk in 1990–1995 the Russian archaeologists Natalia Polos'mak and Vjačeslav Molodin discovered on the high plateau of Ukok, which has an elevation of up to 2,500 m, the graveyards of Ak-Alacha, Verch-Kaldžin and Bertek. At Bertek, petroglyphs from the early Bronze Age[131] show that the site served for a long time as a winter grazing area. Because of strong winds, the Ukok plateau stays free of snow in the winter, when lower valleys lie under a thick layer of snow. The winter grazing lands, to which the nomads returned annually, also served as gravesites for the deceased elite. Especially spectacular discoveries were made in the ice kurgans of Ak-Alacha, which lie in the Russian Altai right on the border with Kazakhstan and China.[132] The graves belong to the Pazyryk Culture, which here superseded the Majemir Culture (900–500 BC). In kurgan 1 of Ak-Alacha 3 an adult woman lay in a wooden casket with large, carved depictions of deer and next to her lay six sacrificed horses in harness. Wooden figurines of deer and ibexes covered with gold leaf adorned the headdress of the deceased. The discovery that the woman was tattooed on both arms with images of animals was unique. Carbon-14 wiggle matching measurements gave a date of around 274 BC for the death of the tattooed woman.[133]

Still more sensational were the discoveries in kurgan 1 of Ak-Alacha 1. In a side chamber of the grave, built from larch wood in a block structure, lay nine ornamented horses, three small wooden shields and three richly decorated felt pelmets. The horses' saddlecloths were each hung with two long predatory fishes called *nalim* cut from felt. These fish were in turn decorated with appliqués of griffins and layered eagle heads. They recall the fish-shaped gold sheets, also attached to saddles, of Arzhan 2 and the mysterious fish-shaped gold plaque found at Vettersfelde, Germany.[134] On the upper half of this fish, scenes of animals fighting are depicted in high relief; on the lower half, a hybrid creature with the body of a fish and the bearded head of a man leads six fishes. A bird of prey flies above the fish's fins, which end in rams' heads. According to two origin myths, the ancestress of the Scythians emerged from an aquatic environment, and such fishes may have served as an apotropaic amulet.

The main chamber of kurgan 1 contained a double burial. In the larger wooden casket lay an armed Europid man wearing a felt cap with earflaps and decorated with small wooden animal figurines. The shape of the cap is very similar to the pointed caps of the Sakan tribute delegation on the Apadana relief of Persepolis. The smaller wooden casket held the remains of a young Europid woman who wore not a skirt but rather trousers made of red woollen cloth. As grave goods she had not only jewellery, a ritual miniature mirror and cowry shells from China or India but also, like the man, a complete set of weapons, consisting of an iron battle axe, an iron akinakes, a quiver, a bow and arrows. Remarkably, these were not ritual weapons unsuitable for combat but actual battle weapons. Like the man, the woman wore a tall felt cap, which ended at the peak in a wooden bird's head covered with gold foil. The sides were

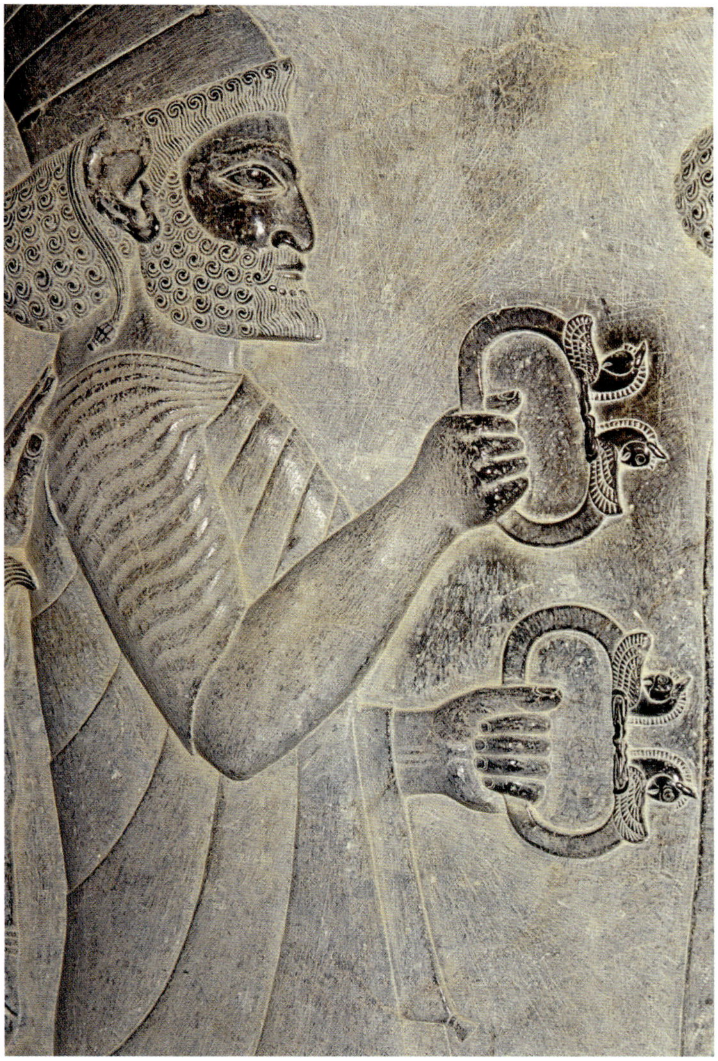

The delegation of the Syrians (or Lydians) also brings armlets with small animal heads, here winged griffins, as tribute gifts for the Achaemenid king of kings. Such gold armbands were rarely worn but rather were traditional honorary gifts of subjected peoples in the Achaemenid Empire. Tribute procession on the Apadana steps to the hypostyle hall of Persepolis, first half of the fifth century BC.

A hybrid creature consisting of a winged carnivore, deer and human being, standing on its hind legs, attacks a phoenix of the same size (not shown). Felt wall hanging, Pazyryk, kurgan 5, Altai, southern Russia, *ca.* 241 BC. The State Hermitage Museum, St. Petersburg.

decorated with two gold-covered horse figurines, a deer statuette and three stylised birds cut from gold foil. Clothing and weapons were identical for both the deceased; the young woman was a warrior who died young. In the neighbouring kurgan 2 lay an eight-year-old boy, who was buried like an adult with a horse and a ritual battle axe. Finally, in kurgan 3 of Verch-Kaldžin 2 a young, tattooed warrior was buried, with clothing and armaments identical to those of the double burial of Ak-Alacha 1.

The double burial of Ak-Alacha, dated to the fourth/third centuries BC,[135] was sensational because it was the first time a female buried with battle weapons had been discovered in north-eastern Central Asia, although finds of weapons in female burials of the Pontic Sythians and Sarmatians from the same time were not unusual.[136] This woman's grave also recalls Herodotus's accounts of Sarmatian women 'taking part in war and wearing the same sort of clothes as men. [...] They have a marriage law which forbids a girl to marry until she has killed an enemy in battle.'[137] But this isolated discovery does not necessarily prove that among the eastern Scythians young women took part in war, as with the Sauromatians and Sarmatians. Presumably this was a unique case, in which the young woman had to take over the tasks of the older man, who was incapable of fighting since he suffered from chronic polyarthritis.

In 2006 explorations east of Ak-Alacha in the high plain of Olon Kurin Gol, at an altitude of 2,500 m in the Mongolian Altai, brought to light first a cenotaph, then a plundered grave and finally the undisturbed kurgan 1 of Olon Kurin Gol from the early third century BC.[138] In front of the kurgan stood a row of nine stone steles, oriented towards the south. In the wooden chamber lay a tattooed, fully clothed warrior, who wore wool trousers and a coat

One of the four hay-stuffed felt figures of a swan that decorated the high-wheeled, collapsible wooden wagon in kurgan 5 of Pazyryk. Altai, southern Russia, around 241 BC. The State Hermitage Museum, St. Petersburg.

made of marmot pelt and sheepskin. His tall felt cap ended, like those of Ak-Alacha, in a wooden bird's head. On the peak of the cap stood a gilded wooden horse figurine with ibex horns. A second horse figurine, this one with deer antlers, was found on the front above the forehead, and the sides were decorated with very realistic, somewhat larger horse figurines. Also particularly interesting was the completely preserved, 120-cm-long asymmetrical composite bow, whose different parts were covered with animal skin. Its length and shape anticipated the Hunnic bow.

In summary it may be concluded that the eastern Scythians in Tuva and the Altai responded to the changing climate by developing a new form of economy, ideally suited to the new conditions. At the same time a hierarchically structured and militarised society arose. The elite members of this society accumulated wealth and created independent forms of art, thanks to long-distance trade with China, the Tarim Basin and especially the Medes and Persians of Iran. North-eastern Central Asia soon became too confining for the nomadic horsemen and individual tribal bands struck out for the south and west.

1.5 Stockbreeding cultures of north-eastern Kazakhstan and the western Siberian forest steppe

The cultural phase of Arzhan 1 extended at least 750 km to the south, where in eastern Kazakhstan in the ninth–seventh centuries BC the early Iron Age cultural phase of the **Zebakino-Čilikta phase** flourished. After this followed the **Čilikta phase** (seventh–fifth centuries BC), which corresponds to the Aldy Bel' Phase of Arzhan 2. Simultaneous with the Pazyryk Culture developed the **Bukon phase** (fifth–third centuries BC).[139] In kurgan 5 of Čilikty (seventh century BC) articles of gold jewellery with colourful inlays of

Wall hanging made of thick felt with sewn-on fine felt appliques, Pazyryk, kurgan 5, Altai, southern Russia, *ca.* 241 BC. The mysterious scene, repeated several times, presumably portrays the Scythian goddess Tabiti holding a tree of life and conferring upon the rider the investiture as ruler. The State Hermitage Museum, St. Petersburg.

Massive gold armlet with two winged griffins, Oxus Treasure, fifth–fourth centuries BC. Such magnificent armlets are also depicted in the tribute procession on the Apadana steps in Persepolis. The British Museum, London.

artificial gemstones made of glass-like coloured paste came to light. The kurgan also held figurines of boars on tiptoe, cut from thin gold sheets. Also striking is the pyramidal shape of a few kurgans with four steeply sloping sides, reminiscent of the kurgan of Barsučij Log.[140]

About 1,300 km north-west of Čilikty, near the Ishim River, lies the necropolis of **Bajkara**, dominated by the enormous kurgan 1.[141] The kurgan contained no royal tomb, however, but was rather a Scythian-era cenotaph with a shrine over it from the fifth/fourth centuries BC, which had been built in four stages. In a first stage a dromos (entrance corridor) was made from the eastern edge of the planned circular kurgan, leading to a never-used central burial chamber. Stairs led then to the exterior, where, in the western part of the plot, twelve wooden posts of unknown purpose stood. In a second stage the dromos and tomb were filled in, the posts removed, and the site covered with several layers of birch bark and encircled by a stone wall. Then the actual kurgan was constructed out of sod, thick layers of clay and finally a stone shell. The kurgan still contained a central chamber, to which three low corridors led. In the fourth stage the corridors were intentionally brought to collapse, and on the western part of the mound, where the side was steepest, a stone platform was built, on which was constructed a small pyramid, visible from afar, made of a reddish mixture of clay and sand, which recalls the kurgan of Barsučij Log. The entrance to the pyramid and thus to the purported shrine ran over the gently sloping eastern side of the kurgan.[142]

The leading archaeologist in the excavation of Bajkara, Anatoli Nagler, associated the kurgan with Herodotus's account of the Scythian cult of their god of war, whom he called Ares: 'In every district, at the seat of government, Ares has his temple [set up in the form of a mound]. On top, the heap is levelled off [to] a square, like a platform, accessible on one side but rising sheer on the other three. [...] On the top of it is planted an ancient iron sword which serves for the image of Ares. Annual sacrifices of horses and cattle are made to this sword [... also] prisoners of war, [...] one man is chosen out of every hundred.'[143] The kurgans of Bajkara and Barsučij Log, as well as other Scythian kurgans with flattened domes may well have been used as shrines dedicated to the god of war. This is illustrated by the seven Scythian–Maeotian kurgans of Uljap (fifth–fourth centuries BC) and two from Ul (sixth–fifth centuries BC) in the region of Kuban in the Russian northern Caucasus. Here human skeletons as well as piles of animal and human bones recall corresponding ritual sacrifices. In the centre of the dome of kurgan 5 of Uljap Alexander Leskov discovered a quadrangular platform with an ancient sword – clear evidence that 'this shrine was associated with the cult of the war god Ares, whose symbol was the sword'.[144] Similar shrines may be traced back in Kuban as far as the early Scythian period of Kelermes (seventh century BC). Over half a millennium after the construction of the shrines of Uljap the Sarmatian Alans, relatives of the Scythians, venerated a sword as the symbol of their god of war, according to the Roman officer and historian Ammianus Marcellinus (*ca.* 330–395 AD), who noted that 'a bare sword is stuck in the ground according to barbarian custom, and [the Alans] worship this believing it to be the god of war and guardian of the territory they inhabit'.[145]

The sword-worship of the Scythians and the Alans is also echoed in the Ossetian version of the Nart saga. This originally presented the code of honour of the warrior nobles of the Iranian-speaking Ossetians, who lived in the Caucasus and who were descended from the Sarmatian Alans.[146] In the saga the chief of the legendary warrior people of the Narts, the demigod hero Bartraz, whose life is existentially linked with a sword, is venerated. As a young warrior he pulled his sword out of a tree root and as an aged, mortally wounded warrior he can die only after a comrade throws his sword into the sea, where it is immediately taken up by a water deity. Parallels to the saga of King Arthur and his sword Excalibur ought not to be overlooked. Perhaps the 5,500 Sarmatian cavalrymen from the tribe of the Iazyges, whom Emperor Marcus Aurelius sent to the Roman province of Britannia after 175 AD to guard Hadrian's Wall, carried this mythological heritage to Great Britain.[147]

In the western Siberian forest steppe between the lower Tobol and the Irtysh the **Sargat Culture**, strongly influenced by the Scythians and Sarmatians, spread from the fifth century BC to the fourth century AD, following the late phases of **Irmen** (1450–800 BC) and **Baitovo** (850–500 BC). A notable witness to the late Bronze Age Irmen Culture was the fortified settlement of Čiča on the

Gold belt buckle with a ram, unknown provenance, presumably southern Siberia, *ca.* fifth–third centuries BC. Private collection, USA.

Gold belt buckle with a scene of animal combat: a winged and horned leopard attacks a horse, with the croup of each animal turned 180 degrees, so the hind legs of the defeated horse point upwards and those of the cat are turned away from the head. Siberian collection of Tsar Peter I (unknown provenance), fifth–fourth centuries BC. The State Hermitage Museum, St. Petersburg.

eastern edge of the Irmen cultural territory between Omsk and Novosibirsk. The settlement boasted a systematic arrangement of rows of over 100 houses with streets lying between them, which required overall planning.[148]

Scythian and Saka tribes had advanced in the direction of the Urals from the eighth century BC and around 500 BC there suddenly appeared, in addition to the small earthen tumuli of the forest steppe inhabitants, enormous kurgans.[149] The Sargat Culture had a mixed population, made up of a settled majority of native forest steppe people, who spoke a Finno-Ugric language, and a nomadic, Iranian-speaking upper class of heavily armed horsemen of Sakan heritage. Beginning in the sixth century BC two factors increased the migration of Saka nomadic horsemen from north-eastern Central Asia to southern Siberia. The first was a renewed drying of the climate, which led to a withering of grazing lands, and the second was pressure arising from the Achaemenid expansion to the north-east.[150]

Most representatives of the Sargat Culture were settled stockbreeders, who also practised hunting and fishing. They lived in mostly unfortified settlements on the banks of rivers and lakes, but also had ringforts. However, the grave goods from the kurgans suggest a heavily armoured horse-riding elite that wore iron scale armour and helmets with neck guards, and carried long iron swords and lances. The bow was no longer the short Scythian recurve bow but rather the superior so-called asymmetrical Hunnic composite bow, 120 cm or longer, which was also used by the Sarmatians.[151] The appearance of such armoured riders, called *kataphraktoi* by the Greeks, confirms the dominant position of the Sarmatians here. Many discoveries of polychrome gold jewellery from western and eastern Central Asia, Chinese mirrors, coins and silk fabrics, Roman coins and artefacts with Aramaic and Choresmian inscriptions attest to active long-distance trade, whose security was protected by the ringforts.[152]

On the western edge of the Sargat Culture the Iron Age culture of **Ananyino** (700–250 BC) flourished in the forest steppes between the Kama and Volga rivers. As a result of increasing pressure from the Sarmatian nomadic horsemen, who had successfully infiltrated and overthrown the neighbouring territory of the Sargat Culture, a high level of militarisation marked the society of Ananyino. This took the form of extensive production of weapons and numerous fortresses and defensive settlements, and led to the term the 'Age of Fortresses'.[153] The stockbreeders, hunters and fishermen adopted certain elements of the Irano-Sarmatian culture, as indicated by by both the burials – the dead were either stripped of their soft tissue or cremated – and the grave

Fish-shaped gold fitting from Vettersfelde, discovered in 1882 by chance in Lusatia 100 km south-east of Berlin. This fitting, likely used to decorate a shield, was part of a hoard deposited *ca.* 500 BC for unknown reasons. Portrayed on the sheet are animal scenes from air, land and water; presumably it had an apotropaic function. Workshops in the Hellenised north-western Pontic region may be assumed as the place of origin. Antiquities Collection, State Museum of Berlin.

goods made of animal bone and decorated in the Scytho–Siberian style. However, depictions of animals of the forest steppe such as bears, elk, wolves and boars replaced the usual steppe animals such as horses, deer and birds of prey.[154]

1.6 Achaemenid invasions in the territory of the Saka: The beginning of a 2,500-year-long conflict between nomadic horse-riding peoples and states of settled societies

While Herodotus maintained that 'the Persians call all Scythians Saka', Pliny the Elder (23–79 AD) stated more precisely that the Persians called only those Scythians who bordered their empire Saka.[155] For ancient historians all Saka belonged to the Scythians but not all Scythians were Saka. Both ethonyms are collective terms for the Iron Age, Iranian-speaking nomadic horsemen of the steppes of Eurasia. In modern scholarship the term Scythian refers to the Pontic group west of the Urals; the term Massagetae, to the nomadic horsemen around the Aral Sea; and the Saka, the remaining groups in eastern Central Asia.[156] Both the etymology and the localisation of individual Saka peoples are debated.

The words 'Scythians' and 'Scoloti' and the name of the first ruler 'Scolaxaïs' may have different roots from the word 'Saka'. The former words probably trace back to the northern Iranian term *skuða*, which means 'archer'.[157] The ethonym 'Saka' and the corresponding Chinese name 'Sai', in contrast, derive either from *skuða* or from the Iranian root *sag*, which means 'deer' in Ossetian, which could indicate that the deer was the totem of the Saka.[158]

Identifying the individual peoples of the Saka, as they are listed in six Achaemenid stone inscriptions, is difficult, as is the correlation with the ethonyms of Herodotus and with his tax register of Persian satrapies.[159] The most informative are the grave inscriptions of Darius I of Naqsh-i Rustam, which were made at the latest in 486 BC, and the so-called Daiva inscription of Xerxes I (r. 486–465 BC) from Persepolis. Both lists of the peoples belonging to the Persians name the *Saka haumavarga* (haoma-worshipping Saka), the *Saka tigraxauda* (pointed cap Saka) and the *Saka tayaiy paradraya* (Saka on the other side of the sea). The Daiva inscription also listed the *Daha*, the Dahae, whereby four Saka peoples were named (see table opposite).

The Achaemenid Empire, which at its height stretched from Egypt and Anatolia in the west as far as Central Asia and Pakistan in the east, arose from the alliance of the Indo-Iranian, originally Central Asian peoples of the Medes and the Persians. Around 672 BC the Medes, who lived in western Iran, managed with the help of bands of Cimmerian warriors to overthrow Assyrian rule. In 655 BC they also conquered the Persian tribes, but they came under the domination of the Scythians from *ca.* 644 BC till 616 BC (or 652 to 624 BC). As Herodotus reported, King Cyaxares II (r. *ca.* 624–584 BC) drove out the Scythians after he had their

Illustration based on the excavation of the woman with a tall headdress buried in kurgan 1 of Ak-Alacha 3, Russian Altai.

military elite murdered at a banquet,[160] and in 612 BC, with his Babylonian allies and Scythian mercenaries he stormed the Assyrian capital, Nineveh. Afterwards the Medes undertook the first campaigns toward the east against Parthia and Hyrcania, both south-east of the Caspian Sea. In 553 BC, however, the Persian vassal prince Cyrus II (ruled as Achaemenid ruler 550–530/29 BC),[161] who had married a daughter of the Mede king Astygates, rebelled against his father-in-law, defeating him decisively three years later. With the uniting of the Persians and the Medes, Cyrus founded the empire of the Achaemenids.[162] In light of the lack of Achaemenid chronicles the only sources of information on the Achaemenid regime in Central Asia, besides archaeological finds, are the few royal proclamations and the Greek historians, above all Herodotus. However, even Herodotus tended to mention the Persians only when their history involved Greeks or Scythians.

After Cyrus II had conquered Elam, Lydia and its king Croesus, as well as the Ionian cities, he divided his army: 'While Harpagus was turning upside-down the western part of Asia, Cyrus was engaged with the north and east, bringing into subjection every nation without exception.'[163] The details of Cyrus's campaign to consolidate and expand Persian power in eastern Central Asia are unknown. The chronological reference points are the fall of the Lydian capital of Sardis and the Ionian cities in 547–546 BC, as well as the conquest of Babylon in 539 BC by Cyrus himself, so the first Central Asian campaign took place *ca.* 545–540 BC. The most important geographical evidence is provided by the Bisotun inscription, since it lists the 23 lands and peoples that Ahura Mazda bequeathed to Darius I as the legitimate heir of his predecessors Cyrus II and Cambyses I (r. 530/29–522 BC). It remains unclear, however, which regions Cyrus had already defeated and which Darius I conquered later. If one follows the inscription, Cyrus incorporated the following regions from the east into the empire: *Parthava* (Parthia and Hyrcania), *Margush* (Margiana), *Uvarazmish*

Identification of the Saka peoples mentioned in the Achaemenid inscriptions[164]

	TERRITORY	NOTES
Saka tayaiy paradraya	Pontic region (southern Ukraine)	Identical to Herodotus's Scythians
Saka tigraxauda	East of the Caspian Sea as far as Semirechie (western to south-eastern Kazakhstan including Choresmia)	Herodotus's Massagetae belonged to the *Saka tigraxauda*
Saka haumavarga	Fergana, Alai, Pamirs (Tajikistan, eastern Uzbekistan)	Identical to Herodotus's Amyrgians
Dahae	Syr Darya delta (east of the Aral Sea)	A sub-tribe of the Dahae, the Parni, conquered Parthia *ca.* 239/38 BC and later Iran

(Choresmia), *Saka* (Saka), *Suguda* (Sogdia) and *Baxtrish* (Bactria), where he built a chain of fortresses to defend the border. One of these fortresses was Kyrshkata (Cyropolis) near the modern city of Istaravshan in north-western Tajikistan, which Alexander the Great captured in 329 BC.[165] Whether there existed in Bactria a pre-Achaemenid empire that was connected to a king called Vistaspa, the purported patron of Zarathustra, is debatable. The archaeologists A. Askarov and V. Masson have argued in favour of a pre-Achaemenid Empire; however G. Gnoli, M. Dandamayev and the majority of scholars remain sceptical.[166] The inscription of Bisotun also listed the following south-eastern regions: *Haraiva* (Latin Aria, the province of Herat in western Afghanistan), *Zraka* (Sistan in south-eastern Iran and south-western Afghanistan), *Harauvatish* (Arachosia in the province of Kandahar in southern Afghanistan), *Gadara* (Gandhara in south-eastern Afghanistan and northern Pakistan) and *Tathagush* (Sattagydia, Punjab in central and eastern Pakistan?).[167]

After the conquest of Babylon Cyrus decided to secure the north-eastern border by means of a second Central Asian campaign against the Massagetae, who belonged to the Scythians. Herodotus reported this campaign in detail.[168] As mentioned above, the Massagetae had an armoured cavalry, worshipped the sun and sacrificed horses to it. At that time their king had died and his wife Tomyris served as regent for her son Spargapises. In 530 or 529 BC. Cyrus, with the help of a pontoon bridge, crossed a river called Araxes by Herodotus – presumably the Uzboy – and, on the advice of Croesus, set a trap for the Massagetae. He retreated with his army and left behind abundant baggage, guarded by only a few soldiers. When a third of the Massagetaean army plundered the baggage and became drunk from the wine contained there, Cyrus returned and killed many of his enemies or took them prisoner, among these Tomyris's son. After this Tomyris gave Cyrus an ultimatum: 'Give me back my son and get out of my country with your forces intact, and be content with your triumph over a third part of the Massagetae. If you refuse, I swear by the sun our master to give you more blood than you can drink, for all your gluttony.'[169] But Cyrus had no thought of return and Spargapises took his own life out of shame. In the subsequent battle Cyrus fell and Tomyris made good on her terrible oath by placing his severed head in a wineskin filled with human blood.

Even if details of Herodotus's accounts are mythological, the fact remains that the founder of the Achaemenid Empire, Cyrus, fell in battle with a Scytho–Sakan people. The two Central Asian

Computer reconstruction of the final building phase of cenotaph 1 of Bajkara, northern Kazakhstan, fifth/fourth centuries BC.

As described by Herodotus (IV, 62), the Scythians worshipped their war god in the form of an iron sword, which they placed on an artificially built mound. Shown here as representatives are the three monumental swords of the Vikings at Hafrsfjord, Stavanger, Norway.

campaigns of Cyrus marked the start of a more than millennium-long conflict between nomadic and settled societies of Indo–Iranian peoples who were related to one another. This struggle is reflected in the Avesta and celebrated in the *Shahname* of Firdausi (940–1020 AD). There it is reported that the ancestor of the Iranian peoples, King Fereydun, bequeathed the Arian Empire to his three sons as follows: to the eldest, Salm, intent on security, he gave Asia Minor; to the middle, reckless son, Tur, Central Asian Turan; and to the youngest, the noble Iraj, the homeland of Iran. The two older brothers were so envious that they murdered their younger brother. One of Fereydun's grandsons avenged Iraj and confirmed the dominion of Iran but the rivalry between the settled urban civilisation of Iran and the nomadic Turanians, those 'with the swift horses', continued for centuries. In the end the *Shahname* epic is about a fratricidal war between two related peoples, one of whom lived sedentarily and the other nomadically.[170]

Cyrus II was followed by Cambyses I, who conquered Egypt. He died in 522 BC during the return to Ektabana, today's Hamadan, where a revolution was in progress. In the subsequent chaos a distant relative of Cyrus and Cambyses, named Darius, prevailed and put down one revolt after another. On the Bisotun inscription Darius I (r. 522–486 BC) proclaimed his victory over the usurper Gautama and the nine rebellious 'kings of lies', among them Frada from Margiana and Skunkha, chief of the Saka tigraxauda. While the loyal satrap (civil governor) of Bactria defeated the insurgent Frada at the end of 522 BC, Darius personally led the campaign against the rebellious Saka in 519 BC: 'I marched with my army to the land of Saka [...] who wore pointed caps. [...] I smote part of the Saka exceedingly, and the other part was captured. [...] Their leader, by the name of Skunkha, was taken prisoner and led to me. Then I appointed another leader and the land became mine.'[171]

But as Alexander the Macedonian must also have experienced later, the Saka horsemen did not allow themselves to be easily subdued; again and again they made raids into the Achaemenid Empire. Thus Darius decided in 513/12 BC to attack the Saka from the west and close in on them. As Herodotus reported, the king failed spectacularly in the face of Scythian stalling tactics and a strategy of 'scorched earth.' The Pontic Scythians under King Idanthyrsos denied the attackers an open battle and retreated far into the territory of disloyal tribes. They 'retired in the direction of those nations who had refused to join the alliance, with the idea of involving them in the war against their will, if they would not fight on their own initiative. [...] The wagons which served as houses for the women and children, and all the cattle [...] were ordered to move northward at once, in advance of their future line of retreat.'[172]

Darius crossed the Bosporus at Byzantion and went on to conquer Thrace. He then advanced across the Danube and encountered the land of the Scythians, now empty. The Scythians had filled in their wells, burned their food stores and trampled down their pastures; their army retreated in lockstep with the advancing Persians, at a day's remove. Like the Russians who, more than two millennia later, led Napoleon into empty lands, the Scythians knew how to make optimal use of the barren steppe. They lured the Persians to the Don (Greek Tanaïs) and then turned northwards into the forest steppe of the neighbouring Budini. There stood here the large, fortified city of Gelonos, built entirely of wood, whose inhabitants were a Greek–Budini mix who spoke a Scythian–Greek

View from the ancient citadel of Cyropolis at the modern city of Istaravshan, north-western Tajikistan. The citadel was founded by the Achaemenid king Cyrus II between 545 and 540 BC; it was destroyed in 329 BC by Alexander the Great and in 1220 by Genghis Khan's troops. Excavations of the citadel confirm an early Achaemenid cultural layer.

language. When the Persians reached 'the wooden fortified town of Gelonos, abandoned and empty of defenders, [they] burnt it'.[173] Gelonos is identified today with the one-time fortified city of Bel'sk on the Vorskla, a tributary of the Dnieper, whose extensive 33-km system of walls surrounded an area of 4,000 ha and linked together three fortresses. Archaeological investigations have revealed that the site, founded in the mid-seventh century BC, was completely burned down at the end of the sixth century BC – that is, at the time of the Persian invasion. Gelonos was one of the most powerful of over 100 ringforts that stood on the waterways and roads of the forest steppe. They served Greek and Scythian traders, as well as local farmers, as places to conduct business and store goods.[174]

Darius was unable to subjugate the aggressive Scythians. On the contrary, they mocked him several times and adopted a guerrilla campaign in which they 'attacked [the Persians] whenever they found them foraging'.[175] Only with great effort were Darius and his exhausted army able to withdraw from the Scythians' lands. They escaped thanks only to a strategic error by the Scythians, who had failed to destroy the Persian pontoon bridge across the Danube.

In 518 BC Darius undertook a series of far-reaching reforms. He divided the empire into 20 satrapies, on which he imposed rigid taxes.[176] Each satrapy had a two-part leadership: a satrap with far-ranging civil functions and a military commander under the direct authority of the king. All central power remained in the hands of the king, however, so the Persian government cannot be compared to medieval feudalism. The most important administrative units of Central Asia were the twelfth satrapy of Bactria and Margiana, the fifteenth satrapy with the Saka and the Caspians, and the huge sixteenth satrapy with Parthia, Choresmia, Sogdia and Aria. For the first time Central Asia was anchored in a political structure that was also active in the direction of Europe.

In order to strengthen the unity of the enormous, multi-ethnic empire, Darius implemented use of the Aramaic language and script as the official language of government, which made Aramaic the lingua franca throughout the empire. Aramaic was not only the first script of Central Asia but also, after Latin, the second most productive script in the world, with 250 derivative systems of writing.[177] Over the course of the subsequent centuries the Aramaic alphabet served the development of writing for widely varied languages of Central Asia. Among these were the Parthian, Choresmian, Sogdian and Bactrian scripts; the last of which was first written with the help of Greek, and then the Manichaean, Nestorian, Uyghur, Mongolian and Manchurian scripts. The Old Turkish rune writing was also derived from the Aramaic alphabet. In addition, Indic languages and Indic-influenced dialects of south-eastern Central Asia, such as Gandhari of the Bamyan type, were put in writing by means of derivatives from Aramaic, out of which developed important scripts such as Brahmi and Kharoshthi.

Ivory fitting on a dagger sheath, on which a lion standing upright holds a small deer in its paws, Oxus Temple Takht-i Sangin, southern Tajikistan, sixth–fifth centuries BC. National Museum of Antiquities of Tajikistan, Dushanbe.

Darius then constructed a network of roads and founded a state postal service that had its own relay stations and was protected by watchtowers in strategic locations. He introduced a unified coinage with standardised coins in gold and silver, which brought coins to Central Asia for the first time. In the Central Asian satrapies, however, silver bars predominated. To encourage trade in his empire, Darius not only built caravan routes but also ordered the seafarer Skylax to open a sea lane that called at the ports along the southern border of the empire. Skylax sailed the Indus and reached the Indian Ocean, whereupon he followed the Iranian coast and then sailed around the Arabian Peninsula until he came to the Red Sea.[178] In order to foster commerce, Darius provided funds for the construction of an irrigation system and the building or expansion of important cities such as Cyropolis, Maracanda (Samarkand) and the neighbouring Kök Tepe, Merv (the site of Erk Kala), Bactra (Balkh, also called Zariaspa),[179] Herat, Kabura (Kabul), Taxila, etc. Finally, Darius created a standing army, which consisted primarily of Persian, Median, Sogdian and Bactrian units. In the event of war the additional bands of horsemen from Bactria, Sogdia and the Saka formed fearsome units and the composite bow of the Central Asian nomadic riders became one of the most important weapons of the entire army.

Darius's greatness lay not only in his military successes – apart from the failed campaign against the Pontic Scythians – but also in his creation of a governmental structure that encompassed the most varied peoples and economies and established both widespread internal peace and relative prosperity for almost two centuries. In comparison, the empire of Alexander, which largely corresponded to the conquered Achaemenid Empire, collapsed a few years after his death and led to the bloody war of the Diadochi. The Achaemenids also set new standards in the area of art. In their monumental architecture they adopted influences from Mesopotamia, Egypt and Greece, and in relief sculpture they perfected Elamite and Assyrian forerunners. Since in Central Asia there were rapidly decaying clay rather than stone buildings, corresponding examples, aside from exceptions such as the Oxus temple Takht-i Sangin, are difficult to retrace. In the area of sculpture, toreutics and painting, by contrast, Achaemenid influences marked the art of Bactria and Sogdia, which reached its zenith in the early Buddhist cave paintings of the northern Tarim Basin and the pre-Islamic murals of Sogdia from the sixth to eighth centuries AD. The Achaemenid Empire enabled easier East–West contact. It also anchored south-eastern Central Asia into the Iranian cultural realm and later the Iranian–Muslim cultural realm. This remained the case until the invasion of the region by tsarist Russia in the second half of the nineteenth century.

Zoroastrianism and its symbol, Faravahar

In the Bisotun inscription Darius used for the first time the symbol of Zoroastrianism and its spirit, called Faravahar. We know almost nothing about the personal beliefs of Darius; presumably he chose faith in the one true god Ahura Mazda for political reasons, in order to give the multi-ethnic empire a unifying state religion. In this way Darius pursued a tolerant religious policy, since as long as people recognised Ahura Mazda as the highest imperial god, they were free to privately worship their own gods. Darius borrowed a symbol from Neo-Assyrian iconography, which had been influenced by Egypt – namely, the image of a man standing in a winged ring, which in the Neo-Assyrian context symbolised the god of the sun and justice Shamash.[180]

In the Faravahar the human figure represents the connection to the Spirit and the three layers of feathers on each wing, the three ethical principles of 'correct thought', 'correct speech' and 'correct action'. By contrast, the lower part of the Faravahar symbolises the 'incorrect thought', 'incorrect speech' and 'incorrect action' that lead to destruction. The loop that falls forward from the ring stands for the good to which we should orient ourselves, and the loop behind the ring represents the evil on which we should turn our backs. The circle in the centre of the Faravahar symbolises the eternity of the Spirit. Finally, the hand gesturing upwards shows the path to true knowledge, while the ring in the other hand refers to loyalty to Zoroastrian principles.[181]

Zarathustra was a priest of an ancient Aryan religion, but it is not known when he lived and where he came from. Presumably he lived at some time between the twelfth and eighth centuries BC and came from south-eastern Central Asia, more precisely Bactria, where, according to tradition, he is said to have preached and died in Balkh.[182] He was a reformer who elevated Ahura Mazda, the 'wise lord', to the only god, and understood all other, functional deities, to whom were assigned particular phenomena such as rain, wind, sun or war, as abstract aspects of Zarathustra's omnipotence and declared the erstwhile gods, the 'daevas', as false gods. Tribal deities and angels also became superfluous. The principle of light and goodness, Ahura Mazda, symbolised by all-purifying fire, was, however, opposed by the opposite principle of darkness and evil, Ahriman. Ahura Mazda's omnipotence is only temporally limited by Ahriman, but he needs the help of humanity to regain it. Zoroastrian dualism is not absolute but rather of a temporal and ethical nature.

In order to defeat Ahriman, Ahura Mazda created the universe as the battlefield for a titanic 'war of the gods'. Thus the human

Faravahar symbol, eastern door of the tripylon (central building) of Persepolis, fifth century BC.

being, who has free will, must decide within the context of the cosmic struggle whether to support good or evil. The human being, as a microcosmic image of the macrocosmic universe, is both stage and actor in the battle of good against evil. As an aid to orientation, the human being is served by the three fundamental principles of 'correct thought', 'correct speech' and 'correct action'. Zarathustra's teaching demands from believers ethical conduct, coupled with a conscious sense of responsibility, but neither hollow rituals nor animal sacrifices. Zarathustra argued vehemently against senseless animal sacrifice, especially the sacrifice of cattle in honour of Mithra. It would be better to use the cattle to plough the fields than to slaughter them in a wild fury. Thus he represented a religious doctrine that contradicted the traditional beliefs and burial rituals of the Indo–Iranian nomadic horsemen in northern Central Asia such as the Scythians, Saka and Massagetae.

Insofar as all human beings, regardless of their status or birth, could participate in the cosmic struggle of good against evil and thus were fundamentally equal before Ahura Mazda, Zarathustra's teaching was revolutionary and diametrically opposed to the caste system emerging under the Aryans of India. In addition, Zoroastrian anthropology, like its cosmology, is fundamentally optimistic, as it teaches the perfection of creation and the triumph of the good at the end of the eschatological process. But because the living are considered pure and the dead impure, the natural elements of earth, water and fire must not be contaminated by corpses. For this reason all soft tissue and flesh had to be removed by natural means by predatory animals or birds before the bones were placed in an ossuary, a custom that had appeared in Sogdia and Bactria even before Zarathustra. Zoroaster's radical ideas regarding the sole reign of Ahura Mazda did not prevail, however, and Artaxerxes (r. 404–358 BC) officially reintroduced the cult of the god of justice Mithra and the goddess of water, love and war, Anahita.[183] The cult of the intoxicant drink *haoma*, banned by Zarathustra, also soon returned to cultic practice, as did animal sacrifices in honour of Mithra, although to a limited extent.

This heterogeneous character of Zoroastrianism was also reflected in the Avesta, its collection of sacred scripture. The oldest extant fragment of the Avesta contains the prayer *Ashem Vohu* in the Sogdian language from the ninth/tenth centuries AD. It was acquired by the British archaeologist Sir Aurel Stein in 1907 in Dunhuang in north-western China.[184] The oldest complete manuscript comes from the thirteenth century AD, so it is not surprising that the existing Avesta consists of texts from different epochs. The earliest collection of the Avesta, as it had been transmitted orally, may have been commissioned by the Parthian ruler Vologases IV (r. 147–191 AD),[185] and others followed under the Sassanids (224–651 AD). The 17 *gathas* (songs), which are part of the 72-chapter *Yasna* (worship), may have come from Zarathustra himself. The *Yasna* represents only one of the five books of the Avesta, however, which makes it clear how small the part of the text ascribed to Zarathustra actually is. The *Visparad*, which forms a kind of appendix to the Yasna, consists of a collection of 24 prayers. The *Vendidad* (also *Videvdad*), the 'law against the demons', is very heterogeneous and contains both a late creation saga and the archaic myth of Yima, the first ruler of the golden age. In the *Yashts* (songs of praise) 21 gods, nature deities and archangels, banished by Zarathustra from his teachings, reappear, with Mithra prominent among them. The Yashts are associated with the Indian Rig Veda and include much pre-Zoroastrian content. In them it becomes clear how strongly the Zoroastrian doctrine was merged with ancient Iranian ideas. The *Khordeh* (small) *Avesta,* finally, consists of excerpts from the Avesta for the daily use of the laity.[186]

The heterogeneous character of the sacred scripture of Zoroastrianism is unsurprising in view of its long history: no less than 3,000 years passed between the first oral tradition of the Indo–Iranians of the second millennium BC and the oldest extant written text.

1.7 Nomadic and settled cultures between the 'Land of Seven Rivers' and Choresmia

In the 'Land of Seven Rivers' in south-eastern Kazakhstan, called *Semirechie* in Russian and *Zhetysu* in Kazakh, the Saka continued to pursue their nomadic lifestyle, even though the Persian advances as far as the Syr Darya and in Choresmia led to the establishment of urban forms of culture in those places. The grass steppes of the Land of Seven Rivers, named for seven rivers that flow out of the mountains of the Dzungarian Alatau and the north-western Tian Shan, were a preferred territory for the Iron Age nomadic horsemen of the Saka, who left behind thousands of kurgans. One of the most important kurgan necropolises lies on the northern bank of the Ili River about 130 km north-east of Almaty. The cemetery of Besschatyr, which means 'five tents', consists of 31 kurgans, up to 17 m in height, of which 21 are made of stone and the remainder of earth and crushed rock. In individual kurgans an aboveground blockhouse-like wooden chamber was built over the tomb, yet it remained covered by the stone barrow.[187] The largest kurgan, 106 m in diameter, was surrounded by 94 stone megaliths arranged in a spiral. Remains of fire and calcined bones found near the stones indicate animal sacrifices and fire rituals. Unfortunately, the graves, dated to the fifth–third centuries BC, have been plundered.[188]

The necropolis of Issyk, 50 km east of Almaty, which numbers 67 kurgans, comes from the same cultural phase of **Issyk-Besschatyr** (fifth–third centuries BC). A side chamber of one of the large kurgans contained the undisturbed burial of a young, 17- or 18-year-old

On the Bisotun inscription, carved around 516 BC, Darius I announces his victory not only over the Saka rebel Skunkha but also over the rebellious ruler of Margiana named Frada, after which he expanded the important city of Margush (Merv). Here, a fortified gate of Merv in the south-western corner of Gyaur Kala displays three different construction layers: at left Seleucid (3rd century BC), in the centre Parthian (*ca.* 2nd/1st century BC) and on top Sassanian (3rd–4th centuries AD).

Saka chief in full parade armour from the fifth century BC. This 'Golden Man of Issyk', discovered in 1969, wore a red jacket and red boots, which were decorated with thousands of small gold discs, as well as an iron sword and dagger in sheaths covered in gold leaf. On one of the two finger rings was engraved a male face with a ray-like headdress. Most notable was the pointed headpiece, about 60 cm tall. At the top stood a golden figurine of an ibex, and beneath it were gilded statuettes of horned or winged horses, birds sitting in trees, snow leopards on a background of craggy mountain peaks, ibexes and 30-cm-long gold-covered arrows. The arrangement of trees with the birds in mountain valleys and the predatory cats against jagged peaks lend the composition a realistic, three-dimensional appearance.[189] The young chief wore on his head the most important elements of the mythical universe of the Saka. Just as unique was the discovery of a silver dish with a rune-like inscription in two lines. The oldest known Saka inscription, this has not been deciphered to this day; the symbols show a certain similarity to the Old Turkish inscriptions of Mongolia and southern Siberia, derived from Aramaic but much later. Some 30 inscriptions with comparable symbols have been identified to date.[190] The Saka also built a great necropolis north of Besschatyr in the valley of the Koksu near the Bronze Age petroglyphs of Eshki Olmes.[191] In contrast to the Bronze Age cist graves placed close beside one another, the large kurgans here stood far removed from one another, as though they wanted to take possession of the landscape.[192]

At the necropolises of **Tagisken South** and **Ujgarak**, north-west of Semirechie, a pronounced fire cult characterised the burial rites and shaped the culture.[193] These necropolises were abandoned in the middle of the first millennium BC, when an arm of the Syr Darya river, and with it the settlements and encampments that lay along it, shifted to the west. Here the **Čirikrabat Culture** (500–200 BC) developed.[194] After this shift of the river's course no more Saka memorials appeared in the broad delta of the Syr Darya. Presumably one group of the Saka migrated to another region and another adapted to the Persian-influenced culture of Čirikrabat, as the region around the mouth of the Syr Darya belonged to the fifteenth Achaemenid satrapy. Among the most striking witnesses to the sudden Persian influence are widely placed irrigation systems and fortified smaller urban centres such as Čirikrabat. They display the typical Central Asian city plan, consisting of a strong surrounding wall guarded by towers, the residential quarters called in the Middle Ages *shahristan* and the fortified citadel called *Kala* with its monumental buildings.[195]

A similar development can be seen in Iron Age Choresmia, where a settled population of farmers and traders lived alongside semi-nomadic stockbreeders. Their only remaining traces are the kurgans of the **Kujusaj Culture** (seventh–second centuries BC), an Iranian-speaking culture related to the early Saka.[196] Parallel to this nomadic culture the urban **Old Choresmian Culture** flourished from the seventh/sixth century BC to the first century AD. The archaeologist Sergei Tolstov (1907–1976) explored here from 1938 to 1964. The pioneer Tolstov was, with Sir Aurel Stein (1862–1943), one of the first archaeologists to use aerial reconnaissance to systematically investigate unfamiliar territory. In this manner he discovered dozens of unknown cities and fortresses in Choresmia.[197] The Old Choresmian culture had Achaemenid influences and belonged to the sixteenth satrapy. However, the local political authorities were able as early as 400 BC to liberate themselves from the Achaemenid Empire and found an independent state. Thus in the winter of 329/28 BC the Choresmian king Pharasmanes provided troops and logistical support to Alexander the Great in anticipation of a campaign against his northern enemies, the Massagetae and the Scythians on the Black Sea.[198] Although Alexander concluded the alliance, the campaign did not come to pass.

Presumably there were three decisive reasons why Alexander did not pursue the terms of the alliance: first, he had to secure his south-eastern flank in Bactria and, second, he dreamed of an advance – in Cyrus's footsteps, so to speak – into the Indus Valley. Third, he must have taken seriously the warnings of two delegations of Pontic Scythians in autumn of 329 BC and spring of 328 BC.[199] In 331 BC the Pontic Scythians had completely destroyed the attacking Macedonian army of Alexander's governor, General Zopyrion, at Olbia and had killed him. Zopyrion's failed offensive had presumably been part of a strategic plan that foresaw first the overthrow of the Pontic Scythians and then a union with Alexander's troops in northern Bactria.[200] According to reports

One of the 31 Sakan kurgans of Besschatyr, south-eastern Kazakhstan, fifth–third centuries BC.

Model according to archaeological data of the 'golden man of Issyk', from the fifth century BC. Southern Kazakhstan. Margulan Archaeological Institute of Kazakhstan, Almaty.

by the Roman historian Quintus Curtius Rufus (first century AD) the second Scythian delegation presented Alexander with an outright threat: 'You proudly claim that you have come in pursuit of bandits, but to all the people you have visited *you* are the bandit. [...] We guard both Asia and Europe. We border on Bactria [where Alexander had troubles quelling Bactrian and Sogdian revolts] except that the Tanaïs [here: the Syr Darya] separates us. We inhabit territory beyond the Tanaïs and all the way to [the Macedonian province of] Thrace and they say Macedonia stands next to Thrace. We are neighbours to both your empires. Consider whether you want us to be your enemies or your friends.' Alluding to the routs of Cyrus II and Darius I, the Scythian added boldly, 'Just cross the Tanaïs and you will discover the extent of Scythian territory – but you will never catch the Scythians. [...] When you think we are far away, you will see us inside your camp. We pursue and retreat at equal speed.'[201] The Scythian threat was twofold: if Alexander were to attack, the Scythians would lure him into the emptiness of their steppes and at the same time mount a campaign against his homeland Macedonia. Alexander abandoned the idea of advancing to the north and contented himself with a victorious skirmish against the Saka north-east of Khujand.

The ancient Choresmian culture had been preceded by the **Amirabad Culture** (*ca.* 1400–750 BC). The settlements of the time consisted of both small, sunken 'single-family houses' of a standard size and longhouses 70 m in length. These were divided into small residential units, each with its own hearth. The tradition of the longhouses was further developed in the Old Choresmian Culture into 'settlements within ramparts' as they were placed together in rectangular or circular complexes. These settlements were surrounded by strong walls made of clay bricks and fortified with towers, and in the interior of these walls narrow, vaulted and corridor-like rooms were concealed. The city of Kjuzeligyr, built in the early Old Choresmian **Kjuzeligyr phase** (seventh/sixth–fourth centuries BC) and located 80 km south-west of today's city of Nukuz, had within its defensive walls three parallel residential corridors, and the neighbouring city of Kalaligyr, 7,000 x 1,000 m in extent, had two.[202] Thousands of people lived in such settlements and the unbuilt sections of the cities offered shelter for herds of cattle in the event of war. In the first half of the fourth century BC a building boom began in Choresmia and many fortified cities arose for protection against the raids of nomadic horsemen in the north. Among these were Ajaz Kala and Gyaur Kala north of the Amu Darya, Gyaur Kala near Mizdajkan, Janbas Kala, the large and the small Qirq Qiz Kala, Qurgashin Kala and Zamakhsha.[203] Vadim Masson very aptly described Old Choresmia as 'a small island of urban culture in an endless sea of nomadic tribes'.[204] At the start of the **Kangju phase** (fourth century BC–first century AD) there appeared within the cities fortified citadels with separate palaces for the rulers and fire shrines, such as Toprak Kala. Towards the end of the Kangju phase and in the subsequent Kushan phase (second–third centuries AD) the social unity of the settlements collapsed, as rulers and nobles remained in the well-fortified cities, while merchants and farmers lived in separated fortified villages, such as Kyzyl Kala.[205]

A unique structure of Old Choresmia was the circular, or, more precisely, 18-sided site of Koi Krylgan Kala (fourth century BC–fourth century AD), which had two concentric ring walls, respectively 87 and 44 m in diameter. The outer defensive wall, 7 m thick and reinforced by nine towers, contained nine connected rooms. The inner wall protected the two-storey central structure, originally about 10 m tall and vaulted with clay. The complex served first as a royal gravesite where rituals associated with an ancestor and sun cult, and perhaps also an astral cult, were performed. Near the complex archaeologists discovered numerous ossuaries filled with charred bones. As mentioned above, this circular gravesite recalls both older gravesites of the Central Asian steppe, such as Anchil Chon or Arzhan 1, and the mythical city of Var.[206] Perhaps the cylindrical central structure represents a forerunner of the future Zoroastrian 'towers of silence', *dakhma*. In any case, Choresmia in the Kjuzeligyr phase was familiar with the burial of mortal remains in ossuaries after the corpse was burned or had decayed. A few ceramic ossuaries from Koi Krylgan Kala took the form of a life-size seated man, with the individually crafted heads presumably reproducing the facial features of the deceased.[207] Another ossuary had the shape of a camel, possibly a symbol of the Iranian god of victory Verethraghna.[208] Around the first century BC radially laid out houses filled the space between the two walls and the gravesite became a fortified settlement, surrounded by an intensively cultivated agricultural zone.[209]

Portable incense altar with openwork base made of copper, Issyk, southern Kazakhstan, fifth–third centuries BC. Central State Museum of the Republic of Kazakhstan, Almaty.

1.8 Mountain, steppe and desert stockbreeders between the Pamirs and Altyn Tagh

1.8.1 Fergana and the Pamirs

The Fergana valley in south-eastern Uzbekistan and south-western Kyrgyzstan, as well as the eastern Pamir Mountains in eastern Tajikistan, were home to the Saka haumavarga from about the seventh century BC. Although these people are listed in Achaemenid inscriptions as belonging to the Empire, this is highly unlikely. In Fergana the Saka abandoned the oases and city-like settlements of the settled populace and moved into the higher elevations as nomads. They maintained their cult of the dead and their burial rituals, as can be seen in the kurgans.[210] The Saka also settled the valleys and high plateaus of the Pamirs on Fergana's southern border. They left behind hundreds of kurgans at an elevation of up to 4,000 m, such as those in the valleys of Alichur, Aksu, Jalang and Shurali and on the southern banks of Karakul Lake, 4,040 m above sea level. In the last three of these places, the Saka created spectacular geoglyphs beside and between their kurgans.

The geoglyphs of the Pamirs are geometric figures on the surface of the earth, which consist of light and dark stones placed over a large area and against a contrasting background. The graveyard of Kara Art on the bank of Karakul Lake, not far from the Chinese border, has 25 kurgans and 19 geoglyphs from the seventh to the second centuries BC, and that of Shurali, seven kurgans and 26 geoglyphs. At both sites nearly all the geoglyphs are oriented toward the south-east; two geoglyphs mark the summer and winter solstices and another the spring and fall equinoxes.[211] Like the kurgans of southern Siberia, the necropolises in the Pamirs were both gravesites and cultic places.

Saka tribes also lived in the eastern foothills of the Pamirs, in what is now the Chinese mountain region of Tashkurgan, as can be seen in the necropolises of the **Xiangbaobao Culture** in Xiangbabei, Xiangbaobao and Mingtiegai from the sixth to the fourth centuries BC.[212] Of the 40 graves of Xiangbabei, 21 were burials of corpses and 19 were cremations.[213] Probably even at that time groups of Saka were advancing farther east into the southern Tarim Basin, where the Sakan oasis culture of Khotan developed later in the second century BC. At that time large groups of Saka fled the attacking Yuezhi to the southern Tarim Basin.[214]

The Saka haumavarga continued the territorial advance begun by their forerunners and, together with tribes of the Saka tigraxauda, attacked Bactria and Margiana around 293–292 BC. They overran garrisons of the Seleucids and plundered several cities, such as Merv, which went up in flames. After that King Seleucus (r. 305–281 BC) sent General Demodamas from Milet to the north-eastern satrapies, who drove out the Saka and advanced to the Jaxartes River (Syr Darya). In view of the threat posed by the restive Saka, Seleukos appointed his son Antiochus, the future Antiochus I (r. 281–261 BC), as viceroy of the eastern satrapies, with the strategically important regions of Margiana and Bactria coming under his rule. Antiochus lived for a time in Bactria, presumably in Bactra, and led the reconstruction of the cities from there. Among these cities were Alexandria Eschate (Khujand), which he renamed Antiochia-in-Scythia, Maracanda (Samarkand) and Merv, which from then on was called Antiochia-in-Margiana. The older, Achaemenid settlement was turned into a citadel and the city now covered an area of 4 km^2.[215] In order to protect the agricultural zones around Merv from plundering nomads, Antiochus surrounded them with a 278-km-long defensive wall.[216] In the mid-third century BC Merv fell to the Greco–Bactrian Kingdom, and, a century later, to the Parthians.[217]

The Choresmian fortress and settlement complex of Ayaz Kala in central Uzbekistan traces back to the late Kjuzeligyr Phase of the Old Choresmian Culture (seventh/sixth–fourth centuries BC). Shown here: in the foreground, ruins of a palace from the fourth century AD; to the rear left, the fortified city of Ayaz Kala I, founded in the fourth century BC; and to the right, the ruler's residence Ayaz Kala II (sixth–eighth centuries AD).

The two-storey Old Choresmian graveyard and later fortified settlement of Koi Krylgan Kala, south-western Uzbekistan, fourth century BC–fourth century AD.

1.8.2 The Chinese Altai and regions north of the Tian Shan Mountains

The area between the mountains of the Altai and the Dzungarian Desert in northern Xinjiang, with its lush pastures, offered ideal living conditions for stockbreeding nomads. Stone engravings on the southern edge of the Altai Mountains attest to their presence from the Bronze Age on. Three types of gravesites from pre-Christian times may be found: large khirigsuurs with deer stones of the second type (900–700 BC), decorated with boars, horses and deer on tiptoe, as well as tomahawks, beside them; simple pit graves, all belonging to the **Dalongku Culture** (*ca.* 800–200 BC). Quite different are the mysterious graves of the **Ke'ermuqi** cultural group (*ca.* second half of the second millennium BC).[218] These consist of one or more cist graves, which are surrounded by a stone enclosure made of upright stone slabs. These enclosures are usually rectangular but occasionally circular. Next to the majority of these graves or grave groups stand anthropomorphic stone steles of heights from 60 to over 150 cm. The steles are almost rectangular or oval in cross-section and from the shoulders the neck moves seamlessly into the broad head. The slightly sculpted, schematically portrayed

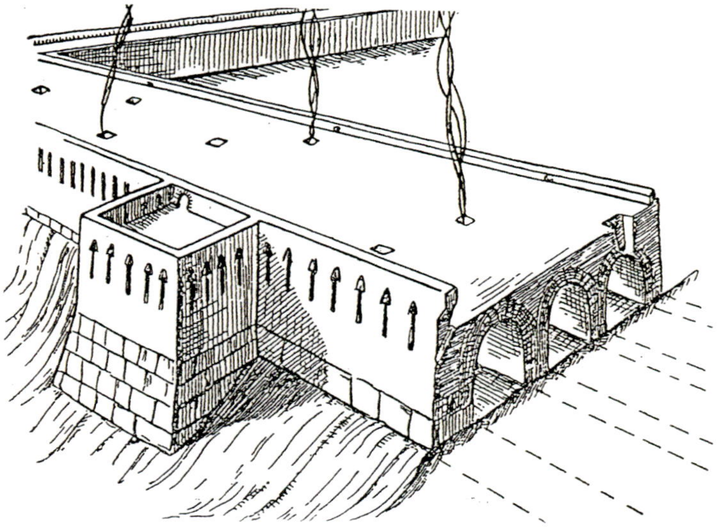

Sketch of the defensive walls with three parallel corridors of the Old Choresmian city of Kjuzeligyr, western Uzbekistan. According to Sergei Tolstov *Drevniy Choresm*, 1948, p. 81.

Mt. Shurali Mozkol, standing 5,119 m above sea level, Gorno-Badakhshan, north-eastern Tajikistan.

face is often surrounded by a torus; sometimes the statue wears a neckring and sometimes sculpted triangular patterns mark the cheeks, as at the complex of Kayina'er about 40 km west of the district town Altay.[219]

The burials and especially the stone steles have been assigned widely varying dates, from the late Afanasievo Culture (second half of the third millennium BC) to the Old Turkish period (fifth–eighth centuries AD).[220] Individual characteristics of the steles rule out a dating to the Old Turkish epoch, since they lack the typical Turkish weapons of that time, the pointed moustache and, in particular, the vessel held in the hand of the warrior portrayed. An analysis of the grave goods shows that in several complexes the graves come from different cultures, ranging from the Okunev to the time of the Saka. We date the Ke'ermuqi cultural group provisionally to the late second millennium BC, hence to the late Bronze Age. Finally, the very slender, 26-cm-tall stone figure from grave 21 is notable, since it is very similar to the almost equally slender stone statues of Kan'ergou in the district of Hutubi.[221] Perhaps the creators of the nearby petroglyphs of Quergou belonged to a cultural circle related to Ke'ermuqi.

The kurgans of the **Tiemulike Culture** (sixth–third centuries BC), which lie on the upper valley of the Ili and its tributaries the Künäs He and the Terek He, recall the Saka nomadic horsemen. After the Saka other nomadic peoples such as the Indo-European Wusun and Yuezhi, the Xiongnu, Xianbei, Rouran and Ashina, which made up the leading clans of the Gök Turks ('blue Turks'), used the lush grazing lands. The Ili was rich not only in pastures that could be used almost year-round but also in sources of ore, such as the copper mines of Nileke near the Nulasai Mountains, where ore was smelted right on site.[222] In the early 1980s a 21-kg ball-shaped copper cauldron with three feet was found on the southern bank of the Künäs He in the district of Xinyuan. This

▶ One of the 26 geoglyphs of Shurali in the Pamirs, Gorno-Badakhshan, north-eastern Tajikistan, seventh–second centuries BC. Saka horsemen created the geoglyphs next to their kurgans.

Yaks enjoy a cooling bath in Lake Karakul at the foot of Muztagata, rising 7,546 m above sea level. Xinjiang, north-western China.

cauldron resembled the kettles of the Land of Seven Rivers. The three-footed cauldron of the Saka should however be distinguished from the cauldron of the Scythians, the so-called Hunnic cauldrons, which stood on a conical foot. The cauldrons not only had a cultic function but also served in daily life as vessels for cooking meat. For the nomads the cooking pot and shared mealtimes were a unifying activity within the extended family or clan. The square bronze table, by contrast, served purely cultic purposes involving burnt offerings. Two bronze neckrings with two winged griffin figurines on the front reveal the close connection to the Russian Altai.[223] The most spectacular discovery from Xinyuan, however, is a bronze statue of a kneeling warrior, wearing a short skirt, who originally held in his hands a sword, lance or banner. His face has Europid features and he wears a helmet with a point bent forward, a so-called 'Phrygian cap', common among the Scythians.

◀ **Anthropomorphic stone steles at the grave complex of Kayina'er in the Chinese Altai, Xinjiang, north-western China. The complex belongs to the Ke'ermuqi cultural group from the second half of the second millennium BC.**

This statue, from the fourth–third centuries BC, could portray a Saka tigraxauda, a 'pointed cap Saka', although with his bare upper body and short skirt, the warrior looks more like a Greek than a Saka. Perhaps the artist had been inspired by a Bactrian statue.[224]

In the second half of the first millennium BC the cultural territory of the Saka extended over Semirechie, Kyrgyzstan, the Pamirs and the Chinese watershed of the Ili as far east as the north-eastern foothills of the Tian Shan and perhaps even the Turfan Depression. Archaeological finds indicate that at the time the boundary between Iranian-speaking Saka and Tocharian-speaking Tocharians ran along a line extending from Niya on the southern edge of the Tarim Basin to the Turfan Depression, where the two ethnicities converged. About 100 km south of Urumqi and west of Turfan lies the necropolis of Alwighul (Chin. Alagou) with two types of Iron Age graves. Burials referred to as Alagou I are pebble graves, so called because the walls of the shaft-like graves are covered with pebbles. The grave goods in these multiple-person graves from the sixth/fifth–third centuries BC display a connection to the necropolis of Jiaohe Gou near Turfan, as well as to the

Three Tajik women in traditional garb in front of the fortress of Tashkurgan, last restored in 1895, Xinjiang, north-western China. In the second half of the first millennium BC Saka lived here, controlling the trade route to the Indus Valley and migrating from here into the eastern Tarim Basin.

cemeteries of Subexi and Yanghai in the south-eastern part of the Turfan Depression. Together these formed the settled **Aidinghou Culture**, which obviously had contacts with the culture of Pazyryk. The slightly later wooden chamber graves of Alagou II (fourth–second centuries BC) were covered with piles of stones, and the skulls of the dead, buried singly or in pairs, were covered with red ochre. The gold jewellery and a bronze table on a square base with a standing pair of winged lions, buried with them, as well as the gold jewellery of Jiaohe Gou, indicate affiliation with the cultural circle of the Saka and the early Wusun of the Künäs valley and Semirechie.[225] Several Europids were buried in the shaft and catacomb graves of Subexi (fifth–third centuries BC); these people presumably belonged to the Tocharians. Among the discoveries was a well-preserved, 121-cm asymmetrical recurve bow, an intact wooden saddle with harness and three women's wool caps, about 50 cm tall, with broad brims and tapered points, which recall the still taller headdresses of Pazyryk.[226]

1.8.3 Oasis cultures south of the Tian Shan Mountains

North of the city of Korla lies the **Charwighul Group** (*ca.* 1000–400 BC) which consists of five necropolises and over 2,000 graves, where stockbreeding, largely sedentary Europids were buried.[227] Horse bits and cheek pieces found in the graves, as well as jewellery decorated in animal style with depictions of coiled animals, show that representatives of this culture were riders who had contact with the Scythian world of southern Siberia. Related to Charwighul is the group of **Qunbake** (800–250 BC) west of Korla. Wooden beams and grass mats were laid over the burial chambers, and these were ritually set on fire before the construction of round or oval kurgans. In isolated cases a wooden house-like construction stood above the grave, similar to the burials of Besschatyr in the Land of Seven Rivers and of Satma Mazar on the lower reaches of the Keriya River. Among the grave goods of the deceased were also the heads of sacrificed horses, camels, sheep, goats and dogs.[228]

At the beginning of the Iron Age the extensive cultural complex of **Zaghunluq-Jumbulakum/Satma Mazar** (tenth–third centuries BC) arose in the southern half of the Tarim Basin. On the southern edge of the Taklamakan Desert near Qiemo lay the necropolis of Zaghunluq, numbering over 1,000 shaft graves, which had its heyday from the tenth to the sixth centuries BC.[229] Unfortunately, even before the start of excavations it had been 90 percent plundered. In one of the undisturbed graves a man and three women were buried. The 2,800-year-old Europid man lay on his back with bent knees, dressed in a burgundy wool robe, shirt and trousers, colourful striped knee socks and knee-high leather boots. He had light brown hair and his face had been painted after death with yellow and red ochre. The painting covered the forehead, temples and upper halves of the cheeks down to the beard like a half-mask; it took the form of rays on each side, like a sun. Two of the female mummies were poorly preserved; the third had spiral-like sun symbols on her cheeks and nose like the man. In an adjacent grave lay an infant wrapped in a crimson woollen cloth, who wore an indigo-coloured blue felt cap and whose eyes were covered with two bluish stones. Of note among the grave goods of this man were a leather saddle, a horse skull, a front hoof and a horsehide.

That he was a rider is also suggested by his trousers – an invention of Central Asian horse-riding peoples – which featured a gusset in the waistband, making it easier to straddle a horse.[230] Representatives of the culture of Zaghunluq were in contact with the steppe peoples of today's Mongolia, eastern Kazakhstan and the Altai, as can be seen in a variety of wooden vessels in which animal figures in the Scytho-Siberian animal style are engraved. Comparable objects in the Tarim Basin are known from Yanghai east of Turfan, Jumbulakum and Satma Mazar in the ancient delta of the Keriya River.[231] Four mummies also lay in another grave. The main person was an older woman, whose left hand was tattooed. She wore short boots made of bearskin and was wrapped in a blue blanket. The excavators interpreted the other corpses, a baby, a

Asymmetrical recurve bow from Subexi I, grave M 27, Turfan district, Xinjiang, north-western China, fifth–third centuries BC. Xinjiang Uyghurs Autonomous Region Museum, Urumqi.

Bronze statue of a warrior with European facial features, who, with his naked upper body and short skirt appears, despite his Sakan pointed cap tipped forward, more Greek than Saka. Xinyuan in the region of the upper Ili, Xinjiang, north-western China, fourth–third centuries BC. Xinjiang Uyghurs Autonomous Region Museum, Urumqi.

Female Europid mummy from the necropolis of Subexi III, grave M 6; Turfan district, Xinjiang, north-western China, fifth–third centuries BC. Museum of the Archaeological Institute of Xinjiang, Urumqi.

one-year-old boy and a 20-year-old woman with amputated legs and arms, as human sacrifices.[232] Whether the earlier burials of Zaghunluq were those of proto-Tocharians is an open question.

Three hundred and fifty kilometres north-west of Zaghunluq stand the ruins of the city of Jumbulakum (Chin. Yuan Sha) on an ancient delta of the Keriya River. About 4,000 years ago, the Keriya Darya, which originated in the Kun Lun Mountains, flowed northward across the Taklamakan Desert, 670 km as the crow flies, until it reached the Tarim River. It formed a broadly branching, meandering delta about 200 km south of the Tarim. The Bronze Age settlement of Sebier and the necropolis of Ayala Mazar lay on such arms of the river.[233] Towards the end of the second millennium BC climatic changes caused a drop in the river's volume, which led to the disappearance of the Bronze Age settlements. Life shifted to the south, and the 7-ha fortified city of Jumubulakum arose around the sixth century BC about 73 km south-west of Sebier. The name of the settlement, first discovered in 1994, means 'round sand' and refers to the layout, in the shape of an irregular hexagon. The city wall, 995 m long, 4 m high and 5 m thick at the base, had entrance gates on the south and east sides. On the exterior the wall was made up of crude clay bricks, 66 x 40 x 11 cm in size, which corresponded to standard Achaemenid bricks and indicates an influence from the Persian satrapies. On the interior of the wall, by contrast, local construction methods were used, since the wall consists of several layers of irregular clay bricks, which were reinforced horizontally by tamarisk branches and vertically by poplar posts. The many traces of burning on the walls bear witness to troubled times.[234]

The settled inhabitants had a mixed economy. They raised sheep, goats, dogs, cattle and camels and, thanks to artificial irrigation, cultivated millet, barley and wheat. They mastered ironworking, produced both crude ceramic and wooden vessels and engaged in trade with central China, as can be seen in the copper cowry shells which served as a medium of exchange there. They also undertook trade with India, from where they obtained carnelian jewellery and dyes, and with Persian satrapies, which supplied glass beads, as well as with the steppe cultures of the north. In the six small cemeteries that surrounded the city a total of 43 dead rested in timber graves or in narrow buried cist-shaped wooden structures. The style of burial and the grave goods display parallels to both Zaghunluq and the Scythian-era sites of the Altai. Among the grave goods were textiles, copper decorations on pointed caps, and round copper adornments, in the form of coiled animals, used on horse gear.[235] The grave MC, close to the city, in which two men lay head-to-toe, their heads shot through

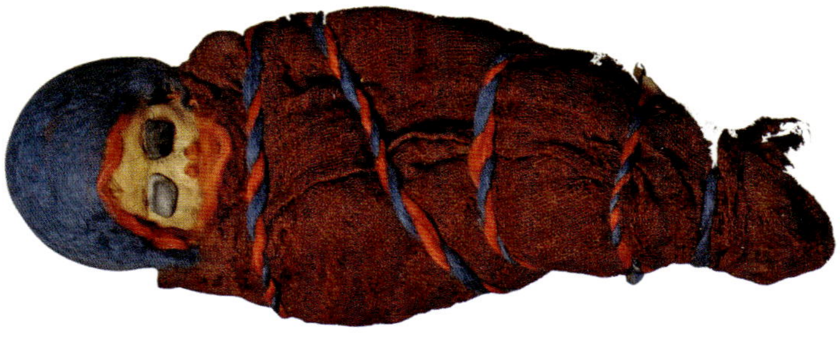

Mummy of an approximately 10-month-old infant, wrapped in a red cloth, with red wool stuffed in its nose and two blue stones placed on its eyes. Side grave M 1 next to grave M 2 in the necropolis of Zaghunluq, where the rider with sun symbols painted on his temples as well as three women were buried. Xinjiang, north-western China, *ca.* 800 BC. Xinjiang Uyghurs Autonomous Region Museum, Urumqi.

with several arrows fired at close range, remains mysterious. Was it a blood sacrifice or an execution? Jumbulakum was abandoned around the third or second century BC because of a water shortage.

Anthropological studies of the naturally mummified corpses reveal that they belonged to a dolichocephalous Europid population. Since the dead of Jumbulakum are assigned culturally to the community of the early Saka and Scythians of the Altai, it may be assumed that they were more or less distant relatives of the Saka. These migrants gave up their earlier, nomadic lifestyle in favour of settled stockbreeding and farming, which they adopted from their presumably proto-Tocharian forerunners. In the last quarter of the first millennium BC additional Saka immigrants practised a settled hybrid culture in the oasis of Khotan, as can be seen in the discoveries at the necropolis of Shanpula.[236]

In autumn 2009, 12 km north-east of Jumbulakum, the author discovered the cemetery of Satma Mazar, which offered further evidence of the cultural connection of the Iron Age population of the Keriya Darya to the steppe world of the Saka. While the northern half of the graveyard, which numbered at least 21 burials, had been plundered, the southern half remained undisturbed. Its layout is trapezoidal with two 630-cm long sides and breadths of 460 cm and 320 cm. Walls up to 2 m in height and made of still-standing poplar posts, which were covered on the exterior with a meshwork of tamarisk branches and rough clay plaster, surrounded the southern section.[237] A 110-cm-high and 120-cm-wide entrance stood there, with a gate made of parallel, V-shaped tamarisk meshwork. The structure, unique for this region and reminiscent of the above-ground wooden chambers of Besschatyr in Semirechie, earned it the Uyghur name *Satma Mazar*, meaning 'house grave'.

Here three corpses lay under a mat made of a meshwork of parallel, diagonally arranged, thin tamarisk branches. There were two juvenile females, whose dolichocephalous skulls showed no signs of violence, and a man, over 190 cm tall, lying on his back. Near the heads of the two women lay grey ceramic jugs with wave-shaped, red-white striped decoration and broad, protruding, beak-shaped spouts, resembling the ceramics of Charwighul,[238] as well as nine flat wooden vessels. The man was laid in a dark red wool blanket, fragments of which still surround his leg bones.

Illustration based on archaeological excavations of the Iron Age city of Jumbulakum (Yuan Sha) on the former middle section of the River Keriya, central Taklamakan Desert, Xinjiang, north-western China.

The women were wrapped in brown wool blankets with a striped pattern, which were presumably woven on a flat loom. The lower legs of one woman were covered with a fine, carmine red wool cloth, presumably a skirt. Analysis of an identical piece from Jumbulakum revealed the use of the animal dye of cochineal coccid (Porphyrophora),[239] so it may have been an import. Beside it lay fragments of a long, tricoloured wool weft faced twill tapestry, presumably part of a decorative band on a skirt. The pattern, which resembles a stylised animal, is made up of two rows of alternating colours arranged so that one is blue-red and the opposing row is blue-yellow. Similar pieces of tapestry of the same age were found at kurgan 2 of Pazyryk[240] and slightly later bands from the last quarter of the first millennium BC were discovered in the necropolis of Shanpula.[241] Next to these fragments lay an 18-cm-long strip made up of a variety of animal fibres. One end of the strip is wrapped in blue and red thread, and at the other end the strip is split into five cords trimmed with red and blue tassels. Similar pieces have been found not only in Jumbulakum but also in Ak-Alacha in the Russian Altai.[242]

Further evidence of contact with nomadic steppe cultures north of the Tian Shan Mountains is provided by a fragment of a bronze buckle in the form of a small horse head, 3 x 3 cm, and a wooden barrel 50 cm high and 20 cm wide. A deer on tiptoe is engraved on two opposite sides of the barrel. In both animals a volute design forms the transition from the body to the forelegs and back legs. In the Iron Age culture of the steppe, such volute designs on animal figures belonged to the syntax of the animal style, and the tiptoe gait had been common in eastern Scythian art since Arzhan 1.[243] Depictions of animals carved into wooden vessels are also known in Xinjiang from Jumbulakum,[244] Zaghunluq[245] and Yanghai[246] east of Turfan. This dynamic representation of cervids in petroglyphs with volute designs and the tiptoe gait of Scythian steppe art spread even further south, to the Changtang (byang thang) high-altitude steppe plateau in north-western Tibet, especially to the Ruthog county, to neighbouring Ladakh and to the Upper Indus Valley in northern Pakistan.[247] The pieces of plaited hairpieces placed near the corpses at Satma Mazar call to mind similar habits among the Saka of the Altai,[248] a ritual symbolising the mourning for the deceased later also adopted by the Xiongnu.[249] In this context of Scythian steppe cultures the discovery of three 6- to 12-cm-long phallic symbols made of wood and stone was surprising and recalls the fertility cult of the Ayala Mazar-Xiaohe Culture, more than a millennium older. An AMS ^{14}C measurement of human hair sampled from the southern section of the cemetery confirmed a calibrated date between 390 BC and 200 BC at a 95.4% probability.[250]

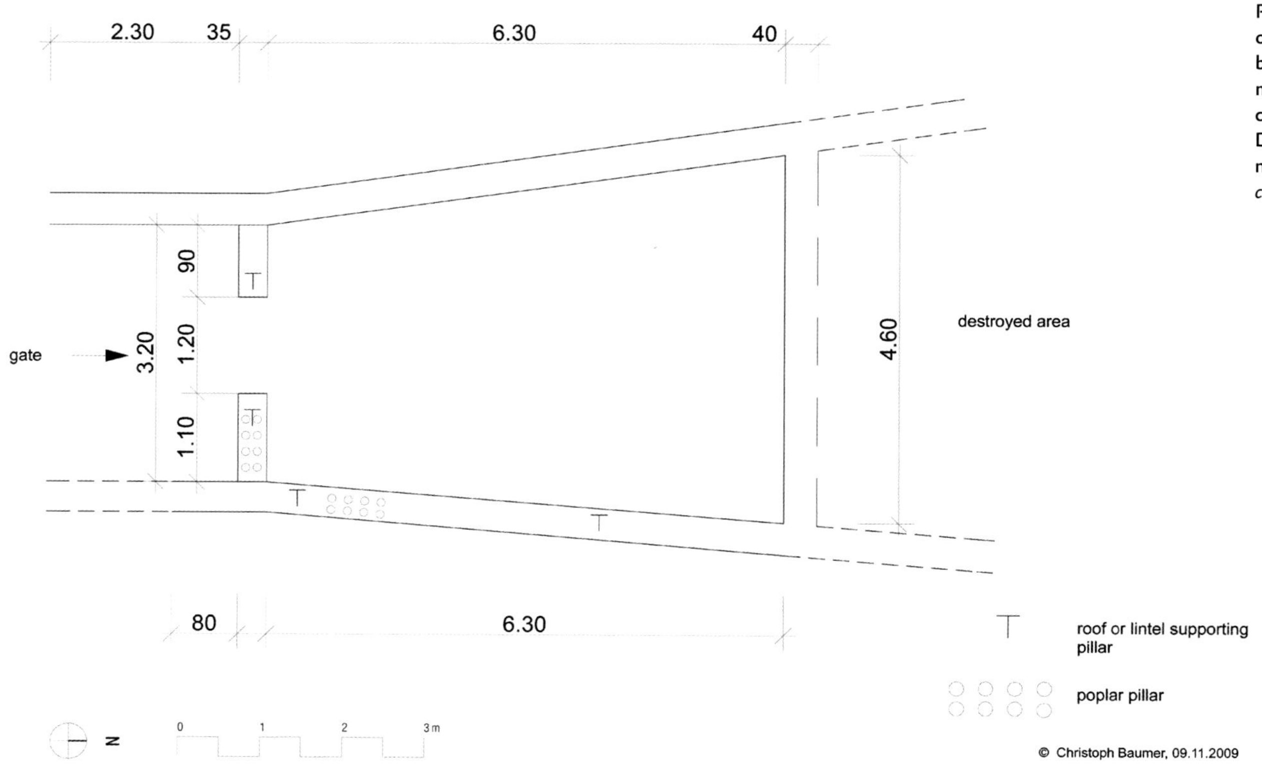

Plan of the necropolis of Satma Mazar, whose boundaries were marked by poplar posts, central Taklamakan Desert, Xinjiang, north-western China, *ca.* 390–200 BC.

Southern half of Satma Mazar during the excavation; to the upper right, a protective mat made of tamarisk wickerwork divided the lower burial area from the upper; in the centre, flat wooden vessels and a grey ceramic vessel painted with red and white stripes, central Taklamakan Desert, Xinjiang, north-western China, *ca.* 390–200 BC.

The just under 50-cm-tall wooden tub had a leather or wooden bottom, which was sewn onto the base of the vessel. The deer on tiptoe and the spiral-shaped depiction of thighs and shoulders carved into both sides are formal elements of the Scytho-Siberian animal style. Cemetery of Satma Mazar, central Taklamakan Desert, Xinjiang, north-western China, *ca.* 390–200 BC.

Grey jugs with beak-shaped spout. The jugs are decorated with incised triangles dotted inside with tiny points, and painted at the neck with wave-shaped red and white stripes. Cemetery of Satma Mazar, central Taklamakan Desert, Xinjiang, north-western China, *ca.* 390–200 BC. Similar jugs were found at Jumbulakum and in the northern section of the Charwighul graveyard north of Korla and dating from the Iron Age.

Tricoloured wool weft faced twill tapestry, whose pattern suggests stylised animals; presumably it was part of a decorative band on a skirt. Cemetery of Satma Mazar, central Taklamakan Desert, Xinjiang, north-western China, *ca.* 390–200 BC.

Fragment of a bronze belt buckle in the Scytho-Siberian animal style. House 4 at Gäze near Satma Mazar, central Taklamakan Desert, Xinjiang, north-western China, *ca.* fifth–third centuries BC.

Southern entrance to the Iron Age cemetery of Satma Mazar, central Taklamakan Desert Xinjiang, north-western China, *ca.* 390–200 BC. The wooden structure over the grave is very similar to corresponding grave structures of the Saka at Besschatyr in south-eastern Kazakhstan and suggests cultural connections.

Satma Mazar was used parallel to the heyday of Jumbulakum, perhaps not by inhabitants of that city but by the sprawling village of Gäze, 13 km farther north. This agricultural settlement extended over 13 km along both banks of an approximately 300-m-wide winding riverbed, and most of its 11 identified residential complexes included stables. Stone mills, piles of ceramics and bronze and iron objects lying between the individual complexes indicate that the region was once more densely populated than the ruins suggest.

Another reference to early eastern Scythian culture is found 300 km south of Jumbulakum at a height of 2,850 m above sea level in the northern Kun Lun Mountains. The necropolis of Liushui, discovered in 2002, lies at the confluence of the Keriya and Liushui rivers and contains 52 graves with multiple burials. It was used from the late tenth to the early eighth centuries BC, contemporaneously with the earliest burials of Zaghunluq. A mound of river stones was plac ed over 13 of the grave chambers; the rest of them had stone circles arranged on the ground. Unusual features on the femurs of a few of the skeletons and healed fractures attest to intensive riding. Both the grave types and the discovery of bronze horse-gear, knives and two-winged arrowheads with sockets show connections to the Kamennyi Log Culture on the Yenisei and early Scythian cultural forms. It remains surprising that the earliest burials in the Kun Lun Mountains belonged to a presumably semi-nomadic rider community that had close contact with distant steppe cultures.[251]

2. Nomadic riding peoples on the north-western periphery of Central Asia

> At the sound of horsemen and archers every town takes to flight. [...] 'People of Israel,' declares the LORD, 'I am bringing a distant nation against you – an ancient and enduring nation, a people whose language you do not know, whose speech you do not understand. Their quivers are like an open grave. [...] Look, an army is coming from the land of the north. [...] They are armed with bow and spear; they are cruel and show no mercy. They sound like the roaring sea as they ride on their horses.'
>
> **Prophet Jeremiah** about the attacking, most likely Scythian warrior horsemen[252]

Thanks to Assyrian and Greek sources we are relatively well informed about the early nomadic horsemen of Eastern Europe, even if the various timelines cannot always be reconciled. The history of the pre-Christian cultures of Iranian-speaking riding peoples may be divided into three periods:

I. **Cimmerians and early Scythians:** Toward the end of the eighth century BC the Cimmerians from the north arrived in the Near East. Presumably a drying of the climate of the northern Pontic region, which began in the eleventh/tenth centuries BC, forced the Cimmerians to leave their homeland there, cross the Caucasus and descend upon the Near East.[253] Three or four decades later bands of Scythian riders invaded the Near East, while the Cimmerians advanced into Anatolia. The economic foundation of the nomadic horsemen active in the Near East consisted of war, raids and the imposition of tribute. The 'means of production', or rather of destruction, of the nomadic warrior were his horse and weapons.

II. **Pontic Scythians:** In the first half of the sixth century BC the Scythians of the Near East returned to other Scythian groups in the region of Kuban and began soon thereafter to occupy the northern Pontic steppe. At the same time new waves of Scythian nomadic horsemen advanced from the east into what is now Ukraine. Here they subjected the farming population of the forest steppes and controlled trade with the Bosporan Kingdom and Greece.

III. **Sarmatians**: While the Sauromatians, presumably ancestors of the Sarmatians, supported the Scythians in the war against the Persian king of kings Darius, towards the beginning of the third century BC Sarmatian tribes began to pressure the Scythians on their eastern border. The advance to the west brought the Sarmatian tribes into a centuries-long conflict with the Bosporan Kingdom and with Rome, during the course of which individual tribes of Sarmatians reached England and North Africa. In this way peoples and cultures originating in Central Asia extended as far as the Atlantic.

2.1 Cimmerians and early Scythians

Akkadian sources from the Neo-Assyrian Empire (911–612 BC) about the archaeologically elusive Cimmerians and early Scythians are especially valuable since they were produced during the time of Assyria's conflicts with the Cimmerians, in contrast to the Greek sources, which were composed at a later time. Additionally, the Akkadian texts were current espionage reports, administrative documents and questions for soothsayers, all of which concerned concrete military problems. The Assyrian texts also consistently distinguish the Cimmerians from the Scythians, although the lifestyle and material culture of the two Iranian-speaking peoples were very similar. The Cimmerians' name in Akkadian was *Gimmirai*, while the Scythians called themselves *Ašguzâi, Iškuzâi*.[254]

The background for the emergence of the Cimmerian people was the climatic fluctuation in the northern Pontic region between the Dnieper and the Volga towards the end of the second millennium BC and the extensive land utilisation of the Srubnaya Culture. The rapidly decreasing productivity of the pastures and fields led to both an out-migration of the population and a transition to nomadic herding. At the same time, the successor culture to Srubnaya, the culture of **Belozerka** (1200–950 BC), came to an end and with it disappeared most of the settlements on the Black Sea steppes. Ukrainian archaeologists propose that around the tenth–ninth centuries BC pre-Scythian, Iranian-speaking nomadic horsemen advanced from Kazakhstan and Siberia into the Pontic steppes, which sped the development of an economy based on nomadic stockbreeding, in which horses played a prominent role. The bimetallic battle pick, common among the Cimmerians, which had its origin in the early Tagar Culture of the Minusinsk Basin, provides one piece of evidence for a hypothetical migration from the east.[255]

The Cimmerians appear in the Assyrian texts for the first time in the year 714 BC, when the Assyrian crown prince Sanherib

Equipment of a Scythian warrior of the fifth–fourth centuries BC, reproduced according to archaeological finds. For defence, the warrior wore, over a linen garment, a scale helmet with cheek and neck guards, armour for breast and thigh, and a rectangular lamellar shield. His offensive weapons were his lance, a bow and an iron sword. This equipment weighed a total of 23 kg. Reconstruction by O.I. Minzhulin.

informed his father, Sargon II (r. 721–705 BC), that the king of Urartu, Rusa I (r. 735–*ca.* 714 BC), whose army was based on war chariots, had attacked the land of the Gimmirai and suffered a devastating defeat. The Cimmerian base Gamir lay in the southern Caucasus, which means that these first nomadic horsemen on the south-western edge of Central Asia must have left their northern Pontic homeland, at least in part, by the last quarter of the eighth century BC at the latest. Since Sargon attacked and destroyed the arch-enemy of Urartu in the same year, coordinated action between the Cimmerians and Assyrians is probable.[256] If there was an alliance against Urartu, it was short-lived, because Sargon fell in a battle 'in the land of the Cimmerians'.[257] After Sargon's death the Cimmerians disappeared from Assyrian texts for a quarter-century and emerged again only around 679 BC, simultaneously with the Scythians, who appear for the first time. According to the 'Annals of Asarhaddon' and the stele of Tell Ahmar, Asarhaddon (r. 680–669 BC) defeated Cimmerians led by King Teušpa in eastern Anatolia in 679/78 BC. A few graves on the upper Euphrates with stone bases and horse sacrifices may be connected to Cimmerian nomads who were active in the area.[258]

The Cimmerian defeat in no way dampened their desire to attack, however, as the Greek historian Strabo reported that in 676–675 BC the Cimmerians assailed the kingdom of Phrygia in central and western Anatolia, their erstwhile ally against Assyria. When the Phrygian capital of Gordion stood on the brink of collapse, King Midas II is said to have chosen suicide by drinking bull's blood.[259] After their victory the Cimmerians extended their military campaigns farther west and attacked the kingdom of Lydia. Here the sources differ: Herodotus speaks of a single Cimmerian raid against Lydia and its capital, Sardes, at the end of the reign of the Lydian king Ardys II (d. *ca.* 629 BC) around the years 633–629 BC. Strabo, however, mentions two Cimmerian campaigns against Sardes, the first of which took place shortly before 660 BC.[260] Since Strabo's accounts accord more closely with Assyrian reports, these two sources are favoured in this case. Assyrian texts report that the Lydian king Gûgu (Gyges) submitted to the Assyrian king Assurbanipal (r. 669–631/627 BC) around 660 BC and asked him for military aid against the Cimmerians who were destroying his land. Thanks to Assyrian help Gyges was able to expel the Cimmerians and sent two captured Cimmerian leaders to Assyria. In revenge the Cimmerians plundered and occupied the regions of Amurru in Syria and Palestine, which belonged to Assyria.

When Pharaoh Psammetichus I (r. 664–610 BC) threw off the Assyrian yoke after 658 BC, however, Gyges changed fronts and supported the rebellious pharaoh with troops against Assurbanipal.

The pharaoh was able to defend the regained sovereignty of Egypt; Gyges paid for his treachery with death. The Cimmerians attacked Sardes under their king Lygdamis in 652 BC at the latest, conquered the city and killed Gyges. A text of Assurbanipal states: 'When he [Gûgu] sent his troops to support Tušamilki [Psammetichus], who had thrown off the yoke of my rule, I implored Assur and Ishtar, "May his corpse be thrown down before my enemy." [...] And so it came to pass. His corpse was thrown before his enemy and his remains were dragged away. The Gimmirai, which he had subjugated through my name [help], rose up and subdued this whole land. After him his son [Ardys II] assumed the throne.'[261] After this victory the Cimmerian king Lygdamis [Dugdammê], whom the Assyrians called 'spawn of hell',[262] undertook an unsuccessful attack on Ephesus on the Ionian coast, where he had the temple of Artemis set on fire. Then he turned to Cilicia in south-eastern Anatolia, where he was twice subjugated by Assyrian troops and met his death. His son and successor Šandakšatru continued the war without success and from this point on the Cimmerians disappear from Assyrian texts. The Cimmerians who remained in Asia Minor were finally destroyed by the Lydian king Alyattes (r. 619/05–560 BC) with the help of Scythian mercenaries.[263]

One of the few archaeological traces of the Cimmerians may be found in the city of Sardes, where a massive layer of burnt remains may date to the time of King Gyges's death.[264] But no Cimmerian settlements have been found in the Near East, the Caucasus or the northern Pontic region, and it appears that the Cimmerians usually buried their dead rulers and warriors in older kurgans from the Bronze Age. Among the kurgans dating from the pre-Scythian period were those of Vysokaja Mogila (graves 2 and 5: 1000–800 BC) and Steblev 15 (late eighth century BC), dated using ^{14}C analysis.[265] The grave gifts of weapons and horse-gear found in the northern Caucasus and the Ukraine were decorated with geometric patterns of spirals, coving, rhombi, squares and crosses, but not with animal-style motifs. The Cimmerian burial culture continued the practice of erecting rudimentarily anthropomorphic stone steles that were decorated with belts of armour and weapons, but again these show no elements of animal style.[266]

Towards the end of the eighth century BC Europid and Iranian-speaking proto-Scythians from eastern Central Asia crossed the Urals and the Volga and advanced into the northern Caucasus, where they subjugated the remaining Cimmerians and the native Maeotae.[267] A few groups of these nomadic horsemen settled in the Kuban and the northern Caucasus, which they chose as their heartland and the base for their campaigns in the Near East. Other groups of Scythian warriors crossed the Caucasus, referred to by the

Adornment of a horse bridle, Oghuz Kurgan, southern Ukraine, last quarter of the fourth century BC.

Greek poet Aeschylus as the 'Scythian road',[268] and, on the trail of the Cimmerians, advanced toward the northern border of Assyria. At first the Scythians, called the Iškuzâi, under the leadership of their king Išpakaia formed an alliance with the Mannaeans. The Mannaeans lived east of Lake Urmia, bordering Assyria, which was also at war with the Cimmerians. The leader of the Assyrians, Asarhaddon, succeeded not only in defeating the Iškuzâi of King Išpakaia but also in establishing an alliance with his successor, Bartatua. It is known from a question Asarhaddon asked an oracle that he considered giving the Scythian king an Assyrian princess as a wife. Whether the Scytho–Assyrian alliance by marriage occurred is unknown, but from then on the Scythians pursued a pro-Assyrian policy and in 673 BC supported Asarhaddon in a war against the Medes. Presumably after this a few Scythians bearing rich spoils of war returned to the Caucasus. Evidence for this is seen in the gold objects made in the Assyrian–Median style from the first royal kurgans of Kelermes (660–640 BC).[269]

This first appearance of the Scythians in the Near East around 679 BC; that is, 35 years after the first Cimmerian attack of 714 BC, does not match up with Herodotus's account of events at the time. He says that the Cimmerians fled their northern Pontic homeland without a fight in advance of the invading Scythians, and that the Cimmerian elite committed mass suicide.[270]

If we believe another account by Herodotus, the Scythian–Assyrian alliance came into effect again at the time of Assurbanipal.[271] Around 644 BC the Medes, who had become independent from Assyria, advanced deep into the Assyrian Empire and besieged its capital, Nineveh. The Median king 'fought a successful battle against the Assyrians, but while he was besieging the town he was attacked by a large Scythian army under the command of King Madyas, son of Protothyes [Bartatua].' Perhaps Madyas was in fact a nephew of Assurbanipal and rushed to aid his embattled uncle, or he took advantage of the invasion to extend his rule over a large part of the Near East. Herodotus continues: 'The Medes were defeated and lost their power in Asia, which was taken over in its entirety by the Scythians. The Scythians next turned their attention to Egypt, but were met in Palestine by Psammetichus, the Egyptian king, who by earnest entreaties supported by bribery managed to prevent their further advance.'[272]

A battle of four young Scythians against two older warriors is portrayed on the 'gold helmet' of Perederijewa Mogila. In the picture, an older warrior has seized the hair of a younger fighter, who has fallen to his knees, in order to finish him off with his sword. Perederijewa Mogila, kurgan 2, Donetsk region, eastern Ukraine, fourth century BC. Ukrainian Museum of Historical Treasures, Kiev.

According to Herodotus Madyas's victory in 644 BC heralded a 28-year rule by the Scythian nomadic riders in the Near East.[273] During their three decades of dominance the Scythian warrior horsemen didn't create a structured empire. Instead, they profited from the collapse of the first Median kingdom, which they subjected to a kind of tribute-granting vassal state, and from their alliance with the still militarily strong Assyrians. The contact with the Assyrians fostered further development of the Scythian military. For one, they adopted the scale armour, which consisted of a leather underlay covered with rows of small iron discs, which provided a fish scale-like outer layer that was both strong and flexible. This innovation was necessary because the introduction of new arrowheads with greater penetrating power required warriors to be better protected. While the Assyrians limited use of the metal discs to armour for the upper body, the Scythians began to fit out weapon belts, thigh coverings, leg pieces and shields using this technology. In a few cases they also protected their horses with breast armour. Somewhat later the scale helmet with protection for the cheeks and neck replaced the heavy, cast bronze helmet. The rectangular, oval or half-moon-shaped lamellar shield, which likewise developed later, was attached to the back and both underarms of the rider. In this way the hands remained free and, by turning his arm and shoulder, the rider could change the position of the shield.

The Scythians also divided their army, following the example of the Medes and Assyrians, into specialised weapon types. While poor Scythians and auxiliaries made up the infantry, the cavalry represented the key formation of the army. This was divided into a light cavalry outfitted with bows, which showered the enemy with a heavy barrage of arrows at the start of a battle, but avoided close combat. After the enemy lines were in disarray, the heavy cavalry followed, consisting of professional warriors. First they assailed the enemy once more with arrows – a practiced archer could shoot up to 12 arrows a minute, and his quiver held 200 to 300 arrows. Then they attacked their opponents with thrown spears and finally engaged in close combat with lances. As soon as the order of the enemy was broken and they began to flee, the light cavalry pursued them in flight. The Scythian cavalry was no wild mob; it maintained its cohesion, so that it could also separate itself from the enemy during a battle, regroup and attack a second enemy unit from another direction. The Scythians began to create the complex system of differently armed, highly mobile and yet very disciplined cavalry units, which first the Avars and then the Mongols would perfect two millennia later. This disciplined behaviour required intensive and ongoing training. The maxim of the Roman historian Flavius Josephus that

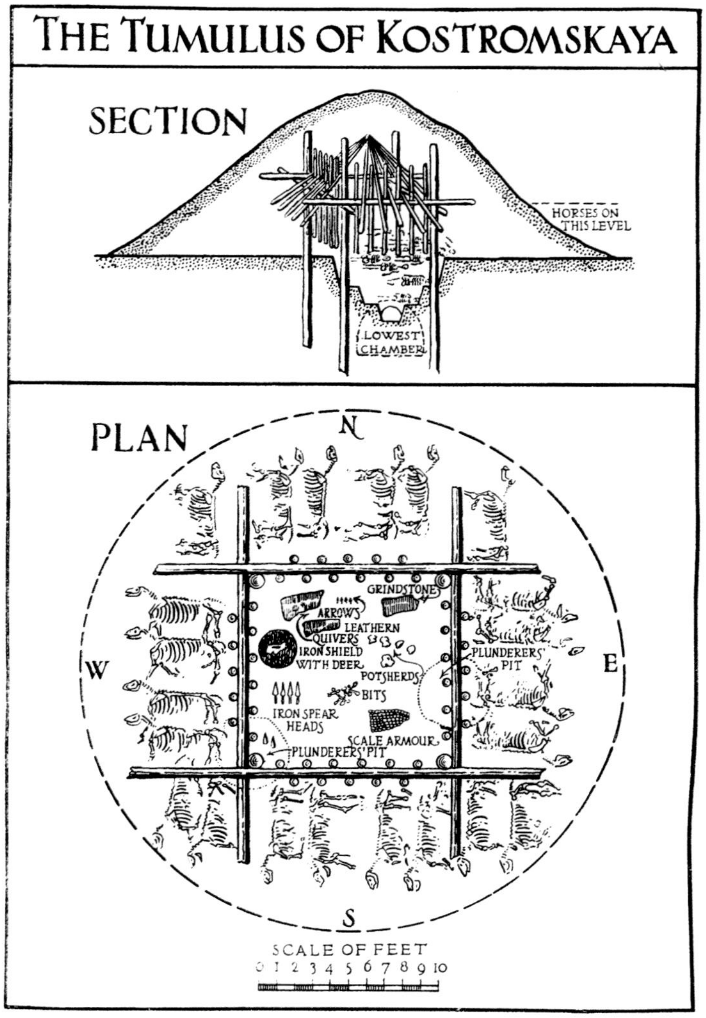

Elevation and plan of the kurgan of Kostromskaya, Kuban region, southern Russia, *ca.* 600 BC. The elevation illustrates the tent-like wooden structure erected over the grave; the plan shows the 22 sacrificed horses, laid out symmetrically. According to: M. Rostovtzeff, *Iranians and Greeks in South Russia,* 1922, p. 46.

the drills of Roman soldiers were bloodless battles and their battles were bloody drills also applies to the Scythian cavalry.[274]

Around the year 616 (or 624) BC the Median king Cyaxares II (r. 624–584 BC) succeeded in shaking off the Scythian yoke. According to Herodotus he did this by getting the Scythian elite drunk at a banquet and then murdering them.[275] In this way the Scythian army was deprived of leadership and Assyria lost its allies. Soon thereafter Cyaxares made a pact with Babylonia and attacked Assyria with the help of Scythian mercenaries. The fall of Nineveh in 612 BC dealt the Assyrian Empire a deathblow.[276] Although the Scythian army presumably split into several groups after the murder of its leaders, they continued to cause unrest in the Near East and, according to Herodotus, provoked a war between Media and Lydia. Cyaxares is said to have insulted a group of Scythians, to whom he had entrusted the military education of his sons, when they returned from a hunt without any prey. In revenge the Scythians 'decided to kill one of their young pupils, chop him up, dress the pieces in the ordinary way like meat [and] serve them to Cyaxares as a dish of game. [...] Cyaxares and the guests at his table ate some of the meat'.[277] The Scythians fled to the Lydian king Alyattes (r. 619/05–560 BC), who refused to surrender his guests. The five-year-long Median-Lydian war ended on 28 May 585 BC at the eastern Anatolian river Halys, when a solar eclipse interrupted the battle, whereupon the opponents made peace and deemed the Halys their shared border.

The majority of the Scythians who had remained in the Near East returned to their homeland in the northern Caucasus after 585 BC. In this way the first wave of nomadic horsemen from Central Asia, who had attacked the settled cultures on their south-western edge and spread to them Central Asian forms of culture and economy, came to an end. The Scythian adventure in the Near East finally foundered on the inability of the nomadic horsemen to create their own stable, state-like structure that could also withstand blows to personnel, such as the massacre of their military leaders by Cyaxares, as well as on the lack of political unity among the tribes. In addition, the Scythians encountered in the Medes a militarily equal opponent, with a tradition of nomadic riders and a strong cavalry armed with bows. Like other nomadic horsemen, the Median riders wore close-fitting clothing and carried half-moon-shaped shields, and they preferred to fight with bows and lances. Presumably the Scythians were vastly outnumbered by their Near Eastern enemies.

In the following centuries battle-tested nomadic riding peoples surged on the heels of the Scythians into the settled cultures of western Central Asia. These peoples included the Sarmatians, Alans, Huns, Magyars, Seljuks and other Turkic peoples, as well as the Mongols, who also attacked China. Only the convergence of several factors in Western Europe in the fifteenth century brought an end to the Central Asian expansion and slowly turned the tide. These factors were material inventions such as gunpowder, the development of centrally governed states, economic interests and the search for resources like spices and precious metals. Most important, however, was a new intellectual attitude in the west marked by curiosity and a thirst for scientific knowledge increasingly freed from religious dogma. At the same time, the Central Asian states largely failed to modernise accordingly. This technological and political stagnation culminated in the nineteenth century in the extensive conquest of Central Asia by tsarist Russia.

2.2 Scythians in the Kuban region

The Scythian veterans returning from the Near East encountered unexpected resistance. Herodotus's florid report says that the returning Scythians 'found trouble waiting for them hardly less serious than their struggle with the Medes. This was in the shape of a large hostile army, which opposed their entrance; for the Scythian women, wearied with their husbands' protracted absence, had intermarried with the slaves', and their sons now set themselves against the returning soldiers.[278] After a few engagements the veterans resorted to deceit and, armed only with riding crops, ripped into the young warriors, at which point they noticed 'that they are slaves'. The trick worked and the young fighters surrendered. This story was popular among Scythians, as can be seen in the so-called 'golden helmet' of Perederieva Mogila in the Ukrainian Donezk region. This helmet depicts an older, bearded warrior grabbing the hair of a younger, beardless warrior in order to run him through with his sword. The tradition indicates that the Scythians were not a homogeneous people but rather made up a heterogeneous federation of nomads. Presumably Herodotus's tribe of Royal Scythians, who ruled over the other Scythian tribes, descended from the victorious Near East veterans.

The Scythians left behind few material traces in the Near East, apart from the many finds of Scythian arrowheads and pieces of horse harnesses. The famous golden hoard of Ziwiyeh from the region of the Mannaeans, which displays Assyrian, Urartian and Scythian influences and which has been associated with the grave of a Scythian military commander, is unfortunately mute and scientifically worthless. The objects, purchased by museums from the antiquities market, come from illicit or commercial excavations, so that neither their provenance nor their relationship as a group are documented; furthermore, the authenticity of several objects is doubtful.[279]

The two most significant early Scythian necropolises in Kuban, Kostromskaya and Kelermes do, however, show obvious influences from the Near East. At Kostromskaya the Scythians removed the topmost part of the dome of a Bronze Age kurgan and put in the now flat platform a wooden pit, which was covered by a tent-like timber structure. As at the kurgans of Barsučij Log, Tagisken South and Ujgarak in eastern Central Asia, the wooden tent was ritually set on fire before the earthen mound above the tomb was built. In the kurgan archaeologists discovered the skeletons of 22 sacrificed horses outside the tomb and, within the tomb, 13 human skeletons, intentionally broken weapons and ceramic vessels, and a 700 g gold emblem of a deer, which once adorned a gorytos or a shield.[280] The deer, which has huge antlers covering its back, appears to flee from a predator, such as a large cat. This calls to mind the equally large golden panther found in kurgan 1 of the neighbouring Kelermes necropolis, which seems to be catching a scent with its flared nostrils. Ten small, coiled panthers form the paws and the tail of the cat. The third representative of the animal triad of the Scythians of Tuva and the Altai, the bird of prey, was found in the likewise early Scythian kurgan of Melgunov–Litoi west of the Dnieper in the form of golden discs of a bird with symmetrically spread wings. With deer, big cat and bird of prey, the three most prominent animals of the art of the Central Asia steppe appeared in north-eastern Europe in complete form as early as the seventh century BC. This underscores the close contact between the Tuvinian homeland of the animal style and the northern Pontic and northern Caucasian regions.

At the necropolis of Kelermes two different grave types met, reflecting the community of two peoples with their own customs. Members of the upper class of the native, agrarian populace of the Maeotae were buried in flat graves; the neighbouring kurgans held the remains of representatives of the ruling Scythian military elite.[281] The most important princely kurgans of Kelermes, and with them their contents, date from the second and third quarters of the seventh century BC, and thus are somewhat older than Arzhan 2 in Tuva.[282] Many of these objects display Near Eastern characteristics. Among them are the aforementioned bimetallic mirror

Gold clothing plaque of a bird of prey. Melgunov-Litoi Kurgan, central Ukraine, second half of the seventh century BC. The State Hermitage Museum, St. Petersburg.

Gold plaque of a recumbent deer. This 31.7-cm-long plaque originally adorned a gorytos or a shield. Kurgan of Kostromskaya, Kuban region, southern Russia, *ca.* 600 BC. The State Hermitage Museum, St. Petersburg.

Gold plaque of a panther whose paws and tail are formed from coiled panther kittens. The 32.6-cm-long plaque presumably decorated a shield. Kurgan 1 of Kelermes, Kuban region, southern Russia, *ca.* 675–625 BC. The State Hermitage Museum, St. Petersburg.

from kurgan 4, whose eight triangular electrum segments show both Ionian–Lydian and Assyrian influences.[283] And then the gold diadem with a griffin's head from kurgan 3; this headdress, common among pre-Scythian warriors, was not adopted by male Scythians but was used later by Sarmatian women.

Other influences from the Near East strongly shaped Scythian art. They are found on the sumptuous gold ceremonial weapons of chiefs and army commanders who had fought in the Near East and were buried in the Kuban. Among them was a gold-covered battle axe from kurgan 1 of Kelermes with a portrayal of two ibexes, standing on their hind legs on either side of a tree of life. One splendid akinakes, also from kurgan 1, has a gold sheath showing winged deities standing before the tree of life – both Assyrian motifs. Additional decorations on this sword sheath also come from the Assyrian–Urartian visual world: they are bow-wielding, four-legged hybrid creatures with lion or raptor heads and pacing predators with the heads of goats or ibexes. All these creatures are being bitten on their front legs by fish. In these fantastical hybrids all three realms of life – air, earth and water – are united in a single being; their idea was most likely the inspiration for the depictions of hybrid creatures among the northern Pontic Scythians and Saka.

With the adoption of Near Eastern elements in Scythian toreutics, there began the second of the five periods of Scythian art:

I. **Archaic period** (ninth–eighth centuries BC): It encompasses the beginnings of the Scytho-Siberian animal style, as it manifested itself in perfected form at Arzhan 1 and developed out of petroglyphs and deer stones of the Minusinsk Basin and western Mongolia.

II. **Kuban period** (seventh–first half of the sixth century BC): The portrayal of the 'holy' animal triad of bird of prey, deer and predatory cat was enriched by elements from Assyria and Urartu, and novel hybrid creatures emerged, such as winged bulls and lions as well as S-shaped wings bent upward. Other Near Eastern motifs, such as the tree of life flanked by two winged deities, were not adopted into the repertoire of Scythian art.

III. **Classical period** (second half of the sixth century–fifth century BC): The Near Eastern elements were developed into a mature, self-contained syntax, which concentrated on the portrayal of the ur-Scythian animals: the bird of prey, the predatory cat and the deer, as well as corresponding hybrids like griffins; other animals, such as wolves and boars, receded into the background. While scenes of animals fighting and coiled animals were popular, depictions of human beings were almost nonexistent and Greek borrowings such as the owl remained rare. The stronger adherence to original Scythian themes resulted from the new waves of Iranian-speaking nomads from eastern Central Asia.

IV. **Greco–Scythian period** (fourth–third centuries BC): Beginning around 400 BC Scytho-Greek artistic contacts developed into a symbiosis. In this regard it is hardly relevant whether Greek goldsmiths living in the Bosporan Kingdom crafted ceremonial objects for their Scythian customers or Scythian artisans living in the steppe created the objects after an apprenticeship with Greek masters. Now human beings, such as Scythian and Greek warriors, Amazons, Greek heroes like Achilles, and Scythian deities appeared beside the animals in toreutics. In a few cases warriors were shown not in battle but rather in scenes from everyday life. At the same time the animal style experienced a softening as the animals were portrayed more naturalistically and domestic animals like cattle and sheep were also depicted.

V. **Late Scythian Crimean period** (second century BC–third century AD): In their last historical phase the Scythians sought refuge from the Sarmatians and Alans on the Crimean peninsula. During this time traditional Scythian mythological content as well as animals largely disappeared from their art.

As Ludmilla Galanina emphasises, Kelermes had a very large number of horse burials: there were 24 horses in kurgan 1, 21 in kurgan 3 and 16 in kurgan 2. The number of horses present is comparable only with the 22 horses at Kostromskaya.[284] These ritual horse sacrifices are not only consistent with the horse burials of Arzhan but they also recall Herodotus's description of a dreadful ritual. One year after the burial of a king, 50 young men were strangled and, as macabre sentries, placed on 50 killed, stuffed and harnessed horses, which were impaled on lances set at an angle in the ground.[285] The 50 horse skeletons found at kurgan 1 at Ul'skji Aul (fourth century BC) on a platform over the central grave correspond to Herodotus's account and show that this ritual continued to be practised after Herodotus.[286] The collections of human and horse bones found at regularly spaced intervals and the at least 50 horse harnesses in the mound at the foot of the royal kurgan of Čertomlyk confirm the pervasiveness of this ritual.[287]

In light of the size and wealth of ceremonial objects in these early Scythian royal kurgans the question arises of whether the royal necropolis of Gerrhos referred to by Herodotus should be sought in the Kuban instead of, as Herodotus states, at the rapids of the Dnieper.[288] Although large royal kurgans with rich gold grave goods lie within a 100-km radius of the rapids, they date to either around or after 400 BC; that is, after Herodotus's death in 424 BC.

Akinakes with gold hilt and gold-plated sheath from kurgan 1 of Kelermes, Kuban region, southern Russia, *ca.* 675–625 BC. The figures, from the Assyrian–Urartian imaginative world, represent two winged deities in front of a tree of life as well as four-legged hybrid creatures, some shooting with bows, which are being bitten by flying fish. The recumbent deer depicted in the upper indentation looks typically early Scythian. The State Hermitage Museum, St. Petersburg.

The huge kurgans along the Dnieper tributary of the Sula, however, come from the seventh–sixth centuries BC and may also be identified with the Scythian 'valley of the kings'.[289]

In the seventh and sixth centuries BC the Kuban represented the military and cultural heart of the European Scythians. As a consequence of the violent seizure of the northern Caucasian homeland by the veterans from the Near East, however, an extended conflict presumably smouldered. This led in the second half of the sixth century BC to an emigration of the Scythian warrior elite and a majority of the tribes to the west, to the lower and middle reaches of the Dnieper. This migration and takeover of the land in the northern Pontic steppe must have occurred before Darius's invasion of 513/12 BC, since King Idanthyrsos's centre of power was found there. Two factors encouraged the geographic shift of the Scythian centre of power and economy: for one, the climate in the northern Black Sea region became wetter,[290] giving rise to rich pastureland, and, for another, the trade of the northern Pontic farming societies with the emerging Bosporan Kingdom and with Greece – Athens was at the time dependent on the Ukraine for imports of grain[291] – could be conveniently controlled from there. The heyday of the western Scythians ran parallel to this optimal climate and the zenith of the Greek–Ionian economy, before it fell victim to the advancing Sarmatians. The Royal Scythians had rich grazing lands for their herds and subjugated the farmers of the forest steppes, from whom they extracted tribute. They also dominated the trade with the Greek and Bosporan cities. In the Kuban, however, Scythian influence receded, even as large kurgans, such as that of Uljap, were being built according to Scythian custom.

2.3 The Pontic Scythians

Two of the legends of the origins of the Scythians transmitted by Herodotus place their homeland in a region near the Dnieper. According to one, the foremother of all Scythians is the daughter of the river god Borysthenes (Dnieper), and according to the other, Hercules fathered the three ancestors of the Scythian tribes with the snake woman in Hylaia, a forested area on the eastern bank of the Dnieper. Two of the six Scythian peoples mentioned by Herodotus lived here, the 'Royal Scythians', who ruled over all of Scythia and whose forefathers lived in Kuban and had probably fought in the Near East, and the stockbreeding 'Nomadic Scythians'.[292] Both groups were most likely Iranian-speaking. The explosive increase in large kurgans north of the Black Sea beginning at the end of the sixth century BC attests to this migration. The Royal Scythians did not establish a fixed governing structure, however; Scythia remained an unstable federation of tribes under the leadership of the royal tribe. That Scythian mounted warriors had advanced into the forest steppes west of the Dnieper long before the end of the sixth century BC is suggested by the 11-m-high Perepiat'ycha kurgan south of Kiev, from the end of the seventh century BC. A chief was buried in the since-plundered kurgan with a 14-member entourage and horses, strongly recalling the contemporaneous kurgan of Arzhan 2 in Tuva.[293]

From the end of the sixth to the end of the fourth century BC, Scythia extended from the Danube to the Don and from the northern Black Sea coast and the Kuban to about as far as Kiev. The sedentary 'Farmer Scythians' settled west of the Nomadic Scythians, and, to the west of the former, the Callipidae and Alazones, two Hellenised Scythian tribes, and the corn growing 'Ploughing Scythians', who provided grain to the trading settlements of the

Bosporan Kingdom.[294] Presumably these four 'Scythian tribes' were barely related to the Iranian-speaking Scythians and ought to be considered instead proto-Slavs who adopted particular 'Scythian' customs under the influence of the Royal Scythians.[295] The Sauromatians, relatives of the Scythians, lived east of the Don, and the Maeotae lived in the Kuban.

When the Kuban Scythians reached the northern Pontic region, they encountered prosperous Greek–Ionic trading settlements and colonies, such as the cities of Borystenes and Olbia, founded in the delta of the Bug River in 645/44 and 633 respectively, the two most important ports for the export of wheat to Athens.[296] The subjugation of the farmers made it possible for the Scythians to base their economy less on war and raids and much more on trade. They exported wheat, cattle, leather, animal hides, wax, honey and prisoners of war, and imported gold objects, ceramics and wine. In a few cases Scythians also served as mercenaries, notably in Athens as mounted police.[297]

In order to secure both their rule and their trade routes, the Scythians built over 100 fortified settlements and fortresses, many of them along navigable rivers. Among the largest of the walled settlements were Bol'šhoe Chodosovskoe gorodišče near Kiev (2,000 ha), Karatul'skoe gorodišče (6,000 ha) and Bel'sk gorodišče (4,000 ha).[298] The last is probably identical to Herodotus's Gelonos, which Darius I burned down. The Scytho–Greek city stood on a northern tributary of the Dnieper and was more than 400 km distant from Olbia as the crow flies. It served as a reloading point for both Scythians and Greek merchants and its 33-km-long and up to 10-m-high walls not only connected three fortresses but also protected many workshops and cultic sites.[299] Still more important was the city of Kamenskoje gorodišče, fortified with strong walls, which lay immediately south of the rapids of the Dnieper which blocked ship traffic at the time. The port was a first-class unloading point for Scythian trade with Olbia and Borystenes and had several weapon-makers, who worked with top-quality iron ore from the nearby mines. On an elevated spot stood an especially well-fortified stronghold, which may have served as the seat of a Scythian chieftain or even king. In any case, the heyday of Kamenskoje gorodišče coincided with the rule of the Scythian king Atheas (r. *ca.* 390–339 BC), when the population also increased significantly. Necropolises lay near Kamenskoje gorodišče on both sides of the Dnieper, containing the royal kurgans of Solocha and Čertomlyk. These sites underscore the importance of this trading city, which was also a significant crossroads.[300] These strong walled sites were not built by local people to protect themselves from belligerent nomadic horsemen. Quite the opposite: they served the Scythian elite as the cornerstone of the consolidation of their power and the channelling of the profitable flow of trade.

Clay model of a two-axle wagon with a yurt-like dwelling erected on top. Kerch, Crimea, Ukraine, first–second centuries AD. The State Hermitage Museum, St. Petersburg.

Another key region for trade between Scythia, the Greek–Ionian trading settlements on the northern Black Sea coast and north-eastern Central Asia was the Sea of Azov, in particular the broadly branching delta of the Don. As early as the third quarter of the seventh century BC Greek merchants founded the port of Taganrog west of the mouth of the Don, which was replaced a century later by the inland port of Elizavetovka in the delta of the Don, used by both Scythians and Greeks. The originally Scythian settlement soon served as a Greek emporium and was also a centre for Greek artisans. The nearby kurgan complex of Piat' Brat'ev ('Five Brothers') underscores the importance of Elizavetovka for the Scythians. At the time of the Bosporan king Eumelos I (r. 310/09–305/04 BC) Elizavetovka was built up into a strongly fortified city. This did not, however, not prevent its destruction around 270 BC by the Sarmatians advancing from the east.[301]

A few years before the burning of Elizavetovka the Bosporan king Pairisades II (r. 280–275 BC) founded the city of Tanaïs north-west of it. The Sarmatian Bosporan king Sauromates I (r. 93/4–123/4 AD) had the city rebuilt in magnificent style after its destruction in 8 AD. Then Tanaïs grew into an important crossroads, where

Bosporan and Roman sailors encountered traders from the Iranian-speaking Aorsi, a Sarmatian group. Strabo reported that the camel caravans of the Aorsi were in trade contact with eastern Central Asia, the Kushans in northern India, Mesopotamia, Armenia and Media.[302] One of the most important transcontinental trade routes of the time ran through the southern Russian steppe, not least because Rome's arch-enemy Iran either levied high taxes on trade between East Asia with Rome or aspired to cut it off.

2.3.1 The Scythian pantheon

Apart from epigrams and inscriptions on coins the Scythians left behind no written sources, so we must rely on Herodotus to reconstruct their religious beliefs.[303] He lists the following eight deities:

- **Tabiti** (Greek Hestia). Herodotus presents the deity of the hearth Tabiti as the highest deity, whom King Idanthyrsos called 'Queen of the Scythians'. Presumably Tabiti symbolised not so much the domestic hearth as the sacred element of fire, which also played a prominent role in the burial rituals of the Scythians.
- **Papaios** (Zeus) and **Api** (Gaïa). After Tabiti followed the primordial parents of all life, the sky god Papaios and the earth and water goddess Api. Papaios and Api were also the primal ancestors of the Scolotoi, since Targitaos was Papaios's son, and the daughter of the river god Borysthenes is to be understood as an aspect of Api.[304] Related to her is the snake woman, who had a human upper body and snake-like legs and was impregnated by Hercules. In some depictions the snake-like legs become plant motifs, turning her into a tendril-limbed semi-human female related to the tree of life. Plants and snakes have a few similarities, as they both live under as well as above the ground and both renew themselves annually, so they symbolise cyclical polarities of death and rebirth. The motif of the snake- and tendril-limbed woman presumably had its origin among the early northern Pontic Scythians and spread quickly both among the Celts and in the Greco–Roman Mediterranean region.[305]
- **Goitosyros** (Apollo). Goitosyros was presumably associated with Mithra; he served as sun god and divine archer, soothsayer and guardian of the herds.
- **Argimpasa** (Aphrodite). Like Goitosyros, Argimpasa had Oriental features and is comparable to both the fertility and war goddess Ishtar and the 'mistress of animals', as she is depicted on the mirror of Kelermes. It is conceivable that the Scythians became familiar with this goddess during their Near Eastern campaigns, even if the idea of a mistress of animals was already known in eastern Central Asia.[306]

Woman's headdress from kurgan 8 of Piat' Brat'ev, Don River delta, southern Russia, second half of the fourth century BC. On the tiny clothing discs the female face may represent for Greeks Demeter or her daughter Persephone, for Scythians Tabiti or Api. Regional museum of Rostov.

- **Thagimasadas** (Poseidon). Only the Royal Scythians worshipped this god, presumably as the personification of the life-giving rivers of Scythia and as the guardian of horses.
- **Hercules.** This god, whose Scythian name is not given by Herodotus, also served the Scythians as primordial ancestor, since he had fathered with the snake woman who lived in the forest steppes Scythes, the mythical ancestor of the Scythian kings, and two other tribal forefathers named by Herodotus as Agathyrsos and Gelonos.[307]
- **Ares.** The Scythians must have had a special devotion to the war god, to whom Herodotus devoted more space than all other Scythian deities combined. He was the only god with a shrine

dedicated to him alone in every district, in which an upright iron sword symbolised his presence. He was also the only god who had people as well as animals killed in his honour – every hundredth prisoner of war was sacrificed to Ares. Archaeological discoveries in kurgan 5 of Uljap and in Bajkara have confirmed Herodotus's account.[308] While Herodotus clearly identifies Ares as the god of war, the role of Hercules, apart from his function as ancestor, is unclear. For an explanation Lebedynsky draws on the Indo–Iranian pantheon, in which male, militaristic contents are assigned to two gods: Verethraghna, or Indra, was a god of thunder and embodied victory in war, so Ares would be comparable to him. Vayu, by contrast, symbolised immense strength, which Hercules could represent.[309]

Although the Scythians had no permanent temples with images of their gods and goddesses, they portrayed their deities in toreutics on gold sewn-on discs and vessels. Perhaps occasional depictions of animals symbolised deities in a coded way, so that we can no longer recognise them. Despite considerable speculations to the contrary, there is no evidence of shamanism or nature religion among the Scythians. Neither the Scythians of Tuva or the Saka nor the Scythians of Eastern Europe seem to have been familiar with the role of a shaman, who would move into invisible worlds and spheres inhabited by spirits to resolve a conflict between humans and powerful spirits or to ensure a successful hunt. The Scythians were equally unfamiliar with an organised clergy intermediating between humans and gods, as rituals and sacrifices were performed

Bronze pole top with the highest god of the Scythians, Papaios, crowned by a bird of prey, in the centre and four more raptors on the ends of the branches arranged in the shape of a cross. Chance discovery at Lysaja gora, Dnepropetrovsk, central Ukraine, fifth–fourth centuries BC. National Museum of the History of the Ukraine, Kiev.

by the leaders of the time.[310] As a 'religious' profession the Scythians had only soothsayers, who, if one believes Herodotus, led dangerous lives. If they were incorrect in their attempt to diagnose an ill king, both they and their sons were executed.[311]

The Scythians also seem to have been remorseless when it comes to enforcing religious conformity. Herodotus told of two prominent Scythians of royal blood who suffered the death penalty on account of dissenting beliefs. One was the legendary philosopher Anacharsis, who ostensibly lived in Athens in the second half of the sixth century and was numbered among the 'Seven Sages' there. When he was seen rendering homage to Cybele on his return to Scythia, his brother, King Saulius, killed him with an arrow shot.[312] The second Scythian chief who died as a consequence of worshipping Greek gods was the mid-fifth-century BC king Scylas. He repudiated his royal duties in three ways, as he sacrificed to Greek gods, participated in the Dionysian mysteries and preferred a settled life in the city to a nomadic one on the steppe. The military court deposed him and appointed his half-brother Octamasadas as his successor, after which the latter executed Scylas.[313] Perhaps the Scythian warrior elite feared that the comforts of urban life might weaken their king and make him unfit for military command. By taking up such a lifestyle, Scylas forfeited his authority.

As described by Herodotus (IV, 70), the Scythians swore blood brotherhood with the shared drinking of a mixture of their own blood and wine. Gold plaque from Kul Oba Kurgan, Crimea, Ukraine, *ca.* 350 BC. The State Hermitage Museum, St. Petersburg.

2.3.2 War and burial customs

It is not surprising that a people as militaristic as the Scythians had special war rituals. In order to strengthen cohesion, pairs of warriors would swear blood brotherhood. They mixed their blood with wine in a cup, dipped their weapons in it and drank it in the presence of witnesses.[314] On the battlefield young warriors also drank the blood of the first enemy killed, in order to incorporate his strength. Since a warrior's share of the spoils was determined by the number of heads of decapitated enemies, they collected these and brought them to their king or chieftain. The collecting of heads on the battlefield brought not only spoils but also honour, since the district rulers gathered all the warriors annually and each warrior who had killed at least one enemy was honoured with a cup of wine. The unsuccessful, however, 'have to sit by themselves in disgrace'.[315] The Scythians further 'made use' of fallen enemies by making drinking vessels out of their skulls and clothing out of their tanned scalps or tying the scalps on the reins of their horses.

As reported by Herodotus and largely confirmed by archaeology, the burial of kings followed a precisely defined, multi-step ritual which lasted more than a year.[316] This ensured that the

Two Scythians fight back to back, presumably a symbol for a blood brotherhood. Gold clothing plaque from Kul Oba Kurgan, Crimea, Ukraine, *ca.* 350 BC. The State Hermitage Museum, St. Petersburg.

king's attendants were able to bid farewell to their ruler and that he was ensured a secure transition into the afterlife. At the same time the ritual legitimised the chosen successor. First the deceased was mummified, placed on a wagon and led in solemn procession through the districts of his realm for 40 days. During these 40 days his soul remained by his corpse and his attendants hosted banquets, mourned him and mutilated their heads and hands as signs of grief. On the fortieth day the funeral procession returned to the royal necropolis, after which the corpse was laid in the prepared grave, together with selected companions. These strangled people were 'a concubine, his butler, his cook, his groom, his steward and his chamberlain' [messenger], as well as horses and cattle.[317] To complete the royal household, gold and bronze vessels, weapons and wine amphorae were also placed with the dead. The kurgan was then erected over the grave. The dead were not cremated but rather buried as corpses, with the tent-like wooden structure over the grave sometimes set on fire before the final burial.

Members of the warrior elite enjoyed similar burials, although on a more modest scale and usually without human sacrifice. With regard to grave goods, horses were included in normal burials of deceased chieftains and mounted warriors, and wagons in the case of aristocratic women. It appears that in the Scythian imagination 'warriors rode horses into the afterlife, and women rode there on a wagon'.[318] This gender-specific distinction occurred practically independently of the function of the buried women, since in the more than one hundred excavated graves of female warriors in Scythia weapons are in fact only found in a single case, from the seventh/sixth century BC, where there was a horse buried as well.[319]

Sketch of a kurgan with an anthropomorphic stone statue standing on its top, near the village of Pervomaievka, eastern Ukraine. Sketch after Kornjienko.

While the early northern Pontic graves were quite simple, beginning in the sixth century BC the so-called catacomb graves represented complex arrangements, which differed from the much earlier catacomb graves of the Bronze Age. In the Scythian kurgans a steep shaft ran 10 to 15 m into the ground, from which corridors up to 30 m long led to various grave chambers containing the bodies of the 'grave inhabitant', his attendants and sacrificed horses. Although the subterranean chamber system of the catacomb graves was complex many kurgans were plundered as early as the Scythian and subsequent Sarmatian periods. Sometimes the tunnels collapsed on the grave robbers and archaeologists found their skeletons two millennia later.[320] Among the grave chambers, the enormous Oguz royal kurgan (second half of the fourth century BC), originally 21 m high, in the northern Pontic region, is an exception, since there was no wooden structure over the grave but rather the floor, walls and a corbelled vault consisted of worked limestone plates layered over one another. Such stone chambers are otherwise known only from the Bosporan Kingdom, where they developed under Greek influence.[321]

The kurgan was topped by an anthropomorphic stone statue of an armed and armoured Scythian warrior. More than 100 such stone warriors, produced between the seventh and fourth centuries BC, have been found. They carry a long sword on the right side and an akinakes on the front. On the left thigh hangs a gorytos with a bow and arrows.[322] The stone men, in some cases more than 2 m tall, were often interpreted as ancestors, yet the hand putting a drinking horn to the mouth strongly recalls the scene on the felt hanging of Pazyryk and the gold discs on which a standing or mounted warrior receives a rython from a seated deity, so the figure more likely symbolises the acceptance of the deceased into the pantheon of heroes. The custom of placing a Scythian stone warrior on the dome of the kurgan was later continued by the Crimean Scythians, the Sarmatians and the Old Turks. The Turkic Polovtsy, by contrast, who dominated the northern Pontic steppes from the eleventh to the thirteenth centuries AD, erected both male and female stone statues.

After a year the soul of the deceased had reached the afterlife and the final sacrificial ritual took place. Fifty young men were

The ruins of Pantikapaion, the ancient capital of the Bosporan Kingdom in the foreground; in the background the modern city of Kerch, eastern Crimea.

Olbia and the Bosporan Kingdom

The Bosporan Kingdom and the port city of Olbia were neighbours and the most important trading partners of the Scythians. While the city-state of Olbia, founded by the Ionian city of Miletus and located at the mouth of the Bug, emphasised its Greek identity and tried to keep its autonomy, around 480 BC several Greek cities that lay on both sides of the Strait of Kerch in the east of the Crimean peninsula and in the west on the opposite peninsula of Taman, began to unite to form a centrally governed defence alliance, from which the Bosporan Kingdom emerged. Presumably the withdrawal of the Scythians from the Kuban facilitated the establishment of Ionian cities in the second half of the sixth century BC on the bordering Taman peninsula. The Strait of Kerch, which at the time was called the Cimmerian Bosporus, was strategically important, since it controlled the trade routes to the north through the Sea of Azov. As Herodotus reported, in the winter Scythian bands from south-eastern Crimea sometimes advanced over the frozen Strait of Kerch against the Sindi in south-western Kuban.[323]

The cities on the Strait of Kerch that had been founded by Ionian Greeks in the sixth century BC at the latest came under pressure from the Scythians after their victory over Darius in 513/12 BC. The strengthened nomadic horsemen, who benefited from the influx of new immigrants from Central Asia, undertook raids not only against the likewise expansive Thracian empire of the Odrysians but also against the Greek colonies. Scythian tribes had already gained a foothold in the north-eastern Crimea as early as the seventh and sixth centuries BC, however, as can be seen in the corresponding burials.[324] While the Scythians spread into the steppes of the Crimea, in the foothills farther south and in the mountains lived native herdsmen, the Tauri. These people were feared by the Greeks because, as Herodotus relates, 'It is the custom of the Tauri to sacrifice to the Maiden Goddess all shipwrecked sailors and such Greeks as they happen to capture upon their coast.'[325]

Around 480 BC three new alliances were formed. The Greek cities of the Cimmerian Bosporus formed a symmachy, a defensive alliance, analogous to the Delian League, from which the Bosporan Kingdom developed. The Scythian king Ariapeithes (r. *ca.* 490–460 BC) then made peace with the Odrysian king Teres, who gave him one of his daughters as a wife.[326] The marriage produced the future Scythian king Octamasadas. For its part, shortly after 480 BC Olbia placed itself under the protection of the Royal Scythians. This protected

The prytaneion of *Pantikapaion* in the lower Acropolis. The ancient seat of the city's government was abandoned and destroyed in the late fifth century BC. when a new ruler took power and concentrated all executive powers in the royal palace on the upper acropolis (Vladimir Tolstikov, *Pantikapaion*, 2002, p. 52).

status continued into the time of King Scylas (r. 460–440 BC), since Olbia was the favoured place of residence for this Scythian king.

At the time of Herodotus's visit around 460 BC, three different lifestyles coexisted in the city-state of Olbia: the urban and maritime culture of a classical Greek polis, the agrarian culture of native tribes and a steppe culture of nomadic horsemen. A century later in 331 BC the Scythians destroyed the Macedonian army of Alexander's governor of Thrace, Zopyrion, when he besieged the city of Olbia. Shortly thereafter Olbia slipped from the dominion of the flagging Scythians, whereupon their hinterland was battered by successive raids. In its distress Olbia turned in the third quarter of the second century BC to the king of Lesser Scythia, Skiluros, who ruled over the western part of the Crimean peninsula. Olbia became a vassal of Skiluros, as can be seen in the coins he had minted in Olbia. After a short period of prosperity under Mithridates VI of Pontus (r. 116/13–63 BC), Olbia was plundered by the king of the Getae, Burebista, around 55 BC and a century later came under the rule of the Sarmatians. In the third century AD first the Sarmatians (232–35 AD) and finally the Goths (269–70) destroyed the port city for good.[327] Notable in Olbia's history is the fact that Scythians, who were a superior power for a long time, never attacked and destroyed

Bosporan tombstone with two mounted archers. The Greek epigram declares: 'Isiôn, son of Papios, farewell!' Regional Museum, Simferopol.

Olbia but rather left it as a Greek island inside their empire. The warrior horsemen understood that it was more rewarding to extract tribute from a wealthy city than to plunder and destroy it.

The Bosporan cities initially placed themselves under the leadership of the Milesian noble line of the Archaeanactidae. Four decades later the Scythians, the Thracians and the Bosporan Kingdom moved closer together when dynasties friendly to Thrace seized power among the Royal Scythians as well as in the Bosporan capital of Pantikapaion, the modern city of Kerch. In 438 BC the dynasty of the Spartocids, who were of Thracian descent, superseded the Archaeanactidae in Pantikapaion and among the Royal Scythians Octamasadas, who was related to the Thracian king Sitalces, supplanted as king the philhellenic Scylas around 440 BC. It was surely no coincidence that rulers friendly to Thrace came to power among the Scythians and in the Bosporan Kingdom practically simultaneously. The Scythian dynasty was from then on related by marriage to the Thracian dynasty, and the Istros River, the Danube, formed their common border.[328]

That the Scythians had good relations with the Bosporan Kingdom at least for a time can be seen in the dozens of kurgans on the edges of its capital Pantikapaion. These include the kurgans of Altyn Oba, whose name means 'golden hill', those at Kul Oba, the large group at Juz Oba, the Zarskij Kurgan and the Melek Chesmen Kurgan in the centre of modern Kerch, all of them dating from the fourth or early third century BC. Under the large earthen tumulus of Kul Oba kurgan lay the central grave with the burials of a man and a woman with rich gold grave goods, as well as a sacrificed stable boy and a horse. The woman rested in a wooden sarcophagus whose inner sides were decorated with paintings showing, among other things, a winged Nike driving a quadriga and a lioness attacking a bull.[329] As at the Oguz kurgan, a dromos led to the grave chamber which consisted of dressed stone blocks, held together by fasteners made of lead, over which stood a corbelled vault. While the structure shows some features of Thracian grave architecture, the grave goods correspond to a Hellenised Scythian style. The buried man was probably a Hellenised Scythian chief who was associated with the Bosporan court.[330]

Towards the end of the third century BC a change in the trading patterns of Greece toward Asia Minor and Egypt sent the Bosporan Kingdom into an economic crisis. At the same time the weakened Scythians surrendered their homeland between the Dnieper and the Don to the Sarmatians more or less without a fight and partly retreated to western Crimea. Why the Scythians collapsed militarily in the third century BC remains unclear. Perhaps the dominance

The kurgan of Kul Oba west of Pantikapaion dated *ca.* 350 BC. Soldiers had found the burial vault by chance in 1830 when searching for large stones for construction purposes. It was one of the first large Scythian barrows to be officially excavated in modern times, but was plundered during the excavations when the armed guards were bribed to leave the site during night. Some of the stolen pieces were later bought back by the Russian government on the local antiques market (Paul Du Brux, *Rackopi kurgana Kul-Oba*, 1830, p. 167).

of the Royal Scythians broke down after the death of King Agaros around 300 BC, but such a fall would not explain the lack of resistance to the Sarmatians by the remaining Scythian groups. Perhaps the centuries-long relationship with the Greek cities and their material seductions had made the warrior horsemen soft.

In Crimea, King Skiluros (r. *ca.* 135–114/13 BC) initiated aggressive raids against Tauric Chersonesos and the Bosporan cities while entering an alliance with the Sarmatian Roxolani. Chersonesos, located near modern Sevastopol in the south-west of the peninsula, was founded by Doric Greeks in the fifth century BC and was a booming trading centre till the encroachments by the Scythians of Neapolis Scythica. The eastern part of the Bosporan Kingdom was also under threat, as the Sarmatian Siraces had formed a military alliance with the Maeotae.[331] Chersonesos then sought an alliance with the Bosporan Kingdom and its last Spartocid king, Pairisades V (r. *ca.* 140–109 BC), requested finally help from the Pontic king Mithridates VI. Mithridates's general, Diophantos, defeated the king of Lesser Scythia, Palakos (r. 113–*ca.* 111/110), and his allies, the Sarmatian Roxolani, in several battles.[332] The Bosporan Scythian Saumakos (r. 108–107 BC) then killed Pairisades V and seized power in the Bosporan Kingdom, but Diophantos quickly ended his rule.[333] The Pontic protectorate did not return the Bosporan cities to prosperity, however; quite the opposite, as Mithridates's wars against Rome had given rise to crushing taxes. When Mithridates fled Crimea in the face of Pompey in 63 BC the Bosporan cities rose up, and with them Mithridates's son Pharnaces. Mithridates, besieged in Pantikapaion, was driven to suicide. The new king, Pharnaces II (r. 63–47 BC), believed he could take advantage of the Roman civil war between Pompey and Caesar and attack Asia Minor, but Caesar completely defeated him and his Sarmatian cavalry in 47 BC at Zela, a victory recalled in the famous words, 'Veni, vidi, vici'.[334]

Shortly after the start of the Christian era, King Aspurgos (r. 14–38 AD) founded the Sarmatian dynasty of Bosporan rulers, who remained in power until the mid-fourth century. With this, two erstwhile nomadic riding peoples divided power in Crimea: in the west, called 'Lesser Scythia', the Scythians ruled, and in the east, their arch-enemies, in the form of a Sarmatian dynasty. The stability of the Bosporan Kingdom depended on Rome's military support, however, so it resembled a Roman protectorate. When the newly strengthened Crimean Scythians besieged Chersonesos, Emperor Nero sent Roman troops in 63 AD, who fought off the Scythian attackers. Now Roman garrisons were stationed in Crimea and a Roman fleet patrolled the Black Sea. Thanks to Roman backing, the power struggle between the Bosporans and the Crimean Scythians was decided in favour of the former under their kings Sauromates I (r. 93/4–123/4), Cotys II (r. 123/4–132/33), Sauromates II (r. 173/4–210/1) and Rhescuporis III (r. 210/1–226/7). The end of the Bosporan cities coincided with the start of the 'barbarian migration', when Goths and Alans after 240 and Huns around 375, left the cities, with the exception of Chersonesos, in ruins.[335]

▲ Gold torque with coloured gold incrustations and two Scythian rider protomes. Kul Oba Kurgan, Crimea, Ukraine, *ca.* 350 BC. The State Hermitage Museum, St. Petersburg.

▶ Marble plaque of the Roman legate of Tanais called Tryphon as a Sarmatian armoured rider with long scale armour, cone-shaped helmet and lance. Tanais on the Don, Rostow region, southern Russia, second half of the second century AD. The State Hermitage Museum, St. Petersburg.

◀ One of the two entrance gates in the western façade of a basilica founded in the sixth century and rebuilt in the tenth/eleventh century AD at Tauric Chersonesos, south-western Crimea.

strangled and seated on 50 killed and stuffed horses, which were impaled on lances in a circle around the kurgan. They formed a gruesome vigil at the final resting place of the dead king. That the kurgan with all its grave goods represented a symbolic replica of the familiar world of the king can also be seen in the construction of the mound. Unlike Bronze Age mounds it was not made of the material dug out of the grave or earth from nearby but rather out of sod from special, black earth that was sometimes brought from a great distance. The earthen tumulus represented a heavenly pasture for the sacrificed horses and the cattle of the deceased, so that the king symbolically took his grazing lands into the afterlife with him.[336] A Scythian kurgan for kings and warriors represented a ritually planned cosmic world of the dead; the kurgan and the bodyguard protected the dead from the world of the living and, conversely, it from him.

The gold comb of Solocha, lower Dnieper region, southern Ukraine, *ca.* 390 BC. A scene of battle among three Scythian warriors is depicted. The rider is presumably the Scythian king Octamasadas; his opponent, fighting on foot after having been thrown, his philhellenic half-brother and predecessor Scylas; and the warrior following the rider on foot, Octamasadas's loyal half-brother Orikos. The State Hermitage Museum, St. Petersburg.

2.3.3 Chronology of the Scythian kings

Since the Scythians produced no chronicles, a reconstruction of their regime depends on foreign sources and interpretations of archaeological finds. Despite this limitation, three royal dynasties can be determined: the first was based in the Kuban at the time of the campaigns in the Near East; the second ruled over classical Scythia; and the third retreated to Crimea.[337]

I. **The dynasty in Kuban** (*ca.* 700–550 BC). The first Scythian king known by name was **Ishpaka** (Išpakaia), who was defeated by the Assyrian Asarhaddon shortly after 680 BC. Ishpaka's successor **Bartatua** changed sides and established a pro-Assyrian policy, which bore fruit in the Scytho–Assyrian victory over the Medes in 673 BC. Bartatua was succeeded by his son **Madyas**, who may have been a nephew of Assurbanipal on his mother's side. In any case, in 644 BC he defeated the Medes when they besieged the Assyrian capital of Nineveh. This victory gave the Scythians a free hand to demand tribute from various peoples of the Near East. Around 616 BC the Median king Cyaxares II had the Scythian leaders murdered. The veterans returning to their homeland had to establish their dominance in Kuban through armed warfare against the clans that had stayed behind.

II. **The dynasty between the Don and the Dnieper** (*ca.* 550–third century BC). The first Scythian king of the northern Pontic steppe mentioned by Herodotus was **Spargapeithes**, who was succeeded by his son **Lykos**, followed in turn by his own son **Gnuros**.[338] Regarding Gnuros's son and successor, King **Saulius**, Herodotus reported that he killed his brother, who was numbered among the 'seven sages' of Greece, when the latter paid homage to Greek gods after his return from Athens. All these kings ruled before 513/12 BC, when the Scythians were faced with the invasion of the Achaemenid king Darius I. The then Scythian king and commander of the Scythian tribes **Idanthyrsos** and his viceroys **Skopasis** and **Taxakis** succeeded in forcing the attackers into retreat by means of clever guerrilla tactics. A Scythian delegation tried in vain to form a military alliance with the king of Sparta, Cleomenes, against the Achaemenids.[339] When exactly King **Ariantas** ruled and whether he was a king or a viceroy is unknown. In any case, Herodotus refers to his census, for which he ordered that every Scythian had to personally deposit an arrowhead in a particular location.[340] **Ariapeithes** (r. *ca.* 490–460 BC), who concluded a peace treaty with the Thracian king Teres around 480 BC and took a daughter of Teres as his wife, ruled at the start of the fifth century BC. The marriage produced the future Scythian

The reconstructed mausoleum of the Scythian king Skiluros at Neapolis Scythica was originally built *ca.* 120 BC.

king Octamasadas. The Thracians and their culture developed as a blend of two different peoples and cultures, when in the mid-fourth century BC nomadic stockbreeders of Indo-European origin moved from the northern Pontic steppe into the agrarian region on the west coast of the Black Sea. Their descendants created a settled culture of aristocratic warrior horsemen and charioteers.[341]

Ariapeithes had at least two additional wives, the Scythian Opoia, who gave birth to Orikos, and a Greek from the Greek colony of Istria in the Danube delta, whose son was Scylas.[342] Ariapeithes's successor was **Scylas** (r. *ca.* 460–440 BC), who pursued a philhellenic policy and neglected his duties as king of a riding people. He was deposed and replaced by his half-brother **Octamasadas** (r. *ca.* 440–390 BC). When Scylas fled to the Thracian king Sitalces (r. 445–424 BC), whose brother had sought refuge with Octamasadas, the Scythian king marched to Thrace and met Sitalces at the Danube. There Sitalces had the following message delivered to Octamasadas: 'Give me back my brother, and I will do the same with Scylas; then neither of us need risk his army in an engagement.'[343] They exchanged the disliked brothers and Octamasadas promptly beheaded his half-brother. This rapprochement between Scythians and Thracians, as well as the coming to power of the Thracian Spartocids in the Bosporan Kingdom, led to a political stabilisation among these three regional powers and led to a period of economic prosperity.

The epic tragedy of Scylas also appeared in art, as can be seen in a gold comb from an intact side chamber of the kurgan of Solocha on the eastern bank of the Dnieper. The comb was discovered by the archaeologist Vesselovski in 1913.[344] It depicts three warriors fighting: one rider raises his lance against an enemy fighting on foot, whose mortally wounded horse lies on the ground. The warrior on foot wears a Thracian ridge helmet and holds an akinakes in his right hand and a half-moon-shaped shield in his left. The rider wears Scythian trousers, a breastplate and a Corinthian helmet; he is protected by a Scythian back shield. The rider is supported by an unarmoured second combatant on foot with an akinakes and shield. It is conceivable that the middle rider and the fighter following him on foot, who have both lost their bows, represent Octamasadas and Orikos, and the unseated rider the defeated Scylas.[345] In light of the fine grave goods in the side burial in the 19-m-high Solocha kurgan, it is undoubtedly a royal burial, as was the unfortunately plundered central grave chamber.[346] Today it is presumed that in the central chamber the loyal half-brother of Octamasadas, Orikos, who died around 410 BC, found his final resting place, and in the undisturbed side chamber lay Octamasadas, who died around 390 BC and next to whose head lay the golden comb.[347]

The presumed successor of Octamasadas was King **Atheas** (r. *ca.* 390–339 BC).[348] Atheas, whose capital may have been Kamenskoje gorodišče, oriented himself towards the south in a time of increasing pressure from the Sarmatians on the eastern flank of Scythia. It is unclear in this regard whether the Sarmatian threat moved him to expand Scythian holdings on the Danube or whether neglect of the eastern border first enabled the Sarmatian invasion. The king tried to provide modern structures for Scythia, as he minted coins bearing images of Hercules and Artemis on the obverse and himself on horseback on the reverse.[349] Atheas's advance to the south-west forced him into conflict with the powerful king of Macedonia, Philip II (r. 359–336 BC). Although the two kings invaded Thrace together in 346 BC, when Atheas later refused to appoint Philip as his successor as he had promised, Philip attacked the Scythian army stationed south of the Danube in 339 BC. The Macedonian won a surprising victory and the 90-year-old Atheas fell in the battle.[350] Atheas's unnamed successor (**'Anonymous I'**) succeeded, however, in completely defeating the Macedonian army led by Zopyrion, Alexander's governor, before Olbia, after which he sent a first delegation to Alexander in Bactria. He died soon thereafter, in 328 BC, and may have had his final resting place in the Oguz kurgan.[351] His brother, another anonymous Scythian ruler (**'Anonymous II'**), apparently ruled only briefly, followed by **'Anonymous III'**[352] or King **Agaros** (d. *ca.* 300 BC). The latter suffered a serious defeat in 313 BC by the Macedonian warlord of Thrace, Lysimachus. Agaros then intervened in the fratricidal Bosporan war of 310/09 BC, when he provided Scythian troops to Satyros in the battle against the latter's younger brother Eumelos. Satyros won the battle but died from a wound.[353]

Stone relief found in 1830 at Neapolis Scythica with the presumed representation of the Scythian kings Skiluros (left) and Palakos (right). The original was lost in the 1890s, and only a gypsum copy remains.

III. **The late Scythian dynasty of Crimea** (*ca.* 170 BC–third century AD). The classical age of Scythia ended with Agaros. Beset in the east by the Sarmatians and in the west by the Thracians and the Galatians, Scythian territory shrank to the western part of Crimea and the Isthmus of Perekop in the north.[354] Those Scythians who were not absorbed by the Sarmatians retreated to Crimea, where they came into conflict with Chersonesos, which had expanded its territory into the north-west of the peninsula toward the end of the fourth century BC.[355] The Crimean Scythians represented a multicultural mixture and they had cities reinforced with strong walls, such as Neapolis Scythica, Chabeion and Palacium, practised farming and raised cattle. The Crimean Scythians no longer sought protection in the wide open steppes, like nomadic horsemen, but rather behind walls, as settled peoples. Their culture was shaped by a consistently increasing Hellenisation. Adaptation to new conditions could also be seen in royal burials. While horses and, in a few cases, servants were sacrificed as before, and stone stelae were put up, the mounding up of earth, which required much space, was now largely given up. The hybrid culture of Scythia Minor represented less the final stage of classic Scythian culture than an amalgamation of Scythian, Thracian and Greek elements.

The first known King of the Late Crimean Scythians was **Argotos**, son of Idanthemidos. He rose to power in the second quarter of the second century BC after having entered a matrimonial alliance with the Bosporan Kingdom by marrying Kamasarye, the widow of King Pairisades III (d. *ca.* 170 BC) and mother of Pairisades IV (r. *ca.* 170–150 BC). Argotos established his residence at Neapolis Scythica in south-western Crimea, close to the modern city of Simferopol. After Argotos, King **Skiluros** (r. *ca.* 135–114/13), who may have been of Sarmatian stock, initiated an aggressive policy. He obliged Olbia to pay tribute, conquered the western Crimean ports of Kerkinitis and Kalos Limen, attacked the hinterland of Chersonesos and forged

Inside the basilica reconstructed in the tenth/eleventh century AD at Tauric Chersonesos. When the city was under threat from the Scythian king Skiluros in 114 BC it sought military assistance from the Bosporan and Pontic Kingdoms.

Gold pectoral, 30.6 cm in diameter, from the kurgan of Tolstaya Mogila, lower Dnieper region, southern Ukraine, around 350 BC. The three sections between the four twisted bands show: in the outer space, scenes of animal combat; in the centre, vegetable ornament; and in the inner space scenes of daily life. Ukrainian Museum of Historical Treasures, Kiev.

an alliance with the Sarmatian Roxolani against the Bosporan Kingdom. At the same time, Skiluros reconstructed Neapolis Scythica, which had been devastated by fire around 130 BC, probably in the wake of a Sarmatian attack. On the acropolis he built a heroon, a shrine in the shape of a Greek temple, in honour of his predecessor Argotos, a fortified palace and his own mausoleum which was later converted into a tower as part of the fortifications.[356] But both Chersonesos and the Bosporan Kingdom appealed to Mithridates VI of Pontus for help against Skiluros. Mithridates responded by sending an army under his general, Diophantos. Skiluros died before the onslaught in 114/13 and his son and successor **Palakos** (r. 113–111/110) was no match for the Pontic army. As Strabo reports,[357] he and his Roxolani allies suffered several crushing defeats by Diophantos who relieved Chersonesos, conquered Kerkinitis and Kalos Limen and utterly destroyed Neapolis Scythica.

By minting his own coins Skiluros had tried to give his unstable 'empire' more secure structures. It was also Skiluros who came up with the famous metaphor of an unbreakable sheaf of arrows or spears as a symbol of unity. As Plutarch reported, when Skiluros appointed Palakos as his designated successor, he called together his 80 sons or tribal leaders. He first asked them to break 80 arrows bundled together, a test they all failed. After this he effortlessly broke each arrow individually and told them that united, they would be invincible but individually they were easy to defeat.[358] Skiluros and possibly also Palakos were buried in the large mausoleum of Neapolis Scythica, where in 1946 72 other buried persons were found.[359] The final Scythian ruler known by name was **Saumakos**, who briefly took power in the Bosporan Kingdom in 108–107 BC, before Diophantos ousted him. After defeats against the Bosporan king Aspurgos (r. 10/11–37/8 AD), against the Roman legate Silvanus around 63 AD,[360] and against the Sarmatian kings of the Bosporan Kingdom, Lesser Scythia and the settled late Scythian culture vanished from history. It was previously believed that the Goths delivered Neapolis Scythica the final death blow in 255/56, but the archaeologist directing its excavation since 1999, Juri Zaytsev, attributes its final destruction to Alan groups in the year 218.[361]

2.3.4 Greek influences on Scythian toreutics and grave architecture

The intensive contact between Scythians, later Sarmatians, and Greeks shaped the art of the nomadic horsemen, especially their goldsmithing. As a result a dazzling kaleidoscope of cultural artefacts developed in the region around the Bosporan Kingdom, which brought together Greek–Ionic, Thracian and Scytho–Sarmatian cultural elements. Under Greek influence Scythian depictions of animals became more naturalistic, not least through their representation in semi-profile; in this way they lost some of the earlier distinctiveness of the animal style with its ability to emphasise significant characteristics of the animal portrayed.

Additionally, the animal figures were supplemented with anthropomorphic motifs, which had been largely absent from the early Scytho–Siberian animal style. The Greco–Scythian depictions of humans showed a markedly authentic and detailed reproduction of facial features, which set them apart from the more idealised and elevated Greek portrayals. In terms of content, griffins and winged horses increasingly appeared in Greco–Scythian toreutics, as did newly domestic animals such as cows and dogs as part of scenes of daily life. An outstanding example of these innovations is the gold pectoral of Tolstaya Mogila. Between the four twisted coils of the pectoral are, in the outer space, scenes of animals fighting; in the middle, vegetable ornamental patterns; and in the inner space, peaceful scenes of daily life, such as milking cows and sheep and making clothes. Among the anthropomorphic images Scythian deities such as Tabiti, Papaios, Hercules or snake women predominate; to these are added elements from Greek mythology like gorgons, sphinxes, maenads, hippocamps and satyrs. Depictions of

Gold gorytos plate from the Melitopol Kurgan, southern Ukraine, second half of the fourth century BC. The gorytos plate is one of four plates made from the same wooden mould. The two centre friezes show episodes from the life of the Greek hero Achilles; they begin to the left in the upper frieze: The young Achilles is taught how to shoot with a bow; Achilles, dressed as a woman among the daughters of Lykomedes, is exposed by Odysseus as he grabs a sword at the sound of the trumpet; Deidameia, daughter of Lykomedes, in tears; Achilles and Lykomedes. Lower frieze: Deidameia's mother and sisters bid farewell to Achilles; Achilles with Odysseus, Diomedes and Agamemnon at Troy; Achilles's mother Thetis with the urn of her son, who fell at Troy. Ukrainian Museum of Historical Treasures, Kiev.

The 37 m long, 2.8 m wide and 7.14 m high dromos made from worked limestone plates leading to the central vault of Zarskij Kurgan near Kerch, eastern Crimea, first half of the fourth century BC.

Illustration of the vault of the Zarskij Kurgan near Kerch looking outwards to the dromos; painted by Carlo Bossoli (1815–1884). Paul Du Brux, *Oeuvres* (2010) Vol. II, p. 289.

warriors were also very popular, whether in battle or in peaceful situations such as fraternising, conversing, tending to a wounded comrade or receiving dental treatment, as can be seen in the gold vase of Kul Oba.[362] The Scythians also occasionally adopted the common Greek depiction of naked or barely clothed warriors, as can be seen on the gold scabbard of Čertomlyk and the gold gorytos cover plates with scenes presumed to be from the life of Achilles, in particular his discovery by Odysseus on the island of Skyros.[363]

Both plates are striking not only because of the vitality of the depictions but also because of the fact they were made with identical moulds. The scabbard with a battle scene between Greeks and 'barbarians', perhaps Persians, was discovered in three versions, the gorytos cover plate in four, namely, in the royal kurgans of Ilintsy (south-west of Kiev), Čertomlyk (north-west of Kamenskoje gorodišče), Melitopol (south-west of Kamenskoje gorodišče) and in the eighth kurgan of Piat' Brat'ev ('Five Brothers,' near Rostow on the Don). These all date from 350–300 BC and were found far apart from one another. These four gorytoses were crafted in the same, presumably Greek, goldsmith shop, according to Scythian taste. A similar gorytos cover plate made of gold was found in the purported grave of Philip II of Macedonia near Vergina in northern Greece, and it is identical to the silver gorytos of Karagodeuashkh in the Kuban, preserved in fragmentary form.[364]

The question of why five different Scythian chiefs had virtually identical objects with a motif from Greek mythology placed in their graves remains unanswered. Were they diplomatic gifts of Bosporan kings or the ruler of Olbia to their powerful neighbours? Or did Scythian leaders identify with Achilles, whose final resting place was said to be on the island of Leuce near Olbia? As Arrian reported in his *Periplus Ponti Euxini*, a temple dedicated to Achilles stood on Leuce, so Olbia served as the last homeland of the greatest Greek hero.[365] In both cases the legend of the war hero Achilles was a shared link between Greeks and Scythians. Given that identical objects have been found in geographically distant but temporally comparable Scythian burials, the hypothesis of A. Shcheglov and V. Katz that the sheaths represent diplomatic gifts to various Scythian tribal chieftains seems plausible.[366]

Scythian grave architecture in Crimea also adopted Hellenistic influences, as had already been revealed in the Oguz kurgan on the Dnieper. At the kurgans from the fourth to third centuries BC within the chora of Pantikapaion a dromos made from smoothed limestone plates layered over one another led to a central crypt with a corbelled vault. Here the dead rested in a huge sarcophagus built of stone. Despite these innovations, the traditional grave goods of weapons and sacrificed horses were not abandoned and the earthen tumuli remained huge. The Zarskij Kurgan for example was 17 m high and had a diameter of 80 m. In a few graves of Neapolis Scythica the Scythians even adopted the Hellenistic and Thracian custom of decorating the walls with paintings. In the paintings, which have been poorly preserved if at all, hunting and sacrifice scenes predominate, as well as solemn depictions of mourners.[367]

A unique piece of Scytho–Greek cultural amalgamation was discovered in 1965 in the largest of the Kurgani Trëkh Bratev, the 'Three-Brothers-Kurgans', located west of Nymphaion which had been conquered by the Bosporan Kingdom in the late fifth century BC. In tomb 1 of kurgan 1 dating from *ca.* 300 BC a noble Scythian woman was buried, together with a sacrificed juvenile servant and a horse. Within the burial chamber made from limestone plates

Stone stele from the 'Three-Brothers-Kurgan' in eastern Crimea, *ca.* 300 BC. The stele, 286 cm high, 165 cm wide and weighing 1.4 tons, was erected in honour of a noble Scythian woman and shows the presumed consecration of a dead warrior as hero by a female deity, possibly Demeter. Lapidarium, Kerch.

Sarmatian armoured rider with a long lance held with two hands, called a kontos, and two armoured warriors on foot (left) in combat against a likewise armoured and an unarmoured rider (right); in the centre a fallen attacker lies on the ground. Mural on the southern side of the grave chamber of the 'Kurgan of 1872', Kerch, Crimea, Ukraine, first century AD. Watercolour by M.V. Farmakovskij from 1909.

Mural on the eastern wall of the grave chamber of Anthesterios, Kerch, Crimea, Ukraine, first century AD. The murals, discovered on private property in 1877 and then sketched, were intentionally destroyed by the owner of the property and the vault of the grave chamber was deliberately brought to collapse. An armoured rider is portrayed approaching a tent with a long lance leaning against it. At the left a gorytos hangs from a tree branch. Two figures sit in the tent and a woman is enthroned beside it while two children bid the rider welcome. Further to the right a second armoured rider holds a lance and a spare horse. The scene may symbolise the return home of a fallen warrior. Tinted drawing by F.I. Groß from 1877. Archive of the Museum of Kerch.

she rested on a stone bed, a *klinai*. She wore a kalathos, the typical high headgear of Scytho–Sarmatian aristocratic women, and was adorned with rich golden jewellery. She was given offerings of meat and a Pantikapaian coin as obolos for Charon. To the east of the vault, on the lower slope of the tumulus about 2 m above the antique ground level, stood a stone altar and a huge limestone stele. The stele is 286 cm high (including the plug), 165 cm wide and weighs 1.4 tons.[368] It depicts a woman wearing a short kalathos and standing on a quadriga under a funeral *naiskos*, a Greek votive shrine ending in a triangular pediment with an eagle spreading its wings in the centre. Parts of the naiskos show remains of red and yellow painting. A groom leads the four horses drawing the quadriga. From the right side a mounted warrior approaches and the woman hands him a vessel, now lost. Behind the rider stands a column with goryt suspended from it. This is a symbol of the transition from this world to the nether world. The scene is reminiscent of similar representations on small gold plaques and, especially, on the famous felt carpet from Pazyryk. It may represent a chthonic deity such as Demeter welcoming a deceased chief into the afterlife and consecrating him as hero. One may surmise that the buried noblewoman was a priestess and that the wooden wagon that was usually part of an aristocratic female Scythian burial in the Pontic area, but absent here, was represented by the quadriga.

Conversely, cultural elements from the nomadic riders also entered Bosporan art, especially during the time of the Sarmatians. In several graves of Hellenistic design on both sides of the Cimmerian Bosporus from the era around the birth of Christ not only are there grave goods from the world of the Scythians such as sacrificed horses and dogs, harnesses, light wagons and weapons but murals painted in a late Hellenistic style showing, beside classical

Greek scenes such as the abduction of Persephone by Hades, many motifs from the worlds of the nomadic horsemen. Among these are duels of Sarmatian mounted warriors armed with long lances, combat between cavalry units, and mounted archers. They also depict the return of dead armoured riders to their tent, with a lance leaning against its top and a gorytos with a bow hanging from a nearby branch.[369]

Scythian cultural influences spread further to the west in the seventh to the fourth centuries BC, whether though contact in the region on the lower Danube inhabited by Thracians or through immigration into the Danube–Tisza region in what is now Hungary. Here the elements of the Scythian triad – horse harnesses, weapons and animal-style objects – are found in many kurgans of the elite of the warrior horsemen. In view of the nearby rich sources of gold, it may be presumed that local goldsmiths produced the gold objects following examples of steppe art. With the invasion of the Celts this distant offshoot of the steppe art of the nomadic riders disappeared.[370]

2.4 Sarmatians, Alans and Amazons

> The Sarmatians do not live in cities; they do not even have fixed residences. They are a warlike tribe, free, unconquered and so cruel and barbaric that even the women take part in war just as the men.
>
> **Pomponius Mela**, first century AD[371]

The presumable forerunners of the largely Indo-European Sarmatians, who were not a unified ethnic group or even a federation but rather a loose group of Iranian-speaking tribes, were the Sauromatians referred to by Herodotus, who lived east of the Don; that is, east of Scythia. At the time of the Persian invasion of Darius I they were allies of the Scythians and placed themselves under the command of the Scythian viceroy Skopasis.[372] In the seventh–fourth centuries BC the Sauromatians and early Saka who lived between the Don and the Ustyurt Plateau of western

Chalk formation called 'Tchink' at twilight, near Bozzhira on the Ustyurt Plateau, Mangyshlak Peninsula, western Kazakhstan.

Kazakhstan formed the hinge between the Siberian Scythians and Saka on one side and the northern Pontic Scythians on the other. The militaristic character of the Sauromatians and their relation to the Scythians can be seen in the origin myth recounted by Herodotus. According to this myth, Greeks in Asia Minor defeated Amazons at the Thermodon River, 50 km east of the modern city of Samsun, taking many of them prisoner and carrying them off in ships. The Amazons broke free, however, and threw the Greeks into the sea, after which they landed on the northern coast of the Sea of Azov. There they stole horses and plundered the area. When the Scythians noticed that the armed invaders were women, they sent young men to seduce them. They joined together and occupied the steppe east of the Don. The women maintained their warrior lifestyle, however, and their masculine garb, and the Sauromatians emerged from their union with the Scythians.[373]

2.4.1 Sauromatians and early Sarmatians between the Volga and the Ustyurt Plateau

Like the Scythians, the Sauromatians and early Sarmatians had no written language, so we are dependent on Greek and Roman sources, as well as archaeological evidence. The group of early Sarmatians furthest to the east lived nomadically on the Mangyshlak Peninsula and the adjacent Ustyurt Plateau, where the landscape 2,500 years ago was less barren than today. At the time one of the trade routes that linked the Don and the Volga with Choresmia and Bactria ran through the corridor between the Caspian Sea and the Aral Sea. Presumably these early Sarmatians were related to Herodotus's Massagetae and the tribal federation of the Dahae. In the mid-third century BC the Parni, a member of the federation of the Dahae, moved south under the leadership of Arsaces and conquered Parthia, where they founded the dynasty of the Arsacids and later began the conquest of Iran.

Sarmatian stone statue with girded akinakes and a rider wearing a reproduction of Sarmatian equipment. Baite, Mangyshlak Peninsula, western Kazakhstan, fourth–third centuries BC.

The most visible traces of the early Sarmatians are over 100 large masculine stone statues. Some of these are life size, while others are up to 4 m tall. The stone figures stand in the steppe near a dozen circular stone shrines, either alone, paired or in groups of up to 32 statues. Presumably they represent honourable deceased people, who were venerated as ancestors and to whom sacrifices were brought. Two groups of statues may be distinguished. In the older type the figure is quite flat, the head is tilted slightly to the side and the bent arms frame the upper body; an akinakes hangs from the belt. The Kazakh archaeologists Samashev and Astafjev associate these stone warriors, which sometimes stood beside an altar of sacrifice within a kurgan-shaped stone shrine with a domed roof, as at Tubezik 2, with the Massagetae of the fifth–fourth centuries BC.[374] The stone men of the second type from the Sarmatian period, such as at Teren, Konaj, Kyzylujik and Baite, come from the fourth–third centuries BC and are strongly reminiscent of Scythian stone statues. They wear flat caps and have moustaches, and from their belts hang an akinakes in front, a double-edged, straight long sword on the right and a gorytos with a bow on the left.[375] A few of the stone statues are decorated with typical Sarmatian *tamgha*, the tribal sign or seal used by stockbreeders to brand cattle or lay claim to a pasture, spring or shrine.

The princely necropolis of Filippovka at the confluence of the Ilek and Ural rivers, about 150 km south-west of Orenburg, comes from the transition period between the Sauromatian and early Sarmatian cultural phases at the turn from the fifth to the fourth century BC.[376] Perhaps the representatives of the culture of Filippovka were also related to the mysterious Issedones of Herodotus.[377] The arrangements of the kurgans in the landscape was not coincidental; if one connects the 18 kurgans in the centre with a line, it forms the outline of a strung bow with an arrow aimed to the north. The largest kurgan 1 forms the notch at the end of the arrow and kurgan 17 its head.[378] The kurgans were family crypts, which were reopened as needed. Despite earlier grave robbing, archaeologists found spectacular gold objects in kurgan 1, including 26 deer-like hybrid creatures. The creatures, up to 52 cm tall, were made of sheets of gold covering a wooden core.[379] They consist of the body of a deer or a big cat and the head of a teeth-baring wolf and have large antlers with volute-like points that sometimes culminate in birds' heads. Spiral patterns form the transition from the body to the fore- and hind legs. In this way these fantastical, majestic hybrids unite the three most important animals of the Scythian Altai; namely, the deer, the predatory cat and the bird of prey, and they must have had a special symbolic significance. Even though these creatures recall similar hybrids from Pazyryk and Berel, they exude a uniqueness.

Deer-like hybrid animal with the body of a carnivore and a huge wolf's snout. Gold leaf applied over a wooden core. Filippovka, kurgan 1, eastern bank of the Ural River, central Russia, early fourth century BC. Archaeological Museum Ufa.

In burial 2 of kurgan 4 a fully armed warrior was found displaying the equipment of a heavily armed Early Sarmatian horseman. He wore iron scale armour and an iron helmet with nose and cheek protections. His offensive weapons consisted of a composite bow and a quiver filled with more than 200 arrows, an iron akinakes with a golden, butterfly-shaped crosspiece and a gilded handle decorated in the Animal Style featuring hunting and sacrifice scenes, an iron battleaxe and a 3.2 m long spear with a massive iron head.[380]

Gold leaf applied over a wooden core of a wild sheep. Filippovka, kurgan 1, eastern bank of the Ural River, central Russia, early fourth century BC. Archaeological Museum Ufa.

2.4.2 Sarmatians and Alans on the Black Sea and in the Roman Empire

The fourth century BC saw the final wave of migration of Iranian-speaking Indo-European tribes from the east to the west. The migration lasted half a millennium and carried a few of them as far as England and North Africa. The collective term 'Sarmatian' does not characterise a specific ethnicity but rather numerous tribes of nomadic horsemen who spoke the same language and had comparable lifestyles, weapons and handicrafts, which differentiated them from the Scythians. The triggers for this migration, which expanded the territory of the originally Central Asian nomadic riders as far as the Atlantic, were many. Among the 'push factors' were the Central Asian expedition of Alexander, the spread of the Xiongnu mounted warriors to the west, a drying of the climate of the northern Caspian region and perhaps demographic pressure. The most important 'pull factor' was the power vacuum among the Pontic Scythians following the death of King Agaros. This westward movement became discernable when Sarmatian tribes of the Prokhorovo Culture west of the Urals crossed the Don and infiltrated the regions of the Kuban and the northern Pontic steppe.[381] In the Kuban the Sarmatians coexisted with the native Maeotae; in the northern Pontic region they assimilated the majority of the Scythian tribes that did not flee to Crimea.

Over the course of the centuries scanty Greek, Bosporan and Roman sources recorded some two dozen names of Sarmatian tribes. A snapshot from the mid-second century BC reveals the following picture:[382] The Siraces occupied the Kuban from the fourth century BC until about 200 AD.[383] North of the Siraces, between the Don and the middle Ural, lived the Aorsi, who, according to Strabo, could mobilise more than 200,000 mounted warriors. Around the time of the birth of Christ they were partially assimilated by the Alans, who were related to them and were advancing out of the Syr Darya region. West of the Aorsi, between the Don and the Dnieper, lived the Roxolani, whose name means 'bright Aryans' or 'bright Alans', and north-west of them, on the right bank of the middle Dnieper, the Urgi. The Saii and the 'Royal Sarmatians', who may have had a level of sovereignty over all Sarmatian tribes west of the Dnieper, settled south of the Urgi.

The Iazyges lived south-west of the Royal Sarmatians, in the delta of the Bug, and thus on the border of Lesser Scythia. In the first century BC the Iazyges began advancing towards the south-west and reached the Hungarian plain between the Tisza and the Danube in the mid-first century AD.

The Kuban region was populated by a mixture of people consisting of Greek immigrants, Sarmatian Siraces and the various native tribes of Maeotae, who were mostly settled and practised farming. A few of the Maeotae tribes, such as the Ixomates, were notorious for their bellicosity.[384] The story told by the Greek rhetorician Polyainos (second century AD) about Queen Tirgatao

The grave, discovered in 1987, of a princess of the Sarmatian Aorsi killed by an arrow. Kobiakovo near Rostov, southern Russia, end of the first/beginning of the second century AD.

Gold torque of the princess of Kobiakovo near Rostov, southern Russia, end of the first/beginning of the second century AD. In the centre of the piece of jewellery, made in the polychrome animal style of the Sarmatians, a bearded man sits on a carpet with a chequerboard pattern; a sword rests on his thighs. On each side three anthropomorphic figures with monkey heads wrestle playfully with a winged dragon, which could indicate a Chinese influence. Regional museum of Rostov.

exemplifies their abilities in battle. After the Bosporan king Satyros I (r. 393/92–389/88 BC) had enabled the deposed king of the Sindi, another tribe of the Maeotae, called Hekataios, to return to the throne, he gave him one of his daughters as a wife. Satyros then ordered Hekataios to kill his first wife, Tirgatao. Tirgatao fled to her tribe, the Ixomates, and roused them to war. The Ixomates laid waste to the land of the Sindi and sacked the Bosporan city of Georgippia. Only when Satyros and Hekataios paid an enormous tribute did Tirgatao agree to make peace.[385]

Siraces: The Siraces interfered with the politics of the Bosporan Kingdom several times, first in 310/09 in the above-mentioned fratricidal war between the legitimate crown prince Satyros and the rebel Eumelos. Although Eumelos, who had the support of the king of the Siraces, lost the battle against his older brother and his Scythian allies, Satyros died soon thereafter and Eumelos assumed the throne.[386] This war showed that the Bosporan Kingdom threatened to devolve into a pawn of Scythian and Sarmatian interests. The Siraces were the most Hellenised of the Sarmatian tribes; many of them were settled and carried out intensive trade with the Bosporan cities and, via the Armenians, with Mesopotamia and India. In the later wars the Siraces were often on the losing side, first in 47 BC at the battle of Zela, where their king Abeakos and his ally King Spadinos of the Aorsi fell to Caesar. Around the time of the birth of Christ the Siraces had to move southward hard pressed by the more numerous Aorsi, so they fought another intra-Bosporan war against their northern neighbours in 40 AD. In the brutal war they supported the Bosporan Mithridates VIII, who opposed Rome, against the alliance with Rome and the king of the Aorsi Eunones formed by the challenger Cotys I. In 45 AD the army of Rome and the Aorsi won an overwhelming victory and the Siraces quickly became insignificant.[387]

Aorsi: The victory of Rome and the Aorsi in 45 AD secured the supremacy of the Aorsi. They lived in the broad delta of the Don and the northern forest steppe, where in the early third century BC they had driven out the Scythians and destroyed their fortified settlements.[388] The Aorsi were the largest Sarmatian tribe and constituted their own federation. Archaeological discoveries suggest that the Iranian-speaking Aorsi advanced in more than one wave from the territory of the Massagetae, between the Caspian Sea and the lower reaches of the Syr Darya, to the Don and thus spread their Central Asian culture, which included Chinese elements in the decoration of weapons, to Northern Europe. During the early seizures of land the Aorsi often buried their deceased leaders in existing Scythian kurgans,[389] but beginning in the mid-first century AD they built their own earthen tumuli over individual graves. The dead were placed diagonally in square grave chambers, whose corners were oriented to the four cardinal directions, with their heads pointing south. The Sarmatians, like the Scythians, worshipped the sword. Despite their clearly militaristic character, however, the Sarmations rejected human sacrifices at burials, and largely abandoned animal sacrifices as well.[390]

Among the most famous of the kurgans of the later Aorsi are those of Datchi south of Azov, Kobiakovo near Rostow and Khokhlach north of Azov, all of which were erected from the end of the first to the start of the second centuries AD. Aristocratic women were buried in the latter two. In Kobiakovo the grave is that of a princess killed by an arrow, and a Chinese mirror was placed within it.[391] The grave in Khokhlach is that of a noblewoman who may have had a religious role.[392] These and other elaborate burials of women of the Aorsi underscore the high status of women in Sarmatian society.

As Rostovtzeff was the first to point out in the 1920s, the polychrome animal style of the Sarmatians, particularly that of the Aorsi and the Alans, should be distinguished from the classical animal style of the Scythians.[393] The polychrome gold work continued the technique, begun with the gold figurines of Čilikty and further developed with the appliqués of Pazyryk, of emphasising certain body parts such as eyes, ears, hooves, paws, shoulders and pelvic muscles with colourful inlays of garnet, carnelian, coral, turquoise and coloured glass. Added to these were hump-shaped depictions of animals as additional decorative elements, of which the dagger sheath from Datchi 1 is a fine example, as is the decoration of the knob of long cavalry swords with jade inlays. Other swords had a disc-shaped knob made of quartz or chalcedony. These innovative knob decorations were

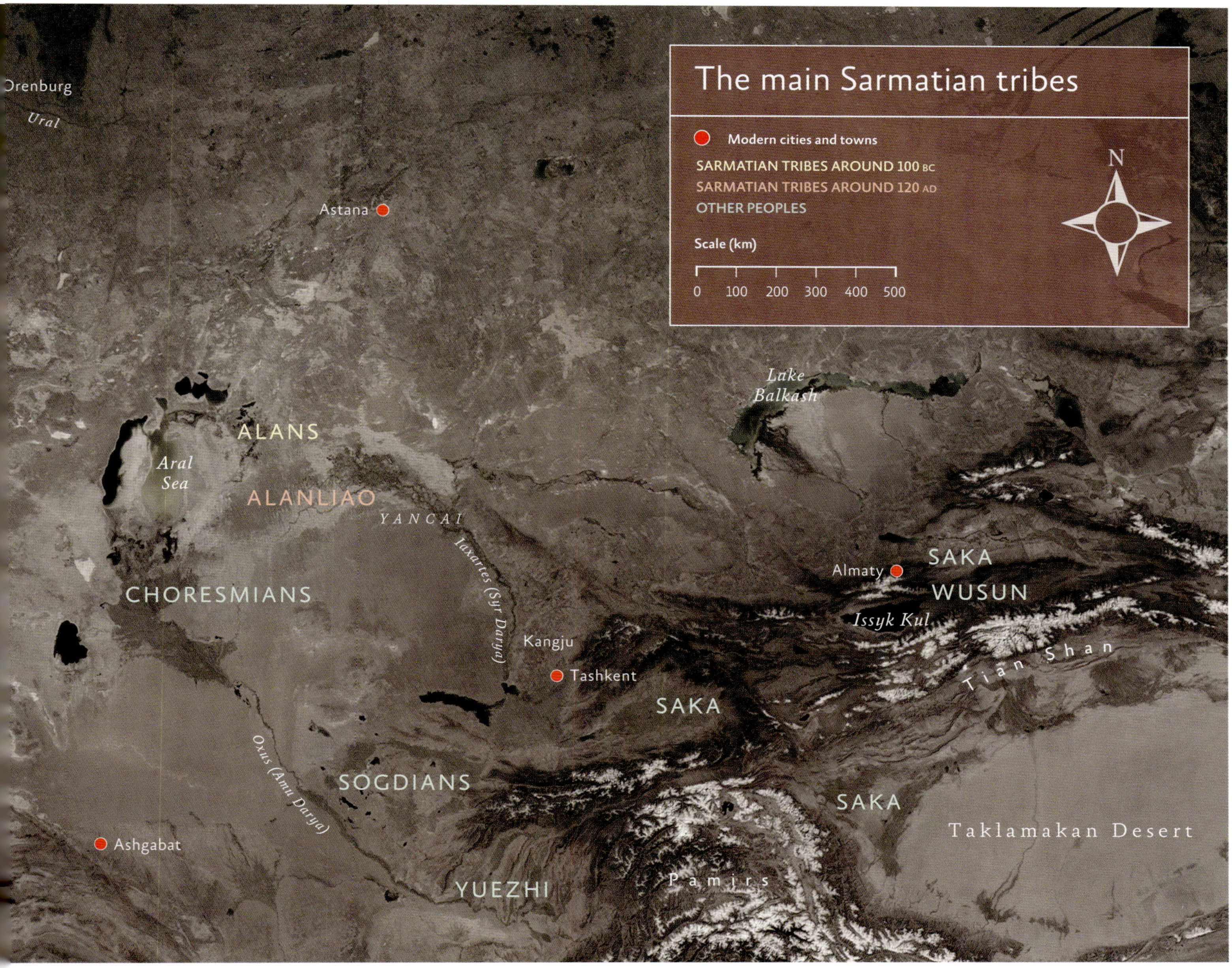

found more frequently among the Aorsi and Alans beginning in the second century AD and indicate influence from China.[394] The custom of intentionally deforming the skull by flattening the back and raising the forehead, seen at the same time among members of the upper class of the Aorsi, also had its origins in eastern Central Asia.[395]

Alans: The nomadic horsemen who immigrated in the first century AD were the Europid Alans. They assimilated the Aorsi settled on the Don and, drawn by new pastures and potential targets for pillaging, spread westwards together. The scenario is suggested not only by Ptolemy (*ca.* 100–175 AD), who wrote about Ἀλανορσοι, 'Alanorsoi', but also by Chinese sources. In the *Shiji* Sima Qian (*ca.* 145–*ca.* 87 BC) described the land of Yancai: 'Yancai lies some 2,000 li [832 km] north-west of Kangju [whose capital was near present Tashkent]. The people are nomads ... and the country has over 100,000 archer warriors, and borders on a great shoreless lake.'[396] The delta of the Syr Darya River, which empties into the Aral Sea and where the homeland of the Massagetae lay, is exactly 830 km away from Tashkent. The chronicle called the *Hou Hanshu*, which records the events of the Eastern Han Dynasty (25–220 AD), adds: 'The kingdom of Yancai has changed its name to the kingdom of Alanliao.'[397] Thanks to the Chinese chronicles it is clear that the Alans, who were originally called 'Yancai' and in the first half of the first century AD changed their name to 'Aryan' or 'Alan', came from Central Asia; their modern descendants are the Caucasian Ossetians. The relative geographic proximity of Alanliao to China and a joint Sino–Alanian military campaign against the Xiongnu conducted in 36 BC[398] explains why the Alans were aware that members of the Chinese elite decorated the knobs of their swords with jade inlays.

Early on, around 73 AD, the Alans laid waste to Media and Armenia. When they again plundered Armenia 60 years later and threatened Asia Minor, they were driven out in 135 AD by the historian and governor of Cappadocia Arrian. Arrian was helping Emperor Hadrian (r. 117–138) to expand the Roman army, which consisted almost exclusively of infantry, by adding units of heavy cavalry. The Alans must have been seen by the Romans as the most dangerous of mounted warriors, since Arrian wrote a work on strategy called *Acies contra Alanos*, the 'Order of Battle against the Alans'.[399] Thanks to their military power, the Alans controlled the trade routes of the steppes with the east. The Alans buried their dead in narrow grave chambers and laid them on benches with their heads oriented toward the north.[400]

Roxolani, Saii and Iazyges: The Roxolani, the 'bright Aryans', lived between the Don and the Dnieper, and west of them lived the Saii, the Royal Sarmatians and the Iazyges, who in the third and second centuries BC either assimilated the Scythians or drove them into Crimea. Like the eastern Sarmatian tribes they intervened with varying success in the fortunes of the Bosporan Kingdom. In 179 BC the king of the Saii, Gatalos, succeeded in demanding tribute from the city-state of Olbia, but the strengthened Scythians were soon able to return Olbia to their sphere of influence.[401] However, in 113–111/110 BC, the Siraces, the Roxolani and their Scythian ally Palakos suffered severe defeats from Diophantos. Under pressure first from the Aorsi and later from the Alans, the western Sarmatian tribes began at the end of the first century BC to cross the Danube and test the defences of the Roman Empire. The first invasions of the Iazyges took place in Macedonia in 18 BC, after which they drove the Dacians out of the Hungarian plain between the Danube and the Tisza and established themselves there as a Roman client state. With the Iazyges for the first time an originally Central Asian tribe settled in the Roman Empire; others soon followed. Rome hoped to be able to defend itself against other threatening barbarian invasions with the help of the Iazyges.

On the heels of the Iazyges followed the Roxolani, who were defeated by the Roman legate Silvanus in 60–63 AD, and 100,000 of whom settled north of the Danube. The Roxolani remained restless; in 69 they were defeated in Moesia south of the Danube, after which they supported the Dacians in the second Dacian war of 101–106. Iazygian units fought on both sides, with one group

Sarmatian gold vessel with a zoomorphic handle from the Khokhlach Kurgan of Novocherkassk, Rostov Oblast, southern Russia, end of the first/beginning of the second century AD. The elk turned toward the rim of the vessel had an apotropaic function and symbolically guarded the contents. The State Hermitage Museum, St. Petersburg.

Small gold figure with inlaid turquoise of a wild sheep from the kurgan of Čilikty, eastern Kazakhstan, seventh–sixth centuries BC. Central State Museum of the Republic of Kazakhstan, Almaty. The gold objects with incrustations of semiprecious stones show that the Sarmato-polychrome animal style developed in eastern Kazakhstan as early as the seventh–sixth centuries BC.

Complete copy after the original of the diadem, discovered in 1864, of Khokhlach Kurgan at Novocherkassk, Rostov Oblast, southern Russia, end of the first/beginning of the second century AD. The diadem, made in the Sarmato-polychrome animal style for a noblewoman of the Aorsi, reveals an influence from the Alans, who had migrated from the delta of the Syr Darya. The diadem's band is decorated with garnets, turquoise, pearls and coloured glass; in the centre is an amethyst bust of a woman, while on the upper rim deer approach trees of life. The woman may have worn the diadem during religious rituals. The State Hermitage Museum, St. Petersburg.

aiming to remove itself from the Roman sphere of influence and the other serving Rome as valued mercenaries. Emperor Trajan (r. 98–117) defeated both Sarmatian tribes, the Iazyges and the Roxolani, and celebrated his success on 'Trajan's column', erected in Rome in 113. In the first Marcomannic war (166–175) the Iazyges allied themselves with the Germanic Marcomanni, Quadi and Vandals against Rome. Emperor Marcus Aurelius (r. 161–180) dealt them a severe defeat on the frozen Danube in 174, after which the Iazyges surrendered and deposed their king, Bana. From then on Marcus Aurelius called himself *Sarmaticus* and the new king of the Iazyges, Zanticus, had to provide 8,000 troops, 5,500 of whom Marcus Aurelius posted to Britain.[402]

About 60 years later the Roman Senate conferred the title *Sarmaticus* on Emperor Maximus Thrax (r. 235–238) as well, after a triumph over the rebellious Iazyges. In the subsequent 150 years groups of Iazyges and Roxolani repeatedly attacked the Roman Empire with varying success; other groups settled throughout the empire, obtained Roman citizenship and served as heavy cavalrymen in Rome's armies. At the end of the fourth century they lost their cultural identity but remained active as mercenary units.

At the start of the third century AD a new power appeared in the northern Black Sea region, the eastern Germanic Goths, who first destroyed the cities of Olbia, Gorgippia and Tanaïs and in 271 occupied the province of Dacia, which had been evacuated by Emperor Aurelian (r. 270–275). Thus they formed a wedge in the territory of the Iranian-speaking tribes and separated the Sarmatians living in the Hungarian plain from the Aorsi and Alans who remained on the Don. 300,000 Sarmatians are said to have fled from the Danube region to the Roman Empire in around 334, settling in several Roman provinces.[403] Less than 40 years later another warlike riding people emerged from Central Asia, the Huns.[404] They were, for the first time, not an Indo-European people advancing from Central Asia to the west but rather an Altaic one. The tribal group of the Huns displayed a marked Mongolid heritage and were presumably led by the elite of a Turkic tribe. The Alans were the final Iranian-speaking Europids to migrate from east to west; the Huns were the first Altai-speaking Turko-Mongolids doing this. Even before 375 they defeated the Alans on the Don, who fled to the northern Caucasus. The Huns, purportedly led by King Balamber, incorporated the remaining Alans into their army and advanced farther westwards. In the years 375–76 they defeated first Ermanaric, king of the Ostrogothic Greuthungi, and then his successor, Vithimir. The defeated Greuthungi moved into the territory of the Visigothic Thervingi, who fled to the Roman Empire. Rome's consent for the fleeing Thervingi to cross the imperial border proved to be a catastrophic mistake. The Roman administration was overstrained by the integration of the armed Thervingi, so the latter soon revolted. In 378 the Thervingi and the allied Alans dealt Rome a crushing defeat at the battle of Adrianople, at which Emperor Valens (r. 364–378) and all the high-ranking officers fell.[405]

Under pressure from the Huns advancing into the Hungarian plain, the Alans living there fled, simultaneously with the Vandals, farther west and on 31 December 406, under the leadership of their king, Respendial, they crossed the frozen Rhine at Mainz. The

Alans then pillaged and laid waste to Gaul for three years, after which they split into two groups. One remained in Gaul and in 451 fought on the side of the Roman general Flavius Aetius and the Visigoths at the important Battle of the Catalaunian Fields near Troyes. Together they defeated the Hun king Attila, who had to halt his campaign. Still today the place names such as *Alainville* and *Alaincourt* recall the originally Central Asian Alans, so the written traces of the Alans extend from the almost 2,000-year-old Chinese chronicles to the contemporaneous place-name signs of France.[406] The other Alans moved on in 409 to Spain, where between 416 and 418 they were annihilated by the Visigoths allied with the Western Roman Empire. After the death of their king Attaces the surviving Alans placed themselves under the protection of the Vandal king Gunderic, who from then on called himself *rex Vandalorum et Alanorum*. Ten years later the united Vandals and Alans advanced to North Africa, where they expelled the Romans and founded the North African Vandal state with Carthage as its capital, which stood from 429 to 534.[407] The Alans, who had originally come from the delta of the Syr Darya east of the Aral Sea, were indeed 'well-travelled' and had over the course of some 20 generations covered more than 9,000 km. They left behind a cultural legacy in the form of military innovations and the art of goldsmithing.

Armoured horsemen wearing a 'spangenhelm' on the victory column of Emperor Trajan in Rome, dedicated in the year 113 AD. The very close-fitting armour of riders and horse, as well as the armour on the horse's legs, are an artistic exaggeration.

2.4.3 Military innovations

The military successes of the Sarmatians and the Alans were essentially grounded in their new offensive and defensive weaponry. Although the Scythians had already adopted the principle of scale armour from the Assyrians, it was the Sarmatian elite horsemen who extended this technology to create full-body armour. Members of the elite, who made up the heavy cavalry, protected their bodies with iron scale armour; those of the light cavalry, which consisted of common free warriors, used armour made of horn or hardened leather.[408] The Sarmatian riders protected not only themselves but also their horses with scale armour, which covered the horses' bodies and their heads. As Herodotus had already reported about the Massagetae, 'they give their horses bronze breastplates'.[409] The Greeks called them *Hippeis de kataphraktoi*, 'completely armoured horsemen'. Except for arrows shot at close range, iron scale armour protected against arrows shot from a short recurve bow.

This armour offered good protection but also had two significant disadvantages. First, it was enormously heavy, as a warrior's armour weighed up to 30 kg and that of a horse around 45 kg, which impeded the horse's mobility. For this reason armoured riders preferred larger horses than the small and very tough steppe horses.[410] Because of the great weight, horses threatened either to fall on slippery ground or to fall through the ice when crossing frozen bodies of water. As the Roman historian Tacitus (*ca.* 58–120) said on the occasion of a defeat of the Roxolani, the horses foundered on the thawing, swampy ground and the fallen riders could not get up again.[411] Secondly, heatstroke and dehydration threatened the armoured horses, especially in warmer latitudes, which is why the Romans called their fully armoured cavalry units *Clibanarii*, 'oven men'.[412]

Another innovation, the riveted plate helmet called the *Spangenhelm*, appeared among the Sarmatians around the time of the birth of Christ. It consisted of a thick metal band on which were affixed four to six metal strips, the *spangen*, between which were placed triangular metal plates. Metal cheek flaps and a neck-guard made from chain mail offered additional protection.[413] It remains unclear whether the Sarmatians were really the inventors of this type of helmet.

While the composite bow was the main weapon of the light cavalry, the heavy cavalry sported a cavalry sword, up to 130 cm in length, and a lance as long as 5 m, wielded with both hands, called the *kontos*. During a frontal attack the horsemen, riding close to one another, spurred their horses and held their lances level, with the tips far in front of the horses' heads and the ends of the shafts secured by loops to the horses' shanks. According to Plutarch (*ca.* 45–125), an attacking *Kontopharos* could impale two opponents, one behind the

Stone relief of a fully armoured Sassanian rider with helmet, shield and lance. The heavy cavalry of the *Kataphraktoi* were an important military branch not only among the Sarmatians and Romans beginning in the second century AD but also among the Iranian Sassanians (224–651 AD). The stone relief of Takht-i Bostan in the Iranian province of Kermanshah presumably portrays the king of kings Khosrau II (r. 590–628 AD).

other, with a single thrust of the lance. As the chief weapon of the heavy cavalry of the Sarmatians and the Alans was the lance, Arrian called them *Kontophoroi*, 'lance-bearers', rather than *Kataphraktoi*. The Greek light cavalry lance *xyston* or the heavy phalanx lance called the *sarissa* may have served as examples for the early Sarmatians.[414] The Sarmatian armoured horsemen abandoned the Scythian strategy of rapid attacks and retreats accompanied by hails of arrows, in favour of an attack carried out as quickly as possible in order to ensure the shortest possible exposure to enemy arrows. The Sarmatian cavalry units resembled a mounted phalanx. In this way they anticipated the military strategy of the medieval knights, as well as their fundamental weakness, in that a frontal attack could succeed only if the enemy remained in place and engaged them.

The mounted archers adopted three additional tools: the slingshot and the lasso, which Sarmatian female warriors and later the Huns also used, and the windsock, which showed the archers the direction of the wind. It consisted of a lance with a metallic dragon, snake or wolf head at its tip, from which hung a colourful windsock made of cloth. Like the Parthians and Sassanids, the Romans adopted the Sarmatian windsock as a battle standard; they called the bearer of this standard the *Draconarius*.[415] Although the Romans had been confronted with armoured enemy cavalry as early as 190 BC at the battle of Magnesia against the Seleucid king Antiochus III, it was more than two centuries before they formed their own cataphract units. While until Emperor Trajan the Romans had found Sarmatian mercenaries sufficient, Emperor Hadrian established cataphracts as an independent unit of the Roman army for the first time. Now the Roman army, which also adopted the Sarmatian long sword called the *spatha*, used the same weapon system as the menacing mounted warriors of the steppe

Roman marble sarcophagus with scenes of an Amazonomachy, origin unknown, around 200 AD, Harvard Art Museum, Boston.

The Amazons – myth and reality

The Sauromatians 'have a marriage law which forbids a girl to marry until she has killed an enemy in battle'.[416] With this description of young Sauromatian women, who were said to be maternally descended from the Amazons, Herodotus confirmed the myth that female warriors lived in foreign Scythia. The source of this legend goes back to around the end of the eighth century BC, the time of Homer's *Iliad*, in which the Amazons appears only as a footnote to the Trojan War. Only in the post-Homeric epic *Aithiopis* (*ca.* seventh century BC) do the Amazons become more clearly defined, in the form of their queen Penthesilea, a daughter of the god of war, Ares. She fights with her Amazon army on the side of the Trojans against the Greeks, but falls in a duel with Achilles. At that time their homeland was localised on the south-eastern coast of the Black Sea near the Thermodon River.[417] Greek exploration of the Black Sea soon deprived the myth of its basis, so the 'man-killing'[418] Amazons were relocated to the distant Sauromatians even before Herodotus, and the Scythian Amazon myth replaced the Greek one. In Greek art, especially vase-painting, the warrior women were no longer portrayed in Greek clothing but rather in Scythian garb. Now they wore long, patterned trousers, long-sleeved jackets and tall felt caps and were armed with battle axes and bows.[419]

To what extent can archaeology confirm the myth of the Amazons? Did women fighters live in the Pontic region and is there evidence for bands of female warriors, who even formed their own communities that lived independently of men? The oldest evidence of a female warrior comes from the Caucasus, where in 1927 at Semo-Awtchala, Georgia, archaeologists discovered the grave of a 30- to 40-year-old woman, who had been given grave goods of a bronze sword, iron spearheads and a horse's head to accompany her into the afterlife. The woman, who had died at the end of the second millennium BC, had a serious skull wound that could not have resulted from post-mortem trepanning, since the injury had healed before her death. This reveals that she was a genuine warrior and that the weapons had not been laid in her grave in a purely ceremonial context.[420] This female warrior remains an anomaly in the Caucasus, however, like the above-mentioned warrior woman of Ak-Alacha in the Altai.

Discoveries from the Scytho–Sarmatian territory are more revealing. Between the lower Volga and the Ural about 20% of all burials with weapons and horse-gear from the Sauromatian period were of women. In these graves, such as those in the cemetery of Pokrovka 2 in the southern Urals, light weapons like akinakes and arrowheads predominate. Since the female skeletons show clear battle wounds only in isolated cases, it often cannot be determined whether the deceased were hunters or warriors. A greater percentage of armed women, as measured by all female burials, are found in Scythia, where some 130 graves of women from the fifth and fourth centuries BC included weapons as grave goods. About one quarter of the excavated female burials of Scythia contained weapons. Frequent signs of injuries such as serious blows or stabs to the skull or arrowheads stuck in bones show that these dead, who belonged to the tribal elite, were women warriors and often died in battle.[421] The Alans, for their part, did not have female fighters; only in the seventh–eighth centuries AD did weapons begin to appear in the graves of Alan women in the forest steppes along the Don.[422]

In contrast to the graves of Sauromatian female warriors and hunters, the burials of Scythian warrior women often contained, in addition to arrows and daggers, heavy weapons such as spears, lances and axes. Iron swords have been found in only three graves, however, as have iron scale belts. Two Scythian graves of female warriors are exceptions: in kurgan 5 of Zelenoje three young female warriors were buried, with the main person given a spear, a javelin, a helmet and scale armour with an iron lamellar shield. This is the only grave of a woman warrior with the complete equipment of heavy cavalry. In kurgan 35 of Bobrica from the seventh–sixth centuries BC, however, a sacrificed horse was placed in the grave of a female warrior.[423]

From these discoveries it may be concluded that although there were neither Amazon armies or Amazon communities in the northern Pontic region, there were indeed female warriors in the light cavalry, who participated in military engagements. The large percentage of female warriors who died young indirectly confirms Herodotus's assertion that Sauromatian women had to perform military service before marriage. But, in the absence of men, married women must also have taken up weapons to defend their herds and grazing lands. Two archaeological observations indicate that female warriors had no special status. Burials of women warriors did not include any splendid ceremonial weapons and no proper weapons were found in the elaborate single burials of women.[424] In Sarmatian and Scythian graves with an opulent female burial as the primary burial, weapons, much less opulent weapons, were hardly ever included as grave goods, but rather costly jewellery and symbols of prestige. Among the latter were the diadem with a tree of life from Khokhlach (first/second centuries AD) and, in particular, the iron ceremonial staff with four deer protomes from the grave of Pestchanyi (first century BC).[425] These women, who belonged to the nobility, may also have had a religious role. Additional evidence of a possible religious task for some aristocratic women is suggested by the portable stone tables whose three legs were decorated with mythical creatures. These tables, mostly found in Sauromatian female graves of the southern Urals, presumably served as altars of sacrifice.[426]

and the Parthians in the east. Although the infantry remained the strategic core of the Roman army, the heavy cavalry increased steadily in importance.[427]

The use of heavy armour was called into question as early as 100 AD, when a few Sarmatians and Alans began using the 120-cm-long, asymmetrical composite bow called the Hunnic bow with its bonded bone reinforcements, whose arrows, mounted with heavy iron arrowheads, could penetrate scale armour. Presumably it was this development that inspired some Sarmatians and Alans to trade the heavy scale armour for the lighter ring armour, the chain mail.[428] Ring armour offered less protection from arrows but was significantly lighter and allowed the rider sufficient mobility to use the powerful Hunnic bow. The clear superiority of the light-armoured Hunnic mounted warriors, who relied on their long composite bow and had mastered the tactic of attack, feigned retreat and renewed attack, over the lumbering Sarmatians could be seen in the ease with which they were able to drive the various Sarmatian tribes from the Don to the Rhine. In his famous military handbook *Strategikon*, the Byzantine emperor Maurice (r. 582–602) aptly described the battle style of the Avars, whom he compared to the Huns, as follows: 'They prefer battles fought at long range, ambushes, encircling their adversaries, simulated retreats and sudden returns, and wedge-shaped formations ... When they make their enemies take to flight, ... they are not content, as the Persians and the Romans, and other peoples, with pursuing them a reasonable distance and plundering their goods, but they do not let up at all until they have achieved the complete destruction of their enemies.'[429] The Huns fought in exactly the same way. Maurice warned further that Central Asian mounted warriors never give up in the face of a looming defeat: 'If the battle turns out well, do not be hasty in pursuing the enemy or behave carelessly. For this nation [the steppe nomads] does not, as others do, give up the struggle

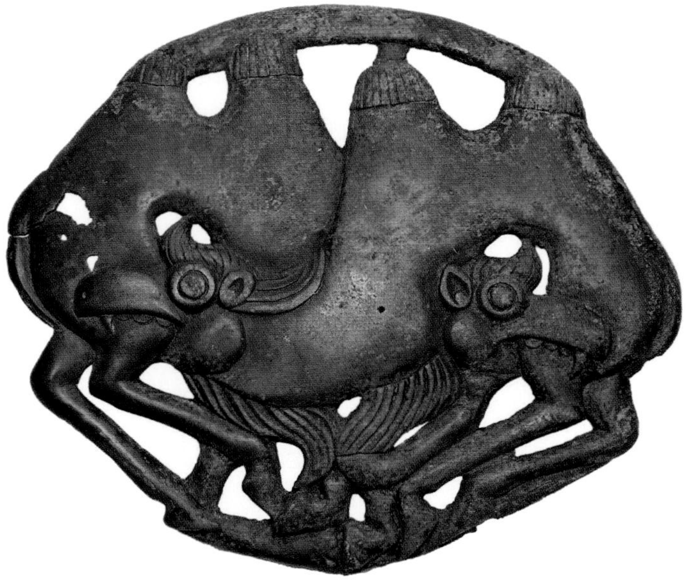

Bronze phalera (decorative plaque on a horse bridle) with two fighting camels. Filippovka, kurgan 1, eastern bank of the Ural River, central Russia, early fourth century BC. Archaeological Museum of Ufa.

Part of the gold diadem of Kargaly near Almaty, southern Kazakhstan, second–first centuries BC. The diadem, placed in a woman's grave, represents a further development of Sarmato-polychrome goldworking by the Wusun; it does not illustrate a scene of animals fighting but rather a magical world of winged humans and animals, suggesting influences from China. Central State Museum of the Republic of Kazakhstan, Almaty.

when worsened in the first battle. But until their strength gives out, they try all sorts of ways to assail their enemies.'[430] The renaissance of heavily armoured cavalry came with the Avars who introduced to western Central Asia and Europe the iron stirrups which formed part of the standard equipment of Roman cavalry by the end of the sixth century.[431]

With the downfall of the Sarmatians, the epoch of Iranian-speaking Europids spreading elements of Central Asian culture into Europe came to an end. Their nomadic riding successors were Altaic-speaking Turko–Mongols, whose advance ended only in 1683 at the gates of Vienna. The obvious wealth of the Scythian and Sarmatian elites, which endured for centuries, was not based only on war and raiding but probably to a greater extent on trade, whether the exchange of goods with the Bosporan Kingdom, Olbia and Rome or the taxing of goods that passed through their territory in transit along the trade routes between east and west.

◀ Ceremonial dagger from Datchi, crafted in the Sarmato-Alan polychrome animal style, kurgan 1, Rostov Oblast, southern Russia, end of the first century AD. The knob and the sheath with the four indentations are made of gold and decorated with turquoise and carnelian. On the knob a Bactrian camel is portrayed, and beneath it a griffin lunges at a standing camel; on the sheath a griffin attacks a kneeling camel four times. The dagger, found in Datchi, displays great similarity to the dagger from grave 4 at Tillya Tepe, northern Afghanistan (40–70 AD) and is an import from the homeland of the Alans on the Syr Darya, Kazakhstan. Azov History, Archaeology and Palaeontology Museum.

2.4.4 The polychrome animal style

Like the Scytho–Siberian animal style, the Sarmatian polychrome animal style, with its coloured inlays, had its roots in Asia and appeared for the first time in the gold animal statuettes of Čilikty from the seventh century BC and, in rudimentary form, in the gold panther of Kelermes, which once had coloured stones in its ears and paws.[432] When enhancing metalwork with inlays of semiprecious stones and glass paste, artists at first found it sufficient to emphasise individual body parts on the head and extremities. In the Sarmatian period they started, as a first step, to draw attention to joints and muscles as well. In a true 'horror vacui', they began in a second step to cover the entire body with coloured glass or stone inlays and finally they added hump-shaped depictions of animals to flat dagger sheaths. Garnet, carnelian, coral, topaz, turquoise and coloured glass served as inlays. In contrast to Scythian toreutics the Sarmatians outside of the Bosporan Kingdom remained largely free of Greek influence, although the diadem of Khokhlach with the female bust made of amethyst represents a spectacular exception.

The Sarmatian polychrome animal style introduced to toreutics not only new techniques but also new contents. Among these were scenes of fierce animal combat, whose subjects were given a strong dynamism, and animals not previously known in the Scythian art of northern Europe such as camels and dragons. While in the southern Urals and in western Kazakhstan images of camels appeared in the animal style as early as the sixth century BC, in the northern Pontic region they emerged four centuries later. It was the Sarmatians who introduced the Bactrian camel into the northern Black Sea region. The numerous discoveries of camel bones, such as those found near the Sarmato–Bosporan trading city of Tanaïs, attest to their proliferation at that time.[433]

One of the most spectacular depictions of camels can be seen on the golden dagger of Datchi from the end of the first century AD, which was discovered in 1986 in kurgan 1 south of Azov. On the front of the rounded knob stands a battle-ready two-humped camel with an open mouth; on the hilt a griffin lunges at a standing camel and bites it between the humps. A plant motif decorates the reverse of the knob and hilt. On the sheath, in scenes repeated four times, a griffin attacks a buckled camel, which bites its attacker on the left wing. On the lower end of the sheath and in three other bulges, a griffin bites a cowering camel, while in the upper indentation to the left a griffin portrayed in profile watches in an attacking pose. All the animals are decorated with carnelians and turquoise.[434] Comparable in both form and content is one of the two golden daggers from grave 4 of Tillya Tepe in northern Afghanistan. In the small necropolis from the second to third quarter of the first century AD a chief of the Alans from Kangju was buried with at least five women.[435] The dagger, crafted in opulent Sarmato–Alanic polychrome style, likewise has a golden sheath with four side indentations. Although a standing bear rather than a camel adorns the knob and a procession of hybrid creatures, each stalking the one before it and biting it on the croup or hind leg, is portrayed on the sheath, an allegory of the cycle of life and death is depicted on both dagger sheaths. As Schiltz noted in her analysis of the dagger of Tillya Tepe, the animals on the knob symbolise life and those on the sheath remind us that without death renewal and life are not possible. On the reverse of both knobs, plant motifs suggesting a tree of life mediate between the antitheses of life and death.[436] The dagger of Tillya Tepe presumably came from an Alanic goldsmith on the Syr Darya and that of Datchi perhaps also from Alanliao (Kangju) or Kazakhstan.

Gold clothing plaques in the form of geometric bulls' heads, Khokhlach Kurgan of Novocherkassk, Rostov Oblast, southern Russia, end of the first/beginning of the second century AD. Such strongly schematised depictions of horned animals kept their original semantics. The State Hermitage Museum, St. Petersburg.

Features of the finds from Tillya Tepe also appear on the neck ring from the grave of the princess of Kobiakovo, not far from Datchi, from the first/second centuries AD. However, there are also signs of influence from Kazakhstan and even China. In the centre of the neck ring sits a bearded man with his sword on his knees. On both sides two-legged, ape-like beings wrestle or play with winged dragons.[437] Depictions of dragons are also found in Tillya Tepe on a dagger sheath from grave 4 and on a pair of golden pendants with images of a lord of the animals taming two dragons from grave 2.[438] Dragons are also seen on the diadem of Kargaly in southern Kazakhstan. This diadem, found not far from Almaty, dates from the second/first centuries BC, a time when the nomadic herders of the Wusun lived in the Ili valley. A few decades earlier the Yuezhi had expelled the Saka from the Ili valley, after which they in turn were displaced by the Wusun, their former neighbour in Gansu, north-western China, whom they had destroyed *ca.* 173 BC. The gold diadem, adorned with carnelians, almandine and turquoise, displays a further development of the polychrome animal style, since neither animal fights nor normal humans are depicted but rather ethereal fantastical creatures in fleet-footed, playful movement. Clear influences from China can also be seen. The diadem shows a landscape with winged horses and winged, feathered men, who, with long flying hair, ride astride winged dragons, lions, buffalos and ibexes, passing other animals like bears, deer and birds. Presumably depicted here are Daoist immortals at play with fantastical hybrid creatures. In the Chinese context dragons are never menacing but rather animals well disposed to humans, which symbolise spring and life-giving water.[439]

Two Sarmatian women's graves from the southern Ukraine, which both show striking parallels to Tillya Tepe, more than

The tradition of portraying horned animals symbolically in extremely abstract forms remains alive today in the production of felt and wool carpets by nomads in Kazakhstan, Kyrgyzstan and western Mongolia. Nomads near Khar Noor Lake, Bayan Ölgyi Aimag, western Mongolia, make such felt carpets.

3,000 km away, illustrate how permeable the Eurasian steppe was at that time and how large the Saka–Sarmatian cultural territory. In both graves from the first century AD, one of Nogajčik (Crimea) and the other of Sokolova Mogila (southern Bug), the hands of the dead rested on silver bowls, a custom also encountered in Tillya Tepe, where two plates were golden and one silver. The woman buried at Nogajčik, whose kurgan was doused with petroleum and set on fire after the end of the funeral solemnities, had golden spiral bands around her ankles, as at Tillya Tepe.[440]

The Sarmatian animal style came up with still more innovations. Among them were forest scenes, such as two wrestlers in a forest, a boar hunt or a warrior resting in the lap of a woman beneath a tree.[441] In Sarmatian toreutics there was also a kind of counter-movement to the baroque opulence, as expressed in the diadem of Khokhlach, in the form of a geometrisation of the portrayal of animals. Horned animals in particular were portrayed on golden discs sewn onto clothing either in extremely stylised form or, in line with the principle of 'pars pro toto', reduced to antlers or horns. Such abstract and geometrical portrayals of animals can still be seen today on Kazakh, Kyrgyz and western Mongolian felt carpets.[442] Finally, the Sarmatian armoured horsemen introduced phalerae as a new decorative element in horse-gear. The hemispheric breast phalera and the round side phalerae had diameters of up to 15 cm, were made of gold or silver and often decorated with agates, turquoise or garnets.[443] In the late Sarmatian period of the second to fourth centuries AD the animal style gave way to a Greco-Roman polychrome style, but Sarmatian goldsmithing with inlays of semiprecious stones was adopted and further developed by Germanic peoples such as the Goths, Vandals and Franks.[444] It should be noted in conclusion that for a few centuries Saka–Sarmatian toreutics represented a transcontinental artistic style, which extended from western China to the Eastern Roman Empire.

▶ Pair of phalerae from kurgan 1 of Datchi, Rostov Oblast, southern Russia, end of the first century AD. A gold setting decorated with garnets, turquoise and rose coral surrounds a veined agate. Azov History, Archaeology and Palaeontology Museum.

VIII

Greeks in Central Asia

Possession achieved by the sword is not of long duration, but gratitude for kindness is everlasting. If we wish to hold Asia and not merely pass through it, we must impart our clemency to these people [the conquered Bactrians and Sogdians] – it is their loyalty which will make our empire stable and enduring.

ALEXANDER THE GREAT in 327 BC. Quoted by Quintus Curtius Rufus[1]

SCYTHIANS
Black Sea
Caucasus
Casp
Se
Pella
Granikos
Gordion
Athens
Sardes
Ephesos
Halikarnassos
Side
Issos
Nisibis
Gaugamela
Arbil
Ectabana
Seleucia
Zagros
Byblos
Damascus
Mediterranean Sea
Tyros
Babylon
Susa
Gaza
Alexandria
Siwa Oasis
Memphis
ARABIA
The campaign of Alexander the Great, 334–323 BC
Cities and towns
Route
N
Scale (km)
0
200
400
600

Aral Sea
MASSAGETAE
Iaxartes (Syr Darya)
SAKA
Oxus (Amu Darya)
Alexandria Eschate (Khujand)
Cyropolis (Istaravshan)
Maracanda (Samarkand)
Nautaka (Shahr-i Sabz)
Kurgansol
Pamirs
Alexandria Oxeiana (Termez/Kampyr Tepe)
Eucratidia (Aï Khanum)
Merv
Oxeiana (Takht-i Sangin)
Bactra (Balkh)
Aornos (Kunduz)
Hekatompylos
Paropamisos (Hindu Kush)
Alexandria ad Caucasum (Begram)
avir Desert
Alexandria in Aria (Herat)
Kabul
Khyber Pass
Taxila
Bucephalia (Jhelum)
Prophtasia (Farah)
Lahore
Alexandria in Arachosia (Kandahar)
Alexandria on the Hyphasis (river Beas)
polis
Alexandria on the Indus (Uch)
Alexandria Carmania (Golâshkerd)
Rhambacia (Bela)
ian
lf
Karachi
Patala
ut Desert
Indian Ocean

The wise saying attributed to Alexander, which anticipates Talleyrand's admonition of Napoleon, 'the only thing you cannot do with a bayonet is sit on it', does not disguise the fact that the Macedonian was a brutal and ruthless commander, who left behind in Bactria and Sogdia a bloody trail of destruction. Although he attempted to repair the rift between the victorious Macedonians and the vanquished Persians as well as the combative Bactrians by means of symbolic gestures such as arranged mass weddings between Macedonian officers and Asian women, he also tended towards excessive violence. Examples included the murder of his close friend Cleitos in Maracanda (Samarkand) and a series of systematic massacres of the civilian populace in rebellious Sogdia and Bactria. The extraordinarily rich influences that Greek art imparted to Central Asian cultures had nothing to do with the campaigns of Alexander but were rather associated with the subsequent Seleucids, the Greco–Bactrian Kingdom and Buddhism.

The Hellenistic period of Central Asia north of the Hindu Kush[2] lasted in a political sense for two centuries, from 329 to 145/30 BC, but in terms of culture it endured for a thousand years, as evidenced in the use of the Greek script and Buddhist sculpture in the Gandhara style, which extended from Central Asia as far as Korea and Japan in the first millennium AD. As a consequence of the incorporation of parts of Central Asia into the empire of the Achaemenids, the first contact between Central Asia and the Hellenistic world took place long before Alexander. For one, Greek architects, politicians, generals and soldiers were in service to the Persian rulers, and, for another, a Greek community had lived in southern Uzbekistan between the cities of Termez and Samarkand since the beginning of the fifth century BC. The Branchidae, descendants of the priests of the Greek oracle of Apollo at Didyma of Miletus, lived in this city. When Xerxes I (r. 486–465 BC) destroyed the shrine in 479 BC, the priests voluntarily surrendered the temple's

Pair of golden clasps featuring two warriors, holding a lance and a shield. Each wears a Greco–Bactrian helmet with a tiny bull's ear, as is seen on coins featuring Alexander or Bactrian kings; the bull's ear symbolising Dionysos, the alleged conqueror of India. Both soldiers wear a breastplate and a Greek griffin-hilted sword, and are surrounded by a frame consisting of plants, birds and dragons, which places the Hellenistic warriors in a typical setting of the art of the steppes. The clasps date from the second century BC and probably stem from an older Bactrian site. Tillya Tepe, grave 3, 40–70 AD. National Museum Afghanistan.

Although Alexander the Great did not reach the Wakhan Corridor in far north-eastern Afghanistan, in 329 BC he had to surmount similarly forbidding mountain chains in the Hindu Kush between Kabul and Bactra. Aerial view of the Afghan Pamir.

treasures to him. Fearing revenge from the Miletian Greeks, the Branchidae fled during the retreat of the Persian army and Xerxes resettled them on the Sogdian–Bactrian border. When Alexander reached the Branchidae city 150 years later, the inhabitants greeted him with joy, but his reaction was a harbinger of the coming massacre: 'The phalanx had been ordered to surround the city walls and, when the signal was given, to sack this city which had provided refuge for traitors, killing the inhabitants to a man. [...] Finally the Macedonians dug down to the foundations of the walls in order to demolish them and leave not a single trace of the city.' Curtius Rufus commented on this barbarity as follows: 'The guilt of their ancestors was being atoned for by descendants who had never seen Miletus and accordingly could not possibly have betrayed it to Xerxes.'[3]

The ruins of the round fort of Talashkan I, reinforced by 15 defensive towers, may be identical to the city of the Branchidae.[4] The fortress lay between the city of Termez on the Oxus and the so-called 'Iron Gates', a 10-km-long complex of two narrow mountain passes, which guarded the advance from Termez to Samarkand. Toward the end of the third century BC, when the Greco–Bactrian Kingdom lost Samarkand to the nomadic horsemen, the 'Iron Gates' were built up into a barrage as a defence against these dangerous neighbours.[5] The strongly fortified settlement of Talashkan I was built at the start of the fifth century BC and at the time of Alexander's campaign was set on fire and completely destroyed.

1. The campaign of Alexander the Great

Although Alexander (r. 336–323 BC) maintained that with his Asian campaign he was avenging the past Persian invasions of Greece from the fifth century BC, it was in fact a war of conquest, which his father, Philip II, had already begun with the deployment of General Parmenion to Asia Minor. At the same time the common military efforts of the Greek states, which had traditionally been at odds with one another, were united under the leadership of Alexander, who saw himself in the role of a second Achilles. In three great battles he defeated the Achaemenid army: namely on the river Granicus not far from Troy (334 BC), at Issus in Cilicia (333 BC) and at Gaugamela in the northern Iraqi plain of Arbil (331 BC). In all three battles Alexander started off defensively with his infantry phalanx, in order to tie up enemy power, then turned the tables with his heavy cavalry, which attacked in a wedge formation as soon as a gap appeared in the Persian line. Then, with his elite horsemen, he personally attacked the enemy commander; at Granicus half the Persian commanders fell; at Issus and Gaugamela the outclassed Achaemenid king Darius III (r. 336–330 BC) had to flee. Although outnumbered, the Macedonian army was superior, as it consisted of veterans and was divided into clear weapon divisions, which, thanks to their discipline, were able to carry out

During his pursuit of the Achaemenid usurper Bessus, Alexander the Great reached the plain of Kabul, where he wintered in 330/329 BC and founded the city of Alexandria ad Caucasum, today Bagram, north of Kabul. Fortress of Bela Hissar in Kabul, Afghanistan. Photo taken by John Burke in 1879. National Army Museum, London.

complicated manoeuvres in battle; in addition, they were led by a bold military genius. The Persian army, by contrast, was a mix of ethnicities of varying quality. Although Darius also had powerful units, such as the Sogdian and Bactrian cavalry led by the Bactrian satrap Bessus, as well as the mounted archers commanded by the Saka king Mauaces, the Persian army lacked coordination.[6]

Darius fled from the pursuing Alexander to the east, where he hoped to find safety and muster a new army. But he had lost all authority and during his flight, in July of 330 BC, the satraps of the Central Asian provinces took him prisoner. When Alexander came within range of the fleeing group, Bessus had Darius killed and declared himself the new king under the name Artaxerxes V.[7] Alexander, who had himself declared the legitimate successor to the defeated Darius and ordered his ceremonial burial, now pursued the murderer of the unfortunate ruler. This undertaking turned into one of the most spectacular chases in history and led Alexander into the heart of Central Asia. Bessus fled to the capital of his Bactrian satrapy, Zariaspa (Balkh in northern Afghanistan), where he believed himself to be protected from Alexander by the Hindu Kush – a mistake. Alexander wanted to capture Bessus before the latter could muster another army, as he had observed the military might of the Bactrian and Sogdian cavalry at Gaugamela. He continued his pursuit.

In order to stabilise the conquered empire, Alexander confirmed the satraps in their offices in several places, on condition that they surrendered and swore loyalty to him. In order to protect his back, during his advance through Central Asia he founded fortified cities and military bases, where he installed strong garrisons and Greek

settlers. These settlements, which often bore the name Alexandria, were arrayed along his route like a string of pearls; when Alexander left Bactria in 327 BC, he had covered Central Asia with a net of military installations manned by a total of about 23,000 soldiers and mercenaries. Thanks to the bematists, who measured distances with their steps, we are quite well informed about the distances covered and cities founded by Alexander's army.

After Alexander had Persepolis burned to the ground, he turned to the north-east, to Hyrcania, on the south-eastern rim of the Caspian Sea, and to Parthia (north-eastern Iran), and then to the south-east and across the satrapies of Aria (western Afghanistan), Drangiana (western Afghanistan and south-eastern Iran) and Arachosia (south-eastern Afghanistan and western Pakistan). On the way Alexander founded Alexandria in Aria (Herat); Prophtasia in Drangiana (Phrada, modern Farah), where Alexander had to put down the first conspiracy of some of his most trusted officers;[8] Alexandria in Arachosia (Kandahar); and Alexandria ad Caucasum (Bagram north of Kabul), where the army spent the winter in 330/329 BC.[9] Before them towered the Hindu Kush, reaching a height of up to 7,700 m, which the Greeks called Parapamisos. This name was derived from the Persian 'uparisana', which means roughly 'where the eagle does not fly'.[10] In the meantime, Bessus had not managed to assemble the hoped-for large army, as the odour of a regicide clung to him, so he adopted a 'scorched earth' strategy. As ancient historians mention neither Persian garrisons nor an Achaemenid government, it may be assumed that the satrap did not have his own troops but rather depended on the loyalty of Bactrian and Sogdian nobles.

In contrast to the Afghans, who were accustomed to the cold and high elevations, Alexander's soldiers suffered greatly under such conditions in the spring of 329 BC. A caravan of Afghan Kirghiz crosses from Afghanistan to Pakistan to reach the valley of Chapursan in northern Pakistan.

In order to avoid an enemy ambush in the mountains, in the spring of 329 BC Alexander crossed the snow-covered and icy Khawak Pass at an elevation of 3,540 m, where his soldiers suffered awful privations. The British lieutenant John Wood, who searched for the source of the Oxus in 1837/38, wrote about the Khawak Pass: 'Firm footing began to fail the horses. The depth of snow was about four feet; and most of the animals, after floundering till exhausted, sunk in up to their bellies.'[11] After the misery of the ice desert came that of the sand desert. Curtius Rufus describes northern Bactria between Bactra and the Oxus as follows: 'A large area of the country is engulfed by desert sands. [...] When the wind blows ... all traces of roads that existed before are obliterated. Consequently, people crossing the plains follow the practice of sailors, watching the stars at night and plotting their course by their movement. [...] The area is impossible to traverse by day, because one finds no track to follow and the light of the celestial bodies is hidden in a misty darkness.'[12]

The cities of Aornos (Kunduz) and Bactra (Balkh) fell to Alexander without a fight, as Bessus had fled in a panic to Nautaka (Shahr-i Sabz south of Samarkand) in Sogdia. Although Bessus had destroyed his pontoon bridge over the Oxus, the powerful river did not represent an insurmountable barrier for the Macedonian army. Alexander 'distributed to the men ... skins stuffed with straw. Lying on these the men swam the river. In this way Alexander deposited the entire army on the far bank in five days.'[13] On account of Bessus's weakness his allies let him fall, and the Sogdian noble Spitames, who would soon become a bitter enemy of Alexander, took him prisoner. While Alexander was waiting for Spitames to

bring him the naked and bound Bessus, he ordered the murder of the Branchidae. Bessus, however, was whipped and crucified after his ears and nose had been cut off.[14] After this Alexander marched to Maracanda (Samarkand), one of the most important cities in Sogdia, and further north-east to Cyropolis (Istaravshan in north-western Tajikistan). This march to the east was no blind drive for conquest; rather Alexander wanted to strengthen the north-eastern border of the empire, which was constantly threatened by the Saka. To help defend against them, he ordered the building of the fortified city of Alexandria Eschate, 'the most distant Alexandria' (present Khujand), north-east of Cyropolis. The city rapidly developed into a crossroads on the trade routes between Sogdia and China and Rome and, as Curtius Rufus reports, it maintained its Greek identity into the first century AD.[15]

While Alexander was pressing ahead with the building of Alexandria Eschate, news reached him of a widespread rebellion in Bactria and Sogdia. It marked the start of a brutal guerrilla war, which cost tens of thousands of civilian lives and left the region in ruins. Only decades later did the two Seleucid rulers Seleucus I (r. 305–281 BC) and Antiochus I (r. 281–261 BC) begin to reconstruct the cities and infrastructure there. Alexander responded to the rebellion with his usual speed. First he conquered the seven rebellious cities on the Syr Darya, which were not able to defend themselves against Greek catapults and mobile siege machines; the men were killed and the women sold into slavery. Then he sent a 4,000-man relief army under General Menedemus to break Spitames's siege of Maracanda. But Spitames lured Menedemus into an ambush and crushed his troops. In the meantime the first

Cotton harvest between Samarkand and Tashkent, Uzbekistan. Cotton was first cultivated in Pakistan during the Indus Valley Civilisation (*ca.* 2800–1800 BC) and spread slowly to Central Asia, where Greeks became familiar with it during the campaign of Alexander the Great.

of two Scythian delegations had reached Alexander's camp and warned him against mounting a campaign against Scythia, since the Scythians could quickly attack his homeland of Macedonia.[16] Nevertheless, Alexander crossed the Syr Darya and successfully attacked a division of Saka mounted warriors with his cavalry. Although Alexander retreated immediately to the southern river-bank, the Saka remained peaceful from then on and Choresmia offered him an alliance. The Macedonian then broke the siege ring around Maracanda and carried out a bloodbath in the valley of the Zerafshan River. 'Alexander divided his forces and ordered the burning of the countryside and the execution of men of military age', reported Curtius Rufus.[17] The army spent the winter in Balkh.[18]

In the spring of 328 BC Alexander continued his strategy of terror against supporters of Spitames and had inhabitants of rebellious cities between Bactra and Samarkand systematically killed. The cities were set on fire and razed to the ground, as is shown by the widespread archaeological traces of fire.[19] This strategy of making a terrible example of rebellious cities foreshadowed that of Genghis Khan. Alexander's brutality was possibly one of the reasons for the development of an early Sogdian diaspora in eastern Central Asia, first in the direction of the Tarim Basin and Gansu, much later throughout northern and central China as far as the capitals of Luoyang and Chang'an.[20] This Sogdian emigration created the necessary conditions for the later dominant position of the Sogdians as traders along the Silk Roads.

Alexander first marched north-east from Bactra to the Oxus (Amu Darya), which he reached east of the location of the future Oxus temple of Takht-i Sangin. The temple lies on the northern bank of the Oxus, about 6 km south-west of the confluence of the ancient Oxus (today's Vakhsh) with the Ochos (today's Panj).[21] Here he divided the army into five divisions: Hephaestion followed the Panj, which today forms the border between Tajikistan and Afghanistan till Dzong, to about 60 km upstream from the future Greek city of Eucratidia (Aï Khanum). Ptolemy purged the valley of the Vakhsh, and Perdiccas that of the Kafirnigan, both in southern Tajikistan, while Coenos and Arzabazos pursued the rebels in the broadly branching valley of the Sukhan Darya. Finally, Alexander 'crossed the Ochus and Oxus rivers and came to the city of Margiana [or Marginia], in the vicinity of which sites for six towns were chosen'.[22]

The city of Margiana that Curtius Rufus refers to is equated with either Termez[23] or with the smaller Kampyr Tepe, 30 km farther west, which could be identical with Alexandria Oxeiana.[24] Of the six military stations established by Alexander, one was discovered near Kurgansol in 2003/4. The fortress of Kurgansol stands about 100 km north of Termez high above an ancient route that linked the Oxus with Maracanda. The fortress, built at the time of Alexander's campaign, contained exclusively Hellenistic ceramics. It was fortified on its north-western and north-eastern sides with six strong, round towers, while on the southern and south-western side vertically sloping precipices ensured its security. The fortress withstood at least one severe attack, but it was abandoned at the start of the third century BC when the region had been sufficiently pacified.

While Alexander received the second Scythian delegation in Maracanda and, in frenzy, murdered his own friend Cleitos, Spitames, whose troops were bolstered by 800 mounted warriors of the Massagetae, succeeded in destroying a Greek division, but he suffered a bitter defeat against General Coenos. While Spitames prepared to flee, the Bactrians and Sogdians deserted him, after which the Massagetae took him prisoner. When they heard that Alexander was pursuing them, they decapitated Spitames and sent his head to the Macedonian as a peace offering. Thus Spitames suffered the same fate that he had inflicted upon Bessus. But a few nobles barricaded themselves in their mountain fortresses, so Alexander had to stay, and he made his winter camp in Nautaka (Shahr-i Sabz) in 328/27 BC.[25]

In the spring of 327 BC Alexander captured the last Bactrian mountain fortresses, including the 'Sogdian cliffs' of the noble Oxyartes.[26] After the surrender the wives and daughters of Oxyartes and other nobles fell into the conqueror's hands. One of these was Roxana, the 13-year-old daughter of Oxyartes, with whom Alexander fell in love. Instead of taking her as a concubine, he promised her a royal wedding. When the Macedonians grumbled that their king was marrying a woman of lower birth, he admonished them, saying that 'intermarriages of Persians and Macedonians would serve to consolidate the empire, that only thus could the conquered lose their shame and the conquerors their pride'.[27] Whether love was really involved is unknown, but the marriage was a politically brilliant move. The Bactrian nobles were impressed by Alexander's treatment of the prisoners and became steadfast allies of Oxyartes's son-in-law. 'Alexander was no longer viewed as a foreign invader, but instead became a Bactrian king.'[28] The resistance collapsed, and Alexander left the region via Kabul in the direction of the Indus, reinforced by Massagetae cavalry units. Presumably Alexander wanted to reach the end of the world, traditionally imagined as disc-shaped, which was surrounded by the world ocean Okéanos, although Greek scholars like Pythagoras (*ca.* 570–510 BC) or his teacher Aristotle (384–322 BC) knew the earth was a sphere. But Alexander must have noticed that the Okéanos was always on the horizon, no matter how far he marched.

For Alexander Central Asia was no sideshow but rather the place he stayed the longest and had to fight the most difficult battles. In the short term Alexander's campaign was a destructive episode for Central Asia; in the long term its consequences changed the political and cultural landscape of the region, and, with regard to art, the canon of Greek sculpture gave emergent

Near the confluence of the Rivers Pamir and Wakhan, which form at Dzong the River Panj, a feeder of the Oxus. Gorno-Badakhshan, southern Tajikistan.

During his Bactrian campaign Alexander's armies had to conquer several practically impregnable fortresses. The fortress of Zamr-i Atish Parast near the village of Yamchun in Gorno-Badakhshan, southern Tajikistan, founded at the end of the Kushan period (first–third centuries AD), protected the trade route that ran along the northern bank of the Oxus. In the background is the Hindu Kush Range.

Buddhism a visual face. The reconstruction of Bactria by the early Seleucids cleared the way for the splendid Greco–Bactrian culture, and when the nomadic horsemen of the Saka and Yuezhi threatened Bactria beginning in 145 BC, Hellenistic artists fled south into the region of Gandhara. Here, along with itinerant Roman artists and local sculptors, they founded the aesthetic style of Gandhara Buddhist sculpture.

Just two years after Alexander's withdrawal there was a mutiny by the Greek mercenaries and veterans who had remained behind in Bactria but still longed for their homeland. Alexander either had them massacred by loyal Macedonian troops or removed them from the army.[29] This episode suggests that the chief threat to the young empire of Alexander came not from outside but rather from within. In fact, immediately after Alexander's death in 323 BC, the wars of the Diadochi broke out.

2. The Greco–Bactrian Kingdom

No sooner had news of Alexander's death reached the 23,000 forcibly settled Greek mercenaries and settlers in Central Asia than they rebelled again and planned the return to their homeland. But the imperial regent Perdiccas (d. 320 BC) sent General Peithon (*ca.* 355–315 BC), son of Crateus, to Bactria with Macedonian troops, who quickly quelled the revolt and accepted the surrender of the rebels. But the Macedonian army ignored Peithon's pact with the surrendered Greeks and massacred them ruthlessly.[30] In the western part of the empire the wars between Alexander's former commanders took their course; at times the five kings, Antigonus, Ptolemy, Seleucus, Lysimachus and Cassander claimed Alexander's legacy as their own. Conflict developed among the Diadochi, the 'successors', because Alexander's two heirs to the throne were minors: Alexander's half-brother Philip III was feeble-minded and his own son, the future Alexander IV, was not yet born. Cassander had Alexander IV and his mother Roxana poisoned in 310 BC. The war within the Macedonian elite came to an end only with the victory of Seleucus over Antigonus in 301 BC.

In Central Asia, Oxyartes, the father of Roxana, continued to rule as satrap of Paropamisadae and the other Greek satrapies were assigned to army officers: Arachosia to Sibyrtius, Aria and Drangiana to Stasanor and Bactria and Sogdiana to Philip, son of Balakros.[31] In 317 BC the satraps of Central Asia entered the Diadochi conflicts. First they repulsed Peithon, who was expanding to the east, and then supported Eumenes in the war against Antigonus. As a result of the betrayal of his two Macedonian generals, Eumenes could not take advantage of two victories. The Argyraspides, the so-called 'silver shield' that had constituted Alexander's personal guard, later handed Eumenes over to Antigonus. He left the satraps of Central Asia, who had fought against him, in their offices after subjugation.[32] Towards the end of the fourth century BC Antigonus (*ca.* 382–301 BC), who ruled in Asia Minor, and Seleucus I (b. *ca.* 358; r. 305–281 BC) remained as the chief rivals. Before Seleucus carried out the decisive attack on Antigonus, he wanted to secure his eastern flank, so in 307 BC he took off to Central Asia, which nominally belonged to his territory but whose satrapies had been virtually autonomous since Peithon's campaign. Seleucus succeeded without great effort in getting Bactria, Sogdia, Margiana and Aria to recognise his authority. The Macedonian Seleucus was well served not only by his military and diplomatic skills but also by the fact that he was married to

The southernmost tower of the citadel of Zamr-i Atish Parast near Yamchun in Gorno-Badakhshan, southern Tajikistan.

While for the Greeks and Macedonians of the time the campaigns of Alexander and the Seleucids represented adventurous but real undertakings in genuinely existing lands, a millennium later in medieval Europe, on account of a loss of geographic knowledge, they entered the realm of fantasy, inhabited by dragons, horse-headed people, giants and other monsters. The Alexander Romance declares that: 'King Alexander and his army battled against dragons with large emeralds on their foreheads.' Manuscript 78.C.1 from France in the 1290s. Kupferstichkabinett Preußischer Kulturbesitz Berlin.

Apama, the daughter of the Sogdian resistance fighter Spitames. Apama and their son, the future Antiochus I (b. 324; r. 281–261 BC), accompanied him, which contributed to the benevolent attitude of the Sogdian and Bactrians.

South of the Hindu Kush, where Greek authority had been eroding gradually since 316 BC, an entirely different opponent awaited Seleucus, namely Chandragupta (d. 297 BC), founder of the Maurya Empire. Instead of subjecting himself to a possible defeat by a numerically far superior foe, Seleucus chose the path of negotiation. He was also aware that in the event of a victory he would have been unable to hold on to the Indus Valley after his return to the Near East. Thus in 303 BC he recognised the de facto rule of Chandragupta over Gedrosia, Paropamisadae and Arachosia (southern Afghanistan and northern and central Pakistan). In return he gained 500 war elephants, which two years later contributed substantially to his decisive victory over Antigonus at Ipsus in Phrygia. About 80 percent of Alexander's empire now stood under Seleucus's control.[33]

With the peace treaty between Seleucus and Chandragupta the Greek colonies south of the Hindu Kush were under Indian foreign rule for a century, until the Greco–Bactrian king Demetrius I (r. *ca.* 195–171/70 BC) reconquered northern India. Thanks to the good relations between the Seleucids and the Maurya, which included the exchange of diplomatic missions, the Greek colonies and their culture flourished even under Indian suzerainty, as can be seen, for instance, in the edicts of Emperor Ashoka (r. 268–234/32), which were also written in Greek,[34] and in the Greek funerary epigram for a man called Sophytos from Kandahar.[35]

As mentioned above, around 293/92 BC Margiana, Bactria and Aria became targets of a powerful invasion of Saka horsemen, who belonged to the confederation of the Dahae; General Demodamas drove them back to the Jaxartes, however.[36] In order to secure Seleucid rule in Central Asia, Seleucus sent his half-Sogdian son Antiochus, whom he appointed viceroy of the eastern satrapies, to Bactria to oversee the reconstruction of the cities and the renovation and construction of irrigation projects. Antiochus promoted the immigration of Macedonian and Greek settlers and supported a rapprochement between Greeks and Bactrians. He replaced Aramaic with Greek as the official administrative language and opened a royal mint, the first in Central Asia, in the newly founded city of Aï Khanum. It produced a full range of gold, silver and bronze coins, in the name first of Seleucus, later of Seleucus and Antiochus and, beginning in 281 BC, of Antiochus alone. It is above all the bronze coins of low value, used in everyday transactions, which show the degree of monetisation of an economy. Central Asia, particularly Bactria, experienced under the first two Seleucids an unparalleled economic boom, founded on the three pillars of flourishing agriculture, lively intercontinental trade and increased urbanisation – not for nothing did ancient authors like Pompeius Trogus and Strabo call Bactria the 'land of a thousand cities'.[37] The navigability of the Oxus – along which, according to Strabo, 'Indian goods ... could easily be transported to Hyrcania [on the Caspian Sea]'[38] – also contributed to the economic upswing. When Seleucus was murdered in 281 BC, Antiochus returned to western Asia, where he immediately had to defend himself from attacks by the Egyptian Ptolemys and the Celtic Galatians.

In order to secure for himself the important resources of Central Asia in the struggle with his enemies in the west, Antiochus I (r. 281–261 BC) appointed his son Seleucus viceroy of the eastern satrapies around 279 BC. Antiochus's wars in the west led him to neglect the eastern satrapies, however, and moreover, his incessant demands for their economic resources weakened their military readiness against the omnipresent threat of the Saka nomads. While the north-eastern satrapies were able to stave off the invasion of 293/92 thanks to the help of the central government, ten years later they were not only forced to fight on their own but also had to provide the government with troops. At that time the region of Maracanda made an agreement with the encroaching nomads, who left the city undisturbed, and Maracanda became independent from the Seleucid Empire.[39] Presumably the viceroy Seleucus also planned the independence of the eastern satrapies, because in around 268/66 Antiochus had his son, who had begun to mint his own coins, executed for conspiracy.[40]

Head of a presumably Greco-Bactrian prince from the Oxus temple of Takht-i Sangin, southern Tajikistan, painted unfired clay, third–second centuries BC. National Museum of Antiquities of Tajikistan, Dushanbe.

Unfortunately only sparse and fragmentary written sources exist for the history of Greco-Bactria, since most relevant works of history have been lost, so the reconstruction of Greco-Bactrian history is based on numismatics and archaeological data.[41] Antiochus I's successor, Antiochus II (r. 261–246 BC) was constantly embroiled in wars in the Near East, which the Greek satraps of Bactria, Diodotus (*ca.* 285–235 BC), and Parthia, Andragoras (d. *ca.* 238 BC) took advantage of in order to gradually secede from the Seleucid Empire. In the turbulent time around Antiochus's death in 246 BC both satraps declared themselves independent and minted coins in their own names; presumably Diodotus opened a second mint in Bactra.[42] While **Diodotus I** (r. *ca.* 246–235 BC) founded the Greco-Bactrian Kingdom, which included the satrapies of Bactria, Sogdia, Margiana and perhaps eastern parts of Aria; that is, southern Uzbekistan, north-western Afghanistan and south-eastern Turkmenistan, his ally Andragoras was unable to assert himself. Around 239 or 238 BC Arsaces (d. 218 or 211 BC), a leader of the Sakan Parni, who belonged to the confederation of the Dahae, first attacked Diodotus in Bactria. Diodotus was, however, able to drive Arsaces out. Arsaces then descended upon Parthia, killed Andragoras and settled his Parni there. He founded the dynasty of the Parthians, which slowly advanced westwards after 190 BC or after 176 BC and in 141 BC captured the Seleucid capital of Seleucia, near the modern city of Baghdad.[43] Although Parthia lay between Bactria and Greece, Greco-Bactria was in no way isolated, as can be seen in the flow of trade by land and by water.

▶ From 208 to 206 BC the Seleucid king Antiochus III besieged the strongly fortified city of Zariaspa (Bactra) in vain, after which he made a compromise with the Greco-Bactrian king Euthydemos I: Antiochus recognised Euthydemos as king and received in return his war elephants. Shown here are Bactra's walls from the late medieval period, after both Genghis Khan (in 1220) and Tamerlane (in the fourteenth century) had destroyed the city.

Silver tetradrachm of the Greco–Bactrian king Eucratides (r. 171/70–145 BC) with a portrait of the king wearing a Greco–Bactrian helmet decorated with Alexander's tiny bull's ear. Private collection, USA.

Silver tetradrachm of the Greco–Bactrian king Eucratides (r. 171/70–145 BC) with the Dioscuri on horseback and the inscription ΒΑΣΙΛΕΩΣ ΜΕΓΑΛΟΥ ΕΥΚΡΑΤΙΔΟΥ, great king Eucratides. Private collection, USA.

King Diodotus I died around 235 BC, and was succeeded by his son **Diodotus II** (r. *ca.* 235–225 BC). When Seleucus II (r. *ca.* 246–225 BC) advanced into Central Asia before 227 BC, to reconquer the renegade satrapies, Diodotus II and Arsaces formed an alliance and staved off the attack.[44] Around 225 BC Diodotus became the victim of a bloody military putsch by his ostensible satrap of Sogdia, **Euthydemos I** (r. *ca.* 225–195 BC), who had the entire royal family murdered. Widespread traces of fire at Aï Khanum from the year 225 BC suggest that Euthydemos captured the city, which lay at the confluence of the Panj and the Kokcha, by violent means.[45] In 209 BC Parthia and Greco–Bactria found themselves again confronted by a Seleucid attempt at reconquest, as Antiochus III (r. 223–187 BC) had stabilised his empire in the west to the point that he could advance to the east with a powerful army. After the conquest of the Parthian capital of Hekatompylos south-east of the Caspian Sea and the subjugation of Arsaces II (r. 218 or 211–191 BC) Antiochus destroyed the Bactrian cavalry of Euthydemos, who sought refuge in his strongly fortified capital, Zariaspa, and withstood a two-year siege from 208 to 206 BC.[46]

Antiochus then sent an intermediary to Euthydemos, who informed the Seleucids of the nomadic threat in the north. He emphasised that a strong Greco–Bactria represented an ideal bulwark against the barbarians, and for this reason he was also protecting the eastern flank of the Seleucid Empire. Moreover, Euthydemos threatened to open the northern border, which would give the nomadic horsemen, who also ruled Maracanda, unimpeded access to the Seleucid Empire. In a peace treaty Antiochus confirmed Euthydemos as the Bactrian king and relinquished claims to tribute. In response Euthydemos handed his war elephants over to Antiochus, who then turned to the south. He crossed the Hindu Kush and occupied Paropamisadae, where the Indian king Sophagasenus, perhaps a descendant of the Maurya dynasty, subjugated himself without opposition. Antiochus confiscated his war elephants, demanded a large tribute and returned to Seleucia stronger than before.[47] Euthydemos and his son Demetrius surely noticed the lack of opposition among the northern Indians and understood that, in light of this power vacuum, a rich bounty awaited their conquest. If one believes a report by Strabo, who quotes Apollodoros, Euthydemos also exploited Antiochus's withdrawal to expand his territory to the north-east to Fergana as far as 'Seres' and the 'Phryni'. Presumably 'Seres' refers to the Tarim Basin and the Phryni may be equated with the Xiongnu, who subjugated the north-eastern part of the Tarim Basin at the start of the second century BC.[48] It is conceivable that General Demodamas had occupied parts of Fergana as early as around 290 BC and that Euthydemos's northern campaign advanced along one of the trade routes as far as Kashgar or Aksu.

Around 195 BC Euthydemos's son and hitherto co-regent **Demetrius I** (r. *ca.* 195–171/70 BC) became the sole ruler of Greco-Bactria and continued the conquests south of the Hindu Kush that had been begun by his father. Demetrius annexed the provinces of Gandhara with the valley of Kabul, Arachosia and Drangiana and thus reconquered the regions with Greek colonies that the Seleucids had lost between 316 and 303 BC. Demetrius advanced further south to Taxila, 35 km north-west of the modern Pakistani capital of Islamabad, where he founded the city of Sirkap. The successful expansion of the Greco-Bactrian Kingdom south of the Hindu Kush marked the start of the Indo-Greek calculation of time in the year 186/85 BC.[49] Demetrius was presumably the first and also the last Greco-Bactrian king who ruled unchallenged on both sides of the Hindu Kush. Numismatic studies from 189 to 171 BC provide the names of six different kings, however. Either they ruled in rapid succession, which seems unlikely, or Demetrius was the most powerful king and the others were regional viceroys.

Pendant with the 'Lord of Animals' holding two dragons, whose rear legs are twisted 180 degrees, a typical motif of eastern steppe art. Gold decorated with turquoise, garnet, lapis lazuli, carnelian and pearls. Tillya Tepe, grave 2, *ca.* 40–70 AD. National Museum Afghanistan.

Among them were Pantaleon, Agathocles and Apollodoros I, who ruled in the newly conquered regions. A few of these rulers had bilingual coins minted in Greek/Brahmi and Greek/Kharoshthi.[50]

Around the year 171 BC, when Demetrius was south of the Hindu Kush, **Eucratides I** (r. 171/70–145 BC), who may have been allied with the Seleucid ruling family,[51] staged a coup in the Bactrian heartland. It rapidly developed into a bloody civil war. The first victim was the ostensible viceroy of Bactria, Euthydemos II. Demetrius marched northwards and, after an initial success, fell in the second battle. After the victory over Demetrius Eucratides killed the viceroy Antimachos I and presumably captured the city of Aï Khanum, which he renamed Eucratideia.[52] Immediately after this Eucratides turned to the north, crossed the Oxus, marched through the 'Iron Gate' and reconquered Maracanda, which was under the control of the nomads of the Kangju federation, and had the city walls fortified.[53] Greco-Bactria was now split in two: Eucratides ruled north of the Hindu Kush, and three viceroys of the defeated Demetrius ruled to the south. In order to re-establish imperial unity, Eucratides crossed the Hindu Kush to the south, where he vanquished Pantaleon, Agathocles and Apollodoros I and presumably pressed on to Sirkap. Here he encountered the successor of Apollodoros, the Indo-Greek king Menandros I (r. *ca.* 165/155–130 BC), the future conqueror of northern India and great champion of Buddhism.[54] Far from his Bactrian power base, Eucratides had to recognise Menandros's domain and returned empty-handed to Bactria, where he fell victim to an attack in 145 BC. Shortly before his death the Parthian king Mithridates I (r. 171–138 BC) succeeded in seizing several areas in western Greco-Bactria, presumably including Margiana.[55]

The circumstances surrounding Eucratides's murder are mysterious. According to Justin, who cited the work of Pompeius Trogus, now lost, Eucratides 'was killed on his march [back to Bactria] by his son, with whom he had shared the throne, ... and who drove his chariot through his blood and ordered his body to be cast out unburied.'[56] Who was the alleged parricide? Several authors incriminate either Heliocles, the last Greco-Bactrian king north of the Hindu Kush, or his brother Plato, who is said to have ruled for only a short time, presumably as viceroy.[57] But Tarn proposed as long ago as 1938 that Eucratides was not killed by his own son but rather by Demetrius II, son of Demetrius I, who had been defeated by Eucratides in 171/70 BC, with the help of the Parthians. Tarn's view is shared by Sidky.[58] Eucratides's son or brother **Heliocles** (r. *ca.* 145–130 BC), perhaps in alliance with **Eucratides II** (r. *ca.* 145–?) and the viceroy of southern Bactria **Plato I** (r. *ca.* 145–140 BC) overthrew **Demetrius II** (r. 145 BC–?), who may have been appointed by

Mithridates.[59] The disappearance of copper coins during the time of these four kings reveals a collapse of the monetisation of the Bactrian economy and the urban trade structures.[60]

Heliocles quickly began to lose control of the northern regions. The civil war provoked by Eucratides, the costly campaign to Gandhara, the loss of Margiana to the Parthians, and Eucratides's murder resulted in a tremendous weakening of the Greco–Bactrian Kingdom, with dramatic consequences. Nomadic riders from the north took advantage of the chaos following Eucratides's death and promptly attacked. In the next 15 years Greco–Bactria suffered an onslaught of nomadic riding peoples at least twice. Both attacks were the result of a domino-like migration of peoples, brought about the conflicts between the Chinese empire and the Xiongnu nomadic horsemen. After the Xiongnu had dealt three serious defeats to the nomadic horsemen of the Yuezhi, who lived in north-western China, in the years 207, 176, and 162 BC, the latter left their homeland for the west.[61] The majority settled in the fertile valley of the Ili, driving out the Saka who lived there. As the Han Shu records, the 'Sai [Saka] tribes split and separated'.[62] One group of Saka moved into the western Tarim Basin, in particular the oasis of Khotan, another to Sogdia and Bactria, and a third further south: 'The King of the Sai [Saka] moved south, crossed over the Suspended Crossing'[63] and 'established himself as master of Chipin.'[64] The frightening Suspended Crossing, called in Chinese *xuandu,* was located in the Upper Hunza Valley. The path was only 50 to 100 cm wide and consisted of flat stones placed upon sticks jammed into cracks in bare cliffs, often hanging dozens of metres over a stormy river. Having mastered the Suspended Crossing, these Saka established themselves in Kashmir.[65]

In 133 or 132 BC the Wusun nomads, who had once been oppressed by the Yuezhi, attacked the Yuezhi with the help of the Xiongnu and drove them out of the Ili valley.[66] Most of the Yuezhi fled to the south and crossed Fergana and Kangju unopposed, after which they forced the Saka out of the former Greco–Bactria.[67] The Saka then attacked the eastern part of the Parthian Empire, where they defeated and killed the two Parthian kings Phraates II (r. 138–128 BC) and Artabanos I (r. 128–123 BC). Mithridates II (r. 123–88/87) was finally able to resettle some of the Saka in Sakastan, today's Sistan, and force others into the Indus Valley.[68]

The second group of those Saka fleeing the Ili valley *ca.* 160 BC from the invading Yuezhi attacked first Maracanda and then Aï Khanum around the year 145 BC. The attackers systematically plundered the city and set the palace on fire, burning it to the ground. Around 130 BC the Yuezhi moved in and plundered the city again.[69] When the Chinese ambassador Zhang Qian (195–114 BC) visited northern Bactria and the city of Bactra in 128 or 127 BC, to recruit the Yuezhi for an alliance against the Xiongnu, he found them firmly established on the northern bank of the Oxus, while they also ruled the part of Bactria south of the river, although they did not occupy it. He reported: 'Daxia [Bactria] is situated over 2,000 li (*ca.* 800 km) southwest of Dayuan [Fergana], south of the Gui [Oxus] river. It has no great ruler but only a number of petty

Cupids riding a dolphin or catfish. A pair of golden clasps decorated with turquoise and mother of pearl. Tillya Tepe, grave 3, *ca.* 40–70 AD. National Museum Afghanistan.

chiefs ruling the various cities. The people are poor in the use of arms and afraid of battle, but they are clever at commerce. After the Great Yuezhi moved west and attacked and conquered Daxia, the entire country came under their sway. The capital is Lanshi [Bactra] where all sorts of goods are bought and sold.'[70] It appears that the new nomadic rulers interfered with neither trade nor agriculture.[71]

Zhang Qian's report makes no mention of a great king, an army or a unified government. The state structures established by the Greeks had evidently disappeared. Heliocles I, who died around 130 BC, was the last Greek ruler of Bactria; south of the Hindu Kush the last Greek, Hermaios, ruled until about 70 BC, and in the eastern Punjab Strato II, a distant descendant of Manandros I, ruled until about 10 AD.[72] The former territory of Greco-Bactria north of the Hindu Kush underwent a transition to an age of semi-settled stockbreeding of nomadic origin.

3. Bactrian art of the steppe, Hellenism and Zoroastrianism

The art of Greco-Bactria developed unique syntheses between nomadic art, Greek, Iranian and local stylistic elements, as well as between Hellenistic and Central Asian architectural principles.

3.1 The golden treasure of Tillya Tepe

One of the most spectacular archaeological discoveries of the twentieth century in Central Asia was left behind by nomadic horsemen of Bactria who had become settled. In 1969 an Afghan-Soviet expedition under the leadership of Viktor Sarianidi began work at Emshi Tepe in northern Afghanistan, about 100 km west of Bactra. Here they uncovered a 20-ha round city from the first century AD.[73] In 1978 Sarianidi set his spade to Tillya Tepe, the mound 500 m south of Emshi Tepe, where he first exposed a village from the third century BC and under that a fortified hall from the late second millennium BC, which he interpreted as a temple. On 15 November one of the Afghan workers made a completely unexpected discovery of gold, which came from the grave of a young woman, on the west side of the small fortress. Between then and 7 February 1979 the team revealed six extremely rich graves, the burials of a chief and five noblewomen. A seventh grave was resealed since Sarianidi had planned his return for autumn of 1979. He handed the find, including the 21,618 gold objects, over to the Afghan National Museum. Unfortunately, due to the worsening civil war and the Soviet invasion at the end of December 1979, the planned continuation of the excavation never took place.

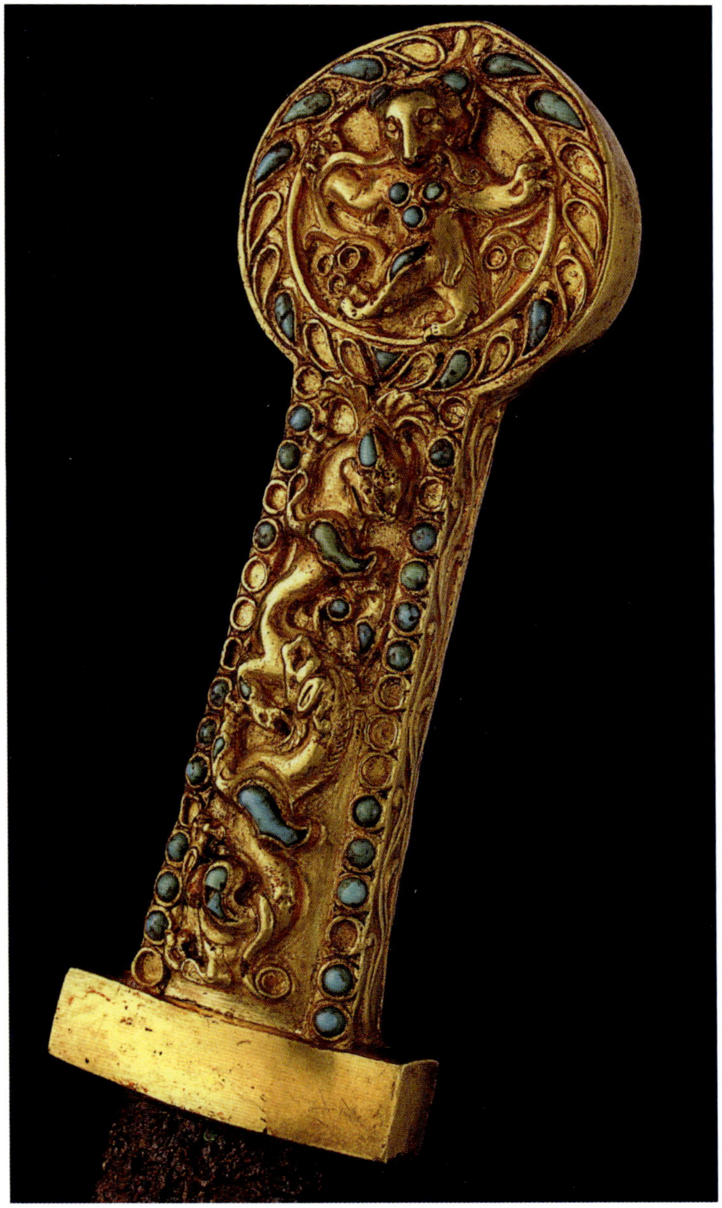

Golden handle of an iron akinakes decorated with turquoise. A dancing bear holding a vine branch in his mouth is shown on the pommel. Tillya Tepe, grave 4, *ca.* 40–70 AD. National Museum Afghanistan.

Looking back, Sarianidi wrote, 'The seventh grave had not yet been examined, and the eighth emerged [in 1979] with the rains, as we sat in Moscow. Since then, darkness has again engulfed the treasures. Soldiers we had trusted apparently looted the two unexcavated graves left in the necropolis. The next spring [1980] there turned up in Kabul's shopping district gold ornaments highly reminiscent of those recovered from Tillya Tepe.' Prophetically he advised the reader: 'Look well on these pieces of the Bactrian masterpieces that follow. Who knows when they will be seen again?'[74] The treasures came within a hair's breadth of falling victim to the chaos of war and the destructive zeal of the Taliban. In 1981 the museums of Hadda and Jalalabad were completely plundered, as was the National Museum in Kabul in 1992, 1994 and 1996, after which the Taliban destroyed most of the statues there in 2001. Fortunately the treasure of Tillya Tepe had been placed securely in a safe in the national bank in 1988 and thus, thanks to the discretion of those few people who knew of it, eluded the grasp of the Taliban. In April 2004 the collection was again secured in the presence of Sarianidi.

According to Sarianidi's description,[75] a young woman lay in grave 1, holding in her hand a coin of the Kushan chief Heraios (r. *ca.* 0–30 AD), the presumed father of the dynastic founder Kujula Kadphises. Her clothing was decorated with seven gold appliqué plates, which show a male figure with snake-like legs, analogous to the primordial mother of all Scythians. This figure carries on his shoulders a huge fish, probably a catfish, and he most likely represents a water god.

In grave 2 lay a 30–40-year-old woman with a Chinese mirror, two daggers decorated in the animal-style and an iron battle axe. Whether the weapons represented a status symbol or identified the woman as a warrior remains unknown. She wore a caftan-like dress with more than 1,500 gold discs and a gold appliqué of a winged 'Aphrodite' or rather Psyche, a pair of gold bracelets ending in the heads of antelopes, which probably date to the third or second century BC,[76] a tall conical headdress decorated with gold discs and a pair of golden pendants in the Sarmato-Alanic style set with semiprecious stones and each showing a 'lord of animals' taming two dragons. To these were added two gold clasps, likewise set with semiprecious stones and depicting a cupid riding on a dolphin or catfish, and three rings, of which two intaglios portray the Greek goddess Athena. In the coffin there also lay tiny amulets made of semiprecious stones in the form of a hand, a foot or animal teeth. Similar amulets were placed in tombs 3, 5 and 6.

Grave 3 also contained the body of a young woman, her head resting on a golden plate. This grave was also rich in grave goods. Although it had not been disturbed by grave robbers, it had been damaged by rodents, who took small gold objects into their lairs and scattered them about the area around the necropolis, which led to the graveyard's local name 'Tillya Tepe', 'Hill of Gold'. Among the grave goods were a silver mirror with Chinese characters and a second mirror with a handle made of ivory, which had been imported from northern India, as well as an Indian ivory comb. There were also two large clasps, each with a warrior in Greco-Bactrian gear and two smaller clasps with cupids riding on dolphins or catfishes, a gold collar, two armbands and two hair pins, three fingerings and a pair of gold shoe soles. Finally, two coins were placed with the woman, a silver Parthian one of Mithridates II (r. 123–88/87 BC) and a gold coin of Emperor Tiberius (r. 14–37 AD). The latter is the oldest Roman coin found in Bactria and provides the terminus post quem, the earliest possible date, not only for the grave but also most likely for the entire necropolis, which is dated to between 40 and 70 AD.

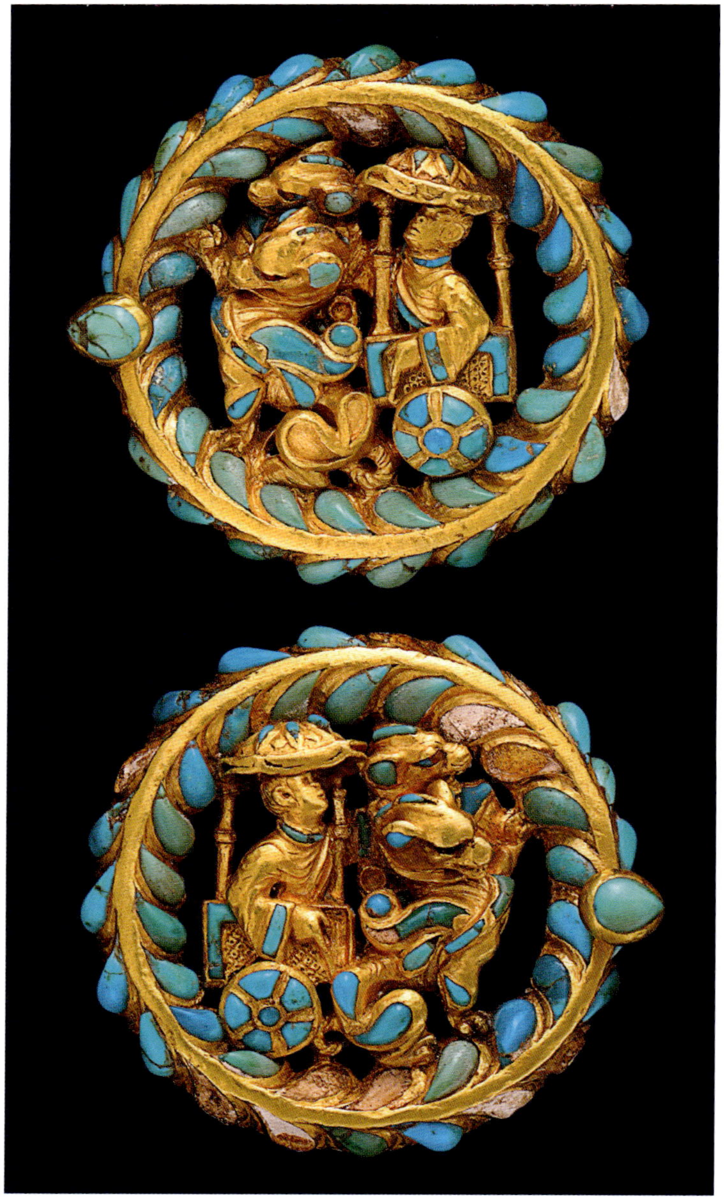

Golden shoe buckles with turquoise and carnelian. They show a man sitting in a chariot under a parasol and pulled by two winged lions. Tillya Tepe, grave 4, *ca.* 40–70 AD. National Museum Afghanistan.

In the main grave 4 lay an adult man, 30 years old, whose head rested on a golden bowl. He was armed with a long iron sword, two daggers, two bows and two full quivers and who was followed into the grave by a sacrificed horse. He was clearly a chieftain, who had either led the life of a mounted warrior or at least been buried according to the traditional customs of nomadic horsemen. One dagger is the one described above,[77] made in the Sarmato-Alanic polychrome style, whose knob is decorated with a bear and whose gold sheath, adorned with turquoise, has one bottom and four side bulges in the form of a coiled, winged carnivore. It is very similar to the dagger of Datchi, as is the second ceremonial dagger from grave 4, on whose gold sheath a winged dragon attacks a predatory creature with a wolf's head and deer antlers. On the rim of this second sheath, 18 swastikas made of blue glass paste surround the scene of animal combat. This second iron dagger has an ivory knob; two small knives are stuck in the back of the sheath, a combination familiar from Tuva and the Altai. With the predator with deer antlers, the dragon and the swastikas, the dagger unites artistic elements from southern Siberia, China and India. Also crafted in opulent Sarmato-Alanic polychrome style were two shoe buckles with two winged lions pulling a chariot, on which sits an aristocratic man under a baldachin. The scene is framed by a double row of rotating turquoise droplets. This portrayal suggests associations with a silver platter from Aï Khanum, on which two lions pull Cybele's chariot,[78] and the type of light, covered chariot recalls one that was discovered in the grave T1 of a chief of the Xiongnu at Gol Mod in northern central Mongolia and that, analogous to Tillya Tepe, dates to the second quarter of the first century AD.[79] As Markus Mode hypothesises, adoption of the theme of the ascension of Alexander by means of griffins in flight is also conceivable.[80] Both buckles were most likely crafted by a local artisan.

Equally spectacular is a golden belt, consisting of an eight-part flexible band and nine medallions, on which a fully sculpted female figure rides a panther. She holds in one hand a cup and with the other one of her breasts in the direction of the cup. The figure could represent the Bactrian goddess Nana, also worshipped by the Kushan people, on her lion, or Cybele who was also venerated in Greco-Bactria. The deceased wore a tall felt or leather cap decorated with a gold moufflon figurine, a headdress decoration similar to those from Arzhan 2 and from the Altai, and a small gold tree, recalling both the diadem of Khokhlach and Chinese money trees.

Also highly notable was a tiny gold medallion that shows on its front a pacing man, rolling an eight-spoked wheel before him; above it is written in Kharoshthi, 'He who puts in motion the

Golden Indian medallion of 1.6 cm diameter showing a man, most probably Buddha Shakyamuni in a yet non-canonical representation, pushing the eight-spoked Wheel of Law in front of him. Tillya Tepe, grave 4, *ca.* 40–70 AD. National Museum Afghanistan.

Wheel of Law'. On the back stands a lion and a second Kharoshthi inscription: 'The lion has driven out fear'. Both sides show key scenes of Buddhism. The setting in motion of the Wheel of Law signifies the first sermon of the Buddha in Sarnath near Varanasi; the eight-spoked wheel, the eightfold path of enlightenment. The lion symbolises the spiritual power of the fearless Buddha and his roar awakens people to the call of the dharma. It appears that the front of the medallion represents one of the oldest, pre-canonical depictions of the Buddha.[81]

In the less richly appointed grave 5 was buried a woman no older than 20, who was given as grave goods a gold collar set with semiprecious gems and two intaglios, one depicting a griffin and the other the Greek goddess of victory Nike. The intaglio with the griffin is the oldest piece found at Tillya Tepe and dates from the fifth to fourth century BC. She wore gold bands on her wrists and ankles and had a sceptre like the corpse in grave 6. To these were added a mirror with a handle, a lidded silver cosmetics box, a silver dish and a bronze bell.

In grave 6 the most distinguished of the five women found her final resting place. The skull of the woman, about 20 years old at death, had been artificially shaped after birth, as was the custom among the nobility of a few Sarmatian tribes, and it lay on a silver dish – two distinguishing features of the contemporaneous 'princess

Foldable golden crown featuring five stylised trees with two tiny birds perched on the upper branches of four of them. The five removable trees are secured with golden tubes to the headband. The lower band is decorated with 20 rosettes having six leaves each. Tillya Tepe, grave 6, *ca.* 40–70 AD. National Museum Afghanistan.

of Kök Tepe', 30 km north of Samarkand, as well.[82] The woman in tomb 6 held in her left hand a gold coin, which was a Bactrian reproduction of a Parthian silver coin of Gotarzes I (r. *ca.* 90–81/80? BC) and in her mouth was a Parthian silver coin of Phraates IV (r. 37–2 BC) with a countermark of a Yuezhi chief. This is reminiscent of the Greek burial ritual of placing a coin under the tongue of the deceased so they can pay Charon, the ferryman of the underworld, to cross the Styx, the river of the dead.[83]

The head of the deceased was adorned with a golden, five-part crown that could easily be folded up and carried in a saddlebag. This crown is decorated with small, stylised trees, similar to those of grave 4, with tiny birds sitting in the upper branches. The branches and twigs of these trees are formed by twisted gold wires hung with thin, sequin-like gold leaves. The Saka and Sarmatians often decorated headdresses with birds and trees of life, as can be seen in the discoveries at Issyk, Khokhlach and Kobiakovo. This splendid crown suggests that the deceased was the main wife of the chieftain. Astonishingly, this crown is very similar to the Korean gold crowns of Silla, also made of sheets of gold and decorated with stylised trees, from the fifth–sixth centuries AD.[84] Presumably Xianbei nomadic horsemen of eastern Mongolia and Manchuria adopted the style and technique of such crowns from the Central Asian Sarmatians and Alans and passed them on to artisans of the northern Korean kingdom of Goguryeo, who in turn passed them on to Silla in the south.

The woman was further adorned with a pair of pendants set with turquoise, each showing a 'mistress of animals' holding a monstrous animal with a wolf's head and gaping jaws and a kind of fishtail, on top of which a raptor sits within the surrounding frame. Sarianidi interprets the figure as Anahita, the Zoroastrian goddess of water and fertility, who in the Avesta lent her name to the Oxus River.[85] The long, caftan-like dress of the deceased was decorated with a gold figurine of a winged 'Aphrodite' or Psyche with a nude upper body, and on the two gold clasps Dionysus and Ariadne ride a bearded griffin, typical of steppe art. In front of the griffin on the ground sits Silenus, associated with Dionysus, with his pointed, horse-like ears. He presents Dionysus with a rython, which the god fills with wine from his cup. Nike hovers behind the couple, holding a wreath above their heads. As Véronique Schiltz observed, 'this kind of explicit unity between man and woman is unknown in the iconography of both the Greeks and the settled Iranians, but seems to fit more naturally into the world of the nomads'. Perhaps this symbolises 'the woman's status as consort to the leader and her apotheosis in death'.[86] As in tomb 3, a silver mirror with Chinese characters lay on her breast and also a mirror with a ivory handle was found. Finally, the deceased wore a gold necklace, two bracelets ending in lions' heads from the third or second century BC, and two simple anklets made of gold. The necklace consisted of ten spherical and two elongated, 25-mm-thick gold beads, whose surface was divided into eight segments by rows of gold filigree, with every other segment decorated with a heart-shaped turquoise. These two goldsmithing techniques were also found in Silla, which is why the expert in Korean art of the Silla period, Young-sook Pak, stated, 'the Tillya Tepe jewelleries [look] as if they were the prototypes for Silla goldsmiths'.[87]

The man, buried in grave 4 in the centre of the small cemetery, may have been a chief of the neighbouring city of Emshi who had maintained the old customs of the nomads and whom five women had to follow into death. Since Bactria was part of a trade network at the time, the treasure of Tillya Tepe brought together objects from every direction: coins and glass from Rome and Parthia, ivory and an early Buddhist medallion from India, silver mirrors from China and motifs of hybrid creatures, weapons and the Sarmato–Alanic polychrome style from the northern steppes. Individual objects, such as the intaglios, came from the Greco–Bactrian period, but the great majority attest to the eclecticism of the local goldsmiths. At the same time the gold objects form a link between the Hellenistic art of Greco–Bactria and the early Buddhist art of the Kushan, as can be seen, for instance, in the clasps from grave 3, where the Macedonian warrior's clothing also appeared in Buddhist sculpture.[88]

To which nomadic group did the princely family of Tillya Tepe belong? Sarianidi proposed one of the five tribes of the Yuezhi, from which the Kushan descended; other scholars, a group of Saka.[89] The Sarmato–Alanic polychrome style of the toreutics, which is not found among the Saka or the Yuezhi, suggests that neither theory is correct. The obvious affinity of the goldwork of Tillya Tepe with the contemporaneous work of the late Sarmatians and Alans of the northern Pontic region, whose homeland lay in Alanliao/Yancai in the delta of the Syr Darya and who were at that time, as the Chinese annals *Hou Hanshu* report, a 'dependency of Kangju', leads to the hypothesis that a chieftain of the Alans, who belonged to the tribal group of Kangju, was buried here.[90]

Two ancient authors reported that, besides the Yuezhi and the Saka, at least one other nomadic tribe played an important role there.[91] Referring to the Scythians, Strabo wrote around the time of the birth of Christ: 'The best known nomads [east of the Massagetai and Sakai] are those who took away Bactriana from the Greeks. I mean the Asii, Pasiani, Tochari and Sacarauli, who originally came from the country on the other side of the Jaxartes River [Syr Darya] that adjoins that of the Sacae and the Sogdiani and was occupied by the Sacae.'[92] The Sacarauli, called 'Sacaraucae' by Pompeius Trogus,[93] may be identified with those Saka who attacked Maracanda and Aï Khanum around 145 BC and, under pressure from the Yuezhi, invaded the eastern Parthian Empire just after 130 BC. The Tochari are the same as the Yuezhi of Chinese sources, whom Zhang Qian encountered on the northern bank of the Oxus in 128 or 127 BC and who, after 200 years of migration through half of Central Asia, founded the Kushan Empire.[94] The

Golden figurine of a winged woman nicknamed 'Aphrodite', but rather representing Psyche. Based on a stylistic analysis it may be dated to the third to second century BC. Tillya Tepe, grave 6, 40–70 AD. National Museum Afghanistan.

Asii and Pasiani are one and the same people, whom Pompeius Trogus called 'Asiani', and to whom he attributed the 'annihilation of the Sacaraucae'.[95] These Asii/Asiani cannot be equated with the Wusun, as Lebedynsky suggests,[96] because after the expulsion of the Yuezhi from the Ili valley, the Wusun settled there in 132 BC and did not pursue the fleeing Yuezhi. As proposed first by Vernadsky and Maenchen-Helfen and later by Grenet, de la Vaissière and Rapin, the Asii/Asiani may be identified with a later group of Alans.[97] In those days around the birth of Christ these Alans belonged to the federation of Kangju.

Since Pompeius Trogus also referred to a victory of the Asiani over the Tochari, the Alans of Kangju not only defeated those Saka who still lived in northern Bactria but also exerted strong pressure against the Yuezhi. The Alans' traces are found in Kök Tepe, and they are different from those of the Sacaraucae.[98] Around the time of Tillya Tepe or shortly thereafter the Kushan forced the nomads belonging to the Kangju northwards and re-established the 'Iron Gate' as border fortification.[99] The Kushan memorialised their triumph over the nomadic bands of Kangju in the great painted clay statues in the palace of Khalchayan north of Termez.[100] The contemporaneous elaborate Alanic graves of the northern Pontic region and of Tillya Tepe from the first century AD reflect the expansion of the Alans to the west and south.

3.2 Aï Khanum – a Greek city in northern Afghanistan

On 18 March 1838 Lieutenant John Wood, who had also discovered one of the sources of the Oxus in the Pamirs, climbed a tall hill in the northern Afghan province of Kunduz. 'From the summit of I-khanam we had a glorious view of the surrounding country. At the foot of the hill was the junction of two rivers. From the point of confluence the Kokcha could be traced to its exit from the mountains on the south, while the eye followed the Oxus westward. [...] Here, we were informed, stood an ancient city. [...] The appearance of the place, however, does indicate the truth of their tradition that an ancient city once stood here.'[101] Wood was the first European to see the ruins of Aï Khanum, but its significance eluded him, as it did the French archaeologist Jules Berthoux when he visited the site in 1926.[102] The honour of recognising the outstanding importance of Aï Khanum is due to the Afghan king Muhammed Zahir Shah (r. 1933–73, d. 2007), when he coincidentally stopped there during a hunt in 1961, noticed the outline of a sunken city and spotted a Corinthian capital in a nearby house. He immediately asked the *Délégation archéologique française en Afghanistan (DAFA)*, which was working in Afghanistan, to investigate the site. Unfortunately the Soviet invasion in late 1979 brought an end to the excavations, which had uncovered only a quarter of the lower city.[103] In the 1990s Aï Khanum was systematically plundered, the excavated monuments were destroyed and the unexplored sections ravaged to such an extent that today the land looks like the surface of the moon. In 2002 a few Ionic and Corinthian capitals as well as columns appeared in neighbouring villages, in one case serving as roof beams in a tea house.[104]

The city, founded by Seleucus I[105] and renamed Eucratideia by Eucratides I around 170 BC, lay in a strategically significant location at the confluence of two rivers near mines for semiprecious gems and on a trade route linking Bactria with China and India. The importance of Aï Khanum as a trading city can be seen in the discovery of 676 Indian silver coins here.[106] An Achaemenid city once stood just 2 km away. Aï Khanum has a triangular plan. The sides along the banks of the Panj and the Kokcha measured 1.8 and 1.5 km respectively, and the third, landward side, 2.6 km, two-thirds of which was protected by tall hills, where the acropolis was located.[107] A strong defensive wall made of unfired clay, 7 m thick

Plan of the Hellenistic city of Aï Khanum in northern Afghanistan, which lay at the confluence of the rivers Panj and Kokcha. To the left is the lower city with the great palace and public buildings; to the right, the sparsely built upper city. According to B. Staviskij, *La Bactriane sous les Kushans*, 1986, p. 162 (illustration J.-Cl. Liger).

Illustrations according to archaeological discoveries of the Hellenistic city of Aï Khanum in northern Afghanistan. From left to right and front to back: The River Ochus (Panj); a patrol of the prodromoi, the light cavalry; the city walls; the gymnasium complex; a mausoleum; the theatre; the palace complex; the temple dedicated to Zeus and the upper city.

in exposed sections and fortified with rectangular towers, surrounded the entire city. In contrast to the conventional defensive walls of Central Asia, such as those of Maracanda, which were caved to offer protection for people, those of Aï Khanum were solid in order to withstand the assaults of large siege machines.

Most of the buildings stood in the lower city, which was less exposed to the wind than was the upper city; a long, straight street ran through the lower city. Among the most notable buildings were a spacious palace, a temple, a public gymnasium with an adjacent bath, a classical theatre that offered space for 5,000 spectators – the easternmost in Hellenistic Asia – an arsenal and two heroii (memorial monument) – all markers of a classical Greek polis. The palace, built at ground level out of fired bricks and above that of unfired clay bricks, reveals a fascinating synthesis of Greek and traditional Central Asian architectural principles. The floor plan of the great halls and the supporting columns corresponded to Greek models, as the latter consisted exclusively of stone, the shaft rested on an Attic base and it was topped by a Corinthian capital. The columns were constructed without mortar but secured by iron bolts – also a typically Greek practice. In the traditional architecture of the region, by contrast, shaft and capital were made of wood, which gave the structure greater flexibility in earthquake-prone Central Asia. On the other hand, the buildings did not have Greek pitched roofs but rather Central Asian flat roofs. They did, however, have two rows of Greek tiles on the edges for decoration, as did the roofs at Khalchayan. Roof tiles only make sense for pitched roofs; they are out of place on flat roofs, as they only add unnecessary weight.

The Oxus treasure

The history of the Oxus treasure, which includes about 180 objects and 500 coins and which can be seen in the British Museum, is just as spectacular as the objects themselves.[108] In the nineteenth century, near the ancient fortress of Takht-i Kuwad, at a ford through the Oxus in southern Tajikistan, local treasure-hunters were looking for gold and silver objects on the riverbank. Around 1877 a few of them made a discovery near the fortress, which is not far from the confluence of the Vakhsh and the Panj. In 1880 they sold a large portion of the hoard to three merchants from Bukhara, who intended to sell the goods in the metropolis of Rawalpindi.[109] At the Afghan border and at sentry points they had to give soldiers individual items, mostly gold and silver coins, as 'tolls', so their treasure slowly dwindled, but they reached Kabul safely. Between Kabul and Peshawar, however, they were set upon by local villagers, robbed and carried off to nearby caves. But one servant escaped and at nightfall alerted the British political officer F.C. Burton, who set out immediately with two orderlies. 'Towards midnight [he] made an unexpected appearance among the bandits, who had already been quarrelling over their plunder. Four of them were lying wounded on the floor.'[110] The thieves handed the officer their loot. Returning to his camp, Burton declared the start of a punitive operation, whereupon other villagers returned more of the goods. Thus the three merchants, who had been freed in the meantime, got back three-quarters of their possessions.

Soon the gold and silver objects in question were being traded by the merchants of Rawalpindi, where they were subject to further dangers. A few merchants supplemented their supply with additional objects of other provenance; others offered hastily produced copies and kept the originals. The odyssey of the Oxus treasure came to an end when Major General Sir Alexander Cunningham, director of the Archaeological Survey of India, bought up the objects and pressured them to sell him the originals, too. Later Sir A.W. Franks acquired Cunningham's collection and bequeathed it to the British Museum in 1897. The museum believes that the objects are authentic.[111] Among the most outstanding finds are a pair of golden armlets with horned griffin protomes,[112] a miniature golden chariot pulled by four horses with a charioteer and a passenger,[113] a silver statue of a naked youth,[114] a golden akinakes sheath with Assyrian-looking motifs,[115] a gold vessel in the shape of a fish and about 40 thin golden plaques, on which is embossed a standing man, in profile, holding either a barsom or a lotus blossom.[116] The barsom has a cultic connection to Zoroastrianism, as it is a consecrated bundle of twigs that priests hold during the reading of the Avesta. Other round gold plaques feature a bearded face similar to the Egyptian god Bes.

Immediately after the publication of Dalton's catalogue in 1905, a lively discussion began about the treasure, which focused on the following questions: Was the treasure a unified collection and was it discovered in a single location or did the discoverers assemble it between 1877 and 1880? Did objects and coins belong together? Were they real? How should the discoveries be dated and where did they come from? Did the hoard have a function? Today most scholars believe that the majority of the objects are genuine[117] and were discovered, and thus had been buried, in the same place, while many items had found their way into other collections or been melted down. The coins presumably belonged to the hoard, but only a third of the original number of about 1,500 made it to the British Museum. Except for some of the inexpertly produced local gold discs, a large number of the objects came from the Achaemenid period[118] and were probably of western Iranian provenance.[119] A few pieces, such as the silver statues of a naked youth, show Greek

Gold disc with a man in Median clothing armed with an akinakes and holding a barsom; presumably he is a priest or worshipper at a fire temple. Oxus Treasure, fifth–fourth centuries BC. The British Museum, London.

influence, and others were produced nearby in Greco–Bactria. A unique gold badge came from the steppe territory.[120]

Like the objects, the coins are of varied origin and period; they came from: Athens (fifth century BC), Macedonia (500–323 BC), Ionian Asia Minor (fifth–fourth centuries BC), Achaemenid royal mints (fifth–fourth centuries BC), Achaemenid satrapies of Asia Minor (400–332 BC), Central Asian satrapies under Greek rule (321–300 BC), Bactra (fourth century BC), Seleucids (312–246 BC), the rulers Andragoras and Wahshuwar (fourth–third centuries BC) and Taxiles (fourth century BC), Greco–Bactria (256–170 BC). The Seleucid and Greco–Bactrian coins made up by far the largest single group.[121] The coins and objects thus define a hypothetical time frame for the hoard from the early fifth to the beginning of the second century BC. The gold plaques, depictions of animals and miniature models of chariots were most likely votive gifts, which suggest a temple origin. Since 1976, with interruptions archaeologists have been excavating a fire temple 5 km upstream near Takht-i Sangin, also dedicated to the river god Oxus.[122] These factors led to the hypothesis that the Oxus collection was originally the treasure of the Oxus temple and had been buried at Takht-i Kuwad. Why and when the hoard was buried remains unknown; it is likely that the looming invasion of the Saka or, soon after, the Yuezhi was a factor.[123]

As in Greece the dead were buried outside the city in family crypts in a cemetery; the construction of a heroon within the city was permitted only in extraordinary cases. Two Greek inscriptions were engraved on one of the two memorial monuments of Aï Khanum. One names Kineas as one of the city fathers; the second comes from the philosopher Clearchus of Soli (*ca.* 340–250 BC), a student of Aristotle who visited Aï Khanum and had the 150 'maxims of Delphi', attributed to the Seven Sages, engraved there. The extant fragment reads:

As a child, be well-behaved.
As a youth, be self-controlled.
As an adult, be just.
As an elder, be wise.
As dying, don't regret.[124]

The sojourn of a pupil of Aristotle in Aï Khanum shows that a lively intellectual exchange took place between the Greek homeland and this outpost of Greek culture in Central Asia.

Aï Khanum had three shrines, whose architecture featured few Greek elements. The main temple, with a square plan of 20 x 20 m, stood in the lower city and within it was a seated statue of Zeus, under whose guise presumably Ahura Mazda or Mithra was worshipped simultaneously.[125] The statue was an acrolith, and it consisted of a combination of materials: head, hands and feet were made of marble, and the torso was sculpted out of clay over a wooden frame.[126] In the temple, the above-mentioned silver plate featuring Cybele, dated to the third century BC, was found. The goddess of nature stands on a light chariot pulled by two lions. The winged goddess Nike is her charioteer, behind her a priest holds a parasol and a second priest makes an incense offering on a altar with high steps; in the sky Helios, the moon and a star observe the scene.[127] The plate is a typical example of hybrid Greco–Oriental art: while the two goddesses standing on a chariot drawn by lions and Helios are Hellenistic motifs, the priest holding a parasol above Cybele's head and the shape of the altar are eastern.

Outside the city, not far from the city gate, stood a second temple and, on the acropolis, a monumental open-air altar. As reported by ancient authors, Iranians tended to worship their deities in such elevated places. While Greco–Bactria adopted many Central Asian elements into its architecture, in the minting of coins it remained faithful to the Greek models. On the coins it can be seen that the official pantheon consisted exclusively of Greek deities, predominantly Zeus, Apollo, Hercules, Poseidon, Athena, Artemis and the Dioscuri. However, the occasional appearance of non-Greek attributes, such as rays of light, indicates that Asiatic gods were being worshipped in the form of a Greek deity, such as Mithra in the form of Zeus or Hercules and Anahita in that of Artemis.[128]

The city of Saksanochur in what is today southern Tajikistan, built a few decades later than Aï Khanum and 40 km north of it, demonstrates that Aï Khanum was not an isolated case. Like Aï Khanum, the city, which still existed in the third century AD, had a palace and temple complex with stone columns and Corinthian capitals.[129] Similar, smaller Hellenistic towns flourished north of the Oxus near Dalverzin Tepe (valley of the Sukhan Darya), which was destroyed by the Saka at the same time as Aï Khanum and rebuilt at the start of the Kushan dynasty, as well as near Kalai Mir (valley of the Kafirnigan Darya).[130] Dilbergine Tepe stood south of the Oxus, 40 km north-west of Bactra. It was one of the many Achaemenid settlements intended to secure the trade routes, but it was destroyed by Alexander. Early Greco–Bactrian kings rebuilt it, fortifying it with strong defensive walls and building a temple dedicated to the Dioscuri, as can be concluded from a mural of the twins Castor and Pollux riding a white horse.[131]

The fire temple of Takht-i Sangin on the northern bank of the Oxus (Amu Darya) in southern Tajikistan was also dedicated to the river god Oxus. From back to front: propylon, temenos (temple plaza area), passageway to the aiwan, aiwan eight-columned room. The central four-columned room was reburied in 1990.

3.3 The Oxus temple

The Oxus temple, which today is called Takht-i Sangin, meaning 'stone throne', may correspond with the ancient settlement of Oxeiana, as it is recorded on the seventh Asian map of Ptolemy.[132] The large temple, 51 x 51 m in extent, and the city, which extended over 2 km south and north of it along the northern bank of the Oxus, were likely to have been built by the Seleucid Antiochus I at the start of the third century BC in his capacity as viceroy of the eastern satrapies.[133] Today the shrine stands in the centre of a citadel 238 x 167 m in extent, which was built toward the end of the Greco–Bactrian Kingdom when invasions threatened from the north.

The temple, built of unfired clay bricks, displays an Iranian layout. One entered through a propylon (gate) into the temenos, the temple plaza, and proceeded through a passageway to a rectangular, covered courtyard, with two side structures connected to the short sides. The hall, enclosed on three sides, remained fully open to the front and formed an *aiwan*, a type of structure later very common in Central Asia and Iran. The flat roof was supported by eight columns, which rested on double plinths and culminated in Ionic capitals.[134] On one plinth nomads had drawn so-called *tamga* symbols, indicating use of the temple for profane purposes during the interruption in temple activity between the end of Greco-Bactria and the early Kushan.[135] In each of two symmetrically placed rooms north and south of the eight-columned hall there stood a fire altar and the sacred ashes were also kept in special pits here. The excavators Litvinsky and Pitschikjan assert that these small complexes, are 'the real hallmark of Iranian fire temples'.[136] For Pitschikjan the Oxus temple represents 'of all the known fire temples in both the territory of middle or Central Asia and Achaemenid Iran, the most complete and least damaged of this type of complex'.[137]

From this eight-columned hall a passage led to the central, square, four-columned room, which was surrounded by long corridors on three sides. This entire complex was again enclosed by long corridors, created when the later enclosure with strong defensive walls and corner towers was built. Under the floor of the central hall archaeologists found pits containing consecrated temple offerings. The bones of sacrificed animals and votive gifts, some ritually shattered, had also been placed in the long corridors surrounding the room.[138] Among the thousands of votive offerings were sculptures made of unfired clay and covered with colourfully painted plaster, of which two impressive portraits of Seleucid or Greco–Bactrian rulers and a third representation of a local chieftain are especially outstanding. To these were added a statue of a seated woman, ivory figurines and objects produced in Bactria, jewellery, coins and gold plaques similar to those found in the Oxus treasure. In the second period, during the time of the Kushan (first–third centuries AD), more weapons of all types appeared in the collection of temple offerings, among them spears, lances and arrowheads, miniature swords and replicas, which suggests a change in cultic activity or in the temple clientele and their concerns.

The most important discovery, however, is the 16-cm-tall bronze statue of Silenus playing an *aulos*, a Greek double flute, from the third/second century BC. Silenus stands on a limestone base with the Greek inscription, 'Following a vow, Atrosokes dedicated [this] to the Oxus'; that is, the river god of the same name.[139] From this inscription it can be concluded that the temple was also consecrated to the river god Oxus. With regard to the geographic location of the shrine, it stood at the 'birthplace' of the river, the confluence of the Vakhsh and the Panj. The small votive statue also illustrates a 'synthesis of Iranian–Bactrian and Greek traditions: the venerated

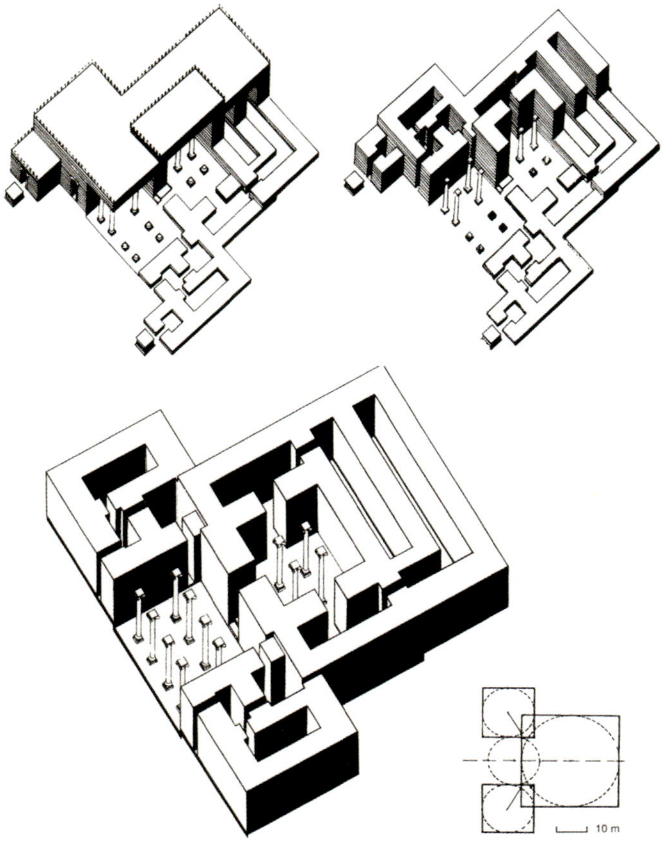

Elevation of the Oxus temple (Taxt-i Sangin), southern Tajikistan: the eight-column aiwan with two side-chapels and the central four-column hall with surrounding corridors. According to: B. Litvinskij, I. Picikjan, *Taxt-i Sangin*, 2002, p. 93, illustration. I. Picikjan, G. Arzumanov.

A Greek inscription on the edge of a mould for a bronze cauldron found in the temple plaza of Takht-i Sangin, southern Tajikistan, confirms that the temple was dedicated to the river god Oxus. Second century BC. National Museum of Antiquities of Tajikistan, Dushanbe.

A winged hippocamp with a female torso and forelegs of a horse holds an oar. Painted ivory with bronze inlays, Takht-i Sangin, southern Tajikistan. Second century BC. National Museum of Antiquities of Tajikistan, Dushanbe.

Oxus is local Bactrian, the name of the donor is of Iranian origin and the inscription and the iconography of the figurine are clearly Greek'.[140] A small ivory statuette of a female hippocamp in the shape of the upper body of a winged woman with the lower body of a fish and the forelegs of a horse was also appropriate for the environs of a river god.[141]

Two additional inscriptions from the first half of the second century BC confirm the interpretation of the shrine as an Oxus temple. One is on the rim of a fragment of a stone bowl and the other on the casting mould for a bronze cauldron found in 2007 in a pit in the temple plaza. The inscription, in mirror image in the mould, reads, 'Seiromios, son of Nemiskos of Molpalres, placed the bronze cauldron [of] seven talents [weight] (approx. 180–250 kg) as a votive gift in the temple of the newly arisen Oxus'.[142] It is likely that both Bactrians and Greeks visited the temple. As both fire and water were worshipped in this temple in the guise of the river god Oxus, it recalls the temple of Jarkutan, more than a millennium older.[143] The temple was destroyed at the same time as Aï Khanum after 145 or around 130 BC, rebuilt at the start of the Kushan period in the first century AD and remained in use into the third century.

Although 27 excavation campaigns have already been carried out at Takht-i Sangin, several questions remain unanswered, not least the one of who deposited the Seleucid votive gifts discovered in the temple. Litvinsky and Pitschikjan assume that there was an earlier, Achaemenid shrine, not yet found, from which the pre-Seleucid votive gifts were transferred to the Seleucid Oxus temple.[144]

IX

Outlook

For the first time the states of the north-[west, that is Central Asia] came into communication with Han-[China]. It was [Zhang] Qian who had pioneered the way between 139 and 115 BC.

SSU-MA CH'IEN (SIMA QIAN)[1]

A lone traveller in the Badain Jaran Desert, Inner Mongolia, northern China.

This volume, the first of four, has addressed the emergence of early Central Asian cultures, which were initially based for many millennia on a hunter-gatherer economy. The first Neolithic revolution made possible the first steps towards a transition to farming in southern and north-western Central Asia. This led to the establishment of larger settlements and proto-urban centres. Later on, metallurgy, horsemanship, the wheel and the wagon revolutionised life in the northern half of Central Asia – it was the moment of birth for an extensive stockbreeding economy, from which nomadic lifestyles later evolved. In these epochs animals played a leading role in religious thought and in forms of artistic expression.

About 5,000 years ago Indo-European languages started to crystallise and a spectacular expansion of Indo-European people began, until they had spread as far east as the border with China and south to the Indian subcontinent. Around 1000 BC the highly mobile nomadic riding peoples of the Scythians and the Saka, as well as related groups, appeared, shaping history and culture in Central Asia for a millennium. Superior weaponry, mastery of horsemanship and marked tactical skill ensured their political dominance.

In the second half of the last pre-Christian millennium on the periphery of Central Asia there appeared stable, centralised states of settled societies with professional armies or at least elite corps. In conflicts with Achaemenids, Macedonians and Romans the Central Asian riders were able to hold the invading forces in check, assimilate them or contribute to their defeat.

The second volume tells the thousand-year history of the age of the classical Silk Roads (*ca.* 200 BC–900 AD), from the establishment of the first nomadic empire by the Xiongnu to the kingdom of the Uyghurs in eastern Turkestan (Xinjiang). Around 200 BC the empire of the Xiongnu nomadic horsemen formed as a response to increasing pressure from the Chinese empire, united for the first time. The expansion of the Xiongnu led to successive waves of migrations of peoples towards the south-west and west, including the Yuezhi, Wusun and Ili-Saka, who advanced as far as Kashmir. These migrations also marked the start of almost 2,000 years of migratory movements of Turko-Mongolian peoples out of eastern Central Asia to China, Turkestan, Iran and Europe. The Huns were the prelude, followed by the Xianbei and the Turkic peoples, who founded two empires in eastern Central Asia and undertook diplomatic relations with Iran and the Eastern Roman Empire.

The beginning of the first millennium bore witness to the expansion of Buddhism in eastern Central Asia and from there to China and Mongolia. The trade routes of Central Asia were travelled not only by caravans laden with exotic goods but also by artistic ideas and further world religions. Among the former was the Buddhist style of Gandhara, a synthesis of elements from Indian, Iranian and Greco-Roman art, and among the latter were Manichaeism and 'Nestorian' Christianity. With the Sogdians, who originated in the region around Samarkand and conducted much of the trade that ran through Central Asia, Iranian cultural assets spread to Turkestan and China. The epoch of the Silk Roads was also the age of the Chinese pilgrim monks who crossed Central Asia in order to study at the Buddhist universities of India and bring Buddhist sutras back to their homeland. The travel diaries of Faxian and Xuanzang in particular provide valuable information about the cultural history of Central Asia which archaeology has confirmed countless times.

In Central Asia the first Christian millennium was shaped not only by a creative and enriching exchange of culture and ideas but also by clashes of great powers such as the two Turkic empires, China, Tibet, Iran and, beginning in the late seventh century, the Arabs. The Arabs distinguished themselves from all other conquerors in that they imposed their own beliefs on those they subjected. Christianity, Judaism and Zoroastrianism were, with limitations, tolerated, but Buddhism was eradicated. Additionally, Islamic iconoclasm represented the first cultural earthquake that shook eastern Central Asia.

The millennium covered in the second volume was an age in which the states on the periphery of Central Asia decisively determined its fortunes. On the other hand, eastern Central Asia was a continuing source for the migration of Turko-Mongolian peoples to the south and west. They ruled northern China from the fourth to the sixth centuries AD; in Central Asia they founded several kingdoms and, towards the end of the first millennium, began to push back the Iranian dominance that had existed until then with regard to ethnicity and language. The expansion of Turkic peoples, which led to a Turkicisation of the previously Indo-European steppes, reached its first climax with the capture of Baghdad in 1055 and its most spectacular triumph in 1453 with the conquest of Constantinople; in 1683 they stood at the gates of Vienna.

An intriguing mixture of ethnicities developed in the Tarim Basin particularly, mostly Buddhist cultures, flourished in the oases. Thanks to itinerant artists from Gandhara, Bactria, Sogdia and China, there were fascinating and at the same time harmonious syntheses of corresponding styles, which reached their zenith in the cave paintings of Kizil and Kumtura on the northern rim of the Tarim Basin and in the neighbouring province of Gansu at the Mogao cave paintings of Dunhuang. The visual transmission of important Buddhist content contributed essentially to the spread of Buddha's teaching and achieved in Central Asia pinnacles of expressiveness and spiritual power.

Appendix: The most important prehistoric and early historic cultures of Central Asia

	WEST OF THE URALS	EAST OF THE URALS	EASTERN KAZAKHSTAN	MINUSINSK
NEOLITHIC	**Elshanka** Volga, 7000–6000 BC			
	Bug–Dniester 6500–5200 BC	**Atbasar and Makhandzhar** northern Kazakhstan 5500–3000 BC		
	Dnieper–Donets I 5700–5200 BC	**Kitoi** West-Baikalia, 5500–4250 BC **Isakovo + Serov** 4250–3250 BC		
	Dnieper–Donets II 5200–4200 BC	**Glazkovo** West-Baikalia, 3250–2100 BC		
CHALCOLITHIC AND EARLY BRONZE AGE	**Cucuteni-Tripolye** Ukraine + eastern Romania, 5200–2800 BC			
	Samara Volga, 5000–4500 BC			
	Khvalynsk Volga, 4700–3800 BC **Late Khvalinsk** 3800–3300 BC			
	Sredny Stog Dnieper, 4500–3500 BC			
	Maikop Kuban, 3750–3000 BC	**Botai** northern Kazakhstan, 3700–3000 BC		
	Repin Don, 3600–2900 BC			
	Usatovo 3300–2800 BC			
	Yamnaya 3300–2250 BC	**Afanasievo** 3300–2350 BC		**Afanasievo** 3300–2350 BC
MIDDLE AND LATE BRONZE AGE	**Poltavka** 2700–2100 BC	**Samus** 2400–1750 BC		**Okunev** 2400–1750 BC
	Katakombnaya 2450–1950 BC	**Andronovo complex** 2200–1250 BC **Sintashta*** 2200–1700 BC **Petrovka*** 2200–1700 BC **Tashkovo** 2200–1700 BC		**Andronovo** 1750–1400 BC (within Minusinsk only)
	Abashevo 2200–1900 BC	**Alakul*** 2100–1400 BC		
	Srubnaya 1950–1200 BC	**Fyodorovo*** 1850–1250 BC		**Karasuk** 1450–1000 BC
	Belozerka 1200–950 BC	**Irmen** 1450–800 BC **Baitovo** 850–500 BC		**Kamennyi Log** 1400–1000 B
IRON AGE	**Cimmerians** 714–600 BC **Kuban Scythians** 700–550 BC **Pontic Scythians** 550–250 BC **Crimean Scythians** 170 BC–218 AD **Sauromatians** 650–400 BC **Sarmatians** 400 BC–400 AD **Alans** 0–400 AD	**Ananyino** 700–250 BC **Sargat** 500 BC–350 AD	**Zebakino-Čilikta** 850–650 BC **Čilikta** 650–450 BC **Bukon** 450–200 BC **Issyk-Besschatyr** 450–200 BC	**Tagar** 1000–200 BC **Bainov** 1000–800 BC **Podgornovo** 800–450 BC **Saragash** 450–200 BC
				Tes 200 BC–50 AD
				Tashtyk 50–500 AD

* Part of the Andronovo Culture

A	MONGOLIA, ALTAI	XINJIANG	SOUTH-EAST
			Hissar 6200–1200 BC
			Kelteminar Choresmia 5500–2400 BC
			Jeitun 6500–4500 BC
			Anau I A 4800–4000 BC
			Namazga I 4000–3500 BC
			Namazga II 3500–3100 BC
			Sarazm I 3500–3200 BC
			Namazga III 3100–2500 BC **Sarazm II** 3200–2900 BC **Sarazm III** 2900–2500 BC
			Zamanbaba Choresmia 2400–1500 BC
	Karakol 2400–1750 BC		**Namazga IV** 2500–2200 BC **Namazga V** 2300/2200–1900 BC **Sarazm IV** 2500–1500 BC **BMAC** 2300/2200–1500 BC
		Ayala Mazar-Xiaohe 2000–1400 BC	**Namazga VI** 2000/1900–1500 BC **Sapalli/Jarkutan** 1700–1350 BC
		Ke'ermuqi 1400–1000 BC	
	Khirigsuur 1400–300 BC		**Jaz I** 1500–1000 BC **Chust** 1400–900 BC
	Slab Grave 1250–100 BC **Deer Stone** 1400–500 BC	**Wupu** 1300–900 BC **Quergou** 1250–1000 BC	**Kuzali, Molali** 1350–900 BC **Beshkent-Vaksh** 1100–900 BC
a 1 850–700 BC **el'** 700–500 BC **azy** 500–200 BC	**Majemir** 900–500 BC **Pazyryk** 400–200 BC	**Charwighul** 1000–400 BC **Dalongkou** 800–200 BC **Qunbake** 800–250 BC **Zaghunluk-Jumbulakum/Satma** **Mazar** 900–200 BC **Xiangbaobao** 550–350 BC **Tiemulike** 550–200 BC **Aidinghou** 500–150 BC	**Jaz II** 1000–800 BC **Jaz III** 800–329 BC **Amirabad** 1450–750 BC **Tagisken South/Ujgarak** 750–480 BC **Čirikrabat** 500–200 BC **Kujusaj** 650–100 BC **Old Choresmia** 600 BC–100 AD **Kjuzeligyr** 600–350 BC **Kangju** 350 BC–100 AD **Kushan** 100–300 AD
			Achaemenids 550–330 BC
			Macedonians 330–307 BC **Seleucids** 307–246 BC **Greco-Bactria** 246–130 BC **Saka/Yuezhi/Alanliao** 130 BC–100 AD

Notes

Introduction

1. We largely abstain from using the term 'civilisation', as in the past it has often been used, from a Eurocentric outlook, to imply a superiority over so-called 'barbarians' or 'uncivilised' ways of life.
2. The 'Han Shu' was begun around 36 AD by the historian Ban Biao, further developed by his son Ban Gu, and completed by the latter's sister Ban Zhao around the year 110.
3. *History of Civilizations of Central Asia* (Unesco Publishing, Paris, 1992–2005).

I. Geography, Climate and Prehuman History of Central Asia

1. Ellsworth Huntington, *The Pulse of Asia* (Boston, 1907), pp. 15, 359.
2. Alexandre de Humboldt, *Asie Centrale. Recherches sur les chaînes des montagnes et la climatologie comparée* (Paris, 1843).
3. This book takes the view that the origin of the Proto-Indo-European language is to be found in the region north-east of the Black Sea. See p. 135.
4. Akiner Shirin, 'Silk Roads, Great Games and Central Asia', *Journal of the Royal Society for Asian Affairs*, London, Vol. XLII, No. 3, November 2011, p. 392.
5. 'Inner Asia' is a purely geographical term and encompasses Xinjiang, Outer Mongolia, Tibet and Tuva in southern Siberia.
6. Roy Chapman Andrews, *Under a Lucky Star* (1943) 2009, p. 3.
7. Andrews, *Under a Lucky Star*, p. 9.
8. Elicio Colin, *L'oeuvre du P. Licent et la Mission paléontologique française en Chine du Nord* (Paris, 1926), p. 287.
9. Andrews, Roy Chapman, *The new conquest of Central* Asia (New York, 1932), p. 39.
10. Ibid.
11. Ibid, p. 162.
12. Ibid, p. 208. A few shell fragments had already been found in 1859 and 1869 in France and tentatively identified as coming from dinosaurs, but Andrews' expedition was the first to find complete eggs with dinosauric embryos inside.
13. Walther Heissig and Claudius Müller, *Die Mongolen* (Frankfurt, 1989), p. 11.
14. Andrews, *The new conquest of Central Asia*, pp. 255f, 268, 413.
15. Ibid, pp. 433ff.
16. Andrews, *Under a Lucky Star*, p. 251.
17. *History of civilizations of Central Asia.* Vol. I. (Paris, 1992), pp. 29–37.
18. Inner Mongolia refers to the Inner Mongolia Autonomous Region in northern China, and Outer Mongolia to the independent Republic of Mongolia.
19. A striking exception were the early Xiongnu rulers, who valued control over strategic territories as essential. For example, when the founder of the Xiongnu Empire, Maodun Chanyu, was asked after 209 BC by his powerful eastern neighbours, the Dong Hu, to hand over his favourite horse and later his favourite consort, he immediately obliged. But when the Dong Hu asked for some eastern parts of the Gobi Desert, 'Maodun flew into a rage [saying]: "Land is the basis of a nation".' Then he attacked and destroyed the Dong Hu (Ssu-ma Ch'ien. *Shih chi.* Translated by Burton Watson, 1971, Vol. II, p. 162). See also Vol. II of the present work.
20. Philipp Johann von Strahlenberg, *Das Nord- und Östliche Theil von Europa und Asia, in so weit solches das gantze Russische Reich mit Siberien und der großen Tartarey in sich begreiffet* (Stockholm, 1730), pp. 91–112.
21. Ancient geographers and historians had already located the boundary between Europe and Asia along the Don; e.g., Arrian around 131/32 AD in his *Periplus Ponti Euxini*, 19.1.
22. Ursula Markus and Ursula Eichenberger, *Augusto Gansser: Aus dem Leben eines Welt-Erkunders*, (Zurich, 2008), p. 44.
23. According to the modern cladistic classification, the dinosaurs include the ancestors of birds, which descended from small theropod dinosaurs.
24. Blount, Kitty, Maggie Crowley et al. (eds), *Encyclopedia of Dinosaurs & prehistoric life* (New York, 2001).
25. Rothe, Peter, *Die Erde* (Damstadt, 2008), supplement.
26. The Greek physician and founder of the science of medicine Hippocrates (*ca.* 460–370 BC) had already postulated a connection between climatic and geographical factors on the one hand and the human constitution and societal structures on the other (E. Kuzmina, *The Prehistory of the Silk Road* (Philadelphia, 2008), p. 8).
27. Robin Dennell, *The Palaeolithic Settlement of Asia* (Cambridge, 2009), pp. 52, 325.
28. The Arctic Circle runs along 66° 34' north latitude.
29. Although the larger share of rain occurs on the windward side, the orographic lift has also a significant effect on the leeward, northern edge of Kopet Dag.
30. Christoph Baumer, *The Ayala Mazar – Xiaohe Culture*, 2010; J.P. Mallory and Victor H. Mair, *The Tarim Mummies* (London, 2000); Songqiao Zhao and Xuncheng Xia, 'Evolution of the Lop Desert and the Lop Nor,' The *Geographical Journal*, cl/3 (1984), p. 311. See here p. 123.
31. Dennell, *The Palaeolithic Settlement of Asia*, pp. 256–258, 464.
32. Huntington, *The Pulse of Asia*.
33. Frank Sirocko, *Wetter, Klima, Menschheitsentwicklung* (Darmstadt, 2010), p. 83.
34. The following explication of climate-influencing factors is taken largely from Sirocko, *Wetter, Klima, Menschheitsentwicklung*, pp. 53–59.
35. Sami Solanki et al., 'Unusual activity of the Sun during recent decades compared to the previous 11,000 years', *Nature*, 28 October 2004, pp. 1084–1087.
36. Dennell, *The Palaeolithic Settlement of Asia*, p. 10.
37. Rothe, *Die Erde*, p. 77.
38. http://en.wikipedia.org/wiki/Permian
39. http://en.wikipedia.org/wiki/Triassic
40. Gingerich, Philip D. *Environment and evolution through the Palaeocene–Eocene thermal maximum* (2006) pp. 246–253; *Mammalian faunal succession through the Palaeocene–Eocene thermal maximum (PRTM) in western North America* (Beijing 2010) pp. 308–327.
41. James Lee, *Climate Change and Armed Conflict* (Oxon, 2009), p. 49.
42. T.H. Barrett, 'Climate Change and Religious Response: The Case of Early Medieval China', *Journal of the Royal Asiatic Society* 3rd series, xvii/ part 2 (April 2007), p. 141.

II. The Settlement of Central Asia in the Palaeolithic

1. Charles Darwin, *The Descent of Man* (London, 1871), Vol. I, p. 199.
2. Robin Dennell, *The Palaeolithic Settlement of Asia* (Cambridge, 2009), p. 438; Johannes Krause et al.,

'The complete mitochondrial DNA genome of an unknown hominin from southern Siberia', *Nature* 10:1038/08976 (advance publication) (2010).

3. Anatoli Derevyanko, for instance, postulated that the Mongolid race began to emerge 'several hundred thousand years ago' (Anatoly Derevyanko (ed.), *The Palaeolithic of Siberia* (Urbana and Chicago, 1998), pp. 333ff).
4. Donald Johanson, *Origins of Modern Humans: Multiregional or Out of Africa?* (Washington, 2001); Martin Kuckenberg, *Als der Mensch zum Schöpfer wurde* (Stuttgart, 2001), pp. 56–71, 188, 197. See also: Dennell, *The Palaeolithic Settlement of Asia*, pp. 456f, 470 note 12.
5. The discoverer of the human fossils of Dmanisi, David Lordkipanidze, sees connections to the still older *Homo habilis*, which is why he introduced the taxon *Homo georgicus* – which is not recognised internationally – and positioned it between *Homo habilis* and *Homo ergaster*, the African *Homo erectus* (David Lordkipanidze and Jean Gagnepain, *La Géorgie, berceau des Européens* (Quinson, 2003), p. 4, 24ff; Paule Valois, 'Quand l'homme a peuplé la terre,' *Archéologia* no. 480 (2010), pp. 53ff). However, still older traces of *ca.* 2-million-year-old hominins are reported to have been discovered in central Syria near Hummal and Aïn al-Fil (Valois, *Quand l'homme a peuplé la terre*, p. 53).
6. Dennell, *The Palaeolithic Settlement of Asia*, pp. 128, 167–176, 183f. The fossils of the purportedly 2.0-million-year old 'Wushan Man' of Longgupo, central China, were from a non-human ape. See: Russell Ciochon, 'The mystery ape of Pleistocene Asia,' *Nature* 2009, pp. 910f. The meagre collection of pebble tools, alleged to be 1.9 million years old, discovered at Riwat, northern Pakistan, are disputed, in part because they were not found in their original context (Dennell, *The Palaeolithic Settlement of Asia*, pp. 84, 123ff, 136ff, 321).
7. Henri de Lumley, 'Les premiers homes en Chine', *Dossiers d'Archéologie* no. 292 (2004), pp. 14f; Jean-Jacques Bahain, 'Les premiers homo erectus en Chine', *Dossiers d'Archéologie* no. 292 (2004), p. 37; 'Les gisements d l'Homme de Lantian', *Dossiers d'Archéologie* no. 292 (2004), pp. 45f.
8. Dennell, *The Palaeolithic Settlement of Asia*, pp. 98–113. *Homo erectus* presumably also invented the raft, in order to cross the Red Sea and to reach the island of Flores.
9. Lanpo Jia and Weiwen Huang, *The Story of Peking Man* (Oxford, 1990), pp. 17, 26, 48–50.
10. Dennell, *The Palaeolithic Settlement of Asia*, pp. 397–418, 444ff; Lanpo and Huang, *The Story of Peking Man*.
11. The pebble tools found by the Soviet palaeontologists Okladnikov and Dervyanko in the Altai and Mongolia, which are purportedly as old as two million years, are highly disputed. See: Derevyanko, *The Palaeolithic of Siberia*, pp. 338ff; V.A. Ranov et al., 'Lower Palaeolithic cultures', in *History of Civilizations of Central Asia*, Vol. 1 (Paris 1992), p. 56f.
12. Dennell, *The Palaeolithic Settlement of Asia*, pp. 326–330; Vadim Ranov, 'Tout commence au paléolithique', *Découverte des civilisations d'Asie Centrale. Les dossiers d'archéologie*, Nr. 185 (1993), pp. 5f. Good surveys of the Palaeolithic sites of inner Central Asia as of 1979 and 1984, respectively, are offered by: Vadim Ranov, 'Toward a new outline of the Soviet Central Asian Palaeolithic', *Current Anthropology* xx/2 (1979), pp. 249–270, and Ranov, 'Zentralasien', in *Neue Forschungen zur Altsteinzeit* (Munich, 1984), pp. 299–343.
13. R. Masov et al. (eds), *National Museum of Antiquities of Tajikistan* (Dushanbe, 2005), pp. 47–55; Joachim Schäfer et al., 'Neue Untersuchungen zum Lösspaläolithikum am Obi-Mazar, Tadžikistan', in *Römisch-Germanisches Zentralmuseum*, Jg. 26, Heft 2 (1996), pp. 97–109; 'Das Altpaläolithikum aus dem 4. Paläobodenkomplex von Obi-Mazar (Tadschikistan),' in *Erkenntnisjäger. Kultur und Umwelt des frühen Menschen. Veröffentlichungen des Landesamtes für Archäologie Sachsen-Anhalt 57* (Festschrift Dietrich Mania) (2003); Leonid Vishnyatsky, 'The Palaeolithic of Central Asia', *Journal of World Prehistory* xiii/1 (March 1999), p. 96f.
14. Dennell, *The Palaeolithic Settlement of Asia*, pp. 329f, 453; Ranov, 'Tout commence au paléolithique', pp. 6ff; Vishnyatsky, 'The Palaeolithic of Central Asia', p. 94.
15. Jiri Chlachula, 'Pleistocene climate change, natural environments and Palaeolithic occupation of East Kazakhstan', *Quaternary International Science Reviews*, ccxx/1–2 (June 2010), p. 83; Zainolla Samashev et al., *Treasures from the Ustyurt and Mangystau* (Almaty, 2007), pp. 34ff; Michael Shunkov, 'The characteristics of the Altai (Russia) Middle Palaeolithic in regional context', *Indo-Pacific Association Bulletin* 25 (2005), p. 72.
16. A good overview is provided by Vishnyatsky, 'The Palaeolithic of Central Asia', pp. 69–122. See also: Ranov et al., 'Lower Palaeolithic cultures', pp. 45–63.
17. Jiri Chlachula et al., 'Palaeolithic occupation in the Angara region, East Central Siberia, in the context of Pleistocene climate change', *Journal of Geological Sciences* no. 25 (2004), p. 35; Anatoly Derevyanko and Zun Lü Zun, 'Upper Palaeolithic cultures', in *History of Civilizations of Central Asia*, Vol. 1 (Paris 1992), pp. 89–101; Vjačeslav Scelinskij and Vladimir Sirokov, *Höhlenmalerei im Ural* (Sigmaringen 1999), p. 8f; A.P. Okladnikow, 'Inner Asia at the dawn of history', in *The Cambridge history of Early Inner Asia* (Cambridge, 1990), pp. 44ff.
18. Yves Coppens et al., 'Discovery of an archaic Homo sapiens skullcap in Northeast Mongolia', *C.R. Palevol* vii (2008), pp. 51–60; Lionel Crooson, 'L'homme de Salkhit a parlé', *National Geographic*, French edition (November 2010), pp. 48–57.
19. Vishnyatsky, 'The Palaeolithic of Central Asia', p. 77.
20. Lumley, 'Les premiers hommes en Chine', pp. 15f.
21. Anatoly Derevyanko et al., 'The stratified cave site of Tsagaan Agui on the Gobi Altai (Mongolia)', *Archaeology, Ethnology & Anthropology of Eurasia* 1 (2000), pp. 23–36.
22. Gerd-Christian Weniger, 'Wie modern waren Neanderthaler?', *Eurasia Antiqua* xiv (2008), p. 1.
23. Dennell, *The Palaeolithic Settlement of Asia*, pp. 279–287, 453; Johanson, *Origins of Modern Humans*.
24. The approximately 800,000-year-old 'Ceprano Man', discovered south of Rome in 1994, remains to this day an isolated discovery; his name does not constitute a taxon. He is considered an early form of *Homo heidelbergensis* (Francesco Mallegni et al., 'Homo cepranensis sp. nov. and the evolution of African-European Middle Pleistocene hominids,' *Comptes Rendus Palevol* ii/2 (2003), pp. 255–259).
25. *Homo antecessor*, at least 780,000 years old, is disputed as a taxon. Most palaeontologists consider it to belong to *Homo erectus* or as an early form of *Homo heidelbergensis* (Dennell, *The Palaeolithic Settlement of Asia*, p. 458).
26. Kuckenberg, *Als der Mensch zum Schöpfer wurde*, pp. 67–72.
27. Katerina Harvati, '100 years of Homo heidelbergensis – life and times of a controversial taxon', *Mitteilungen der Gesellschaft für Urgeschichte* xvi (2007), pp. 85–91.
28. J. Desmond Clark et al., 'Stratigraphic, chronological and behavioural contexts of Pleistocene Homo sapiens from Middle Awash, Ethiopia', *Nature* cdxxiii (2003); Jamie Shreeve, 'Sur la route de l'évolution', *National Geographic* (2010); Tim White et al., 'Pleistocene Homo sapiens from Middle Awash, Ethiopia', *Nature* cdxxiii (2003).
29. Dennell, *The Palaeolithic Settlement of Asia*, p. 458; Richard Green et al., 'Analysis of one million base pairs of Neanderthal DNA', *Nature* 10:1038/05336, no. 444 (2006); David Reich et al., 'Genetic history of an archaic hominin group from Denisova Cave in Siberia', *Nature* 10:1038/09710 (December 2010), p. 1053.
30. Mitochondrial DNA (mtDNA) is located in organelles called mitochondria which convert chemical energy from food into a form adapted for the cell. mtDNA is maternally inherited. Non-mtDNA is mostly located in the cell nucleus.
31. Reich et al., 'Genetic history of an archaic hominin group', p. 1057.
32. Willerslev Eske, Rasmussen Morten et al., 'An Aboriginal Australian genome reveals separate human dispersals into Asia', *Science*, Vol. 333, pp. 1689ff, 23 September 2011.
33. Reich et al., 'Genetic history of an archaic hominin group', p. 1059.
34. Green Richard et al., 'A Draft Sequence of the Neanderthal Genome', *Science*, Vol. 328 (7 May 2010), p. 721.
35. Kuckenberg, *Als der Mensch zum Schöpfer wurde*, pp. 93–103.
36. David Christian, *A History of Russia, Central Asia and Mongolia. Vol. I, Inner Eurasia from Prehistory to the Mongol Empire* (Oxford, 1998), 30–33.
37. Frank Sirocko, *Wetter, Klima, Menschheitsentwicklung* (Damstadt, 2010), pp. 71f, 77ff.
38. James Lee, *Climate Change and Armed Conflict* (Oxford, 2009), p. 30.
39. Adrian Briggs et al., 'Targeted Retrieval and Analysis of Five Neandertal mtDNA Genomes', *Science* 325 (17 July 2009); Beat Müller, *Geburt war schon bei Neandertalern schwierig*, Informationsdienst Wissenschaft der Universität Zürich (2008).

40. Bridget Allchin, 'Middle Palaeolithic culture', in *History of Civilizations of Central Asia,* Vol. 1 (Paris 1992), pp. 65–88; Ranov et al., 'Lower Palaeolithic cultures', pp. 45–63; 'Tout commence au paléolithique,' p. 9.
41. Analyses of the lithic material from Obi-Rakhmat led a few researchers to posit a gradual development from Middle Palaeolithic to Upper Palaeolithic stone tools, from which they postulated a region inhabited simultaneously by Neanderthals and sapiens. See: Andrei Krivoshapkin and Jeffrey Brantingham, 'The Lithic industry of Obi-Rakhmat Grotto, Uzbekistan', *Actes du XIV Congres UISPP, 2–8 septembre 2001. BAR International Series 1240* (2001), pp. 203, 214; Vishnyatsky, 'The Palaeolithic of Central Asia', p. 98.
42. Vishnyatsky, 'The Palaeolithic of Central Asia', p. 112.
43. Hallam Movius, 'Teshik-Tash: A Mousterian Cave Site in Central Asia', in *Société Royale Belge d'Anthropologie et de Préhistoire, en l'honneur du Professeur Hamal-Nandrin* (Brussels, 1953), pp. 75, 79.
44. The oldest known burial sites in the world are those in the cave of Qafzeh near Nazareth in the Levant. Here modern humans of the species *Homo sapiens* were intentionally buried 115,000 (+/-15,000) years ago. Well documented by the stratigraphy are the double grave of a young woman with a young child and the grave of a youth whose hands held a deer antler (H.P. Schwarcz, 'ESR dates for the hominid burial site of Qafzeh in Israel', *Journal of Human Evolution* xvii (1988), pp. 733, 736); Bernard Vandermeersch, 'The excavation of Qafzeh: Its contribution to knowledge of the Mousterian in the Levant', *Bulletin du Centre de recherche français de Jérusalem* x (2002), pp. 66ff.
45. Vadim Masson and Victor Sarianidi, *Central Asia: Turkmenia before the Achaemenids* (London, 1972), p. 22.
46. Allchin, 'Middle Palaeolithic culture', p. 86.
47. Ralph S. Solecki, 'Shanidar cave: a Palaeolithic site in northern Iraq', *Annual Report of the Smithsonian Institution* (1954), pp.389–425; Ralph S. Solecki and P. Agelarakis Anagnostis, *The Proto-Neolithic Cemetery in Shanidar Cave* (Texas A&M University Press, 2004). A tenth Neanderthal, who died very young, was discovered by Melinda Zeder in 2006.
48. The thesis proposed by Steven Churchill in 2009 that Shanidar III was killed by a modern sapiens because the Neanderthals ostensibly were unfamiliar with the spear is unsustainable. Neanderthals certainly used spears and, secondly, no contemporaneous signs of sapiens have been found in Kurdistan (Steven Churchill and Robert Franciscus, 'Shanidar 3 Neandertal Rib Puncture Wound and Palaeolithic Weaponry,' *Journal of Human Evolution* lvii/2 (August 2009)).
49. Other researchers believe, however, that the flower pollen could have been brought into the cave by a rodent, such as a jerboa.
50. Based on the discovery of Palaeolithic tools which are supposed to have been manufactured by modern *Homo sapiens* at Jebel Faya, United Arabian Emirates, it has been claimed in January 2011 that *Homo sapiens* crossed the then almost dry straits of Bab al Mandeb already some 130,000 to 125,000 years ago. It remains so far unproven that these tools were made by modern humans (Armitage Simon J. et al., *The Southern Route 'Out of Africa': Evidence for an Early Expansion of Modern Humans into Arabia,* Science 2011).
51. Dennis Etler: 'Based on the fact that modern human Upper cave remains from Zhoukoudian [China], dated to *ca.* 20,000 ya, cannot be identified as belonging to any particular living "racial" group, I would conclude that the differentiation of modern ethnicities in Asia is relatively recent, most likely only within the last 10–12,000 years.' Letter of Professor Dennis Etler, Cabrillo College, Aptos, USA, to the author dated 8 April 2010; Nicole Maca-Meyer et al., 'Major genomic mitochondrial lineages delineate early human expansions', *BMC Genetics* ii/13 (2001); Stephen Oppenheimer, *The real Eve: Modern Man's Journey Out of Africa* (London, 2003), pp. 195–242; E.D. Phillips, *The Royal Hordes. Nomad Peoples of the Steppes* (Thames & Hudson, 1965), p. 14.
52. Krause et al., 'The complete mitochondrial DNA genome of an unknown hominin from southern Siberia'.
53. Sergei Vasil'ev et al., 'Radiocarbon-based chronology of the Palaeolithic in Siberia and its relevance to the peopling of the New World', *Radiocarbon* xliv/2 (2002), pp. 503, 511f. Dolitsky, by contrast, believes that an earlier migration over the Bering land bridge took place in the Kargin Interglacial, 30,000 to 33,000 years ago (Alexander Dolitsky, 'Siberian Palaeolithic Archaeology', *Anthropology* xxvi/3 (1985), p. 367).
54. Higham Thomas et al. Testing models for the beginnings of the Aurignacian and the advent of figurative art and music: The radiocarbon chronology of Geißenköcherle. In: *Journal of Human Evolution*, Vol. XXX, 2012, pp. 1–13. doi:19.1016/j.jhevol.2012.03.003.
55. The ostensible 230,000- to 280,000-year-old 'Venus' statues of Berekhat Ram (Golan Heights, Syria) and Tan-Tan (Morocco) are in author's opinion most likely naturally occurring pseudo-artefacts. Paul Bahn, *Prehistoric Art* (Cambridge, 1998), p. 87; Kuckenberg, *Als der Mensch zum Schöpfer wurde*, pp. 125–142, 158f.
56. Nicholas Conrad et al. (eds), *Eiszeit, Kunst und Kultur* (Stuttgart, 2009), 228ff.
57. The paintings of the abri of Zaraut Kamar (Uzbekistan), once dated to the Upper Palaeolithic or Mesolithic, are of a much more recent date and are presumably just a few centuries old. The same holds for the ostensibly Upper Palaeolithic paintings of Shishkino and Tal'ma in Siberia. Robert Bednarik, 'Pleistocene rock art in Central Europe?' *International newsletter on rock art INORA*, No. 45 (2006), p. 29; Andrzej Rozwadowski, 'The forgotten art of ancient Uzbekistan', *The Times of Central Asia* iii/4 (26 January 2001).
58. Ranov, 'Zentralasien', pp. 316, 329.
59. Jacques, Jaubert, 'The decorated cave of Hoït Tsenkher Agui', *International newsletter on rock art INORA*, no. 17 (1997); Jaubert Jacques, Eleonora Novgorodva et al., *Ulangom. Ein skythenzeitliches Gräberfeld in der Mongolei* (Wiesbaden, 1982), pp. 38–51.
60. Vicomte Edmond de Poncins, *Chasses et Explorations dans la Région des Pamirs* (Paris, 1897), pp. 54f.
61. Observations of the author in 2008. See also: K. Tashbayeva et al., *Petroglyphs of Central Asia* (Samarkand, 2001), pp. 128f.
62. Vadim Ranov, 'L'exploration archéologique du Pamir', *Bulletin de l'Ecole française de d'Extrême Orient* lxxiii (1984), pp. 76f, 88, 94.
63. Tashbayeva et al., *Petroglyphs of Central Asia*, pp. 129ff. The dating by the Chinese scholar Wang Binghua of a few red ochre cave drawings in the Chinese Altai Mountains to the late Palaeolithic seems highly doubtful to us. Wang Binghua, 'The Polychrome Rock Paintings in the Altay Mountains', *The Silk Road Journal* iii/1 (2005).
64. Tashbayeva et al., *Petroglyphs of Central Asia*, pp. 18f.
65. Christian, *A History of Russia, Central Asia and Mongolia*, p. 30.
66. Scelinskij and Sirokov, *Höhlenmalerei im Ural*, p. 34.
67. Andreï Alexeev et al., *Trésors des Steppes* (Hauterive, 2006), pp. 19ff; Mikhail Gladkih et al., 'Mammoth-Bone Dwellings on the Russian Plain', *Scientific American* ccli/5 (November 1984), pp. 165–175. Lioudmilla Iakovleva, 'Les habitats en os de mammouth des chasseurs paléolithiques d'Ukraine', *Dossiers d'Archéologie no. 266, L'or des rois Scythes* (2001); Lioudmilla Iakovleva and François Djindjian, 'New data on Mammoth bone settlements of Eastern Europe in the light of the new excavations of the Gontsy site Ukraine', *International Science Reviews*, 126–128 (2005); I.H. Pidoplichko, *Upper Palaeolithic Dwellings of Mammoth Bones in the Ukraine: Kiev-Kirillovskii, Gontsy, Dobranichevka, Mezin and Mezhirich* (Oxford, 1998); Randall White, *Prehistoric Art: The symbolic journey of mankind* (New York, 2003), pp. 128, 147.
68. Iakovleva, 'Les habitats en os de mammouth des chasseurs paléolithiques d'Ukraine', p. 45.
69. Conrad, *Eiszeit, Kunst und Kultur*, pp. 192–195.
70. I.H. Pidoplichko, *Meziritchiskie jilicha iz kosteï* (Kiev, 1976), pp. 162, 169, 174, 180, 183.
71. Pidoplichko, *Upper Palaeolithic dwellings of mammoth bones*, pp. 161, 164, 167.
72. Gladkih et al., 'Mammoth-Bone Dwellings on the Russian Plain', pp. 170, 175; Iakovleva, 'Les habitats en os de mammouth des chasseurs paléolithiques d'Ukraine', pp. 46ff; Pidoplichko, *Meziritchiskie jilicha iz kosteï*, pp. 204, 206, 212; Pidoplichko, *Upper Palaeolithic Dwellings of Mammoth Bones in the Ukraine,* pp. 213f.
73. Scelinskij and Sirokov, *Höhlenmalerei im Ural*, pp. 94–132.
74. Ibid, pp. 136f.
75. White, *Prehistoric Art*, pp. 136–146.
76. Bahn, *Prehistoric Art*, pp. 89ff. A crude clay figure, about 16,000 years old and 9.6 centimetres tall, was also found in southern Siberia near the Maiyna settlement, on the western bank of the Yenisei River. http://vm.kemsu.ru/en/palaeolith/plastic/maina.html
77. Derevyanko, *The Palaeolithic of Siberia*, p. 8.

78. Alexeev et al., *Trésors des Steppes*, pp. 22ff; Derevyanko, *The Palaeolithic of Siberia*, pp. 8–12, 132–135; Jakov Sher, 'Pétroglyphes de Russie', *Archéologia* no. 395 (2002), p. 62; White, *Prehistoric Art*, pp. 145f. Astonishingly, the grave at Malt'a is one of a very few graves in Siberia from this epoch; perhaps the dead were left in forests or 'buried' high in trees, a custom still practised at the start of the twentieth century.
79. Sirocko, *Wetter, Klima, Menschheitsentwicklung*, pp. 86, 88; White, Randall, *Prehistoric Art*, 2003, p. 146.
80. Gaëlle Rosendahl et al., 'Le plus vieil arc du monde?', *L'Anthropologie* cx/3 (2006), pp. 371f, 375, 379f.
81. Volker, Alles (ed.), *Reflexbogen: Geschichte und Herstellung* (Ludwigshafen, 2009), pp. 13ff.
82. See p. 42.
83. Alles, *Reflexbogen: Geschichte und Herstellung*, pp. 13–17, 22.
84. Ibid, p. 23.
85. Renate Rolle, *Die Welt der Skythen* (Lucerne, 1980), p. 73.
86. Maurice, Byzantine Emperor, *Strategikon*, 1984, VIII, 48 (p. 87).
87. David Anthony, *The Horse, the Wheel and Language: How Bronze-Age riders from the Eurasian Steppes shaped the modern world* (Princeton, 2007), pp. 223f; David Anthony and Dorcas Brown, *Harnessing Horsepower. Horses and Humans in Antiquity* (2007).
88. Konstantin Čugunov, Hermann Parzinger and Anatoli Nagler, 'Der skythische Fürstengrabhügel von Arzhan 2 in Tuva, Vorbericht der russisch-deutschen Ausgrabungen', *Eurasia Antiqua* ix (2003), pp. 135ff; *Der Goldschatz von Arzhan* (Munich, 2006), pp. 14, 122; *Der skythenzeitliche Fürstenkurgan Aržhan 2 in Tuva* (Mainz, 2010), pp. 216–231.
89. Vjačeslav Molodin, 'Das skythenzeitliche Kriegergrab aus Olon-Kurin-Gol, Mongolischer Altaj', *Eurasia Antiqua* xiii (2008), p. 261.
90. Chengyuan Ma, *Archaeological treasures of the Silk Road in Xinjiang Uygur Autonomous Region* (Shanghai, 1998), pp. 104, 254; Alfred Wieczorek and Christoph Lind (eds), *Ursprünge der Seidenstraße* (Stuttgart, 2007), p. 177.
91. Zhao Feng and Yu Zhiyong (eds), *Legacy of the Desert King* (Hong Kong, 2000), p. 48.

III. A Global Climatic Warming Ushers in the Mesolithic

1. A.P. Okladnikow, *Der Hirsch mit dem goldenen Geweih* (Wiesbaden, 1972), p. 7.
2. Frank Sirocko, *Wetter, Klima, Menschheitsentwicklung* (Darmstadt, 2010), pp. 93, 100–102.
3. We will not use the term 'Epipalaeolithic', sometimes equated with the Mesolithic, because the former term is defined differently, depending on the author. The epoch between the Palaeolithic and the Neolithic is sometimes called the Epipalaeolithic for cultures of southern regions that were never affected by ice ages. In the archaeology of Russia and northern Europe, the term 'Mesolithic' predominates.
4. Vadim Ranov, 'Toward a new outline of the Soviet Central Asian Palaeolithic', *Current Anthropology* xx/2 (1979), p. 258; Georg Renner and Christa Selic, *Abseits der großen Minarette* (Leipzig, 1992), p. 29.
5. Esther Jacobson (ed.), *Répertoire des pétroglyphes d'Asie Centrale. Fascicule 6: Mongolie du Nord-Ouest, Tsagaan Salaa/Baga Oigor*, Vol. I (Paris, 2001), pp. 9–11.
6. The first scholars to give attention to the stone engravings were two Chinese: the philosopher Han Fei (289–233 BC) and the geographer Li Daoyuan (fifth century AD) (Paul Bahn, *Prehistoric Art* (Cambridge, 1998), pp. 1–3). An interpretation of Bronze Age petroglyphs as Shamanistic is problematic since we do not know if a Siberian type of Shamanism existed at that period. Also the alleged first millennium BC petroglyphs of men beating a drum along the Middle Yenissei River are not conclusive, since their dating is unsure and the representation of a drum does not in itself provide evidence of 'Shamanism'. For pictures see: Ekaterina Devlet. *Rock Art and the material culture of Siberian and Central Asian Shamanism* (London, 2001) p. 47, Fig. 3.5.
7. Two exceptions may be the wagons shown in the top view, which could recall a view of an open grave with a wagon burial, as well as possible portrayals of a horse sacrifice. See photos pp. 85 and 92.
8. Jacobson, *Répertoire des pétroglyphes d'Asie Centrale. Fascicule 6*, p. 7; Esther Jacobson and James Meacham, *Archaeology and Landscape in the Mongolian Altai: An Atlas* (Redlands, CA, 2010), pp. 22f.
9. Esther Jacobson, 'The Rock Art of Mongolia', *The Silk Road Journal*, iv/1 (2006), p. 7.
10. Interpretations of the mushroom-shaped head coverings as bronze helmets decorated with feathers seem improbable, since such helmets, discovered in Mongolia, date to a later time, *ca.* eleventh–eighth century BC. In a few battle scenes from the late Bronze Age, this interpretation may be correct. See: D. Erdenebaatar, 'Burial materials related to the history of the Bronze Age in the territory of Mongolia', in Katheryn Linduff (ed.), *Metallurgy in ancient Eastern Eurasia from the Urals to the Yellow River* (Ceredigion, 2004), p. 197.
11. Goryachev A.A., Mariyashev A.N. *Petroglyphs of Semirechye*. Fort inform 1999.
12. Skiing has been practised in northern Eurasia for millennia; 4,500-year-old skis made of ash wood have been discovered (Andreï Alexeev, *Trésors des steppes* (Hauterive, 2006), p. 27).
13. Baumer, *Traces in the Desert*, p. 69f.
14. Camels pulling wagons are not found in Tsagaan Salaa but are in Kazakhstan, as, for instance, in Arpa Uzen.
15. See p. 157.
16. Jakov Sher et al. (eds), *Répertoire des pétroglyphes d'Asie Centrale. Fascicule 1: Sibérie du Sud 1. Oglakhty I–III* (Paris, 1994).
17. Natalia Blednova et al. (eds), *Répertoire des pétroglyphes d'Asie Centrale. Fascicule 2: Sibérie du Sud 2. Tepsej I–III, Ust'-Tuba I–VI* (Paris, 1995).
18. N. Batbold (ed.), *Petroglyphs of Aral Tolgoi (Mongolia)* (Ulaan Baatar, 2007).
19. Christoph Baumer, *Traces in the Desert: Journeys of Discovery across Central Asia* (London, 2008), pp. 69–72; Jacobson, *Répertoire des pétroglyphes d'Asie Centrale, Fascicule 6*. For a good selection of photos, see also: http://depts.washington.edu/silkroad/archaeology/mongolia/bagaoigor/bagaoigor.html
20. Baumer, *Traces in the Desert*, p. 59.
21. Eleonora Novgorodva, *Alte Kunst der Mongolei* (Leipzig, 1980), pp. 50–54.
22. Anatoly Derevyanko and D. Dorj, 'Neolithic tribes in northern parts of Central Asia', in *History of civilizations of Central Asia*, Vol. I (Paris, 1992), pp. 170ff; John Maringer, *Contribution to the prehistory of Mongolia*, Reports from the scientific expedition to the north-western provinces of China under the leadership of Dr. Sven Hedin (Stockholm, 1950), pp. 201–208.

IV. The Economic Revolution of the Neolithic

1. Nicholai Przhevalsky, *Mongolia: The Tangut county and the solitudes of Northern Tibet: Being a narrative of three years travel in Eastern High Asia* (London, 1876), p. 120.
2. While the camel was only domesticated around 2600 BCE, Przhevalsky's statement applies to most animals domesticated in the Neolithic.
3. In Western scholarship the new methods of production are the prerequisite for designating a culture as Neolithic. In Soviet and Russian scholarship, however, knowledge of ceramics most often defines the start of the Neolithic, so that a hunter-gather society that produced ceramics and refined stone tools would be described as Neolithic, while in traditional Western accounts it would be considered Mesolithic. Since in the Eurasian steppe the people remained hunter-gatherers but had advanced stone tools and ceramics many centuries after sedentariness and food production had begun in Old Europe and the Near East, we follow Parzinger in adopting the Russian view. According to classic Western scholarship, these steppe cultures would have experienced no Neolithic phase and would have jumped from the Mesolithic directly to the Chalcolithic. David Anthony, *The Horse, the Wheel and Language: How Bronze Age riders from the Eurasian Steppes shaped the modern world* (Princeton, 2007), pp. 125f; Hermann Parzinger, *Die frühen Völker Eurasiens: Vom Neolithikum bis zum Mittelalter* (Munich, 2006), pp. 41f.
4. Vadim Ranov, 'Toward a new outline of the Soviet Central Asian Palaeolithic', *Current Anthropology* xx/2 (1979), pp. 255, 259f.
5. Vadim Ranov, 'Les énigmes de la culture de Hissar', *Découverte des civilisations d'Asie Centrale. Les dossiers d'archéologie* no. 185 (1993), pp. 14–21.
6. Boroffka, Nikolaus. *Klima und Besiedlungsgeschichte am Aral-See, Kasachstan und Usbekistan*, in Boroffka, Nikolaus, Hansen Svend (eds). *Archäologische Forschungen in Kasachstan, Tadschikistan, Turkmenistan und Usbekistan*. Eurasien-Abteilung, Deutsches Archäologisches Institut, Berlin 2010, p. 39.
7. Sergei Tolstov, *Auf den Spuren der altchoresmischen Kultur* (Berlin, 1953), p. 75.

8. René Létolle et al., 'Uzboy and the Aral regression', *International Science Reviews* 123–174 (2007). pp. 125–136; Vadim Masson, 'The Decline of the Bronze Age Civilization and Movements of the Tribes', in *History of civilizations of Central Asia*, Vol. I (Paris, 1992), p. 337.
9. Delmar Morgan and C. Coote, *Early voyages and travels to Russia and Persia by Anthony Jenkinson and other Englishmen*, Vol. 1 (London, 1886), p. 70.
10. Vadim Masson and Victor Sarianidi, *Central Asia: Turkmenia before the Achaemenids* (London, 1972), p. 73f; Victor Sarianidi, 'Food-producing and other Neolithic communities in Khorasan and Transoxiana', in *History of civilizations of Central Asia*, Vol. I (Paris, 1992), p. 121ff; A.P. Okladnikow, 'Inner Asia at the dawn of history', in Denis Sinor (ed.), *The Cambridge history of Early Inner Asia* (Cambridge, 1990), p. 64.
11. Sarianidi, 'Food-producing and other Neolithic communities', p. 115f.
12. Other origination sites for agriculture later arose independently in China, Central America, the Andes of South America, and central Africa.
13. Steven Mithen, *After the ice: A global human history 20.000–5000 BC* (Cambridge, 2003), pp. 406–415; Sarianidi, 'Food-producing and other Neolithic communities', pp. 124f.
14. Sarianidi, 'Food-producing and other Neolithic communities', p. 118.
15. The covering of the dead with ochre presumably had not only a symbolic but also a functional component, since ochre possesses a certain anti-inflammatory and antiseptic effect. Perhaps the people believed they could stop the decomposition of the corpse by sprinkling it with ochre. Paul Bahn, *Prehistoric Art* (Cambridge, 1998), p. 72.
16. Grégoire Frumkin, *Archaeology in Soviet Central Asia* (Leiden, 1970), p. 130; Frederik Talmage Hiebert et al., *A Central Asian Village at the Dawn of Civilization, excavations at Anau, Turkmenistan* (Philadelphia, 2003), pp. 15ff; Masson and Sarianidi, *Central Asia*, pp. 33–46; Sarianidi, 'Food-producing and other Neolithic communities', pp. 112–121.
17. Anatoly Derevyanko and D. Dorj, 'Neolithic tribes in northern parts of Central Asia', in *History of civilizations of Central Asia*, Vol. I (Paris, 1992), pp. 169–181.
18. A kurgan is a burial mound, of varying size, made of earth or stone and having a circular shape, which is erected over one or more burial chambers. The Russian word курган comes from Old Turkic.
19. Walther Heissig and Claudius Müller (eds), *Die Mongolen* (Innsbruck, 1989), p. 15.
20. Whether the red ochre found for millennia in the burials of Central Asia was really understood as a symbol of the sources of life or the 'blood of the dead' remains unknown. Denis Sinor, *The Cambridge History of Early Inner Asia* (Cambridge, 1990), p. 67.
21. Hermann Parzinger, *Die frühen Völker Eurasiens: Vom Neolithikum bis zum Mittelalter* (Munich, 2006), pp. 79–89; Sinor, *The Cambridge History of Early Inner Asia,* pp. 67f.
22. Aleksandr Kislenko and Nataliya Tatarintseva, 'The Eastern Ural Steppe at the End of the Stone Age' in Marsha Levine et al., *Late prehistoric exploitation of the Eurasian steppe* (Cambridge, 1999), pp. 185–197.
23. Anthony, *The Horse, the Wheel and Language*, pp. 132, 138.
24. Ibid, pp. 138, 145–149.
25. The dating of the earliest Elshanka finds must perhaps be corrected to about 500 years later, to 6500 BC, which would shift the introduction of ceramics to 6200 BC (Anthony, *The Horse, the Wheel and Language*, pp. 149, 480, note 19).
26. Anthony, *The Horse, the Wheel and Language*, pp. 148, 154. See p. 135.
27. Ibid, pp. 151, 159.
28. See here p. 78.
29. Anthony, *The Horse, the Wheel and Language*, pp. 138–159; D. Telegin et al., 'Settlement and economy in Neolithic Ukraine: a new chronology', *Antiquity* lxxvii/297 (2003), pp. 457ff.
30. Anthony, *The Horse, the Wheel and Language*, pp. 155–159, 174, 182.
31. Telegin et al., 'Settlement and economy in Neolithic Ukraine', pp. 459, 465.
32. Anthony, *The Horse, the Wheel and Language*, pp. 160f, 181f, 185, 234f, 254.

V. The Chalcolithic and the Early Bronze Age

1. Herodotus, I, 216. The English translation is taken from: Herodotus, *The Histories* (London 2003).
2. David Anthony, *The Horse, the Wheel and Language. How Bronze-Age riders from the Eurasian Steppes shaped the modern world* (Princeton, 2007), pp. 123f.
3. The term 'Metal Age', sometimes used as an alternative, unnecessarily obscures important differences in the development of a culture and between contemporaneous cultures.
4. The Copper Stone Age is also called the Eneolithic. The frequently encountered term 'Copper Age' is actually wrong, since this period was characterised by the use of both copper and stone objects. In archaeology one speaks of the 'Chalcolithic' only when proper copper objects appear, not only copper sheets.
5. Evengy Chernykh, 'Ancient metallurgy in northeast Asia: From the Urals to the Saiano-Altai', in Katheryn Linduff (ed.), *Metallurgy in ancient Eastern Eurasia from the Urals to the Yellow River* (Ceredigion, 2004), p. 16; Evengy Chernykh, 'The "Steppe Belt" of stockbreeding cultures in Eurasia during the Early Metal Age', *Trabajos de Prehistoria* lxvi/2 (2008), pp. 75ff; Philip Kohl, *The making of Bronze Age Eurasia* (Cambridge, 2007), pp. 29ff.
6. The term 'circumpontic' derives from the Greek name for the Black Sea, *Póntos Euxeinos* (Πόντος Εὔξεινος), meaning 'hospitable sea'. At first, however, it was called *Póntos Áxeinos* (Πόντος Ἄξεινος), which means 'inhospitable sea'. The original name was presumably chosen by the Greeks on account of the often stormy swells and the fearsome coastal inhabitants. After the founding of colonies it became the 'hospitable' sea.
7. Chernykh, 'Ancient metallurgy in northeast Asia', pp. 16f, fig. 1.1; Ludmila Koryakova and Andrej Epimakkhov, *The Urals and Western Siberia in the Bronze and Iron Ages* (Cambridge, 2007), pp. 26–33.
8. Evengy Chernykh, 'Kargaly: The largest and most ancient metallurgical complex on the border of Europe and Asia', in Linduff (ed.), *Metallurgy in ancient Eastern Eurasia*, p. 224.
9. Kohl, *The making of Bronze Age Eurasia*, pp. 57–83. On the Maikop Culture, see also here p. 92. Other scholars believe that the technology of bronze alloying arose in Mesopotamia (Anthony, *The Horse, the Wheel and Language*, pp. 287ff).
10. Anthony, *The Horse, the Wheel and Language*, p. 125; Koryakova and Epimakkhov, *The Urals and Western Siberia*, p. 32.
11. Kohl, *The making of Bronze Age Eurasia*, pp. 85, 110, 144.
12. See here p. 148.
13. Koryakova and Epimakkhov, *The Urals and Western Siberia*, pp. 39f.
14. Georg Renner and Christa Selic, *Abseits der großen Minarette* (Leipzig, 1982), p. 73.
15. Koryakova and Epimakkhov, *The Urals and Western Siberia*, pp. 190–193.
16. Raphael Pumpelly (ed.), *Explorations in Turkestan: Expedition of 1904: Prehistoric civilizations of Anau* (Washington, 1908), pp. XXIII–XXXV, 15f.
17. Fredrik Hiebert, *A Central Asian Village at the Dawn of Civilization, excavations at Anau, Turkmenistan* (Philadelphia, 2003), pp. 125f, 162.
18. Pumpelly (ed.), *Explorations in Turkestan*, Vol. I; Hiebert, *A Central Asian Village at the Dawn of Civilization*, p. 172.
19. Hiebert, *A Central Asian Village at the Dawn of Civilization*, pp. 162–72.
20. L.B Kirtcho, 'The earliest wheeled transport in southwestern Central Asia: New finds from Altyn-Depe', *Archaeology, Ethnology & Anthropology of Eurasia* xxxvii/1 (2009), pp. 25–32; Masson, *Altyn-Depe*, p. 99, pl. XIX.
21. Daniel Potts, 'Bactrian Camels and Bactrian-Dromedary Hybrids', *The Silk Road Journal* iii/1 (2005), p. 53.
22. Grégoire Frumkin, *Archaeology in Soviet Central Asia* (Leiden, 1970), pp. 132f; Hiebert, *A Central Asian Village at the Dawn of Civilization*, pp. 15–23; Kohl, *The making of Bronze Age Eurasia*, pp. 201f, Vadim M. Masson, *Altyn-Depe* (Philadelphia, 1988), p. 15; Hermann Müller-Karpe, *Neolithisch-kupferzeitliche Siedlungen in der Geoksjur-Oase, Süd-Turkmenistan* (Munich, 1984), p. 40; Viktor Sarianidi, 'Margiana in the Bronze Age', in Philip Kohl (ed.), *The Bronze Age Civilization of Central Asia: Recent Soviet discoveries* (New York, 1981), pp. 188ff.
23. Daniel Potts, 'Bactrian Camels and Bactrian-Dromedary Hybrids', *The Silk Road Journal* iii/1 (2005), p. 53.
24. Kirtcho, 'The earliest wheeled transport in southwestern Central Asia', pp. 25, 32.
25. Vadim Masson and Victor Sarianidi, *Central Asia: Turkmenia before the Achaemenids* (London, 1972), p. 51; Vadim Masson, 'The Bronze Age in Khorasan and Transoxiana', *History of Civilizations of Central Asia*, Vol. I (Paris, 1992), pp. 225ff.
26. Masson and Sarianidi, *Central Asia*, p. 59. Ulug Depe has the deepest prehistoric stratigraphy of all Central Asian settlements; Olivier Lecomte, 'Ulug Dépé: 4,000 ans d'évolution entre plaine et désert', *Dossiers d'Archéologie* no. 317 (2006), p. 17.
27. Masson and Sarianidi, *Central Asia*, 1972, p. 61.

28. Müller-Karpe, *Neolithisch-kupferzeitliche Siedlungen*, pp. 9f, 55, 85f.
29. See pp. 123ff.
30. Müller-Karpe, *Neolithisch-kupferzeitliche Siedlungen*, pp. 18, 42f.
31. Ibid, pp. 12, 74–84.
32. Vadim Masson, *Das Land der tausend Städte: Die Wiederentdeckung der ältesten Kulturgebiete in Mittelasien* (Munich, 1982), pp. 69ff, 77, 92, 129.
33. S.G. Kljastornyj and T.I. Sultanov, *Staaten und Völker in den Steppen Eurasiens: Altertum und Mittelalter* (Berlin, 2006), pp. 41f. See p. 72.
34. Masson, *Altyn-Depe*, pp. 55–80.
35. Stephen Bourke, *The Middle East: The cradle of civilization revealed* (London, 2008), pp. 96f; R. Ghirsman, *Fouilles de Sialk près de Kashan* (Paris, 1938).
36. Bruno Bioul, *Jiroft*, (2003), pp. 67, 74, 76, 92.
37. Joan Aruz, *Art of the first cities* (New York, 2003), p. 349; Maurizio Tosi et al., 'The Bronze Age in Iran and Afghanistan', *History of civilizations of Central Asia* Vol. I (Paris, 1992), pp. 199, 206f, 215; The SHAHR-I-SOKHTA ONLINE project. http://www.bradypus.net/sis-online/.
38. A. Dani and B. Thapar, 'The Indus Civilization', *History of civilizations of Central Asia* Vol. I (1992), p. 298; Gabriele Rossi-Osmida, *Adji Kui Oasis, III–II mill.* BC (Venice, 2007), p. 147. See here p. 78f.
39. Aruz, *Art of the first cities*, p. 357.
40. Gabriele Rossi-Osmida, *Adji Kui Oasis, III–II mill.* BC (Venice, 2007), p. 153.
41. Masson and Sarianidi, *Central Asia*, pp. 129–136; Masson, *Altyn-Depe*, pp. 86ff. See also Aruz, *Art of the first cities*, p. 164.
42. There is also evidence of a local snake cult in the delta of the Tejen River (Rossi-Osmida, *Adji Kui Oasis*, p. 149).
43. Toreutics are objects of artistic metalworking.
44. Bourke, *The Middle East*, p. 337.
45. Masson, *Das Land der tausend Städte*, pp. 34f; Masson, *Altyn-Depe*, pp. IV, 68–76, plate XXIII.
46. Masson, *Das Land der tausend Städte*, pp. 40, 45; *Altyn-Depe*, 1988, p. 89, plate XVII.
47. *Avesta*, yasna IX, 25–27 (2006, Vol. II. p. 71); J.P. Mallory and D.Q. Adams (eds), *Encyclopedia of Indo-European Culture* (London, 1997), p. 259.
48. Masson, *Das Land der tausend Städte*, p. 26; Masson, *Altyn-Depe*, pp. 40, 51, 105.
49. The influence of the proto-Elamite culture that may be observed in Altyn Tepe and other oasis cities of Kopet Dag can be traced back to this trade contact and not to a sometimes postulated mass emigration out of Mesopotamia or Iran. On this thesis see: Masson and Sarianidi, *Central Asia*, 1972, pp. 51, 81, 85, 89.
50. Masson, *Altyn-Depe*, p. 121; Colin Renfrew, 'Die Indoeuropäer aus archäologischer Sicht', in Richard Breuer (ed.), *Die Evolution der Sprachen: Spektrum der Wissenschaft*, Dossier 2 (Heidelberg, 2007), p. 48.
51. A.I. Isakov, 'Sarazm et la civilisation de l'Asie centrale', *Découverte des civilisations d'Asie Centrale: Les dossiers d'archéologie* no. 185 (1993), p. 26.
52. Anthony, *The Horse, the Wheel and Language*, pp. 419f; Isakov, 'Sarazm et la civilisation de l'Asie centrale', pp. 28–35; A.I. Isakov, 'Sarazm: An Agricultural Center of Ancient Sogdiana', *Bulletin of the Asia Institute* viii (1994), pp. 1–12; Rauf Razzakov, *Sarazm* (Dushanbe, 2006), pp. 22–28.
53. Isakov, 'Sarazm', p. 3; Razzakov, *Sarazm*, pp. 26, 36. figs. 136–138.
54. Isakov, 'Sarazm et la civilisation de l'Asie centrale', 1993, pp. 34f; Isakov, 'Sarazm', p. 6; Tatiana Kiatkina, 'Le population de l'Asie Moyenne ancienne', *Découverte des civilisations d'Asie Centrale: Les dossiers d'archéologie* no. 185 (1993), pp. 37f.
55. Anthony, *The Horse, the Wheel and Language*, p. 420.
56. Pierre Amiet, *L' âge des échange inter-iraniens 3500–1700 avant J.-C. (Paris, 1986), pp. 182f;* Masson, 'The Bronze Age in Khorasan and Transoxiana', pp. 232f; Tosi et al., *The Bronze Age in Iran and Afghanistan*, p. 208.
57. Henri-Paul Francfort, *Fouilles de Shortugaï*, Vol. I (Paris, 1989), pp. 76, 131–135, 144, 165–168.
58. Francfort, *Fouilles de Shortugaï*, Vol. I, pp. 283, 286ff. On the Bronze Age culture of Bactria, see p. 114.
59. Warwick Ball, *The Monuments of Afghanistan: History, archaeology and architecture* (London, 2008), p. 265.
60. Jonathan Kenoyer, *Ancient cities of the Indus Valley Civilization* (Oxford, 1998), p. 17.
61. Ibid, pp. 15–69.
62. Kenoyer. *Ancient cities*, pp. 69–80; Deo Prakash Sharma, *Indus Script on its way to decipherment* (Delhi, 2000).
63. Irene Good, J.M. Kenoyer and R.H. Meadow, 'New evidence for early silk in the Indus civilizations', Archaeometry 1 (2009), p. 1f.
64. Good, Kenoyer and Meadow, 'New evidence for early silk', pp. 3–8.
65. Nüzhet Dalfes, George Kukla and Harvey Weiss (eds), *Third Millennium* BC *Climate Change and Old World* Collapse (Berlin, 1997), p. 231.
66. James Lee, *Climate Change and Armed Conflict: Hot and Cold Wars* (Oxon, 2009), pp. 31ff; Holly Pittman, *Art of the Bronze Age: Southeastern Iran, Western Central Asia and the Indus Valley* (New York, 1984), pp. 81f.
67. Asif Raza Morio, *Moen Jo Daro: Mysterious City of Indus Valley Civilization* (Larkana, 2007), pp. 35, 92f.
68. Frank Sirocko, *Wetter, Klima, Menschheitsentwicklung* (Damstadt, 2010), pp. 119, 127f.
69. Frumkin, *Archaeology in Soviet Central Asia*, 1970, p. 141; Masson and Sarianidi, *Central Asia*, pp. 93f, 103.
70. The Cucuteni Culture of Romania and the Tripolye Culture of the Ukraine were originally treated as separate cultures; today they are considered as a single unit.
71. Vladimir Zbenovic, *Siedlungen der frühen Tripol'e-Kultur zwischen Dnestr und Südlichem Bug* (Espelkamp, 1996), pp. 35–38.
72. Krzystof Ciuk (ed.), *Mysteries of ancient Ukraine* (Toronto, 2008), pp. 27f, 58f, 145ff; Kohl, *The making of Bronze Age Eurasia*, p. 44.
73. Ciuk (ed.), *Mysteries of ancient Ukraine*, p. 60.
74. 'Apotropaic' means warding off evil.
75. Anthony, *The Horse, the Wheel and Language*, pp. 170ff; Ciuk (ed.), *Mysteries of ancient Ukraine*, p. 14.
76. Ciuk (ed.), *Mysteries of ancient Ukraine*, pp. 19, 147, 167. See p. 90.
77. Ciuk (ed.), *Mysteries of ancient Ukraine*, p. 64.
78. The hypothesis formulated by Marija Gimbutas in the 1970s of a brutal destruction of the peaceful, egalitarian, and matrilineally organised agrarian culture of 'Old Europe' by militaristic and patriarchal Indo-European rider hordes from the east has been laid to rest. There is also no evidence that Chalcolithic agrarian culture was matriarchal and egalitarian, nor that steppe peoples had an armed cavalry as far back as the fifth/fourth millennium BC. It is true, however, that the semi-nomadic herders had an armed elite and erected kurgans.
79. Anthony, *The Horse, the Wheel and Language*, pp. 229f, 346. On the proto-Indo-European language family PIE and on the problem of associating a prehistoric culture that finally consists of a cluster of particular archaeological discoveries with specific languages and these then with ethnicities, see note 151 and p. 135.
80. Anthony, *The Horse, the Wheel and Language*, pp. 268ff. 355f; Ciuk (ed.), *Mysteries of ancient Ukraine*, pp. 12, 30f, 37, 45, 232.
81. Anthony, *The Horse, the Wheel and Language*, p. 234.
82. Ibid, pp. 338f, 355; Ciuk (ed.), *Mysteries of ancient Ukraine*, pp. 31, 37, 45, 138f; Iaroslav Lebedynsky. *Les Indo-Européens* (Errance, 2006), pp. 124f.
83. Renate Rolle et al., *Gold der Steppe: Archäologie der Ukraine* (Schleswig, 1991), pp. 44f; D. Telegin and J.P. Mallory, *The Anthropomorphic Stelae of the Ukraine: The Early Iconography of the Indo-Europeans* (Washington, 1994), pp. 10–14.
84. Telegin and Mallory, *The Anthropomorphic Stelae of the Ukraine*, pp. 29f, 55ff.
85. See p. 157.
86. Anthony, *The Horse, the Wheel and Language*, pp. 360, 368, 380.
87. Ibid, p. 189.
88. Ibid, p. 182.
89. Ibid, pp. 185f, 235, 254.
90. Anthony, *The Horse, the Wheel and Language*, pp. 182, 275, 299f, 317; David Christian, *A History of Russia, Central Asia and Mongolia, Vol. I, Inner Eurasia from Prehistory to the Mongol Empire* (Oxford, 1998), p. 100; Parzinger et al., 'Das mehrperiodige Gräberfeld von Suchanicha bei Minusinsk', *Eurasia Antiqua* xv (2009), p. 195.
91. Mallory and Adams, *Encyclopedia of Indo-European Culture*, pp. 540f.
92. Anthony, *The Horse, the Wheel and Language*, pp. 98ff, 245; Christian, *A History of Russia, Central Asia and Mongolia*, p. 86; J.P. Mallory, *In Search of the Indo-Europeans: Language, Archaeology and Myth* (London, 1989), pp. 182, 241f, 264.
93. Anthony, *The Horse, the Wheel and Language*, pp. 43–49, 57, 100, 251, 259, 262; Kristian Kristiansen, 'La diffusion préhistorique des langues indo-européennes', *Dossiers d'Archéologie* no. 338 (2008), p. 42.
94. Anthony, *The Horse, the Wheel and Language*, p. 185; Kohl, *The making of Bronze Age Eurasia*, p. 140; E. Kuzmina, *The Prehistory of the Silk Road* (Philadelphia, 2008), p. 25.
95. Anthony, *The Horse, the Wheel and Language*, pp. 213–215.
96. Robert Drews, *Early Riders: The beginnings of mounted warfare in Asia and Europe* (New York, 2004), p. 13.

97. Anthony, *The Horse, the Wheel and Language*, pp. 216–220; Anatoly Derevyanko and D. Dorj, 'Neolithic tribes in northern parts of Central Asia', in *History of civilizations of Central Asia*, Vol. I (Paris, 1992), p. 185; Michael Frachetti, *Pastoralist landscapes and social interaction in Bronze Age Eurasia* (Berkeley, 2008), p. 46; Aleksandr Kislenko and Nataliya Tatarintseva, 'The Eastern Ural Steppe at the End of the Stone Age' in Marsha Levine et al., *Late prehistoric exploitation of the Eurasian steppe* (Cambridge, 1999), p. 203; Hermann Parzinger, *Die frühen Völker Eurasiens: Vom Neolithikum bis zum Mittelalter* (Munich, 2006), pp. 219–230.
98. Whether representatives of the Botai Culture were in fact the first to ride horses remains debated. Levine believes that the horse bones came only from slaughtered wild horses, while Anthony and Christian are inclined to think that the art of riding was known west of the Urals even before the Botai Culture. Anthony, *The Horse, the Wheel and Language*, pp. 221–223, 265; Christian, *A History of Russia, Central Asia and Mongolia*, pp. 82, 85; Levine et al., *Late prehistoric exploitation of the Eurasian steppe*, p. 53.
99. Drews, *Early Riders*, pp. 32f.
100. Ibid, pp. 85, 88–91, 94, 97.
101. Ibid, pp. 66, 100.
102. Georges Roux and Johannes Renger, *Irak in der Antike* (Mainz, 2005), p. 194.
103. Five carbon-14 analyses gave a date of *ca.* 1000 BC for this grave, but aspects of the ceramic typology have led some scholars to propose a date of around 800 BC. Elizabeth Barber, *The mummies of Ürümchi* (London, 1999), p. 37, plate I; Christoph Baumer, *Southern Silk Road* (Bangkok, 2003), p. 31; Victor Mair (ed.), *Secrets of the Silk Road* (Santa Ana, CA, 2010), p. 36; Binghua Wang et al., *The ancient corpses of Xinjiang* (Xinjiang Renmin Chubanshe, 2001), pp. 79–94; Alfred Wieczorek and Christoph Lind (eds), *Ursprünge der Seidenstraße* (Stuttgart, 2007), pp. 183–187, 201.
104. Albert Dien, 'The stirrup and its effect on Chinese military history', *Ars Orientalia* xvi (1986); Philip de Souza (ed.), *The ancient world at war* (London, 1980), p. 260.
105. Walter Pohl, *Die Awaren. Ein Steppenvolk in Europa 567–822 n.Chr.* (Munich, 2002), pp. 89, 171ff.
106. Herodotus I, 215; Renate Rolle (ed.), *Amazonen: Geheimnisvolle Kriegerinnen* (Speyer, 2010), pp. 153–157. Whether the Massagetae had leather stirrups is debated. E.D. Phillips, *The Royal Hordes: Nomad Peoples of the Steppes* (London, 1965), pp. 93, 107; Véronique Schiltz, *Die Skythen und andere Steppenvölker* (Munich, 1994), p.405.
107. R. Brzezinski and M. Mielczarek, *The Sarmatians 600 BC – AD 450* (London, 2002), pp. 16ff; Iaroslav Lebedynsky, *Les Sarmates* (Errance, 2002), pp. 163, 166. See here p. 262.
108. Ch'ien Ssu-ma, *Records of the grand historian of China*, Vol. II (New York, 1971), p. 155.
109. Drews, *Early Riders*, pp. 139–147.
110. Brian Todd Carey, *Warfare in the Ancient World* (Barnsley, 1988), pp. 64–77; Ruth Sheppard, *Alexander der Grosse und seine Feldzüge* (Stuttgart, 2009), pp. 77–184; Souza, *The ancient world at war*, pp. 119–126.
111. Joseph Maran, 'Die Badener Kultur und ihre Räderfahrzeuge', in Mamoun Fansa and Stefan Burmeister (eds), *Rad und Wagen* (Mainz, 2004), pp. 265–282; Joseph Maran, 'Kulturkontakte und Wege der Ausbreitung der Wagentechnologie im 4. Jahrtausend v. Chr.', in Fansa and Burmeister, *Rad und Wagen*, p. 429.
112. Jan Albert Bakker, 'Die neolithischen Wagen im nördlichen Mitteleuropa', in Fansa and Burmeister, *Rad und Wagen*, pp. 283, 288.
113. Helmut Schlichtherle, 'Wagenfunde aus den Seeufersiedlungen im zirkumalpinen Raum', in Fansa and Burmeister, *Rad und Wagen*, pp. 295ff.
114. Stefan Burmeister, 'Neolithische und bronzezeitliche Moorfunde aus den Niederlanden, Nordwestdeutschland und Dänemark', in Fansa and Burmeister, *Rad und Wagen*, pp. 329ff.
115. Ciuk (ed.), *Mysteries of ancient Ukraine*, pp. 147, 167; Maran, 'Die Badener Kultur und ihre Räderfahrzeuge', pp. 275, 279; Maran, 'Kulturkontakte und Wege der Ausbreitung der Wagentechnologie', pp. 437ff.
116. Anthony, *The Horse, the Wheel and Language*, p. 295; Viktor Trifonov, 'Die Majkop-Kultur und die ersten Wagen in der südrussischen Steppe', in Fansa and Burmeister, *Rad und Wagen*, pp. 168ff.
117. Andrej Belinskij and Aleksej Kalmykov, 'Neue Wagenfunde aus der Katakombengrab-Kultur im Steppengebiet des zentralen Vorkauskasus', in Mamoun Fansa and Burmeister, *Rad und Wagen*, p. 201; Aleksandr Gej, 'Die Wagen der Novotitarovskaja-Kultur', in Fansa and Burmeister, *Rad und Wagen*, pp. 177, 188; Trifonov, 'Die Majkop-Kultur und die ersten Wagen', pp. 173f; Michail Tureckij, 'Wagengräber der grubengrabzeitlichen Kulturen im Steppengebiet Osteuropas', in Fansa and Burmeister, *Rad und Wagen*, p. 192.
118. Shen Chen, *Anyang and Sanxingdui: Unveiling the Mysteries of Ancient Chinese Civilizations* (Toronto, 2002), p. 75.
119. J.P. Mallory and Victor H. Mair, *The Tarim Mummies* (London, 2000), p. 325. See here p. 122.
120. Christopher Pare, 'Die Wagen der Bronzezeit in Mitteleuropa', in Fansa and Burmeister, *Rad und Wagen*, p. 358.
121. Tureckij, 'Wagengräber der grubengrabzeitlichen Kulturen', p. 196ff. Other scholars, such as Victor Trifonov, remain committed to the earlier hypothesis, according to which Maikop adopted the technology of wagon construction from Mesopotamia (Trifonov 'Die Majkop-Kultur und die ersten Wagen', pp. 171–174f).
122. Maran, 'Kulturkontakte und Wege der Ausbreitung der Wagentechnologie', pp. 437ff; M. Primas, 'Innovationstransfer vor 5000 Jahren: Knotenpunkte an Land- und Wasserwegen zwischen Vorderasien und Europa', *Eurasia Antiqua* xiii (2007), pp. 4ff.
123. This was during the Subboreal (3700–450 BC).
124. Christian, *A History of Russia, Central Asia and Mongolia*, p. 142; Kuzmina, *The Prehistory of the Silk Road*, p. 65.
125. Rolle (ed.), *Amazonen. Geheimnisvolle Kriegerinnen*, pp. 105f.
126. Mallory and Adams, *Encyclopedia of Indo-European Culture*, p. 628.
127. Anthony, *The Horse, the Wheel and Language*, pp. 397, 402; Kuzmina, *The Prehistory of the Silk Road*, pp. 44ff. A single-axle cart with a light body from the great kurgan of Ipatovskij in the region of Stavropol, south-western Russia, is about 100 years older than the earliest from Sintashta, but the type of wheel cannot be determined. Belinskij and Kalmykov, 'Neue Wagenfunde aus der Katakombengrab-Kultur', 2004, p. 215f.
128. On the Sintashta-Petrovka Culture see pp. 141ff.
129. Herodotus I, 216. See here p. 200.
130. See pp. 141ff.
131. *Rig Veda*, Book 2, II:3 (zweiter Liederkreis, 1. Gruppe, 2.2.3.) (English text is from http://www.sacred-texts.com/hin/rigveda/rv02002.htm.)
132. Herodotus, IV 71; Rostovtzeff, M., *La peinture décorative antique en Russie méridionale* (1913–1914) (Paris, 2004), pp. 80f.
133. A. Kantorovic A. and E. Maslov, 'Eine reiche Bestattung der Majkop-Kultur aus einem Kurgan der stanica Mar'inskaja, Kreis Stavropol, Nordkaukasien', *Eurasia Antiqua*, xiii (2008), p. 159.
134. Contrary to popular belief, not all lapis lazuli must stem from the famous Sar-i Sang-mine in Badakhshan, northern Afghanistan, although it is the largest and longest exploited mine; other lapis lazuli mines exist in the Pamirs, in the Chagai Hills in Baluchistan, Pakistan, and at the southern shore of Lake Baikal in southern Siberia. Furthermore, other feldspathoid such as sodalite and lazurite which can be found in several other sites in Central and Southeast Asia may be confused with true lapis lazuli. Hence caution is advised when deducing from the find of a lapis lazuli or related feldspathoid a trade connection with Badkhshan (Good, Irene, *When East met West: Interpretative Problems in Assessing East-West Contact and Exchange in Antiquity*, in Vth ICAANE Congress, Madrid. Edited by Allison Betts and Fiona Kidd (Louvain 2008) pp. 28–30).
135. Andreï Alexeev et al., *Nomades des Steppes* (Paris, 2001); Andreï Alexeev et al., *Trésors des Steppes* (Hauterive, 2006), pp. 45–51; Anthony, *The Horse, the Wheel and Language*, pp. 287–289.
136. Aruz, *Art of the first cities*, pp. 94, 120; Jeremy Black and Anthony Green, *Gods, Demons and Symbols of Ancient Mesopotamia* (Austin, 2000), p. 104f; Richard Zettler and Lee Horne (eds), *Treasures from the Royal Tombs of Ur* (Philadelphia, 1998), pp. 21–38, 48f.
137. Kohl, *The making of Bronze Age Eurasia*, p. 74.
138. Ibid, pp. 165, 222f.
139. The classification of cultures by types of tombs was introduced by the Russian archaeologist Vasilij Gorodcov in 1905 (Leskovar Jutta, Zingerle Maria-Christina (eds), *Goldener Horizont* (2010), p. 22).
140. Anthony, *The Horse, the Wheel and Language*, pp. 274f.
141. Ibid, pp. 254, 274f, 300ff; Jurij Rassamakin, 'The Eneolithic of the Black sea Steppe: Dynamics of Cultural and Economic Development 4500–2300 BC', in Marsha Levine et al., *Late prehistoric exploitation of the Eurasian steppe* (Cambridge, 1999), pp, 151–54.
142. Since in both preceding and subsequent cultures graves were sprinkled with ochre, this term is unspecific and unhelpful.
143. Anthony, *The Horse, the Wheel and Language*, pp. 317, 343f, 361.

144. Ibid, pp. 57f, 100f, 305, 344, 349.
145. See here pp. 264f.
146. Christian, *A History of Russia, Central Asia and Mongolia*, p. 101.
147. Frachetti, *Pastoralist landscapes and social interaction*, p. 45.
148. Anthony, *The Horse, the Wheel and Language*, pp. 264f, 305, 308; Christian, *A History of Russia, Central Asia and Mongolia*, p. 101; Michael Frachetti, 'Bronze Age Exploitation and Political Dynamics of the Eastern Eurasian Steppe Zone', in Marsha Levine et al., *Late prehistoric exploitation of the Eurasian steppe* (Cambridge, 1999), p. 164. See also: N.A. Bokovenko, 'Malinovyj Log. Ein Gräberfeld der Afanas'evo-Kultur', *Eurasia Antiqua* vi (2000), p. 31.
149. Kislenko and Tatarintseva, 'The Eastern Ural Steppe', pp. 209f.
150. Mallory, *In Search of the Indo-Europeans*, pp. 223ff. Mallory and Adams, *Encyclopedia of Indo-European Culture*, p. 4.
151. Brian Hemphill and J.P. Mallory, 'Horse-mounted invaders from the Russo-Kazakh Steppe or agricultural colonists from Western Central Asia? A craniometric investigation of the Bronze Age settlements of Xinjiang', *American Journal of Physical Anthropology* cxxiv/ 3 (2004), p. 202; Keyser Christine et al. *Tracking back ancient south Siberian population history using mitochondrial and Y-chromosome SNPs*, 2008, pp. 343–345. We will use the term 'Europid' in an ethnic sense, which should be distinguished from the linguistic term 'Indo-European'. Not all Europids spoke Indo-European languages, and not all Indo-European-speakers were Europids. While the two terms can be congruent, they need not be. Regarding the historically loaded term 'Aryan', the Rig Veda, one of the four canonical scriptures of Hinduism, makes clear that Aryan is a cultural-linguistic category, not a racial one. Anyone who offers the proper rituals to the right gods and recites the appropriate hymns is an Aryan. The same holds true with regard to the Avesta, the most sacred book of Zoroastrianism. Here we add that blond hair and light skin are in no way inherent distinguishing features of Nordic Europids, but rather the result of depigmentation as a consequence of a colder climate and less UV-radiation. See: Lebedynsky, *Les Indo-Européens*, p. 91.
152. Douglas Adams, 'Mummies', in Victor H. Mair (ed.), *The Mummified Remains Found in the Tarim Basin*, *Journal of Indo-European Studies* xxiii/3&4 (1995), pp. 410f; Hemphill and Mallory, 'Horse-mounted invaders from the Russo-Kazakh Steppe', pp. 200–202; Mallory, *In Search of the Indo-Europeans*, pp. 61, 226; Mallory and Mair, *The Tarim Mummies*, p. 293. See p. 135.
153. Cists are tombs made of stone slabs.
154. Burchard Brentjes, 'Frühe Steinstelen Sibiriens und der Mongolei', *Central Asiatic Journal* xl (1996), p. 22; Vladimir Kubarev, *Drevnie rospisi Karakola* (Novosibirsk, 1988), pp. 28–31, 39–42, 50, 60, 69f, 168–172.
155. Nikolaj Leon'ev and Vladimir Kapel'ko, *Steinstelen der Okunev-Kultur* (Mainz, 2002), figs. 3, 7, 32, 174. See p. 137.
156. Karl Baipakov and A.N. Mariashev, *The Eshkiolmes Rock's Petroglyphs* (Almaty, 2005), p. 118.
157. Henri-Paul Francfort, 'Central Asian petroglyphs: between Indo-Iranian and shamanistic interpretations', in Christopher Chippindale and Paul Taçon (eds), *The Archaeology of Rock-Art* (Cambridge, 1998), p. 309.
158. A.N. Mar'jasev et al. (eds), *Répertoire des pétroglyphes d'Asie Centrale. Fascicule 5: Kazakhstan 1. Choix de pétroglyphes du Semirech'e* (Paris, 1998), figs. 1–7; A.A. Goryachev, A.N. Mariyashev. *Petroglyphs of Semirechye*, 1999; Andrzej Rozwadowski, *Symbols through Time: Interpreting the Rock Art of Central Asia* (Poznan, 2004), pp. 65ff.
159. Marianna Devlet, 'Felsbilder von Aldy-Mozag, Tuva', *Eurasia Antiqua* v (1999), pp. 604f.
160. E. Kuzmina, 'Les steppes de l'Asie centrale à l'époque du bronze, Découverte des civilisations d'Asie Centrale', *Les dossiers d'archéologie*, No. 185 (1993), p. 89.
161. *Rig Veda*, Book 4, 4.13.2; Book 7, 7.61.1, 7.63.5, 7. 65.1,7,12.
162. *Avesta*, VII, XXVI (10) 17ff; (2006, Vol. III. pp. 9, 89–102)
163. Baumer, *Southern Silk Road*, p. 31. See here photo p. 83.
164. Rozwadowski, *Symbols through Time*, pp. 57ff. On the symbolism of a horse with horns or deer antlers accompanying the dead into the afterlife, see p. 187.
165. Herodotus, I, 216.
166. See p. 146.
167. *Rig Veda*, Book 1, 14.1.162f; Anthony, *The Horse, the Wheel and Language*, pp. 370–375, 405–411; Rozwadowski, *Symbols through Time*, pp. 38–42.V. The Chalcolithic and the Early Bronze Age

VI. The Middle and Late Bronze Age

1. Nicola di Cosmo, *Ancient China and its enemies: The rise of nomadic power in East Asian history* (Cambridge, 2002), p. 13; Sima Guang, *Zizhi tongjian* (Bloomington 2009), pp. 14f; Ssu-ma Ch'ien, *Shih chi. Records of the grand historian of China* (New York 1971), Vol. II, p. 159.
2. The hypothesis of Soviet archaeologists and Claude Rapin is now broadly accepted, that the upper reaches of the ancient Oxus, as defined by the geographers of the classical antiquity, are not identical with the Darya-i Panj, which forms the modern border between Tajikistan and Afghanistan east of Takht-i Sangin as far as Dzong. (East of Dzong the border follows the River Pamir.) Instead, the ancient upper Oxus coincides with the Vakhsh, whose source lies in southern Kyrgyzstan; hence ancient Bactria also included present south-eastern Tajikistan. However, it remains unclear whether the 'Bactria' mentioned by Strabo (*ca.* 63 BC) and Ptolemy was identical with the Bronze Age Bactria. It is unlikely that this was the case. The Darya-i Panj is identical with the ancient Ochus. Askarov Akhmadali, *La Bactriane à l'aube de la civilisation,* 1993, p. 60; Claude Rapin, 'L'Afghanistan et l'Asie Centrale dans la géographie mythique des historiens d'Alexandre et dans la toponymie des géographes gréco-romains', in Osmund Bopearachchi and Marie-Françoise Boussac (eds), *Afghanistan. Ancien carrefour entre l'est et l'ouest* (Turnhout, 2005), p. 144; Ptolemaois Claudios, *Handbuch der Geographie* (2006), VI, 11, 1; 12, 1; Strabo, *Geographica* (2007), II, 1, 15; XI, 8, 8; 12, 1).
3. Viktor Sarianidi, *Margush: Ancient Oriental Kingdom in the Old Delta of Murgab River* (Ashgabat, 2002), p. 86.
4. Despite this limitation we prefer the term 'Bactria-Margiana Archaeological Complex' to the alternative, introduced by H.-P. Francfort, of an 'Oxus Civilisation', because the Murgab River and Margiana do not belong to the natural watershed of the Oxus River, today called the Amu Darya. A more precise description would be 'Murgab-Oxus Civilisation' (Henri-Paul Francfort, 'La civilisation de l'Oxus et les Indo-Iraniens et Indo-Aryens en Asie Centrale,' in Gérard Fussman et al., *Aryas, Aryens et Iraniens en Asie Centrale* (Paris, 2005), p. 253).
5. Gabriele Rossi-Osmida, *Adji Kui Oasis, III–II mill. BC* (Venice, 2007), pp. 72f.
6. Fredrik Talmage Hiebert et al., *Origins of the Bronze Age Oasis Civilization in Central Asia* (Harvard University, 1994), pp. XXXII, 2, 67, 164f; Gabriele Rossi-Osmida, *Margiana: Gonur-depe Necropolis* (Venice, 2002), p. 18.
7. On Margiana: Francfort et al., *Fouilles de Shortugaï*, pp. 379, 459; Hiebert et al., *Origins of the Bronze Age Oasis Civilization*, pp. 77ff; J.P. Mallory and D.Q. Adams, *Encyclopedia of Indo-European Culture*, (London, 1997), pp. 653f; Sarianidi, 'Margiana in the Bronze Age', p. 188. On Bactria: Akhmadali Askarov, 'Southern Uzbekistan in the Second Millennium BC', in Philip Kohl (ed.), *The Bronze Age Civilization of Central Asia: Recent Soviet discoveries* (New York, 1981), p. 261; Vladimir Ionesov, *The struggle between life and death in Proto-Bactrian Culture* (Ceredigion, 2002), pp. 31–80; Temur Sirinov, 'Die frühurbane Kultur der Bronzezeit im südlichen Mittelasien: Die vorgeschichtliche Siedlung Dzarkutan', *Archäologische Mitteilungen aus Iran und Turan* xxxiv (2003), pp. 139ff. Regarding the classification, introduced by Ionesov, of a Sapalli Culture, one should note that the first period is also called Sapalli, while the next three are named for the sites Jarkutan, Kuzali and Molali/Bustan.
8. Hiebert et al., *Origins of the Bronze Age Oasis Civilization*, p. 10; Rossi-Osmida, *Adji Kui Oasis*, p. 21. Sarianidi, *Margush,* p. 87.
9. Henri-Paul Francfort et al., *Fouilles de Shortugaï: Recherches sur l'Asie Centrale protohistorique* (Paris, 1989), p. 379; Hiebert et al., *Origins of the Bronze Age Oasis Civilization*, pp. 40, 75ff; Vadim Masson, *Altyn-Depe* (Philadelphia, 1988), p. 135; Hermann Parzinger, *Die frühen Völker Eurasiens: Vom Neolithikum bis zum Mittelalter* (Munich, 2006), pp. 432f; Viktor Sarianidi, 'Margiana in the Bronze Age,' in Philip Kohl (ed.), *The Bronze Age Civilization of Central Asia: Recent Soviet discoveries* (New York, 1981), pp. 188ff.
10. Hiebert et al., *Origins of the Bronze Age Oasis Civilization*, pp. 62ff; Sarianidi, 'Margiana in the Bronze Age', p. 167ff.
11. Hiebert et al., *Origins of the Bronze Age Oasis Civilization*, pp. 89–107; Sarianidi, *Margush*, pp. 220–223.

12. Viktor Sarianidi, 'Temples of Bronze Age Margiana: traditions of ritual architecture', *Antiquity* lxviii/297 (1994), p. 389; *Margush*, pp. 194ff.
13. Hiebert et al., *Origins of the Bronze Age Oasis Civilization*, pp. 109–129; Sarianidi, *Margush*, p. 194ff.
14. Rossi-Osmida, *Margiana*, pp. 27, 72.
15. Hiebert et al., *Origins of the Bronze Age Oasis Civilization*, p. 129.
16. David Anthony, *The Horse, the Wheel and Language. How Bronze-Age riders from the Eurasian Steppes shaped the modern world* (Princeton, 2007), p. 452; Henri-Paul Francfort, 'La Civilisation de l'Asie Centrale à l'âge du Bronze et è l'âge du Fer', in Osmund Bopearachchi et al. (eds), *De l'Indus à l'Oxus: Archaéologie de l'Asie Centrale* (Lattes, 2003), p. 31; E. Kuzmina, *The Origin of Indo-Iranians* (Leiden, 2007), pp. 238f; Mallory and Adams, *Encyclopedia of Indo-European Culture*, p. 20. On Andronovo see pp. 141ff.
17. Vadim Masson, 'The Decline of the Bronze Age Civilization and Movements of the Tribes', in *History of Civilizations of Central Asia*, Vol. I (Paris, 1992), p. 345. See also: Hiebert et al., *Origins of the Bronze Age Oasis Civilization*, pp. 69f; G.A. Pugachenkova, *Antiquities of Southern Uzbekistan* (Tokyo, 1991), p. 41.
18. Strabo, *Geographica*, XI, 10, 2. See also: A. Dani and P. Bernard, 'Alexander and his successors in Central Asia', in *History of Civilizations of Central Asia*, Vol. II (Paris, 1994), p. 91; Renato Sala, *Historical survey of irrigation practices in West Central Asia* (Almaty, 2004), p. 12. Other authors date this long wall to the Sassanid period (224–651 AD) (V. Gaïbov and G.Kochelenko, *La Margiane*, 2002, p. 48).
19. Hiebert et al., *Origins of the Bronze Age Oasis Civilization*, pp. 71, 113, 130.
20. Francfort, 'La civilisation de l'Oxus et les Indo-Iraniens et Indo-Aryens', p. 274; Rossi-Osmida, *Margiana*, pp. 27–30; Viktor Sarianidi, 'Les tombes royales de Gonur-Dépé', *Archéologia*, No. 420 (2005), pp. 52–59; 'Nouvelles sépultures sur le territoire de la "nécropole royale" de Gonur Dépé', *Arts Asiatiques*, Vol. 65 (2010), pp. 5–26.
21. Viktor Sarianidi, 'Le plus ancien sacrifice de poulain au Proche-Orient', *Dossiers d'Archéologie*, No. 317 (2006), pp. 35f.
22. Hiebert et al., *Origins of the Bronze Age Oasis Civilization*, pp. 141f; Rossi-Osmida, *Adji Kui Oasis*, pp. 152ff, 159, 166–172, 188.
23. Rossi-Osmida, *Adji Kui Oasis*, pp. 173ff, 189ff.
24. Joan Aruz (ed.), *Art of the first cities* (New York, 2003), p. 368; Agnès Benoit, 'Les "princesses" de Bactriane', in *Arts & Cultures* (Geneva, 2005), pp. 38f; Marie-Claude Bianchini, *Afghanistan*, 2002, pp. 94f; Sarianidi, *Margush*, p. 148.
25. Rossi-Osmida, *Margiana*, pp. 39, 104f; Rossi-Osmida, *Adji Kui Oasis*, p. 180.
26. Cluzan, Sophie: *De Sumer à Canaan* 2005, p. 220.
27. Aruz, *Art of the first cities*, pp. 105f; Richard Zettler and Lee Horne (eds), *Treasures from the Royal Tombs of Ur* (Philadelphia, 1998), p. 55.
28. Sarianidi, 'Aegean-Anatolian Motifs', pp. 28ff.
29. www.ancient-wisdom.co.uk/.../gilgamesh1.jpg
30. The claim by the Iranian archaeologist Yousef Majidzadeh that the discoveries support the existence of an independent 'culture of Jiroft' or 'Halil Rud' is controversial (Bruno Bioul, *Jiroft* (2003)).
31. Aruz, *Art of the first cities*, p. 331; Bioul, *Jiroft*, pp. 30, 36f, 43, 99, 109–111, 132.
32. Metropolitan Museum of Art, New York, Ancient Near Eastern Art, no. L. 1994.39.3.
33. Stierlin, *Splendors of Ancient Persia*, pp. 67–71.
34. Equating the mistress of animals with the so-called Venus statues of the Palaeolithic and with female deities of earlier agrarian cultures, as has been proposed by Marija Gimbutas, is not appropriate and obscures the distinctive features of the 'mistress of animals' (Mircea Eliade (ed.), *The Encyclopedia of Religions* (New York, 1993), Vol. 8, pp. 420ff).
35. Various inscriptions seem to indicate that Asherah was also worshipped in Jerusalem until the Babylonian Exile in the year 586 BC. Only then was she condemned as the wife of the 'evil' Canaanite god Baal (Sandra Scham, *The Lost Goddess of Israel*, 2005. pp. 36–40).
36. Michael Maqdissi et al., *Schätze des Alten Syriens* (Stuttgart, 2009), p. 58; *Le Monde de la Bible*, # 149 (Paris, March 2003), p. 14.
37. Geneviève Lüscher, *Die Hydria von Grächwil* (Bern, 2002).
38. The Celts also had an animal-human hybrid, as can be seen on the silver cauldron of Gundestrup, Denmark, from the last pre-Christian centuries, which was probably crafted on the eastern edge of the Celtic world in the Balkans or Anatolia or else in Thrace. On one of the five inner plates a seated man with deer antlers is portrayed, holding a snake and a torque, a neck band open to the front, and surrounded by various animals such as a stag, a goat, a lion and a kind of greyhound (Sabatino Moscati et al. (eds), *The Celts* (Venice, 1991), pp. 538f; http://www.unc.edu/celtic/catalogue/Gundestrup/kauldron.html).
39. Jakov Sher et al. (eds), *Répertoire des pétroglyphes d'Asie Centrale. Fascicule 1: Sibérie du Sud 1. Oglakhty I–III* (Paris, 1994), plate Oglakhty I,10.1.
40. Aruz, *Art of the first cities*, p. 408.
41. L.K. Galanina, *Die Kurgane von Kelermes* (Berlin, 1996), pp. 173–187, plate I.
42. Pierre Cambon, Jean-François Jarrige et al., *Afghanistan, les trésors retrouvés: Collections du musée national de Kaboul* (Paris, 2006), pp. 174, 210, 273, 283.
43. Jean-Paul Barbier, *Art des Steppes* (Geneva, 1996), p. 70; *Le Monde de la Bible*, # 150 (Paris, April 2003), pp. 64f.
44. Aruz, *Art of the first cities*, p. 169; Rossi-Osmida, *Adji Kui Oasis*, p. 178.
45. R. Ghirsman, 'Deux statuettes élamites du plateau iranien', *Artibus Asiae* xxx/2/3 (1968), pp. 243f; Henri Stierlin, *Splendors of Ancient Persia* (Vercelli, 2006), pp. 33f. A similar seated woman, wearing a kaunakes, can be seen on a silver pin from Margiana (Aruz, *Art of the first cities*, p. 367).
46. Rossi-Osmida, *Margiana*, 43ff. There are other such seals from Margiana and Bactria, but of unknown origin. Viktor Sarianidi, 'The Bactrian Pantheon', *Information Bulletin of the International Association for the Study of the Cultures of Central Asia, IASCCA*, No. 10 (1986), fig. 1, nr. 10; Sylvia Winkelmann, *Seals of the oasis from the Ligabue Collection* (Venice, 2004), pp. 71f. Many such metal seals, which appeared on the Chinese antiquities market at the start of the twentieth century, were incorrectly identified as 'Nestorian Ordos crosses', How such seals reached the Ordos, the northern bend of the Yellow River, from the BMAC region remains a mystery (Philip Kohl (ed.), *The Bronze Age Civilization of Central Asia: Recent Soviet Discoveries* (New York, 1981), pp. XXII, XXXVII).
47. Stephen Bourke, *The Middle East: The cradle of civilization revealed* (London, 2008), p. 83.
48. See Vol. II.
49. Holly Pittman, *Art of the Bronze Age. Southeastern Iran, Western Central Asia and the Indus Valley*, (New York, 1994), pp. 72–77.
50. Francfort, 'La civilisation de l'Oxus et les Indo-Iraniens et Indo-Aryens' p. 284; *Images du combat contre le sanglier en Asie centrale (3ème au 1er millénaire av. J.-C.)*, pp. 130–33; Pittman, *Art of the Bronze Age*, p. 73. On another ceremonial axe a silver lion attacks a gilt boar (Bianchini (ed.), *Afghanistan*, 2002, p. 105).
51. Sarianidi, 'The Bactrian Pantheon', fig. 1. Another seal made of soapstone or chlorite, depicting a naked man holding two snakes, is on display at the Metropolitan Museum of Art, New York, Ancient Near Eastern Art, no. 1984.383.29.
52. Hiebert et al., *Origins of the Bronze Age Oasis Civilization*, pp. XXXIII, 60f, 152f; Viktor Sarianidi, 'Aegean-Anatolian Motifs in the Glyptic Art of Bactria and Margiana', *Bulletin of the Asia Institute* viii (1994), pp. 28–32.
53. Jeremy Black and Anthony Green, *Gods, Demons and Symbols of Ancient Mesopotamia* (Austin, 2000), p. 100.
54. Rossi-Osmida, *Adji Kui Oasis*, pp. 21f.
55. Three well-preserved 'foundation pegs', in the forms of a personal patron deity, a lion, and King Shulgi of Ur, are exhibited at the Metropolitan Museum of Art, New York: 1989, 281.5; 1948, 48.180 and Rogers Fund, 1959, 59.41.1. Six additional pegs are on display in the British Museum. See also: Aruz, *Art of the first cities*, pp. 65, 80, 222, 438f.
56. Rossi-Osmida, *Adji Kui Oasis*, pp. 67–120.
57. Sarianidi's interpretation of the citadel as a public temple, in whose necropolis a priestess was buried with a sacrificed man, is debated. Sarianidi, 'Temples of Bronze Age Margiana', p. 391; Sarianidi, *Margush*, pp. 165ff.
58. Hiebert et al., *Origins of the Bronze Age Oasis Civilization*, p. 121. Here as well Sarianidi interprets the complex as an Indo-Iranian temple with archaic fire altars. Traces of ephedra, whose alkaloid ephedrine has stimulant effects, in a few vessels led him to the hypothesis that the sacred intoxicant of the Indo-Aryans called *haoma* (mentioned in the Avesta) or *soma* (in the Rig Veda) was prepared in Togolok 21, and he postulated a connection with the Indo-Europeans who advanced into northern India and the Saka Haumavarga, the 'haoma-worshiping Saka', mentioned by Darius I more than a thousand years later. Hiebert et al., *Origins of the Bronze Age Oasis Civilization*, p. XXXIV; Sarianidi, 'Temples of Bronze Age Margiana', pp. 391–397; Sarianidi, *Margush*, pp. 178–181.

59. See the above overview and note 8.
60. Hiebert, Cambon, *Afghanistan, Crossroads of the Ancient World*, (2011) pp. 67–79.
61. Francfort et al., *Fouilles de Shortugaï*, p. 341.
62. Askarov, 'Southern Uzbekistan in the Second Millennium BC', p. 258f.
63. Askarov, 'La Bactriane à l'aube de la civilisation', p. 63; Kohl, *The Bronze Age Civilization of Central Asia*, p. XXI.
64. Askarov, 'Southern Uzbekistan in the Second Millennium BC', p. 263; Sirinov, 'Die frühurbane Kultur der Bronzezeit', pp. 1–7.
65. A. Askarov and T. Shirinov, 'The "Palace", Temple and Necropolis of Jarkutan', *Bulletin of the Asia Institute* viii (1994), pp. 21, 23; Sirinov, 'Die frühurbane Kultur der Bronzezeit', pp. 43, 65, 79, 82.
66. Rig Veda, Book 2, 2.1.1,6; *The Encyclopedia of Religions*, Vol. 1, p. 134.
67. Sirinov, 'Die frühurbane Kultur der Bronzezeit', p. 150.
68. Barbara Kaim, 'Où adorer les dieux? Un spectaculaire temple du feu d'époque sassanide', *Dossiers d'Archéologie*, No. 317 (2006), pp. 66–71.
69. Boris Litvinskij and Igor Picikjan, 'The Hellenistic Architecture and Art of the Temple on the Oxus', *Bulletin of the Asia Institute* viii (1994), pp. 57f; Boris Litvinskij and Igor Picikjan, *Taxt- Sangin. Der Oxus-Tempel* (Mainz, 2002), pp. 6, 34, 109. See here pp. 300ff
70. Sirinov, 'Die frühurbane Kultur der Bronzezeit', pp. 50, 79.
71. Ibid, p. 73.
72. On burial rituals of Bactria: Askarov, 'Southern Uzbekistan in the Second Millennium BC', pp. 260f; Ionesov, *The struggle between life and death in Proto-Bactrian Culture*, pp. 31–120, 182f; Sirinov, 'Die frühurbane Kultur der Bronzezeit', pp. 9–126.
73. Mike Teufer and Natalija Vinogradova, 'Das Gräberfeld von Gelot, Tadschikistan', in Nikolaus Boroffka and Svend Hansen (eds), *Archäologische Forschungen in Kasachstan, Tadschikistan, Turkmenistan und Usbekistan*, (Eurasien-Abteilung, Deutsches Archäologisches Institut, Berlin) 2010, pp. 28f.
74. Boris Litvinskij and L.T. Pyankova, 'Pastoral Tribes of the Bronze Age in the Oxus Valley (Bactria)', in *History of Civilizations of Central Asia*, Vol. I (Paris, 1992), pp. 382–390; L.T. Piankova, 'Bronze Age settlements of Southern Tadjikistan', in Philip Kohl (ed.), *The Bronze Age Civilization of Central Asia: Recent Soviet discoveries* (New York, 1981), p. 302.
75. Konstantin Čugunov, Hermann Parzinger and Anatoli Nagler, *Der skythenzeitliche Fürstenkurgan Aržhan 2 in Tuva* (Mainz, 2010), pp. 144f.
76. Akhmadali Askarov, 'The beginning of the Iron Age in Transoxania', in *History of Civilizations of Central Asia*, Vol. I (Paris, 1992), p. 444; Čugunov, Parzinger and Nagler, *Der skythenzeitliche Fürstenkurgan Aržhan 2 in Tuva*, p. 319; Wilfried Menghin et al. (eds), *Im Zeichen des goldenen Greifen: Königsgräber der Skythen* (Munich, 2007), pp. 107, 175f; E.D. Phillips, *The Royal Hordes: Nomad Peoples of the Steppes* (London, 1965), pp. 73f.
77. Renate Rolle et al., *Gold der Steppe: Archäologie der Ukraine* (Schleswig, 1991), p. 219.
78. Mahnaz Moazami, 'The dog in Zoroastrian religion: Videvdad Chapter XIII', *Indo-Iranian Journal* xlvi (2006), pp. 127–149.
79. Askarov, 'Southern Uzbekistan in the Second Millennium BC', p. 271; Sven Hansen et al., *Alexander der Große und die Öffnung der Welt: Asiens Kulturen im Wandel* (Mannheim, 2009), pp. 136ff.
80. Parzinger, *Die frühen Völker Eurasiens*, pp. 329–334.
81. Philip Kohl, *The making of Bronze Age Eurasia* (Cambridge, 2007), pp. 192, 200. A connection between the collapse of the Indus Valley Civilisation at the start of the nineteenth century BC and the crisis of the BMAC Culture is doubtful, all the more so since the Indus Valley Civilisation ended about three centuries before the BMAC Culture, although the warrior conquerors of northern India glorified in the Rig Veda came from the north. See: Christopher Beckwith, *Empires of the Silk Road* (Princeton, 2009), pp. 42, 397f, endnote 38; Richard Frye, *The heritage of Central Asia: From Antiquity to the Turkish Expansion* (Princeton, 1996), pp. 54–59.
82. Jianjun Mei, *Copper and Bronze Metallurgy in Late Prehistoric Xinjiang* (Oxford, 2000), pp. 67–69, 75.
83. Francfort et al., *Fouilles de Shortugaï*, pp. 386, 435–41; Vadim M. Masson, *Das Land der tausend Städte: Die Wiederentdeckung der ältestens Kulturgebiete in Mittelasien* (Munich, 1982), pp. 51–56.
84. Francfort et al., *Fouilles de Shortugaï*, 1989, p. 437; Francfort, 'La Civilisation de l'Asie Centrale à l'âge du Bronze et è l'âge du Fer', p. 32.
85. See Vol. II.
86. Hiebert et al., *Origins of the Bronze Age Oasis Civilization*, pp. 49f, 454.
87. Cosmo, *Ancient China and its enemies*, pp. 46f; E. Kuzmina, 'Historical perspectives on the Andronovo and metal use in Eastern Asia', in Katheryn Linduff (ed.), *Metallurgy in ancient Eastern Eurasia from the Urals to the Yellow River* (Ceredigion, 2004), pp. 38–44; Parzinger, *Die frühen Völker Eurasiens*, pp. 437ff.
88. Kuzmina, 'Historical perspectives on the Andronovo and metal use', pp. 40ff; Andrew Sheratt, 'The Trans-Eurasian Exchange: The Prehistory of Chinese Relations with the West', in Victor H. Mair, *Contact and Exchange in the Ancient World* (Honolulu, 2006), pp. 34, 55, note 23.
89. Jianjun Mei and Colin Shell, 'Copper and Bronze Metallurgy in Late Prehistoric Xinjiang', in Victor Mair, *The Bronze Age and Early Iron Age Peoples of Eastern Central Asia* (Pennsylvania, 1998), pp. 581ff, 593; Michael Puett, 'China in Early Eurasian History', in Victor Mair, *The Bronze Age and Early Iron Age Peoples of Eastern Central Asia* (Pennsylvania, 1998), pp. 703f.
90. Craig Benjamin, *The Yuezhi: Origin, Migration and the Conquest of Northern Bactria* (Turnhout, 2007), p. 34.
91. Elizabeth Barber, *The mummies of Ürümchi* (London, 1999), pp. 123, 126, 220; Kuzmina, 'Historical perspectives on the Andronovo and metal use', pp. 47; Iaroslav Lebedynsky, *Les Indo-Européens* (Errance, 2006), p. 91; Alexander Lubotsky, 'Tocharian Loan Words in Old Chinese', in Victor Mair, *The Bronze Age and Early Iron Age Peoples of Eastern Central Asia* (Pennsylvania, 1998), pp. 379–390.
92. Dolkun Kamberi, 'A Century of Tarim Archaeological Exploration (*ca.* 1886–1996)', in Victor Mair, *The Bronze Age and Early Iron Age Peoples of Eastern Central Asia* (Pennsylvania, 1998), p. 808; Puett, 'China in Early Eurasian History', pp. 703, 706.
93. Cosmo, *Ancient China and its enemies*, pp. 134–137; Ssu-ma Ch'ien, *Records of the grand historian of China. Translated from the Shih chi of Ssu-ma Ch'ien by Burton Watson*, Vol. II (New York, 1971), p. 159.
94. See Vol. II.
95. Sir Aurel Stein, *Innermost Asia*, Vol. I (Oxford, 1928), fig. 173, pp. 264, 734–737.
96. Songqiao Zhao and Xuncheng Xia, 'Evolution of the Lop Desert and the Lop Nor', *The Geographical Journal* cl/3 (1984), p. 311.
97. A few mummies are displayed in the new Xinjiang Regional Museum in Urumqi, and a few more are held in the museum of the Archaeological Institute, which is not open to the public. The great majority of the 500 mummies are decomposing because they are kept in poor conditions. Mallory estimates that thousands more mummies were destroyed by neglect or grave robbing (J.P. Mallory and Victor H. Mair, *The Tarim Mummies* (London, 2000), pp. 27, 179–181).
98. Kangxin Han, 'The Physical Anthropology of the Ancient Populations of the Tarim Basin and Surrounding Areas', in Victor Mair, *The Bronze Age and Early Iron Age Peoples of Eastern Central Asia* (Pennsylvania, 1998), pp. 558–568.
99. Han, 'The Physical Anthropology of the Ancient Populations', p. 568.
100. Rubin Han and Shuyn Sun, 'Preliminary Studies on the Bronzes Excavated from the Tianshanbeilou Cemetery, Hami, Xinjiang', in Katheryn Linduff (ed.), *Metallurgy in ancient Eastern Eurasia from the Urals to the Yellow River* (Ceredigion, 2004), pp. 158f.
101. Cosmo, Nicola di, *Ethnogenesis, coevolution and political morphology of the earliest steppe empire: the Xiongnu question revisited*, in Brosseder Ursula, Miller Bryan (eds), *Xiongnu Archaeology*, 2011, p. 41.
102. See Vol. II.
103. As the author knows from personal experience in the Tarim Basin, isolated chance finds of flints, stone weapons and stone tools can hardly be dated with any certainty. Kamberi mentions Palaeolithic discoveries from the oases of Khotan and Turfan; Mair expresses serious doubts which are shared by the author. Kamberi, 'A Century of Tarim Archaeological Exploration', pp. 797, 801; Victor Mair, 'The Archaeology of the Xinjiang Uyghur Autonomous Region', in Victor Mair (ed.), *Secrets of the Silk Road* (Santa Ana, CA, 2010), pp. 27ff.
104. Douglas Adams, 'Mummies', in Victor H. Mair (ed.), *The Mummified Remains Found in the Tarim Basin, Journal of Indo-European Studies* xxiii/3&4 (1995), pp. 410f; Anthony, *The Horse, the Wheel and Language*, pp. 56f, 264f; Crubézy et al., 'Indo-européens et anthropologie biologique', in Charlotte Félix (ed.), *Les Indo-Européens, Dossiers d'Archéologie*, no. 338 (2010), p. 67; Brian Hemphill and J.P. Mallory, 'Horse-mounted invaders from the Russo-Kazakh Steppe or agricultural colonists from Western Central Asia? A craniometric investigation of the Bronze Age settlements of

Xinjiang', *American Journal of Physical Anthropology* cxxiv/ 3 (2004), pp. 200–202; J.P. Mallory, *In Search of the Indo-Europeans: Language, Archaeology and Myth* (London, 1989), pp. 61, 226; Mallory and Mair, *The Tarim Mummies*, pp. 293f, 303, 317ff; Edwin Pulleyblank, 'Why Tocharians?', in Victor H. Mair (ed), *The Mummified Remains Found in the Tarim Basin, Journal of Indo-European Studies* xxiii/3&4 (1995), pp. 415f.

105. Barber, *The mummies of Ürümchi*, pp. 117ff.
106. The dating of the interesting necropolis of Yanbulake near Hami is controversial and ranges from 1700 to 500 BC, so the discoveries there cannot be interpreted. See: Victor Mair (ed.), *Secrets of the Silk Road*, p. 45.
107. Barber, *The mummies of Ürümchi*, pp. 71–80; Christoph Baumer, *Southern Silk Road* (Bangkok, 2003), pp. 26ff; Binghua Wang et al., *The ancient corpses of Xinjiang* (Xinjiang Renmin Chubanshe, 2001), pp. 17, 21f, 42–47.
108. Stein, *Innermost Asia*, Vol. II, fig. 173, p. 734.
109. Han, 'The Physical Anthropology of the Ancient Populations', 1998, pp. 558f.
110. Wang et al., *The ancient corpses of Xinjiang*, pp. 228, 234. See also: Barber, *The mummies of Ürümchi*, p. 81. On the basis of craniometric studies Hemphill and Mallory question this hypothesis and suggest a development of an indigenous population of 'unknown origin' (Hemphill and Mallory, 'Horse-mounted invaders from the Russo-Kazakh Steppe', pp. 214, 218).
111. Abdulressul Idriss et al., 'The Xiaohe Graveyard in Luobupo, Xinjiang', *Chinese Archaeology* viii (2008), p. 95.
112. That these statues were not buried wooden mock-corpses is shown by a photograph from 1905, when E. Huntington documented an 80-cm-tall female wooden statue, standing at the head of a grave, about 50 km north of Xiaohe (Ellsworth Huntington, *The Pulse of Asia* (Boston, 1907), pp. 262f).
113. Christoph Baumer, 'Indo-europäische Mumien im Herzen der Wüste Taklamakan. Die Ayala Mazar-Xiaohe Kultur', in *Antike Welt* (Mainz, 2010). *The Ayala Mazar – Xiaohe Culture. Results from an archaeological exploration of the ancient Keriya Delta, China, in 2009*, Self-published (June 2010) and in *Kristi*, New Delhi, Vol. 3 (2011), pp. 1–23; 'The Ayala Mazar-Xiaohe Culture: New archaeological discoveries in the Taklamakan Desert, China', in *Journal of the Royal Society for Asian Affairs* (London, Vol. XLII, No. 1, March 2011), pp. 49–70.
114. Surprisingly, such a wooden mask is also included in the Otani-Collection assembled before 1914. See: *Central Asian objects brought back by the Otani mission* (Toyko 1971) fig. 84, no provenance given. The piece was most probably sold by the Uighur guide and treasure-hunter Ördek to the Japanese member of the Otani mission Tachibana Zuicho when he guided him in winter 1910/11 in the Lop Nor Desert. More than two decades later Ördek volunteered to lead Folke Bergman to Xiaohe which he called a 'hill covered with a thousand coffins' and admitted that he had visited (and looted) the site many years earlier. This initial visit by Ördek must have taken place before November 1910 (Bergman Folke, *Archaeological researches in Sinkiang* (Stockholm 1939), pp. 51f).
115. On Xiaohe see: Christoph Baumer, 'Die 'Tausend-Särge-Nekropole' von Xiaohe', in *Antike Welt* (Mainz, 2006), pp. 39–49; Idriss, 'The Xiaohe Graveyard in Luobupo, Xinjiang', pp. 85–95; Victor Mair, 'The Rediscovery and Complete Excavation of Ördek's Excavation', *Journal of Indo-European Studies* xxxiv/3&4 (2006), pp. 273–318; Mair, *Secrets of the Silk Road*, pp. 46ff, 160–180.
116. Li Chunxiang et al., 'Evidence that a West-East admixed population lived in the Tarim Basin as early as the early Bronze Age', *BMC Biology* viii (2010), pp. 1–12. Mitochondria are inherited only maternally and y-chromosomes only paternally. A study published in 2004 of 20 mummies, approximately 3,800 years old, from the northern Lop Nor and 11 mummies, about 2,500 years old, from Turfan showed that the mummies from the Bronze Age had significantly more Europid mtDNA lines of descent than the later mummies from the Iron Age (Christopher Thornton and Theodore Schurr, 'Genes, language and culture: an example from the Tarim Basin', *Oxford Journal of Archaeology* xxiii (2004), pp. 93ff).
117. The Uyghur word 'darya' means 'river'. On Jumbulakum see: Corinne Debaine-Francfort, *Keriya. Mémoires d'un fleuve* (Paris, 2001), pp. 120–225.
118. More recently, Victor Mair's March 2010 exhibition catalogue *Secrets of the Silk Road* mentioned on pp. 49–52 a 'northern cemetery' lying 70 km north of Jumbulakum, but no pictures were published. The description suggests that it is Ayala Mazar, which a Uyghur archaeologist had ostensibly already visited briefly in 2008. The first publications of the author occurred in Swiss newspapers on 22 January 2010 (*Thurgauer Zeitung*) and on 14 February 2010 (*Zentralschweiz am Sonntag*). See also note 119.
119. Possnert Göran, Sundström. Result of ^{14}C dating of human hair from Xinjiang, China (Uppsala 11 March 2011).
120. These tiny wooden masks look very different from those found in burials of the Okunev Culture.
121. Two additional residential complexes from the Bronze Age, 'H 16' and 'H 17', are 32 and 37 km from the necropolis respectively.
122. Jianjun Mei and Colin Shell, 'The existence of Andronovo cultural influence in Xinjiang during the 2nd millennium BC', *Antiquity* lxxiii (1999), pp. 575ff; Jianjun Mei and Colin Shell, 'Metallurgy in Bronze Age Xinjiang and its cultural context', in Katheryn Linduff (ed.), *Metallurgy in ancient Eastern Eurasia from the Urals to the Yellow River* (Ceredigion, 2004), p. 183.
123. Mei, *Copper and Bronze Metallurgy*, pp. 14, 25, 28ff, 36, 72, 89, 119, 123, 142.
124. Presumably there were other, still unknown sites of this culture between the Keriya Darya and Lop Nor in the inland deltas of the former Niya, Andier or Karamiran rivers.
125. The fact that the craniometric studies of Hemphill and Mallory, which compared material from the Tarim Basin, the steppe, south-eastern Central Asia, and the Near East, showed no great affinity between skulls from the Lop Nor and from Bactria–Margiana is not an argument against the 'Bactria hypothesis', as their sample contained no material from the Keriya delta and a transfer of technology does not imply a mass migration. See: Hemphill and Mallory, 'Horse-mounted invaders from the Russo-Kazakh Steppe', pp. 214f.
126. Mei, *Copper and Bronze Metallurgy*, 2000, pp. 11f; Mair, *Secrets of the Silk Road*, p. 44; Wang et al., *The ancient corpses of Xinjiang*, pp. 63–68.
127. See photo p. 83.
128. Emmanuel Anati, 'Le grand sanctuaire rupestre d'Hutubi', *Archéologia*, no. 356 (1999), pp. 57f; Qi Xiaoshan and Bo Wang, *The ancient culture in Xinjiang along the Silk Road* (Urumqi, 2008), pp. 214f.
129. Jean-Paul Demoule, 'Deux siècles à la recherche des Indo-Européens', in *Les Indo-Européens. Dossiers d'Archéologie,* No. 338 (2010), pp. 7f.
130. Lebedynsky, *Les Indo-Européens*, p. 12.
131. Marsha Levine et al., *Late prehistoric exploitation of the Eurasian steppe* (Cambridge, 1999), p. 2.
132. Anthony, *The Horse, the Wheel and Language*, pp. 12–101; Lebedynsky, *Les Indo-Européens*, pp. 80ff, 100; Mallory and Adams, *Encyclopedia of Indo-European Culture*, pp. 290–311.
133. Beckwith, *Empires of the Silk Road*, p. 368.
134. Frantz Grenet, 'An Archaeologist's Approach to Avestan Geography', in Vesta S. Curtis and Sarah Stewart (eds), *The Idea of Iran*, Vol. 1, (London, 2005), pp. 35f.
135. John Curtis, *Ancient Persia* (London, 2000), pp. 20–25; Henri-Paul Francfort, 'La « culture de Marlik » et l'arrivée des Indo-Iraniens', in Laurence Mattet (ed.), *Le Profane et le Divin: Arts de l'Antiquité de l'Europe au Sud-Est Asiatique* (2008), pp. 143, 145; Igor Khlopin, 'L'Hyrcanie Antique', *Découverte des civilisations d'Asie Centrale. Les dossiers d'archéologie*, no. 185 (1993), p. 47; Iaroslav Lebedynsky, *Les Cimmériens* (Errance, 2004), pp. 153f. The idea that the ancestors of the Medes and Persians came from the Srubnaya Culture and advanced into Iran via the Caucasus is obsolete.
136. Frye, *The heritage of Central Asia*, pp. 68f; Mallory, *In Search of the Indo-Europeans*, pp. 52f, 229f.
137. Only in the Rig Veda can the term *asura* also refer to the 'good' or 'highest spirit'.
138. Lebedynsky, *Les Indo-Européens*, p. 167.
139. Colin Renfrew, *Archaeology & Language: The puzzle of Indo-European origins* (London, 1987); Colin Renfrew, 'Die Indoeuropäer aus archäologischer Sicht', in Reinhard Breuer (ed.), *Die Evolution der Sprachen* (Heidelberg, 2007); Colin Renfrew, 'Le problème Indo-européen et l'hypothèse anatolienne', *Dossiers d'Archéologie,* No. 338 (2010).
140. Mallory, *In Search of the Indo-Europeans*, in J.P. Mallory (ed.), *The Oxford introduction to Proto-Indo-European and the Proto-Indo-European World* (Oxford, 2006); J.P. Mallory, 'L'hypothèse des steppes', *Dossiers d'Archéologie,* No. 338 (2010); Mallory and Adams, *Encyclopedia of Indo-European Culture.*
141. Kuzmina, *The Origin of Indo-Iranians.*
142. Anthony, *The Horse, the Wheel and Language*, pp. 75–81; Lebedynsky, *Les Indo-Européens*, pp. 109f; Mallory and Adams, *Encyclopedia of Indo-European Culture*, pp. 298f; Mallory, *L'hypothèse des steppes*, p. 34. The suggestion for a merger of the two theories, according to which as a first step the Neolithic farmers of Anatolia spread PIE to Eastern Europe, where it was, in a second step, adopted by steppe peoples in the sphere of

the Tripolye Culture and thus spread further, is unable to answer all the unresolved questions. Kohl, *The making of Bronze Age Eurasia*, p. 236; Bernhard Victorri, 'Die Debatte um die Ursprache', in Reinhard Breuer (ed.), *Die Evolution der Sprachen* (Heidelberg, 2007) p. 18.

143. Anthony, *The Horse, the Wheel and Language*, pp. 99f, 317, 343, 369, 464.
144. Michail Grjaznov, *Südsibirien* (Geneva, 1970), pp. 64ff; Parzinger, *Die frühen Völker Eurasiens*, pp. 302–308; Denis Sinor, *The Cambridge history of Early Inner Asia* (Cambridge, 1990), p. 81.
145. Anatolj Nagler, 'Waren die Träger der Okunev-Kultur Nomaden?', *Eurasia Antiqua* v (1999), pp. 22, 25.
146. Grjaznov, *Südsibirien*, pp. 67f, fig. 7.
147. I.V. Kovtun, 'The bear image in Western Siberian art of the 2nd Millennium BC and its relevance for delimiting the eastern periphery of the Samus Culture', *Archaeology, Ethnology & Anthropology of Eurasia* xxxv/3 (2008), p. 100).
148. As shown by a three-line Old Turkish runic inscription, Okunev steles were still being reused in the mid-first millennium AD (Nikolaj Leon'ev and Vladimir Kapel'ko, *Steinstelen der Okunev-Kultur* (Mainz, 2002), p. 87, fig. 223.
149. On the Okunev steles see: Burchard Brentjes, 'Frühe Steinstelen Sibiriens und der Mongolei', *Central Asiatic Journal*, xl (1996), pp. 34–42; Leon'ev and Kapel'ko, *Steinstelen der Okunev-Kultur*, with 300 sketches.
150. Vladimir Kubarev, *Drevnie rospisi Karakola* (Old paintings of Karakol) (Novosibirsk, 1988).
151. Leon'ev and Kapel'ko, *Steinstelen der Okunev-Kultur*, p. 48.
152. See pp. 157ff, 175ff.
153. Parzinger et al. 'Das mehrperiodige Gräberfeld von Suchanicha bei Minusinsk', *Eurasia Antiqua* xv (2009), pp. 187–203
154. Parzinger, *Die frühen Völker Eurasiens*, p. 354.
155. Ludmila Koryakova and Andrej Epimakkhov, *The Urals and Western Siberia in the Bronze and Iron Ages* (Cambridge, 2007), p. 64.
156. Parzinger, *Die frühen Völker Eurasiens*, p. 350.
157. Ibid, pp. 350f.
158. Leskovar Jutta, Zingerle Maria-Christina (eds), *Goldener Horizont* (2010), pp. 32; Mallory and Adams, *Encyclopedia of Indo-European Culture*, p. 92.
159. Mallory and Adams, *Encyclopedia of Indo-European Culture*, pp. 439f.
160. Anthony, *The Horse, the Wheel and Language*, pp. 437f; Parzinger, *Die frühen Völker Eurasiens*, p. 440.
161. Koryakova and Epimakkhov, *The Urals and Western Siberia*, pp. 111, 116, 122f; Parzinger, *Die frühen Völker Eurasiens*, pp. 439ff.
162. On account of its non-Indo-Iranian sponsorship affiliation, we do not consider the Okunev Culture part of the Andronovo cultural complex. The phenomenon of Seima Turbino, sometimes referred to as a forest steppe culture, was not a culture but rather an industry of high-quality objects made of tin bronze found in several cultures of northern Central Asia.
163. Kuzmina, *The Origin of Indo-Iranians*, pp. 237ff; E. Kuzmina, *The Prehistory of the Silk Road* (Philadelphia, 2008), pp. 76f; Parzinger, *Die frühen Völker Eurasiens*, pp. 417ff.
164. V.T. Kovalyova and O.V. Ryzhkova, 'Circular Settlements in the Lower Tobol Area (Tashkovo Culture)', in Karlene Jones-Bley and D.G. Zdanovich, *Complex Societies of Central Eurasia from the 3rd to the 1st Millennium BC* Vol. I (Washington DC, 2002), p. 291.
165. Parzinger, *Die frühen Völker Eurasiens*, pp. 251ff.
166. Lumley Henri de. *Arkaïm*, 2010, pp. 12–17. A mildly similar architectural concept is found in Anatolia at Mersin, Demircihöyük and Pulor. Since these three settlements date from the last quarter of the fifth millennium to the mid-third millennium BC, they are considerably older than Sintashta or Akraim, which rules out an (already improbable) influence (S.A. Grigoryev, *Ancient Indo-Europeans* (Chelyabinsk, 2002), pp. 31–34).
167. On the settlements of Sintashta: Grigoryev, *Ancient Indo-Europeans*, pp. 20–105; Koryakova and Epimakkhov, *The Urals and Western Siberia*, pp. 37f, 68–75, 89; Parzinger, *Die frühen Völker Eurasiens*, pp. 251ff.
168. Henri de Lumley, *Arkaïm: Une cité de l'âge du Bronze dans les steppes de l'Oural* (Tende, 2010), p. 18.
169. http://terra-x.zdf.de/ZDFde/inhalt/25/0,1872,8011225,00.html
170. Anthony, *The Horse, the Wheel and Language*, pp. 391, 435.
171. Jettmar's interpretation of Sintashta as a 'ceremonial village' with uninhabited houses, which he calls 'cabins', is untenable. Karl Jettmar, 'Sintashta – ein gemeinsames Heiligtum der Indo-Iraner', *Eurasia Antiqua* ii (1996), p. 221. Jettmar's later interpretation of Akraim as a 'ceremonial town', where clans annually performed ritual battles, is equally unfounded ('Bemerkungen zu Arkaim', *Eurasia Antiqua* iii (1998), pp. 251f).
172. Anthony, *The Horse, the Wheel and Language*, pp. 393–306; Lumley Henri de. *Arkaïm*, 2010, pp. 22f.
173. Grigoryev S.A. *Ancient Indo-Europeans*, 2002, pp. 43, 58; Lumley, *Arkaïm*, pp. 24, 30.
174. D.G. Zdanovich and L.L. Gayduchenko, 'Sintashta Burial Sacrifice: The Bolschekaragansky Cemetery in Focus', in Karlene Jones-Bley and D.G. Zdanovich, *Complex Societies of Central Eurasia*, p. 206.
175. Zdanovich and Gayduchenko, 'Sintashta Burial Sacrifice', p. 202.
176. Lumley Henri de. *Arkaïm*, 2010, pp. 28–31; Koryakova and Epimakkhov, *The Urals and Western Siberia*, pp. 75–96.
177. *Rig Veda*, Book 6, 6.75.6f.
178. *Rig Veda*, Book 9, 9.53.2.
179. *Rig Veda*, Book 5, 5.66.3.
180. *Rig Veda*, Book 2, 1st group, 2.2.3.
181. *Rig Veda*, Book 2, 2nd group, 2.17.4. Book 10, 10.138.3.
182. *Rig Veda*, Book 10, 10.91.14. On horse sacrifices: Book 1, 14th group, 1.162.
183. *Rig Veda*, Book 10, 10.14.10f. English from http://www.sacred-texts.com/hin/rigveda/rv10014.htm.
184. *Rig Veda*, Book 10, 10.16.1.
185. *Rig Veda*, Book 10, 10.18.11ff. English from http://www.sacred-texts.com/hin/rigveda/rv10018.htm
186. Baimatowa Nasiba, *5000 Jahre Architektur in Mittelasien: Lehmziegelgewölbe vom 4./3. Jt. v.Chr. bis zum Ende des 8. Jhs. n.Chr.* (Mainz, 2008), pp. 178–189. T.S. Malyutina, '"Proto-towns" of the Bronze Age in the South Urals and Ancient Khorasmia', in Karlene Jones-Bley and D.G. Zdanovich, *Complex Societies of Central Eurasia*, pp. 161, 166; A. Medvedev, 'Avestan "Yima's Town" in Historical and Archaeological Perspective', in Karlene Jones-Bley and D.G. Zdanovich, *Complex Societies of Central Eurasia*, p. 57.
187. Anthony, *The Horse, the Wheel and Language*, p. 408.
188. *Avesta*, Vendidad, Fargard 2. *Avesta: Die heiligen Schriften der Parsen*, Vol. I, trans. by Friedrich Spiegel (Leipzig, 1859; reprint by Elibron Classics, 2006), pp. 70–77.
189. N.A. Bokovenko, 'Das karasukzeitliche Gräberfeld Ančil Čon in Chakassien', *Eurasia Antiqua* vi (2000), pp. 244ff; Parzinger, *Die frühen Völker Eurasiens*, p. 468. *Der skythenzeitliche Fürstenkurgan Aržhan 2 in Tuva*, p. 7. See also here photo p. 178.
190. Kohl. *The making of Bronze Age Eurasia*, p. 149.
191. Kovalyova and Ryzhkova, 'Circular Settlements in the Lower Tobol Area', pp. 283f, 287.
192. Parzinger, *Die frühen Völker Eurasiens*, p. 318.
193. Koryakova and Epimakkhov, *The Urals and Western Siberia*, p. 82.
194. Ibid, p. 37.
195. Evengy Chernykh reports that Seima Turbino cemeteries consisted largely of cenotaphs. Evengy Chernykh, 'Ancient metallurgy in northeast Asia: From the Urals to the Saiano-Altai', in Katheryn Linduff (ed.), *Metallurgy in ancient Eastern Eurasia from the Urals to the Yellow River* (Ceredigion, 2004), p. 26; Evengy Chernykh, 'The "Steppe Belt" of stockbreeding cultures in Eurasia during the Early Metal Age', *Trabajos de Prehistoria* lxv/2 (2008), pp. 85f.
196. Koryakova and Epimakkhov, *The Urals and Western Siberia*, p. 39.
197. Ibid, pp. 106ff.
198. Parzinger posits the origin of this specific type of knob in the bronze needles with heads featuring figurative decoration from Bactria in the Namazga V/VI stages (Hermann Parzinger, 'Sejma-Turbino und die Anfänge des sibirischen Tierstils,' *Eurasia Antiqua* iii (1997), pp. 239–241).
199. See photo p. 152.
200. Chernykh, 'Ancient metallurgy in northeast Asia,' pp. 26, 28; Koryakova and Epimakkhov, *The Urals and Western Siberia*, pp. 108f.
201. Chernykh, 'The 'Steppe Belt' of stockbreeding cultures', p. 88; Michael Frachetti, *Pastoralist landscapes and social interaction in Bronze Age Eurasia* (Berkeley, 2008), p. 42; Mallory and Adams, *Encyclopedia of Indo-European Culture*, p. 20; Parzinger, *Die frühen Völker Eurasiens*, pp. 257, 259, 426.
202. A recent study is Kiryushin Yu.F. and Solodovnikov K.N., *The origins of the Andronovo (Fedorovka) population of Southwestern Siberia, based on a Middle Bronze Age cranial series from the Altai forest-steppe zone*, 2011, pp. 136–140.
203. Grjaznov, *Südsibirien*, pp. 93f; S.G. Kljastornyj and T.I. Sultanov, *Staaten und Völker in den Steppen Eurasiens: Altertum und Mittelalter* (Berlin, 2006), pp. 23ff; Kuzmina, *The Origin of Indo-Iranians*, pp. 163–198.
204. Eleonora Novgorodva, *Alte Kunst der Mongolei* (Leipzig, 1980), pp. 84f, 98f.
205. *Rig Veda*, Book 10, 10.18.4. English from http://www.sacred-texts.com/hin/rigveda/rv10018.htm.

206. Frachetti, *Pastoralist landscapes and social interaction*, p. 32f; Grjaznov, *Südsibirien*, p. 96; Koryakova and Epimakkhov, *The Urals and Western Siberia*, pp. 127, 218.
207. Malyutina, '"Proto-towns" of the Bronze Age', p. 165.
208. Olga Korochkova and Vladimir Stafano, 'The Trans-Ural Fedorovo Complexes in relation to the Andronovo', in Katheryn Linduff (ed.), *Metallurgy in ancient Eastern Eurasia from the Urals to the Yellow River* (Ceredigion, 2004), pp. 94ff; Zainolla Samashev, *Treasures from the Ustyurt and Mangystau* (Almaty, 2007), pp. 123–126.
209. Grjaznov, *Südsibirien*, p. 101.
210. Koryakova and Epimakkhov, *The Urals and Western Siberia*, pp. 134f.
211. Parzinger, *Die frühen Völker Eurasiens*, pp. 443–463, supplement II.
212. Parzinger, *Die frühen Völker Eurasiens*, pp. 456–462.
213. Whether the ostensible culture of Kamennyi Log represents a late phase of Karasuk lasting into the eighth century BC, as postulated by Grjaznov and Askarov, or whether it developed essentially parallel to Karasuk, as Parzinger argues, remains an open question. Akhmadali Askarov, 'Pastoral and nomadic tribes at the beginning of the first millennium BC,' in *History of Civilizations of Central Asia*, Vol. I (Paris, 1992), p. 459. Grjaznov, *Südsibirien*, 1970, p. 132. Parzinger, *Die frühen Völker Eurasiens*, p. 464. Parzinger, 'Das mehrperiodige Gräberfeld,' pp. 198f.
214. Grjaznov, *Südsibirien*, p. 135 [English is from Mikhail P. Gryaznov, *The Ancient Civilization of Southern Siberia*, trans. from the Russian by James Hogarth (New York: Cowles Book Company, Inc., 1969), p. 104.]
215. Emma Bunker, *Ancient Bronzes of the Eastern Eurasian Steppes from the Arthur M. Sackler Collections* (New York, 1997), pp. 184, 294.
216. Askarov, 'Pastoral and nomadic tribes', pp. 460f; Sophie Legrand, 'Karasuk Metallurgy: Technological development and regional influence', in K.K. Linduff, *Metallurgy in Ancient Eastern Eurasia from the Urals to the Yellow River* (Lampeter, 2004), pp. 146f.
217. Grjaznov, *Südsibirien*, p. 130; A.P. Okladnikow, 'Inner Asia at the dawn of history', in Denis Sinor (ed.), *The Cambridge history of Early Inner Asia* (Cambridge, 1990), p. 84.
218. Bokovenko, 'Das karasukzeitliche Gräberfeld Ančil Čon', p. 244.
219. Ibid, p. 246.
220. Igor Lazaretov, 'Spätbronzezeitliche Denkmäler in Südchakassien', *Eurasia Antiqua* vi (2000), p. 277f.
221. Novgorodva, *Alte Kunst der Mongolei*, pp. 100ff, fig. 61–69; Parzinger, *Die frühen Völker Eurasiens*, pp. 474–477, 631–635.
222. D. Erdenebaatar, 'Burial materials related to the history of the Bronze Age in the territory of Mongolia', in Katheryn Linduff (ed.), *Metallurgy in ancient Eastern Eurasia from the Urals to the Yellow River* (Ceredigion, 2004), pp. 194f.
223. Parzinger, *Die frühen Völker Eurasiens*, p. 635.
224. See p. 178.
225. Erdenebaatar, 'Burial materials', pp. 190f; N. Mamonova, 'Die Paläoanthropologie des Gräberfelds Ulangom', in Eleonora Novgorodva et al., *Ulangom: Ein skythenzeitliches Gräberfeld in der Mongolei* (Wiesbaden, 1982), pp. 140, 151; Eleonora Novgorodva et al., *Ulangom: Ein skythenzeitliches Gräberfeld in der Mongolei* (Wiesbaden, 1982), pp. 31ff.
226. Mamonova, 'Die Paläoanthropologie des Gräberfelds', p. 148; Novgorodva et al., *Ulangom*, p. 34.
227. Jérôme Magail, 'Tsatsiin Ereg, site majeur du début du Ier millénaire en Mongolie', in Archéo-steppe.com., Mission archéologique Monaco Mongolie (2009). http://archeo-steppe.com/content/view/73/195/lang,french/. Other estimates assume 2,000 deer stones. William Fitzhugh, 'The Mongolian deer stone-khirigsuur complex: dating and organisation of a late Bronze Age menagerie', in Jan Bemmann et al., *Current archaeological research in Mongolia* (Bonn, 2009), p. 183.
228. Aruz, *Art of the first cities*, pp. 37, 217; Joan Aruz (ed.), *The Golden Deer of Eurasia: Perspectives on the Steppe Nomads of the Ancient World* (New York, 2006), p. 170.
229. See p. 254.
230. See Vol. II.
231. See Vol. III.
232. Wilhelm Radloff, *Aus Sibirien*, Vol. II (Leipzig, 1893), p. 92.
233. Novgorodva, *Alte Kunst der Mongolei*, pp. 146f, fig. 104–108.
234. Nagler Anatoli. *O stilisovannych isobrajenniach olenei na olennix kamniach Zentralnoy Asii*, 2012.
235. Novgorodva, *Alte Kunst der Mongolei*, pp. 131–169; Eleonora Novgorodva, 'Archäologische Funde, Bestattungsplätze und Skulpturen', in Walter Heissig and Claudius Müller (eds), *Die Mongolen* (Innsbruck/Frankfurt, 1989), p. 16. See also: William Fitzhugh, 'Stone Shamans and Flying Deer of Northern Mongolia: Deer Goddess of Siberia or Chimera of the Steppe?', *Arctic Anthropology* xlvi/1–2 (2009), p. 78.
236. Menghin et al., *Im Zeichen des goldenen Greifen*, p. 123, fig. 6; Véronique Schiltz, *Die Skythen und andere Steppenvölker* (Munich, 1994), p. 268.
237. Goryachev A.A., Mariyashev A.N. *Petroglyphs of Semirechye*, 1999.
238. One stele can be found in the museum of the nearby village of Mörön. When fallen deer stones were put back up, most were incorrectly oriented to the south instead of the east.
239. The numbering follows Novgorodva, who was one of the first to explore the area. *Alte Kunst der Mongolei*, pp. 133–149. In her reconstruction she presents three rows of steles, although there were presumably just two (Shu Takahama et al. (eds), 'Preliminary Report of the Archaeological Investigations in Ulaan Uushig I (Uushigiin Övör) in Mongolia', *Bulletin of archaeology*, University of Kanazawa, no. 28 (2006), p. 84).
240. Takahama et al., 'Preliminary Report', pp. 76, 79.
241. Novgorodva, *Alte Kunst der Mongolei*, pp. 115f.
242. Henri-Paul Francfort, 'Les pétroglyphes de Tamgaly', *Bulletin of the Asia Institute* ix (1995), pp. 185–197.
243. Aruz, *The Golden Deer of Eurasia*, p. 50.
244. Claudia Chang (ed.), *Of Gold and Grass: Nomads of Kazakhstan* (Bethesda, 2006), p. 55; Menghin et al., *Im Zeichen des goldenen Greifen*, p. 164, fig. 3; Marie-Catherine Rey (ed.), *Kazakhstan, hommes, bêtes et dieux de la steppe* (Versailles, 2010), pp. 80, 82.
245. Čugunov, Parzinger and Nagler, *Der skythenzeitliche Fürstenkurgan Aržhan 2 in Tuva*, plate 45, 4.
246. Aruz, *The Golden Deer of Eurasia*, p. 193.
247. Alexander Leskov, *The Maikop Treasure* (Philadelphia, 2008), p. 53; Menghin et al., *Im Zeichen des goldenen Greifen*, p. 210, fig. 6.
248. Chang, *Of Gold and Grass*, pp. 66f, 126; Menghin et al., *Im Zeichen des goldenen Greifen*, p. 129, fig. 14; Sergei Rudenko, *Frozen tombs of Siberia: The Pazyrik Burials of Iron Age Horsemen* (London, 1970), plates 119–124; Zainolla Samashev et al., 'Le kourgane de Berel dans l'Altaï kazakhstanais', *Asiatiques* 1 (2000), pp. 13, 18; Schiltz, *Die Skythen und andere Steppenvölker*, p. 275, fig. 206.
249. Chang, *Of Gold and Grass*, p. 120; Menghin et al., *Im Zeichen des goldenen Greifen*, p. 153; I. Molodin et al., 'Das skythenzeitliche Kriegergrab aus Olon-Kurin-Gol. Neue Entdeckungen in der Permafrostzone des mongolischen Altaj', *Eurasia Antiqua* xiv (2008), p. 258.
250. Menghin et al., *Im Zeichen des goldenen Greifen*, p. 134.
251. V. Schiltz hypothesises a connection between this burial and an Indo-Iranian functionary in service to the Mitanni state (Schiltz, *Die Skythen und andere Steppenvölker*, p. 269.)

VII. The Iron Age

1. Johann Georg Kohl, *Reisen in Südrussland* (1841, reprint in 3 vols. from the 3rd edition 1847, Elibron Classics, 2008), p. 189.
2. Hermann Parzinger, *Die Skythen* (Munich, 2004), p. 13.
3. Ludmila Koryakova and Andrej Epimakkhov, *The Urals and Western Siberia in the Bronze and Iron Ages* (Cambridge, 2007), pp. 44, 190–193.
4. V.G. Dirksen, 'Mid to late Holocene climate change and its influence on cultural development in South Central Siberia', in *Impact of the Environment on Human Migration in Eurasia* (2004), pp. 304f; B. van Geel, 'The sun, climate change and the expansion of the Scythian culture after 850 BC', in *Impact of the Environment on Human Migration in Eurasia* (2004), pp. 151–153.
5. G.I. Zaitseva, 'The occupation history of the southern Eurasia steppe during the Holocene', in *Impact of the Environment on Human Migration in Eurasia* (2004), pp. 76, 78.
6. Herodotus, *Histories* IV, 127.
7. Ibid, 98, 136–142.
8. Michail Grjaznov, *Südsibirien* (Geneva, 1970), p. 156. The English is from *South Siberia*, translated from the Russian by James Hogarth (Barrie & Rockliff: The Cresset Press, London, 1969), p. 132.
9. Véronique Schiltz, *Histoire de kourganes: La redécouverte de l'or des Scythes* (Paris, 1991), pp. 42f.
10. Hermann Parzinger, *Die frühen Völker Eurasiens: Vom Neolithikum bis zum Mittelalter* (Munich, 2006), pp. 623, 751, 760; Parzinger et al., 'Das mehrperiodige Gräberfeld von Suchanicha bei Minusinsk', *Eurasia Antiqua* xv (2009), pp. 200–203.
11. Grjaznov, *Südsibirien*, pp. 235–241. Grjaznov's division is still valid today, but it has been shifted about two centuries earlier by Parzinger. See here note 10.

12. Burchard Brentjes and R. Vasilievsky, *Schamanenkrone und Weltenbaum: Kunst der Nomaden Nordasiens* (Leipzig, 1989), p. 92; Parzinger, *Die frühen Völker Eurasiens*, p. 625.
13. Grjaznov, *Südsibirien*, pp. 236, 240; Parzinger, *Die frühen Völker Eurasiens*, p. 627. S.V. Kiselev has never published the full results of his excavation of the great Salbyk Kurgan and in 2000 a German-Russian project to restart the excavations was cancelled for unclear reasons. Earlier sonic measurements indicated a still-unexplored grave chamber.
14. Hermann Parzinger and Anatoli Nagler, ‚Der tagarzeitliche Großkurgan von Barsučij Log in Chakassien', *Eurasia Antiqua*, Vol. 16/2010, Deutsches Archäologisches Institut, Berlin; Philipp von Zabern, Mainz 2010, pp. 222–229, 236–246, 262–276.
15. Wilfried Menghin, Hermann Parzinger, Anatoli Nagler and Manfred Nawroth (eds), *Im Zeichen des goldenen Greifen: Königsgräber der Skythen* (Munich, 2007), pp. 107f, 172–176.
16. Parzinger and Nagler, ‚Der tagarzeitliche Großkurgan von Barsučij Log in Chakassien', pp. 215, 250, 262.
17. Brentjes and Vasilievsky, *Schamanenkrone und Weltenbaum*, pp. 94f; Grjaznov, *Südsibirien*, photo 54; Parzinger, *Die frühen Völker Eurasiens*, p. 752.
18. Alfred Wieczorek and Christoph Lind, *Ursprünge der Seidenstraße* (Stuttgart, 2007), p. 260.
19. Andreï Alexeev, *Trésors des Steppes* (Hauterive, 2006), p. 93; Iaroslav Lebedynsky, *Les Saces* (Errance, 2006), p. 122; Eileen Murphy, 'Mummification and Body Processing: Evidence from the Iron Age in Southern Siberia', in *Kurgans, Ritual Sites and Settlements* (2000), p. 282.
20. Parzinger, *Die frühen Völker Eurasiens*, pp. 755–759.
21. Renate Rolle, *Gold der Steppe: Archäologie der Ukraine* (Schleswig, 1991), p. 46.
22. Herodotus, *Histories* IV, 11.
23. As in the case of Marco Polo, a few scholars doubt that Herodotus really undertook the travels he refers to and consider him a mere armchair scholar. Others reject comparisons between archaeological discoveries and his accounts for obscure methodological reasons.
24. Herodotus, *Histories* IV; 76. Renate Rolle, *Die Welt der Skythen* (Lucerne, 1980), pp. 14, 139
25. On the location of Gerrhos see pp. 231f.
26. Herodotus, *Histories* IV, 6.
27. The usual transliteration of Σκολάξάϊς as Kolaxaïs appears to be a mistake (Christopher Beckwith, *Empires of the Silk Road* (Princeton, 2009), pp. 377f).
28. The fact that only Scolaxaïs was able to hold the glowing gold may indicate that he was a blacksmith. A millennium later, the forefathers of the first Gök Türk rulers were also believed to have been blacksmiths.
29. Herodotus, *Histories* IV, 5–7.
30. Ibid, 78–80.
31. Ibid, 120.
32. Ibid, 66.
33. Ssu-ma Ch'ien. *Records of the grand historian of China* (1971), Vol. II, p. 163.
34. Herodotus, *Histories* IV, 8–10.
35. Julian Baldick, *Homer and the Indo-Europeans* (London, 1994), pp. 137–141.
36. Menghin et al., *Im Zeichen des goldenen Greifen*, p. 281.
37. Herodotus, *Histories* IV, 11–12. On the Cimmerians see p. 224.
38. Herodotus, *Histories* IV, 13–32. Herodotus was sceptical about some of Aristeas's information.
39. Herodotus, *Histories* IV, 24.
40. Parzinger, *Die Skythen*, pp. 25f.
41. According to Herodotus, the Persians called all the Scythians they dealt with Saka (*Histories* VII, 64).
42. Herodotus, *Histories* IV, 27.
43. Lebedynsky, *Les Saces*, p. 34; Menghin et al., *Im Zeichen des goldenen Greifen*, p. 301.
44. See p. 111. Esther Jacobson, *The Art of the Scythians* (Leiden, 1995), pp. 156, 185.
45. A.I. Melyukova, 'The Scythians and Sarmatians', in *The Cambridge history of Early Inner Asia* (Cambridge, 1990), p. 90.
46. Michail Grjaznov, *Der Großkurgan von Arzhan in Tuva, Südsibirien* (Munich, 1984), p. 9; Konstantin Čugunov, Hermann Parzinger and Anatoli Nagler, 'Der skythische Fürstengrabhügel von Arzhan 2 in Tuva, Vorbericht der russisch-deutschen Ausgrabungen', *Eurasia Antiqua* ix (2003), p. 114.
47. Grjaznov, *Der Großkurgan von Arzhan*, pp. 57f.
48. Rolle, *Die Welt der Skythen*, p. 44.
49. Véronique Schiltz, *Die Skythen und andere Steppenvölker* (Munich, 1994), p. 251.
50. Grjaznov, *Der Großkurgan von Arzhan*, pp. 11–69.
51. A. Abetekov et al., 'Ancient Iranian nomads in western Central Asia', in *History of civilizations of Central Asia*, Vol. II, p. 28.
52. Grjaznov, *Der Großkurgan von Arzhan*, pp. 25–57; Parzinger, *Die frühen Völker Eurasiens*, p. 609; Rolle, *Die Welt der Skythen*, p. 41. Schiltz, *Die Skythen und andere Steppenvölker*, pp. 252–255.
53. Schiltz, *Die Skythen und andere Steppenvölker*, pp. 253.
54. Boris Piotrovsky, *L'art scythe* (Leningrad, 1986), pl. 13–15; Schiltz, *Die Skythen und andere Steppenvölker*, pp. 78–80.
55. Schiltz, *Die Skythen und andere Steppenvölker*, p. 81.
56. Konstantin Čugunov, *Der skythenzeitliche Fürstenkurgan Aržhan 2 in Tuva*. (Mainz, 2010), p. 174; Parzinger, *Die frühen Völker Eurasiens*, p.609.
57. L.K. Galanina, *Die Kurgane von Kelermes* (Berlin, 1996), Vol. I, p. 187.
58. Hermann Parzinger, *Die Skythen der ukrainischen Steppe und ihre Stellung in der Welt der eurasischen Reiternomaden* (2010), p. 58.
59. Contrary hypotheses, according to which the Scythian nomadic horsemen emerged in the northern Pontic region (Heine-Geldern) or the region of the Volga (Jettmar) and spread from there to southern Siberia, are thus refuted (Nicola di Cosmo, *Ancient China and its enemies: The rise of nomadic power in East Asian history* (Cambridge, 2002), p. 35).
60. Georg Kossack, 'Mittelasien und skythischer Tierstil', in *Beiträge zur allgemeinen und vergleichenden Archäologie* 2 (Mainz, 1980), p. 91.
61. Emma Bunker, *Ancient Bronzes of the Eastern Eurasian Steppes from the Arthur M. Sackler Collections* (New York, 1997), p. 194; Emma Bunker, *Nomadic Art of the Eastern Eurasian Steppes* (New Haven, 2002), p. 24; Gu Fang, *The harmonious beauty of jade* (2008), p. 74; Mayke Wagner and Herbert Butz, *Nomadenkunst* (Mainz, 2007), pp. 46f.
62. An example of speculative interpretations is put forth by Ivan Marazov, 'The "coiled-up carnivore": visual etymology of the motif', in *Silk Road Art and Archaeology*, Vol. 8 (Kamakura, 2002).
63. Kossack, 'Mittelasien und skythischer Tierstil', pp. 91f.
64. M. Rostovtzeff, *The Animal Style in South Russia and China* (Princeton, 1929), p. 68. See also: M. Rostovtzeff, *Iranians and Greeks in South Russia* (Oxford, 1922), p. 197; Parzinger, *Die Skythen*, pp. 35ff, 99f.
65. Bunker, *Nomadic Art of the Eastern Eurasian Steppes*, 2002, p. 17.
66. Ellis Minns, *Scythians and Greeks: A survey of ancient history and archaeology on the north coast of the Euxine from the Danube to the Caucasus* (Cambridge, 1913), pp. 241, 252, 267f, 278. At first Rostovtzeff sharply attacked Minns on account of this hypothesis and rejected any connection between Scythian and Siberian toreutics of the Iron Age. In 1922 he changed his opinion and adopted Minns's view (Gregory Bongard-Levin, 'E.H. Minns and M.I. Rostovtzeff: Glimpses of a Scythian friendship', in *Scythians and Greeks* (Exeter, 2005), p. 17).
67. Herodotus, *Histories* IV, 71. Askold Ivantchik has shown that 15 of the 17 characteristics of a Scythian royal burial listed by Herodotus have been substantiated by archaeology (Menghin et al., *Im Zeichen des goldenen Greifen*, p. 241).
68. Menghin et al., *Im Zeichen des goldenen Greifen*, p. 239.
69. Renate Rolle, *Totenkult der Skythen* (Berlin, 1979), Vol. I. p. 100; *Gold der Steppe*, pp. 62f. The additional 50 horse skeletons found on a platform at Ul'skji Aul correspond to Herodotus's description of a memorial ceremony one year after the burial, at which 50 horses and 50 young men were sacrificed (*Histories* IV, 72).
70. The explanations of Arzhan 2 are based on the following sources: Konstantin Čugunov, Hermann Parzinger and Anatoli Nagler, 'Der skythische Fürstengrabhügel von Arzhan 2 in Tuva. Vorbericht der russisch-deutschen Ausgrabungen', in *Eurasia Antiqua* 9 (2003), pp. 113–162; Konstantin Čugunov, *Der skythenzeitliche Fürstenkurgan Aržhan 2 in Tuva*, (Mainz, 2010); Menghin et al., *Im Zeichen des goldenen Greifen*, pp. 69–100; Parzinger, *Die frühen Völker Eurasiens*, pp. 611–614.
71. Menghin et al., *Im Zeichen des goldenen Greifen*, p. 55; Sergei Rudenko, *Die sibirische Sammlung Peters I*, 1962, pp. 9–15.
72. Schiltz, *Histoires de kourganes*, pp.30–33.
73. Menghin et al., *Im Zeichen des goldenen Greifen*, pp. 55, 57.
74. Koryakova and Epimakkhov, *The Urals and Western Siberia*, p. 332; Menghin et al., *Im Zeichen des goldenen Greifen*, p. 56
75. Iaroslav Lebedynsky, *De l'Épée Scythe au Sabre Mongol* (Errance, 2008), pp. 38–49.
76. Natascha Polos'mak, 'Die „Amazone" von Pazyryk', in *Amazonen* (2010), p. 134.
77. Vjačeslav Molodin, 'Das skythenzeitliche Kriegergrab aus Olon-Kurin-Gol. Neue Entdeckungen in der Permafrostzone des mongolischen Altaj', in *Eurasia Antiqua* 14 (2008), pp. 243, 258.
78. Claudia Chang (ed.), *Of Gold and Grass: Nomads of Kazakhstan* (Bethesda, 2006), p. 112.

79. Wieczorek and Lind, *Ursprünge der Seidenstraße*, pp. 180f.
80. Nikolaj Leon'ev and Vladimir Kapel'ko, *Steinstelen der Okunev-Kultur* (Mainz, 2002), pp. 15, 24.
81. Menghin et al., *Im Zeichen des goldenen Greifen*, pp. 158f.
82. Renate Rolle, *Königskurgan Čertomlyk: Ein skythischer Grabhügel des 4. vorchristlichen Jahrhunderts* (Mainz, 1998), Vol. I, p.102.
83. Herodotus, *Histories* IV, 71.
84. Iaroslav Lebedynsky, *Les Scythes* (Errance, 2001), p. 198; Wolfgang Scharlipp, *Die frühen Türken in Zentralasien* (Darmstadt, 1992), p. 27.
85. See p. 116. Not all the stone circles are extant; on the south-west side, where a tarred road runs through the landscape, they are missing entirely.
86. On account of a 16-kg (?) gold ring found on the upper Indus in Pattan in northern Pakistan, Parzinger extends this cultural territory even as far as the southern foot of the Karakorum (Čugunov, *Der skythenzeitliche Fürstenkurgan Aržhan 2 in Tuva*, pp. 311–317). It seems questionable that a single discovery could suffice to expand a cultural range so significantly.
87. Wilhelm Radloff, *Aus Sibirien* (Leipzig, 1893), Vol. II, p. 167.
88. I thank Mr Jürg Rageth of Riehen, Basel, for the evidence for this new dating (I. Hajdas, G. Bonani et al., 'Chronology of Pazyryk 2 and Ulandryk 4 Kurgans based on high resolution radiocarbon dating and dendrochronology – a step towards more precise dating of Scythian burials', in *Impact of the Environment on Human Migration in Eurasia* (2004), p. 114). Despite this more precise dating, Parzinger maintains an earlier dating: 'Pazyryk I and II belong accordingly in the fifth and Pazyryk V at the turn of the fifth to the fourth centuries BC' (*Die frühen Völker Eurasiens*, p. 599).
89. The most important source on Pazyryk is Rudenko Sergei, *Frozen Tombs of Siberia: The Pazyrik Burials of Iron Age Horsemen* (London, 1970). The book also contains 180 illustrations. See also: Grjaznov, *Südsibirien*, pp. 158–220; Menghin et al., *Im Zeichen des goldenen Greifen*, pp. 118–131; Parzinger, *Die frühen Völker Eurasiens*, pp. 586–596; Schiltz, *Die Skythen und andere Steppenvölker*, pp. 260–289.
90. P.B. Konovalov, *The Burial vault of a Xiongnu prince at Sudzha (Il'movaia Pad', Transbaikalia)*, 2008, pp. 46f. See Vol. II. of the present work.
91. Herodotus, *Histories* IV, 64. The Greeks called scalping *aposkythizein*, which means roughly 'to de-Scythify' (Rolle, *Die Welt der Skythen*, p. 91).
92. Herodotus, *Histories* IV, 71.
93. For illustrations see: Rudenko, *Frozen Tombs of Siberia*, pp. 109, 111.
94. Boris Litvinskij, *Antike und frühmittelalterliche Grabhügel im westlichen Fergana-Becken, Tadzikistan* (Munich, 1986), pp. 98f.
95. Chang, *Of Gold and Grass*, pp. 66f.
96. Polos'mak, 'Die 'Amazone' von Pazyryk,' p. 132.
97. Menghin et al., *Im Zeichen des goldenen Greifen*, p. 153; Hermann Parzinger et al., 'New discoveries in the Mongolian Altai: The warrior grave of the Pazyryk Culture at Olon-Güüriin-Gol 10', in *Current archaeological research in Mongolia* (Bonn, 2009), p. 213.
98. Chang, *Of Gold and Grass*, pp. 1, 4, 35f, 42, 66, 126; Zainolla Samashev et al., 'Le kourgane de Berel dans l'Altaï kazakhstanais', in *Arts Asiatiques. Musée national des Arts asiatiques-Guimet* 55 (2000), p. 13.
99. Joan Aruz (ed.), *The Golden Deer of Eurasia: Scythian and Sarmatian treasures from the Russian steppes* (New York, 2000), p. 261.
100. The assertions sometimes found in the literature that the tattoos and the ubiquity of animal images are 'shamanistic' are untenable, as there is no evidence of Scythian shamanism.
101. Rudenko, *Frozen Tombs of Siberia*, plate 92.
102. R.D. Barnett, 'The art of Bactria and the treasure of the Oxus', in *Iranica Antiqua*, Vol. VIII (1968), pl. VIII.
103. O.M. Dalton, *The treasure of the Oxus with other examples of early oriental metal-work* (London, 1964), p. 33, plate 1; John Curtis and Nigel Tallis, *Forgotten Empire: The world of Ancient Persia* (London, 2005), pp. 137–143.
104. Gerold Walser, *Die Völkerschaften auf den Reliefs von Persepolis* (Berlin, 1966), pl. 8, 13, 18, 47, 49, 57.
105. Piotrovsky, *L'art scythe*, fig. 45–46.
106. Schiltz, *Die Skythen und andere Steppenvölker*, fig. 145.
107. Menghin et al., *Im Zeichen des goldenen Greifen*, pp. 252f; Piotrovsky, *L'art scythe*, fig. 150.
108. Schiltz, *Die Skythen und andere Steppenvölker*, fig. 296.
109. Igor Pitschijan, *Oxos-Schatz und Oxos-Tempel* (Berlin, 1992), p. 37.
110. Rudenko, *Frozen Tombs of Siberia*, pp. 191f, 224.
111. Aruz, *The Golden Deer of Eurasia*, p. 267.
112. Rolle, *Die Welt der Skythen*, p. 102; *Gold der Steppe*, p. 157.
113. Herodotus, *Histories* IV, 73–75.
114. Richard Frye, *The heritage of Central Asia: From Antiquity to the Turkish Expansion* (Princeton, 1996), p. 82.
115. Menghin et al., *Im Zeichen des goldenen Greifen*, p. 123.
116. Radiocarbon testing gave an even older date from the eighth to seventh centuries BC for a fragment of a knotted wool carpet from Central Asia (Antoine de Moor, Chris Verhecken-Lammens and André Verhecken, *3500 years of textile art* (Tielt 2008) p. 226).
117. Rudenko, *Frozen Tombs of Siberia*, pp. 149, 173.
118. In the Achaemenid Empire the lotus blossom was a royal or divine attribute. Later, in Central Asian Buddhism, holding a lotus bud or blossom represented the respectful greeting of a Buddha or bodhisattva and expressed the hope of being reborn in the paradise of the future Buddha Amitabha, Sukhavati (Christoph Baumer, 'Sogdian or Indian Iconography and Religious Influences in Dandan Uiliq (Xinjiang, China)?', in *Proceedings of the International Seminar 'The Art of Central Asia and the Indian Sub-Continent in Cross-Cultural Perspective'* (New Delhi, 2008), p. 175).
119. Rudenko, *Frozen Tombs of Siberia*, pp. 289f.
120. Herodotus, *Histories* IV, 127.
121. Aruz, *The Golden Deer of Eurasia*, p. 69.
122. Herodotus, *Histories* IV, 59; Lebedynsky, *Les Scythes*, p. 181; Menghin et al., *Im Zeichen des goldenen Greifen*, pp. 251, 278, 283, 296; Rolle, *Gold der Steppe*, pp. 308f, 378f, 394; Wilfried Seipel (ed), *Gold der Steppe* (Leoben, 2009), p. 176.
123. Henri-Paul Francfort, 'Observation sur la toreutique de la civilisation de l'Oxus'; in *Afghanistan: Ancien carrefour entre l'est et l'ouest* (2005), p. 23; Sylvia Winkelmann, *Seals of the oasis from the Ligabue Collection* (Venice, 2004), p. 16.
124. Jutta Frings (ed.), *Die Thraker: Das goldene Reich des Orpheus* (Mainz, 2004), pp. 180, 230.
125. Sabine Kaufmann (ed.), *Die Wikinger* (Speyer, 2008), p. 288.
126. Sergei Rudenko, *Die Kultur der Hsung-Nu und die Hügelgräber von Noin Ula* (Bonn, 1969), fig. 48, plates XLi–XLv.
127. Dominik Keller and Regula Schorta, *Fabulous Creatures from the Desert Sands* (Riggisberg, 2001), fig. 15. See here Vol. II.
128. Dalton, *The treasure of the Oxus with other examples of early oriental metal-work*, pp. XLivf, Lviii; Menghin et al., *Im Zeichen des goldenen Greifen*, pp. 163–165; Marie-Catherine Rey (ed.), *Kazakhstan, hommes, bêtes et dieux de la steppe* (Versailles, 2010), pp. 82f.
129. Minns, *Scythians and Greeks*, pp. 281f; Rostovtzeff, *Iranians and Greeks*, pp. 14, 124, 190; *The Animal Style*, pp. 43–46.
130. Finds in the neighbouring necropolises of Bashadar and Tuekta (Russian Altai), as well as Berel' (Kazakh Altai) add to the picture of a prosperous nomadic elite. Discoveries made between 1990 and 2006 at greater elevation in the permafrost high plains brought to light additional spectacular finds, among them the grave of an armed female warrior and a warrior with remarkably well-preserved clothing (Menghin et al., *Im Zeichen des goldenen Greifen*, pp. 118ff, 132–139).
131. Vjačeslav Molodin, 'Petroglyphs of the Ukok Plateau', *Archaeology, Ethnology & Anthropology of Eurasia* 4 (32) (2007), p. 93.
132. The following sources were used for the discoveries on the Ukok Plateau: Natascha Polos'mak and Mathias Seifert, 'Menschen aus dem Eis Sibiriens: Neuentdeckte Hügelgräber (Kurgane) im Permafrost des Altai', in *Antike Welt* 1996/2, pp. 87–108; Polos'mak, 'Die „Amazone" von Pazyryk', pp. 129–137; Parzinger, *Die frühen Völker Eurasiens*, pp. 599–604.
133. Mathias Seifert, 'Zur absoluten Datierung der Hügelgräber der Pazyryk-Kultur', in *Amazonen* (2010), p. 139.
134. This gold fish plaque weighed no less than 609 g. The golden hoard of Vettersfelde was discovered in 1882 about 100 km south of Berlin and had originally been produced around the sixth/fifth centuries BC in the northern Pontic region (Menghin et al., *Im Zeichen des goldenen Greifen*, pp. 318–327).
135. The kurgan was originally dated by Polos'mak and Seifer to 'the fifth century or at the latest at the start of the fourth century', and likewise by Parzinger in 2006. Parzinger, *Die frühen Völker Eurasiens*, pp. 599–604. Polos'mak and Seifert, 'Menschen aus dem Eis Sibiriens', 1996, p. 106. In 2010 Polos'mak dated kurgan 1 of Ak-Alacha 1 to the fourth/third centuries BC ('Die "Amazone" von Pazyryk', p. 140f).
136. See pp. 264f.
137. Herodotus, *Histories* IV, 116f.

138. Molodin, 'Das skythenzeitliche Kriegergrab', pp. 241–265.
139. Parzinger, *Die frühen Völker Eurasiens*, pp. 654–658.
140. Chang, *Of Gold and Grass*, pp. 51–55; Menghin et al., *Im Zeichen des goldenen Greifen*, pp. 163ff.
141. Hermann Parzinger, *Der große Kurgan von Bajkara* (Mainz, 2003).
142. Between 150 and 50 BC Sarmatians used the kurgan for a magnificent reburial.
143. Herodotus, *Histories* IV, 62; Parzinger, *Der große Kurgan von Bajkara*, p. 220.
144. Alexander M. Leskov, *Grabschätze der Adygeen: Neue Entdeckungen im Nordkaukasus* (Munich, 1990), p. 37.
145. Marcellinus Ammianus. *The Later Roman Empire (AD 354–378)*, book 31.2. (London, 2004), p. 414. Rolle, *Gold der Steppe*, p. 152.
146. Vladimir Kouznetsov and Iaroslav Lebedynsky, *Les Alains* (Errance, 2005), pp. 26f; Parzinger, *Der große Kurgan von Bajkara*, p. 220.
147. Iaroslav Lebedynsky, *Les Sarmates* (Errance, 2002), pp. 50, 54, 58, 243.
148. Vjačeslav Molodin, 'Čiča – eine befestigte Ansiedlung der Übergangsperiode von der Spätbronze- zur Früheisenzeit in der Barabinsker Waldsteppe', in *Eurasia Antiqua*, Vol. 8/2002, pp. 185–236.
149. Molodin, 'Čiča – eine befestigte Ansiedlung', pp. 185–236.
150. Koryakova and Epimakkhov, *The Urals and Western Siberia*, pp. 294ff.
151. R. Brzezinski and M. Mielczarek, *The Sarmatians 600 BC – AD 450* (London, 2002), p. 34; Koryakova and Epimakkhov, *The Urals and Western Siberia*, pp. 306, 309.
152. Aruz, *The Golden Deer of Eurasia*, p. 111; Koryakova and Epimakkhov, *The Urals and Western Siberia*, pp. 310, 332.
153. Koryakova and Epimakkhov, *The Urals and Western Siberia*, pp. 253f, 258.
154. Ibid, pp. 259f.
155. Herodotus, *Histories* VII, 64; Plinius Gaius, *Naturalis Historia,* VI, 19, 50.
156. M. Dandamayev, 'Media and Achaemenid Iran', in *History of civilizations of Central Asia*, Vol. II, p. 37.
157. Beckwith, *Empires of the Silk Road,* pp. 61, 377f, 389.
158. Beckwith, *Empires of the Silk Road,* pp. 377f; Lebedynsky, *Les Saces*, p. 8; Schiltz, *Die Skythen und andere Steppenvölker*, p. 52. The ethonym Massagetae is interpreted as 'great Saka' or 'deer people' (Lebedynsky, *Les Saces*, p. 10).
159. Herodotus, *Histories*, III, 89–94. Walser, *Die Völkerschaften auf den Reliefs von Persepolis,* pp. 27–49. We will refrain from using the Persian chronicle of the Greek doctor and historian Ktesias of Knidos (late fifth–early fourth centuries BC), as his accounts are extremely unreliable when not outright fabrications.
160. Herodotus, *Histories,* I, 106. The dates of Scythian rule over the Medes are debated.
161. Cyrus was king of the Persians of Anshan from 559 BC and, after his victories over the Medes, he declared himself king of the Persians and Medes in 550 BC.
162. Dandamayev, 'Media and Achaemenid Iran', pp. 37ff.
163. Herodotus, *Histories*, I, 177.
164. On the localisation of Sakan peoples: Abetekov et al., 'Ancient Iranian nomads in western Central Asia', pp. 24f; M. Dandamayev, 'Media and Achaemenid Iran', p. 44; Frye, *The heritage of Central Asia*, pp. 81ff; Lebedynsky, *Les Saces*, pp. 41–44; Boris Litvinskij, *La civilisation de l'Asie centrale antique* (Espelkamp, 1998), p. 36; J.P. Mallory and Victor H. Mair, *The Tarim Mummies* (London, 2000), pp. 41, 108.
165. David Christian, *A History of Russia, Central Asia and Mongolia* (Oxford, 1998), p. 164; Dandamayev, 'Media and Achaemenid Iran', p. 43; Litvinskij, *La civilisation de l'Asie centrale antique*, p. 36. Other authors locate Cyropolis at the nearby city of Khudjand. The discovery of Achaemenid ceramics at the citadel of Istrafshan corroborates the first hypothesis (Personal communication from Dr Sharofuddin Kurbanov, Panjikant, in 2008).
166. Akhmadali Askarov, 'The beginning of Iron Age in Transoxania', in *History of Civilizations of Central Asia*, Vol. I (Paris, 1992), p. 457; Dandamayev, 'Media and Achaemenid Iran', p. 41f; Vadim M. Masson, *Das Land der tausend Städte: Die Wiederentdeckung der ältestens Kulturgebiete in Mittelasien* (Munich, 1982), p. 58.
167. Walser, *Die Völkerschaften auf den Reliefs von Persepolis*, p. 29.
168. Herodotus, *Histories,* I, 201–215.
169. Ibid, 212.
170. E. Kuzmina, 'Les steppes de l'Asie centrale à l'époque du bronze', in *Découverte des civilisations d'Asie Centrale* (1993), p. 83; Shapur Shanbazi, 'Iranian mythology', in *Encyclopaedia Iranica* http://www.iranica.com/articles/iraj. Only much later, when the Arabs conquered Iran and Turkic peoples began to advance into the Turan Basin, did the term 'Turanians' come to refer to Turkic ethnic groups.
171. Christian, *A History of Russia, Central Asia and Mongolia,* p. 165.
172. Herodotus, *Histories,* IV, 120f.
173. Ibid, 108, 123.
174. Rolle, *Die Welt der Skythen*, pp. 124ff; Rolle, 'Das Burgwallsystem von Bel'sk (Ukraine): Eine frühe stadtartige Anlage im skythischen Landesinnern', *Hamburger Beiträge zur Archäologie* 18 (1996), pp. 69, 76.
175. Herodotus, *Histories,* IV, 128.
176. Herodotus's listing of the 20 satrapies can be reconciled with the lists of Persian peoples only with difficulty and reservations, all the more so since Herodotus mentions certain peoples twice, assigning them to different satrapies (Walser, *Die Völkerschaften auf den Reliefs von Persepolis*, pp. 42–49).
177. Harald Haarmann, *Universalgeschichte der Schrift* (Frankfurt, 1998), p. 501.
178. Herodotus, *Histories,* IV, 44.
179. While Strabo and most modern historians accept the identification of Zariaspa with Bactra/Balkh, Ptolemy clearly differenciates between Zariaspa and Bactra. Ptolemaios Claudios, *Handbuch der Geographie* (Basel, 2006), VI, 11, 7 + 9 (Vol. II, p. 649); Strabo, *Geographica* (Wiesbaden, 2007), XI, 8, 11. The absence of Achaemenid findings at Bactra/Balkh and the recent discovery of a major Achaemenid site at Chesm-e Shafa 24 km south-east of Balkh raises the question of whether Chesm-e Shafa could be identical with Achaemenid Zariaspa (Lawler Andrew, 'Edge of an Empire. An ancient Afghan fortress offers rare evidence of Persia's forgotten territories', *Archaeology*. Archaeological Institute of America, Boston September/October 2011, pp. 42–47).
180. Georges Rougemont and David Stronach, 'On the Date of the Oxus Gold Scabbard and other Achaemenid Matters', *Bulletin of the Asia Institute* 12 (1998), p. 235.
181. This information was taken from a sign in a fire temple in Yazd, Iran, in 2001.
182. Frye, *The heritage of Central Asia*, pp. 67–69.
183. Frantz Grenet, 'Les religions dans l'Empire perse', in *Le monde de la Bible* (2009), p. 28.
184. The manuscript is found in the British Library, London. http://www.bl.uk/onlinegallery/sacredtexts/ashem.html
185. Sergei Tolstov, *Auf den Spuren der altchoresmischen Kultur* (Berlin, 1953), p. 98. Other scholars credit Vologases I (r. 51–78 AD) with the first codification of the Avesta (G.A. Koshelenko and V.N. Pilipko, 'Parthia', in *History of civilizations of Central Asia*, Vol. II, p. 149).
186. *Avesta: Die heiligen Schriften der Parsen* (Leipzig, 1859; 2006); Frye, *The heritage of Central Asia*, pp. 69–72; Litvinskij, *La civilisation de l'Asie centrale antique*, pp. 32f, 164–168.
187. P.B. Konovalov, *The Burial vault of a Xiongnu prince at Sudzha (Il'movaia Pad', Transbaikalia)*, 2008, pl. 32.
188. Menghin et al., *Im Zeichen des goldenen Greifen*, pp. 164. Parzinger, *Die frühen Völker Eurasiens*, pp. 659f. Rolle, *Totenkult der Skythen*, Vol. I., p. 45, note 45.
189. K.A. Akishev, *Issyk Mound: The art of Saka in Kazakhstan* (Moscow, 1978); Chang, *Of Gold and Grass*, pp. 29–34, 57–70.
190. Lebedynsky, *Les Saces*, p. 217f.
191. Michael Frachetti, *Pastoralist landscapes and social interaction in Bronze Age Eurasia* (Berkeley, 2008), pp. 141f.
192. In 1988 in the village of Zalauly near Almaty a group of schoolchildren made a surprising discovery when they found a sack with 649 gold objects weighing 1.5 kg. The pieces date to the eighth–third centuries BC and had presumably been stolen from various kurgans around Almaty in the nineteenth century and hidden in Zalauly. Several objects are decorated with coloured paste inlays and semiprecious gems, similar to the discoveries from Čilikty (Menghin et al., *Im Zeichen des goldenen Greifen*, pp. 163–165).
193. See p. 116.
194. Parzinger, *Die frühen Völker Eurasiens*, pp. 670–73.
195. Sven Helms, 'Ancient Choresmia: The Northern Edge of Central Asia from the 6th Century BC to the mid-4th Century AD', in *Worlds of the Silk Roads: Ancient and Modern* (Turnhout, 1998), p. 89; Tolstov, *Auf den Spuren der altchoresmischen Kultur*, pp. 108ff.
196. Helms, 'Ancient Choresmia', p. 89; Tolstov, *Auf den Spuren der altchoresmischen Kultur*, pp. 108ff.
197. Sergei Tolstov, *Drevniy Choresm* (Moscow, 1948); Tolstov, *Auf den Spuren der altchoresmischen Kultur.*
198. Lucius Flavius, *The Campaigns of Alexander* (London, 1971), pp. 227f; Quintus Curtius Rufus, *The History of Alexander* (London, 2004), Viii, 1;

Masson, *Das Land der tausend Städte*, p. 165; N. Negmatov, 'States in north-western Central Asia', in *History of civilizations of Central Asia*, Vol. II, p. 455; Yuri Rapoport, 'The palaces of Topraq-Qal'a', *Bulletin of the Asia Institute* 8 (1996), p. 161.

199. Arrian, *The Campaigns of Alexander* (London, 1971), pp. 201, 227.
200. Arrian confirms that Alexander was planning an attack on the northern Pontic Scythians. Alexander is said to have sent spies to the Scythians and to have announced to Pharasmanes a joint campaign against the Scythians after the conquest of India. Arrian, *The Campaigns of Alexander*, pp. 201, 227; Quintus Curtius Rufus, *The History of Alexander*, Vii, 6, 12.
201. Quintus Curtius Rufus, *The History of Alexander*, Vii, 8, 19–30. See also: Rolle, *Königskurgan Čertomlyk*, Vol. I, pp. 176–178. Like the early historians of Alexander, Curtius Rufus mistakes Herodotus's River Tanaïs, which formed the border between Europe and Asia for Greek historians and corresponds to today's Don, with the Jaxartes, the Syr Darya, which he also describes as the border between Europe and Asia (Vii, 6,7). Arrian, however, was aware of this confusion and differentiated between the two rivers (Arrian, *The Campaigns of Alexander*, p. 199). Likewise confusing is the reference in several ancient authors to the Hindu Kush as the 'Indian Caucasus' (Claude Rapin, 'L'Afghanistan et l'Asie Centrale dans la géographie mythique des historiens d'Alexandre et dans la toponymie des géographes gréco-romains', in *Afghanistan: Ancien carrefour entre l'est et l'ouest*, pp. 149ff).
202. Helms, 'Ancient Choresmia', pp. 87ff; Litvinskij, *La civilisation de l'Asie centrale antique*, pp. 41f; Parzinger, *Die frühen Völker Eurasiens*, p. 677; Boris Staviskij, *Kunst der Kuschan* (Leipzig, 1979), pp. 31f; Tolstov, *Auf den Spuren der altchoresmischen Kultur*, pp. 104ff.
203. Nasiba Baimatowa, *5000 Jahre Architektur in Mittelasien: Lehmziegelgewölbe vom 4./3. Jt. v.Chr. bis zum Ende des 8. Jhs. n.Chr.* (Mainz, 2008), pp. 178–189, 201–204, 233–238; David Richardson, *The Karakalpaks* (2005), http://www.karakalpak.com/anckoy.html
204. Masson, *Das Land der tausend Städte*, p. 164.
205. See Vol. II.
206. See pp. 147, 178.
207. Parzinger, *Die frühen Völker Eurasiens*, p. 678; Richardson, *The Karakalpaks*. http://www.karakalpak.com/anckoy.html. A similar, somewhat later ossuary is pictured in: Staviskij, *Kunst der Kuschan*, fig. 149.
208. David Richardson, *The Karakalpaks*.
209. Baimatowa, *5000 Jahre Architektur in Mittelasien*, pp. 178–189; T.S. Malyutina, '"Proto-towns" of the Bronze Age in the South Urals and Ancient Khorasmia', in *Complex Societies of Central Eurasia from the 3rd to the 1st Millennium BC*, Vol. I (Washington, DC, 2002), p. 166; Tolstov, *Auf den Spuren der altchoresmischen Kultur*, pp. 35f, 123, 131f.
210. Litvinskij, *Antike und frühmittelalterliche Grabhügel*, pp. 127f.
211. R. Masov et al. (eds), *National Museum of Antiquities of Tajikistan* (Dushanbe, 2005), pp. 221, 223.
212. As Hermann Parzinger emphasises, the classification of cultures of Iron Age Xinjiang is debated and varies from four (Chen/Hiebert) to 14 (Jianjun Mei) different cultural phases. Kwang-tzuu Chen and Fredrick Hiebert, 'The Late Prehistory of Xinjiang in Relation to its neighbours', *Journal of World Prehistory* 9.2 (1995), pp. 250, 272–283; Jianjun Mei, *Copper and Bronze Metallurgy in Late Prehistoric Xinjiang* (Oxford, 2000), pp. 15–24; Parzinger, *Die frühen Völker Eurasiens*, pp. 700ff. We generally accept Parzinger's classification into seven groups, and we try, when possible, to assign the cultures to ethnic groups.
213. Yong Ma and Wang Binghua, 'The culture of the Xinjiang region', in *History of civilizations of Central Asia*, Vol. II, p. 210; Wang Binghua, *Recherches historiques préliminaires sur les Saka du Xinjiang ancien* (1987), pp. 40f.
214. See Vol. II.
215. Antiochia-in-Margiana is today called Gyaur Kala. Arrian, *The Campaigns of Alexander*; Frye, *The heritage of Central Asia*, pp. 104–107; V. Gaïbov and G. Kochelenko, 'La Margiane', in *Les Parthes* (Quétigny, 2002), p. 48; Litvinskij, *Antike und frühmittelalterliche Grabhügel*, 1986, pp. 128f; Masson, *Das Land der tausend Städte*, pp. 141–147; H. Sidky, *The Greek Kingdom of Bactria: From Alexander to Eucratides the Great* (Lanham, 2000), pp. 132f; V.A. Zavyalov, 'The Fortifications of the City of Gyaur Kala, Merv', in *After Alexander. Central Asia before Islam* (London, 2007), pp. 313–326.
216. Strabo, *Geographica*, XI, 10,2; A. Dani and P. Bernard, 'Alexander and his successors in Central Asia', in *History of civilizations of Central Asia*, p. 91. As already mentioned, other authors attribute these fortifications to the Sassanids (Gaïbov and Kochelenko, 'La Margiane', p. 48).
217. Zavyalov, 'The Fortifications of the City of Gyaur Kala, Merv', pp. 313, 325f.
218. Tei Hatakyama, *The Tumulus and Stag Stones at Shiebar-kul in Xinjiang, China* (2002); Ma and Wang, 'The culture of the Xinjiang region', pp. 222–225' Bo Wang, 'Hirschsteine in Xinjiang', *Eurasia Antiqua*, Vol. 7 (2001), pp. 105–132.
219. Another oval stone statue with two triangles on the cheeks was discovered in the Mongolian province of Khovd, bordering on Xianjiang (Alexej Kovalëv and Diimaazhav Erdenebaatar, 'Discovery of new cultures of the Bronze Age in Mongolia according to the data obtained by the International central Asian Archaeological Expedition', in *Current archaeological research in Mongolia* (Bonn, 2009), pp. 155, 157).
220. Alexej Kovalëv, 'Überlegungen zur Herkunft der Skythen aufgrund archäologischer Daten', *Eurasia Antiqua*, Vol. 4 (1998), pp. 265ff; 'Die ältesten Stelen am Ertix', *Eurasia Antiqua*, Vol. 5 (1998), pp. 162, 171; 'Discovery of new cultures of the Bronze Age in Mongolia', pp. 158f; Mei, *Copper and Bronze Metallurgy in Late Prehistoric Xinjiang*, pp. 14f; Xiaoshan Qi and Bo Wang, *The ancient culture in Xinjiang along the Silk Road* (Urumqi, 2008), pp. 220f.
221. Kovalëv, 'Die ältesten Stelen am Ertix', pp. 162, 169; Qi and Wang, *The ancient culture in Xinjiang*, pp. 215, plate 7, 220, 4. The find of two iron knives indicates that the graveyard was also used in the Iron Age.
222. Wang, *Recherches historiques préliminaires sur les Saka du Xinjiang ancien*, pp. 36ff; See also: Mei, *Copper and Bronze Metallurgy in Late Prehistoric Xinjiang*, pp. 50–57.
223. Chengyuan Ma and Feng Yue, *Archaeological treasures of the Silk Road in Xinjiang Uygur Autonomous Region* (Shanghai, 1998), pp. 244f; Mei, *Copper and Bronze Metallurgy in Late Prehistoric Xinjiang*, p. 21; Wang, *Recherches historiques préliminaires sur les Saka du Xinjiang ancien*, p. 35. Wieczorek and Lind, *Ursprünge der Seidenstraße*, pp. 300f.
224. Victor Mair (ed.), *Secrets of the Silk Road* (Santa Ana, Calif., 2010), p. 155; Wieczorek and Lind, *Ursprünge der Seidenstraße*, pp. 54, 290, 300. The helmets of the Thracians also looked like Phyrgian caps cast in metal. See: Frings, *Die Thraker*, pp. 128f, 294.
225. Ma and Yue, *Archaeological treasures of the Silk Road*, pp. 213–220; Mei, *Copper and Bronze Metallurgy in Late Prehistoric Xinjiang*, pp. 18f; Qi and Wang, *The ancient culture in Xinjiang*, p. 123; Wang, *Recherches historiques préliminaires sur les Saka du Xinjiang ancien*, pp. 33–35.
226. Ma and Yue, *Archaeological treasures of the Silk Road*, pp. 104f, 254f; Wang et al., *The ancient corpses of Xinjiang* (2001), pp. 98–111; Wieczorek and Lind, *Ursprünge der Seidenstraße*, pp. 174–181.
227. Chen and Hiebert, *The Late Prehistory of Xinjiang*, pp. 274ff. Kangxin Han, 'The Physical Anthropology of the Ancient Populations of the Tarim Basin and Surrounding Areas', in *The Bronze Age and Early Iron Age Peoples of Eastern central Asia* (Pennsylvania, 1998), pp. 564f; Mei, *Copper and Bronze Metallurgy in Late Prehistoric Xinjiang*, p. 16.
228. Chen and Hiebert, *The Late Prehistory of Xinjiang*, p. 278f; Mei, *Copper and Bronze Metallurgy in Late Prehistoric Xinjiang*, p. 16.
229. Despite five carbon-14 analyses giving a date around 1000 BC, the earliest undisturbed graves date to around 800 BC. Elizabeth Barber, *The mummies of Ürümchi* (London, 1999), p. 37, pl. I; Christoph Baumer, *Southern Silk Road* (Bangkok, 2003), p. 31; Mair, *Secrets of the Silk Road*, p. 36. Wang et al., *The ancient corpses of Xinjiang*, pp. 79–94; Wieczorek and Lind, *Ursprünge der Seidenstraße*, pp. 182–201.
230. Barber, *The mummies of Ürümchi*, pp. 46–54; Wang et al., *The ancient corpses of Xinjiang*, pp. 79–84
231. Christoph Baumer, 'The Ayala Mazar – Xiaohe Culture. Results from an archaeological exploration of the ancient Keriya Delta, China, in 2009' (2010). See here p. 220.
232. Dexiu He, 'A Brief Report on the Mummies from the Zaghunluq Site in Chärchän County', in *The Bronze Age and Early Iron Age Peoples of Eastern central Asia* (Pennsylvania, 1998), pp. 169–174; Wang et al., *The ancient corpses of Xinjiang*, pp. 84f, 89, 92.
233. See. p. 129.
234. Investigations of the author in October 2009. See also: Corinne Debaine-Francfort, *Keriya: Mémoires d'un fleuve* (Paris, 2001), pp. 120–225.
235. Debaine-Francfort, *Keriya*, pp. 135ff, 156, 172, 189, 210; Henri-Paul Francfort, 'De l'art des steppes au sud du Taklamakan', *Bulletin of the Asia Institute* 12 (1998), pp. 45–57.

236. See Vol. II.
237. About 80 pillars originally surrounded the grave. For Satma Mazar see: Christoph Baumer, 'Indo-europäische Mumien im Herzen der Wüste Taklamakan', *Antike Welt* (2010), pp. 18–28; 'The Ayala Mazar – Xiaohe Culture' (2010); *The Ayala Mazar-Xiaohe Culture* (2011), pp. 49–70.
238. Debaine-Francfort, *Keriya*, p. 173.
239. Debaine-Francfort, *Keriya*, p. 216; Yue Feng (ed.), *A grand view of Xinjiang's Cultural Relics and Historic Sites* (Urumqi, 1999), p. 169.
240. Sergei Rudenko, *Frozen Tombs of Siberia* (London, 1970), Fig. 157. I thank Jürg Rageth from Riehen, Basel, who brought this parallel to my attention.
241. Dominik Keller and Regula Schorta (eds), *Fabulous Creatures from the Desert Sands* (Riggisberg 2001), Figs. 89, 115.
242. Debaine-Francfort, *Keriya*, p. 165; Rolle Renate. *Amazonen*, 2010, p. 142.
243. Čugunov, *Der skythenzeitliche Fürstenkurgan Aržhan 2 in Tuva*, pp. 28, 30f, 130–141, 163. Grjaznov, *Der Großkurgan von Arzhan*, p. 58. Kossack, 'Mittelasien und skythischer Tierstil', pp. 102ff. See also: Aruz, *The Golden Deer of Eurasia*, pl. 1–4, 84–91, 169.
244. Debaine-Francfort, *Keriya*, p. 172.
245. Yue Feng, *Collection of the historical culture of Xinjiang* (Urumqi, 2009), p. 50; Qi and Wang, *The ancient culture in Xinjiang*, p. 44f.
246. Yue Feng, *Collection of the historical culture of Xinjiang*, p. 37, 40f; Wieczorek and Lind, *Ursprünge der Seidenstraße*, p. 216.
247. I thank John Vincent Bellezza from the University of Virginia, Charlottesville, for drawing my attention to the Iron Age petroglyphs in the Changtang (byang thang). John Vincent Bellezza, *Antiquities of Northern Tibet,* 2001, pp. 211–215, figs. 10:52–10:59; *Zhang Zhung. Foundations of Civilization in Tibet*, 2007, pp. 191–193, figs. 293–296, 358–359; Hauptmann Harald (ed.), *Die Felsbildstation Thalpan*, 2003, plates 8 (13:3, 69:1), 58 (30:231), 62 (30:226), 89 (30:CC), XIII (69A), XXVI (30:190).
248. Peter Tomka, *Über die Bestattungen der Hunnen*, 2007, p. 254.
249. Sergei Rudenko, *Frozen Tombs of Siberia,* 1970, p. 80.
250. Göran Possnert, *Sundström. Result of* ^{14}*C dating of human hair from Xinjiang, China* (Uppsala 11 March 2011.)
251. Michael Schultz, 'Ergebnisse der paläopathologisch-anthropologischen Untersuchung der menschlichen Skelettfunde aus dem Grab 26 von Liushui, Xinjiang China', in *Eurasia Antiqua* 13 (2007), pp. 181–197; Xinhua Wu et al., 'Das protoskythische Gräberfeld Liushi im Kun Lun-Gebirge, NW-China', *Eurasia Antiqua* 12 (2006), pp. 173–191; *Major archaeological discoveries in China in 2005* (Beijing, 2006), pp. 48–52.
252. Jeremiah 4.29; 5.15–16; 6.22–23. English is from NIV.
253. S. Makhortykh, 'The Northern Black Sea steppes in the Cimmerian epoch', in *Impact of the Environment on Human Migration in Eurasia* (2004), pp. 37ff.
254. Askold Ivantchi, *Kimmerier und Skythen* (Berlin, 2001), pp. 17–19, 280; Iaroslav Lebedynsky, *Les Cimmériens* (Errance, 2004), p. 20.
255. It is highly improbable that the Thracian populace belonged to the Cimmerian groups, as the Thracians were sedentary and the Cimmerians nomadic. The only commonality was that each had elite warrior horsemen. Ivantchik, *Kimmerier und Skythen*, pp. 48f, 279; Esther Jacobson, *The Art of the Scythians* (Leiden, 1995), pp. 37f; Lebedynsky, *Les Cimmériens*, pp. 19, 73–76, 104f, 116, 152; Renate Rolle et al., *Gold der Steppe: Archäologie der Ukraine* (Schleswig, 1991), pp. 49, 58.
256. Ivantchik, *Kimmerier und Skythen*, pp. 55, 61; Hermann Sauter, *Studien zum Kimmerierproblem* (Bonn, 2000), pp. 219, 222, 247, 251.
257. Whether Sargon really fell in a battle against the Cimmerians remains debated (Lebedynsky, *Les Cimmériens*, p. 30).
258. Ivantchik, *Kimmerier und Skythen*, pp. 21ff, 42–49; Sauter, *Studien zum Kimmerierproblem*, pp. 226, 247.
259. Lebedynsky, *Les Cimmériens*, pp. 17, 31, 126f; Sauter, *Studien zum Kimmerierproblem*, 2000, p. 167. Whether there was one Phrygian king with the name Midas or two is debated, and it is also uncertain whether the King Midas mentioned in 738 BC is the same as the Midas who took his own life 63 years later.
260. Herodotus, *Histories* I, 15; Sauter, *Studien zum Kimmerierproblem*, pp. 166, 171f, 249. Strabo, *Geographica*, XIII, 4, 8.
261. Sauter, *Studien zum Kimmerierproblem*, p. 232. See also: Lebedynsky, *Les Cimmériens*, p. 45.
262. Hermann Parzinger, *Die Skythen* (Munich, 2004), p. 19.
263. Ivantchik, *Kimmerier und Skythen*, p. 71; Lebedynsky, *Les Cimmériens*, pp. 19, 33, 45, 169; Parzinger, *Die Skythen*, p. 23. The historian Callisthenes (*ca.* 370–327 BC) refers to a second conquest of Sardes by the Lycians and the Treri, and, in another context, Strabo calls the Treri a Cimmerian people (Sauter, *Studien zum Kimmerierproblem*, pp. 166, 171, 235, 248).
264. Ivantchik's interpretation of a single bone disc putatively in the shape of a coiled animal, found in Sardes in a building layer from the mid-seventh century BC, as a material trace of the Cimmerians and as evidence that they were familiar with the early Scythian animal style is unpersuasive (Ivantchik, *Kimmerier und Skythen*, pp. 72–79).
265. Andreï Alexeev et al., 'Some problems in the study of the chronology of the ancient nomadic cultures of Eurasia (9th–3rd centuries BC),' *Geochronometria* 21 (2002), pp. 144f. To what extent the pre-Scythian material cultures of Chernogorovka (tenth–ninth centuries BC) and Novocherkassk (late ninth–eighth centuries BC) were associated with the Cimmerians remains debated. Jacobson, *The Art of the Scythians*, pp. 36. Elke Kaiser, *Begraben, aber nicht vergessen. Katakomben – Eine neue Grabkonstruktion in den Grabhügeln.* Jutta Leskovar and Maria-Christina Zingerle (eds), *Goldener Horizont: 4000 Jahre Nomaden der Ukraine* (Weitra, 2010), pp. 42–48. Hermann Parzinger, *Die frühen Völker Eurasiens: Vom Neolithikum bis zum Mittelalter* (Munich, 2006), pp. 705–707.
266. Lebedynsky, *Les Cimmériens*, pp. 84f; Iaroslav Lebedynsky, *De l'Épée Scythe au Sabre Mongol* (Errance, 2008), pp. 27–30; D. Telegin and J. P. Mallory, *The Anthropomorphic Stelae of the Ukraine: The Early Iconography of the Indo-Europeans* (Washington, DC, 1994), pp. 59–67.
267. Lebedynsky, *Les Cimmériens*, p. 166; Renate Rolle, *Königskurgan Čertomlyk: Ein skythischer Grabhügel des 4. vorchristlichen Jahrhunderts* (Mainz, 1998), Vol. I, p. 168.
268. L.K. Galanina, *Die Kurgane von Kelermes* (Berlin, 1996), p. 13.
269. Galanina, *Die Kurgane von Kelermes*, pp. 187, 203; Lebedynsky, *Les Cimmériens*, pp. 31, 44; Rolle, *Gold der Steppe*, p. 59.
270. Herodotus, *Histories*, IV, 11–12.
271. The Assyrian texts mention neither Nineveh's siege by the Medes nor the intervention of the Scythians. Sauter, *Studien zum Kimmerierproblem*, 2000, p. 231.
272. Herodotus, *Histories*, I, 103–105.
273. Sauter dates the Scythian rule over the Medes somewhat earlier to 652–625 BC (*Studien zum Kimmerierproblem*, 2000, p. 98).
274. Philip de Souza (ed.), *The ancient world at war* (London, 2008), p. 201.
275. Herodotus, *Histories*, I, 106.
276. David Christian, *A History of Russia, Central Asia and Mongolia* (Oxford, 1998), p. 163; Wilfried Menghin, Hermann Parzinger, Anatoli Nagler and Manfred Nawroth (eds), *Im Zeichen des goldenen Greifen: Königsgräber der Skythen* (Munich, 2007), p. 228.
277. Herodotus, *Histories*, I, 73f.
278. Herodotus, *Histories*, IV, 3f.
279. Oscar White-Muscarella, '"Ziwiye" and Ziwiye: The Forgery of a Provenience [sic]', *Journal of Field Archaeology* 4.2 (1977), pp. 197–219.
280. Menghin et al., *Im Zeichen des goldenen Greifen*, p. 199; E.D. Phillips, *The Royal Hordes: Nomad Peoples of the Steppes* (1965), pp. 73f.
281. Galanina, *Die Kurgane von Kelermes*, pp. 195, 197, 207.
282. Ibid, p. 187.
283. All the objects from Kelermes mentioned here are pictured in: Galanina, *Die Kurgane von Kelermes*, plates 1–44. Unfortunately, the first excavator of Kelermes, the mining engineer D.G. Schultz, proved to be a grave robber, who surreptitiously melted down over 3 kg of gold objects (Ibid, pp. 17–25).
284. Galanina, *Die Kurgane von Kelermes*, pp. 35, 55, 59, 71, 83.
285. Herodotus, *Histories* IV, 72.
286. Alexander M. Leskov, *Grabschätze der Adygeen: Neue Entdeckungen im Nordkaukasus* (Munich, 1990), pp. 15–17. As Radlov reported, in the second half of the nineteenth century AD southern Siberian peoples such as the Teleuts and the Altaians still practised the custom of impaling sacrificed horses on lances (Wilhelm Radloff, *Aus Sibirien* (Leipzig, 1893), Vol. I, pl. 9; Vol. II, pl. 1). Around 1291 the Dominican missionary Riccoldo da Monte di Croce observed the same custom among the Mongols (Iaroslav Lebedynsky, *Les Scythes* (Errance, 2001), p. 200).
287. Rolle, *Königskurgan Čertomlyk*, Vol. I, pp. 65–67.
288. Herodotus, *Histories* IV, 71.
289. The kurgans on the Sula are, however, more than 200 km away from the former rapids, which today are flooded over (Lebedynsky, *Les Scythes*, pp. 206, 210).
290. Rolle, *Königskurgan Čertomlyk*, Vol. II, part III, p. 58.
291. Ellen Reeder, *Scythian Gold: Treasures from ancient Ukraine* (New York, 1999), p. 33.

292. Herodotus, *Histories*, IV, 17–21.
293. Sergej Skoryj, 'Der Kurgan Perepjaticha', *Hamburger Beiträge zur Archäologie* 18 (1996), pp. 102–105.
294. Herodotus, *Histories* IV, 17f.
295. Reeder, *Scythian Gold*, pp. 32, 94.
296. Vledilen Anochin, 'Die Münzen der skythischen und sarmatischen Könige', *Hamburger Beiträge zur Archäologie* 18 (1996), p. 141. Pericles's visit to Olbia in the 430s BC underscores Olbia's importance for Athens (David Braund and S. Kryzhitskiy, *Classical Olbia & the Scythian World* (London, 2007), pp. 3, 34).
297. Parzinger, *Die Skythen*, p. 14.
298. Rolle, *Gold der Steppe*, p. 79.
299. V. Yu Murzin, 'Key points in Scythian history', in *Scythians and Greeks* (Exeter, 2005), p. 37; Renate Rolle, 'Das Burgwallsystem von Bel'sk (Ukraine): Eine frühe stadtartige Anlage im skythischen Landesinnern', *Hamburger Beiträge zur Archäologie* 18 (1996), pp. 57–84.
300. Renate Rolle, *Totenkult der Skythen* (Berlin, 1979), pp. 160–166; Renate Rolle, *Die Welt der Skythen* (Lucerne, 1980), pp. 135–138.
301. Larenok Pavel and Dally Ortwin, 'Taganrong', in *Das Bosporanische Reich* (Mainz 2002), p. 90; Véronique Schiltz (ed.), *L'or des Amazones* (Paris, 2001), pp. 40–44, 56–59, 102f, 109–126.
302. Strabo, *Geographica*, 2007. XI, 5, 8 (p. 731). See also: Schiltz, *L'or des Amazones*, pp. 47, 143.
303. In light of the complete rejection of Greek gods and religious cults by the Scythians it is out of the question that they worshipped their deities, which were presumably related to the Indo-Iranian culture, under Greek names (Herodotus, *Histories*, IV, 59–62). See also: Andreï Alexeev et al., *Nomades des Steppes* (Paris, 2001), pp. 102–106; Lebedynsky, *Les Scythes*, pp. 178–181; Parzinger, *Die Skythen*, pp. 96f.
304. In Avestan the name 'Api' means water (Véronique Schiltz, *Die Skythen und andere Steppenvölker* (Munich, 1994), p. 184).
305. Yulia Ustinova, 'Snake-limbed and tendril-limbed goddesses in the art and mythology of the Mediterranean and Black Sea', in *Scythians and Greeks* (Exeter, 2005), p. 75.
306. See p. 110.
307. Herodotus, *Histories*, IV, 8–10.
308. See p. 173.
309. Lebedynsky, *Les Scythes*, p. 180.
310. Ibid, pp. 146, 188. In light of the obvious lack of a clergy, interpretations of women's graves with finds of (symbolic) weapons, mirrors and possibly portable altars as 'proof' of 'warrior princesses' and a female priestly caste are pulled out of thin air. For examples of such interpretations see: Jeannine Davis-Kimball, 'Amazons, Princesses and other Women of Status: Females in Eurasian Nomadic Societies', in *Silk Road Art and Archaeology*, Vol. 5 (1997/98), pp. 1–50; Jeannine Davis-Kimball, *Warrior women* (New York, 2002).
311. Herodotus, *Histories*, IV, 67–69.
312. Ibid, 76.
313. Ibid, 78–80.
314. Ibid, 70.
315. Ibid, 66.
316. Ibid, 71–75.
317. These sacrificial animals belonged to the dead and were not consumed at the funeral feast.
318 Rolle, *Königskurgan Čertomlyk*, Vol. I, p. 66. See also: Jurij Boltrik and Elena Fialko, 'Der Oghuz Kurgan: Die Grabanlage eines Skythenkönigs zur Zeit nach Ateas', *Hamburger Beiträge zur Archäologie* 18 (1996), p. 121.
319. Renate Rolle et al. (eds), *Amazonen: Geheimnisvolle Kriegerinnen* (Speyer, 2010), pp. 105, 120, 125.
320. Rolle, *Totenkult der Skythen*, Vol. I, pp. 11f, 155–158. A few scholars propose that 'a large percentage of the Scythian kurgans were plundered some five to twenty-five years after the burials took place' (Rolle, *Gold der Steppe*, p. 182).
321. Boltrik and Fialko, 'Der Oghuz Kurgan', pp. 109, 119; Rolle, *Totenkult der Skythen*, Vol. I, p. 151; Vol. II, p. 98, folding map 11.
322. V. Olkhovsky and G. Evdokimov, *Skifskie izvajanija VII–III vv. do n.e,* (Moscow, 1994); P.N. Schulz, 'Skifskiye izvayanina', in *Khudozhestvennaya kul'tura i arkheologiya antichnogo mira* (Moscow, 1976), pp. 218–231; Telegin and Mallory, *The Anthropomorphic Stelae of the Ukraine*, pp. 68–76; Rolle, *Die Welt der Skythen*, pp. 21–24.
323. Herodotus, *Histories*, IV, 28.
324. Thomas Werner, *Unbekannte Krim*, 1999, p. 22.
325. Herodotus, *Histories*, IV, 103.
326. Jutta Frings (ed.), *Die Thraker: Das goldene Reich des Orpheus* (Mainz, 2004), p.118.
327. Braund and Kryzhitskiy, *Classical Olbia & the Scythian World*, pp. 87, 151–153, 157, 161–164, 169.
328. Fornasier and Böttger, *Das Bosporanische Reich*, p. 4; Frings, *Die Thraker*, p. 119; Herodotus, *Histories*, IV, 80; Alexander Podossinov, 'Am Rande der griechischen Oikumene', in *Das Bosporanische Reich* (Mainz 2002) p. 26f; Vladimir Tolstikov, 'Pantikapaion', in *Das Bosporanische Reich* (Mainz 2002) p. 51.
329. Du Brux Paul, *Oeuvres* (St Petersburg 2010) Vol. I, p. 171, Vol. II, p. 115.
330. Menghin et al., *Im Zeichen des goldenen Greifen*, pp. 276–282; Ellis Minns, *Scythians and Greeks: A survey of ancient history and archaeology on the north coast of the Euxine from the Danube to the Caucasus* (Cambridge, 1913), pp. 194–206; Véronique Schiltz, *Histoire de kourganes: La redécouverte de l'or des Scythes* (Paris, 1991), pp. 60–72.
331. Ekatarina Alexeeva, 'Gorgippia', in *Das Bosporanische Reich* (Mainz 2002) p. 100.
332. Anochin, 'Die Münzen der skythischen und sarmatischen Könige', pp. 146f.
333. P. Foucart, 'Décret de la ville de Chersonésos en l'honneur de Diophantos, général de Mithridate', *Bulletin de correspondance hellénique* 5 (1881), pp. 70–87.
334. Ekatarina Alexeeva, 'Gorgippia', pp. 101f; Alexander Podossinov, 'Am Rande der griechischen Oikumene', in *Das Bosporanische Reich* (Mainz 2002) p. 31.
335. Ekatarina Alexeeva, 'Gorgippia', pp. 108, 111; Burkhard Böttger, Jochen Fornasier and Tatjana Arseneva, 'Tanais am Don', in *Das Bosporanische Reich* (Mainz 2002) p. 82; Alexander Podossinov, *Am Rande der griechischen Oikumene*, pp. 32–34, 37; Rolle, *Gold der Steppe*, p. 211.
336. Earlier, the Hittites had also understood the location of a king's afterlife as a kind of heavenly pasture. Boltrik and Fialko, 'Der Oghuz Kurgan', p. 112; Rolle, *Totenkult der Skythen*, Vol. I, p. 42; Rolle, *Die Welt der Skythen*, p. 34.
337. The following section is a chronological overview of kings and events that have already been mentioned, so we will forgo reference to sources and rely on the index, as long as no new facts are involved. See also: Andreï Alexeev, 'Scythian kings and "royal" burial-mounds of the fifth and fourth centuries BC', in *Scythians and Greeks* (Exeter, 2005), pp. 39–55; Herodotus, *Histories*, IV, 4.76, 78.
338. Herodotus, *Histories*, VI, 76.
339. Ibid, 84.
340. Herodotus, *Histories*, IV, 81.
341. David Anthony, *The Horse, the Wheel and Language: How Bronze-Age riders from the Eurasian Steppes shaped the modern world* (Princeton, 2007), pp. 260f; Frings, *Die Thraker*, pp. 15f, 31, 95.
342. Herodotus, *Histories*, IV, 78.
343. Ibid, IV, 80.
344. More precisely, the son of the president of the imperial archaeological commission Bobrinskoï found the comb at the end of the excavation (Schiltz, *Histoires de kourganes*, p. 124).
345. Menghin et al., *Im Zeichen des goldenen Greifen*, p. 246f; Schiltz, *Histoires de kourganes*, p. 93.
346. Contrary to the view encountered in the earlier literature that an armed woman was the main person buried in the central chamber of Solocha, it is in fact a man (Menghin et al., *Im Zeichen des goldenen Greifen*, p. 250).
347. Alexeev et al., *Nomades des Steppes*, pp. 130f; 'Some problems in the study of the chronology of the ancient nomadic cultures', p. 15; Menghin et al., *Im Zeichen des goldenen Greifen*, pp. 250f.
348. It remains debated whether Atheas was a chief king or a western viceroy.
349. Anochin, 'Die Münzen der skythischen und sarmatischen Könige', pp. 145f, plate 19.3.
350. Ibid, pp. 144–146; Lebedynsky, *Les Scythes*, pp. 44f.
351. Arrian, *The Campaigns of Alexander* (London, 1971), p. 227; Boltrik and Fialko, 'Der Oghuz Kurgan', p. 129. See also: Alexeev, 'Scythian kings and 'royal' burial-mounds', p. 47.
352. The number of anonymous kings is debated (Alexeev, 'Scythian kings and "royal" burial-mounds', pp. 40, 44f).
353. E.V. Cernenko et al., *The Scythians 700–300 BC.* (London, 1983), pp. 31f; Rolle, *Königskurgan Čertomlyk*, Vol. I, pp. 172–175.
354. M. Rostovtzeff, *Iranians and Greeks in South Russia* (Oxford, 1922), pp. 98, 147.
355. A.N. Shcheglov and V.I. Katz, 'A fourth-century BC Royal Kurgan in the Crimea', *Metropolitan Museum Journal* 26 (1991), p. 117.
356. P.N. Schultz and V.A. Golovkina, 'Neapolis des Scythes', in *Ourartou, Neapolis des Scythes, Kharezm* (Paris, 1954), pp. 67–103; C.A. Tur, *Neapol Skyfsji*, Universum, 2011; Juri Zaytsev, 'Skilur and his Kingdom', in *Ancient Civilisations from Scythia to Siberia* (Leiden), Vol. 7, No. 3–4, 2001, pp. 239–271; *The Scythian Neapolis (2nd century BC to 3rd century AD)*, 2004; 'Scythian Neapolis – the Capital of the Kingdom of Skiluros', in Friederike Fless and Mikhail Treister, *Bilder und Objekte als Träger kultureller Identität und interkultureller Kommunikation im Schwarzmeergebiet* (Rahden 2005), pp. 141–144.

357. Strabo, *Geographica*, 2007. VII, 3, 17 (p. 430).
358. Schultz and Golovkina, 'Neapolis des Scythes', pp. 95f. The analogy was also known to the Sogdians, Iranians, Mongols and Aesop (Christoph Baumer, *Traces in the Desert: Journeys of Discovery across Central Asia* (London, 2008), p. 198, part II, note 4).
359. Valery Olkhovsky, *Scythian Culture in the Crimea*, 1995, p. 76; Schultz and Golovkina, 'Neapolis des Scythes', pp. 83–96; Rolle, *Die Welt der Skythen*, pp. 146f.
360. The Roman legate Silvanus established a naval base for the Ravenna fleet at Charaks, east of Chersonesos (Werner, *Unbekannte Krim*, p. 45).
361. Tur, *Neapol Skyfsji*, pp. 10–14; Zaytsev, *The Scythian Neapolis*, pp. 37–39.
362. Boris Piotrovsky et al., *L'art scythe* (Leningrad, 1986), pl. 184–187.
363. Both objects can be seen in: Rolle, *Königskurgan Čertomlyk*, pl. 19–15. It is occasionally argued that it is not episodes from Achilles's life portrayed on the gorytos but rather scenes from the lives of Scythian heroes (Menghin et al., *Im Zeichen des goldenen Greifen*, pp. 243f).
364. Jacobson, *The Art of the Scythians*, p. 225. Rolle; *Königskurgan Čertomlyk*, pp. 137ff. A few scholars propose that several moulds were combined with one another (Reeder, *Scythian Gold*, p. 71). The gorytos in the alleged grave of Phillip II was presumably war booty. The third, slightly different sword sheath is held by the Metropolitan Museum of Art, New York; it presumably came from a kurgan in north-western Crimea (Shcheglov and Katz, 'A fourth-century BC Royal Kurgan', pp. 97–122).
365. Arrian, *Periplus Ponti Euxini*, 20–23.
366. Shcheglov and Katz, 'A fourth-century BC Royal Kurgan', pp. 115f.
367. Schultz and Golovkina, 'Neapolis des Scythes', pp. 83–98.
368. Patric-Alexander Kreuz, *Norm und Sonderweg: Grabstelen klassischer und frühhellenistischer Zeit aus den Städten des Bosporanischen Reichs und das Relief aus dem Drei-Brüder-Kurgan bei Nymphaion*, (Rahden, 2005) pp. 43–52; *Das Relief aus dem Drei-Brüder-Kurgan* (Bonn, Simferopol 2008) pp. 131–140; E.A. Savostina, 'Tema nadgrobnoj stelu iz Trechbratnego kurgana v kontekste antičnogo mirfa', in *Istoriko-archeologičeskij almanach 1* (Armarir, Moskva 1995), pp. 110–119; Mikhail Treister, *Die Drei-Brüder-Kurgane* (Bonn, Simferopol 2008).
369. Most of these grave paintings had already been destroyed by the end of the nineteenth century (M. Rostovtzeff, *La peinture décorative antique en Russie méridionale* (Paris, 1913–1914; 2004)).
370. Menghin et al., *Im Zeichen des goldenen Greifen*, pp. 306–323; Parzinger, *Die Skythen*, p. 199ff.
371. Wilfried Seipel (ed.), *Gold der Steppe* (Leoben, 2009), p. 105.
372. Herodotus, *Histories*, IV, 21, 119f.
373. Ibid, 110–117.
374. Zainolla Samashev, *Treasures from the Ustyurt and Mangystau* (Almaty, 2007), pp. 186–203, 208.
375. Samashev, *Treasures from the Ustyurt and Mangystau*, pp. 213–215, 232–259. See also: V. Olkhovsky, 'Baité: Un ensemble culturel', in *Les Scythes* (1994), pp. 54–57; V. Olkhovsky, 'Ancient Sanctuaries of the Aral and Caspian Regions', in *Kurgans, Ritual Sites and Settlements* (2000), pp. 33–42.
376. The calibrated radiocarbon dates of 832–774 BC for kurgan 1 of Filippovka reported by Alekseev et al. are improbable, since Achaemenid art objects from the fifth century BC were found in kurgan 1. Alexeev, 'Some problems in the study of the chronology of the ancient nomadic cultures of Eurasia', p. 148; Joan Aruz (ed.), *The Golden Deer of Eurasia: Scythian and Sarmatian treasures from the Russian steppes* (New York, 2000), p. 61, pl. 93–95; Leonid T. Yablonsky, 'New excavations of the early nomadic burial ground at Filippovka (Southern Ural Region, Russia)', in *American Journal of Archaeology*, Vol. 114, Jan. 2010, pp. 129, 131, 141f.
377. It is difficult to estimate the extent to which Sauromatian culture is related to the Sauromatians or Issedones of Herodotus.
378. Aruz, *The Golden Deer of Eurasia*, p. 74. The necropolis consits of 29 kurgans of which 17 were excavated in 1986–90. While 9 additional kurgans were investigated 2004–2007, severe looting, even with the use of heavy equipment, occurred between both campaigns and also in 2005. Yablonsky, 'New excavations of the early nomadic burial ground at Filippovka (Southern Ural Region, Russia)', pp. 129, 132ff.
379. Aruz, *The Golden Deer of Eurasia*, pl. 1–4, 84–91.
380. Yablonsky, 'New excavations of the early nomadic burial ground at Filippovka (Southern Ural Region, Russia)', pp. 136f, 142; 'L'épée dorée de Filippovka', in *Archéologia* (Editions Faton, Dijon, no. 494, 2011), pp. 50ff.
381. Ludmila Koryakova and Andrej Epimakkhov, *The Urals and Western Siberia in the Bronze and Iron Ages* (Cambridge, 2007), p. 244.
382. R. Brzezinski and M. Mielczarek, *The Sarmatians 600 BC – AD 450* (London, 2002), p. 7; J. Harmatta, *Studies in the History and Language of the Sarmatians* (Szeged, 1979), pp. 10, 36; Iaroslav Lebedynsky, *Les Sarmates* (Errance, 2002), p. 39.
383. In the literature the Ixomates are classified as either Maeotian or Sauromatian (Lebedynsky, *Les Sarmates*, p. 33).
384. The term Maeotae is a collective name for native tribes of the Kuban, who adopted cultural influences from the Cimmerians; it is uncertain whether they were Iranian-speaking.
385. Alexeeva, 'Gorgippia', p. 96; Schiltz, *L'or des Amazones*, pp. 54f.
386. Schiltz, *L'or des Amazones*, p. 58.
387. Braund and Kryzhitskiy, *Classical Olbia & the Scythian World*, p. 166; Vladimir Kouznetsov and Iaroslav Lebedynsky, *Les Alains*, (Errance, 2005), p. 51; Schiltz, *L'or des Amazones*, pp. 68ff.
388. Aleksandr Medvedev, *Hügelgräber und befestigte Siedlungen der sarmatischen Zeit am oberen Don*, 2007, pp. 260, 272, 276.
389. Seipel, *Gold der Steppe*, p. 85
390. Lebedynsky, *Les Sarmates*, pp. 78f, 196.
391. Schiltz, *L'or des Amazones*, pp. 219f.
392. Lebedynsky, *Les Sarmates*, pp. 111f; Seipel, *Gold der Steppe*, p. 64. The burials of Kobiakovo and Khokhlatch, as well as the square burial chambers, are sometimes attributed to the Alans instead of the Aorsi (Schiltz, *L'or des Amazones*, p. 70).
393. Rostovtzeff, *Iranians and Greeks in South Russia*, pp. 43–46; *The Animal Style in South Russia and China*, 1929, pp. 124–126, 178–190.
394. Lebedynsky, *Les Sarmates*, pp. 118f; *De l'Épée Scythe au Sabre Mongol*, pp. 84–86, 98. See here p. 266.
395. According to Zenobius (first half of second century AD) the Siraces already elected as their king the man with the longest skull (Lebedynsky, *Les Sarmates*, pp. 18f, 113ff, 221).
396. Ssu-ma Ch'ien, *Shih chi*, Book 123, 1971, Vol. II, p. 267.
397. John Hill, *Through the Jade Gate to Rome. An annotated translation of the Chronicle on the 'Western regions' in the Hou Hanshu*, 2009, p. 33. It is unclear whether a single principality was called 'Alanliao' or if two principalities called Alan and Liao are meant. The chronicle *Weilüe*, written between 239 and 265 AD and quoted in 429, states only that 'Yancai' changed its name to 'Alan' (Ibid, pp. 380–391).
398. Pan Ku, *The History of the Former Han Dynasty, Vol. II* (Baltimore, 1944), p. 331; Sima Guang, *Zizhi tongjian* (Bloomington, 2009), pp. 375–380.
399. Ann Hyland, *Training the Roman Cavalry*, 1993, pp. 5, 80–83, 93; Souza, *The ancient world at war*, pp. 200f.
400. Schiltz, *L'or des Amazones*, p. 73.
401. Harmatta, *Studies in the History and Language of the Sarmatians*, p. 19.
402. Brzezinski and Mielczarek, *The Sarmatians 600 BC – AD 450*, pp. 5, 9; Lebedynsky, *Les Sarmates*, pp. 50–55, 248–250.
403. Alexeeva, 'Gorgippia', p. 111. Podossinov, 'Am Rande der griechischen Oikumene', p. 37. Kouznetsov and Lebedynsky, *Les Alains*, p. 58; Lebedynsky, *Les Sarmates*, pp. 50f, 249.
404. See Vol. II.
405. Lebedynsky, *Les Sarmates*, pp. 63–65, 232f; Kouznetsov and Lebedynsky, *Les Alains*, pp. 58f, 90–96; Souza, *The ancient world at war*, pp. 203–207.
406. Kouznetsov and Lebedynsky, *Les Alains*, pp. 101–105, 115.
407. Ibid, pp. 120f.
408. Lebedynsky, *Les Sarmates*, pp. 167–70.
409. Herodotus, *Histories*, I, 215. One of the best preserved remains of such iron armour from the third century BC was found at Aï Khanum in northern Afghanistan (Frederik Hiebert and Pierre Cambon, *Afghanistan, Crossroads of the Ancient World* (London 2011) p. 102).
410. Lebedynsky, *Les Sarmates*, p. 163.
411. Ibid, p. 164.
412. An alternative etymology sees as the root the Middle Persian word *griwban*, which means essentially 'iron neck-guard' (Ann Hyland, *Training the Roman Cavalry: From Arrian's Ars Tactica* (London, 1993), pp. 85, 87). Valerii Nikonorov, 'Cataphracti, Catafractarii and Clibanarii: Another look at the old problem of their identifications', in: *Military Archaeology* (St. Peterburg, 1998), p. 132.
413. Matthias Pfaffenbichler, *Spangenhelme*, 2007, pp. 245, 249.
414. Brzezinski and Mielczarek, *The Sarmatians 600 BC – AD 450*, pp. 16, 18, 23f; Lebedynsky, *Les Sarmates*, pp. 90, 105, 108; *De l'Épée Scythe au Sabre Mongol*, pp. 50f, 64; Souza, *The ancient world at war*, p. 177.
415. Lebedynsky, *Les Sarmates*, p. 175; Souza, *The ancient world at war*, p. 225.

416. Herodotus, *Histories*, IV, 117.
417. Jochen Fornasier, *Amazonen: Frauen, Kämpferinnen und Städtegründerinnen* (Mainz, 2007), pp. 37ff; Renate Rolle, 'Amazonen in der archäologischen Realität', in *Kleist-Jahrbuch 1986* (Berlin, 1986), pp. 49f; *Amazonen*, pp. 17, 27, 39.
418. Herodotus, *Histories*, IV, 119.
419. Fornasier, *Amazonen*, pp. 54f; Rolle, *Amazonen*, pp. 40–42, 93.
420. Rolle, *Amazonen*, pp. 23, 154, 174.
421. Davis-Kimball, *Warrior women*, pp. 57, 54; Lebedynsky, *Les Scythes*, pp. 53f, 151; *Les Sarmates*, pp. 155ff; *Les Saces*, 2006, p. 178; Rolle, *Die Welt der Skythen*, pp. 97f; *Amazonen*, pp. 103, 119f.
422. Kouznetsov and Lebedynsky, *Les Alains*, pp. 130, 174.
423. Rolle, *Amazonen*, pp. 120f, 125, 156f.
424. Lebedynsky, *Les Scythes*, p. 151; Rolle, *Totenkult der Skythen*, Vol. I, p. 134. The 'Princess of Kobiakovo', who was killed by an arrow, was also given no ceremonial weapons as grave gifts, only an iron axe.
425. Schiltz, *L'or des Amazones*, p. 168.
426. Lebedynsky, *Les Sarmates*, pp. 78–80, 88.
427. Hyland, *Training the Roman Cavalry*, pp. 78–83, 90; Lebedynsky, *De l'Épée Scythe au Sabre Mongol*, p. 112.
428. Brzezinski and Mielczarek, *The Sarmatians 600 BC – AD 450*, pp. 19, 34; Lebedynsky, *De l'Épée Scythe au Sabre Mongol*, pp. 63f.
429. Maurice, Byzantine Emperor, *Strategikon* (Philadelphia, 1984), XI, 2 (p. 117).
430. Ibid, p. 118.
431. Maurice, Byzantine Emperor, *Strategikon*, I, 2 (p. 13).
432. See photo p. 231.
433. Joan Aruz (ed.), *The Golden Deer of Eurasia: Perspectives on the Steppe Nomads of the Ancient World* (New York, 2006), pp. 196, 199, 206f; Jean-Yves Cozan, Pierre Amandry and Véronique Shiltz, *L'Or des Sarmates: Nomades des steppes dans l'Antiquité* (1995), pp. 18, 30; Schiltz, *L'or des Amazones*, p. 143.
434. Cozan, Amandry and Schiltz, *L'Or des Sarmates*, pp. 74–79; Schiltz, *L'or des Amazones*, pp. 214, 218; Seipel, *Gold der Steppe*, pp. 74–83. Similar, somewhat later daggers were found in Gorgippia, Kuban, Kossika on the Volga and in Mskheta, Georgia. W.A. Nabatschikow, *Gold und Kunsthandwerk vom antiken Kuban* (Stuttgart, 1989), pl. 46; Schiltz, *L'or des Amazones*, p. 218.
435. An attribution of the necropolis to the Yuezhi, as proposed by its discoverer Sarianidi, is improbable, on the basis of the Alano-Sarmatian-style toreutics. Claude Rapin, 'Nomads and the shaping of Central Asia', in *After Alexander: Central Asia before Islam* (London, 2007), pp. 58, 62; Sarianidi, *The Golden Hoard of Bactria*, p. 18. See here p. 293.
436. Véronique Schiltz, 'Notule sur un ours énigmatique', in *Afghanistan* (2005), pp. 296f. See also: Sarianidi, *The Golden Hoard of Bactria*, pp. 212–219; Seipel, *Gold der Steppe*, pp. 296f.
437. Cozan, Amandry and Schiltz, *L'Or des Sarmates*, pp. 6, 72f; Schiltz, *L'or des Amazones*, pp. 224–226.
438. Sarianidi, *The Golden Hoard of Bactria*, pp. 98–103, 220–223. See here photo p. 289, p. 292.
439. K.A. Akishev, *Ancient gold of Kazakhstan* (Almaty, 1983), pp. 41f, 158–169; John Boardman, 'Central Asia: West and East', in *After Alexander* (2007), pp. 14–21; M. Rostovtzeff, *The Animal Style in South Russia and China* (Princeton, 1929), pp. 33, 56; James Watt, 'The legacy of Nomadic Art in China and Eastern Central Asia', in *Nomadic Art of the Eastern Eurasian Steppes* (New York/New Haven, 2002), p. 202; Y.A. Zadneprovskiy, 'The nomads of Northern Central Asia after the invasion of Alexander', in *History of civilizations of Central Asia*, Vol. II, pp. 461f.
440. Leskovar and Zingerle, *Goldener Horizont*, p. 126; Rolle, *Gold der Steppe*, pp. 219–226.
441. Phillips, *The Royal Hordes*, pp. 95–98.
442. Seipel, *Gold der Steppe*, pp. 70ff, 241ff.
443. Rostovtzeff, *Iranians and Greeks in South Russia*, pp. 129ff; Seipel, *Gold der Steppe*, pp. 221–229.
444. Rostovtzeff, *Iranians and Greeks in South Russia*, pp. 14, 124, 190; *The Animal Style in South Russia and China*, pp. 43–46. Whether a distant connection exists between the animal style and genres of medieval Western European art such as the Irish book arts or Romanesque capitals remains debated (Andreï Alexeev, *Trésors des Steppes* (Hauterive, 2006), p. 124). In the sixth to ninth centuries AD the *Permian animal style* developed along the Kama, a tributary of the Volga. The Permian style evinces no connection to the Sarmatian animal style. See Vol. II.

VIII. Greeks in Central Asia

1. Curtius Rufus, *The History of Alexander*, VIII, 8, 11–12
2. The last Greco-Bactrian king north of the Hindu Kush was Heliocles I (r. *ca.* 145–130 BC), and the last Indo-Greek king south of the Hindu Kush was Strato II (r. *ca.* 25 BC–10 AD). Osmund Bopearachchi et al., *De l'Indus à l'Oxus* (Lattes, 2003), pp. 98, 130f, 139; Frank Holt, *Thundering Zeus: The making of Hellenistic Bactria* (Berkeley, 1999), p. 135; H. Sidky, *The Greek Kingdom of Bactria: From Alexander to Eucratides the Great* (Lanham, 2000), pp. 192, 226–228.
3. Curtius Rufus, *The History of Alexander*, VII, 5, 32–35.
4. Nasiba Baimatowa, *5000 Jahre Architektur in Mittelasien: Lehmziegelgewölbe vom 4./3. Jt. v.Chr. bis zum Ende des 8. Jhs. n.Chr* (Mainz, 2008), pp. 167–172; Anatoli Sagdullaev and Shakir Pidaev, 'L'âge du Fer en Bactriane', in *La Bactriane de Cyrus à Timour* (Quétigny, 1999), pp. 26f.
5. Claude Rapin, Muxammedzon Isamiddinov and Mutallib Khasanov, 'La tombe d'une princesse nomade à Koktepe près de Samarkand', *Académie des inscriptions et belles-lettres* 145.1 (2001), p. 76; Claude Rapin, Aymon Baud et al., *Les recherches sur la région der Portes de Fer de Sogdiane* (Samarkand, 2006), pp. 48–59.
6. Arrian, *The Campaigns of Alexander* (London, 1971), p. 160.
7. Ibid, pp. 182ff; Sidky, *The Greek Kingdom of Bactria*, pp. 26–29, 39.
8. Arrian, *The Campaigns of Alexander*, pp. 191–193.
9. Claude Rapin, 'L'Afghanistan et l'Asie Centrale dans la géographie mythique des historiens d'Alexandre', in *Afghanistan: Ancien carrefour entre l'est et l'ouest* (Turnhout, 2005), pp. 147–167; Sidky, *The Greek Kingdom of Bactria*, pp. 39–47.
10. Georg Renner and Christa Selic, *Abseits der großen Minarette* (Leipzig, 1982), p. 115.
11. John Wood, *A journey to the source of the River Oxus* (London, 1872), p. 274.
12. Curtius Rufus, *The History of Alexander*, VII, 4, 27–29. On the logistical issues see: Donald Engels, *Alexander the Great and the Logistics of the Macedonian Army*, 1978.
13. Curtius Rufus, *The History of Alexander*, VII, 5, 17f.
14. Arrian, *The Campaigns of Alexander*, pp. 197f; Curtius Rufus, *The History of Alexander*, VII, 5, 23–43.
15. Curtius Rufus, *The History of Alexander*, VII, 6, 27.
16. See pp. 207f.
17. Curtius Rufus, *The History of Alexander*, VII, 9, 22.
18. Arrian, *The Campaigns of Alexander*, pp. 201–226; Curtius Rufus, *The History of Alexander*, VII, 6, 13–9, 22.
19. For example, at Djandavlat, Dilbergine and Talashkan Tepe. Pierre Leriche, 'Bactria: Land of thousand cities', in *After Alexander* (2007), p. 128; Shakir Pidaev and Pierre Leriche, 'Quelques villes moyennes de Bactriane', in *La Bactriane de Cyrus à Timour* (Quétigny, 1999), pp. 52–55.
20. Annette Juliano and Judith Lerner (eds), *Monks and Merchants. Silk Road treasures from Northwest China*, 2001, p. 315, n. 2. De la Vaissière questions this hypothesis and dates the beginning of the Sogdian trade with China to the first century BC (Étienne de la Vaissière, *Sogdian Traders* (Leiden 2005) pp. 22f, 38–41).
21. While Soviet research consistently identified the ancient Oxus with the Vakhsh, western scholarship of the twentieth century mostly saw the Panj as the Oxus. Today the Soviet interpretation has prevailed. Bopearachchi et al., *De l'Indus à l'Oxus*, p. 115. Frantz Grenet and Claude Rapin, 'Alexander, Aï Khanum, Termez: Remarks on the Spring Campaign of 328', *Bulletin of the Asia Institute* 12 (1998), p. 80; Rapin, 'L'Afghanistan et l'Asie Centrale dans la géographie mythique', pp. 144.
22. Arrian, *The Campaigns of Alexander*, pp. 228f; Curtius Rufus, *The History of Alexander*, VII, 10, 13–16. The city of Margiana mentioned here cannot, as so often assumed, be identified with the city of Merv, more than 600 km further west, but rather should be sought near Termez. Such a far march away from the nucleus of Spitames' revolt made no military sense and the six fortified cities near 'Margiana' mentioned by Curtius Rufus as being 'all...founded on high hills', 'spaced only a short distance apart' (VII, 10) cannot be located near Merv as its environment is flat. Grenet and Rapin believe that 'Margiana' is a spelling mistake and should read 'Marginia'. Grenet and Rapin, 'Alexander, Aï Khanum, Termez,' pp. 79–85; Rapin, 'L'Afghanistan et l'Asie Centrale dans la géographie mythique', p. 167.
23. http://claude.rapin.free.fr/3GeogrPF1_2002.htm Rapin, Baud et al., *Les recherches sur la région der Portes de Fer de Sogdiane, p. 49.*
24. Leriche and Rtveladze identify Alexandria Oxeiana with Kampyr Tepe. Leriche, 'Bactria: Land of thousand cities,' (2007) p. 133. Edvard Rtveladze, 'Kampyr Tepe-Pandokheïon', in *La Bactriane de Cyrus à Timour* (Quétigny, 1999),

pp. 56f; Edvard Rtveladze, 'Kampyr Tepe-Pandokheïon – Alexandria Oxiana', in *Alexander der Große und die Öffnung der Welt: Asiens Kulturen im Wandel* (Mannheim, 2009), pp. 169–175.

25. Arrian, The Campaigns of Alexander, pp. 213–17, 227–230; Curtius Rufus, The History of Alexander, VIII, 1–3.
26. On the identification of the most important mountain fortresses that are described differently by Arrian and Curtius Rufus, see: Rapin, 'L'Afghanistan et l'Asie Centrale dans la géographie mythique', pp. 157f; Rapin, Baud et al., *Les recherches sur la région des Portes de Fer de Sogdiane, pp. 53–56. Route d'Alexandre le Grand et toponymie de la Bactriane-Sogdiane.* http://claude.rapin.free.fr/4GCarte_Asie_centrale.html
27. Curtius Rufus, *The History of Alexander*, VIII, 4, 25.
28. Sidky, *The Greek Kingdom of Bactria*, p. 77.
29. Ibid, pp. 90–93.
30. Ibid, pp. 92–101.
31. A.D.H. Bivar, 'The history of Eastern Iran', in *Cambridge History of Iran*, Vol. 3(1) (Cambridge University Press, Cambridge 1983), p. 185.
32. A. Dani, 'Alexander and his successors in Central Asia', in *History of civilizations of Central Asia*, Vol. II (Paris, 1994), p. 89; Sidky, *The Greek Kingdom of Bactria*, pp. 106f.
33. The Seleucid calculation of time, often encountered in the works of classical authors, begins with Seleucus'sinvasion of Babylon, according to the Macedonian calendar on 1 October 312 BC and according to the Babylonian calendar on 1 April 311 BC (Sven Hansen et al. (eds), *Alexander der Große und die Öffnung der Welt: Asiens Kulturen im Wandel* (Mannheim, 2009), p. 116).
34. Dani, 'Alexander and his successors in Central Asia', pp. 89–90; Sidky, *The Greek Kingdom of Bactria*, pp. 103–122.
35. Hiebert, Cambon, *Afghanistan, Crossroads of the Ancient World*, (2011) pp. 96f.
36. See p. 210.
37. Richard Frye, *The heritage of Central Asia: From Antiquity to the Turkish Expansion* (Princeton, 1996), pp. 104–107; Holt, *Thundering Zeus*, pp. 26, 36f; Vadim M. Masson, *Das Land der tausend Städte: Die Wiederentdeckung der ältesten Kulturgebiete in Mittelasien* (Munich, 1982), p. 16; Strabo, *Geographica* (Wiesbaden, 2007), XV, 1, 3.
38. Strabo, *Geographica*, II, 1, 15.
39. B. Lyonnet, 'Les Grecs, les nomades et l'indépendance de la Sogdiane', *Bulletin of the Asia Institute* 12 (1998), p. 152.
40. Boris Litvinskij, *La civilisation de l'Asie centrale antique* (Espelkamp, 1998), p. 50.
41. On sources see Holt, *Thundering Zeus*, pp. 55–60, 79f, 174–184. Modern forgers, who invent new types of coins and create their own minting equipment, make the work of historians even more difficult. For an overview of Greco-Bactrian coins, see: Osmund Bopearachchi, 'Les successeurs d'Alexandre le Grand en Asie centrale et en Inde: les Gréco-Bactriens', in *De l'Indus à l'Oxus*, pp. 81–108; Osmund Bopearachchi, 'Indo-Grecs, Indo-Scythes, Indo-Parthes', in *De l'Indus à l'Oxus*, pp. 129–168; Joe Cribb, 'The Greek kingdom of Bactria, its coinage and its collapse', in *Afghanistan: Ancien carrefour entre l'est et l'ouest*, pp. 207–225; Percy Gardner, *The coins of the Greek and Scythic Kings of Bactria and India in the British Museum* (Chicago, 1966); Holt, *Thundering Zeus*; A.K. Narain, *The Indo-Greeks* (Delhi, 1953, 2003), pp. 307–349; Hatto H. Schmitt and Ernst Vogt (eds), *Lexikon des Hellenismus* (Wiesbaden, 2005), pp. 185–190; R.B. Whitehead, *Catalogue of coins in the Panjab Museum* (Varanasi, 1914, 1971).
42. Holt, *Thundering Zeus*, p. 125.
43. Ibid, pp. 61, 64, 99; Sidky, *The Greek Kingdom of Bactria*, pp. 149–150. For the Parthian Empire see Vol. II. The Chinese name for Parthia, *Anxi*, is presumably derived from Arsaces' name (Iaroslav Lebedynsky, *Les Saces* (Errance, 2006), p. 54).
44. Holt believes, however, that Diodotus II entered into the alliance with Arsaces not because of the Seleucid threat but rather in light of the impending rebellion of Euthydemos. Holt, *Thundering Zeus*, pp. 62ff, 105; Sidky, *The Greek Kingdom of Bactria*, pp. 151f.
45. Holt, *Thundering Zeus*, pp. 43, 54.
46. French archaeologists searched in vain for Hellenistic remains in Balkh in 1924–25 and in the 1950s, but in 2002 Greek capitals and plinths appeared in the bazaar of Balkh.
47. Holt, *Thundering Zeus*, 1999, pp. 127–130, 182; Sidky, *The Greek Kingdom of Bactria*, pp. 167f, 171–174.
48. John Gardiner-Garden, *Apollodoros of Artemita and the Central Asian Skythians* (Bloomington, Ind., 1987), pp. 23, 29; Sidky, *The Greek Kingdom of Bactria*, p. 176; W.W. Tarn, *The Greeks in Bactria & India* (Chicago, 1938, 1951, 1997), pp. 83–87.
49. Richard Salomon, 'The Indo-Greek era of 186/5 BC in a Buddhist reliquary inscription', in *Afghanistan: Ancien carrefour entre l'est et l'ouest*, pp. 365, 370. Joe Cribb, however, dates the start of the Indo-Greek period to the year 174 BC (Cribb, 'The Greek kingdom of Bactria, its coinage and its collapse', p. 214).
50. Craig Benjamin, *The Yuezhi: Origin, Migration and the Conquest of Northern Bactria* (Turnhout, 2007), pp. 178f; Sidky, *The Greek Kingdom of Bactria*, pp. 199, 208–213.
51. Tarn, *The Greeks in Bactria & India*, pp. 196f.
52. Sidky, *The Greek Kingdom of Bactria*, pp. 199, 209, 215.
53. Claude Rapin, 'La Sogdiane d'Alexandre le Grand aux derniers Gréco-Bactriens', in *Samarcande* (Quétigny, 2010), p. 31.
54. For Menandros see Vol. II. Benjamin, *The Yuezhi*, p. 179; Sidky, *The Greek Kingdom of Bactria*, p. 216.
55. Masson, *Das Land der tausend Städte*, p. 148; Sidky, *The Greek Kingdom of Bactria*, p. 221. A first attack of the Parthians on the province of Aria may have happened as early as the 160s BC. Phraates II (r. 138–129/28 BC) was the first to have coins minted in Merv (V. Gaïbov and G. Kochelenko, 'La Margiane', in *Les Parthes* (Quétigny, 2002), p. 50).
56. Sidky, *The Greek Kingdom of Bactria*, p. 221. In another place, however, Justin attributes the death of Eucratides to the victorious Parthians (Tarn, *The Greeks in Bactria & India*, pp. 219f).
57. Narain, *The Indo-Greeks*, pp. 88–90.
58. Sidky, *The Greek Kingdom of Bactria*, pp. 225f. Sidky gives 160 BC as the death date of Eucratides (Tarn, *The Greeks in Bactria & India*, pp. 220–222).
59. For an overview of various chronologies of kings, see: Cribb, 'The Greek kingdom of Bactria, its coinage and its collapse', p. 216; Holt, *Thundering Zeus*, 25.
60. Cribb, 'The Greek kingdom of Bactria, its coinage and its collapse', p. 212f.
61. Benjamin, *The Yuezhi*, pp. 64–74. John Hill lists in his book *Through the Jade Gate to Rome: An annotated translation of the Chronicle on the 'Western regions' in the Hou Hanshu* (Australia, 2009) on pp. 312–314 the same three Xiongnu victories over the Yuezhi, but on p. 577 he adds a fourth one in '166 BCE at the latest'.
62. A.F.P. Hulsewé and M.A.N. Loewe, *China in Central Asia. The Early Stage: 125 BC – AD 23. An Annotated Translation of Chapters 61 and 96 of the History of the Former Han Dynasty* (Leiden 1979) 96A 10B.
63. Hulsewé and Loewe, *China in Central Asia*, 96B 1B. It remains unclear if the Chinese term *Sai wang* is to be understood literally as 'king of the Sai' or if it names a tribe called Royal Sai.
64. Hulsewé and Loewe, *China in Central Asia*, 96A 10B.
65. Benjamin, *The Yuezhi*, pp. 110f; I.V. Piankov, 'The Ethnic History of the Sakas', in *Bulletin of the Asia Institute*, Vol. 8 (Bloomfield Hills 1996) p. 38.
66. Benjamin, *The Yuezhi*, pp. 114f.
67. For the conflict between the Xiongnu and the Yuezhi see Vol. II, chapter I and Benjamin, *The Yuezhi*, pp. 48–151.
68. Gardiner-Garden, *Apollodoros of Artemita and the Central Asian Skythians*, pp. 34, 57, 60; G.A. Koshelenko and V.N. Pilipko, 'Parthia', in *History of civilizations of Central Asia*, Vol. II (Paris, 1994), p. 132.
69. Benjamin, *The Yuezhi*, pp. 179–189; Lyonnet, 'Les Grecs, les nomades et l'indépendance de la Sogdiane', 143. The last inscription found in Aï Khanum dates to the year 147 BC (Pierre Leriche, 'Aï Khanoum', in *La Bactriane de Cyrus à Timour*, p. 39).
70. Ssu-ma Ch'ien, *Shih chi*, Book 123 (New York, 1971), Vol. II, p. 269.
71. Boris Staviskij, *Kunst der Kuschan* (Leipzig, 1979), p. 60.
72. Paul Bernard, 'The Greek kingdoms of Central Asia', in *History of civilizations of Central Asia*, Vol. II, p. 103.
73. The most important sources for Tillya Tepe are: Pierre Cambon, Jean-François Jarrige et al., *Afghanistan, les trésors retrouvés: Collections du musée national de Kaboul* (Paris, 2006); Pierre Cambon, *Hidden Afghanistan* (2007); Viktor Sarianidi, *The Golden Hoard of Bactria: From the Tillya-tepe Excavations in Northern Afghanistan* (New York, 1985); Viktor Sarianidi, 'The golden hoard of Bactria', *National Geographic* 177.3 (1990).
74. Sarianidi, *The Golden Hoard of Bactria*, p. 16; 'The golden hoard of Bactria,' p.65.
75. Sarianidi, *The Golden Hoard of Bactria*, pp. 19–55. See also: Cambon, *Hidden Afghanistan*, pp. 155–227.
76. Referring to some objects we follow the dates given in the exhibition at the British Museum rather than those in the catalogues.
77. See p. 268, photo p. 291.
78. Cambon, *Hidden Afghanistan*, p. 138.
79. Jean-Paul Desroches et al., *Mongolie, le premier empire des steppes* (Paris, 2003), pp. 112, 120, 124, 130f.

80. Markus Mode, *Hunnen, Sogder und das Erbe Alexanders in Mittelasien* (2008), p. 106.
81. Cambon, *Hidden Afghanistan*, p. 206.
82. A Chinese mirror and three incense holders made of clay were also found in the grave (Rapin et al., 'La tombe d'une princesse nomade', pp. 42ff, 48–50, 61).
83. A few corpses with coins placed in their mouths were also discovered in the Bactrian cemeteries of Tulkhar and Tup-Khona in southern Tajikistan, a custom that was common not only in ancient Greece but also in China. Judith Rickenbach (ed.), *Oxus: 2000 Jahre Kunst am Oxus-Fluss in Mittelasien* (Zurich, 1989), pp. 55f; Boris Staviskij, *La Bactriane sous les Kushans* (Paris, 1986), pp. 178, 186.
84. Roger Goepper and J. Lee-Khalisch, *Korea. Die alten Königreiche* (Zurich, 2000), pp. 150–153; Young-Sook Pak, 'The Origins of Silla Metalwork', *Orientations Magazine* (September 1988), pp. 45–52; Staffan Rosén, 'Korea and the Silk Roads', *The Silk Road Journal* 6/2 (2009), pp. 3–5.
85. S.G. Kljastornyj and T.I. Sultanov, *Staaten und Völker in den Steppen Eurasiens: Altertum und Mittelalter* (Berlin, 2006), pp. 30–33; Sarianidi, *The Golden Hoard of Bactria*, p. 49.
86. Véronique Schiltz. 'Tillya Tepe Catalog', in Hiebert and Cambon, *Afghanistan, Crossroads of the Ancient World* (2011) p. 286.
87. Pak, 'The Origins of Silla Metalwork', p. 52.
88. Staviskij, *La Bactriane sous les Kushans*, p. 183.
89. Cambon, *Hidden Afghanistan*, p. 63; Lebedynsky, *Les Saces*, p. 147; Sarianidi, *The Golden Hoard of Bactria*, p. 18.
90. John Hill, *Through the Jade Gate to Rome: An annotated translation of the Chronicle on the 'Western regions' in the Hou Hanshu* (Australia, 2009), p. 33.
91. Strabo quotes extensively from the now-lost history *Parthika* of Apollodoros of Artemita (first century BC); the likewise lost work of Pompeius Trogus (age of Augustus) *Historiae Philippicae* is quoted by Justin. The *Parthika* of Apollodoros presumably also served as a source for Trogus (Gardiner-Garden, *Apollodoros of Artemita and the Central Asian Skythians*, pp. 1–10).
92. Strabo XI, VIII, 2. English from: Gardiner-Garden, *Apollodoros of Artemita and the Central Asian Skythians*, p. 35.
93. The name Sacaraucae means essentially 'Royal Saka'. Whether they are the same as the Sai Wang of Chinese chronicles is somewhat unclear, although that term likewise means 'Royal Saka'.
94. The identification of these four nomadic peoples has been the subject of controversy since the eighteenth century. See: Craig Benjamin, 'The Yuezhi and their Neighbours: Evidence for the Yuezhi in the Chinese Sources *ca.* 220 - 25 BCE', in *Realms of the Silk Roads: Ancient and Modern* (Turnhout, 2000), pp. 184–189; G. Enoki, A. Koshelenko and Z. Haidary 'The Yüeh-chih and their migrations', in *History of civilizations of Central Asia*, Vol. II, pp. 173, 180; Gardiner-Garden, *Apollodoros of Artemita and the Central Asian Skythians*, pp. 35–60; Staviskij, *La Bactriane sous les Kushans*, p. 118.
95. Pompeius Trogus/Justin, *Prologi*, XLI, in Gardiner-Garden, *Apollodoros of Artemita and the Central Asian Skythians*, p. 35. Gardiner-Garden is inclined, however, to identify the *Pasianoi* with the *Apasiakai*, the 'water Scythians', from whom Arsaces may have descended. Ibid. pp. 42f.
96. Lebedynsky, *Les Saces*, p. 63.
97. Gardiner-Garden, *Apollodoros of Artemita and the Central Asian Skythians*, p. 40; Claude Rapin, 'Nomads and the shaping of Central Asia', in *After Alexander: Central Asia before Islam* (London, 2007), p. 59. Also Bivar's identification of the Asiani with the early Kushans having conquered the four other Yuezhi tribes is problematic since the Chinese *Hou Han Shu* (118.9a) attributes the conquest of the Yuezhi tribes to Kujula Kadphises who came to power not before 25 to 30 AD, but Strabo died in 24 AD (A.D.H. Bivar, 'The history of Eastern Iran', in *Cambridge History of Iran*, Vol. 3 (1) (Cambridge University Press, Cambridge 1983), p. 197).
98. Rapin et al., 'La tombe d'une princesse nomade', p. 77.
99. Ibid, pp. 77, 90f.
100. Boris Staviskij, *Kunst der Kuschan* (Leipzig, 1979), p. 103. See also Vol. II.
101. Wood, *A journey to the source of the River Oxus*, pp. 259f.
102. Paul Bernard, 'Aï Khanoum en Afghanistan hier (1964–1978) et aujourd'hui', in *Académie des Inscriptions & Belles-Lettres, Paris. Comptes rendus des scéances de l'année 2001* (2001), pp. 978f. Jules Bartoux was not really an archaeologist but rather a geologist and his real name was Jules Couyat (Zamariallai Tarzi, 'Jules Bartoux: le découvreur oublié d'Aï Khanoum', in *Académie des Inscriptions & Belles-Lettres, Paris. Comptes rendus des scéances de l'année 1996* (1996)).
103. Bernard, 'Aï Khanoum en Afghanistan', pp. 971–975; Holt, *Thundering Zeus*, p. 16.
104. Bernard, 'Aï Khanoum en Afghanistan', pp. 994–1008; Marie-Claude Bianchini (ed.), *Afghanistan: Une histoire millénaire* (Paris, 2002), p. 86.
105. The hypothesis that Aï Khanum was founded by Seleucus I is based on the numerous discoveries of coins from Seleucus I and Antiochus I; other scholars attribute the establishment of the city to Alexander's general Hephaestion (Sidky, *The Greek Kingdom of Bactria*, pp. 131f).
106. Staviskij, *Kunst der Kuschan*, p. 55.
107. On Aï Khanum: Paul Bernard, 'L'architecture religieuse de l'Asie Centrale à l'époque hellénistique', in *Akten des XIII. Internationalen Kongresses für Klassische Archäologie, Berlin 1988* (1990); Bernard, 'The Greek kingdoms of Central Asia'; Bernard, 'Aï Khanoum en Afghanistan'; Guy Lecuyot and O. Ishizawa, 'La restitution virtuelle d'Aï Khanoum. Une cité hellénistique en Afghanistan', in *Archéologia* no. 420 (Dijon, 2005); Guy Lecuyot and O. Ishizawa, 'Aï Khanum Reconstructed', in *Proceedings of the British Academy* 133 (2007); Staviskij, *La Bactriane sous les Kushans*, pp. 163–172.
108. The adventurous-sounding but finally unverifiable story was reconstructed by the first buyer of the objects, Sir Alexander Cunningham. O.M. Dalton, *The treasure of the Oxus with other examples of early oriental metal-work* (London, 1964); Boris Litvinskij, *Taxt- Sangin: Der Oxus-Tempel* (2002), pp. 1–12; Igor Pitschikjan, *Oxos-Schatz und Oxos-Tempel* (Berlin, 1992), pp. 61–67.
109. What happened to the objects during the three years from 1877 to 1880 is unknown.
110. Dalton, *The treasure of the Oxus*, p. XIV.
111. John Curtis, *Ancient Persia* (London, 2000), p. 62. Igor Pitschikjan's claim that a 'collection' of about 2,500 (!) precious metal objects offered for sale on the antiquities market in 1993 and acquired by the Miho Museum, which opened in 1997, represents the 'second part of the Oxus Treasure' is unfounded ('Rebirth of the Oxus Treasure: Second part of the Oxus Treasure from the Miho Museum Collection', in *Ancient Civilizations from Scythia to Siberia*, Vol. 4, No. 4 (Leiden, 1997)). The authenticity of the Miho collection is uncertain.
112. See photo p. 196.
113. See photo p. 87.
114. Curtis, *Ancient Persia*, p. 64.
115. Georges Rougemont and David Stronach, 'On the Date of the Oxus Gold Scabbard and other Achaemenid Matters', *Bulletin of the Asia Institute* 12 (1998), pp. 232f.
116. A standing woman, a camel or a horse are depicted on another dozen discs (Dalton, *The treasure of the Oxus*, pl. XIV, XV, pp. 19–26).
117. Recently the controversial researcher Muscarella strongly questioned the authenticity of the Oxus treasure (Oscar White Muscarella, *The lie became great*, 2000, pp. 208f, note 30; *All that glisters isn't gold*, 2003).
118. For some objects a pre-Achaemenid, Median dating is considered, for example for the akinakes sheath. Rougemont and Stronach, 'On the Date of the Oxus Gold Scabbard'; Pitschikjan, *Oxos-Schatz und Oxos-Tempel*, p. 80.
119. How individual objects got from western Iran to the Oxus remains unclear. Pitschikjan's hypothesis that they were carried to the Oxus as war trophies of the invading Macedonian army cannot be substantiated (*Oxos-Schatz und Oxos-Tempel*, 1992, pp. 85, 92, 100).
120. Curtis, *Ancient Persia*, p. 65.
121. Pitschijkan, *Oxos-Schatz und Oxos-Tempel*, pp. 69f.
122. The first explorations in Takht-i Sangin by B. Denike from 1926 to 1928 were never published, and in 1956 A.M. Mandelshtam did not dig deep enough to yield any finds (Litvinskij, *Taxt- Sangin*, p. 7). The excavations lasted from 1976 to 1991 and started again in 1998.
123. Given the later coins, significantly earlier dates, such as the invasion of Alexander, the campaign of Seleucus I or the threat from the north mentioned by Euthydemos I, either are impossible or negate the inclusion of the coins in the hoard. Grenet and Rapin, 'Alexander, Aï Khanum, Termez', 89; Litvinskij, *Taxt- Sangin*, p. 38; Pitschijkan, *Oxos-Schatz und Oxos-Tempel*, pp. 71, 74, 93.
124. Slightly adapted from: Holt, *Thundering Zeus*, p. 175.
125. Bernard, 'Aï Khanoum en Afghanistan', p. 1021.
126. Osmund Bopearachchi, 'A Faience Head of a Graeco-Bactrian King from Aï Khanum', *Bulletin of the Asia Institute* 12 (1998), p. 24.
127. Hiebert and Cambon, *Afghanistan, Crossroads of the Ancient World*, (2011) p. 118.
128. Bernard, 'The Greek kingdoms of Central Asia', pp. 114ff.
129. Litvinskij, *La civilisation de l'Asie centrale antique*, pp. 54ff.
130. Holt, *Thundering Zeus*, p. 66.

131. Pidaev and Leriche, 'Quelques villes moyennes de Bactriane', pp. 53ff; Staviskij, *La Bactriane sous les Kushans*, pp. 268–272. Bernard believes that the temple was dedicated to Zeus and the Dioscuri were merely his attendant deities ('L'architecture religieuse de l'Asie Centrale à l'époque hellénistique', p. 55).
132. Ptolemaios Claudios, *Handbuch der Geographie* (Basel, 2006), VI, 12, 5; VIII, 23, 11 (Vol. II, pp. 653, 877, 880f); Anjelina Drujinina, *Wohnen im hellenistischen Baktrien – Wohnhäuser in der Stadt Oxeiane (Tachti Sangin)*, (Mannheim, 2009), p. 177.
133. On the Oxus temple: Anjelina Drujinina, 'Gussform mit griechischer Inschrift aus dem Oxos-Tempel', in *Archäologische Mitteilungen aus Iran und Turan* 40 (Berlin, 2008); Anjelina Drujinina, 'Excavations of Takht-i Sangin City, Territory of Oxus Temple, in 2006', *Bulletin of Miho Museum, Koka* 9 (March 2009); Gunvor Lindström, 'Graeco–baktrische Symbiose', in *DAMALS, Kontadin, Leinfelden-Echterdingen* 1 (2009); Boris Litvinskij, 'The Hellenistic Architecture and Art of the Temple on the Oxus', *Bulletin of the Asia Institute* 8 (1994); Litvinskij, *Taxt- Sangin*; Pitschijkan, *Oxos-Schatz und Oxos-Tempel*.
134. Litvinskij, 'The Hellenistic Architecture and Art of the Temple on the Oxus,' figs. 6.–9.
135. Litvinskij, *Taxt- Sangin*, pl. 17.
136. Ibid, p. 96.
137. Pitschijkan, *Oxos-Schatz und Oxos-Tempel*, p. 20. Gignoux and Litvinsky however speculated in 1996 that the Oxus Temple wasn't a fire temple, but that the 'temple of the god Oxus at Takht-i Sangin merely had two chapels reserved for the worship of fire' (Ph. Gignoux and B.A. Litvinsky, *Religions and religious movements I,* 1996, p. 410).
138. For images of the objects see: Hansen et al., *Alexander der Große und die Öffnung der Welt*, pp. 351–368; R. Masov et al. (eds), *National Museum of Antiquities of Tajikistan* (Dushanbe, 2005), pp. 97–106.
139. Hansen et al., *Alexander der Große und die Öffnung der Welt*, p. 354.
140. Ibid.
141. Litvinskij, 'The Hellenistic Architecture and Art of the Temple on the Oxus', p. 59.
142. Drujinina, 'Gussform mit griechischer Inschrift', pp. 124–133. It is unclear how to interpret the phrase 'newly arisen Oxus': Had the temple been restored or did it refer to a kind of myth of rebirth?
143. See p. 114.
144. This hypothetical older shrine could also have served as a storage site for the pre-Seleucid objects from the Oxus treasure (Litvinskij, *Taxt- Sangin*, pp. 104, 107, 112).

IX Outlook

1. Ssu-ma Ch'ein, Shih chi, 123 (New York, 1971), Vol. II, p. 274.

Bibliography

Abdullaev, K.A. et al. (ed.). *Culture and Art of Ancient Uzbekistan*. Vneshtorgizdat, Moscow 1991.

Abetekov, A., Yusupov, H. 'Ancient Iranian nomads in western Central Asia', in *History of civilizations of Central Asia*, Vol. II., 1994, pp. 23–33.

Abrazov, Rafis. *The Palgrave concise historical atlas of Central Asia*. Palgrave, New York 2008.

Adams, Douglas. 'Mummies', in Victor H. Mair (ed.), 'The Mummified Remains Found in the Tarim Basin', *Journal of Indo-European Studies*, Washington, Vol. 23, No. 3&4, 1995, pp. 399–413.

Agrawal, D.P., Kharakwal, J.S. *Bronze and Iron Ages in South Asia*. Aryan Books, New Delhi 2003.

Akiner, Shirin. 'Silk Roads, Great Games and Central Asia', *Journal of the Royal Society for Asian Affairs*, London, Vol. XLII, No. 3, November 2011, pp. 391–402.

Akishev, K.A. *Issyk Mound. The art of Saka in Kazakhstan*. Iskusstvo Publishers, Moscow 1978.

— *Ancient gold of Kazakhstan*. ONER, Almaty 1983.

Alemany, Agusti. *Sources on the Alans. A critical compilation*. Brill, Leiden 2000.

Alexeev, Andreï et al. *Nomades des Steppes*. Editions Autrement, Paris 2001.

— 'A chronology of the Scythian antiquities of Eurasia based on new archaeological and ^{14}C Data', in *Proceedings of the 17th International ^{14}C Conference*, edited by Carmi I., Boaretto E., *Radiocarbon*, Vol. 43, No. 2B, 2001, pp. 1085–1107. University of Arizona, Tucson.

— 'Some problems in the study of the chronology of the ancient nomadic cultures of Eurasia (9th–3rd centuries BC)', in *Geochronometria*, Gliwice, Vol. 21, 2002, pp. 143–150. www.geochronometria.pl/pdf/geo_21/geo21_17.pdf

— 'Scythian kings and "royal" burial-mounds of the fifth and fourth centuries BC', in Braund, David (ed.). *Scythians and Greeks*. University of Exeter Press, Exeter 2005, pp. 39–55.

— *Trésors des Steppes*. Laténium, Hauterive 2006.

Alexeeva, Ekatarina. 'Gorgippia. Geschichte einer griechischen Polis an der Stelle der heutigen Stadt Anapa', in Fornasier Jochen, Böttger Burkhard (eds). *Das Bosporanische Reich*. Philipp von Zabern, Mainz 2002, pp. 92–112.

Allchin, Bridget. 'Middle Palaeolithic culture', in History of civilizations of Central Asia. Vol. I. Unesco Publishing, Paris 1992, pp. 65–88.

Alles, Volker (ed.). *Reflexbogen. Geschichte und Herstellung*. Hörnig, Ludwigshafen 2009.

Amiet, Pierre. *L'âge des échanges inter-iraniens 3500–1700 avant J.-C.* Editions de la Réunion des musées nationaux, Paris 1986.

Anati, Emmanuel. 'Le grand sanctuaire rupestre d'Hutubi', *Archéologia*. Editions Faton, Dijon, No. 356, 1999, pp. 52–58.

— 'Parable of the Mask', in *Arts & Cultures*, 2005, pp. 54–73. Musées Barbier-Mueller, Geneva 2006.

André, Guilhem. 'Une tombe princière Xiongnu à Gol Mod, Mongolie. Campagnes de fouilles 2000–2001', *Arts Asiatiques*. Musée national des Arts asiatiques-Guimet, 57/2002, pp. 194–205. Paris.

Andrews, Roy Chapman. *On the trail of ancient man*. Putnam's Sons, New York 1926.

— *The new conquest of Central Asia. A narrative of the explorations of the Central Asiatic expeditions in Mongolia and China, 1921–1930*. Natural History of Central Asia, Vol. I. The American Museum of Natural History, New York 1932.

— *Under a Lucky Star. A Lifetime of Adventure*. Borderland (1943) 2009.

Anke, Bodo et al. 'Ausgrabungen auf dem Gräberfeld von Süttü-Bula, Raj. Kočkorka, Kyrgyzstan', *Eurasia Antiqua*, Vol.3/1997, pp. 513–570. Deutsches Archäologisches Institut, Berlin; Philipp von Zabern, Mainz 1998.

Anke, Bodo et al. (eds). *Attila und die Hunnen*. Historisches Museum der Pfalz Speyer, Theiss Verlag Stuttgart 2007.

— *Hunnen zwischen Asien und Europa. Aktuelle Forschungen zur Archäologie und Kultur der Hunnen*. Beier & Beran, Langenweißbach 2008.

Anochin, Vledilen. 'Die Münzen der skythischen und sarmatischen Könige', *Hamburger Beiträge zur Archäologie*, Vol. 18, pp. 47–56. Philipp von Zabern, Mainz 1996.

Anthony, David. *The Horse, the Wheel and Language. How Bronze-Age riders from the Eurasian Steppes shaped the modern world*. Princeton University Press, Princeton, 2007.

— *The Lost World of Old Europe. The Danube Valley, 5000–3500 BC*. Princeton University Press, Princeton 2010.

Anthony, David, Brown, Dorcas. *Harnessing Horsepower. Horses and Humans in Antiquity*. 2007. ttp://users.hartwick.edu/anthonyd/harnessing/horsepower.html

Anthony, David et al. *The Samara Valley Project. Late Bronze Age Economy and Ritual in the Russian Steppes*. No date. http://users.hartwick.edu/anthonyd/opening.html

Argent, Gala. 'Do the clothes make the horse? Relationality, roles and statuses in Iron Age Inner Asia', *World Archaeology*, 42:2, pp. 157–174, Routledge, London 2010.

Armitage, Simon J. et al. 'The Southern Route "Out of Africa": Evidence for an Early Expansion of Modern Humans into Arabia', *Science*, Vol. 331, pp. 453–446, 28 January 2011. American Association for the Advancement of Science, New York 2011.

Arrian, Lucius Flavius. *Arrian's history of the expedition of Alexander the Great, and conquest of Persia*. Translated by Mr. Rooke. Davis, London 1812.

— *The Campaigns of Alexander. (Anabasis Alexandri)*. Translated by Aubrey de Sélincourt. Penguin Books, London 1971.

— *Periplus Ponti Euxini.* Translated by A. Liddle. Bristol Classics, London 2003.

Aruz, Joan (ed.). *The Golden Deer of Eurasia. Scythian and Sarmatian treasures from the Russian steppes.* The Metropolitan Museum of Art, New York 2000.

— *Art of the first cities.* The Metropolitan Museum of Art, New York 2003.

— *The Golden Deer of Eurasia. Perspectives on the Steppe Nomads of the Ancient World.* The Metropolitan Museum of Art, New York 2006.

Askarov, Akhmadali. Southern Uzbekistan in the Second Millennium BC', in Kohl, Philipp (ed.). *The Bronze Age Civilization of Central Asia. Recent Soviet discoveries.* Sharpe, New York 1981, pp. 256–272.

— 'The beginning of Iron Age in Transoxania', in *History of Civilizations of Central Asia*, UNESCO Publishing, Paris, Vol. I, 1992, pp. 441–458.

— 'Pastoral and nomadic tribes at the beginning of the first millennium BC', in *History of Civilizations of Central Asia*, UNESCO Publishing, Paris, Vol. I, 1992, pp. 458–472.

— 'La Bactriane à l'aube de la civilisation', *Découverte des civilisations d'Asie Centrale. Les dossiers d'archéologie.* Faton, Dijon, Nr. 185, 1993, pp. 60–69.

Askarov, A., Shirinov, T. 'The "Palace", Temple and Necropolis of Jarkutan', *Bulletin of the Asia Institute*, Vol. 8, 1994, pp. 13–26. The Asia Institute, Bloomfield Hills 1996.

Atkinson, Thomas Witlam. *Oriental and Western Siberia.* Harper Brothers, New York 1858.

Atwood, Christopher. *Encyclopedia of Mongolia and the Mongol Empire.* Facts on File, New York 2004.

Autio, Eero. *The Permian Animal Style.* Folklore Vols. 18 & 19, 162–186. Folk Belief and Media Group, Tartu 2001. www.haldjas.folklore.ee

Avesta. Die heiligen Schriften der Parsen. Übersetzt von Friedrich Spiegel. Engelmann, Leipzig 1859. Reprint by Elibron Classics, 2006.

Bahain, Jean-Jacques. 'Les premiers homo erectus en Chine', *Dossiers d'Archéologie* No. 292, 2004, pp. 30–37.

— 'Les gisements de l'Homme de Lantian', *Dossiers d'Archéologie* No. 292, 2004, pp. 44–46.

Bahn, Paul. *Prehistoric Art.* Cambridge University Press, Cambridge 1998.

— *Prehistoric Rock Art. Polemics and progress.* Cambridge University Press, Cambridge 2010.

Baimatowa, Nasiba. *5000 Jahre Architektur in Mittelasien. Lehmziegelgewölbe vom 4./3. Jt. v.Chr. bis zum Ende des 8. Jhs. n.Chr.* Philipp von Zabern, Mainz 2008.

Baipakov, Karl, Nasyrov, Rakip. *Along the Great Silk Road.* KRAMDC Publishers, Almaty 1991.

Baipakov, Karl. *Ancient gold collection.* Didar Publishing, Almaty 1998.

Baipakov, Karl, Mariashev, A.N. *Petroglyphs of South Kazakhstan and Semirechye.* Margulan Archaeology Institute, Almaty 1994.

— *Petroglyphs in the Kulzhabasy Mountains.* Margulan Archaeology Institute, Almaty 2004.

— *The Eshkiolmes Rock's Petroglyphs.* Margulan Archaeology Institute, Almaty 2005.

— *Petroglyphs of Ak-Kainar site.* Margulan Archaeology Institute, Almaty 2009.

— *Archaeological cultural heritage of Almaty.* Margulan Archaeology Institute, Almaty 2010.

Bakker, Jan Albert. 'Die neolithischen Wagen im nördlichen Mitteleuropa', in Fansa, Mamoun, Burmeister, Stefan. *Rad und Wagen.* Philipp von Zabern, Mainz 2004, pp. 283–294.

Baldick, Julian. *Homer and the Indo-Europeans.* I.B.Tauris, London 1994.

— *Animals and Shaman. Ancient Religions of Central Asia.* I.B.Tauris, London 2000.

Balint, Csanad. *Die Archäologie der Steppe.* Böhlau, Wien 1989.

Ball, Warwick. *The Monuments of Afghanistan. History, archaeology and architecture.* I.B.Tauris, London 2008.

Ban Biao, Ban Gu and Ban Zhao: see Pan Ku.

Barber, Elizabeth. *The mummies of Ürümchi.* Macmillan, London 1999.

Barbier, Jean-Paul. *Art des Steppes.* Musée Barbier-Müller, Geneva 1996.

Barrett, T.H. 'Climate Change and Religious Response: The Case of Early Medieval China', *Journal of the Royal Asiatic Society*, 3rd series, Vol. 17, part 2, April 2007, pp. 139–156.

Barnett, R.D. 'The art of Bactria and the treasure of the Oxus', *Iranica Antiqua*, Vol. VIII, pp. 34–53, Brill, Leiden1968.

Batbold, N. (ed.) *Petroglyphs of Aral Tolgoi (Mongolia).* Mongolia Academy of Sciences, Ulaan Baatar 2007.

Batsaihan, J. (ed.) *National Museum of Mongolian History.* Decom Studio, Ulaan Baatar c. 2000.

Baumer, Christoph. *Southern Silk Road.* Orchid Press, Bangkok, 2003.

— *The Church of the East. An illustrated History of Assyrian Christianity.* I.B.Tauris, London 2006.

— 'Die „Tausend-Särge-Nekropole' von Xiaohe', *Antike Welt*, Philipp von Zabern, Mainz 2006/6, pp. 39–49

— *Traces in the Desert. Journeys of Discovery across Central Asia.* I.B.Tauris, London 2008.

— 'Sogdian or Indian Iconography and Religious Influences in Dandan Uiliq (Xinjiang, China)?', in *Proceedings to the International Seminar 'The Art of Central Asia and the Indian Sub-Continent in Cross-Cultural Perspective'.* Aryan Books International, New Delhi, 2008.

— 'Indo-europäische Mumien im Herzen der Wüste Taklamakan. Die Ayala Mazar-Xiaohe Kultur', *Antike Welt*, Philipp von Zabern, Mainz 2010/4, pp. 18–28.

— *The Ayala Mazar – Xiaohe Culture. Results from an archaeological exploration of the ancient Keriya Delta, China, in 2009.* Self-published June 2010 and in: *Kristi*, New Delhi, Vol. 3, 2011, pp. 1–23.

— 'The Ayala Mazar-Xiaohe Culture: New archaeological discoveries in the Taklamakan Desert, China', *Journal of the Royal Society for Asian Affairs*, London, Vol. XLII, No. 1, March 2011, pp. 49–70.

Bausum, Ann. *Dragon, Bones and Dinosaur Eggs. A photobiography of Explorer Roy Chapman Andrews.* National Geographic Society, Washington 2000.

Becker, Alexander, Kalinowski, Ruth (translators). *Lebende Vergangenheit. Prähistorische Ausgrabungen.* Rütten & Loening, Berlin 1954.

Beckwith, Christopher. *Empires of the Silk Road.* Princeton University Press, Princeton 2009.

Bednarik, Robert. 'Pleistocene Rock Art in Central Europe?', *International newsletter on rock art INORA*, No. 45, pp. 27–30. Foix 2006.

Beijing, Cultural Relics Research Institute. *Yan State cemetery of the Western Zhou period at Liulihe.* Cultural Relics Publishing House, Beijing 1995.

Belenickij, Alesandr. *Zentralasien.* Nagel, Genf 1968.

Belinskij, Andrej, Kalmykov, Aleksej. 'Neue Wagenfunde aus der Katakombengrab-Kultur im Steppengebiet des zentralen Vorkauskasus', in Fansa, Mamoun, Burmeister, Stefan. *Rad und Wagen.* Philipp von Zabern, Mainz 2004, pp. 201–220.

Bell-Fialkoff, Andrew (ed.). *The Role of Migration in the History of the Eurasian Steppe.* Macmillan, Basingstoke 2000.

Bellezza, John Vincent. *Antiquities of Northern Tibet. Pre-Buddhist archaeological discoveries on the high plateau.* Adroit, Delhi 2001.

— *Zhang Zhung. Foundations of Civilization in Tibet.* Österreicherische Akademie der Wissenschaften, Wien 2007.

Belli, Oktay. *Stone Balbals and statues in human form in Kirghizistan*. Arkeoloji ve sanat yayinlari, Istanbul 2003.

Bemmann, Jan et al. *Current archaeological research in Mongolia*. R.F.W.-Universität, Bonn, 2009.

Bendezu-Sarmiento, J.-C. et al. 'La fouille de kourganes dans les Tianshan et dans l'Altaï', *Eurasia Antiqua*, Vol. 12/2006, pp. 193–210. Deutsches Archäologisches Institut, Berlin; Philipp von Zabern, Mainz 2007.

— 'Post-mortem mutilations of human bodies in Early Iron Age Kazakhstan and their possible meaning for rites of burial', *Antiquity* 82, pp. 73–86, York 2008.

Benjamin, Craig. 'The Yuezhi and their Neighbours: Evidence for the Yuezhi in the Chinese Sources *ca*. 220 – *ca*. 25 BCE', in Christian, David, Benjamin, Craig (eds). *Silk Road Studies IV. Realms of the Silk Roads: Ancient and Modern*, pp. 105–160. Brepols, Turnhout 2000.

— 'The Yuezhi Migration and Sogdia', in *Eran ud Aneran*. Webfestschrift Marshak 2003. http://www.transoxiana.org/Eran/

— 'The Yuezhi. Origin, Migration and the Conquest of Northern Bactria', *Silk Road Studies* XIV. Brepols, Turnhout 2007.

Benoit, Agnès. 'Les "princesses" de Bactriane', in *Arts & Cultures*, 2005, pp. 36–45. Musées Barbier-Mueller, Geneva 2005.

Benton, Michael. *The story of life on earth*. Grisewood & Dempsey, London 1986.

Berchem, Max van. *Amida. Matériaux pour l'Épigraphie et l'Histoire Musulmanes du Diyar-Bekr*. Carl Winter's Universitätsbuchhandlung, Heidelberg 1910.

Bergman, Folke. *Archaeological researches in Sinkiang*. Reports from the scientific expedition to the north-western provinces of China under the leadership of Dr. Sven Hedin. Publication 7. Thule, Stockholm 1939.

Bernard, Paul. 'Le monnayage d'Eudamos, satrape grec du Panjab et 'maître des éléphants', in *Orientalia Iosephi Tucci memoriae dicata*, pp. 65–94. IsMEO, Istituto italiano per il Medio ed Estremo Oriente, Roma 1985.

— 'L'architecture religieuse de l'Asie Centrale à l'époque hellénistique', in *Akten des XIII. Internationalen Kongresses für Klassische Archäologie, Berlin 1988*, pp. 51–59. Philipp von Zabern 1990.

— 'The Greek kingdoms of Central Asia', in *History of civilizations of Central Asia*. Vol. II. Unesco Publishing, Paris 1994, pp. 99–129.

— 'Aï Khanoum en Afghanistan hier (1964–1978) et aujourd'hui', in Académie des Inscriptions & Belles-Lettres, Paris. Comptes rendus des scéances de l'année 2001, fasc. II, pp. 971–1029; 2001.

Bianchini, Marie-Claude (ed.). *Afghanistan. Une histoire millénaire*. Réunion des musées nationaux, Paris 2002.

— *Afghanistan, les trésors retrouvés. Album de l'exposition*. Réunion des musées nationaux, Paris 2006.

Binder, Franz. *Mittelasien*. Hirmer, München 2004.

Bivar, A.D.H. 'The history of Eastern Iran', in *Cambridge History of Iran*, Vol. 3 (1), Cambridge University Press, Cambridge 1983, pp. 181–231.

Black, Jeremy, Green, Anthony. *Gods, Demons and Symbols of Ancient Mesopotamia*. University of Texas Press, Austin 2000.

Blount, Kitty, Crowley, Maggie et al (eds). *Encyclopedia of Dinosaurs & prehistoric life*. DK Publishing New York in association with the American Museum of Natural History, New York 2001.

Boardman, John et al. 'A Faience Head of the Graeco-Bactrian King from Aï Khanum', *Bulletin of the Asia Institute*, Vol. 12, 1998, pp. 23–30. The Asia Institute, Bloomfield Hills 2001.

— 'Central Asia: West and East', in Cribb Joe. *After Alexander*, 2007, pp. 9–25.

Bogdanov, E. 'Zur Kunst des skythisch-sibirischen Kulturkreises. Raubtierdarstellungen in Werken der Nomaden Zentralasiens', *Eurasia Antiqua*, Vol. 13/2007, pp. 199–214. Deutsches Archäologisches Institut, Berlin; Philipp von Zabern, Mainz 2008.

Bokovenko, N.A. 'Malinovyj Log. Ein Gräberfeld der Afanas'evo-Kultur', *Eurasia Antiqua*, Vol. 6/2000, pp. 209–248. Deutsches Archäologisches Institut, Berlin; Philipp von Zabern, Mainz 2000.

— 'Das karasukzeitliche Gräberfeld Ančil Čon in Chakassien', *Eurasia Antiqua*, Vol. 6/2000, pp. 13–33. Deutsches Archäologisches Institut, Berlin; Philipp von Zabern, Mainz 2000.

— 'Migrations of Early Nomads of the Eurasian Steppe in a context of Climatic Changes', in E. Scott et al. *Impact of the Environment on Human Migration in Eurasia*. Kluwer, Dordrecht 2004 pp. 21–33.

Boltrik, Jurij, Fialko, Elena. 'Der Oghuz Kurgan. Die Grabanlage eines Skythenkönigs zur Zeit nach Ateas', *Hamburger Beiträge zur Archäologie*, Vol. 18, pp. 107–130. Philipp von Zabern, Mainz 1996.

Bongard-Levin, Gregory, Minns, E.H., Rostovtzeff, M.I. 'Glimpses of a Scythian friendship', in David Braund, *Scythians and Greeks*. University of Exeter Press, Exeter 2005, pp. 13–32.

Bopearachchi, Osmund. 'A Faience Head of a Graeco–Bactrian King from Aï Khanum', *Bulletin of the Asia Institute*, Vol. 12, 1998, pp. 23–30. The Asia Institute, Bloomfield Hills 2001.

— *De l'Indus à l'Oxus. Archaéologie de l'Asie Centrale*. Association IMAGO, Lattes 2003.

— 'Les successeurs d'Alexandre le Grand en Asie centrale et en Inde: les Gréco-Bactriens', in Bopearachchi, Osmund et al. *De l'Indus à l'Oxus*. IMAGO, Lattes 2003, pp. 81–108.

— 'Indo-Grecs, Indo-Scythes, Indo-Parthes', in Bopearachchi, Osmund et al. *De l'Indus à l'Oxus*. IMAGO, Lattes 2003, pp. 129–168.

Bopearachchi, Osmund, Boussac, Marie-Françoise (eds) *Afghanistan. Ancien carrefour entre l'est et l'ouest*. Brepols, Turnhout 2005.

Boroffka, Nikolaus, Hansen, Svend (eds). *Archäologische Forschungen in Kasachstan, Tadschikistan, Turkmenistan und Usbekistan*. Eurasien-Abteilung, Deutsches Archäologisches Institut, Berlin 2010.

Boroffka, Nikolaus. 'Klima und Besiedlungsgeschichte am Aral-See, Kasachstan und Usbekistan', in Boroffka, Nikolaus, Hansen, Svend (eds), *Archäologische Forschungen in Kasachstan, Tadschikistan, Turkmenistan und Usbekistan*. Eurasien-Abteilung, Deutsches Archäologisches Institut, Berlin 2010, pp. 38–41.

Bosinsky, Gerhard. 'Seite an Seite – Frühe Menschen und Säbelkatzen', *Antike Welt* 2005/1, pp. 55–61. Philipp von Zabern, Mainz, 2005.

Böttger, Burkhard, Fornasier, Jochen, Arseneva, Tatjana. 'Tanais am Don. Emporion, Polis und bosporanisches Tauschhandelszentrum', in Fornasier, Jochen, Böttger, Burkhard (eds), *Das Bosporanische Reich*. Philipp von Zabern, Mainz 2002, pp. 69–85.

Bourgeois, Ignace et al. *Ancient nomads of the Altai Mountains*. Royal Museums of Art and History, Brussels 2000.

Bourke, Stephen. *The Middle East. The cradle of civilization revealed*. Thames & Hudson, London 2008.

Boyle, Katie, Renfrew, Colin & Levine, Marsha (eds), *Ancient interactions: east and west in Eurasia*. McDonald Institute for Archaeological Research, University of Cambridge, Cambridge 2002.

Braund, David, Kryzhitskiy, S. *Classical Olbia & the Scythian World*. The British Academy, London 2007.

Braund, David (ed.). *Scythians and Greeks. Cultural interactions in Scythia, Athens and the Early Roman Empire (sixth century BC-first century AD)*. University of Exeter Press, Exeter 2005.

Bregel, Yuri. *An Historical Atlas of Central Asia*. Brill, Leiden 2003.

Brentjes, Burchard. *Mittelasien. Eine Kulturgeschichte der Völker zwischen Kaspischem Meer und Tien-Schan*. Tusch, Wien 1977.

— *Der Tierstil in Eurasien*. Seemann Verlag, Leipzig 1982.

— *Die Ahnen Dschingis-Chans. Eurasien und das Werden Europas*. Tusch, Wien 1988.

— 'Frühe Steinstelen Sibiriens und der Mongolei', *Central Asiatic Journal*, Vol. 40, p. 21–55. Harrassowitz, Wiesbaden 1996.

Brentjes, Burchard, Vasilievsky, R. *Schamanenkrone und Weltenbaum. Kunst der Nomaden Nordasiens*. Verlag Seemann, Leipzig 1989.

Breuer, Reinhard (ed.). *Die Evolution der Sprachen*. Spektrum der Wissenschaft, Dossier 2/2007. Heidelberg 2007.

Briggs, Adrian et al. 'Targeted Retrieval and Analysis of Five Neandertal mtDNA Genomes', *Science*, Vol. 325, pp. 318–321, 17 July 2009. American Association for the Advancement of Science, New York 2010.

Brosseder, Ursula, Miller, Bryan (eds) *Xiongnu Archaeology*. Rheinische Friedrich-Wilhelms-Universität Bonn, 2011.

Brzezinski, R., Mielczarek, M. *The Sarmatians 600 BC – AD 450*. Osprey, London 2002.

Bujskich, Alla. 'Die Gründung von Olbia im Lichte jüngster archäologischer Untersuchungen', *Eurasia Antiqua*, Vol. 11/2005, pp. 15–35. Deutsches Archäologisches Institut, Berlin; Philipp von Zabern, Mainz 2006.

Bunker, Emma, et al. *Ancient Bronzes of the Eastern Eurasian Steppes from the Arthur M. Sackler Collections*. The Arthur M. Sackler Foundation, Abrams, New York 1997.

— *Nomadic Art of the Eastern Eurasian Steppes*. The Metropolitan Museum of Art, New York, Yale University Press, New Haven 2002.

— 'Northern China in the First Millennium BC: Beifang Artefacts as Historical Documents', *Arts & Cultures*, 2005, pp. 90–103. Musées Barbier-Mueller, Geneva 2006.

Burkett, Mary. *The Art of the Felt Maker*. Abbot Hall Art Gallery, Kendal, 1979.

Burmeister, Stefan. 'Neolithische und bronzezeitliche Moorfunde aus den Niederlanden, Nordwestdeutschland und Dänemark', in Fansa, Mamoun, Burmeister, Stefan. *Rad und Wagen*. Philipp von Zabern, Mainz 2004, pp. 321–340.

Bussagli, Mario. *Die Malerei in Zentralasien*. Skira, Geneva 1963.

Cambon, Pierre et al. *L'Asie des steppes, d'Alexandre le Grand à Gengis Khan*. Réunion des Musées nationaux, Paris 2000.

Cambon, Pierre, Jarrige, Jean-François et al. *Afghanistan, les trésors retrouvés. Collections du musée national de Kaboul*. Réunion des musées nationaux, Paris 2006.

Cambridge History of Iran. The Seleucid, Parthian and Sasanian periods. Vol. 3 (1), edited by Ehsan Yarshater. Cambridge University Press, Cambridge 1983.

Carey, Brian Todd. *Warfare in the Ancient World*. Pen and Sword, Barnsley 1988.

Carlson, Roy. 'Diring Yuriakh. An early palaeolithic site of the Lena River, eastern Siberia', *Indo-pacific prehistory association bulletin* 212, Melaka Papers, Vol. 5, pp. 132–137. Australian National University, Canberra 2001.

Carrier, Michel. '2500 years ago. An Ice Maiden in Siberia', *Arts & Cultures*, 2005, pp. 36–53. Musées Barbier-Mueller, Geneva 2006.

Casin, Jack. *Archaeological pre-history of Turkmenistan*. Weaving Art Museum and Research Institute. www.weawingartmuseum.org

Central Asian objects brought back by the Otani mission. National Museum, Toyko 1971.

Cernenko, E.V. et al. *The Scythians 700–300 BC*. Osprey, London 1983.

Chaliand, Gerard. *Nomadic Empires. From Mongolia to the Danube*. Transaction Publishers, New Brunswick 2004.

Chang, Claudia (ed.) *Of Gold and Grass: Nomads of Kazakhstan*. The Foundation for International Arts & Educations, Bethseda 2006.

Chen, Kwang-tzuu, Hiebert, Fredrick, The Late Prehistory of Xinjiang in Relation to its Neighbours', *Journal of World Prehistory*, Vol. 9, No. 2, pp. 243–300. Plenum Press, New York 1995.

Chen, Shen. *Anyang and Sanxingdui. Unveiling the Mysteries of Ancient Chinese Civilizations*. Royal Ontario Museum, Toronto 2002.

Chen, Xiejun, Wang Qingzheng (eds). *Treasures on Grassland: archaeological finds from the Inner Mongolia Autonomous Region*. Shanghai Museum, Shanghai 2000.

Cheremisin, D.V. 'The meaning of representations in the animal style and their relevance for the reconstruction of Pazyrik ideology', in *Archaeology, Ethnology & Anthropology of Eurasia*, Vol. 3, No. 31, pp. 87–102. Elsevier, Amsterdam 2007.

Chernykh, Evengy. 'Ancient metallurgy in northeast Asia: From the Urals to the Saiano-Altai', in Linduff, Katheryn (ed.). *Metallurgy in ancient Eastern Eurasia from the Urals to the Yellow River*. Mellen, Ceredigion 2004, pp. 15–36.

— 'Kargaly: The largest and most ancient metallurgical complex on the border of Europe and Asia', in Linduff, Katheryn (ed.) *Metallurgy in ancient Eastern Eurasia from the Urals to the Yellow River*. Mellen, Ceredigion 2004, pp. 223–237.

— 'The "Steppe Belt" of stockbreeding cultures in Eurasia during the Early Metal Age', *Trabajos de Prehistoria*, Vol. 65, No.2, 2008, pp. 73–93.

CHIME Chinese Early Metal: Database – Analyses – Applications. Deutsches Archäologisches Institut, Berlin 2010. http://www.dainst.org/chime

Chippindale, Christopher, Taçon, Paul (eds). *The Archaeology of Rock-Art*. Cambridge University Press, Cambridge 1998.

Chlachula, Jiri et al. 'Palaeolithic occupation in the Angara region, East Central Siberia, in the context of Pleistocene climate change', *Journal of Geological Sciences*, Prague 2004, No. 25, pp. 31–49.

— 'Pleistocene climate change, natural environments and Palaeolithic occupation of East Kazakhstan', *Quaternary International Science Reviews*, Vol. 220, No. 1–2, June 2010, Elsevier, Amsterdam pp. 64–87.

Christian, David. *A History of Russia, Central Asia and Mongolia. Vol. I, Inner Eurasia from Prehistory to the Mongol Empire*. Blackwell, Oxford 1998.

— 'State Formation in the Inner Eurasian Steppes', in Christian, David, Benjamin, Craig (eds). *Silk Road Studies II. Worlds of the Silk Roads: Ancient and Modern*, pp. 51–76. Brepols, Turnhout 1998.

Chunxiang, Li et al. 'Evidence that a West-East admixed population lived in the Tarim Basin as early as the early Bronze Age', *BMC Biology*, 2010, Vol. 8. http://www.biomedcentral.com/content/pdf/1741-7007-8-15.pdf

Churchill, Steven, Franciscus, Robert. 'Shanidar 3 Neandertal Rib Puncture Wound and Palaeolithic Weaponry', *Journal of Human Evolution*, Vol. 57, No. 2, August 2009, pp. 163–178. See also: CSI Neanderthal: Interspecies Homicide of Shanidar 3, in *Scientific Blogging*, ION Publishing, 20 July 2009. http://www.scientificblogging.com/news_articles/csi_neanderthal_interspecies_homicide_shanidar_3

Chuvin, Pierre (ed.). *Les arts de l'Asie Centrale*. Citadelles & Mazenod, Paris 1999.

Ciochon, Russell. 'The mystery ape of Pleistocene Asia', *Nature*, 2009, pp. 910f. http://www.nature.com/nature/journal/v459/n7249/full/459910a.html

Ciuk, Krzystof (ed.). *Mysteries of ancient Ukraine*. Royal Ontario Museum, Toronto 2008.

Clark, J. Desmond et al. 'Stratigraphic, chronological and behavioural contexts of Pleistocene Homo sapiens from Middle Awash, Ethiopia', *Nature*, Vol. 423, pp. 747–752, Macmillan Publishers, Basingstoke 2003.

Clottes, Jean. *World Rock Art.* Getty Publication, Los Angeles 2002.

Cluzan, Sophie: *De Sumer à Canaan.* Le Seuil/Musée du Louvre, Paris 2005.

Colin, Elicio. ,L'oeuvre du P. Licent et la Mission paléontologique française en Chine du Nord', *Annales de géographie, Paris,* Vol. 35, No. 195, 1926, pp. 286–288.

Conrad, Nicholas et al (eds). *Eiszeit, Kunst und Kultur.* Ausstellungskatalog des Kunstgebäudes Stuttgart. Thorbecke, Ostfildern 2009.

Coppens, Yves et al. 'Discovery of an archaic Homo sapiens skullcap in Northeast Mongolia', *C.R. Palevol,* Vol. 7, 2008, pp. 51–60.

Cormas, David et al. 'Trading genes along the Silk Road: mtDNA sequences and the origin of Central Asian populations', *American Journal for Human Genetics,* Vol. 63, pp. 1824–1838, The American Society for Human Genetics, Bethesda 1998.

Cosmo, Nicola di. *Ancient China and its enemies. The rise of nomadic power in East Asian history.* Cambridge University Press, Cambridge 2002.

— 'The Origins of the Great Wall', *The Silk Road Journal,* Vol. 4/1, pp. 14–19, 2006. The Silk Road Foundation, Saratoga. http://www.silkroadfoundation.org/newsletter/vol4num1/srnewsletter_v4n1.pdf

— 'Ethnogenesis, coevolution and political morphology of the earliest steppe empire: the Xiongnu question revisited', in Brosseder, Ursula, Miller, Bryan (eds). *Xiongnu Archaeology.* Rheinische Friedrich-Wilhelms-Universität Bonn, 2011, pp. 35–48.

Costermans, Barbara et al (eds). *Les Huns.* Europalia International, Bruxelles 2005.

Cozan, Jean-Yves, Amandry Pierre, Schiltz Véronique. *L'Or des Sarmates. Nomades des steppes dans l'Antiquité.* Abbaye de Daoulas 1995.

Cribb, Joe. 'The Greek kingdom of Bactria, its coinage and its collapse', in Bopearachchi, Osmund, Boussac, Marie-Françoise. *Afghanistan. Ancien carrefour entre l'est et l'ouest.* Brepols, Turnhout 2005, pp. 207–225.

Cribb, Joe, Herrmann, Georgina (eds). *After Alexander. Central Asia before Islam.* The British Academy, London 2007.

Crooson, Lionel. 'L'homme de Salkhit a parlé', *National Geographic.* French edition, Paris Novembre 2010, pp. 48–57.

Crubézy et al. 'Indo-européens et anthropologie biologique', in Félix Charlotte (ed). *Les Indo-Européens. Dossiers d'Archéologie No. 338,* Faton, Quétigny 2010, pp. 62–67.

Čugunov, Konstantin. 'Der skythenzeitliche Kulturwandel in Tuva', *Eurasia Antiqua,* Vol. 4/1998, pp. 273–307. Deutsches Archäologisches Institut, Berlin; Philipp von Zabern, Mainz 1999.

Čugunov, Konstantin, Parzinger, Hermann, Nagler, Anatoli. 'Der skythische Fürstengrabhügel von Arzhan 2 in Tuva. Vorbericht der russisch-deutschen Ausgrabungen', *Eurasia Antiqua,* Vol. 9/2003, pp. 113–162. Deutsches Archäologisches Institut, Berlin; Philipp von Zabern, Mainz 2003.

— *Der Goldschatz von Aržhan. Ein Fürstengrab in der südsibirischen Steppe.* Schirmer/Mosel, München 2006.

— *Der skythenzeitliche Fürstenkurgan Aržhan 2 in Tuva.* Philipp von Zabern, Mainz 2010.

Cui, Yin Qiu et al. 'Analysis of the matrilineal genetic structure of population in the early Iron Age from Tarim Basin, Xinjiang, China', *Chinese Science Bulletin,* Vol. 54, 2009, pp. 3916–3923. http://www.springerlink.com/content/lmk6120014352864/fulltext.pdf

Curtis, John. *Ancient Persia.* British Museum Press, London 2000.

— 'Iron Age Iran and the Transition to the Achaemenid Period, in Curtis Vesta, S., Stewart, Sarah (eds). *The Idea of Iran.* Vol. 1. I.B.Tauris, London 2005, pp. 112–131.

Curtis, John, Tallis, Nigel. *Forgotten Empire. The world of Ancient Persia.* British Museum Press, London 2005.

Curtis, Vesta S., Stewart, Sarah (eds). *The Idea of Iran.* 4 vols. I.B.Tauris, London 2005–2009.

Dalfes, Nüzhet, Kukla, George, Weiss, Harvey (eds). *Third Millennium BC Cli,mate Change and Old World Collapse.* NATO Scientific Affairs Division and Springer Verlag, Berlin 1997.

Dalton, O.M. *The treasure of the Oxus with other examples of early oriental metal-work.* British Museum, London (1905) 1964.

Dandamayev, M. 'Media and Achaemenid Iran', in *History of civilizations of Central Asia,* Vol. II. Unesco Publishing, Paris 1994, pp. 35–65.

Dani, A., Thapar, B. 'The Indus Civilization', in *History of civilizations of Central Asia,* Vol. I. Unesco Publishing, Paris 1992, pp. 283–318.

Dani, A., Bernard, P. 'Alexander and his successors in Central Asia', in *History of civilizations of Central Asia,* Vol. II. Unesco Publishing, Paris 1994, pp. 67–97.

Darwin, Charles. *Die Entstehung der Arten* (German translation of '*On the Origin of Species by Means of Natural Selections, or the Preservation of Favoured Races in the Struggle for* Life' von 1859). Nikol, Hamburg 2008.

— *The Descent of Man, and Selection in Relation to sex.* John Murray, London 1871. Online publication: http://darwin-online.org.uk/pdf/1871_Descent_F937.1.pdf and in German translation: *Die Abstammung des Menschen.* Fischer, Frankfurt 2009.

Dashnyam, L. et al. *Historical and Cultural Monuments of Mongolia.* Mongolian Academy of Humanities, Ulaan Baatar 1999.

David, Bruno, Thomas, Julian (eds). *Handbook of Landscape Archaeology.* Left Coast Press, Walnut Creek 2008.

Davis-Kimball, Jeannine. 'Amazons, Princesses and other Women of Status. Females in Eurasian Nomadic Societies', *Silk Road Art and Archaeology,* Vol. 5, 1997/98, pp. 1–50. Journal of the Institute of Silk Road Studies, Kamakura 1998.

— *Warrior women.* Warner Books, New York 2002.

— Davis-Kimball, Jeannine et al (eds). *Kurgans, Ritual Sites and Settlements. Eurasian Bronze and Iron Age.* British Archaeological Reports, International Series, Archaeopress, London 2000.

Davudov, Omar. 'Kimmerier, Skythen und Dagestan. Ein hochalpines Feuerheiligtum im Kontext der reiternomadischen Vorderasienzüge', *Hamburger Beiträge zur Archäologie,* Vol. 18, pp. 47–56. Philipp von Zabern, Mainz 1996.

Debaine-Francfort, Corinne. 'Keriya. (Xinjiang)', in *Les carnets de l'archéologie, France-diplomatie,* no date, www.diplomatie.gouv.fr/culture/culture_scientifique/archeologie/keriya

Debaine-Francfort, Corinne et al., *Keriya. Mémoires d'un fleuve.* Findakly, Paris, 2001.

— *La Keriya dans tous ses états: modes de peuplement et paléoenvironnements.* IMASIE, Paris 2007. www.reseau-asie.com

— 'The Taklamakan Oases: An environmental evolution shown through georchaeology', in Schneier-Madanes, G., Courel, M.-F. (eds). *Water and Sustainability in Arid Regions.* Springer Netherlands, 2010, pp. 181–202.

Demoule, Jean-Paul. 'Deux siècles à la recherche des Indo-Européens', in *Les Indo-Européens. Dossiers d'Archéologie* No. 338, Editions Faton, Quétigny 2010, pp. 6–13.

Dennell, Robin. *The Palaeolithic Settlement of Asia.* Cambridge University Press, Cambridge 2009.

Dennell, Robin, Roebroeks, Wil. 'An Asian perspective on early human dispersal from Africa', *Nature,* Vol. 438, pp. 1099–1104, Macmillan Publishers, Basingstoke 2005.

Derevyanko, Anatoly (ed.). *The Palaeolithic of Siberia.* University of Illinois Press, Urbana and Chicago 1998.

Derevyanko, Anatoly, Lü Zun. 'Upper Palaeolithic cultures', in *History of civilizations of Central Asia*, Vol. I. Unesco Publishing, Paris 1992, pp. 89–108.

Derevyanko, Anatoly, Dorj, D. 'Neolithic tribes in northern parts of Central Asia', in *History of civilizations of Central Asia*, Vol. I. Unesco Publishing, Paris 1992, pp. 169–189.

Derevyanko, Anatoly et al. 'The stratified cave site of Tsagaan Agui on the Gobi Altai (Mongolia)', in *Archaeology, Ethnology & Anthropology of Eurasia* 1, 2000, pp. 23–36.

http://paleo.sscnet.ucla.edu/DereviankoEtAl2000.pdf

Desroches, Jean-Paul et al. *Mongolie, le premier empire des steppes*. Actes Sud, Paris 2003.

Devlet, Ekaterina. 'Rock Art and the material culture of Siberian and Central Asian Shamanism', in Neil Price (ed.). *The Archaeology of Shamanism*. Routledge, London 2001, pp. 43–55.

Devlet, Marianna. 'Felsbilder von Aldy-Mozag, Tuva', *Eurasia Antiqua*, Vol. 5/1999, pp. 595–655. Deutsches Archäologisches Institut, Berlin; Philipp von Zabern, Mainz 1999.

Dien, Albert. 'The stirrup and its effect on Chinese military history', *Ars Orientalia,* Vol. 16, 1986, pp. 33–56. http://www.silk-road.com/artl/stirrup.shtml

Dirksen, V.G., Geel, B. van. 'Mid to late Holocene climate change and its influence on cultural development in South Central Siberia', in Scott, Marian et al (eds). *Impact of the Environment on Human Migration in Eurasia*, 2004, pp. 291–307.

Dolitsky, Alexander. 'Siberian Palaeolithic Archaeology', *Current Anthropology*, Vol. 26, No. 3, pp. 361–378, Chicago Journals, Chicago 1985.

Dossiers d'Archéologie No. 185, *Découverte des civilisation d'Asie Centrale*. Faton, Quétigny 1993.

— No. 194, *Les Scythes*. Faton, Quétigny 1994.

— No. 212, *Tombes gelées de Sibérie*. Faton, Quétigny 1996.

— No. 247, *La Bactriane de Cyrus à Timour*. Faton, Quétigny 1999.

— No. 266, *L'or des rois Scythes*. Faton, Quétigny 2001.

— No. 271, *Les Parthes* Faton, Quétigny 2002.

— No. 287, *Jiroft. Fabuleuse découverte en Iran*. Faton, Quétigny 2003.

— No. 292, *Premiers hommes de Chine*. Faton, Quétigny 2004.

— No. 317, *Turkménistan, un berceau culturel en Asie Centrale*. Faton, Quétigny 2006.

— No. 338, *Les Indo-Européens*. Faton, Quétigny 2010.

— No. 341, *Samarcande*. Faton, Quétigny 2010.

Dovzhenko, Nadia, Zabashta Rostislav. *Davina skulptura i plastyka Ukrainy (Ancient sculpture of Ukarine)*. Rodovit, Kiev 2009.

Drujinina, Anjelina. 'Gussform mit griechischer Inschrift aus dem Oxos-Tempel', *Archäologische Mitteilungen aus Iran und Turan*, Vol. 40, pp. 121–135. Deutsches Archäologisches Institut Berlin 2008.

— 'Excavations of Takht-i Sangin City, Territory of Oxus Temple, in 2006', *Bulletin of Miho Museum, Koka*, Vol. IX, March 2009, pp. 59–84.

— 'Wohnen im hellenistischen Baktrien – Wohnhäuser in der Stadt Oxeiane (Tachti Sangin)', in Sven Hansen et al. (eds), *Alexander der Große und die Öffnung der Welt: Asiens Kulturen im Wandel* (Mannheim, 2009), pp. 177–181.

Du Brux, Paul. *Oeuvres*. (1811–1835) Compiled and edited by I.V. Tunkina. 2 vols. Kolo, St. Petersburg 2010.

— 'Rackopi kurgana Kul-Oba, 1830 g', in Paul Du Brux. *Oeuvres* (Petersburg 2010) pp. 167–194.

Dueck, Daniela et al. (eds) *Strabo's cultural geography*. Cambridge University Press, Cambridge 2005.

Encyclopedia of Religions, edited by Mircea Eliade. 16 vols. Macmillan, New York, 1993.

Engels, Donald. *Alexander the Great and the Logistics of the Macedonian Army*. University of California Press, Berkeley, 1978.

Enoki, G., Koshelenko, A., Haidary, Z. 'The Yüeh-chih and their migrations', in *History of civilizations of Central Asia*, Vol. II. Edited by Harmatta Janos et al. Unesco Publishing, Paris 1994, pp. 171–189.

Erdenebaatar, D. 'Burial materials related to the history of the Bronze Age in the territory of Mongolia', in Linduff, Katheryn (ed.). *Metallurgy in ancient Eastern Eurasia from the Urals to the Yellow River*. Mellen, Ceredigion 2004, pp. 189–222.

Etler, Dennis. *Implications of new fossil material attributed to Plio-Pleistocene Asian hominidae*. Center for the study of Chinese prehistory, Cabrillo College, Aptos, no date. www.chineseprehistory.com

— 'The fossil evidence for human evolution in Asia', *Annual review of Human Anthropology*, Vol. 25, pp. 275–301, Annual Reviews, Palo Alto 1996.

Fagne, Claude (ed.). *La Route de la Soie*. Europalia, Bruxelles 2009.

Fansa, Mamoun, Burmeister, Stefan (eds). *Rad und Wagen*. Philipp von Zabern, Mainz 2004.

Fay, Marianne et al (eds). *Adapting to climate change in Eastern Europe and Central Asia*. The World Bank, Washington 2010.

Félix, Charlotte (ed). 'Les Indo-Européens', *Dossiers d'Archéologie* No. 338, Editions Faton, Quétigny 2010.

Fitzhugh, William. 'Stone Shamans and Flying Deer of Northern Mongolia: Deer Goddess of Siberia or Chimera of the Steppe?', *Arctic Anthropology*, University of Wisconsin, Vol. 46, No.1–2, 2009, pp. 72–88.

— 'The Mongolian deer stone-khirigsuur complex: dating and organization of a late Bronze Age menagerie', in Bemmann, Jan et al. *Current archaeological research in Mongolia*. R.F.W.-Universität, Bonn, 2009, pp. 183–199.

Fless, Friederike, Treister, Mikhail. *Bilder und Objekte als Träger kultureller Identität und interkultureller Kommunikation im Schwarzmeergebiet*. Verlag Marie Leidorf, Rahden 2005.

Fless, Friederike, Lorenz, Angelika. 'Die Nekropolen von Pantikapaion im 4. Jh. v.Chr', in Fless, Friederike, Treister, Mikhail. *Bilder und Objekte als Träger kultureller Identität und interkultureller Kommunikation im Schwarzmeergebiet*. Verlag Marie Leidorf, Rahden 2005, pp. 17–25.

Fol, Valeria (ed.). *L'or des Thraces*. Éditions Snoeck, Gand 2006.

Fornasier, Jochen. 'Das Pektorale von Tolstaja Mogila. Vergleichende Untersuchungen zur Form und Funktion', in Stähler, Klaus (ed). *Zur graeco-skythischen Kunst*. Archäologisches Kolloquium Münster 1995. Ugarit-Verlag, Münster 1997, pp. 119–146.

— *Amazonen. Frauen, Kämpferinnen und Städtegründerinnen*. Philipp von Zabern, Mainz 2007.

Fornasier, Jochen, Böttger, Burkhard (eds). *Das Bosporanische Reich*. Philipp von Zabern, Mainz 2002.

— 'Das Bosporanische Reich ', in Fornasier, Jochen, Böttger, Burkhard (eds). *Das Bosporanische Reich*. Philipp von Zabern, Mainz 2002, pp. 21–38.

Foucart, P. 'Décret de la ville de Chersonésos en l'honneur de Diophantos, général de Mithridate', *Bulletin de correspondance hellénique*. Vol. 5, 1881, pp. 70–87.

Frachetti, Michael. 'Bronze Age Exploitation and Political Dynamics of the Eastern Eurasian Steppe Zone', in Levine, Marsha et al. *Late prehistoric exploitation of the Eurasian steppe*. McDonald Institute for Archaeological Research, Cambridge, 1999, pp. 161–170.

— *Pastoralist landscapes and social interaction in Bronze Age Eurasia*. University of California Press, Berkeley 2008.

Francalacci, Paolo. 'DNA Analysis on Ancient Corpses from Xinjiang: Further Results', in Mair, Victor. *The Bronze Age and Early Iron Age Peoples of Eastern Central Asia*. The Institute for the Study of Man, Pennsylvania, 1998, pp. 537–547.

Francfort, Henri-Paul et al. *Fouilles de Shortugaï. Recherches sur l'Asie Centrale protohistorique*. Boccard, Paris 1989.

— 'Art rupestre du bassin de Minusinsk: nouvelles recherches franco-russe', *Arts Asiatiques. Musée national des Arts asiatiques-Guimet*, 48/1993, pp. 5–52. Paris.

— 'Les pétroglyphes de Tamgaly', *Bulletin of the Asia Institute*, Vol. 9, 1995, pp. 167–208. The Asia Institute, Bloomfield Hills 1997.

— 'Central Asian petroglyphs: between Indo-Iranian and shamanistic interpretations', in Chippindale Christopher, Taçon Paul (eds). *The Archaeology of Rock-Art*. Cambridge University Press, Cambridge 1998, pp. 302–318.

— 'De l'art des steppes au sud du Taklamakan', *Bulletin of the Asia Institute*, Vol. 12, 1998, pp. 45–58. Bloomfield Hills, 2001.

— 'La Civilisation de l'Asie Centrale à l'âge du Bronze et è l'âge du Fer', in Bopearachchi, Osmund et al. *De l'Indus à l'Oxus. Archaéologie de l'Asie Centrale*. Association IMAGO, Lattes 2003, pp. 29–62.

— 'La civilisation de l'Oxus et les Indo-Iraniens et Indo-Aryens en Asie Centrale', in Fussman, Gérard et al. *Aryas, Aryens et Iraniens en Asie Centrale*, pp. 253–328. Diffusion Boccard, Paris 2005.

— 'Observation sur la toreutique de la civilisation de l'Oxus', in Bopearachchi, Osmund et al. *Afghanistan. Ancien: carrefour entre l'est et l'ouest*, 2005, pp. 21–64.

— 'Images du combat contre le sanglier en Asie centrale (3ème au 1er millénaire av. J.-C.)', *Bulletin of the Asia Institute*, Vol. 16, 2002, pp. 117–142. Bloomfield Hills, 2006.

— 'La «culture de Marlik» et l'arrivée des Indo-Iraniens', in Mattet, Laurence (ed.). *Le Profane et le Divin. Arts de l'Antiquité de l'Europe au Sud-Est Asiatique*, 2008, pp. 138–145.

Frings, Jutta (ed.). *Die Thraker. Das goldene Reich des Orpheus*. Kunst und Ausstellungshalle der Bundersrepublik, Bonn, Philipp von Zabern, Mainz 2004.

Frumkin, Grégoire. *Archaeology in Soviet Central Asia*. Brill, Leiden 1970.

Frye, Richard. *The heritage of Central Asia. From Antiquity to the Turkish Expansion*. Markus Wiener Publishers, Princeton 1996.

Fuhrmeister, Kirsten. 'Zweiergruppen und Brüdermotive', in Stähler Klaus (ed). *Zur graeco-skythischen Kunst*. Archäologisches Kolloquium Münster 1995. Ugarit-Verlag, Münster 1997, pp. 161–176.

Gafurov, B.G. *Central Asia. Prehistoric to pre-modern times*. Shipra Publications, Delhi (1972) 2005.

Gaïbov, V., Kochelenko, G. 'La Margiane', *Dossiers d'Archéologie* No. 271, *Les Parthes*. Editions Faton, Quétigny 2002, pp. 46–53.

Galanina, L.K. *Die Kurgane von Kelermes*. Deutsches Archäologisches Institut, Berlin 1996.

Gall, Hubertus von. 'Das Motiv des „Reiters mit dem Knappen" auf den bosporanischen Grabstelen', *Archäologische Mitteilungen aus Iran und Turan*, Vol. 34, pp. 397–413. Deutsches Archäologisches Institut Berlin 2003.

Gao, Shi Zhu. 'Mitochondrial DNA analysis of human remains from the Yuansha site in Xinjiang, China', *Science in China Series C: Life Sciences*, Vol. 51, No.3, March 2008, pp. 205–213. http://www.scichina.com:8082/sciCe/fileup/PDF/08yc0205.pdf

Gardiner-Garden, John. *Apollodoros of Artemita and the Central Asian Skythians*. Papers on Inner Asia, No. 3. Indiana University, Bloomington 1987.

Gardner, Percy. *The coins of the Greek and Scythic Kings of Bactria and India in the British Museum*. Argonaut Publishers, Chicago 1966.

Geel, B. van et al. 'The sun, climate change and the expansion of the Scythian culture after 850 BC', in Scott Marian et al (eds). *Impact of the Environment on Human Migration in Eurasia*, 2004, pp. 151–158.

Gej, Aleksandr. 'Die Wagen der Novotitarovskaja-Kultur', in Fansa Mamoun, Burmeister Stefan. *Rad und Wagen*. Philipp von Zabern, Mainz 2004, pp. 177–190.

Gentelle, Pierre. 'Une géographie du mouvement: le désert du Taklamakan et ses environs comme modèle', *Annales de Géographie*, Armand Collin, Paris, Vol. 101, nr. 567, 1992, pp. 553–594.

Ghirsman, R. *Fouilles de Sialk près de Kashan. 1933–1937*. 2 vols. Paul Geuthner, Paris, 1938.

— 'Le dieu Zurvan sur les bronzes de Luristan', *Artibus Asiae*, Vol. XXI, pp.37–42. Ascona 1958

— 'Deux statuettes élamites du plateau iranien', *Artibus Asiae*, Vol. XXX, 2/3, pp. 237–247. Ascona 1968.

Gignoux, Ph., Litvinsky, B.A. 'Religions and religious movements I', in *History of civilizations of Central Asia*, Vol. III. Unesco Publishing, Paris 1996, pp. 403–420.

Gingerich, Philip D. 'Environment and evolution through the Palaeocene-Eocene thermal maximum', in *Trends in Ecology and Evolution*, Vol 21, 2006, pp. 246–253.

— 'Mammalian faunal succession through the Palaeocene-Eocene themal maximum (PRTM) in western North America', *Vertebrata PalAsiatica*, Vol. 48, No. 4, pp.308–327, Beijing 2010.

Gladkih, Mikhail et al. 'Mammoth-Bone Dwellings on the Russian Plain', *Scientific American*, Vol. 251, No. 5, November 1984, pp. 165–175.

Goepper, Roger, Lee-Khalisch, J. *Korea. Die alten Königreiche*. Ausstellungskatalog, Museum Rietberg, Zürich 2000.

Golden, Peter. *Central Asia in World History*. Oxford University Press, Oxford 2011.

Golzio, Karl-Heinz. *Kings, Khans and other rulers of Early Central Asia*. Religionswissenschaftliches Seminar der Universität Bonn, Bonn 1984.

Good, Irene. *On the question of silk in pre-Han Eurasia*, 1995. http://harvard.academia.edu/documents/0009/8367/good1995.pdf

— 'When East met West: Interpretative Problems in Assessing East-West Contact and Exchange in Antiquity', in *Vth ICAANE Congress, Madrid*. Edited by Allison Betts and Fiona Kidd. Ancient Near Easstern Monograph series. Peeters, Louvain 2008.

Good, Irene, Kennoyer, J.M., Meadow, R.H. 'New evidence for early silk in the Indus civilizations', *Archaeometry*, University of Oxford, 50, 2009. http://www.scribd.com/doc/11508384/Indussilk

Gorelik, Mikhael. *Warriors of Eurasia*. Montvert, Stockport 1995.

Gorshenina, Svetlana, Rapin, Claude. *De Kaboul à Samarcande. Les archéologues en Asie centrale*. Gallimard, Paris 2001.

Goryachev, A.A., Mariyashev, A.N. *Petroglyphs of Semirechye*. Fort inform 1999. http://tourkz.com/eng/articles/petrogle_3.html

Götzelt, Thomas. *Ansichten der Archäologie Süd-Turkmenistans bei der Erforschung der mittleren Bronzezeit (Periode Namazga V.)* Marie Leidorf, Espelkamp 1996.

Gougouev, Vladimir. 'Tombe d'une reine Sarmate', *Dossiers d'Archéologie*, No. 194, *Les Scythes*, 1994, pp. 76–83.

Govedarica, B. et al. 'Der Grabhügel „Tarasova Mogila' bei der Stadt Prechov', *Eurasia Antiqua*, Vol. 12/2006, pp. 63–112. Deutsches Archäologisches Institut, Berlin; Philipp von Zabern, Mainz 2007.

Green, Richard et al. 'Analysis of one million base pairs of Neanderthal DNA', *Nature*, 10:1038/05336, No. 444, pp. 330–336, Macmillan Publishers, Basingstoke 2006. http://www.nature.com/nature/journal/v444/n7117/full/nature05336.html

— 'A Draft Sequence of the Neanderthal Genome',

Science, Vol. 328, pp. 710–722, 7 May 2010. American Association for the Advancement of Science, New York 2010.

Grenet, Frantz. 'An Archaeologist's Approach to Avestan Geography', in Curtis Vesta, S., Stewart, Sarah (eds). *The Idea of Iran*, Vol. 1, I.B.Tauris, London 2005, pp. 29–51.

— 'Les religions dans l'Empire perse', in *Le monde de la Bible*. Bayard, Montrouge, Nr. 187, 2009, pp. 26–31.

Grenet, Frantz, Rapin, Claude. 'Alexander, Aï Khanum, Termez. Remarks on the Spring Campaign of 328', *Bulletin of the Asia Institute*, Vol. 12, 1998, pp. 79–90. The Asia Institute, Bloomfield Hills 2001.

Grigoryev, S.A. *Ancient Indo-Europeans*. RIFEI, Chelyabinsk 2002.

— 'The Sintashta Culture and the Indo-European Problem', in Jones-Bley, Karlene, Zdanovich, D.G. *Complex Societies of Central Eurasia from the 3rd to the 1st Millennium BC*. Vol. I., Institute for the Study of Man, Washington DC, 2002, pp. 148–160.

Grjaznov, Michail. *Südsibirien*. Nagel, Genf 1970.

— *Der Großkurgan von Arzhan in Tuva, Südsibirien*. C.H. Beck, München, 1984.

Grousset, René. *The Empire of the Steppes*. Rutgers, New Brunswick (1939) 1970.

Haarmann, Harald. *Universalgeschichte der Schrift*. Campus, Frankfurt 1998.

Hajdas, I, Bonani, G. et al. *Chronology of Pazyryk 2 and Ulandryk 4 Kurgans based on high resolution radiocarbon dating and dendrochronology – a step towards more precise dating of Scythian burials*. In Scott, Marian et al. *Impact of the Environment on Human Migration in Eurasia*, 2004, pp. 107–116.

Han, Kangxin. 'The Physical Anthropology of the Ancient Populations of the Tarim Basin and Surrounding Areas', in Mair Victor, *The Bronze Age and Early Iron Age Peoples of Eastern Central Asia*. The Institute for the Study of Man, Pennsylvania, 1998, pp. 558–570.

Han, Rubin, Sun Shuyun. 'Preliminary Studies on the Bronzes Excavated from the Tianshanbeilou Cemetery, Hami, Xinjiang', in Linduff Katheryn (ed.). *Metallurgy in ancient Eastern Eurasia from the Urals to the Yellow River*. Mellen, Ceredigion 2004, pp. 157–172.

Hansen, Sven et al (eds). Alexander *der Große und die Öffnung der Welt. Asiens Kulturen im Wandel*. Reiss-Engelhorn-Museen, Mannheim 2009.

Harmatta, J. *Studies in the History and Language of the Sarmatians*. Acta Universitatis de Attila József Nominatae. Acta antique et archaeologica Tomus XIII. Szeged 1970 http://www.kroraina.com/sarm/jh/index.html

Harvati, Katerina. '100 years of Homo heidelbergensis – life and times of a controversial taxon', *Mitteilungen der Gesellschaft für Urgeschichte. Blaubeuren*, Vol. 16, 2007, pp. 85–94.

Hatakyama, Tei. *The Tumulus and Stag Stones at Shiebar-kul in Xinjiang, China*. 2002. http://web.kanazawa-u.ac.jp/~steppe/sougen13.hatakeyama.html

Hauptmann, Harald (ed.). *Die Felsbildstation Thalpan. Kataloge Chilas-Brücke und Thalpan (Steine 1–30)*. Vol. I. Philipp von Zabern, Mainz 2003.

He, Dexiu. 'A Brief Report on the Mummies from the Zaghunluq Site in Chärchän County', in Mair, Victor, *The Bronze Age and Early Iron Age Peoples of Eastern Central Asi*a. The Institute for the Study of Man, Pennsylvania, 1998, pp. 169–174.

Hebeisen, Kurt Beat. *Spurensuche nach dem Ursprung der Kunst*. Haupt, Bern 2009.

Hedin, Sven. *Through Asia*. Harper, New York, 1899.

— *Der wandernde See*. Brockhaus, Leipzig 1938.

Hedin, Sven et al. *History of the expedition in Asia 1927–1935. Part I–IV.* Reports from the scientific expedition to the north-western provinces of China under the leadership of Dr. Sven Hedin. Publications 23–26. Elanders Boktryckeri Aktiebolag, Göteborg 1943–45.

Heissig, Walther, Müller, Claudius (eds). *Die Mongolen*. Pinguin, Innsbruck/Umschau, Frankfurt 1989.

Helms, Sven. 'Ancient Choresmia. The Northern Edge of Central Asia from the 6th Century BC. to the mid-4th Century AD', in Christian, David, Benjamin, Craig (eds). *Silk Road Studies II. Worlds of the Silk Roads: Ancient and Modern*, pp. 77–96. Brepols, Turnhout 1998.

Helms, Sven et al. 'Five seasons of excavations in the Tash-k'irman oasis of Ancient Chorasmis, 1996–2000. An interim report', *Iran. Journal of the British Institute of Persian Studies*, Vol. XXXIX, pp. 119–144. The British Institute of Persian Studies, London 2001.

Hemphill, Brian, Mallory J.P. 'Horse-mounted invaders from the Russo-Kazakh Steppe or agricultural colonists from Western Central Asia? A craniometric investigation of the Bronze Age settlements of Xinjiang', *American Journal of Physical Anthropology*, Vol. 123, No. 3, 2004, pp. 199–222. http://www3.interscience.wiley.com/journal/105558550/abstract

Herman, Luc. *Les pétroglyphes de Tcholpon-Ata au Kirghizstan*. BoD, Paris 2010.

— *Die Petroglyphen von Tamgaly in Kasachstan*. BoD, Paris 2011.

— *Die Petroglyphen von Usektal in Kasachstan*. BoD, Paris 2011.

Hermanns, Matthias. *Chinas Ursprung*. Missionsdruckerei Yenchowfu, Shantung 1935.

Herodotus. *Geschichten und Geschichte*. Artemis, Zürich 1973.

— *The Histories*. Translated by Aubrey de Sélincourt and revised by John Marincola. Penguin Books, London 2003.

Herrmann, Georgina. *Monuments of Merv*. The Society of Antiquaries, London 1999.

Herrmann, Georgina et al. The international Merv Project. Preliminary report on the ninth year (2000)', *Iran. Journal of the Br itish Institute of Persian Studies*, Vol. XXXIX, pp. 9–52. The British Institute of Persian Studies, London 2001.

Hiebert, Fredrik Talmage et al. *Origins of the Bronze Age Oasis Civilization in Central Asia*. Peabody Museum, Harvard University, 1994.

— *A Central Asian Village at the Dawn of Civilization, excavations at Anau, Turkmenistan*. University of Pennsylvania Museum, Philadelphia 2003.

Hiebert, Frederik, Cambon, Pierre (eds). *Afghanistan, Crossroads of the Ancient World*. The British Museum Press, London 2011.

Higham, Thomas et al. Testing models for the beginnings of the Aurignacian and the advent of figurative art and music: The radiocarbon chronology of Geißenköcherle. In: *Journal of Human Evolution*, Vol. XXX, 2012, pp. 1–13. Elsevier, Amsterdam 2012. doi:19.1016/j.jhevol.2012.03.003.

Hildinger, Erik. *Warriors of the Steppe. A military history of Central Asia 500 BC to 1700 AD* Da Capo Press, Cambridge MA 2001.

Hill, John. *Through the Jade Gate to Rome. An annotated translation of the Chronicle on the 'Western regions' in the Hou Hanshu*. John Hill publication, Australia, 2009.

History of civilizations of Central Asia. Vol. I. The dawn of civilization: earliest times to 700 BC. Edited by Dani A.H., Masson Vadim. Unesco Publishing, Paris 1992.

History of civilizations of Central Asia. Vol. II. The development of sedentary and nomadic civilizations: 700 BC to AD 250. Edited by Harmatta Janos et al. Unesco Publishing, Paris 1994.

History of civilizations of Central Asia. Vol. III. The crossroads of civilizations. AD 250 to 750. Edited by Litvinsky, Boris et al. Unesco Publishing, Paris 1996.

Holt, Frank. *Thundering Zeus. The making of Hellenistic Bactria*. University of California Press, Berkeley 1999.

Höllmann, Thomas, Kossack, Georg. 'Maoqinggou. Ein eisenzeitliches Gräberfeld in der Ordos-Region (Innere Mongolei)', in *Materialien zur Allgemeinen und Vergleichenden Archäologie*, Vol 50, pp. 46–87. Philipp von Zabern, Mainz 1992.

Hrdlicka, Ales. 'Crania of Siberia', *American Journal of Physical Anthropology*, Vol. XXIX, No. 4, pp. 435–481, American Association of Physical Anthropologists, Baltimore (1942) 2005.

Hsü, Kenneth. *Klima macht Geschichte*. Orell Füssli, Zürich 2000.

Hübner, Ulrich et al (eds). *Die Seidenstraße. Handel und Kulturaustausch in einem eurasischen Wegenetz*. EB-Verlag, Hamburg 2001.

Hulsewé, A.F.P., Loewe, M.A.N. *China in Central Asia. The Ealy Stage: 125 BC – AD 23. An Annotated Translation of Chapters 61 and 96 of the History of the Former Han Dynasty*. Brill, Leiden 1979.

Humboldt, Alexandre de. *Asie Centrale. Recherches sur les chaînes des montagnes et la climatologie comparée*. 3 vols. Gide, Paris 1843. *Zentral-Asien. Untersuchungen zu den Gebirgsketten und zur vergleichenden Klimatologie*. Nach der deutsche Übersetzung von 1844, Fischer-Verlag, Frankfurt a.M., 2009.

Huntington, Ellsworth. *The Pulse of Asia*. Houghton, Boston 1907.

Hyland, Ann. *Training the Roman Cavalry. From Arrian's Ars Tactica*. Grange, London 1993.

Iakovleva, Lioudmilla. 'Les habitats en os de mammouth des chasseurs paléolithiques d'Ukraine', *Dossiers d'Archéologie* No. 266, *L'or des rois Scythes*, 2001, pp. 36–47.

Iakovleva, Lioudmilla, Djindjian, François. 'New data on Mammoth bone settlements of Eastern Europe in the light of the new excavations of the Gontsy site Ukraine', *International Science Reviews*, 126–128, 2005, pp. 195–207. Elsevier, Amsterdam.

Idriss, Abdulressul et al. 'The Xiaohe Graveyard in Luobupo, Xinjiang', *Chinese Archaeology*, Vol. 8. China Social Sciences Press, Beijing 2008, pp. 85–95.

Ionesov, Vladimir. *The struggle between life and death in Proto-Bactrian Culture*. Mellen, Ceredigion 2002.

Isakov, A.I. 'Sarazm et la civilisation de l'Asie centrale', in *Découverte des civilisations d'Asie Centrale. Les dossiers d'archéologie*. Faton, Dijon, Nr. 185, 1993, pp. 28–35.

— Sarazm. 'An Agricultural Center of Ancient Sogdiana', *Bulletin of the Asia Institute*, Vol. 8, 1994, pp. 1–12. The Asia Institute, Bloomfield Hills 1996.

Ivanisev, N.D. *Drevnosti vremennoj komisii po razboru drevnich aktov*, Kiev, 1846.

Ivanova, N.O. (ed.) *Materialy po arkheologii i etnografii Iuzhnogo Urala*. Trudymuzeia-zapovednika Arkaim, Cheliabinskii universitet, Cheliabinsk 2006.

Ivantchik, Askold. *Les Cimmériens au Proche-Orient*. Editions Universitaires, Fribourg (Suisse) 1993.

— *Kimmerer und Skythen*. Deutsches Archäologisches Institut, Berlin 2001.

Jacobson, Esther. *The Deer Goddess of Ancient Siberia*. Brill, Leiden 1993.

— *The Art of the Scythians*. Brill, Leiden 1995.

— 'The "bird-woman", the "birthing-woman" and the "woman of the animals": a consideration of the female image in petroglyphs of Ancient central Asia', *Arts Asiatiques. Musée national des Arts asiatiques-Guimet*, 52/1997, pp. 37–59. Paris.

— 'Cultural Riddles: Stylized Deer and Deer Stones of the Mongolian Altai', *Bulletin of the Asia Institute*, Vol. 15, 2001, pp. 31–56. The Asia Institute, Bloomfield Hills 2005.

— 'The Rock Art of Mongolia', *The Silk Road Journal*, Vol. 4/1, pp. 5–13, 2006. The Silk Road Foundation, Saratoga. http://www.silkroadfoundation.org/newsletter/vol4num1/srnewsletter_v4n1.pdf

Jacobson, Esther, Meacham, James. *Archaeology and Landscape in the Mongolian Altai: An Atlas*. ESRI Press, Redlands CA 2010.

Jäger, Ulf. *Reiter, Reiterkrieger und Reiternomaden zwischen Rheinland und Korea: Zur spätantiken Reitkultur zwischen Ost und West, 4.–8. Jh. n. Chr.* Beier & Beran, Langenweißbach 2006.

Jahresbericht 2007, AA 2008/Beiheft. Deutsches Archäologisches Institut, Berlin. Hirmer, München 2008.

Jahresbericht 2008, AA 2009/Beiheft. Deutsches Archäologisches Institut, Berlin. Hirmer, München 2009.

Jahresbericht 2009, AA 2009/Beiheft. Deutsches Archäologisches Institut, Berlin. Hirmer, München 2010.

Jäkel, Dieter, Zhu, Zenda. 'Reports on the 1986 Sino-German Kun Lun Shan Taklimakan-Expedition', *Die Erde, Gesellschaft für Erdkunde Berlin, Ergänzungsheft 6*, 1992.

Jaubert, Jacques. 'The decorated cave of Hoït Tsenkher Agui', *International newsletter on rock art INORA*, No. 17, pp. 23–26. Foix 1997.

Jettmar, Karl. *Die frühen Steppenvölker*. Holle, Baden-Baden 1964.

— *Zwischen Gandhara und den Seidenstraßen. Felsbilder am Karakorum Highway*. Philipp von Zabern, Mainz 1985.

— 'Archäologie in Xinjiang und ihre Bedeutung für Südsibirien – eine Bestandesaufnahme'. in *Beiträge zur allgemeinen und vergleichenden Archäologie*, Vol. 12, pp. 130–151. Philipp von Zabern, Mainz 1992.

— 'Sintashta – ein gemeinsames Heiligtum der Indo-Iraner?', *Eurasia Antiqua*, Vol. 2/1996, pp. 215–228. Deutsches Archäologisches Institut, Berlin; Philipp von Zabern, Mainz 1996.

— 'Bemerkungen zu Arkaim', *Eurasia Antiqua*, Vol.3/1997, pp. 249–254. Deutsches Archäologisches Institut, Berlin; Philipp von Zabern, Mainz 1998.

— *Beyond the Gorges of the Indus*. Oxford University Press, Oxford 2002.

Jettmar, Karl, Kattner, Ellen (eds). *Die vorislamischen Religionen Mittelasiens*. Kohlhammer, Stuttgart 2003.

Jia, Lanpo, Huang Weiwen. *The Story of Peking Man*. Oxford University Press, Oxford 1990.

Johanson, Donald. *Origins of Modern Humans: Multiregional or Out of Africa?* American Institute of Biological sciences, Washington 2001. http://www.actionbioscience.org/evolution/johanson.html

Jones-Bley, Karlene, Zdanovich, D.G. *Complex Societies of Central Eurasia from the 3rd to the 1st Millennium BC*. Vol. I., Institute for the Study of Man, Washington D.C., 2002.

Jones-Bley, Karlene. 'Indo-European Burial, the "Rig Veda" and "Avesta"', in Jones-Bley, Karlene, Zdanovich, D.G. *Complex Societies of Central Eurasia from the 3rd to the 1st Millennium BC*. Vol. I., Institute for the Study of Man, Washington DC, 2002, pp. 68–81.

Juliano, Annette, Lerner Judith (eds). *Monks and Merchants. Silk Road treasures from Northwest China*. Abrams/Asia House, New York 2001.

Kaim, Barbara. 'Où adorer les dieux? Un spectaculaire temple du feu d'époque sassanide', *Dossiers d'Archéologie* No. 317, 2006, pp. 66–71.

Kalashnik, Yuri. *Greek gold. From the treasure rooms of the Hermitage*. Lund Humphries, Aldershot 2004.

Kamberi, Dolkun. 'A Century of Tarim Archaeological Exploration (*ca.* 1886–1996)', in Mair Victor, *The Bronze Age and Early Iron Age Peoples of Eastern Central Asia*. The Institute for the Study of Man, Pennsylvania, 1998, pp. 785–811.

Kaniuth, Kai. 'The metallurgy of the Late Bronze Age Sapalli Culture (Southern Uzbekistan) and its implications for the "tin question"', *Iranica Antiqua*, Vol. XLII, pp. 23–40, 2007. Peeters Publishers, Louvain.

Kantorovic, A., Maslov, E. 'Eine reiche Bestattung der Majkop-Kultur aus einem Kurgan der stanica Mar'inskaja, Kreis Stavropol, Nordkaukasien', *Eurasia Antiqua*, Vol. 13/2008, pp. 151–166. Deutsches

Archäologisches Institut, Berlin; Philipp von Zabern, Mainz 2009.

Karabelnik, Marianne. *Aus den Schatzkammern Eurasiens. Meisterwerke antiker Kunst.* Kunsthaus Zürich 1993.

Karomatov, F.M. et al. *Musikgeschichte in Bildern.* Mittelasien. Brockhaus, Leipzig 1987.

Kaufmann, Sabine (ed.). *Die Wikinger.* Historisches Museum der Pfalz, Speyer 2008.

Keller, Dominik, Schorta, Regula (eds). *Fabulous Creatures from the Desert Sands.* Abegg-Stiftung, Riggisberg 2001.

Kenk, Roman. *Das Gräberfeld der hunno-sarmatischen Zeit von Kokel', Tuva, Süd-Sibirien.* C.H. Beck, München 1984.

Kenk, Roman, auf Grundlage der Arbeit von A.D. Grač. *Grabfunde der Skythenzeit aus Tuva, Süd-Sibirien.* C.H. Beck, München 1986.

Kenoyer, Jonathan. *Ancient cities of the Indus Valley Civilization.* Oxford University Press, Oxford 1998.

Keyser, Christine et al. 'Tracking back ancient south Siberian population history using mitochondrial and Y-chromosope SNPs', *Forensic Sciences International: Genetics Supplements Series 1*, pp. 343–345. Elsevier, Amsterdam, 2008.

Khazanov, Anatoly. *Nomads and the Outside World.* University of Wisconsin Press, Madison 1994.

Khlopin, Igor. 'L'Hyrcanie Antique', in *Découverte des civilisations d'Asie Centrale. Les dossiers d'archéologie.* Faton, Dijon, Nr. 185, 1993, pp. 42–51.

Khrapunov, I.N., Herzen, A.H. (eds). *Ot Kimerijev do Krimchakov.* Dolia, Simferopol 2010.

Kiatkina, Tatiana. 'Le population de l'Asie Moyenne ancienne', in *Découverte des civilisations d'Asie Centrale. Les dossiers d'archéologie.* Faton, Dijon, Nr. 185, 1993, pp. 36–41.

Kirtcho, L.B. 'The earliest wheeled transport in southwestern Central Asia: New finds from Altyn-Depe', *Archaeology, Ethnology & Anthropology of Eurasia* 37/1, pp. 25–33. Elsevier, Amsterdam 2009

Kiryushin, Yu.F., Solodovnikov, K.N. 'The origins of the Andronovo (Fedorovka) population of Southwestern Siberia, based on a Middle Bronze Age cranial series from the Altai forest-steppe zone', *Archaeology, Ethnology & Anthropology of Eurasia*, 38/4 pp. 122–142. Elsevier, Amsterdam 2011.

Kislenko, Aleksandr, Tatarintseva, Nataliya. 'The Eastern Ural Steppe at the End of the Stone Age', in Levine Marsha et al. *Late prehistoric exploitation of the Eurasian steppe.* McDonald Institute for Archaeological Research, Cambridge, 1999.

Kljastornyj, S.G., Sultanov, T.I. *Staaten und Völker in den Steppen Eurasiens. Altertum und Mittelalter.* Schletzer, Berlin 2006.

Koch, Alexander (ed.). *Attila und die Hunnen.* Herausgegeben vom Historischen Museum der Pfalz Speyer, Theiss, Stuttgart 2007.

— *Hunnen zwischen Asien und Europa.* Herausgegeben vom Historischen Museum der Pfalz Speyer. Beier & Beran, Langenweissbach 2008.

Kohl, Johann Georg. *Reisen in Südrussland.* 1841, reprint in 3 vols. from 3rd edition of 1847, Elibron Classics 2008.

Kohl, Philipp (ed.). *The Bronze Age Civilization of Central Asia. Recent Soviet discoveries.* Sharpe, New York 1981.

— *The making of Bronze Age Eurasia.* Cambridge University Press, Cambridge 2007.

Kondakof, N., Tolstoï, J., Reinach, S. *Antiquités de la Russie méridionale.* Ernest Leroux, Paris 1891.

Konovalov, P.B. *The Burial vault of a Xiongnu prince at Sudzha (Il'movaia Pad', Transbaikalia).* Rheinische Friedrich-Wilhelms-Universität Bonn, 2008.

Korochkova, Olga, Stafanov, Vladimir. *The Trans-Ural Fedorovo Complexes in relation to the Andronovo.* in Linduff, Katheryn. Metallurgy in ancient Eastern Eurasia from the Urals to the Yellow River. Mellen, Ceredigion 2004.

Korolkova, E.F. *The Rulers of the Steppe* (in Russian). APC Publishers, St. Petersburg 2006.

Koryakova, Ludmila, Epimakkhov, Andrej. *The Urals and Western Siberia in the Bronze and Iron Ages.* Cambridge University Press, Cambridge 2007.

Koshelenko, G.A., Pilipko, V.N. *Parthia.* in History of civilizations of Central Asia. Vol. II. Unesco Publishing, Paris 1994, pp. 131–150.

Kosintsev, P.A. 'Animals in the Burial Rite of the Population of the Volga-Ural Area in the Beginning of the 2nd Millennium BC', in Jones-Bley, Karlene, Zdanovich, D.G. *Complex Societies of Central Eurasia from the 3rd to the 1st Millennium BC.* Vol. I., Institute for the Study of Man, Washington DC, 2002, pp. 232–247.

Kossack, Georg. *Mittelasien und skythischer Tierstil.* Beiträge zur allgemeinen und vergleichenden Archäologie 2, pp. 91–107. Philipp von Zabern, Mainz 1980.

Kostijuk, O. *Die Galerie der Kostbarkeiten in der Ermitage.* Kunstverlag Iwan Fjodorow, St. Petersburg 2005.

Kotova, Nadezhda. *Early Eneolithic in the Pontic Steppes.* BAR International Series 1735. Oxford, 2008.

— *The Neolithization of Northern Black Sea area in the context of climate changes.* http://arheologija.ff.uni-lj.si/documenta/authors36/kotova.pdf

Kouznetsov, Vladimir, Lebedynsky, Iaroslav. *Les Alains.* Editions, Errance 2005.

Kovalëv, Alexej. 'Überlegungen zur Herkunft der Skythen aufgrund archäologischer Daten', *Eurasia Antiqua*, Vol. 4/1998, pp. 247–271. Deutsches Archäologisches Institut, Berlin; Philipp von Zabern, Mainz 1999.

— 'Die ältesten Stelen am Ertix', *Eurasia Antiqua*, Vol. 5/1999, pp. 135–178. Deutsches Archäologisches Institut, Berlin; Philipp von Zabern, Mainz 1999.

Kovalëv, Alexej, Erdenebaatar, Diimaazhav. 'Discovery of new cultures of the Bronze Age in Mongolia according to the data obtained by the International central Asian Archaeological Expedition' in Bemmann Jan et al. *Current archaeological research in Mongolia.* R.F.W.-Universität, Bonn, 2009, pp. 149–170.

Kovalyova, V.T., Ryzhkova, O.V. 'Circular Settlements in the Lower Tobol Area (Tashkovo Culture)', in Jones-Bley Karlene, Zdanovich, D.G. *Complex Societies of Central Eurasia from the 3rd to the 1st Millennium BC*, Vol. I., Institute for the Study of Man, Washington DC, 2002, pp. 283–395.

Kovtun, I.V. 'The bear image in Western Siberian art of the 2nd Millennium BC and its relevance for delimiting the eastern periphery of the Samus Culture', *Archaeology, Ethnology & Anthropology of Eurasia*, Novosibirsk, 35/3, 2008, pp. 97–104.

Kozemjako, P., Kozomberdieva, E., Kozomberdiev, I. 'Ein Katakombengrab aus der Schlucht Shamsi', *Eurasia Antiqua*, Vol. 4/1998, pp. 451–471. Deutsches Archäologisches Institut, Berlin; Philipp von Zabern, Mainz 1999.

Kozintsev, A.G. 'The "Mediterraneans" of Southern Siberia and Kazakhstan', *Archaeology, Ethnology & Anthropology of Eurasia* 36/4, pp. 140–144. Elsevier, Amsterdam 2009.

— 'Craniometric evidence of the early Caucasoid migrations to Siberia and Eastern Central Asia, with reference to the Indo-European problem', *Archaeology, Ethnology & Anthropology of Eurasia* 37/4, pp. 125–136. Elsevier, Amsterdam 2009.

Krause, Johannes et al. 'Neanderthals in central Asia and Siberia', *Nature*, 10:1038/06193, No. 449, pp. 902–904, Macmillan Publishers, Basingstoke 2007.

— 'The complete mitochondrial DNA genome of an unknown hominin from southern Siberia', *Nature*, 10:1038/08976 (advance publication) Macmillan Publishers, Basingstoke March 2010.

Kreuz, Patric-Alexander. 'Norm und Sonderweg: Grabstelen klassischer und frühhellenistischer Zeit aus den Städten des Bosporanischen Reichs und das Relief aus dem Drei-Brüder-Kurgan bei Nymphaion', in Fless, Friederike, Treister, Mikhail. *Bilder und Objekte als Träger kultureller Identität und interkultureller Kommunikation im Schwarzmeergebiet.* Verlag Marie Leidorf, Rahden 2005, pp. 43–52.

— 'Das Relief aus dem Drei-Brüder-Kurgan', in Treister, Mikhail. *Die Drei-Brüder-Kurgane. Katalog und Analyse der Befunde und Funde einer Grabhügelgruppe auf der östlichen Krim aus der Zeit des 4. bis 3. Jhs. v.Chr.* Universum, Bonn, Simferopol 2008. pp. 131–140.

Krivoshapkin, Andrei, Brantingham, Jeffrey. 'The Lithic industry of Obi-Rakhmat Grotto, Uzbekistan', *Actes du XIV Congres UISPP, 2–8 septembre 2001.* BAR International Series 1240. pp. 203–214. Université de Liège, Liège. (pdf)http://paleo.sscnet.ucla.edu/KrivoshapkingBrantUISPP2004.pdf

Kristiansen, Kristian. 'La diffusion préhistorique des langues indo-européennes', *Dossiers d'Archéologie* No. 338, Editions Faton, Quétigny 2010, pp. 36–43.

Kruta, Vencelas. 'Les racines profondes de l'Europe', in *Clareté-grandes signatures*, 2008/4, pp. 46–59. Editions Faton, Dijon.

Kubarev, Vladimir. *Drevnie rospisi Karakola. (Old paintings of Karakol)* NAUKA Novosibirsk 1988.

— 'Skythische Kurgane aus den Gräberfeldern Bike I und III am mittleren Katun, Sibirien', *Eurasia Antiqua*, Vol. 7/2001, pp. 133–167. Deutsches Archäologisches Institut, Berlin; Philipp von Zabern, Mainz 2001.

— 'Biluut-Tolgoi. A new rock art site in Mongolia', *Archaeology, Ethnology & Anthropology of Eurasia*, 3 (31), pp. 63–68. Elsevier, Amsterdam 2007.

— 'Results and prospects of studying ancient art monuments in Mongolia', in Bemmann, Jan et al. *Current archaeological research in Mongolia*, 2009, pp. 67–81.

Kubarev, Vladimir, Zevendorz, D. 'Steinstelen aus der Westmongolei', *Eurasia Antiqua*, Vol. 3/1997, pp. 571–580. Deutsches Archäologisches Institut, Berlin; Philipp von Zabern, Mainz 1998.

Kuckenberg, Martin. *Als der Mensch zum Schöpfer wurde.* Klett-Cotta, Stuttgart 2001.

Kühn, Herbert. *Wenn Steine reden.* Brockhaus, Wiesbaden 1966.

Kuzmina, E. 'Les steppes de l'Asie centrale à l'époque du bronze', in *Découverte des civilisations d'Asie Centrale. Les dossiers d'archéologie.* Faton, Dijon, Nr. 185, 1993, pp. 82–89.

— 'Cultural connections on the Tarim Basin People and pastoralists of the Asian Steppes in the Bronze Age', in *The Bronze Age and Early Iron Age Peoples of Eastern central Asia*, The Institute for the Study of Man, Pennsylvania, 1998, pp. 63–93.

— 'Historical perspectives on the Andronovo and metal use in Eastern Asia', in Linduff, Katheryn (ed.). *Metallurgy in ancient Eastern Eurasia from the Urals to the Yellow River*, Mellen, Ceredigion 2004, pp. 37–84.

— *The Origin of Indo-Iranians.* Edited by J.P. Mallory. Brill, Leiden 2007.

— *The Prehistory of the Silk Road.* Edited by Mair, Victor, H. University of Pennsylvania Press, Philadelphia 2008.

Kyzlasov, L.R. *Drevniaia Tuva. (Ot paleolita do IX B.)* Icdatelstvo Moskovckovo Universiteta, Moskva 1979.

Larenok, Pavel, Dally, Ortwin. 'Taganrog. Eine frühgriechische Siedlung an den Gestaden des Asowschen Meers', in Fornasier, Jochen, Böttger, Burkhard (eds). *Das Bosporanische Reich.* Philipp von Zabern, Mainz 2002, pp. 86–91.

Lawler, Andrew. 'Central Asia's Lost Civilization', *Discover Magazine*, New York, November 2006 http://discovermagazine.com/2006/nov/ancient-towns-excavated-turkmenistan

— 'Edge of an Empire. An ancient Afghan fortress offers rare evidence of Persia's forgotten territories', *Archaeology.* Archaeological Institute of America, Boston September/October 2011, pp. 42–47.

Lazaretov, Igor. 'Spätbronzezeitliche Denkmäler in Südchakassien', *Eurasia Antiqua*, Vol. 6/2000, pp. 249–280. Deutsches Archäologisches Institut, Berlin; Philipp von Zabern, Mainz 2000.

Lebedynsky, Iaroslav. *Les Scythes.* Errance, Paris 2001.

— *Les Sarmates.* Errance, Paris 2002.

— *Les Cimmériens.* Errance, Paris 2004.

— *Les Saces.* Errance, Paris 2006.

— *Les Indo-Européens.* Errance, Paris 2006.

— *Les Nomades.* Errance, Paris 2007.

— *De l'Épée Scythe au Sabre Mongol* Errance, Paris 2008.

— *Armes et Guerriers du Caucase.* L'Harmattan, Paris 2008.

Lecomte, Olivier. 'Ulug Dépé. 4.000 ans d'évolution entre plaine et désert', *Dossiers d'Archéologie*, No. 317, 2006, pp. 16–23.

Lecuyot, Guy, Ishizawa, O. 'La restitution virtuelle d'Aï Khanoum. Une cité hellénistique en Afghanistan', *Archéologia.* Editions Faton, Dijon, No. 420, 2005, pp. 60–71.

— 'Aï Khanum Reconstructed',. *Proceedings of the British Academy, London*, 133, 2007, pp. 155–162.

Lee, James. *Climate Change and Armed Conflict. Hot and Cold Wars.* Routledge, Oxford 2009.

Legrand, Sophie. 'Karasuk Metallurgy: Technological development and regional influence', in Linduff K.K. *Metallurgy in Ancient Eastern Eurasia from the Urals to the Yellow River.* Edwin Mellen Press, Lampeter, 2004, pp. 139–155.

Leon'ev, Nikolaj. 'Ein Kurgan der Okunev-Kultur am Fluss Černovaja, Chakassien', *Eurasia Antiqua*, Vol. 7/2001, pp. 53–74. Deutsches Archäologisches Institut, Berlin; Philipp von Zabern, Mainz 2001.

Leon'ev, Nikolaj, Kapel'ko, Vladimir. *Steinstelen der Okunev-Kultur.* Philipp von Zabern, Mainz 2002.

Leriche, Pierre. 'Aï Khanoum', *Dossiers d'Archéologie* No. 247, *La Bactriane de Cyrus à Timour.* Editions Faton, Quétigny 1999, pp. 36–42.

— 'Bactria. Land of thousand cities', in Cribb, Joe. *After Alexander*, 2007, pp. 121–153.

Leriche, Pierre, Pidaev, Chakirjan. *Termez sur Oxus. Cité-capitale d'Asie Centrale.* Maisonneuve & Larose, Paris 2008.

Leskov, Alexander M. *Grabschätze der Adygeen. Neue Entdeckungen im Nordkaukasus.* Hirmer, München 1990.

— *Grabschätze vom Kaukasus. Neue Ausgrabungen sowjetischer Archàologen in der Adygee und im nördlichen Ossetien.* Leonardo, De Luca, Roma 1991.

— *The Maikop Treasure.* University of Pennsylvania, Philadelphia 2008.

Leskovar, Jutta, Zingerle, Maria-Christina (eds). *Goldener Horizont. 4000 Jahre Nomaden der Ukraine.* Bibliothek der Provinz, Weitra 2010.

Létolle, René et al. 'Uzboy and the Aral regression: A hydrological approach', *International Science Reviews*, 123–174, 2007, pp. 125–136. Elsevier, Amsterdam.

Levine, Marsha et al. *Late prehistoric exploitation of the Eurasian steppe.* McDonald Institute for Archaeological Research, Cambridge, 1999.

Levis-Williams, David, Pearce, David. *Inside the Neolithic Mind.* Thames & Hudson 2009.

Lindström, Gunvor. 'Graeco–baktrische Symbiose', *DAMALS*, Kontadin, Leinfelden-Echterdingen, 10/2009, pp. 54–57.

Linduff, Katheryn (ed.). *Metallurgy in ancient Eastern Eurasia from the Urals to the Yellow River.* Mellen, Ceredigion 2004.

Litvinskij, Boris. *Antike und frühmittelalterliche Grabhügel im westlichen Fergana-Becken, Tadzikistan.* C.H. Beck, München 1986.

— *La civilisation de l'Asie centrale antique.* Marie Leidorf, Espelkamp 1998.

Litvinskij, Boris, Picikjan, Igor. 'The Hellenistic Architecture and Art of the Temple on the Oxus', *Bulletin of the Asia Institute*, Vol. 8, 1994, pp. 47–66. The Asia Institute, Bloomfield Hills 1996.

— *Taxt-Sangin. Der Oxus-Tempel.* Philipp von Zabern. 2002.

Litvinskij, Boris, Pyankova, L.T. 'Pastoral Tribes of the Bronze Age in the Oxus Valley (Bactria)', in *History of Civilizations of Central Asia*, UNESCO Publishing, Paris, Vol. I, 1992, pp. 379–394.

Lontcho, Frédéric, Melmoth, Françoise (eds). 'Les tombes royales des Thraces', *L'archéologue* No. 86. Archaéologie Nouvelle, Paris 2006.

Lorblanchet, Michel et al (eds). *Chamanisme et arts préhistoriques.* Errances, Paris 2006.

Lordkipanidze, David, Gagnepain, Jean. *La Géorgie, berceau des Européens.* Musée de Préhistoire des Gorges du Verdon, Quinson 2003.

Lubotsky, Alexander. 'Tocharian Loan Words in Old Chinese', in Mair, Victor, *The Bronze Age and Early Iron Age Peoples of Eastern Central Asia.* The Institute for the Study of Man, Pennsylvania, 1998, pp. 379–390.

Lumley, Henri de. 'Les premiers hommes en Chine', *Dossiers d'Archéologie* No. 292, 2004, pp. 7–17.

— *Arkaïm. Une cité de l'âge du Bronze dans les steppes de l'Oural.* Musée des merveilles, Tende, 2010.

Lüscher, Geneviève: *Die Hydria von Grächwil.* Bernisches Historisches Museum, Bern 2002.

Lyonnet, B. 'Les Grecs, les nomades et l'indépendance de la Sogdiane', *Bulletin of the Asia Institute*, Vol. 12, 1998, pp. 141–160. The Asia Institute, Bloomfield Hills 2001.

Ma, Chun Mei et al. *Climate and environment reconstruction during the Medieval Warm Period in Lop Nur of Xinjiang, China.* in Chinese Science Bulletin, Vol. 53, No. 19, 2008, pp. 3016–3027. Co-published with SpringerLink. http://www.springerlink.com/

Ma, Yong, Wang Binhua. 'The culture of the Xinjiang region', in *History of civilizations of Central Asia.* Vol. II. Unesco Publishing, Paris 1994, pp. 209–225.

Maca-Meyer, Nicole et al. 'Major genomic mitochondrial lineages delineate early human expansions', *BMC Genetics*, 2001, 2:13, BioMed Central, London 2001.

Macaulya, Martin et al. 'The emerging tree of West Eurasian mtDNAs: A synthesis of control-region sequences and RFLPs', *American Journal for Human Genetics*, Vol. 64, pp. 232–249, The American Society for Human Genetics, Bethesda 1999

Magail, Jérôme. 'Tsatsiin Ereg, site majeur du début du Ier millénaire en Mongolie', Archéo-steppe.com., Mission archéologique Monaco Mongolie, 2009. http://archeo-steppe.com/content/view/73/195/lang,french/

Mair, Victor H. (ed.). 'The Mummified Remains Found in the Tarim Basin', *Journal of Indo-European Studies*, Washington, Vol. 23, No. 3&4, 1995, pp. 279–445.

— 'Prehistoric Caucasoid Corpses of the Tarim Basin', *Journal of Indo-European Studies*, Washington, Vol. 23, Nr. 3&4, 1995, pp. 281–307.

— *The Bronze Age and Early Iron Age Peoples of Eastern central Asia* (ed.). The Institute for the Study of Man, Pennsylvania, 1998.

— *Contact and Exchange in the Ancient World.* University of Hawaii Press, Honolulu 2006.

— 'The Rediscovery and Complete Excavation of Ördek's Excavation', *Journal of Indo-European Studies*, Washington, Vol. 34, No. 3&4, 2006, pp. 273–318.

— 'The Archaeology of the Xinjiang Uyghur Autonomous Region', in *Secrets of the Silk Road.* Bowers Museum, Santa Ana, California 2010.

— *Secrets of the Silk Road* (ed). Bowers Museum, Santa Ana, California 2010.

Major archaeological discoveries in China in 2005. Cultural Relics Publishing House, Beijing 2006.

Mak, Philip. *Treasures of the Eurasian steppes.* Ariadne Gelleries, New York 1998.

Makhortykh, S. 'The Northern Black Sea steppes in the Cimmerian epoch', in Scott Marian. *Impact of the Environment on Human Migration in Eurasia*, 2004, pp. 35–44.

Mallegni, Francesco et al. '*Homo cepranensis* sp. nov. and the evolution of African–European Middle Pleistocene hominids', *Comptes Rendus Palevol*, Vol. 2, No. 2, Elsevier, Amsterdam, 2003, pp. 153–159.

Mallory, J.P. *In Search of the Indo-Europeans. Language, Archaeology and Myth.* Thames & Hudson, London 1989.

— 'L'hypothèse des steppes', *Dossiers d'Archéologie* No. 338, Editions Faton, Quétigny 2010, pp. 28–35.

Mallory, J.P., Mair Victor, H. *The Tarim Mummies.* Thames & Hudson, London, 2000.

Mallory, J.P., Adams, D.Q. (eds). *Encyclopedia of Indo-European Culture.* Fitzroy Dearborn, London 1997.

— *The Oxford introduction to Proto-Indo-European and the Proto-Indo-European World.* Oxford University Press, Oxford 2006.

Malyutina, T.S. '"Proto-towns" of the Bronze Age in the South Urals and Ancient Khorasmia', in Jones-Bley, Karlene, Zdanovich, D.G. *Complex Societies of Central Eurasia from the 3rd to the 1st Millennium BC.* Vol. I., Institute for the Study of Man, Washington DC, 2002, pp. 161–169.

Mamonova, N. 'Die Paläoanthropologie des Gräberfelds Ulangom', in Novgorodva, Eleonora et al. *Ulangom. Ein skythenzeitliches Gräberfeld in der Mongolei*, 1982, pp. 140–151.

Maran, Joseph. 'Die Badener Kultur und ihre Räderfahrzeuge', in Fansa, Mamoun, Burmeister Stefan. *Rad und Wagen.* Philipp von Zabern, Mainz 2004, pp. 265–282.

— 'Kulturkontakte und Wege der Ausbreitung der Wagentechnologie im 4. Jahrtausend v. Chr', in Fansa, Mamoun, Burmeister, Stefan. *Rad und Wagen.* Philipp von Zabern, Mainz 2004, pp. 429–442.

Maqdissi, Michael et al. *Schätze des Alten Syriens.* Theiss, Stuttgart 2009.

Marazov, Ivan. 'The "coiled-up carnivore": visual etymology of the motif', *Silk Road Art and Archaeology*, Vol. 8, pp. 255–271, Kamakura, 2002.

Marcellinus, Ammianus. The Later Roman Empire (AD 354–378). Translated by Walter Hamilton. Penguin Classics, London 2004.

Maringer, John. *Contribution to the prehistory of Mongolia.* Reports from the scientific expedition to the north-western provinces of China under the leadership of Dr. Sven Hedin. Publications 34. Thule, Stockholm 1950.

— *Gräber und Steindenkmäler in der Mongolei.* Monumenta Serica. Journal of Oriental Studies, undated reprint from Vol. XIV, 1949–1955, pp. 303–339.

Mariyashev, A.N. *Petroglyphs of South Kazakhstan and Semirechye.* Margulan Archaeology Institute Almaty 1994.

Markley, Jonathan. 'Gaozu confronts the Shanyu: The Han Dynasty's First Clash with the Xiongnu', in Benjamin, Craig, Lieu, Samuel (eds). *Silk Road Studies VI. Walls and Frontiers in Inner-Asian History*, pp. 131–140. Brepols, Turnhout 2002.

Markus, Ursula, Eichenberger, Ursula. *Augusto Gansser. Aus dem leben eines Welt-Erkunders.* AS Verlag, Zürich 2008.

Marsadolov, Leonid. 'The Art Images and Ideas along the Great Steppe Road of Eurasia in the IXth–VIIth Centuries BC', *Silk Road Art and Archaeology*, Vol. 8, pp. 221–238, Kamakura, 2002.

Masov, R. et al. (eds) *National Museum of Antiquities of Tajikistan.* Donish Institute of History, Archaeology and Ethnography, Dushanbe 2005.

Masson, Vadim. M. *Das Land der tausend Städte. Die Wiederentdeckung der ältesten Kulturgebiete in Mittelasien.* Udo Pfriemer, München 1982.

— *Altyn-Depe.* University of Pennsylvania, Philadelphia 1988.

— 'The Bronze Age in Khorasan and Transoxiana', in *History of Civilizations of Central Asia*, Unesco Publishing, Paris, Vol. I, 1992, pp. 225–245.

— 'The Decline of the Bronze Age Civilization and Movements of the Tribes', in *History of Civilizations of Central Asia*, Unesco Publishing, Paris, Vol. I, 1992, pp. 337–356.

Masson, Vadim, Sarianidi, Victor. *Central Asia. Turkmenia before the Achaemenids.* Thames and Hudson, London 1972.

Mattet, Laurence (ed.). *Le Profane et le Divin. Arts de l'Antiquité de l'Europe au Sud-Est Asiatique.* Éditions Hazan, Paris 2008.

Maurice, Byzantine Emperor. *Strategikon.* Translated by G.T. Dennis. University of Philadelphia Press, Philadelphia, 1984.

Mayr, Hans, Lehner, Johann. *Gold der Skythen aus der Leningrader Eremitage.* Bundesministerium für Wissenschaft und Forschung der Republik Österreich, Wien 1988.

Medvedev, A. 'Avestan "Yima's Town" in Historical and Archaeological Perspective', in Jones-Bley, Karlene, Zdanovich, DG. *Complex Societies of Central Eurasia from the 3rd to the 1st Millennium* BC. Vol. I., Institute for the Study of Man, Washington DC, 2002, pp. 53–67.

— 'Hügelgräber und befestigte Siedlungen der sarmatischen Zeit am oberen Don', in *Eurasia Antiqua*, Vol. 13/2007, pp. 257–284. Deutsches Archäologisches Institut, Berlin; Philipp von Zabern, Mainz 2008.

Mei, Jianjun. *Copper and Bronze Metallurgy in Late Prehistoric Xinjiang*, Archaeopress, Oxford, 2000.

Mei, Jianjun, Shell, Colin. *Copper and Bronze Metallurgy in Late Prehistoric Xinjiang.* in Mair, Victor, The Bronze Age and Early Iron Age Peoples of Eastern Central Asia. The Institute for the Study of Man, Pennsylvania, 1998, pp. 573–603.

— 'The existence of Andronovo cultural influence in Xinjiang during the 2nd millennium BC', *Antiquity*, 73, pp. 570–578, York 1999.

— 'Metallurgy in Bronze Age Xinjiang and its cultural context', in Linduff, Katheryn. *Metallurgy in ancient Eastern Eurasia from the Urals to the Yellow River.* Mellen, Ceredigion 2004, pp. 173–188.

Meijden, Ella van der (ed.). *Die alten Zivilisationen Bulgariens. Das Gold der Thraker.* Antikenmuseum Basel, Basel 2007.

Melikian-Chirvani, A.S. 'Rostam and Herakles, a Family Resemblance', *Bulletin of the Asia Institute*, Vol. 12, 1998, pp. 171–200. The Asia Institute, Bloomfield Hills 2001.

Melyukova, A.I. 'The Scythians and Sarmatians', in Sinor, Denis (ed.). *The Cambridge history of Early Inner Asia.* Cambridge University Press, Cambridge 1990, pp. 97–117.

Menghin, Wilfied, Parzinger, Hermann, Nagler, Anatoli, Nawroth, Manfred (eds). *Im Zeichen des goldenen Greifen. Königsgräber der Skythen.* Prestel, München 2007.

Mertens, Michaeila. *Spuren alter Besiedlung im Altai-Gebirge und religiöse Vorstellungen der Altai-Völker.* Philipps-Universität Marburg, no date. http://web.uni-marburg.de/geographie/HPGeo.old/personal/Opp/Mittelseminar_Sibirien/altai/mertens/mertens.pdf

Metternich, Alain. *Afghanistan, les trésors retrouvés. Album des plus beaux objets du Musée national de Kaboul.* SFPA, Paris 2006.

Miller, Bryan et al. 'Xiongnu Elite Tomb Complexes in the Mongolian Altai. Results of the Mongol-American Hovd Archaeological Project 2007', *The Silk Road Journal*, Vol. 5/2, pp. 27–36, 2008. The Silk Road Foundation, Saratoga. http://www.silkroadfoundation.org/newsletter/vol5num2/

— 'Xiongnu Constituents of the High Mountains: Results of the Mongol-American Hovd Archaeological Project 2008', *The Silk Road Journal*, Vol. 7, pp. 8–20, 2009. The Silk Road Foundation, Saratoga. http://www.silkroadfoundation.org/newsletter/vol7/

Minaev, Sergei. 'The Excavation of Xiuongnu Sites in the Buryatia Republic', *Orientations Magazine*, Hong Kong, November 1995, pp. 44f.

Minaev, Sergei, Sakharovskaia, Lidiia. 'Investigation of a Xiongnu Royal Tomb Complex in the Tsaraam Valley', *The Silk Road Journal*, Vol. 4/1, pp. 47–54, 2006 and Vol. 5/1, 2007, pp. 44–56. The Silk Road Foundation, Saratoga.

Minaev, Sergei, Elikhina, Julia. 'On the Chronology of the Noyon uul Barrows', *The Silk Road Journal*, Vol. 7, pp. 21–35, 2009. The Silk Road Foundation, Saratoga.

http://www.silk-road.com/newsletter/vol4num1/

Minns, Ellis. *Scythians and Greeks. A survey of ancient history and archaeology on the north coast of the Euxine from the Danube to the Caucasus.* Cambridge University Press, Cambridge 1913.

Mithen, Steven. *After the ice. A global human history 20.000 – 5000* BC. Harvard University Press, Cambridge 2003.

Moazami, Mahnaz. 'The dog in Zoroastrian religion: Videvdad Chapter XIII', *Indo-Iranian Journal*, Vol. 46, 2006, pp. 127–149. http://www.springerlink.com/content/b6312v8779677117/fulltext.pdf

Mode, Markus. 'Sogdian Gods in Exile. Some iconographic evidence from Khotan in the light of recently excavated material from Sogdiana', *Silk Road Art and Archaeology*, Vol. II, pp. 179–214. The Institute of Silk Road Studies, Kamakura 1991/92.

— 'Hunnen, Sogder und das Erbe Alexanders in Mittelasien', in *Hunnen zwischen Asien und Europa.* Herausgegeben vom Historischen Museum der Pfalz Speyer. Beier & Beran, Langenweissbach 2008, pp. 101–108.

Mode, Markus, Tubach Jürgen (eds). *Arms and Armour as Indicators of Cultural Transfer.* Reichert, Wiesbaden 2006.

Molodin, Vjačeslav, Cheremisin, D.V. 'Pétroglyphes de l'Age du Bronze du plateau d'Ukok: à propos des représentations de personnages avec une coiffure fongiforme', *Arts Asiatiques.* Musée national des Arts asiatiques-Guimet, 54/1999, pp. 148–152. Paris.

— 'Bronzezeit im Berg-Altai', in *Eurasia Antiqua*, Vol. 7/2001, pp. 1–52. Deutsches Archäologisches Institut, Berlin; Philipp von Zabern, Mainz 2001.

— 'Petroglyphs of the Ukok Plateau', *Archaeology, Ethnology & Anthropology of Eurasia*, 4 (32) pp. 91–101. Elsevier, Amsterdam 2007. http://www.springerlink.com/content/876332w625462h2x/

Molodin, Vjačeslav et al. 'Čiča – eine befestigte Ansiedlung der Übergangsperiode von der Spätbronze-zur Früheisenzeit in der Barabinsker Waldsteppe. Vorbericht der Kampagnen 1999–2001', *Eurasia Antiqua*, Vol. 8/2002, pp. 185–236. Deutsches Archäologisches Institut, Berlin; Philipp von Zabern, Mainz 2002.

— 'Das skythenzeitliche Kriegergrab aus Olon-Kurin-Gol, Mongolischer Altaj', *Eurasia Antiqua*, Vol. 14/2008, pp. 241–266. Deutsches Archäologisches Institut, Berlin; Philipp von Zabern, Mainz 2009.

Moor, Antoine de, Verhecken-Lammens, Chris, Verhecken, André. *3500 years of textile art.* Lannoo, Tielt 2008.

Morgan, Delmar, Coote, C. *Early voyages and travels to Russia and Persia by Anthony Jenkinson and other Englishmen.* 2 vols, Hakluyt Society, London 1886.

Morio, Asif Raza. *Moen Jo Daro. Mysterious City of Indus Valley Civilization.* Morio Editions, Larkana, 2007.

Moscati, Sabatino et al. (eds). *The Celts.* Bompiani, Venezia 1991.

Movius, Hallam. 'Teshik-Tash: A Mousterian Cave Site in Central Asia', in *Société Royale Belge d'Anthropologie et de Préhistoire, en l'honneur du Professeur Hamal-Nandrin*, pp. 72–83, Bruxelles 1953.

Mukhareva, A.N. 'Camel scenes in the rock art of the Minusinsk Basin', *Archaeology, Ethnology & Anthropology of Eurasia*, 4 (32) pp. 102–109. Elsevier, Amsterdam 2006.

Müller, Beat. *Geburt war schon bei Neandertalern schwierig.* Informationsdienst Wissenschaft der Universität Zürich, 2008. http://idw-online.de/pages/de/news276581

Müller, Claudius, Wenzel, Jacob (eds) *Dschingis Khan und seine Erben. Das Weltreich der Mongolen.* Kunst und Ausstellungshalle der Bundersrepublik, Bonn and Philipp von Zabern, Mainz 2005.

Müller-Karpe, Hermann. *Neolithisch-kupferzeitliche Siedlungen in der Geoksjur-Oase, Süd-Turkmenistan.* C.H. Beck, München 1984.

Murphy, Eileen. 'Mummification and Body Processing. Evidence from the Iron Age in Southern Siberia', in Davis-Kimball, Jeannine et al (eds). *Kurgans, Ritual Sites and Settlements*, 2000, pp. 279–292.

Murzin V. Yu. 'Key points in Scythian history', in Braund, David. *Scythians and Greeks.* University of Exeter Press, Exeter 2005, pp. 33–38.

Muscarella, Oscar White. 'Ziwiye' and Ziwiye. The Forgery of Provenience', *Journal of Field Archaeology*, Boston University, Vol. 4.2, 1977, pp. 197–219.

— *The lie became great. The forgery of ancient Near Eastern Cultures.* Styx Publications, Groningen 2000.

— 'All that glisters isn't gold', *The Sunday Times*, 19 December 2003.

Nabatschikow, W.A. *Gold und Kunsthandwerk vom antiken Kuban.* Theiss, Stuttgart 1989.

Nagler, Anatoli. *Kurgane der Mozdok-Steppe in Nordkaukasien.* Marie Leidorf, Espelkamp 1996.

— 'Waren die Träger der Okunev-Kultur Nomaden?', *Eurasia Antiqua*, Vol. 5/1999, pp. 1–27. Deutsches Archäologisches Institut, Berlin; Philipp von Zabern, Mainz 1999.

— *O stilisovannych isobrajenniach olenei na olennix kamniach Zentralnoy Asii.* (On the stylistic representation of deer on deer stones of Central Asia.) Advance copy. Archaeological Institute and Academy of Sciences, Novosibirsk, 2012.

Narain, A.K. *The Indo-Greeks.* B.R. Publishing Corporation, Delhi (1953) 2003.

Nazarov, Vladimir V. 'Archäologische Untersuchungen auf Berezan', in Stähler, Klaus (ed). *Zur graeco-skythischen Kunst. Archäologisches Kolloquium Münster 1995.* Ugarit-Verlag, Münster 1997, pp. 5–21.

Negmatov, N. 'States in north-western Central Asia', in *History of civilizations of Central Asia. Vol. II. The development of sedentary and nomadic civilizations: 700 BC to AD 250.* Edited by Harmatta Janos et al. Unesco Publishing, Paris 1994, pp. 441–456.

Neumann, Karl. *Hellenen im Skythenlande.* Reimer, Berlin 1855.

Nikolova, Alla, Kaiser, Elke. 'Die absolute Chronologie der Jamnaja-Kultur im nördlichen Schwarzmeergebiet auf der Grundlage erster dendrologischer Daten', *Eurasia Antiqua*, Vol. 15/2009, pp. 209–240. Deutsches Archäologisches Institut, Berlin; Philipp von Zabern, Mainz 2010.

Nikonorov, Valerii. *Cataphracti, Catafractarii and Clibanarii: Another look at the old problem of their identifications.* In: *Military Archaeology. Weaponry and Warfare in the Historical and Social Perspective.* The State Hermitage Museum, St. Peterburg 1998, pp. 131–138.

Novgorodva, Eleonora. *Alte Kunst der Mongolei.* Seemann Verlag, Leipzig 1980.

— 'Archäologische Funde, Bestattungsplätze und Skulpturen', in Heissig, Walther, Müller, Claudius (eds). *Die Mongolen.* Pinguin, Innsbruck/Umschau, Frankfurt 1989, pp. 14–20.

Novgorodva, Eleonora et al. *Ulangom. Ein skythenzeitliches Gräberfeld in der Mongolei.* Harrassowitz, Wiesbaden, 1982.

Očir-Gorjaeva, Maria, *Pferdegeschirr aus Chošeutovo. Skythischer Tierstil an der Unteren Wolga.* Philipp von Zabern, Mainz 2003.

Okladnikow, A.P. *Der Hirsch mit dem goldenen Geweih.* Brockhaus, Wiesbaden 1972.

— 'Inner Asia at the dawn of history', in Sinor Denis (ed.). *The Cambridge history of Early Inner Asia.* Cambridge University Press, Cambridge 1990, pp. 41–96.

Olkhovsky, Valery. 'Baité. Un ensemble culturel', *Dossiers d'Archéologie*, No. 194, *Les Scythes*, 1994, pp. 54–57.

— 'Scythian Culture in the Crimea', in Davis Kimball, Jeannine, Bashilov, Vladimir, Yablonsky, leonid (eds). *Nomads in the Eurasian Steppes in the Early Iron Age.* Zinat Press, Berkeley 1995. pp. 63–81.

— 'Ancient Sanctuaries of the Aral and Caspian Regions', in Davis-Kimball, Jeannine. *Kurgans, Ritual Sites and Settlements*, 2000, pp. 33–42.

Olkhovsky, V., Evdokimov, G. *Scythian Statues VII–III B.C. (Skifskie izvajanija VII–III vv. do n.e; in Russian.)* Russian Academy of Sciences, Institute of Archaeology, Moscow 1994.

Oppenheimer, Stephen. *The real Eve. Modern Man's Journey Out of Africa.* Constable & Robinson, London 2003.

Ovchinnikov, Igor et al. 'Molecular analysis of Neanderthal DNA from the northern Caucasus', *Nature*, Vol. 404, pp. 490–493, Macmillan Publishers, Basingstoke 2000. http://www.nature.com/nature/journal/v404/n6777/pdf/404490a0.pdf

Pak, Young-sook. 'The Origins of Silla Metalwork', *Orientations Magazine*, Hong Kong, September 1988, pp. 44–53.

Palaeoanthropology of Central Asia. No date. www.bookrags.com

Pan, Ku. *The History of the Former Han Dynasty. [The Han Shu]* A critical translation with annotations by Homer H. Dubs. 3 vols. Wawerly Press, Baltimore 1938, 1944, 1955.

Pare, Christopher. 'Die Wagen der Bronzezeit in Mitteleuropa', in Fansa, Mamoun, Burmeister, Stefan. *Rad und Wagen.* Philipp von Zabern, Mainz 2004, pp. 355–372.

Parker, E. *A thousand years of the Tartars.* Kegan Paul, London 2002.

Parzinger, Hermann. 'Sejma-Turbino und die Anfänge des sibirischen Tierstils', *Eurasia Antiqua*, Vol.3/1997, pp. 223–247. Deutsches Archäologisches Institut, Berlin; Philipp von Zabern, Mainz 1998.

— *Der große Kurgan von Bajkara.* Philipp von Zabern, Mainz 2003.

— *Die Skythen.* C.H. Beck, München 2004.

— *Die frühen Völker Eurasiens. Vom Neolithikum bis zum Mittelalter.* C.H. Beck, München 2006.

— 'The "Silk Roads" Concept Reconsidered: About Transfers, Transportation and Transcontinental Interactions in Prehistory', *The Silk Road Journal*, Vol. 5/2, pp. 7–15, 2008 . The Silk Road Foundation, Saratoga. http://www.silkroadfoundation.org/newsletter/vol5num2/

— 'Die Skythen der ukrainischen Steppe und ihre Stellung in der Welt der eurasischen Reiternomaden', in Leskovar Jutta, Zingerle Maria-Christina (eds). *Goldener Horizont*, 2010, pp. 58–66.

Parzinger, Hermann, Nagler, Anatoli et al. 'New discoveries in the Mongolian Altai: The warrior grave of the Pazyryk Culture at Olon-Güüriin-Gol 10', in Bemmann Jan et al. *Current archaeological research in Mongolia.* R.F.W.-Universität, Bonn, 2009, pp. 203–220.

— 'Das mehrperiodige Gräberfeld von Suchanicha bei Minusinsk', *Eurasia Antiqua*, Vol. 15/2009, Deutsches Archäologisches Institut, Berlin; Philipp von Zabern, Mainz 2010, pp. 67–208.

— 'Der tagarzeitliche Großkurgan von Barsučij Log in Chakassien', *Eurasia Antiqua*, Vol. 16/2010, Deutsches Archäologisches Institut, Berlin; Philipp von Zabern, Mainz 2010, pp. 169–281.

Pfaffenbichler, Matthias. 'Spangenhelme', in Koch, Alexander (Hg). *Attila und die Hunnen*. Theiss, Stuttgart 2007, pp. 244–251.

Phillips, E.D. *The Royal Hordes. Nomad Peoples of the Steppes*. Thames & Hudson 1965.

Piankov, I.V. 'The Ethnic History of the Sakas', *Bulletin of the Asia Institute*, Vol. 8, 1994, pp. 37–46. The Asia Institute, Bloomfield Hills 1996.

Piankova, L.T. 'Bronze Age settlements of Southern Tadjikistan', in Kohl, Philipp, *The Bronze Age Civilization of Central Asia. Recent Soviet discoveries*. Sharpe, New York 1981, pp. 287–310.

Pidaev, Shakir, Leriche, Pierre. 'Quelques villes moyennes de Bactriane', in *La Bactriane de Cyrus à Timour. Dossiers d'Archéologie*, Editions Faton, Quétigny 1999, pp. 50–55.

Pidoplichko, I. H. *Meziritchiskie jilicha iz kosteï*. Naukova Dumka, Kiev 1976.

— *Upper Palaeolithic Dwellings of Mammoth Bones in the Ukraine: Kiev-Kirillovskii, Gontsy, Dobranichevka, Mezin and Mezhirich*. BAR International Series 712, J. and E. Hedges, Oxford, 1998.

Pilipko, V.N. 'Excavations at Staraia Nisa', *Bulletin of the Asia Institute*, Vol. 8, 1994, pp. 101–116. The Asia Institute, Bloomfield Hills 1996.

Piotrovsky, Boris et al. *Ourartou, Neapolis des Scythes, Kharezm*. Maisonneuve, Paris 1954.

Piotrovsky, Boris et al. *L'art scythe*. Aurora, Léningrad 1986.

Piotrovsky, Mikhail et al. *The Treasures of the Sarmatians* (in Russian). Museum of Azov 2008.

Pitschikjan, Igor. *Oxos-Schatz und Oxos-Tempel*. Akademie Verlag, Berlin 1992.

— 'Rebirth of the Oxus Treasure: Second part of the Oxus Treasure from the Miho Museum Collection', in *Ancient Civilizations from Scythia to Siberia*, Vol. 4, No. 4. Brill, Leiden 1997, pp. 306–383.

Pittman, Holly. *Art of the Bronze Age. Southeastern Iran, Western Central Asia and the Indus Valley*. The Metropolitan Museum of Art, New York 1984.

Podossinov, Alexander. 'Am Rande der griechischen Oikumene. Geschichte des Bosporanischen Reichs', in Fornasier, Jochen, Böttger, Burkhard (eds). *Das Bosporanische Reich*. Philipp von Zabern, Mainz 2002, pp. 21–38.

Pohl, Walter. *Die Awaren. Ein Steppenvolk in Europa 567–822 n.Chr.* C.H.Beck, München 2002.

Polos'mak, Natascha, Seifert, Mathias. 'Menschen aus dem Eis Sibiriens. Neuentdeckte Hügelgräber (Kurgane) im Permafrost des Altai', *Antike Welt* 1996/2, pp. 87–108. Philipp von Zabern, Mainz 1996.

— 'Die ‚Amazone' von Pazyryk', in Rolle Renate, *Amazonen*, 2010, pp. 129–137.

Pommereau, Claude (ed.). *La vie des hommes de la préhistoire*. Figaro, Beaux Arts magazine, Paris 2008.

Poncins, Vicomte Edmond de. *Chasses et Explorations dans la Région des Pamirs*. Challamel, Paris 1897.

Possnert, Göran, *Sundström. Result of ^{14}C dating of human hair from Xinjiang, China*. Report from The Angström Laboratory, Uppsala Universitet, Uppsala 11 March 2011.

Potts, Daniel. 'Bactrian Camels and Bactrian-Dromedary Hybrids', *The Silk Road Journal*, Vol. 3/1, pp. 49–59, 2005. The Silk Road Foundation, Saratoga. http://www.silkroadfoundation.org/newsletter/vol3num1/7_bactrian.php

Prejevalsky, Nicholai. *Mongolia. The Tangut country and the solitudes of Northern Tibet. Being a narrative of three years travel in Eastern High Asia*. 2 vols. Sampson Low, Marston, Searle & Rivington, London 1876.

Preston, Douglas. *Dinosaurs in the Attic*. St. Martin's Griffin, New York 1986.

Price, Neil (ed.). *The Archaeology of Shamanism*. Routledge, London 2001.

Primas, M. 'Innovationstransfer vor 5000 Jahren. Knotenpunkte an Land-und Wasserwegen zwischen Vorderasien und Europa', *Eurasia Antiqua*, Vol. 13/2007, pp. 1–20. Deutsches Archäologisches Institut, Berlin; Philipp von Zabern, Mainz 2008.

Ptolemaios, Claudios. *Handbuch der Geographie*. Herausgegeben von Alfred Sückelberger und Gerd Grasshoff. 2 Bde. Schwabe, Basel 2006.

Puett, Michael. 'China in Early Eurasian History', in Mair, Victor, *The Bronze Age and Early Iron Age Peoples of Eastern Central Asia*. The Institute for the Study of Man, Pennsylvania, 1998, pp. 699–715.

Pugachenkova, G.A. *Development of architecture in South Turkmenistan for classical and early medieval periods. (Puti razvitiia arhitektur'i iuzhnogo Turmenistana.)* Academy of Sciences, Moscow 1958.

— *Antiquities of Southern Uzbekistan*. Soka University Press, Tokyo 1991.

Pulleyblank, Edwin. 'Chinese and Indo-Europeans', *Journal of the Royal Asiatic Society*, London April 1966, pp. 9–39.

— 'Why Tocharians?', in Mair, Victor H. (ed.). 'The Mummified Remains Found in the Tarim Basin', *Journal of Indo-European Studies*, Washington, Vol. 23, No. 3&4, 1995, pp. 415–430.

Pumpelly, Raphael (ed.). *Explorations in Turkestan. Expedition of 1904. Prehistoric civilizations of Anau*. Carnegie Institute, Washington 1908.

Pyankov, I.V. 'Arkaim and the Indo-Iranian Var', in Jones-Bley, Karlene, Zdanovich, D.G. *Complex Societies of Central Eurasia from the 3rd to the 1st Millennium BC*. Vol. I., Institute for the Study of Man, Washington D.C., 2002, pp. 42–52.

Qi, Xiaoshan, Wang Bo. *The ancient culture in Xinjiang along the Silk Road*. (in Chinese) Xinjiang renmin chubanshe, Urumqi, 2008.

Quintus, Curtius Rufus. *The History of Alexander*. Translated by John Yardley. Penguin Classics, London 2004.

Radloff, Wilhelm. *Aus Sibirien*. 2 vols. Weigel Nachfolger, Leipzig 1893.

Ranov, Vadim. 'Toward a new outline of the Soviet Central Asian Palaeolithic', *Current Anthropology*, University of Chicago Press, Vol. 20. No. 2, 1979, pp. 249–270.

— 'Zentralasien', in Bar-Yosef, O. et al. *Neue Forschungen zur Altsteinzeit*. Beck, München 1984, pp. 299–343.

— 'L'exploration archéologique du Pamir', *Bulletin de l'Ecole française de d'Extrême Orient*, Paris, Vol. 73, 1984, pp. 67–97.

— 'Tout commence au paléolithique', in *Découverte des civilisations d'Asie Centrale. Les dossiers d'archéologie*. Faton, Dijon, Nr. 185, 1993, pp. 4–13.

— 'Les énigmes de la culture de Hissar', in *Découverte des civilisations d'Asie Centrale. Les dossiers d'archéologie*. Faton, Dijon, Nr. 185, 1993, pp. 14–21.

— 'The "Loessic Palaeolithic" in south Tadjikistan, Central Asia: its industries, chronology and correlation', *Quaternary Science Reviews* 14, 1995, pp. 731–745. Elsevier, Amsterdam.

Ranov, Vadim et al. 'Kuldara: Earliest Human Occupation in Central Asia in its Afro-Asian Context', *Current Anthropology*, Tucson, Vol. 36, No.2, 1995, pp. 337–346.

— 'Lower Palaeolithic cultures', in *History of civilizations of Central Asia*. Vol. I. Unesco Publishing, Paris 1992, pp. 45–63.

— *Guide to the principal archaeological sites of the Eastern Pamir (Tajikistan)*. META, Murgab 2003.

Rapin, Claude. 'L'incompréhensible Asie centrale de la carte de Ptolémée. Propositions pour un décodage', *Bulletin of the Asia Institute*, Vol. 12, 1998, pp. 201–226. The Asia Institute, Bloomfield Hills 2001.

— 'L'Afghanistan et l'Asie Centrale dans la géographie mythique des historiens d'Alexandre et dans la toponymie des géographes gréco-romains', in Bopearachchi Osmund, Boussac Marie-Françoise (eds). *Afghanistan. Ancien carrefour entre l'est et l'ouest*. Brepols, Turnhout 2005, pp. 143–172.

— 'Nomads and the shaping of Central Asia', in Cribb, Joe; Herrmann, Georgina (eds). *After Alexander. Central Asia before Islam*. The British Academy, London 2007, pp. 29–72.

— 'La Sogdiane d'Alexandre le Grand aux derniers Gréco-Bactriens', *Dossiers d'Archéologie* No. 341, *Samarcande*. Editions Faton, Quétigny 2010. pp. 28–31.

Rapin, Claude, Isamiddinov, Muxammedzon, Khasanov, Mutallib. 'La tombe d'une princesse nomade à Koktepe près de Samarkand', Académie des inscriptions et belles-lettres, 145e année, N. 1, 2001, pp. 33–92.

Rapin, Claude, Baud, Aymon et al. *Les recherches sur la région der Portes de Fer de Sogdiane. Bref état des questions en 2005*. Istorija Material'noj Kul'tury Uzbekistana, IMKU pp. 48–59, Samarkand, 2006 http://claude.rapin.free.fr/1BiblioTextesGeogrPDF/GeogrPF_IMKU35.pdf

Rapoport, Yuri. 'The palaces of Topraq-Qal'a', *Bulletin of the Asia Institute*, Vol. 8, 1994, pp. 161–185. The Asia Institute, Bloomfield Hills 1996.

Rassamakin, Jurij. 'The Eneolithic of the Black sea Steppe: Dynamics of Cultural and Economic Development 4500–2300 BC', in Levine Marsha et al. *Late prehistoric exploitation of the Eurasian steppe*. McDonald Institute for Archaeological Research, University of Cambridge, Cambridge 1999, pp. 59–182.

— *Die nordpontische Steppe in der Kupferzeit. Gräber aus der Mitte des 5. Jts. bis Ende des 4. Jts. v. Chr.* 2 vols. Philipp von Zabern, Mainz 2004.

Razzakov, Rauf. *Sarazm*. Donish Institute of History, Archaeology and Ethnography, Dushanbe 2006.

Reeder, Ellen. *Scythian Gold. Treasures from ancient Ukraine*. Abrams, New York 1999.

Reger, Gary. *Traders and Travellers in the Black and Aegean Seas*. Pontos Publications 2007. pp. 273–285.

Regzen, G. *Korean-Mongolian joint expedition in Mongolia 1997–2001*. The National Museum of Mongolian History, Ulaan Baatar 2002.

Reich, David et al. 'Genetic history of an archaic hominin group from Denisova Cave in Siberia', *Nature*, 10:1038/09710, Macmillan Publishers, Basingstoke December 2010, pp. 1053–1060.

Renfrew, Colin. *Archaeolgy & Language. The puzzle of Indo-European origins*. Jonathan Cape, London 1987.

— 'Die Indoeuropäer aus archäologischer Sicht', in Breuer, Reinhard (ed.) 'Die Evolution der Sprachen', *Spektrum der Wissenschaft*, Dossier 2/2007, pp. 40–48. Heidelberg 2007.

— 'Le problème indo-européen et l'hypothèse anatolienne', *Dossiers d'Archéologie* No. 338, Editions Faton, Quétigny 2010, pp. 44–53.

Renner, Georg; Selic, Christa. *Abseits der großen Minarette*. Brockhaus Leipzig 1982.

Répertoire des pétroglyphes d'Asie Centrale. Fascicule 1: Sibérie du Sud 1. Oglakhty I–III. Edité par Sher Jakov et al. Diffusion de Boccard, Paris 1994.

Répertoire des pétroglyphes d'Asie Centrale. Fascicule 2: Sibérie du Sud 2. Tepsej I–III, Ust'-Tuba I–VI. Edité par Blednova Natalia et al. Diffusion de Boccard, Paris 1995.

Répertoire des pétroglyphes d'Asie Centrale. Fascicule 3: Sibérie du Sud 3. Kalbak-Tash I. Edité par Kubarev Vladimir et al. Diffusion de Boccard, Paris 1996.

Répertoire des pétroglyphes d'Asie Centrale. Fascicule 4: Sibérie du Sud 4. Cheremushny Log, Ust'-Kulog. Edité par Sher Jakov et al. *Stèles de Khakassie*. Edité par Savinov Dimitri et al. Diffusion de Boccard, Paris 1999.

Répertoire des pétroglyphes d'Asie Centrale. Fascicule 5 :Kazakhstan 1. Choix de pétroglyphes du Semirech'e. Edité par Mar'jasev A.N. et al. Diffusion de Boccard, Paris 1998.

Répertoire des pétroglyphes d'Asie Centrale. Fascicule 6: Mongolie du Nord-Ouest, Tsagaan Salaa/Baga Oigor. Edité par Jacobson Esther et al. 2 vols, Diffusion de Boccard, Paris 2001.

Rey, Marie-Catherine (ed.). *Kazakhstan, hommes, bêtes et dieux de la steppe*. Artlys, Versailles 2010.

Rezepkin, Alexeij. D. *Das frühbronzezeitliche Gräberfeld von Klady und die Majkop-Kultur in Nordwestkaukasien*. Marie Leidorf, Espelkamp 2000.

Richardson, David. *The Karakalpaks*, 2005. http://www.karakalpak.com/index.html

Rickenbach, Judith (ed.). *Oxus. 2000 Jahre Kunst am Oxus-Fluss in Mittelasien*. Museum Rietberg, Zürich 1989.

Rieger, Angelica (ed.). *Der Alexanderroman*. Müller und Schindler, Stuttgart 2002.

Rieu, Jacques. *Trésors de l'Altai Mongol*. Creatica, Santander 2006.

Rig Veda, published by Peter Michel. Marix, Wiebaden 2008.

Rivera, Norberto (ed.). *Shang and Western Zhou Jades*. Throckmorton Fine Art, Inc. New York 2010.

Rogozhinsky, A.E. (ed.). *Rock Art sites of Central Asia*. NIPI PMK, Almaty 2004.

Rolle, Renate. *Totenkult der Skythen*. 2 vols. Walter de Gruyter, Berlin 1979.

— *Die Welt der Skythen*. Bucher, Luzern 1980.

— 'Amazonen in der archäologischen Realität', *Kleist-Jahrbuch* 1986, pp. 38–62. Erich Schmidt Verlag, Berlin 1986.

Rolle, Renate et al. *Gold der Steppe. Archäologie der Ukraine*. Archäologisches Landesmuseum, Schleswig 1991.

— 'Das Burgwallsystem von Bel'sk (Ukraine). Eine frühe stadtartige Anlage im skythischen Landesinnern', in *Hamburger Beiträge zur Archäologie*, Philipp von Zabern, Mainz, Vol. 18, 1996, pp. 57–84.

— *Königskurgan Čertomlyk. Ein skythischer Grabhügel des 4. vorchristlichen Jahrhunderts*. 2 vols. Philipp von Zabern, Mainz 1998.

Rolle, Renate et al. (ed.) *Amazonen. Geheimnisvolle Kriegerinnen*. Historisches Museum der Pfalz, Speyer 2010.

Rosén, Staffan. 'Korea and the Silk Roads', *The Silk Road Journal*, Vol. 6/2, pp. 3–14, 2009. The Silk Road Foundation, Saratoga. http://www.silkroadfoundation.org/newsletter/vol6num2/srjournal_v6n2.pdf

Rosendahl, Gaëlle et al. 'Le plus vieil arc du monde? Une pièce intéressante en provenance de Mannheim, Allemagne', *L'Anthropologie*, Vol. 110, No. 3, Elsevier, Amsterdam, 2006, pp. 371–382.

Rossi-Osmida, Gabriele (ed.). *Turkmenistan. Environment, history, monuments, ethnography*. Centro Studi Ricerche Ligabue, Venezia 1996.

— *Margiana. Gonur-depe Necropolis*. Il Punto, Venice 2002.

— *Adji Kui Oasis, III–II mill. BC*. Centro Studi Ricerche Ligabue, Venezia 2007.

Rostovtzeff, M. *Iranians and Greeks in South Russia*. Clarendon, Oxford 1922.

— *The Animal Style in South Russia and China*. Princeton University Press, Princeton 1929.

— *La peinture décorative antique en Russie méridionale*. Diffusion Boccard, Paris (1913–1914) 2004.

Rothe, Peter. *Die Erde*. WBG, Wissenschaftliche Buchgesellschaft, Damstadt 2008.

Rougemont, Georges, Stronach, David. 'On the Date of the Oxus Gold Scabbard and other Achaemenid Matters', *Bulletin of the Asia Institute*, Vol. 12, 1998, pp. 231–248. The Asia Institute, Bloomfield Hills 2001.

Roux, Georges, Renger, Johannes. *Irak in der Antike*. Philipp von Zabern, Mainz 2005.

Roux, Jean-Paul. *L'Asie Centrale. Histoire et civilisations*. Fayard, Paris 1997.

Rowland, Benjamin. *Zentralasien*. Holle, Baden-Baden 1970.

Rozwadowski, Andrzej. 'The forgotten art of ancient Uzbekistan', *The Times of Central Asia*, 26 January 2001, Vol. 3, No. 4.

— 'Sun gods or shamans? Interpreting the "solar-headed" petroglyphs of Central Asia', in Price, Neil (ed). *The Archaeology of Shamanism.* Routledge, London 2001, pp. 65–86.

— *Symbols through Time. Interpreting the Rock Art of Central Asia.* Adam Mickiewicz University, Poznan 2004.

Rtveladze, Edvard. 'Kampyr Tepe-Pandokheïon', in *La Bactriane de Cyrus à Timour. Dossiers d'Archéologie,* Editions Faton, Quétigny 1999, pp. 56f.

— 'Kampyr Tepe-Pandokheïon – Alexandria Oxiana', in Hansen Sven. *Alexander der Große und die Öffnung der Welt. Asiens Kulturen im Wandel.* Reiss-Engelhorn-Museen, Mannheim 2009, pp. 169–175.

Rudenko, Sergei. *Die sibirische Sammlung Peters I.* Verlag der Akademie der Wissenschaften der UdSSR. Moskau-Leningrad 1962.

— *Die Kultur der Hsung-Nu und die Hügelgräber von Noin Ula.* Habelt, Bonn 1969.

— *Frozen Tombs of Siberia. The Pazyrik Burials of Iron Age Horsemen.* Dent & Sons, London 1970.

Rusanov, D.V. 'The Fortification of Kampir-Tepe: A Reconstruction', *Bulletin of the Asia Institute,* Vol. 8, 1994, pp. 155–160. The Asia Institute, Bloomfield Hills 1996.

Sagdullaev, Anatoli, Pidaev, Shakir. 'L'âge du Fer en Bactriane', La Bactriane de Cyrus à Timour. *Dossiers d'Archéologie,* Editions Faton, Quétigny 1999, pp. 24–27.

Sala, Renato. *Historical survey of irrigation practices in West Central Asia.* Laboratory of Geoarchaeology, Almaty 2004.

Sala, Renato, Deom, Jean-Marc. *Petroglyphs of South Kazakhstan.* Laboratory of Geoarchaeology, Almaty 2005.

Salmony, Alfred. *Sino-Siberian Art in the collection of C.T. Loo.* C.T. Loo Publishers, Paris 1933.

— *Antler and tongue. An essay on ancient Chinese symbolism and its implications.* Artibus Asiae, Ascona 1954.

Salomon, Richard. 'The Indo–Greek era of 186/5 BC in a Buddhist reliquary inscription', in Bopearachchi, Osmund, Boussac, Marie-Françoise. *Afghanistan. Ancien carrefour entre l'est et l'ouest.* Brepols, Turnhout 2005, pp. 359–401.

Samashev, Zainolla. *Petroglyphs of East Kazakhstan as historical sources.* Rakurs, Almaty 1993.

Samashev, Zainolla et al. 'Le kourgane de Berel dans l'Altaï kazakhstanais', *Arts Asiatiques.* Musée national des Arts asiatiques-Guimet, 55/2000, pp. 5–20. Paris.

— *Treasures from the Ustyurt and Mangystau.* Publishing Group 'Archaeology' LLC, Almaty 2007.

Sanders, Alan. *Historical Dictionary of Mongolia.* Scarecrow Press, Lanham 2003.

Sarianidi, Viktor. 'Margiana in the Bronze Age', in Kohl Philipp. *The Bronze Age Civilization of Central Asia. Recent Soviet discoveries.* Sharpe, New York 1981, pp. 165–193.

— *The Golden Hoard of Bactria. From the Tillya-tepe Excavations in Northern Afghanistan.* Abrams, New York 1985.

— 'Le complexe culturel de Togolok-21 en Margiane', *Arts Asiatiques.* Musée national des Arts asiatiques-Guimet, 41/1986, pp. 5–21. Paris.

— 'The Bactrian Pantheon', *Information Bulletin of the International Association for the Study of the Cultures of Central Asia, IASCCA,* No. 10, pp. 5–20, Moscow 1986.

— 'The golden hoard of Bactria', *National Geographic,* Vol. 177, No. 3, March 1990. National Geographic Society, Washington, pp. 50–75.

— 'Food-producing and other Neolithic communities in Khorasan and Transoxiana: Eastern Iran, Soviet Central Asia and Afghanistan', in *History of civilizations of Central Asia.* Vol. I. Unesco Publishing, Paris 1992, pp. 109–126.

— 'Temples of Bronze Age Margiana: traditions of ritual architecture', *Antiquity,* Vol. 68, No. 297, pp. 388–397, York 1994.

— 'Aegean-Anatolian Motifs in the Glyptic Art of Bactria and Margiana', *Bulletin of the Asia Institute,* Vol. 8, 1994, pp. 27–36. The Asia Institute, Bloomfield Hills 1996.

— *Margush. Ancient Oriental Kingdom in the Old Delta of Murgab River.* Türkmendöwlethabarlary, Ashgabat, 2002.

— 'Les tombes royales de Gonur-Dépé', in *Archéologia.* Faton, Dijon, No. 420, 2005, pp. 52–59.

— 'Le plus ancien sacrifice de poulain au Proche-Orient', *Dossiers d'Archéologie,* No. 317, 2006, pp. 34–39.

— 'Nouvelles sépultures sur le territoire de la «nécropole royale» de Gonur Dépé', *Arts Asiatiques.* Musée national des Arts asiatiques-Guimet, 65/2010, pp. 5–26. Paris.

Saunders, Nicholas. *L'âme des animaux.* Albin Michel, Paris 1995.

Sauter, Herrmann. *Studien zum Kimmerierproblem.* Habelt, Bonn 2000.

Savinov, D.G., Chlenova, N.L. 'Zapadnyye predaly rasprostraneniya olennykh kamney i voprosy ikh kul'turno-etnicheskoy prinadlezhnosti', in *Arkheologiya i etnografiya Mongolii.* Novosibirsk 1978, pp. 72–94.

Savostina, E.A. *Tema nadgrobnoj stelu iz Trechbratnego kurgana v kontekste antičnogo mirfa.* Istoriko-archeologičeskij almanach 1. Armarir, Moskva 1995, pp. 110–119.

Schäfer, Joachim et al. 'Neue Untersuchungen zum Lösspaläolithikum am Obi-Mazar, Tadžikistan', *Römisch-Germanisches Zentralmuseum,* Mainz, Jg. 26, Heft 2, 1996, pp. 97–109.

— 'Das Altpaläolithikum aus dem 4. Paläobodenkomplex von Obi-Mazar (Tadschikistan)', in J. Burdukiewicz u. al. (eds), *Erkenntnisjäger. Kultur und Umwelt des frühen Menschen. Veröffentlichungen des Landesamtes für Archäologie Sachsen-Anhalt 57,* 2003 (Festschrift Dietrich Mania), pp. 509–535.

Scelinskij, Vjaceslav, Sirokov, Vladimir. *Höhlenmalerei im Ural.* Thorbecke, Sigmaringen 1999.

Scham, Sandra. 'The Lost Goddess of Israel', *Archaeology.* Archaeological Institute of America, Boston March/April 2005.

Scharlipp, Wolfgang. *Die frühen Türken in Zentralasien.* WBG, Darmstadt, 1992.

Schiltz, Véronique. *Histoires de kourganes. La redécouverte de l'or des Scythes.* Gallimard, Paris 1991.

— *Die Skythen und andere Steppenvölker.* C.H. Beck. München 1994.

— *L'or des Amazones* (ed.). Findakly, Paris 2001.

— 'Notule sur un ours énigmatique', in Bopearachchi Osmund. *Afghanistan,* 2005, pp. 293–305.

Schlichtherle, Helmut. 'Wagenfunde aus den Seeufersiedlungen im zirkumalpinen Raum', in Fansa, Mamoun, Burmeister, Stefan. *Rad und Wagen.* Philipp von Zabern, Mainz 2004, pp. 295–314.

Schmitt, Hatto H., Vogt, Ernst (eds). *Lexikon des Hellenismus.* Harrasowitz, Wiesbaden 2005.

Schultz, Michael. 'Ergebnisse der paläopathologisch-anthropologischen Untersuchung der menschlichen Skelettfunde aus dem Grab 26 von Liushui, Xinjiang China', *Eurasia Antiqua,* Vol. 13/2007, pp. 181–197. Deutsches Archäologisches Institut, Berlin; Philipp von Zabern, Mainz 2008.

Schultz, P.N., Golovkina, V.A. 'Neapolis des Scythes', in Piotrovsky, Boris et al. *Ourartou, Neapolis des Scythes, Kharezm.* Maisonneuve, Paris 1954.

Schulz, P.N. 'Skifskiye izvayanina', in *Khudozhestvennaya kul'tura i arkheologiya antichnogo mira.* Nauka, Moskwa, 1976, pp. 218–231.

Schwarcz, H.P. 'ESR dates for the hominid burial site of Qafzeh in Israel', *Journal of Human Evolution,* 17, Elsevier, Amsterdam, 1988, pp. 733–737.

Scott, Marian et al (eds). *Impact of the Environment on Human Migration in Eurasia*. NATO Scientific Affairs Division and Kluwer Publishers, Dordrecht, 2004.

Seaman, Gary (ed.). *Foundations of empire. Archaeology and Art of the Eurasian Steppes*. University of Southern California, Los Angeles 1992.

Seaman, Gary, Marks, Daniel (eds). *Rulers from the Steppe. State Formation on the Eurasian Periphery*. University of Southern California, Los Angeles 1991.

Seifert, Mathias. 'Zur absoluten Datierung der Hügelgräber der Pazyryk-Kultur', in Rolle Renate et al. *Amazonen,* 2010, p. 138f.

Seipel, Wilfried (ed.). *Gold der Steppe*. Kunsthistorisches Museum, Leoben 2009.

Semonov, Petr Petrovich. *Travels in the Tian-Shan, 1856–1857*. Haklyut Society, London (1946) 1998.

Shanbazi, Shapur. 'Iranian mythology. Iraj', in *Encyclopaedia Iranica*. Columbia University, New York. http://www.iranica.com/articles/iraj

Shao, Qinglong et al. *Genghis Khan – The Ancient Nomadic Culture of the Northern China*. N.D. Beijing 2004.

Sharma, Deo Prakash. *Indus Script on its way to decipherment*. Prakashan, Delhi 2000.

Shcheglov, A.N., Katz, V.I. 'A fourth-century BC Royal Kurgan in the Crimea', *Metropolitan Museum Journal*. New York, Vol. 26, 1991, pp. 97–122.

Sheppard, Ruth. *Alexander der Grosse und seine Feldzüge*. Theiss, Stuttgart 2009.

Sher, Jakov. 'Pétroglyphes de Russie', *Archéologia*. Editions Faton, Dijon, No. 395, 2002, pp. 58–65.

Sheratt, Andrew. 'The Trans-Eurasian Exchange: The Prehistory of Chinese Relations with the West', in Mair, Victor H. *Contact and Exchange in the Ancient World*, 2006, pp. 30–61.

Shreeve, Jamie. 'Sur la route de l'évolution', *National Geographic*, Washington/Paris. July 2010, pp. 2–35.

Shunkov, Michael. 'The characteristics of the Altai (Russia) Middle Palaeolithic in regional context', *Indo-Pacific Association Bulletin* 25, Taipei, 2005, pp. 69–77.

Sidky, H. *The Greek Kingdom of Bactria. From Alexander to Eucratides the Great*. University Press of America, Lanham 2000.

Sima, Guang. *Zizhi tongjian*. 1084. Excerpt titled *Wars with the Xiongnu*, translated by Joseph P. Yap. Author House, Bloomington 2009.

Sima, Qian: see Ssu-ma Ch'ien.

Simonenko, A.V. 'Bewaffnung und Kriegswesen der Sarmaten und späten Skythen im nördlichen Schwarzmeergebiet', *Eurasia Antiqua*, Vol. 7/2001, pp. 187–328. Deutsches Archäologisches Institut, Berlin; Philipp von Zabern, Mainz 2001

— 'Sarmatian relics of the "Eastern Wave" in the North Pontic Region', *Silk Road Art and Archaeology*. Vol. 8, 2002, pp. 1–28. Journal of the Institute of Silk Road Studies, Kamakura 2002.

Sinor, Denis (ed.). *The Cambridge history of Early Inner Asia*. Cambridge University Press, Cambridge 1990.

Sirinov, Temur. 'Die frühurbane Kultur der Bronzezeit im südlichen Mittelasien. Die vorgeschichtliche Siedlung Dzarkutan', *Archäologische Mitteilungen aus Iran und Turan*, Vol. 34, pp. 1–170. Deutsches Archäologisches Institut Berlin 2003.

Sirocko, Frank. *Wetter, Klima, Menschheitsentwicklung*. WBG, Wissenschaftliche Buchgesellschaft, Darmstadt 2010.

Skvorcov, N., Skripkin, A. 'Eine sarmatische Adelsbestattung aus dem Wolgograder Wolgagebiet', in *Eurasia Antiqua*, Vol. 12/2006, pp. 251–268. Deutsches Archäologisches Institut, Berlin; Philipp von Zabern, Mainz 2007.

Skoryj, Sergej. 'Der Kurgan Perepjaticha', in *Hamburger Beiträge zur Archäologie*, Vol. 18, pp. 86–106. Philipp von Zabern, Mainz 1996.

Sokolov, G. *Antique art of the Northern Black Sea coast*. Aurora, Leningrad 1974.

Solanki, Sami et al. *Unusual activity of the Sun during recent decades compared to the previous 11,000 years*, Nature 28 October (2004). http://dx.doi.org/10.1038/nature02995

Solecki, Ralph S. *Shanidar cave: a Palaeolithic site in northern Iraq*. Annual Report of the Smithsonian Institution, 1954: pp. 389–425.

Solecki, Ralph S.; Anagnostis P., Agelarakis (2004). *The Proto-Neolithic Cemetery in Shanidar Cave*. Texas A&M University Press, 2004.

Souza, Philip de (ed.). *The ancient world at war*. Thames & Hudson, London 2008.

Ssu-ma, Ch'ien. *Shih chi. Records of the grand historian of China. Translated from the Shih chi of Ssu-ma Ch'ien by Burton Watson*. Columbia University Press, New York 1971.

Stähler, Klaus (ed.). *Zur graeco-skythischen Kunst. Archäologisches Kolloquium Münster 1995*. Ugarit-Verlag, Münster 1997.

Stark, Sören, Rubinson, Karen (eds.). *Nomads and Networks. The Ancient Art and Culture of Kazakhstan*. Institute for the Study of the Ancient World at New York University, New York, and Princeton University Press, Princeton 2012.

Staviskij, Boris. *Kunst der Kuschan*. Seemann, Leipzig 1979.

— *La Bactriane sous les Kushans*. Maisonneuve, Paris 1986.

Stein, Sir Aurel. *Ruins of Desert Cathay*. Macmillan, London, 1912.

—*Serindia*. Clarendon, Oxford, 1921.

— *Innermost Asia*. Clarendon, Oxford 1928.

Stierlin, Henri. *Splendors of Ancient Persia*. White Star Publishers, Vercelli 2006.

Strabo. *Geographica*. In der Übersetzung und mit Anmerkungen von Dr. A. Forbiger. Marix Verlag, Wiesbaden 2007.

Strahlenberg, Philip Johann von. *Das Nord-und Östliche Theil von Europa und Asia, in so weit solches das gantze Russische Reich mit Siberien und der großen Tartarey in sich begreiffet*. In Verlegung des Autoris, Stockholm 1730.

Stronach, David. 'On the date of the Oxus Scabbard and other Achaemenid Matters', *Bulletin of the Asia Institute*, Vol. 12, 1998, pp. 231–248. The Asia Institute, Bloomfield Hills 2001.

Takahama, Shu et al. (eds). 'Preliminary Report of the Archaeological Investigations in Ulaan Uushig I (Uushigiin Övör) in Mongolia', *Bulletin of archaeology, the University of Kanazawa* No. 28, .pp. 61–102, 2006. http://ci.nii.ac.jp/naid/110006278430/en/

Talbot-Rice, Tamara. *Die Skythen*. Dumont, Köln 1957.

Tarn, W.W. *The Greeks in Bactria & India*. Ares Publishers, Chicago (1938, 1951) 1997.

Tarzi, Zamariallai. 'Jules Bartoux: le découvreur oublié d'Aï Khanoum', in *Académie des Inscriptions & Belles-Lettres, Paris. Comptes rendus des scéances de l'année 1996*, fasc. II, pp. 595–611, 1996.

Tashbayeva, K. et al. *Petroglyphs of Central Asia*. International Institute for Central Asian Studies, Samarkand 2001.

Telegin, D., Mallory, J.P. 'The Anthropomorphic Stelae of the Ukraine. The Early Iconography of the Indo-Europrans', *Journal of Indo-European Studies Monograph No. 11*. The Institute for the Study of Man, Washington 1994.

Telegin, D. et al. 'Settlement and economy in Neolithic Ukraine: a new chronology', *Antiquity*, Vol. 77, No. 297, pp. 456–470, York 2003.

Teufer, Mike, Vinogradova, Natalija. 'Das Gräberfeld von Gelot, Tadschikistan', in Boroffka, Nikolaus, Hansen, Svend (eds). *Archäologische Forschungen in Kasachstan, Tadschikistan, Turkmenistan und Usbekistan*. Eurasien-Abteilung, Deutsches Archäologisches Institut, Berlin 2010, pp. 28–31.

Thornton, Christopher, Schurr, Theodore. 'Genes, language and culture: an example from the Tarim Basin', *Oxford Journal of Archaeology*, Oxford, Vol. 23, 2004, pp. 83–106.

Tolstikov, Vladimir. 'Pantikapaion. Ein archäologisches Porträt der Hauptstadt des Kimmerischen Bosporus', in Fornasier, Jochen, Böttger Burkhard (eds). *Das Bosporanische Reich.* Philipp von Zabern, Mainz 2002, pp. 39–58.

Tolstov, Sergei. *Drevniy Choresm.* Isdanjje MGU, Moscow 1948.

— *Auf den Spuren der altchoresmischen Kultur.* Verlag Kultur und Fortschritt, Berlin 1953.

Tomasello, Michael. *Die kulturelle Entwicklung des menschlichen Denkens.* Suhrkamp, Frankfurt a. M., 2002.

Tomka, Peter. *Über die Bestattungen der Hunnen.* in Koch, Alexander (ed.). Attila und die Hunnen. Theiss, Stuttgart 2007, pp. 252–257.

Tosi, M. et al. 'The Bronze Age in Iran and Afghanistan', in *History of civilizations of Central Asia.* Vol. I. Unesco Publishing, Paris 1992, pp. 191–223.

Treister, Mikhail. *Die Drei-Brüder-Kurgane. Katalog und Analyse der Befunde und Funde einer Grabhügelgruppe auf der östlichen Krim aus der Zeit des 4. bis 3. Jhs. v.Chr.* Universum, Bonn, Simferopol 2008.

Trifonov, Viktor. 'Die Majkop-Kultur und die ersten Wagen in der südrussischen Steppe', in Fansa, Mamoun, Burmeister, Stefan. *Rad und Wagen.* Philipp von Zabern, Mainz 2004, pp. 167–176.

Trofimova, Anna (ed.). *Greeks on the Black Sea.* Paul Getty Museum, Los Angeles 2007.

Tsultem, N. *Mongolian Arts and Crafts.* State Publishing House, Ulaan Baatar 1987.

— *Mongolian Architecture.* State Publishing House, Ulaan Baatar 1988.

— *Mongolian Sculpture.* State Publishing House, Ulaan Baatar 1989.

Tur, C.A. *Neapol Skyfsji.* Universum, Simferopol 2011.

Tureckij, Michail. 'Wagengräber der grubengrabzeitlichen Kulturen im Steppengebiet Osteuropas', in Fansa, Mamoun, Burmeister, Stefan. *Rad und Wagen.* Philipp von Zabern, Mainz 2004, pp. 191–200.

Ustinova, Yulia. 'Snake-limbed and tendril-limbed goddesses in the art and mythology of the Mediterranean and Black Sea', in Braund, David (ed.). *Scythians and Greeks.* University of Exeter Press, Exeter 2005, pp. 64–79.

Vaissière, Étienne de la. 'Huns et Xiongnu', *Central Asiatic Journal*, Vol. 49, pp. 3–26. Harrassowitz, Wiesbaden 2005.

— *Sogdian Traders. A History.* Brill, Leiden 2005.

Valois, Paule. 'Quand l'homme a peuplé la terre. Les récentes découvertes', *Archéologia.* Editions Faton, Dijon, No. 480, 2010, pp. 48–56.

Vandermeersch, Bernhard. 'The excavation of Qafzeh. Its contribution to knowledge of the Mousterian in the Levant', *Bulletin du Centre de recherche français de Jérusalem*, 10, 2002, pp. 65–70. http://bcrfj.revues.org/index1192.html

Vasil'ev, Sergei et al. 'Radiocarbon-based chronology of the Palaeolithic in Siberia and its relevance to the peopling of the New World', *Radiocarbon*, Vol. 44/2, pp. 503–530, University of Arizona, Tucson 2002.

Vedder, James. 'Greeks, Amazons and Archaeology', *The Silk Road Journal*, Vol. 2/2, pp. 17–24, 2004. The Silk Road Foundation, Saratoga. http://www.silkroadfoundation.org/newsletter/vol2num2/greek.html

Vickers, Michael. *Scythian and Thracian antiquities.* Asmolean handbooks, Oxford 2002.

Victorri, Bernhard. 'Die Debatte um die Ursprache', in Breuer, Reinhard (ed.). 'Die Evolution der Sprachen', *Spektrum der Wissenschaft*, Dossier 2/2007, pp. 16–19. Heidelberg 2007

Vishnyatsky, Leonid. 'The Palaeolithic of Central Asia', *Journal of World Prehistory*, Vol. 13, No. 1, March 1999, pp. 69–122.

Vitebsky, Piers. *Les Chamanes.* Albin Michel, Paris 1995.

Wagner, Mayke, Butz, Herbert. *Nomadenkunst.* Philipp von Zabern, Mainz 2007.

Wagner, Mayke, Wang Wei (eds). *Bridging Eurasia.* Philipp von Zabern, Mainz 2010.

Walser, Gerold. *Die Völkerschaften auf den Reliefs von Persepolis.* Teheraner Forschungen, Bd. 2, Mann, Berlin 1966.

Wang, Binghua. 'Recherches historiques préliminaires sur les Saka du Xinjiang ancien', *Arts Asiatiques.* Musée national des Arts asiatiques-Guimet, 42/1987, pp. 31–44. Paris.

— 'The Polychrome Rock Paintings in the Altay Mountains', *The Silk Road Journal*, Vol. 3/1, pp. 16–23, 2005. The Silk Road Foundation, Saratoga. http://www.silkroadfoundation.org/newsletter/vol3num1/srjournal_v3n1.pdf

Wang, Binghua et al. *The ancient corpses of Xinjiang.* Xinjiang Renmin Chubanshe, 2001.

Wang, Bo. 'Hirschsteine in Xinjiang', *Eurasia Antiqua*, Vol. 7/2001, pp. 105–132. Deutsches Archäologisches Institut, Berlin; Philipp von Zabern, Mainz 2001.

Wang, Tao; Wang, Helen. 'The Anau Seal and the questions it raises', *Journal of Inner Asian Art and Archaeology* 2/2007, pp. 143–150. Brepols, Turnhout 2007.

Watt, James. 'The legacy of Nomadic Art in China and Eastern Central Asia', in Bunker, Emma. *Nomadic Art of the Eastern Eurasian Steppes.* The Metropolitan Museum of Art, New York, Yale University Press, New Haven 2002, pp. 199–209.

Weniger, Gerd-Christian. 'Wie modern waren Neanderthaler?', *Eurasia Antiqua*, Vol. 14/2008, pp. 1–18. Deutsches Archäologisches Institut, Berlin; Philipp von Zabern, Mainz 2009.

Wereshagin, Wassilij Wassiljewitch. *Turkestan. Etyudy s natury. (Turkestan. Studien nach der Natur.)* Beggrow, St. Petersburg 1874.

Werming, Jeanette. 'Käwrigul/Gumugou and Xiaohe, Lop Nur Zhen', in Wieczorek, Alfred, Lind, Christoph (eds), *Ursprünge der Seidenstraße.* Theiss, Stuttgart 2007, pp. 102–133.

Werner, Thomas (ed.). *Unbekannte Krim.* Kehrer, Heidelberg 1999.

West, M.L. *Indo-European Poetry and Myth.* Oxford University Press, Oxford 2007.

Wheeler, Mark. 'Back to the Source. A modern-day archaeologist digs deep in Central Asia and excavates a hero', *Huntington Frontiers*, Fall/Winter 2005, pp. 20–24. The Huntington Library, San Marino CA 2005.

White, Randall. *Prehistoric Art. The symbolic journey of mankind.* Abrams, New York 2003.

White, Tim et al. 'Pleistocene Homo sapiens from Middle Awash, Ethiopia', *Nature*, Vol. 423, pp. 742–747, Macmillan Publishers, Basingstoke 2003.

Whitehead, R.B. *Catalogue of coins in the Panjab Museum, Lahore.* (1914), Indic Academy, Varanasi 1971.

Wieczorek, Alfred, Lind, Christoph (eds). *Ursprünge der Seidenstraße.* Theiss, Stuttgart 2007.

Willerslev, Eske, Rasmussen, Morten et al. 'An Aboriginal Australian genome reveals separate human dispersals into Asia', *Science*, Vol. 333, pp. 1689ff, 23 September 2011. American Association for the Advancement of Science, New York 2011.

Williams, James. 'The Tahilt Region: A Preliminary Archaeological Survey of the Tahilt Surroundings to Contextualize the Tahilt Cemeteries', *The Silk Road Journal*, Vol. 5/2, pp. 27–36, 2008. The Silk Road Foundation, Saratoga. http://www.silkroadfoundation.org/newsletter/vol5num2/

Winkelmann, Sylvia. *Seals of the oasis from the Ligabue Collection.* Il Punto, Venice 2004.

Wood, John. *A journey to the source of the River Oxus.* Murray, London 1872.

Wu Rukang, Olsen, John W. (eds) *Palaeoanthropology and Palaeolithic Archaeology in the People's Republic of China.* Left Coast Press, Walnut Creek 2009.

Wu Xinhua et al. 'Das protoskythische Gräberfeld Liushi im Kun Lun-Gebirge, NW-China', *Eurasia Antiqua*, Vol. 12/2006, pp. 173–192. Deutsches Archäologisches Institut, Berlin; Philipp von Zabern, Mainz 2007.

Xinjiang Institute of Archaeology. *New Achievements in archaeological research in Xinjiang during the time span 1990–1996* (in Chinese). Xinjiang Wenwu, Urumqi, 1997.

— 'Investigation and Excavation of the Xiaohe Cemetery in 2002' (in Chinese), in *Cultural Relics of Xinjiang*, Xinjiang Wenwu, Urumqi, 2003/2.

— 'Investigation and Excavation of the Xiaohe Cemetery in 2003' (in Chinese), in *Cultural Relics of Xinjiang*, Xinjiang Wenwu, Urumqi, 2007/1.

Xu Wenkan. 'Xinjiang Mummies and the Origin of the Tocharians', in Mair, Victor H. 'The Mummified Remains Found in the Tarim Basin', *Journal of Indo-European Studies*, Washington, Vol. 23, Nr. 3&4, 1995, pp. 357–369.

Yablonsky, Leonid T. 'New excavations of the early nomadic burial ground at Filippovka (Southern Ural Region, Russia)', *American Journal of Archaeology*, Archaeological Institute of America, Boston, Vol. 114, Jan. 2010, pp. 129–143.

Yablonsky, Leonid T. et al. 'L'épée dorée de Filippovka', *Archéologia*. Editions Faton, Dijon, No. 494, 2011, pp. 50–57.

Yang Juping. 'Alexander the Great and the Emergence of the Silk Road', *The Silk Road Journal*, Vol. 6/2, 2009, pp. 15–22. The Silk Road Foundation, Saratoga.

Yang Xiaoping. 'The oases along the Keriya River in the Taklamakan Desert, China, and their evolution since the end of the last glaciation', *Environmental Geology*, Springer, Berlin 1993, Vol. 41, No. 3–4. pp. 314–320.

Yang Xiaoping et al. 'Late Quaternary environmental changes in the Taklamakan Desert, western China, inferred from OSL-dated lacustrine and Aeolian deposits', *Quaternary International Science Reviews* 25, 2006, pp. 923–932. Elsevier, Amsterdam.

— 'Hydrological changes and land degradation in the southern and eastern Tarim Basin, Xinjiang, China', *Land Degradation & Development*, Vol. 17, No. 4, 2006, pp.381–392. http://www3.interscience.wiley.com/journal/6175/home

— 'Late Quaternary palaeoenvironment change and landscape evolution along the Keriya River, Xinjiang, China: the relationship between high mountain glaciation and landscape evolution in foreland desert regions', *Quaternary International*, Elsevier, Amsterdam, 2002, Vol. 97–98, pp. 155–166.

Yatsenko, Sergey. 'The biggest expedition. Studying the Ancient Iranian World: Chorasmian Expedition of S.P. Tolstov', *Transoxiana* 12, 2007. http://www.transoxiana.org/12/yatsenko-tolstov_chorasmia.php

Yue Feng (ed). *A grand view of Xinjiang's Cultural Relics and Historic Sites.*(in Chinese with English captions). Xinjiang meishu sheying chubanshe, Urumqi, 1999.

— *Collection of the historical culture of Xinjiang* (in Chinese). Xinjiang meishu sheying chubanshe, Urumqi, 2009.

Zadneprovskiy, Y.A. 'The nomads of Northern Central Asia after the invasion of Alexander', in *History of civilizations of Central Asia*. Vol. II. Unesco Publishing, Paris 1994, pp. 457–472.

Zaitseva, G.I., Geel, B. van. 'The occupation history of the southern Eurasia steppe during the Holocene', in Scott, Marian et al (eds). *Impact of the Environment on Human Migration in Eurasia*, 2004, pp. 63–82.

Zavyalov, V.A. 'The Fortifications of the City of Gyaur Kala, Merv', in Cribb, Joe, Herrmann, Georgina (eds). *After Alexander. Central Asia before Islam*. The British Academy, London 2007, pp. 313–329.

Zaytsev, Juri. 'Skilur and his Kingdom', in *Ancient Civilisations from Scythia to Siberia*. Brill, Leiden. Vol. 7, No. 3–4, 2001. pp. 239–271.

— *The Scythian Neapolis (2nd century BC to 3rd century AD). Investigation into the Graeco-Barbarian city on the northern Black Sea coast.* BAR International Series 1219, Oxford 2004.

— 'Scythian Neapolis – the Capital of the Kingdom of Skiluros', in Fless, Friederike, Treister, Mikhail, *Bilder und Objekte als Träger kultureller Identität und interkultureller Kommunikation im Schwarzmeergebiet*. Verlag Marie Leidorf, Rahden 2005, pp. 141–144.

Zbenovic, Vladimir G. '*Siedlungen der frühen Tripol'e-Kultur zwischen Dnestr und Südlichem Bug.* Marie Leidorf, Espelkamp 1996', in Jones-Bley, Karlene, Zdanovich, D.G. *Complex Societies of Central Eurasia from the 3rd to the 1st Millennium BC*. Vol. I., Institute for the Study of Man, Washington D.C., 2002, pp. 121–138.

Zdanovich, D.G, Batanina, I.M. 'Planography of the Fortified Centers of the Middle Brinze Age in the Southern Trans-Urals according to Aerial Photography Data', in Jones-Bley, Karlene, Zdanovich, D.G. *Complex Societies of Central Eurasia from the 3rd to the 1st Millennium BC*. Vol. I., Institute for the Study of Man, Washington D.C., 2002, pp. 121–138.

Zdanovich, D.G., Gayduchenko, L.L. 'Sintashta Burial Sacrifice: The Bolschekaragansky Cemetery in Focus', in Jones-Bley, Karlene, Zdanovich, D.G. *Complex Societies of Central Eurasia from the 3rd to the 1st Millennium BC*. Vol. I., Institute for the Study of Man, Washington D.C., 2002, pp. 202–231.

Zeimal, E.V. 'The political history of Transoxiana', in *Cambridge History of Iran,* Vol. 3 (1), Cambridge University Press, Cambridge 1983, pp. 232–262.

Zettler, Richard, Horne, Lee (eds). *Treasures from the Royal Tombs of Ur.* University of Pennsylvania Museum of Archaeology and Anthropology, Philadelphia 1998.

Zhao Feng, Yu Zhiyong (eds). *Legacy of the Desert King*. ISAT/Costume Squad, Hong Kong 2000.

Zhao Songqiao, Xia Xuncheng. 'Evolution of the Lop Desert and the Lop Nor', *The Geographical Journal*, Vol. 150, No.3, 1984, pp. 311–321. The Royal Geographical Society, London.

Zhou Xuejun, Song Weimin. *Archaeological treasures of the Silk Road in Xinjiang Uygur Autonomous Region.* Shanghai Translation Publishing House. Shanghai 1998.

Zuev, V., Ismagil, E. 'Frühsarmatische Steinstelen von Ustyurt und Mangyshlak, West-Kasachstan', *Antiqua*, Vol. 2/1996, pp. 307–404. Deutsches Archäologisches Institut, Berlin; Philipp von Zabern, Mainz 2007.

List of Maps

Satellite imagery © NASA. http://visibleearth.nasa.gov/

Photo Credits

All photos are by the author with the exception of the following:

American Museum of Natural History Library, New York: pp. 6–7, 9.

Antikensammlung, Staatliche Museen zu Berlin, bpk/Photo: Johannes Laurentius: p. 198.

Archaeological Institute of the Kazakh Ministry of Sciences, Almaty: p. 208.

Archaeological Museum, Ufa: pp. 255, 256, 265.

Azov History, Archaeology and Palaeontology Museum, Azov: pp. 266, 270.

Astavjev Andrej, Aktau: pp. 150, 254.

Blaser Architekten, Basel: p. 220.

British Museum, London: Front jacket, pp. 87, 196, 298.

Central State Museum of the Republic of Kazakhstan, Almaty:
pp. 209, 260 right, 267.

Drujinina Anjelina, Deutsches Archäologisches Institut DAI, Eurasien-Abteiling, Berlin: p. 301.

Ewig Willi, Manilla, Australia: p. 13.

Garrett Kenneth, Broad Run: pp. 102–03, 106, 286–87.

Giancola Donato, Brooklyn: pp. 182–183.

Harvard Art Museum, Arthur M. Sackler Museum, Gift of Edward W. Forbes, 18999.9 + 1932.49. Photo: Katya Kallsen; © President and Fellows of Harvard College: p. 264.

Historical Museum, Abakan: p. 137.

Historical Museum of Dnepropetrovsk: p. 79.

Historical Museum of Uzbekistan, Tashkent: p. 112.

Huang Yan Hong / Redlink Hong Kong: p. x.

Institute for Archaeology of the Russian Academy of Sciences, Moscow: p. 172.

Institute for Archaeology and Ethnography, Novosibirsk: p. 199.

Kubarev Vladimir, Novosibirsk: pp. 59, 91, 186.

Kupferstichkabinett Preußischer Kulturbesitz Berlin/bpk: p. 284.

Lapidarium Kerch: p. 251.

Li Xueliang, Urumqi: pp.120, 121, 122, 123.

Metropolitan Museum of Art, New York, bpk/Photography: MMA: pp. 107, 109, 164.

Möckli Urs, Wetzikon: pp. 126–27, 223.

Museum of Archaeology, National Museum of Sciences of the Ukraine, Kiev: p. 78 right.

Museum zu Allerheiligen Schaffhausen, Sammlung Ebnöther: p. 108 right.

Nagler Anatoli, Deutsches Archäologisches Institut DAI, Eurasien-Abteilung, Berlin: p. 200.

National Army Museum, London, Courtesy of the Council of the N.A.M. Photo John Burke, 1879: pp. 276–77.

National Museum of Afghanistan, Kabul: pp. 274, 289, 290, 292, 293, 294, 295.

National Museum of Antiquities of Tajikistan, Dushanbe: pp. 72, 203, 285, 302.

National Museum of the History of the Ukraine, Kiev: pp. 78 left, 236.

National Museum of Turkmenistan, Ashgabat: pp. 65 top, 66 both, 106, 108 left.

National Museum of Tuva, Kyzyl: pp. 179 left, 181.

Paley Matthieu / paleyphoto.com: pp. 275, 278–79.

Prisma Bildagentur © waldhaeusl.com: p. 201.

Regional Museum of Rostov: p. 235, 257.

Regional Museum of Simferopol: p. 240 bottom.

Rieser Lorenz, Luzern: p. 219.

Shekeyuan, Zhongguo shehuikexue yuan kaogu yanjiusuo kaogudui. 1981–1983 nian Liulihe Xizhou Yan guo mudi fajue jianbao. Kaogu, Beijing 1984, H.5.: p. 84.

State Hermitage Museum, St. Petersburg. Photographs © The State Hermitage Museum/photo by Vladimir Terebenin, Leonard Kheifets, Yuri Molodkovets: pp. 34, 35, 65 bottom, 90, 111, 171, 173, 174, 175, 179 right, 187 both, 188, 189, 191, 194 both, 195, 197, 229, 230 both, 232–33, 234, 237 (both), 243 (both), 244, 260 left, 261, 268.

Stierlin Henri, Geneva: p. 192.

Stuhrmann Jochen, Hamburg: pp. 67, 142–43, 297.

Stuhrmann Jochen, GEO, Picture Press, Hamburg: p. 32.

Throckmorton Fine Art, New York: p. 152.

Tscherne Erik, GEO, Picture Press, Hamburg: p. 21.

Ukrainian Museum of Historical Treasures, Kiev: pp. 227, 248, 249.

Waugh Dan, Shoreline: pp. 28 both, 45, 85.

Weber Therese, Arlesheim, Switzerland: pp. 10, 23, 43 bottom right, 92, 115, 138 bottom.

Wereshagin Wassilij Wassiljewitch. *Turkestan. Etyudy s natury.* Beggrow, St. Petersburg 1874. Tafel 18: p. 169.

Weyl Laurent, Argos, Picturetank, Paris: pp. 14–15.

Wong Adam / Redlink Hong Kong: pp. 304–05.

Xinjiang Uigurs Autonomous Region Museum, Urumqi: pp. 82, 83, 98, 116, 217 both, 218 both.

All efforts have been made to name or identify copyright holders. We will endeavour to rectify any unintended omissions in future editions of this work, upon receipt of evidence of relevant intellectual property rights.

Acknowledgements

This book is based on dozens of expeditions and journeys undertaken in the last three decades. My research was successful only thanks to hundreds of kind people in China, India, Iran, Iraq, Kazakhstan, Kyrgyzstan, Mongolia, Pakistan, Russia, Tajikistan, Tibet, Turkmenistan, Ukraine and Uzbekistan; to all of them I remain grateful. The book itself was produced only with the help of many people. A few preferred to remain anonymous; others are briefly acknowledged here, in alphabetical order.

Mrs Susanne Annen, Kabul, who helped me obtain permission to publish the photos from Tillya Tepe.

Mr John Vincent Bellezza, Charlottesville, for drawing my attention to the Iron Age petroglyphs in the Changtang, Tibet.

Dr Nikolaus Boroffka, Berlin, who indicated a similarity between ceramics from Satma Mazar and Charwighul.

Dr Anjelina Drujinina, Berlin, who put her unpublished material about the Oxus temple at my disposal.

Prof. Denis Etler, Aptos, who suggested a date when modern Asian ethnicities differentiated.

Prof. Don Johanson, Tempe, who put me in touch with Denis Etler.

Dr Sharofuddin Kurbanov, Panjikant, who gave me several valuable indications concerning archaeological facts in Tajikistan.

Dr Anatoli Nagler, Berlin, who shared his wide knowledge about the Scythians and gave me an advance copy of his publication on the stylistic representation of deer on deer stones of Central Asia.

Jürg Rageth, Riehen, who made me aware of the newest dating of the Pazyryk kurgans and gave other valuable inputs concerning Central Asian textiles.

Dr Alexei Savchenko, Kiev, whose inputs in the fields of Central Asian archaeology and religions I highly appreciate.

Dr St. John Simpson, London, who helped me obtain permission to publish the photos from Tillya Tepe.

Mrs Verhecken-Lammens, Antwerp, who provided interesting insights into the textiles discovered at Ayala Mazar and Satma Mazar, Taklamakan Desert.

Prof. Therese Weber, Arlesheim, who accompanied me on numerous journeys and expeditions and contributed to the research results, especially concerning the analysis of ancient textiles.

Dr Judith Wörner-Hasler, Lörrach, who carefully reviewed the German manuscript.

Index: Concepts

Illustrations are indicated by *italic* references. Tables are indicated by *t*.

Index: People

Index: Places

Illustrations are indicated by *italic* references. Tables are indicated by *t*.

The main archaeological sites of Central Asia and present state boundaries